Unphenomenal Shakespeare

Costerus New Series

STUDIES IN ENGLISH WORLDWIDE

Editors

Theo D'haen (*Leiden University, The Netherlands
and Leuven University, Belgium*)
Raphaël Ingelbien (*Leuven University, Belgium*)
Birgit Neumann (*Heinrich-Heine-Universität Düsseldorf, Germany*)
Carmen Birkie (*Philipps-Universität Marburg, Germany*)

VOLUME 232

This titles published in this series are listed at *brill.com/cos*

Unphenomenal Shakespeare

Pending Critical Quarrels

By

Julián Jiménez Heffernan

BRILL

LEIDEN | BOSTON

Cover illustration: Photo taken by the author

Library of Congress Cataloging-in-Publication Data

Names: Jiménez Heffernan, Julián, author.
Title: Unphenomenal Shakespeare : pending critical quarrels / Julián Jiménez Heffernan.
Description: Leiden ; Boston : Brill, 2023. | Series: Costerus ns (new series), 01659618 ; vol. 232 | Includes bibliographical references and index. | Summary: "In the aftermath of New Historicism and Cultural Materialism, the field of Shakespeare Studies has been increasingly overrun by post-theoretical, phenomenological claims. Many of the critical tendencies that hold the field today–post-humanism, speculative realism, ecocriticism, historical phenomenology, new materialism, performance studies, animal studies, affect studies–are consciously or unwittingly informed by phenomenological assumptions. This book aims at uncovering and examining these claims, not only to assess their philosophical congruency but also to determine their hermeneutic relevance when applied to Shakespeare. More specifically, Unphenomenal Shakespeare deploys resources of speculative critique to resist the moralistic and aestheticist phenomenalization of the Shakespeare playtexts across a variety of schools and scholars, a tendency best epitomized in Bruce Smith's Phenomenal Shakespeare (2010)"– Provided by publisher.
Identifiers: LCCN 2022049744 (print) | LCCN 2022049745 (ebook) | ISBN 9789004526617 (hardback) | ISBN 9789004526631 (ebook)
Subjects: LCSH: Shakespeare, William, 1564-1616–Criticism and interpretation. | Phenomenology and literature. | Hermeneutics–Philosophy. | LCGFT: Literary criticism.
Classification: LCC PR2976 .J56 2023 (print) | LCC PR2976 (ebook) | DDC 822.3/3–dc23/eng/20221021
LC record available at https://lccn.loc.gov/2022049744
LC ebook record available at https://lccn.loc.gov/2022049745

Typeface for the Latin, Greek, and Cyrillic scripts: "Brill." See and download: brill.com/brill-typeface.

ISSN 0165-9618
ISBN 978-90-04-52661-7 (hardback)
ISBN 978-90-04-52663-1 (e-book)

Copyright 2023 by Koninklijke Brill NV, Leiden, The Netherlands
Koninklijke Brill NV incorporates the imprints Brill, Brill Nijhoff, Brill Hotei, Brill Schöningh, Brill Fink, Brill mentis, Vandenhoeck & Ruprecht, Böhlau, V&R unipress and Wageningen Academic.
All rights reserved. No part of this publication may be reproduced, translated, stored in a retrieval system, or transmitted in any form or by any means, electronic, mechanical, photocopying, recording or otherwise, without prior written permission from the publisher. Requests for re-use and/or translations must be addressed to Koninklijke Brill NV via brill.com or copyright.com.

This book is printed on acid-free paper and produced in a sustainable manner.

To my cousin Christopher McGann

Contents

Acknowledgements IX

Introduction 1

1 The Unphenomenal
  "This Nothing's More than Matter" 29

2 The Spectre of the Cartesian Subject 60

3 Misrepresentations
  Shakespeare and the Phenomenologists 102

4 What Phenomenology? Kant to Levinas 126

5 Spontaneous Me 161

6 The Harm That Good Men and Women Do 173

7 Affective styles 205

8 A Pastoral Philosophy 221

9 What Matters in Shakespeare? 237

10 Undialing the Dialectic 275

11 The Maladies of Abstinence
   No More Cakes and Ale 297

12 The Naturalization of Reason
   Who Is Afraid of Ferdinand Derrida? 323

13 Doing Shakespeare
   To the Things Themselves 391

14 Reading Shakespeare
   Is There a Text in This Play? 415

15 If Caliban Is a Chimpanzee and Other Posthumanist Conditions   427

16 The Aesthetic Ideology   450

17 The Aesthetic Fallacy   466

18 The Fallacy of Representation   502

19 The Fallacy of Immediacy   529

20 The Fallacy of Presentism   557

Bibliographical References   587
Index of Names   612

Acknowledgements

In sections 7 and 19 I have included material that was published in the review sections of the *Shakespeare Jahrbuch* 151 (2015) and 156 (2020) respectively. I want to thank the editors of these two volumes for allowing me to reproduce it, and especially Stephan Laqué for inviting me to review. I am very grateful to Masja Horn, Clovis Jaillet, and Anita Opdam for their interest in this book and their help during the process of seeing it to press. The two readers at Brill made this difficult manuscript publishable. I am extremely grateful for their careful and generous reading of the original version, their judgement, and suggestions.

During the last three years, while nibbling around the edges of this project, I have been rarely honored with the epistolary friendship of an American scholar. This person has given me more genuine advice than I could translate into visible terms, more intellectual information than I could conceivably master, and more sense of proportion than I knew what to do with. For so much, my apologies, and my lasting gratitude.

Introduction

1

According to Richard Rorty, "the world does not speak. Only we do" (*Contingency* 6). Read today, this dictum runs against—in fact, ruins—the sacred truths currently worshipped by a dominant cult of institutional Shakespeareans, scholars who believe that what the bard wrote is altogether negligible, either because inferior to his non-verbal modes of expressive performance or because subservient to the world's speech—its sensuous noises, sounds and sweet airs. I want to rephrase the maxim—"The non-human world is speechless. Only we speak, and Shakespeare more significantly than most of us"—and disclose its latent coda: speech is a non-phenomenal part of the world, and so is significance. The incontrovertible fact that speech is determined, in the last instance, by writing—that speech *is* writing—may account for this dearth. I use, moreover, the adjective "incontrovertible" to prompt a straight profession of theoretical faith. Rorty was just one card. All are predictable enough, some have already been laid (*détermination, écriture, dernière instance*), and the rest will soon cover the table.[1]

In *Logiques des mondes* (2006), French philosopher Alain Badiou condensed the dogma of contemporary "democratic materialism" in the parallel statements that "there are only bodies and languages, or individuals and communities" and "there are only individuals and communities" and he famously impugned this "natural belief" by protesting that *there are* truths (*Logics* 4, 8; *Logiques* 12, 17). Badiou's absolutist faith in truths, let alone his often repulsive politics (his constant scorn of parliamentary democracy, voting, freedom of opinion …) are not exactly cards I will flaunt in my hand, but his critical discriminations are disarmingly lucid, and I will often use them during the game.[2] In this particular case, the above diagnosis captures much of what is at stake today in early modern studies, a field sadly overpowered by what Badiou, with Humean gusto, calls

---

1 The notion of *écriture* obviously presupposes Derridean assumptions, central to my book. The idea of a *détermination-en-dernière-instance* (*in letzer Instanz*) is a Marx-Engels principle discussed by important French thinkers like Louis Althusser and François Laruelle. See Althusser, "Contradiction and Overdetermination" in *For Marx*, 49–92, especially 74–79; and Laruelle, *Introduction to Non-Marxism*, 41–62.
2 Badiou's political stance informs all his work, but it receives obsequious attention in books like *Metapolitics* or *The Communist Hypothesis*. Unsavory jeremiads against the evils of parliamentary democracy and the democracy of opinion can still be found in his more recent *L'immanence des vérités*, 98–100, 238.

the "natural belief"—a condition, incidentally, that ipso facto redescribes the field as pre-phenomenological, however loud its protestation to the contrary. Let me explain. Although *democratic materialism* is a logo that befits a field glutted with "effects of equality"—a field where "everybody participates in the same intelligence" (Corcoran, "Introduction" to Rancière, *Dissensus* 3–5)—the truth is that in early modern studies languages and individuals went long ago extinct: natural *languages* (especially English) are deemed too abstract, elitist, Western, rational, exclusionary, and undemocratic, and *individuals*, everyone seems to concur, are just liberal aberrations. This leaves us with *bodies* and *communities*, communal bodies (liturgies), bodies in community (networks). And this is, I claim, where we are, in the phenomenal hustle and bustle that marks *le partage* of the Shakespearean *sensible*. The resulting remainder constitutes the prize and treasure of the phenomenal Shakespeare. So, and short of any appeal to truths, however immanent, the de-phenomenalization of the bard could conceivably be conducted through a return to individuals and languages. Or better, to the arch-individual (the poet or literary dramatist Shakespeare) and his natural language (English). Such de-phenomenalization is what in this book I partly intend to encourage, and the reader is right to expect a rather offbeat turning back of the clocks, for my arguments are unabashedly informed by liberal and formalist assumptions. Also humanist: I tend to believe, with Nietzsche, Foucault and Deleuze, that "it is in man himself that we must look for the set of forces and functions which resist the death of man" (Deleuze, *Foucault* 93). And I find no fault in acknowledging that Shakespeare is a man— i.e. a human being, however gendered—if not *the* man.

The present book takes the form of a refutation, though at times the term *diatribe* would seem more apropos. It is also animated by the traditional rhetorical mode of the supplication. In fact, I was tempted to title it, playing on a Pascal title, *Prière pour demander à Dieu le bon usage de Shakespeare*, but there was no point in vexing prospective publishers.[3] All in all, the final title imparts, I hope, the antagonistic nature of my book: I construe and brandish an *unphenomenal Shakespeare* against what I take to be the current phenomenalization of his work. In the "Introduction" to the *Criticism* issue dedicated to "Shakespeare and Phenomenology" (2012), Kevin Curran and David Kearney argue that "one of Husserl's maxims," namely the call "to recover 'things themselves,'" is "an apt description of early modern and Shakespeare studies of the past twenty years" (364). This is very true. But it doesn't follow that the maxim

---

3   Pascal's prayer, *Prière pour demander à Dieu le bon usage des maladies*, was first published as part of a book titled *Divers traités de piété* (Cologne, 1666). It was later included in some editions of his *Pensées*. All references to this text are taken from *Oeuvres complètes*.

INTRODUCTION   3

was correctly understood, let alone applied. The maxim was rather retranslated into terms suited to the drift in literary studies to move away from forms and reengage the real world, a tendency that harks back to the early seventies, when de Man made the following observation:

> To judge from various recent publications, the spirit of the times is not blowing in the direction of formalist and intrinsic criticism. We may no longer be hearing very much about relevance, but we do continue to hear a great deal about reference, about the non-verbal 'outside' to which language refers, by which it is conditioned, and upon which it acts.
> *Allegories of Reading* 3

At the time de Man formulated his diagnosis, phenomenology was only partly responsible for this anti-formalist drive. To be sure, de Man found much to blame phenomenology for (intentionalism, mentalist logicism, expressionist theories of meaning), but the new turn toward reference was spurred from other quarters, especially from those responsive to "history."[4] Today, instead, literary scholarship that craves for the "non-verbal 'outside'" is distinctly informed by "phenomenological" assumptions, some implicit, some explicit, some correct, and some wrong.

2

This book is an attempt to unmask the theoretical insufficiency and hermeneutic poverty of the critical practices that, in their approach to Shakespeare, consciously or unwittingly seek support in phenomenology as a philosophical doctrine, in whichever of its versions—the early Husserl, the late Husserl, Merleau-Ponty's body-oriented phenomenology, Levinasian phenomenology, historical phenomenology. In Section 4 I offer a succinct overview of phenomenology in a historical perspective, from Kant to Levinas: the reader who is not conversant with this philosophical school is invited to start there and then return to this point. Perhaps the most alarming symptom of the poverty I denounce is lodged in a clinging misconstruction: *the matters at hand* (*Sache selbst*) in Husserl's acclaimed maxim have been invariably mistranslated as *things themselves* (*Dinge selbst*), thus prompting the grossly empiricist

---

4   For a sharp reflection on de Man's prophetic gesture, and the ironic aftermaths, see Warminski, "Ending Up/Taking Back (with Two Postscripts on Paul de Man's Historical Materialism)" in *Material Inscriptions*, 159–189.

naturalization of a philosophical method (Husserl's) distinctly characterized by transcendental discretion—whence the return to the "natural belief," to what Husserl called "the natural standpoint [*natürliche Einstellung*]" (*Ideas I* §27). Bruce Smith's book *Phenomenal Shakespeare*, a much-cited landmark in the consolidation of this critical approach to the English poet's work, offers an adept illustration of this particular mode of philosophical incompetence: a text that makes grandiose philosophical claims, vaunts its cutting-edge theoretical novelty, but that, in its sustained inability to assume the formal, transcendental, structural and dialectical demands posed by Saussure and Derrida, falls back into a crude pre-reflective empiricism—what Husserl himself attacked as "naiven Positivität" (*Cartesianische* 179) and thinkers like Hegel, Marx, Nietzsche, Freud and Heidegger worked hard to eradicate. *And all for nothing!* (*Hamlet* 2.2.534).[5] For all intents and purposes, what Smith and his followers promote is "a return to a misunderstood natural life" (Marx, *Grundrisse* 83), to the misconstruction Husserl described as "naturalistische Missdeutung" (*Ideen I* 33). It is important to note, at the outset, that Husserl's unquestionable philosophical originality stemmed largely from his selective ignorance of the history of philosophy. This applies too to the early Wittgenstein, but the Austrian philosopher turned his artlessness into a very powerful weapon. By contrast, Husserl's refusal to come to grips with Hegel's speculative dialectic—a refusal that determined too the "dialectical-speculative inhibition/limitation marking Heideggerian phenomenological ontology" (Johnston 373)—is the "material cause" of the philosophical poverty of soi-disant phenomenological thinkers today. The most visible effect of the workings of naïve positivism is the neglect of holistic presuppositions (considerations of determinations of totality) in favour of some anaemic suppositions, many fanciful positions, peregrine positionings, and a great deal of posing.

The fact that the ontic opulence of the *phenomenal* received bad press already amongst early promoters of the game of phenomenology like Levinas should not overawe us. In his first essay on Levinas, Jacques Derrida rightly observed that the new "discipline of the question" of genuine philosophical origins that the author of *Totalité et infini* had inaugurated was firmly at odds with

---

5 *All for Nothing: Hamlet's Negativity* is the title of Andrew Cutrofello's excellent book on the diverse philosophical reactions to *Hamlet*. The book's focus on negativity reveals an estimation of speculative dialectics that is one of the signature passions of its author, a specialist on Kant-Hegel who is also alert to the contemporary drift of dialectical thought in Žižek or Badiou. All quotations from Shakespeare are from the Norton Edition, based on the Oxford text, edited by Stephen Greenblatt, Walter Cohen, Jean E. Howard, and Katharine Eiseman Maus (New York: Norton, 2007). In the case of *King Lear*, I use the conflated version prepared by Barbara K. Lewalski for this edition.

"the inconceivable tradition of the negative (of negative determination), and [...] is completely previous (*antérieure*) to irony, to maieutics, to *epoché*, and to doubt" (*Writing* 80; *L'écriture* 118). I quote this admonitory aside not only because it helps us grasp how distant from Levinasian prophecy lies Shakespeare's textual world, but also because it offers a germane *a contrario* description of this world, one certainly sustained by the tradition of the negative and riddled by irony, maieutic dialogism, and suspense-promoting doubt. A world, in short, adverse to harmonic and profusive phenomenalization. Shakespeare was a rationalist skeptic, and his meanings are unphenomenal in a radical sense of the word—a sense not contemplated by Levinas' constant outmaneuvering (interruption, reduction, neutralization) of phenomenology in overly transcendent (not transcendental) directions.[6] That is why Derrida's concession that Levinas's "phénomène est une certaine non-phénoménalité, que sa présence (*est*) une certaine absence" (*L'écriture* 135) holds limited value for the argument I put forward in this book.[7] Whereas it may be correct to observe, as Derrida does, that Levinas impugns the helio-politics inherent to Platonic epistemology and ontology—the seemingly necessary correlation between Being, truth, self and light—it is not totally irrelevant to note that *visage*, perhaps the central trope in Levinas eschatological ethics, derives etymologically from *visus* and *videre* (to see).[8] This investment in self-cum-other-centered photo-epistemology seriously compromises the anti-Platonism of the whole venture. Levinas, of course, would have never concurred with Giordano Bruno that *umbra profunda sumus*: his primeval soup is an ethical and metaphysical, at bottom scriptural-mythical, scene of reciprocal seeing, and a little *lumière* is after all required for the ecstasies—Merleau-Ponty would say *flashes*—of face-to-face inspection.[9] Neither would Shakespeare, true enough, whose helio-politics, though inflected by the clinamen of the *perjured eye*, are ontological in the sense despised by the French philosopher—they are, that is, plagued by figures of violence, war, totality, selfishness, reason and systematicity. They are, moreover, post- or pre-metaphysical, and therefore genuinely anti-Platonic, in that they turn "toward the power of metaphor itself to posit a world that lies beyond

---

6   For the Levinasian *interruption* of phenomenology, see Derrida, *Adieu à Emmanuel Levinas*, 95–96. The terms *reduction* and *neutralisation* are used by Derrida: "Violence et métaphysique" in *L'écriture et la différence*, 143.

7   Derrida resumes discussion of the "non-phénoménalisation originaire" in *L'écriture*, 181.

8   Derrida recalls this etymology later in his essay, without registering contradiction: *L'écriture*, 146.

9   Bruno's famous apothegm is drawn from *De umbris idearum* (1582). See Ciliberto, 15–20. According to Merleau-Ponty, "To have a body is to be looked at (it is not only that), it is to be visible—Here the impression of telepathy, of the occult = vivacity in reading the look of the other in a flash—Should we say reading?" (*Visible* 189–190).

phenomenality" (Lukacher, *Daemonic* 73). These figures of violence, reason and totality portend, I submit, Shakespeare's particular way of being unphenomenal, and this is hardly news to those aware that *Shakespeare's Problem Plays*, the title of E.M.W. Tillyard's remarkable book, is a reductionist misnomer because all of Shakespeare's plays are problematic in the sense therein described—they are, that is, bitter, satirical, cynical, and infused with "speculative thought" (*Shakespeare's Problem* 14).[10] Perhaps Heraclitean *polemos* or unphenomenal *waltender Streit* as a conflict that predominates in advance of human and divine wars, as the contraposition (*Ausereinandersetzung*) of immaterial letters opening up the field of writing and culture, comes even closer to the Shakespearean configuration, one where bastard letters speed, and crooked inventions thrive (*King Lear* 1.2.19–20).[11] Did Levinas—the philosopher of non-violence—enjoy *The Tempest*?[12] Did anyone ever *enjoy* it? Are we thrilled by "the very structures of a world in which war would rage— strange conditional—if the infinitely other were not infinity, if there were, by chance, one naked man, finite and alone (*un homme nu, fini, et seul*)" (Derrida, *L'écriture* 107; 158)? Whose visage expresses in *The Tempest* the absolving infinity of this unzipped phenomenology? To whose naked, finite, and lonely body would that face belong? To Prospero's, Caliban's, or Miranda's? Is *enjoy* the verb that best describes our response to the text or performance of *The Merchant of Venice, Troilus and Cressida, Hamlet*, or *The Tempest*? Jouissance vis-à-vis the phenomenal? Really? The fact that Levinas urged repeatedly that Autrui was "irréductible à la phénoménalité" (*Totalité* 233–34), or that Derrida obsequiously glossed his move—away from Husserl—towards *non-phénoménalité*, doesn't make his world-view any more amenable to the *unphenomenal conditions* I shall invoke in this book as specific *to* Shakespeare. But note that unphenomenal doesn't mean unreal or lacking in experience. On the contrary. Nothing describes better Shakespeare's artistic personality than Althusser's

---

10   Perhaps what the *problem plays* share is a decidedly daemonic tropological atmosphere: "The positing power of language to reveal that there is the 'other' of phenomenality, the realm of the hiddenness of the sun's essence, is metaphor in the fundamental sense that Heidegger calls daemonic" (Lukacher, *Daemonic* 73).
11   See Derrida's analysis of Heidegger's translation and comment of fragment 53 of Heraclitus: *Politiques de l'amitié*, 403–404.
12   Levinas' understanding of language as originating in a primeval educational-moral rapport between a subject and its "Maître" may throw light on the brutal scene of instruction (Miranda and Prospero vis-à-vis Caliban) that underpins the *The Tempest*'s improbable sociological ecosystem, but his notion that "la societé est le lieu de la vérité" (*Totalité* 104) is at bottom eminently un-Shakespearean. Derrida holds that for Levinas "phénoménologie et ontologie seraient donc des philosophies de la violence" (136).

account of Marx's "extraordinary theoretical temperament, animated by an insatiable critical passion, an intransigent insistence on reality, and a prodigious feeling for the concrete" (*For Marx* 34). In fact, the best characterization of his social thought can be found in Victoria Kahn's summary of the parallels between Machiavelli and Spinoza: "For both, power was a relation of forces, a shifting calculus, through which individuals and the multitude could exert their wills. Neither was naïve about the virtues of the people or their intelligence" (*Future* 145–46).

3

I understand that there are people who hold beliefs in modes of communication (languages) that deviate from the rational, contingent, arbitrary, negative, and mediation-driven structuredness of most naturales languages, in pre-rational languages informed by the human body (Merleau-Ponty), or anti-rational languages deformed by the tension of an infinite alterity (Levinas). I myself am uninterested in these two forms of communication, but I respect their relevance for others. What I find disturbing is that some Shakespeare scholars seek to persuade us that the bard's genuine language is either pre-rational or anti-rational, or that his real meanings were encoded in either kind of language. This is, may I say, a very silly perversion of academic thought. There may still exist today devout musicologists who protest "Ok, yes, there is Bach's written music (the scores of his cantatas, fugues, oratorios, motets ...), but the music that he really meant, the one that really mattered to him and consequently to us is the music he cherished in his heart, the music of God, which never (alas) received adequate expression," but it is hard to believe they draw much scholarly attention. Things are different with Shakespeare. The scholastic perversion takes on a distinctly acritical modality of presentation—a crude combination of moralism and empiricism: the meaning of Shakespeare's plays, they tell us, is in the *good* Shakespeare *things*, these things being the attending *matters,* the sustaining *affections*, the supporting *communities* of his phenomenal *Lebenswelt*. We thus return to the perverted humanism that Marx and Engels stood up to—"une idéologie morale d'essence religieuse, prêchée par des petits-bourgeois en civil" (Althusser, "La querelle de l'humanisme," *Écrits philosophiques II* 476). Deleuze argued that the originality of Kant's *critical* philosophy sprang from his very early determination to challenge "d'avance les decisions empiriques et les tribunaux théologiques" (*La philosophie critique* 7). The phenomenal Shakespeare I discuss in this book is a tin god uncritically concocted, on the one hand, by the *empiricist decisions* of neo-materialists, historical phenomenologists, and object-oriented scholars, and on the other, by the *theological tribunals* of affect-oriented academics, ethically-turned and face-to-face-leaning scholars, and neo-Puritan critics morally pledged to a strong Idea (group identity, social community, cosmic membership, the *Umwelt*). The empiricists tell us that Shakespeare's meanings are stored in the objectal, corporal, networked, communal matters of the world, and the divines simply see the meanings the empiricists propose, and, behold, they are very good. Derrida's essay on Levinas dates back to 1964, and Deleuze's study of Kant was published only one year earlier. I am writing, I know, a very old book. I wasn't even born when I wrote it.

Because a *phenomenal Shakespeare* is, first and foremost, a non-critical Shakespeare, its refutation demands a reactivation of the Kantian precept to be *nothing if not critical (Othello* 2.1.122).[13] My book, therefore, aims to be critical, and is adversarial and deliberately polemic. It is not, strictly speaking, a book about Shakespeare, but rather about *how we read and how we might* read Shakespeare. I claim that the way we read Shakespeare's texts today is so extensively controlled by vaguely phenomenological assumptions about immediacy, embodiment, intersubjective action, and the life-world, so broadly quickened by the elision of mediation, that these texts are very likely to remain unread. The way, in short, we read Shakespeare now is by not reading his texts—or rather, by *reading into* them so much metaphysical *presence* (aesthetic *representation*, historical *present*, embodied-communal *presentment*, environmental *presents*) that their linguistic-textual dimension—a transcendental structure affording differential spacing, dialectical tension, systemic arbitrariness, and figural mediation—is likely to fade away unrecognized. With it goes, I believe, much of what is truly meaningful in the standard Shakespeare text, not least its dialectically internalized awareness of its being a text. But, of course, the gathering neo-phenomenological armies have no time for dialectics or internalization, not to mention textuality. I characterize their assumptions as "vaguely phenomenological" because they rarely conform to the idealist and transcendental-constitutive spirit of Husserl's original philosophical project. This spirit, I submit, is much more Cartesian than some of Husserl's followers, working under the influence of Merleau-Ponty, are willing to acknowledge. Indeed, to judge the problematic impact of Merleau-Ponty's "phenomenology of the flesh" (Derrida, *On Touching* 184) in early modern studies, and in

---

13   To my mind, *Iago is Shakespeare* is a far less crude overstatement than *Shylock is Shakespeare,* the title of Kenneth Gross's interesting book. Less unrealistic, less candid, and, yes, perhaps, less phenomenal.

INTRODUCTION

particular in Shakespeare studies, is one of this book's attendant goals: if the goal is not fulfilled, I at least contribute, I hope, to identify a pattern.

4

Such influence is discernible in Bruce Smith's important monograph *Phenomenal Shakespeare* (2010), whose title I deliberately tip over in mine, and whose ideas I rather strongly controvert. Smith's theoretical investments become explicit in the way he openly invokes Husserl and phenomenology. But he takes, alas, both names in vain. His misreading of Husserl prompts him to further, related, misconstructions—the misreadings, for instance, of Descartes, Saussure, and Derrida—which have become the stock-in-trade of the early modern literary scholar that aspires to pull off as critically engaged and theoretically attached in the quick-sands of the new millennium. The opening chapter of Smith's book, titled "As It Likes You," presents his "theoretical" argument as a sustained defense of phenomenological "framing," an epistemological strategy that encourages, in his view, the corporal positioning of the knower inside—not before, not outside, not above—an objectal stage. In a distinctively anti-theoretical move, this "theoretical" defense is carried out as a rebuttal of rationalism (Descartes, Hegel, Saussure, Derrida).[14] Most strands of my book are woven through with a *filo rosso* whose aim is to penetrate and deflate the futile premises subtending such rebuttal. I defend Descartes and Derrida from anti-rationalist, vaguely phenomenological charges in sections 2 and 16, respectively. Although in Section 11 I conduct a refutation of Smith's erroneous appropriation of Husserl's ideas, my whole book is animated by a resolve to oppugn what I take to be the gratuitous and gratuitously misguided co-optation of phenomenology by Shakespearean hermeneuts. Smith's misreading of Saussure is also representative of a wider trend of anti-structuralist or anti-theoretical animosity that harkens back at least to Brian Vickers's *Appropriating Shakespeare: Contemporary Critical Quarrels* (1993), a book that devotes seventy prefatory pages to the ideas of the Swiss linguist. Why should misreading Saussure prove so expedient, so necessary and vital, for an effective phenomenalization of Shakespeare is a question I try to answer in section 12, "The Naturalization of Reason." But let me anticipate something: during the seventeen years that elapsed between Vickers's *Appropriating Shakespeare*

---

14 The term *anti-theoretical* is vaguely inspired in Badiou, who often speaks of *anti-philosophers* like Kierkegaard, Wittgenstein, and Lacan.

(1993) and Smith's *Phenomenal Shakespeare* (2010) the tendency either to overlook or despise French structuralist and poststructuralist theory became dominant in Shakespeare studies. Vickers's massive monograph did a service to the field by ridiculing the deluge of sloppy, second-hand, theoretical papers that, pretending to seek support in the tradition of Lacan, Althusser, Foucault, de Man and Derrida, were merely lifting decontextualized concepts from school-text introductions to theory and misapplying (regurgitating) them (on)to Renaissance literary texts. But Vickers in turn cut a slightly ridiculous figure when he sought to cross swords with the thinkers whose work had prompted the deluge. Here he miscalculated his strengths. Not only was his book informed by an odd proprietorial impetus—Vickers condemned the alienation or mis-*appropriation* of Shakespeare by foreign thinkers, implying through a subdued *Jargon der Eigentlichkeit* that there is a *proper* Shakespeare guarded by English pragmatic and philological traditions of common sense. His aim was also imprudently ambitious. By including the Swiss Saussure not only did he assign a strong commander to the French-speaking enemy contingent, already made of French and Belgian soldiers. He placed himself in the risky position to engage in body combat with the author of the *Cours*, and, as I seek to prove in section 12, he didn't exactly leave the field unscathed. But this is just a symptom. The moral of my story is that the *phenomenological turn* in Shakespeare studies could only safely take place once the field had been expurgated of structuralist (what I call speculative-dialectical) theoretical assumptions, and that this expurgation necessarily rested on the denigration of Saussure. The temporal arc that goes from Vickers's to Smith's book covers a critical trajectory (the denigration of Saussure, the expurgation of structuralist assumptions, the turn to phenomenology) that is implicitly reenacted by every scholar (Harris, Curran, Raber, Lupton) whose open or unspoken intention is to champion a *phenomenal Shakespeare*. If I subtitle my book "Pending Critical Quarrels" it is because I believe that the "Contemporary Critical Quarrels" Vickers identified in his book remain still open and unresolved.

Shorn of its theoretical-conceptual ballast, Bruce Smith's *Phenomenal Shakespeare* offers three readings of three particular Shakespeare texts: sonnet 29, *Venus and Adonis* and *King Lear*. Let us consider each of these readings in turn. In the second chapter, titled "How Should One Read a Shakespeare Sonnet?," Smith invites us to read and see sonnet 29 "strangely" (39) by way of a supposedly phenomenological act of "bracketing." This estrangement is achieved, he believes, by means of a presentation of the sonnet that enhances its relation to the human body: first, by considering the material (touchable) reality of the 1609 quarto, second, by speculating on the reader's handwriting of the poem, and third, by carefully examining a version of the sonnet interpreted into American Sign Language. In the three versions (holding the printed quarto, handwriting the poem, watching the poem's signing) there is an evident interaction between the poem and the human hand. Smith argues that the possibility of such exchange is less a contingent possibility built into the poem's reception than evidence of the poem's meaning's constitutive reliance on a body-oriented conceptual competence he describes as "thought-without-speech" or "thought *before* words" (54–55). The existence of such cognitive competence would seriously challenge, he believes, the Saussurean emphasis on the discontinuous "markings of difference": "language begins, not in mental acts of marking, but in movements of the body" (64).

In the second chapter on *Venus and Adonis* he seeks to convince us that the poem cannot be properly understood without considering an ecology of human-nonhuman synergy, awash with "kinesthetic pleasures" (109), the entwining of "human subjects with plants and animals" (128) and gender-fluidity interactions. Part of his argument goes into the demonstration that recursive patterns of "phenomenological framing" (117) ensconced in the poem bring about an effective unframing of the rigid subject-object positioning in conventional reading processes, inviting the reader/sensor to participate as an actant in the poem's represented inter-action. Smith proposes an "ecological reading" of the poem that "will attend not just to the paradigm of characters—world at hand [...] but also to the paradigm of reader—world-at-hand" (86), and to that end mobilizes a "paradigm of phenomenal knowing," with the reader/sensor engaged with the "world-at-hand," to replace an *epistemic scene* dominated by the "third-person observer" with an *aesthetic scene* (an "ambient poetics") ruled by an economy of two (86). The rejected epistemic scene takes in "evidence brought forward in court records, medical books, conduct books, and Saussure-inspired readings of literary texts" (86). The new aesthetic scene frames the poem as a reality that "heightens ambiguity about the boundaries of the self" (86) and produces a "carnal knowledge" that "can be *tasted*" (101).

In the fourth chapter on *King Lear*, titled "Touching Moments," Smith revisits his argument about the centrality of kinesthesia and body-based, integrative, common-sense, in the re-construction of Shakespearean meaning. *King Lear*'s overall "feelingness" (134), a notion Smith coins prompted by Gloucester's claim to see "feelingly" (*King Lear* 4.5.145), is first evinced by the parallel hand-experiments of holding a quarto, touching the "inked signs," and reading a Braille translation of the play. In all three cases tactility mediates the apprehension of a meaning that is quite literally, Smith argues via a putative Husserl echo, "*at hand*" (135). In his view, "*The Tragedy of King Lear* is replete with moments in which words become physical presences" (162), with "words themselves" becoming "assault weapons" (163) and having "their effect on epidermis and nerves" (164). Smith also calls attention to the prominence of "tongue" and "tongues" in the play, which "never lets an audience forget that words are more than signifiers" (166). He contends that the "linguistics" of Saussure and Derrida is not "answerable to the movings of the mind" and that we need "a linguistics that takes into account touch as well as speech, seeing as well as hearing, feeling as well as decoding" (166). Drawing on Artaud, he champions a "language of nature," a kind of "inner speech" based on analogy, not equivalence, whose idea is deeper than the Saussure-inspired construal of language we find in Lacan or deconstruction (170–171). Following theoreticians of gesture-language, Smith invokes an understanding of language that locates meaning-making in "the constantly moving human body" (173). Of course, such focus on meaning, intention and the pre-verbal is parallel to Husserl's assimilation of intention (*Meinen*) to ante-predicative evidence (*Méditations cartésiennes* 30–31).[15]

The theory, in sum, is disappointingly shallow: guided by two phenomenological tools—*framing* and the *world at-hand*—Smith attempts to replace the Saussurean (arbitrary, differential, negative, relational) *langue* with a conjectural *language of nature* or *thought-without-language* that may account for what he takes to be Shakespeare's *ambient poetics*. As I pointed out above, I will carefully consider each of these theoretical problems in upcoming sections. What concerns me at this point is less the congruity of the theoretical articulation than its relevance for the Shakespearean readings that make up his book. Is it necessary to deploy these theoretical (philosophical, linguistic) tools in order to assert a phenomenal "in-between" that is, according to Smith, what is actually "touching" about Shakespeare (XVIII)? My query begs of course the question, for I would certainly oppose the claim that Merleau-Ponty's sentence, "the touching is never exactly the touched," is the maxim that holds the key to Shakespeare's singular significance.[16] Still, this maxim, in its English version, betokens the kind of ambiguity whose dependence on etymology, and therefore on philology, is only imperfectly concealed by Smith. Otherwise put, the best of Smith's readings are his etymological insights, the way he brings to light the hidden physical meaning of a supposedly abstract term. This kind of insight—good old *Etymologie als Denkform* (Curtius)—attended by claims

---

15 I will sometimes use the original French edition of Husserl's text (1931), translated from the 1929 German lectures by Gabrielle Pfeiffer and Emmanuele Levinas.
16 See Merleau-Ponty, *The Visible*, 254. Smith closes his "Prologue" to *Phenomenal Shakespeare* with a gloss of Merleau-Ponty's dictum (*Phenomenal*, xviii). Derrida's deconstruction of Merleau-Ponty's misreading of Husserl apropos of touching can be found in *On Touching*, 159–215. His comments on the above dictum can be found in 213–215.

of deconstructive tropology (Nietzsche, Blumenberg, Derrida, de Man) and framed within a generic reading strategy that contextualizes the text through a cultural poetics sensible to juridical and visual-arts documents would have been enough to render his readings productive.[17] Smith obviously rejects deconstructive tropology, but he deftly, if incompletely, enacts the cultural-poetics reading strategy. This is regrettable, for the former would surely complement the findings of the latter, as well as furnish them with a convenient philological grounding. The reading of *Venus and Adonis*, for instance, is more focused on visual material than on the text itself, and he is at pains to demonstrate that the logic organizing the visual materials (prints by Jacob Matham, Philps Galle, Crispijn de Passe, Van Dyck's double portrait, etc.) obtains too in Shakespeare's poem. In the reading of the sonnet, enhanced philological attention would render more effective the excavation of the latent physical implications of the terms' etymologies, as well as the identification of all the topological coordinates that are mapped out by the interaction of pronouns and spatial deictics. For instance, the probing of the etymology of *state*, realized at the chapter's close, could have been complemented with the etymological elucidation of terms like *outcast*, *remembered*, and *featured*, for all suggest the *manual* operations of the self. But this philological intensification would surely compromise Smith's suggestion that "by attending to pronouns" and "embracing middle voice" we may be able to assume the subject position of "one" that is latent in the term "state" in the line "I alone beweep my outcast *state*" (80–81). As it turns out, few English sonnets invest more strongly on the egological resources of the pronominal markers "I," "my" and "myself." Thought, Smith argues, "is not just words but bodily gesture, an extension of the speaker's body into the ambient space" (80), but this sonnet is an affair of self-centered words, of word-made self-reflection—"and look upon myself" (4)—and "the speaker's body" amounts to a spectral inference, a hauntological rebus reached through the examination of verbal traces, what he calls "marks." Furthermore, Smith seems to forget that a signer is a human that primarily and originally *reads* existing *markings*, and tries to translate them into body-gestures, and not retrieve, let alone produce, pre-differential sense or

---

17   It is surprising that Derrida, who never ceased to pursue etymological paths in order to substantiate speculative insights, should speak in 1964 of "l'empirisme étymologique, racine caché de toute empirisme" (*L'écriture* 204). Still, what he condemns here is the kind of etymological research that remains unaware of the central role of rhetoricity in the constitution of conceptual meaning: "Empiricism is thinking *by* metaphor without thinking the metaphor *as such*" (139).

antepredicative meanings.[18] Smith also forgets that the term *state* is there less to be immediately naturalized than to be mediated by similar artificial-cultural occurrences in Petrarca's *Canzoniere*—"Ma del misero stato oven noi semo" (8.9), "benigna mi redusse al primo stato" (23.135), "né so quant'io mi viva in questo stato" (37.32), "mostrato quale / era 'l mio stato" (97.3) "In questo stato son, donna, per voi" (134.14), "Come m'avete in basso stato messo" (298.14)—and beyond (Garcilaso de la Vega, Du Bellay, Spenser). A *state* is less an organic datum than a cultural, polysemous trope. But anyway: do you need forty-three pages of historical-phenomenological elucidation to reach the conclusion you had originally posited as premise, that "thought is not just words but bodily gesture, an extension of the speaker's body into ambient space" (80)? Is it reasonable or critically legitimate to use sonnet 29 for that demonstration? Does the sonnet really allow you to instrumentalize it for that end, to prove that "difference-marking might not be the beginning of meaning-marking"? And does your "historical-phenomenological" claim about the original sonnet reader's manual contact with the quarto work in fact as further evidence of the soundness of the argument? The implicit claim "Since I can touch the sonnet, the sonnet is also or primarily about touching" strikes me as a deeply naïve inference. It overlooks the structural-transcendental bearing that both language as a system and the literary system, in particular the tradition of the sonnet, have on the private act of reading, then and now, a Shakespeare sonnet. It reminds me of Roy Harris's excellent caricature of Bateson's misreading of Saussure—"It is rather as if one were to describe how tennis is played by insisting that the only part of the game that the two players both share is the trajectory of the ball between one racquet and the other" (*Reading Saussure* 10)—which is pretty much like "responding to Zeno by walking across a room" (McDowell, *Mind* xxi). In other words, something more than the particular game—i.e. internalized rules, structural habits, normative determinacy, arbitrary conventions—is at stake in the particular game. There is something more to space than space—and remember that writing generates space.

In the case of *Venus and Adonis*, Smith's appeal to kinesthetic interactivity is sensible enough, but his reading doesn't add much to the existing scholarship on the poem's Ovidian metamorphic tropology and vagarious eroticism.

---

18   The antiquarian-romantic conception of translation as an operation that restores (or restitutes: *Sinnwiedergabe*) the original meaning (actually, a pure language) buried in the false original is of course a well-known Benjaminian mystification. In "Des tours de Babel," Derrida carefully unpacks the "scholastic-phenomenological" assumptions on which Benjamin's romantic delusion rests. See *Psyché: Inventions de l'autre 1*, 203–235; especially 232–234.

The argument is shot through with inconsistencies. For one, the notion that the third-person position of the voyeur (judge, analyst, witness, reader) is forborne, is contradicted by Smith's constant recourse to a "lascivious gaze" in a "scene of voyeurism" (92), with the voyeur spying "into the fiction from without" (93). To claim that the "final subject position" is *ours*, both that of the poem's protagonists (Venus, Adonis) and that of the reader (98), does not revoke the ironic-rational, inquisitive exteriority of the reader's position: if all characters involved (Venus, Adonis, the eroticized or scandalized or indifferent reader) end up fusing into a consistent *we*, then this plural persona is less a subject of pluri-erotic fusions than an aggregate subject of sadistic observation. *Venus and Adonis* is not, as Smith aims to prove, a parable of "carnal knowledge" staging "the melting of body into body and body into the world-at-hand" (131). It is rather a critical fable of verbal supervision. Smith overlooks the radical *intangibility* claimed by some of Shakespeare's most significant *personae*, characters like Hamlet or Cordelia: their refusal to speak their hearts spells a mode of inviolable pronominal solipsism—a mental *noli me tangere*— that is liable to sociological inspection, as in Richard Wilson's brilliant *Secret Shakespeare*, yet surely not so open as to dissolve into the primordial soup of the phenomenal we/one.[19] Lucrece's and Adonis's tragic resistance to ravishing reads as Shakespeare's early exploration of this problem.

With respect to Smith's interpretation of *King Lear*, it strikes me as fruitlessly reiterative. His notation that the play's words are like weapons that we can actually feel adds little to Bradley's shock at Lear's "appalling imprecations" (*Tragedy* 261) or Wilson Knight's account of the way Lear invokes forces and deities "to execute natural punishment" (*Wheel* 189). Frankly, the mobilization of phenomenological vocabulary does not make the extant "liberal-humanist" interpretation—a reading that remains essentially uncontested—progress in any discernible direction. Besides, you do not need to be Poirot to realize that *King Lear*, like *Wuthering Heights*, "is replete with moments in which words become physical presences" (Smith, *Phenomenal* 162). The physicalizing of words is after all one of the central issues of the play, one that is consciously thematized by agents as well as victims of verbal abuse (insult, curse, repudiation, slander). Still, Shakespeare is not oblivious to the fact that a finite reality poses limits to the finite infinity of figuration, that certain things (say, words and bodies) are simply incommensurable, and that while Lear murders his daughters only figuratively through verbal weapons, Gloucester's eyes are

---

19 Wilson deals with Catholic touching in *Romeo and Juliet* in *Secret Shakespeare*, 148–149. For Hamlet's and Cordelia's recalcitrant resistance to confession and self-revelation, see 22 and 34.

actually pulled out by Cornwall's hands, and the servant slain by his sword. In a play that moves inexorably to its final "gored state" (*King Lear* 5.3.319), one should abstain from pushing the analogy too far. Language doesn't kill. Only we do. If language could kill, *Hamlet* would be a very short comedy.

5

Disinterest in, or ignorance of, a rationalist-dialectical construal of transcendental-materialist mediation that is necessarily indebted to a speculative-dialectical—Gasché would call it "reflexive" (*Mirror* 15)—tradition broadly understood (Plato, Descartes, Kant, Hegel, Marx, Derrida), has led to the kind of ingenuous return to affection-driven empiricism and *Lebenswelt* positivism that Smith's work swimmingly epitomizes. Many of the critical trends I inventory in my book—neo-materialism, ecocriticism, physiological materialism, speculative realism, posthumanism—rely, when making inroads into Shakespeare territory, consciously or unintentionally on similar misrepresentations as well on a parallel disdain for the benefits of dialectical insight. Scholars following these trends are hardly able "to withstand the temptation of naturalism" (Zahavi, *Husserl's Legacy* 6). While it may be wise to respond to a hand touchingly with another hand—"Let me have thy hand … There is my hand" (*Antony and Cleopatra* 2.2.153–156)—it is much wiser, I believe, to reciprocate a mirror (even a broken, convex mirror) with something preferably of a "glassy essence" (*Measure for Measure* 2.2.124). The act of responding to a mirror (the Shakespeare text) with a hand (the phenomenological critic's) that only aspires to caress its embodied surface is bound to lapse into affective, narcissistic, and self-congratulatory silence. Critical masturbation is the other likeliest outcome. The solacing stillness of "a facticity confronted with another facticity" (Kates, *Derrida* 182) is moreover the net result of the moralistic turn of a post-1970s academic intelligentsia that merrily embarked on the cooptation of Shakespeare into group-identity politics of the most diverse nature: ecocritical Shakespeare, posthumanist Shakespeare, communitarian Shakespeare, material Shakespeare, ethical Shakespeare, face-to-face Shakespeare. In 1993 Graham Bradshaw foresaw that "the advance into the Radiant Future of ideological critique can also be seen as a return to the critical Dark Ages" (8). He was right. What he called *ideological critique*, the work then of cultural materialists and neo-historicists, names a flagrant reversal of the good old *Ideologiekritik* (Sloterdijk, *Kritik* 53) and has been replaced by expansive and candid modes of moralistic and increasingly de-theorized critique. Phenomenology is, for most of the scholars therein engaged, not only a prestige-conferring category in a critical scenario progressively bereft of philosophical grounding. It is also a prefabricated conceptual tool-kit allowing them access to the Shakespearean *Sache selbst*. For, of course, their cooptation of Shakespeare can only succeed if the reflexive and dialectical power of his texts has been properly defused in advance. "Always dedialecticize!" thus runs the implicit motto spurring the critical endeavors of a generation of phenomenology-oriented Shakespeare scholars (Bruce Smith, Kevin Curran, Scott Maisano, Jonathan Gil Harris, Karen Raber, Sanford Budick, Joseph Campana, Gabriel Egan). The explicit slogan is, of course, "Always phenomenalize!" or "Forever phenomenal!" The fact that four particularly brilliant Shakespeare critics like Richard Wilson, Julia Lupton, Simon Palfrey, and Paul Kottman, have partly sacrificed their erstwhile dialectical flare for the facile gratifications—embodied presence, immediate intersubjectivity, aesthetic representation, the historical present—of neo-phenomenological exegesis is further proof of the preponderance of anti-speculative methods in Shakespeare studies today. In the present book I conduct some brief close readings of some of what I take to be their recent *misreadings*. I may, of course, be the one who misreads. In fact my claim is not that I am more correct than these brilliant scholars. What I do claim is to identify a trend and to construe what I take to be its attendant hermeneutic misprision in the terms that the contrary trend would parse it. Since formulations of the contrary trend are difficult to come by—or fail to emerge *tout court*—I merely posit an adversarial claim that may lend the contrary arguments a local habitation and a name. In other words, I play the devil's advocate: if phenomenology-oriented readings of Shakespeare are misled, I provide a set of reasons that help elucidate the cause of their shared *Missdeutung*. If, on the contrary, they fare, then one may retain the analytical basis of my intended refutation and proceed to reverse its valence: when you read "This is how it works and is silly" flip it over into "This is how it works and is great." This may sound sophistic, but it is not. There is no sophistry in trying to find out *how* things work, and I only claim to explain how these readings jointly or similarly operate, partly because I favor *critical explanations* over *doctrinal intimations*—what Bradshaw called *ideological critique*, which is never critique—but also because I am surprised at the fact that no scholar working in the field appears to feel the need to do so in this particular case. Perhaps it is useful to add that I am not, have never been, that particular thing, a specialized scholar working in the Shakespeare field. In the humanities, I mistrust narrow specialization, especially that of name-oriented disciplines (Milton Studies, Joyce Studies, Dickinson Studies), and look ahead—in fact, more often back—to the open, un-demarcated fields of English, comparative literature, and literary theory. I told you: this is a very old book.

I was tempted to use "A Refutation" as a subtitle, but this would have been, I am aware, hardly a selling point. This brings me to the second problem I take up in my book, the positive question of *how we might read* Shakespeare, as I contend that there is indeed a tradition of speculative-dialectical readings of the English poet's texts, quite often openly inspired in Hegel, Marx, or Derrida, that may be upheld against phenomenology-oriented hermeneutics. This tradition is best represented by the work of Joel Fineman, Jonathan Goldberg, Stephen Orgel, Richard Halpern, Marjorie Garber, Catherine Belsey, Margreta de Grazia, Nicholas Royle, Ned Lukacher and Andrew Cutrofello. I take Shakespeare's oeuvre to hold a middle ground between philosophy and literature, to span the dialectical continuum where both textual practices continually interact. Just as, according to Adorno, good literature is designed to resist its own meanings—its mimetic figuration, its representations—so genuine philosophy refuses "to clutch at any immediate thing [*an kein Unmittelbares sich klammert*]" (*Negative Dialectic* 15; *Negative Dialektik* 27). The combination, in Shakespeare's playtexts, of philosophical defiance against factual immediacy and literary resistance to mimetic figuration lends them the negative-critical force that accounts for their *impure aesthetics* (Hugh Grady). Such impurity is not to be found solely in the material side of its production—the way it springs from infrastructural overdeterminants—but also in the dialectical dimension of its pre-diction (the way the corpus is inexorably mediated by prior *dicta* and *scripta*), and in the uncanny logic of its reproduction. To read Shakespeare dialectically is an *a contrario* deconstructive exercise in de-phenomenalization. What must be de-phenomenalized is not, however, the already negative and impure Shakespeare. What must be de-phenomenalized is a certain mode of hermeneutics of the Shakespeare text. The bulk of this book consists accordingly in a sustained *pars destruens* (the refutation) where the hermeneutic validity of some phenomenological claims is subject to scrutiny. Although the alternative speculative-dialectical reading of Shakespeare emerges at every turn of the deconstructive argument, the gist of the *pars construens* (the projection) is located in section 1, where I put forward an unphenomenal interpretation of the Ophelia trace in *Hamlet*.

The title of my book registers an intentional inversion of a phrase, *phenomenal Shakespeare*, that Smith's book has done much to legitimize. The Shakespeare I contrastively present is unphenomenal because he fails to give us the expected *realia*. In their mystified attempts to return us to the Shakespearean *things themselves*, to the pastoral bounty of his "cakes and ale" (*Twelfth Night* 2.3.104), phenomenological critics remind me of the efforts of French economists during the reign of Louise XIV, who proposed money should return to "its natural limits [*ses bornes naturelles*]." Marx laughed at their vain attempts "to have mutton and vineyards attain the status of money [*à l'état de monnaie*]" (*Misère* 139). Mutton and vineyards as monetary currency: what would Timon say? In turn these economists evoke the fatuous character in Proust's *Sodome et Gomorrhe* who prizes Charcot's research on pupillary light reflex over the tradition of Socratic philosophy (439). He would have probably upheld the Scholastic belief that, in the sensorial act of seeing, a small-scale image/reproduction of the seen thing is—in an apotheosis of representative immediacy—effectively transferred into the human brain. Something like the theory of "le petit homme qui est dans l'homme" (*Écrits I* 159) that Lacan railed at in his essay on psychic causality. Let me note, incidentally, that the traditional construal of representation as delegate presentation based on resemblance was after all one of Descartes' most enduring targets. He alludes with sarcasm to the belief in "quelques petits tableaux qui s'en formassent en notre tête" when we contemplate "un tableau."[20] *Quelques petits tableaux*, for instance, of phenomenal mutton and vineyards. Very much against Husserl himself, who also reviled such theory of perception by delegation, this Scholastic—i.e. metaphysical and doctrinal—mode of belief has been lately resurrected by critics who make their readings of Shakespeare's plays depend on a transferential mental small-scale internalization of ideal and sensorially lavish performances of these plays—one often has the feeling that the Shakespeare scholar discussing a play tends more often to remember scenes in a film production than pages in a printed edition. One may forgive Žižek for talking about Austen or James without carefully reading their actual novels, but this is unforgivable bad taste, let alone bad manners, in the case of a literary scholar.[21] "Au lieu que nous devons considérer," argues Descartes, "qu'il y a plusieurs autres choses que des images, qui peuvent exciter notre tête; comme par exemple, les signes et les paroles, qui ne ressemblent en aucune façon aux choses qu'elles signifient" (*Dioptrique* in *Œuvres completes III*, 169). To protest that there are more things affecting our senses and minds than are dreamt of in the standard visual imagination, things like signs and words that hold no resemblance whatsoever with the things they signify, is to advance a thesis of semiotic arbitrariness that enlivens the rationalist position at its root, anticipating the claim that all speculative-dialectical thinkers (Descartes, Hegel,

---

20   He repeats the same idea at the opening of his treatise *Le monde*: "Car encore que chacun se persuade communément que les idées que nous avons en notre pensée sont entièrement semblables aux objets dont elles procèdent, je ne vois point toutefois de raison qui nous assure que cela soit; mais je remarque, au contraire, plusieurs expériences qui nous en doivent faire douter" (*Œuvres philosophiques* 315).
21   For Žižek on Henry James, see *Parallax View*, 124–145.

Marx, Derrida) share. To reduce meaningful communication to affection, and affection alone to embodied affection, is to stray inexorably from these positions. The real defense against the propinquity of things that have alarmingly begun to touch us (*auf den Leib gerückt*), a proximity already denounced by Benjamin, is not to assume, as Sloterdijk does, "the a priori of pain [*das Schmerz-Apriori*]" (*Kritik* 19)—I don't intend to replace affection with woeful defection—but rather to celebrate all the forms of distance that *les signes et les paroles* afford.[22] To those who seek the wholesale abolition of "affective distance" (Raber, *Shakespeare* 49), I respond by championing a return to the good old, at bottom liberal, *pathos of distance* (Nietzsche), what Derrida called, in his reading of Kant's third *Critique*, *détachement* (*La vérité en peinture* 47). To the propinquities of close feeling I oppose the distances of close reading.

6

In this book I set out to explore five basic fallacies. The *pastoral philosophy*, which I examine in section 8, is a moral diversion beholden to the metaphysics of origin, and rooted in assumptions of simplicity, spontaneity, and unimpaired intersubjectivity. The *fallacy of immediacy*, examined in section 19, taps the metaphysical resourcefulness of phenomenal givenness (*Gegebenheit*). Section 18 is devoted to the *fallacy of representation*, which rests on claims about symbolic harmony and referential consistency. Finally, I argue in section 20 that the *fallacy of presentism* underpins a hermeneutic of sociological reference and political immediacy. These five fallacies contribute, in my view, to the *Entkunstung* or de-arting (Adorno, *Ästhetische Theorie* 32) of Shakespeare's art, construed as an assortment of political happenings, life-worldly designs, and emotional events. Robert Pippin's phrasing of an aesthetic demand urged by Hegel—"the possibility of sensible embodiment of sharable meaning" (*After the Beautiful* 95)—brings home the stakes involved in the *aesthetic fallacy* I denounce in section 17: the sensible and the embodied, the shareability of meaning, and

---

22 For all his merits, Sloterdijk's objections to critical theory in the "Introduction" to *Kritik der zynischen Vernunft* (17–20) fail to identify the *forte* of thinkers like Adorno. Nobody discusses the latter's valorization of an elitist sensibility, but this gesture is based less on the atrophy of an exalted petit-bourgeois *Empfindlichkeit* than on a sound respect for the mediations of reason. The threat that "the emotional moralism of [middle-class] decency [*Anstandsgefühls*]" (106) poses to critical work remains today as strong as then, with the only difference that the characters of George Sand have now turned into early modern scholars, the curators of their own *akademisches Idyll* (48). More on this in section 8, "A Pastoral Philosophy".

the putative (unconstructed) givenness both of the sensible and of its meaning. Paradoxically, this *Entkunstung* often unfolds as a meretricious re-arting of the poet's work along lines of hyper-mimesis and polymorphic, unqualified, embodiment, which tend to obliterate the negative-determinate dimensions of the poet's dramatic verse.

These fallacies hinge upon a phenomenological grasp of the Shakespeare thing, open to consumption in its "initial stage of natural crudity and immediacy" (Marx, *Grundrisse* 92). The visible and invisible work of phenomenology in Shakespeare studies today will therefore be the object of my continued consideration. Let me recall at the outset that the real enemy of phenomenology is not psychology, as Husserl tirelessly claimed, not even metaphysics, as he also—*pace* Levinas—implied. The true enemy of phenomenology is dialectic—a mode of thought firmly rooted in the philosophical tradition (from Plato to Hegel). The fact that Husserl had a languid and biased grasp of the history of philosophy, an embarrassment denounced very early by Derrida, and remained therefore largely unacquainted with dialectics, marks a legacy of neglect that is worth considering as a cause of subsequent privations and inherited evasions.[23] As I have already pointed out, the critical attempt to grasp the Shakespeare *things themselves* depends on another misconstruction, examined in section 13, i.e. the belief that phenomenology is a science of things, a philosophical method that encourages, contra idealist philosophies, a return to real things. This is a gruesome error. Despite the evolutions it underwent in Husserl's hands, phenomenology started out as a propaedeutic discipline of logical-idealist purifications and transcendentalist reductions. At any rate, the error of those (so many) that have misread Husserl's call to the *Sache selbst* or things themselves as a return to factual material things is but a corollary deduced from Husserl's most basic error: to overlook mediation.

---

23 Husserl was of course intimately acquainted with Descartes, and he returned constantly to Hume and Kant in his courses. Still, an explicit recognition of his unorthodox position in the history of philosophy is also constant in his work. See, for instance, *Ideas* §18, where he conceded he hadn't "made use of traditional or even generally recognized philosophical theories" (33). Yet what he takes as a mark of revolutionary originality is also evidence of disciplinary neglect. And if, as the hermeneutic tradition (Schleiermacher, Dilthey, Heidegger, Gadamer, Derrida) has emphasized, philosophy is indissociable from the history of philosophy, then phenomenology's inability to secure its position in this tradition can be seen as a weakness. Derrida asks in a footnote: "peut-on ici s'autoriser des immenses ignorances de Husserl en matière d'histoire de la philosophie?" (*Genèse* 7). In his "Introduction" to Husserl's *L'origine de la géométrie*, he points out that the *Encyclopedia of Philosophical Sciences* is "un des rares ouvrages hegeliens que Husserl semble d'ailleurs avoir lus" (58).

It doesn't really matter on which side of the polarity one stands (physis-logos, reality-concepts, things-ideas) if one is resolved in advance to ignore both the inescapability of the dialectic and the logic of mediation it devolves to thought as an exigence. Derrida's dialectical recusation of Husserl's phenomenology—what we now call *deconstruction*—was first formulated in the Avant-Propos to his 1954 doctoral dissertation:

> celle-ci, étant à la fois histoire et philosophie, n'est-elle pas vouée, par définition, à une oscillation dialectique, à une réciprocité originelle et indépassable de renvois et de références entre la singularité historique d'une pensée, prise au ras de son discours, de sa lettre, et l'universalité philosophique, considérée ici comme sa prétention, sa signification intentionnelle ?
> *Le problème de la genèse* 5

Like Husserl in his own time, current phenomenology-oriented scholars of Shakespeare studies are still working to ideologically unmask the *philosophical universality* of the bard's texts, but they are no longer attending, as did their neo-historicist predecessors, to the historical singularity of thoughts. They have heard about intentional (body-driven, world-attuned, object-conforming) meanings, and are all ears. They miss no corporal noise, no ambience sound, and no sweet air, but they seem to have forgotten to register the need to take someone's thoughts primarily at textual level—*au ras de son discourse* and *de sa lettre*. In the "Introduction" to his *Treatise of Human Nature*, David Hume denounced the banal dispersion into which genuine philosophical debate had fallen due to the noisy collision of separate and competing sciences. "There is nothing which is not the subject of debate," he complained, and noted, more critically, that "the most trivial question escapes not our controversy." To make things worse, the squandering of research and banalization of dispute lead, in his opinion, to no discernible outcome:

> Disputes are multiplied, as if every thing was uncertain; and these disputes are managed with the greatest warmth, as if every thing was certain. Amidst all this bustle 'tis not reason, which carries the prize, but eloquence; and no man needs ever despair of gaining proselytes to the most extravagant hypothesis, who has art enough to represent it in any favourable colours. The victory is not gained by the men at arms, who manage the pike and the sword; but by the trumpeters, drummers, and musicians of the army. (41)

INTRODUCTION   23

I have quoted this passage at length because I take Hume's diagnosis to apply, almost literally, to the situation of Shakespeare studies today. I would particularly stress three points of equivalence: the trivialization of the selected materials ("things") for study, some of which demand "the most extravagant hypothesis," the collective warmth which travesties uncertainty as certainty, and the eloquence that promotes the trumpeting of falsely contradictory claims. Similarly, I want to argue that Shakespeare criticism has become, in the last thirty years, manneristic, cumulative, neo-baroque, and blandly encyclopedic. Not even a semblance of dispute organizes the indiscriminate hoarding up of increasingly banal theoretical claims. There is much addition, but very little conflict, much compilation, and no real confrontation. The field has become, in short, nearly devoid of dialectical tension. The notion, put forward by Craig Bourne and Emily Caddick Bourne in their "Introduction" to *The Routledge Companion to Shakespeare and Philosophy*, that "Shakespeare is for everyone" and that the area of study he defines is one where "people working with very different methodologies, both within and across disciplines, can talk to each other—an area where there can be genuine cross-disciplinary engagement," has become so commonplace that we no longer sense its inaccuracy. Shakespeare is for everyone only in the way the K-2 is for everyone—for everyone, that is, to try to climb it and fail. And not every discipline trains you properly for the goal. It is puerile to presume otherwise. Students, even doctoral students, in short, should not *only* be given "boldness and aspiring confidence" (*King John* 5.1.). It would do them no harm to become conversant with Shakespeare's "weighty difference" (*All Is True* 3.1.57). This would return tension to the field.

Most scholars, even some of the most theoretically qualified in the discipline—critics like Richard Wilson, Simon Palfrey, Julia Lupton or Paul Kottman—appear to have entered the playgrounds of an institutionalized *pax perpetua*. The problem is not that tacit consensus threatens dissent. The time of dissent for dissent's sake is happily past. The real problem is that it is unlikely that academic discussion devoid of dialectical tension can lead the practitioners of a field to a space of critical revelation. Shakespeare criticism progresses today in a randomly assimilative manner, moving from "Shakespeare and Terrorism" (the 2000s) to "Trumping Shakespeare" (the 2010s) and "Coronal-virus: Infectious Kinghood in Shakespeare" (the 2020s), or from to "Shakespeare's Selfies" (the 2010s) to "Shakespeare, Sherry and the Global Warming of the Blood" (the 2020s). The structure of the arguments shows no inner development: what progresses is the empirical (spatial) or historical (temporal) field to which a slim and stagnant set of theoretical claims is being recursively applied.

So just as Hume was trying to escape, by means of a critique that proved essential to Kant, a morass of impressionistic psychology and dogmatic metaphysics, in the same way it appears expedient to escape the current consensus with a rehabilitation of critical work. I am not familiar with any academic book or article whose defined goal is to denounce the hermeneutic trouble—the *phenomenalization* of the playtexts, i.e. the occlusion of their linguistic-textual dimension—consequent on the current *phenomenologization* of Shakespeare criticism. Nor am I acquainted with essays or books written in opposition to any of the particular trends (posthumanism, new materialism, cognitive performance studies) which, in their adaptation to Shakespeare studies, I succinctly examine in my book. I have encountered, here and there, passing expressions of dissatisfaction with the destitution of high theory that is underway in early modern studies, complaints voiced by Hugh Grady, Jonathan Goldberg, Catherine Belsey, Jean Howard, and Scott Shershow, but there is, I believe, no book-length study where dismay instigates a set of connected arguments. This is why I decided to write this refutation. I believe that lack of internal contestation and genuine methodological debate is proof not only of widespread theoretical insufficiency, but also perhaps of a shared belief among practitioners of these new methods that the theoretical war against formalism was waged and won by others (scholars keen on dissent like Jonathan Dollimore, Stephen Greenblatt, or Bruce Smith) and that their more recent work is therefore exempt from the burden of confutation and counterclaim, and free therefore to declare itself exclusively in the assertive mode—what Cardinal Newman called a *grammar of assent*. Crucial to this belief (perhaps faith) is the mistaking of speculative-dialectical theory (Lacanian Psychoanalysis, Althusserian Marxism, and deconstruction) for an obsolete overelaboration of formalist claims. Also central to this confidence is the assumption that deconstruction lost the war, and that the triumphant army (phenomenology) needs no longer to comport itself antagonistically:

> Actually, as Vincent Descombes has shown, all that deconstruction can "undermine" are the "descriptive ambitions" of phenomenology, in particular "Husserlian descriptions," that is merely "the descriptive façade of phenomenology" (Descombes 1986, p. 62). Phenomenology has survived; one doubts if deconstruction will.
>
> *Appropriating Shakespeare* 168

INTRODUCTION   25

That was Brian Vickers in 1993. Descombes was wrong about the seriousness of the harm inflicted by deconstruction to phenomenology.²⁴ And so was Vickers. But the latter was right about the survival of phenomenology. In the Humanities, where ideological dogma tends to suppress independent study and unaffiliated research, it doesn't really matter who wins what war. What counts is the institutional recognition of victory. In that particular sense, deconstruction has been *almost* defeated. And I guess the claims advanced in this book operate in the residual room this *almost* propitiously affords.

7

Recent theoretical interventions defending the superiority of mediation-sensitive, speculative-dialectical methods over other reading practices applied to Shakespeare are also difficult to come by. There are, however, scholars like Andrew Cutrofello, Nicholas Royle, and Ned Lukacher, whose approach to Shakespeare is distinctly marked by the Hegelian speculative-dialectical tradition, even if they do not necessarily see themselves as working in it, and it is to this work that I turn for support at some strategic points in my book. What my book adds to their work is a resolve to make arguments turn around the dialectical opposition to phenomenological readings of Shakespeare. Apart from these scholars, I have also drawn inspiration from academics of earlier generations whose work on Shakespeare is particularly sensitive to poststructuralist speculation and textual mediation: Christopher Norris, Marjorie Garber, Catherine Belsey, Harold Bloom, A.D. Nuttall, David Scott Kastan, John Kerrigan, Jonathan Goldberg, Stephen Orgel, Margreta de Grazia, David Schalkwyk, Richard Halpern, Graham Bradshaw, and others. I know that most of them would strongly disapprove of the reliance on liberal rationalism that undergirds my arguments, but that doesn't stop me from turning to them for inspiration. The best way to present an *unphenomenal Shakespeare* is by engaging creatively with the momentous critique of phenomenology that, anticipated by Heidegger, was performed independently by the two

---

24 Descombes' claim is self-defeating because in the same sentence he admits to the necessary attention deconstruction pays to the "epistemological requirements" of phenomenological description, here exposed as an instance of the metaphysics of presence. Descombes: "[Deconstruction] does not attempt to rescue the description from epistemological requirements but seeks instead to honor them meticulously, so much so that "the thing itself" will escape forever" (*Objects of All Sorts* 62–63).

thinkers that preside over my book, Theodor Adorno and Jacques Derrida.[25] The intersections between Derrida and Shakespeare have not yet been thoroughly identified and explored, but some powerful research (by Joel Fineman, Christopher Norris, Nicholas Royle, David Schalkwyk, Chiara Alfano) has been invested in the task.[26] In particular, I want to single out four books that offer,

---

[25] Derrida's early engagement with Husserl is a well-known story. Adorno's intellectual relation with phenomenology is less conspicuous. At Frankfurt in 1924 he wrote a thesis on Husserl. In 1940 he publishes "Husserl and the Problem of Idealism" and in 1956, at Oxford, he resumed research on phenomenology, leading to the publication in German of *Against Epistemology—A Metacritique: Studies in Husserl and the Metaphysical Antinomies*. As Stefan Müller-Doohm notes, "This immersion in Husserl's *Formal and Transcendental Logic* and his *Cartesian Meditations* was the means to an end in Adorno's mind. He thought of it as a 'a kind of critical, dialectical, prelude to a materialist logic'" (204).

[26] Chiara Alfano's *Derrida Reads Shakespeare* was published in 2020. The book is interesting, but her framing argument about the originality of Derrida's approach to Shakespeare is vitiated by the preposterous decision to oppose it to Harold Bloom's "bardolatrous" reading of the genius. Alfano has done her homework and read the prefatorial note "To the Reader" and the opening chapter titled "Shakespeare's Universalism" of Bloom's Shakespeare book, where the term and issue of "Bardolatry" are mentioned and briefly discussed. Sadly, the assignment didn't include the reading of the remaining 700 pages of variously attentive reading and speculative interpretation of Shakespeare's plays. Had she done so, she would have realized that Bloom is a much more sophisticated, original, and of course informed, reader of Shakespeare than Derrida, and that the former's analyses far exceed the putative "idealization of the Shakespearean corpus as a seemingly endless well of wisdom and truth" (*Derrida* 33). Seven hundred pages of bardolatry are too many pages, even by Bloomean standards. Derrida on Shakespeare is fascinating because Derrida is nearly always fascinating. But it makes no sense to assess the originality of his take on the English poet by pitting it against the Shakespeare interpretation of a scholar who, despite his declarations to the contrary, is at his best when deploying a speculative (quite often still deconstructive) mode of reading. For instance, Bloom's chapter on *Romeo and Juliet* rehearses exactly the same motifs (mistiming, contingency, chance, serialization, repetition) Derrida urges in his piece on the same tragedy—examined by Alfano in her book—and does it with a richness of literary intertextual implication and sensibility to poetic nuance that is completely missing from Derrida's essay. Sneering at Bloom is a lot easier if you decide not to read him. It may be worth noting that one of the first—if not *the* first—engagements of Derrida with an English-speaking literary author was prompted by Harold Bloom's invitation to write about Shelley's poem *The Triumph of Life* in 1979. And that "English" (literary) engagements were not exactly numerous: Shelley, Joyce, Shakespeare, Hopkins ... Also worth mentioning is the fact that Nicholas Royle, an important Derridean scholar to whose insights on Shakespeare Alfano often appeals, includes in the "Suggestions for Further Reading" of his book on Shakespeare the following recommendation: "For a couple of recent wide-ranging critical studies that are especially thought-provoking, as well as good on the poetic dimensions of Shakespeare's writing, see Harold Bloom's *Shakespeare: The Invention of the Human* and Frank Kermode's *Shakespeare's Language*" (*How to Read* 126). Let me recall that Royle's book was written in 2005, when critical studies on Shakespeare were not exactly lacking. Finally, the absence

in my view, the most sophisticated deconstructive take on Shakespeare to date: Joel Fineman's *Shakespeare's Perjured Eye: The Invention of Modern Subjectivity in the Sonnets* (1986), Marjorie Garber's *Shakespeare's Ghost Writers* (1987), Ned Lukacher's *Daemonic Figures: Shakespeare and the Question of Conscience* (1994), and Jonathan Goldberg's *Shakespeare's Hand* (2003). The search for current Shakespeare scholars with a genuine stake in Adorno is a much more uncertain endeavor. Perhaps Hugh Grady, in *Shakespeare and Impure Aesthetics* (2009) and other scattered essays, is the Shakespeare critic most committed to Adorno's memory, but his work is circumscribed to *Aesthetic Theory*. Paul Kottman has recently written an Introduction to Adorno's *Notes on Literature* (2019), but his readings of Shakespeare do not bear the imprint of this legacy. Actually, the Adorno I engage with and invoke in my book is not the Adorno that reads literature or analyzes art, but rather the Adorno that defends Hegel's speculative insight from the purgation of dialectical reason attempted by high phenomenological thought. Finally, the mobilization of deManian arguments with a view to disclosing the tropological tension and unphenomenal materiality of Shakespearean meaning is a critical maneuver that has never, to my knowledge, been attempted. Maybe the notably illiberal attack against deconstruction (Derrida and de Man, particularly) launched decades ago by Brian Vickers in *Appropriating Shakespeare* had a more lasting effect upon early modern scholars than anyone could have expected. Maybe it is about time to set the record straight.

8

I am not sure that there is a clear-cut opposition between "le privé et le public, le secret et le phenomenal" (Derrida, *De l'hospitalité* 61), but if the limit exists, even if it only exists to be effaced, then I would place Shakespeare's meaning on the side of the private and the secret. The phenomenalization of Shakespeare, the creation of a phenomenal Shakespeare, is part of a futile political strategy to democratize further the bard's significance. The strategy is futile because

---

of references in a book about Derrida on Shakespeare to scholars like Joel Fineman and Jonathan Goldberg—but also Margreta de Grazia, Peter Stallybrass, Ned Lukacher, Jonathan Gil Harris—is, in my opinion, inexcusable (Wilson's *Shakespeare in French Theory* it at least referenced in an endnote). To believe, in short, that the singularity of Derrida's approach to Shakespeare lies in his ability to "dodge philosophical bardolatry" (21) is both to misconstrue the gist of Derrida's speculative take on Shakespeare and to ignore the nature of the critical debates in Shakespeare studies today.

what offers itself to be phenomenally democratized from the vast Shakespeare canon is precisely what is less significant: that Shakespeare and his characters were also embodied human beings, that they had bodies and corporal needs, that they lived in a social environment which encouraged their interaction with others, that they were surrounded by objects inciting them, more or less effectively, to affective, moral, and political action. So what? We are all more or less there, but we are neither Shakespeare nor Shylock, neither Shakespeare nor Edgar, neither Shakespeare nor Ophelia. We are more or less identical with Shakespeare in owning human bodies that are surrounded by other bodies, and we may extend this identity, hypothetically, to his fictional creatures, but this identity is what matters less in the assessment of his characters' singularity, which lies mostly in their difference, in their not being us, not speaking like us, perhaps not even to us.[27] They are but incidents of a verbal excess whose exact meaning eludes us.

Let me say something more about the final claim—about our not being Ophelia, and about our awareness of her not being whomever it was she was up to be. About her secrets, her intractable privacy, her unphenomenality. This liberal scruple informs Derrida's swerve from Levinas, his injunction to adjust the volume of the imperative of separation—of the infinite separate Other—to the Heideggerian philosophies of finitude and mortality that Levinas then, and Badiou today, despise. Derrida beautifully speaks of the "respect non-violent du secret" (182). More on this in the next section.

---

27 Uncertainty about the identity of the person or persons addressed in many of Hamlet's speeches is a recurrent concern in Nicholas Royle's readings of the tragedy. I would extend this uncertainty to Shakespeare's global address.

CHAPTER 1

The Unphenomenal

"This Nothing's More than Matter"

1

The term *unphenomenal*, nowhere to be found in dictionaries, is common in philosophical jargon, especially of a post-phenomenological bent. John Caputo, for instance, dabs "unphenomenal" the mode of time that shuns retention and protention, and is therefore unlived, nonexperiential, extraordinary—"other" (*Prayers* 77). A time, say, for chanting snatches of old tunes in the "scene individable, or poem unlimited" (*Hamlet* 2.2.382) of play. Unphenomenal, for Derrida, is the secret that "exceeds the play of veiling/unveiling, dissimulation/revelation, night/day, forgetting/anamnesis, earth/heaven [...] Its nonphenomenality is without relation, even negative, to phenomenality" ("Passions," qtd. in Lukacher, *Daemonic* 5–6). Concomitantly, Maurice Blanchot calls unphenomenal the space of clandestinity spreading beyond all human relation, as well as the time of "non-appearance" where one "dies unphenomenally, unbeknownst to all and to oneself, wordlessly, without leaving any trace" (*Writing* 35). The French thinker argues that the two Kantian a priori forms of sensibility (space, time) compossibilize, through the invisible, the "essence of suicide." Unphenomenal is, for example, the fact that rather sooner than later "the woman will be out" (*Hamlet* 4.7.161).[1] Out, we may inflect, with Emily Dickinson, "of ground, or air, or ought" (*Complete* 162). But we know Ophelia's death—possibly, suicide—is not without trace, and is surely not wordless. The report of her drowning constitutes one of the most memorable—pointedly narrative (*there, but, there, when, and, but*), lavishly mimetic (*willow, brook, leaves, stream, garlands, boughs, brook, clothes*)—stretches of elegiac verse in Shakespearean drama:

> There is a willow grows aslant a brook,
> That shows his hoar leaves in the glassy stream.
> There with fantastic garlands did she come

---

1 Laertes refers to the loss of his feminine side, but the context doesn't allow us to forget the woman who is really out (Ophelia).

> Of crow-flowers, nettles, daisies, and long purples,
> That liberal shepherds give a grosser name,
> But our cold maids do dead men's fingers call them.
> There, on the pendent boughs her coronet weeds
> Clamb'ring to hang, an envious sliver broke,
> When down her weedy trophies and herself
> Fell in the weeping brook. Her clothes spread wide,
> And mermaid-like a while they bore her up;
> Which time she chanted snatches of old tunes,
> As one incapable of her own distress,
> Or like a creature native and indued
> Unto that element. But long it could not be
> Till that her garments, heavy with their drink,
> Pulled the poor wretch from her melodious lay
> To muddy death.
>
> HAMLET 4.7.137–154

This is, one must admit, a phenomenal report. Neither the tropes (*mermaid-like, dead men's fingers, like a creature*) nor the closing evanescence into growing abstractions (*melodious lay, muddy death*) detract from its emblematic force. But where does the vignette come from? We know who speaks it (the Queen), but we ignore upon what evidence or based on the authority of whose testimony. Nobody seems to have *seen* the most gorgeously *seen* scene in the play; seen or heard, for the possibility that someone heard Ophelia's "snatches of old tunes" and failed or refused to save her from drowning is not to be discarded. Shakespeare's most tendentially ekphrastic moments are often informed by the inscription of erotic violence and death, and by the detached coldness of distanced sadistic overseeing. Like the death of Adonis, Ophelia's drowning is, therefore, an *unphenomenally* phenomenal report. The playgoers cannot see the scene therein evoked, as Shakespeare signally reserved this pastoral composition for offstage denouement: how do you stage a cold maid edging out of ought with a garland of dead men's fingers? So, they cannot see her, but neither can the central characters in the play. Ophelia dies, Blanchot would say, "unbeknownst to all and to oneself." Beyond all human relation. And yet, the words are there, and so are the traces. Are we entitled to phenomenalize her lasting solitude and moralize her lingering retreat? Of course not:

> The daemon is neither good nor evil. It names the barely discernible shadow that falls upon present beings, cast by the flickering withdrawal of the elusive thing that brings things and beings to presence. The

> daemon is the name of the disjunctive conjunctive of their (not) being together. Whatever is present and whatever brings presence to the present are joined by virtue of their very disjunction. The withdrawal, the self-concealment, the self-denial, or refusal of the thing that presences leaves behind only a ghostly, daemonic, uncanny, whisperlike, shadowlike trace.
>
> LUKACHER, *Daemonic* 14–15

In his first brief tribute to Nietzsche, Thomas Mann reminds us that the German philosopher established a distinction between visual and aural persons, and that he saw himself as one of the latter.[2] And Joel Fineman avers that the Lacanian distinction between the Imaginary and the Symbolic rehearses an earlier Freudian contrast "between visual *Sachvorstellungen* and verbal *Wortvorstellungen*" (44). Audience or spectators, readership or spectatorship: the fact that these options are neither symmetric nor straightforward—for a play-reader sees before she internally hears, and a spectator, especially in an early modern performance, hears more than he sees—no doubt instils a sense of phenomenological urgency into the scrutiny of Shakespeare's work. If pursued far enough, however, this scrutiny leads to the dismantling of phenomenological presuppositions, and demands modes of inquiry whose materialist premises prove invitingly simple: Shakespeare's *hand*, his *perjured eye*, his *daemonic figures*, the resulting *ghost writing*.[3] Contemporary physicists teach us that "in order to leave a trace, it is necessary for something to become arrested, to stop moving, and this can happen only in an irreversible process—that is to say, by degrading energy into heat" (Rovelli, *The Order of Time* 100). Or by degrading, say, distress into tunes. Neo-historicists would speak rather of the degradation of dissidence into plays, or of subversion into verse. And Nietzsche and Derrida, in a more generic-transcendental vein, would object

---

2   "Spoken prelude to a musical tribute to Nietzsche" is the title of Mann's speech delivered at the Odeon concert hall during the commemoration of the 80th anniversary of Nietzsche's birth. See, Mann, *Schopenhauer, Nietzsche, Freud*, 98.

3   I am implicitly alluding to the four contemporary masterpieces of Shakespearean criticism mentioned above: Joel Fineman's *Shakespeare's Perjured Eye* (1986), Marjorie Garber's *Shakespeare's Ghost Writers* (1987), Ned Lukacher's *Daemonic Figures* (1994) and Jonathan Goldberg's *Shakespeare's Hands* (2003). These four books share a strong reliance on Derrida's early philosophical work. Their internal connection, duly stressed by Goldberg (viii, 150, 189), is too often missed. Jonathan Gil Harris, for instance, fails to include the books by Fineman, Lukacher and Goldberg in *Shakespeare and Literary Theory*, an omission that shows the prevailing disinterest in—and phenomenological outmaneuvering of—genuinely deconstructive readings of Shakespeare. Symptomatically, however, both Harris and Catherine Belsey accord pride of place to Garber's extraordinary book. See Harris, *Shakespeare* 211; and Belsey, *Shakespeare*, 29.

that the inscription of a trace is contingent on the degradation of sheer *Kraft* into *paroles*. At any rate, we may surmise that the witness of her suicide needed Ophelia to progress towards her final cessation in order to enjoy the phenomenal, if somewhat allegorical, composition of her traces—to *see* the flowers in the garland and *listen* to the tunes. This composes, let me insist, a mode of sadistic aestheticism that, foreshadowed by Lucretius (*De rerum natura* 2.1–19) and studied by Hans Blumenberg in *Schiffbruch mit Zuschauer* (1979), is not alien to Shakespeare's couth sensibility. The resulting composition is one of those "passages of proof" that Claudius, of all people, takes as an illustration of the proviso that, though "love is begun by time," "time" too "qualifies the spark and fire of it" (*Hamlet* 4.7.93–95). It is time indeed that qualifies Ophelia's erotic spark and fire, degrading it into the words and traces of her disappearance. If there is, for her, a "timeless world of play" (Bloom, *Shakespeare* 394), it is only to be found in the temporal play of words. No tragic fall, no *casus*, without a release of energy (Rovelli, *The Order* 18–19). And no time without falls, without words and traces, or words as traces—*écriture*. Beckett didn't need Proust to discover just that: reading *Hamlet* and *King Lear* proved enough. For Derrida, "the trace must be thought before the entity. But the movement of the trace is necessarily occulted, it produces itself as self-occultation" (*Of Grammatology*, 47). In Nicholas Royle's suggestive terms, "the itineracy of the trace will always already have burrowed deeper or elsewhere" (*The Uncanny* 252). Self-occulted, then, Ophelia falls into muddy death, or crashes and breaks her body open against the asphalt [*als der Körper auf dem Asphalt aufschlug*], like Isa, Hans Blumenberg's imaginary student in Sibylle Lewitscharoff's brilliant novel (*Blumenberg* 80)—a late-modernist variation on ghosts, suicide, and the "embodiment of the disembodied" (Garber 20). Derrida:

> What the thought of the trace has already taught us is that it could not be simply submitted to the onto-phenomenological question of essence. The trace is nothing [*la trace n'est rien*], it is not an entity [*elle n'est pas un étant*], it exceeds the question What is? and contingently makes it possible. Here one may no longer trust even the opposition of fact and principle, which, in all its metaphysical, ontological, and transcendental forms, has always functioned within the system of what is. Without venturing up to the perilous necessity of the question on the arche-question "what is," let us take shelter in the field of grammatological knowledge.
> *Of grammatology* 75; *De la grammatologie* 110

In *Hamlet*, the arch-question, the ontological question of essence as phenomenal entity—*la question qu'est-ce que*—is accidentally raised by Polonius,

"What is the matter, my lord?" (2.2.193) and is nowhere better answered than in Laertes' remark on his sister's seeming madness: "This nothing's more than matter" (4.5.172).[4] Ophelia's matter—her bundle of traces, her redelivered remembrances, chanted tunes, and spoken flowers—debuts and lingers as a *nothing* that is more than phenomenal matter. It constitutes the play's central matter insofar as it is the only (no)thing that appears to matter positively to Hamlet. "I loved Ophelia" (5.1.254), he tells his mother, at the critical point when he learns about the girl's death, a confession that, if not true, serves at least to unblock his pragmatic resolve, thus allowing the play to play itself out and become an actual play. A mourning *jeu* (*Trauerspiel*) of differences, of course, with the interplay of presence and absence made possible only by the work of difference as its "obliterated origin [*l'origine oblitérée*]" (*Of Grammatology*, 143; 206). Hamlet, we know, wavers viciously in his responses to Ophelia, from "I did love you once" (3.1.116) to "I loved you not" (3.1.119), only to prove that "since the crime is exposure, the excuse consists in recapitulating the exposure in the guise of concealment" (de Man, *Allegories of Reading*, 286). Because if difference is at one with the obliterated origin, and, in accordance with the logic of confession studied by de Man, this origin can be traced back to the loved girl (Marion for Rousseau) as "the organizing principle" and "hidden center of an urge to reveal" (289), then we may tentatively conclude that Ophelia—as nothing, vagina, non-phallus, and omphalos—is indistinguishable from this erased source (*origo*). Levinas' injunction on the societal condition of Being—"La societé est la presence de l'être" (*Totalité* 198)—leaves Ophelia's claim to being utterly untouched. Her use of language, her talk of nothing, hardly conforms to the French philosopher's view of language as a primeval realm of interpersonal relationality that rescinds the inevitable contract between phenomenality and interiority: "L'existence de l'homme demeure phénoménale, tant qu'elle reste intériorité. Le langage par lequel un être existe pour un autre, est son unique possibilité d'exister d'une existence qui est plus que son existence intérieure" (199). Levinas is wrong. There are, as Ophelia vividly proves, modes of existence in language that defy purposive communication with alterity and yet remain un-interior, unphenomenal. They are all-out modes of being out—being exterior, separate, and alien. She enjoys at most the kind of non-phenomenality Derrida paradoxically reserves for Levinas' Other: "De lui seul on peut dire que son phénomène est une certaine non-phénoménalité, que sa presence

---

4 Jonathan Goldberg's brilliant essay "Hamlet's Hand" closes with Laertes' Delphian sentence (*Shakespeare's Hand*, 131). I believe that, in view of the developments of phenomenological neo-materialism in Shakespeare studies that have followed this 1988 essay, the words of Ophelia's brother take on an even stronger significance.

(*est*) une certaine absence" (*L'écriture* 135). As Saussure suggested, *tous les phénomènes sont des rapports* (*Cours*, Engler's edition 275) revolving around a composite referential absence. Obliterated, self-occulted, vanished, the cold maid pulled from melodious lays to muddy death: termal death as the entropy-increasing and time-engendering fall where tragedies are consummated. But in his *Confessions*, Rousseau could also modulate his voice to achieve latitudes of withdrawal that reach beyond Hamlet into Ophelia's vaporous remoteness:

> I would love society like others, if I were not sure of showing myself [*de m'y montrer*] not only at a disadvantage, but as completely different [*tout autre*] from what I am. The part that I have taken of writing and hiding myself [*Le parti que j'ai pris d'écrire et de me cacher*] is precisely the one that suits me. If I were present [*Moi present*], one would never know what I was worth [*ce que je valais*].
> Les confessions, 179–180.[5]

Although the theatricals behind such longing for absence have been scrutinized *in extenso* by Sartre, Starobinski, Derrida and de Man, there is no denying the force and effect of the pretension to withdraw into oneself through a reflexive labyrinth of non-referential, exclusively discursive, excuses, especially if we insert such longing in a theatrical context, supposedly given to the exaltation of factual, referential, phenomenal, and consensually truth-based, presence. Peter Szondi took such cohabitation of outside and inside, visible and invisible, to pose a relatively unprecedented threat to the modern theatrical system, which eventually cracked under the modernist pressure of a truth that belonged solely in the realm of personal interiority—"die Wahrheit die der Innerlichkeit" (*Theorie* 29). But anti-classical Shakespeare foreshadowed this outcome. Like Prince Hal or Cordelia, we can overhear Ophelia whispering to herself: "If I were present, one would never know what I was worth." But she decided to prelude her definitive absence, her impresence, with a distribution of unlikely *presents*—prospective remembrances, fading flowers, the fleeting names of herbs:

> LAERTES. This nothing's more than matter.
> OPHELIA. There's rosemary, that's for remembrance. Pray, love, remember. And there is pansies; that's for thoughts.

---

5 The reference and page number correspond to the original French edition. I use the English translation as it appears in Spivak's version of *Of Grammatology*, where this Rousseau passage is commented by Starobinski (*Of Grammatology* 142).

LAERTES. A document in madness—thoughts and remembrance fitted.
OPHELIA. There's fennel for you, and columbines. There's rue for you, and here's some for me. We may call it herb-grace o' Sundays. O, you must wear your rue with a difference. There's a daisy. I would give you some violets, but they withered all when my father died. They say he made a good end. (*Song*) For bonny sweet Robin is all my joy. (4.172–182)

This is Ophelia writing and hiding herself, like Rousseau's elusive persona, allowing her wild script to predetermine and constitute an entity (her trace-being) whose essence cannot be staged, represented, or captured by "what is." On the evidence of these dubious words, the girl's death is deemed "doubtful" (5.1.209), her body buried "in ground unsanctified" (5.1.211)—"pas de tombeau visible et phenomenal, seulement une inhumation secrete, une insépulture invisible ..." (Derrida, *De l'hospitalité* 103). These misgivings, which shelter her from what Derrida calls *l'extériorité phénoménale* (105), acknowledge too her liberal triumph. In 1957, the *Report of the Committee on Homosexual Offences and Prostitution* stated very clearly that "there must be a realm of private morality and immorality which is in brief and crude terms not the law's business" (qtd. in Dworkin, *Taking Rights Seriously* 242). If the space is too narrow, the private maid whose "honesty" has been questioned by coercive males, is likely to slip off unnoticed, whether *se offendendo* or *se defendendo*, and vanish. And no critical law sustained in no moral principle, no "great command" (*Hamlet* 5.1.210), no epistemic regime and no moral "order" (211) should work to repair this absence—by throwing "shards" or "maiden strewments" (213–214) into her grave, in a desperate attempt to bring (her) home—to *present* or *represent* a *presentist* (ultra-gendered, racialized, feminist, liturgic-sacrificial, post-human, eco-responsible) Ophelia. Whether as immaculate prostitute or impure angel, Ophelia is always out—"out of the shot of danger and desire" (1.3.35), "out of the air" (2.2.204), "out of the grave" (stage direction at 5.1.250).[6] Trace upon trace, self-differing, underwritten and outsourced, she is also the girl "that out a maid / Never departed more" (4.5.53–54), not because she was deflowered, like the maid in the ballad that Ophelia sings, but because she never quite reached the stage of sexual availability. Unlike the unnamed young woman in the sources (especially, the vamp in Belleforest), she is never "out" in that particular sense. The outing of our unlikely "baker's daughter" (4.5.41),

---

6 The stage direction "*The Attendants part them, and they come out of the grave*" only appears in some editions of the play.

our fishmonger's daughter and self-offender, is far more primordial than that. On this reading, Hamlet's injunction, "Get thee to a nunnery" (3.1.122), may be less a brutal, dishonest command, than a paradoxically sincere piece of advice. But Ophelia is disinclined to fraternize or sororize. Her only possible reply to the prince would have been something resembling what Roxane tells Bajazet: "Rentre dans la néant dont je t'ai fait sortir" (*Bajazet* 2.1.524). For, like the prince, she inhabits her own waxing nothingness, an overspilled "mental space" (Bloom, *Shakespeare* 388) immune to the lures of shared appearances or communal phenomenality. This space is a *camera obscura* where words speed up and deflect their trajectory in accordance with the fluctuations of her moral clinamen. Words (remembrances, tunes, flowers) that line up, for us, who are unable to grasp the totality of other potential configurations, into a plot—the story of *Ophelia disfigured*. Hers is the time of non-appearance. Hers "the Hour of Lead—/ Remembered, if outlived, / As Freezing persons, recollect the Snow—/ First—Chill—then Stupor—then the letting go" (Dickinson 162). I take this non-appearance, this resistance to appear, to be more conspicuous, in Ophelia's case, than the fully thematized, splendidly pictorial motif of her disappearance. Hers is arguably a case of "superfluous death," for nothing in the previous scenes unequivocally confirms her ephemeral theatrical life—only the sarcastic bite at his brother at 1.3.45–51—Julia Lupton rightly speaks of "some capacity to push back" (*Thinking* 87)—betokens genuine moral reactivity.[7] The rest is lethargy or hibernation—"comme un effort de la vie se protégeant elle-même *en différant* l'investissement dangereux, en constituant une réserve (*Vorrat*)" (Derrida, "La différance," *Marges* 19). If, as Lukacher suggests, the real question in *Hamlet* is that of feminine desire—"What does a woman want?" (*Primal* 207)—then Ophelia would appear to call into question that very question by failing to compose such libidinal conundrum. Or maybe her evasion from the scene of desire is but an exacerbation of its primal intractability in the play. At any rate, she fails to survive *because* she hardly lives: the much younger Juliet seems to have experienced more, at least intellectually.[8] Ophelia doesn't really die, she *surdies*. The mode of art Shakespeare executed in his wildly indirect tribute to her is not an *Überlenbenskunst* (Blumenberg 52–64) but rather an *Übertodeskunst*—an art

---

[7] Lupton's attempt to read "a template for a possible polity" (*Thinking* 87), governed by principles of civic virtue, recognition, and equality, into Ophelia's brief response to her brother, is however exorbitant, and is more grounded on the critic's moral passions than on the play's textual evidence.

[8] For the Derridean notion of "life death," and its Freudian context, see Lukacher, *Daemonic*, 59–61.

of surdeath. Such innocuous circularity (from pre-life to post-death) is implied in Gertrude's honed epanalepsis: "sweets to the sweet" (5.1.226). Hamlet's longing for the undoing of his own birth—"it were better my mother had not born me" (3.1.124)—releases the notion of un-creatureliness, best suited to Ophelia, and most eloquently expressed by Laertes' puritanical advice to suppress her presence, fore-wither and un-bloom:

> Fear it, Ophelia, fear it, my dear sister,
> And keep you in the rear of your affection,
> Out of the shot and danger of desire.
> The chariest maid is prodigal enough
> If she unmask her beauty to the moon.
> Virtue itself scapes not calumnious strokes.
> The canker galls the infants of the spring
> Too oft before their buttons be disclosed,
> And in the morn and liquid dew of youth
> Contagious blastments are most imminent. (1.3.33–42)

2

I have argued elsewhere, contra messianic-utopian readings of Shakespeare, that the unique *event* registered in his plays is the birth of human animals, what Hannah Arendt dubbed *natality* and Hugh Grady calls, with a charming Marxian inflection, "the sexual production of children" (*Shakespeare and Impure Aesthetics*, 70).[9] Not because such an occurrence is evental *per se* in the natural order (it is not), but rather because it poses a rare challenge to the social-cultural order: what are the rest of human beings supposed to do with the human "infants of the spring" (*Hamlet* 1.3.39)? How should we refrain to "moralize the spectacle" (*As You Like It*, 2.1.44) of their coming into being, their epigonal late coming, their becoming (human), while securing their entitlement to universal human rights? This may seem a rather démodé, humanist-liberal question, one likely to trouble only human animals concerned with cruelty inflicted on other human animals, unfashionable and fatuous beings like Godwin, Dickens, Mill, Nietzsche, Dostoyevsky, Kafka, Pasolini, or Rorty. The urgent question now is, by contrast, how to go on moralizing the

---

9   For "the miracle of natality" as the "central category of political, as distinguished from metaphysical, thought" see Arendt, *The Human Condition*, 9, 278, 247.

running show of the generic human becoming compulsively particular, of the generic human striving to become post-human, of the non-human (animals, natural environment, objects) becoming ridiculously human, cartoonishly anthropomorphic. I take this moralizing to lie at the root of the social-cultural drive to aestheticize the human along phenomenal lines. Milton figured *Paradise Lost* against his best liberal instincts, and so did Hawthorne in *The Scarlet Letter*, though in the latter case the liberal instincts were unrecoverably buried. Both yielded to phenomenal figuration out of a Puritan yearning to cancel reality, and in that cancellation, they confronted the generic-universal cipher (ought, nought, naught, nothing) that comprises the liberal myth furiously at work in Hegel's paean to a Sein-rooted *Geist* that draws all its sustenance from Nothing. Like Ophelia, Eve and Pearl are figures under erasure, uncannily bound to remain unborn or vanish at every turn of the plot. Only two characters in *Paradise Lost* are granted the privilege to *disappear*: Satan (6.414) and Eve (8.478). Perhaps because at bottom—at the dirty bottom, that is, of the Puritan quagmire—they are looked down upon as the same slimy thing. When the Almighty rips Adam's rib and fashions Eve with his hands, at that much anticipated and climactic instant, something strange occurs:

> She disappeared, and left me dark; I waked
> To find her, or for ever to deplore
> Her loss, and other pleasures all abjure. (8.478–480)

She disappeared. What for this hide-and-seek, wherefore this interlude, to what likely end? Only to reappear three lines later, "When out of hope, behold her, not far off, / Such as I saw her in my dream ..." (481–482)? What is the ground of this interruption, the point of this suspension, the rationale of this suspense? Disappeared [...] loss: (this) appeared lost: para dis lost. The etymology of the term *paradise* leads elsewhere, of course, but "the instance of the letter" (Lacan) is worth exploring for its own sake: *para-* (beside, issuing from, against), *dis-* (lack of, not, opposite of), *lost* (no longer possessed, no longer visible, ruined). In *Hamlet*, the term *lost* nearly always occurs in adjacency to the word *father* (*Hamlet, or, Father is Lost*), a conjuncture that is anything but casual, especially if one is ready, unlike Gertrude, to confront the rationale behind "Ophelia's disturbingly knowledgeable ballads" (Garber 172). Interestingly, moreover, Adam sees or fails to see in the internal, abstract manner that reinstates Hamlet's *mind's eye*: "Mine eyes he closed, but open left the cell / Of fancy, my internal sight; by which / Abstract as in a trance methought I saw" (8.460–62). I am interested in the apparently necessary correlation between the framing operation of an internal sight and the disappearance of the woman, but also intrigued by the abstract, but certain, condemnation of the cruelty unspokenly signified in such disappearance. I am also intrigued by the brutality of a clash between *rational liberalism* and *aesthetic puritanism* not so much as it occurs in Milton, Poe, Hawthorne, James, or Gaddis, but rather as it is prefigured in Shakespeare, and I am intrigued by it because the prevailing neo-phenomenological regimes of reading Shakespeare have sided indefectibly with the Puritan camp, thus depriving his plays of the dialectical tension upon which they are grounded. Current early modernists, including brilliant scholars like Jonathan Goldberg, are still trapped in the delusion that liberalism is inherently opposed to radicalism. This chimera is based on a confusion between political-economic "neoliberalism"—a conjuncture that emerges, historically, in the early 1980s, broadly to replace, in the cultural imaginary, what the sixties radicals called "the military-industrial complex" (see, for instance, Mailer's *The Armies of the Night*)—and traditional liberalism. From its inception in Hobbes, the adversaries of genuine *liberalism* are the Puritans—in all their variety (prophetic, messianic, apocalyptic activists, moral sentimentalists, and upholders of *vivere civile*). The fact that the sixties radicals could hardly conceal their Puritan leanings, their compulsive cathexis to "millennial hope" and American utopia (Bercovitch, "Preface" to *The American Jeremiad* xxiv) in no way alters the logic that opposes an individualist, rational liberalism for which the nation is a pragmatic expedient, and a communitarian, irrational Puritanism for which America is the City of God. Puritans and radicals both strive to *see* the girl (Ophelia), whether dressed up in the habit of a nun or nude like a hippy. Both are involved in the same scopic compulsion to place the girl, for visual consumption, before the mirror of nature, to phenomenalize her as a symbol, say, of a potential liberation or a possible polity. Indifference to her aesthetic presence is not necessarily an exclusive feature of ironic liberals, but it remains a fact, for instance, that Trilling, an admirer of Freud, was scarcely offended by Hamlet's Oedipal attachment to his mother. Leaving Hamlet alone—Hamlet never giving up on his desires, however deviant—is the first step towards unseeing him, reading him, listening to him (*The Liberal Imagination* 52). This will help us tolerate better the scandal of his unphenomenal Ophelia. Bercovitch's moving preface to the reedition of *The American Jeremiad* presses claims that help sustain my point, and it offers the added interest of outlining a recent history of American studies that is bizarrely akin to the recent story of Shakespeare studies: one is left to wonder if America is or hoped ever to become—as free, inventive, and reality-encompassing as—Shakespeare. Remember Locke's hyperbole—"Thus in the beginning all the World was *America*" (*Two Treatises*, 301)—which Johnson tamed into Shakespeare's "drama is the mirror of nature" (265). The fact that so many American Shakespeareans have transformed the bard's works into the very mirror, soil, and habitat of their own beautiful soul/selves—their one locus of face-to-face hospitality, their intersubjective neo-material dwelling, their site of mutual eco-ideological recognition—is not casual. This explains why some of their essays on Shakespeare differ little from interior-design brochures, booklets of self-care, or religious-sect circular letters for spiritual exercises. The genuine opposition, I insist, is that between Puritans and liberals. Think of the difference between Spenser and Hobbes, Richardson and Hume, George Eliot and Darwin. Although *prima facie* Shakespeare would appear best to line up with the first names of these three pairs, he is actually much closer to Hobbes, Hume, and Darwin: as Russell pointed out in 1925, "the good life involves much beside virtue—intelligence, for instance" (*What I believe*, 29). This is not to say, obviously, that Spenser, Richardson, and Eliot were dull, but rather that their intelligence was often befuddled by confounding moral passions. Some of the confuse neo-communitarian configurations of the 1960s are typically neo-Puritan in their hostility to liberal individualism.[10] Puritanism—including pornography—is always *aesthetic* in that it works to embody and phenomenalize what it must energetically condemn. Pornography-consumers and their Puritan detractors, including feminist opponents, are both oblivious to the (liberal) fact, highlighted by J.M. Coetzee, that "the interests and desires of human beings are many times more complex, devious, inscrutable, and opaque to their subjects" (*Giving Offense*, 62) than they would be willing to allow. Note that the cumulating adjectives *complex*, *devious*, *inscrutable*, and *opaque* all gesture toward the *unphenomenal*. The Neoclassical program *aut prodesse aut delectare* is at bottom a Puritan mishmash designed to rationalize the mass production of inquisitorial voyeurism (show me bad girls so that we can censure them and learn to be good) and the serialization of exorcisms of controlled-contained flesh. This may help explain, among other things, the popularity of Ovid in the England of Spenser and the black-suited censors, or the recourse to confounding irony by the author of *Moll Flanders*.

---

10 Most branches of the noisy and lively American Left of the 1960s did not come to grips with rational-dialectical-materialist Marxism, any more than they connected with the Unionist traditions of the good Old Left. This is no discovery. But see Richard Rorty, *Achieving Our Country*, 73–110. Commenting on a book by Himmelfarb, Dworkin notes: "She says, for example, that the radical 'counterculture' celebrates spontaneity, and she therefore claims it as Mill's creature. But she concedes that the language of this 'counterculture' emphasizes community more than individuality. She might have added that its proponents have held liberalism in general, and Mill in particular, in special contempt, and have much preferred such writers as Marcuse, whose hostility to *On Liberty* they find congenial" (261).

But the Neoclassical program that subjected, like Hegel's Hamlet, aesthetic contemplation to moral-doctrinal condemnation, never quite managed to elucidate the writings of the bard. Johnson did his best, which wasn't enough, and Wittgenstein's reaction against the "asymmetry" of Shakespeare's art smacks too of Puritan intolerance.[11] In fact, the way phenomenological critics of Shakespeare remain instructed by his pleasurable phenomena and delighted or very disgusted by his supposedly moral or ideological doctrine (it all depends on what rule is at stake) is proof of an extensive misjudgment, as it runs counter to the Neoclassical embarrassment (Dryden's, Johnson's, Voltaire's) with both Shakespeare's inartistic aesthetics and his very unlikely teachings. Such embarrassment spelled no complete misjudgment: it revealed good critical instinct and sound judgement attended by bigoted prejudice. But fear not: the inveterate tradition of rewriting, correcting and remoralizing Shakespeare is in no danger of declining.

3

The story of a liberal mind illiberally inflicting cruelty on a beautiful young woman, and eventually causing her death, remains a liberal story, even if it carries no discernible "moral purpose": this is hard to swallow for "liberal metaphysicians" (Rorty, *Contingency* 144). Edgar Allan Poe, who was not exactly a liberal ironist, made much fuss of this apparent platitude.[12] And so did Henry James, who turned, in late life, with reactive praise, to *The Tempest*, a play where the girl survives—or dies into marriage, which is the same thing. This permitted James to allay his remorse for having resurrected Ophelia in *Daisy Miller* and *The Wings of the Dove*. Thomas Mann, whose celebration of Nietzsche is signally perspectivized through Ophelia's praise of Hamlet, reminded us that, to the author of *Beyond Good and Evil*, the philosopher's love of life is like the love felt for a woman about whom we are in doubt.[13] I am, I am aware, moving in circles around a center (Ophelia) pulled in opposite directions—liberal

---

11 For Hegel's and Wittgenstein's response to *Hamlet*, and to Shakespeare more generally, see Andrew Cutrofello, *All for Nothing*, 34–41; 131–133.

12 In "The Philosophy of Composition," Poe wrote that "the death, then, of a beautiful woman is, unquestionably, the most poetical topic in the world" (*Essays and Reviews* 19).

13 Mann's longest text on the German philosopher, "Nietzsche in the Light of Modern Experience," opens with a sustained elaboration of Ophelia's praise to Hamlet beginning with the line "O what a noble mind is here o'erthrown!" (*Hamlet* 3.1.149). The above quote is taken from a shorter piece, titled "Spoken prelude to a musical tribute to Nietzsche."

weightlessness and moral-metaphysical weight. Ronald Dworkin contended that "liberals are suspicious of ontological luxury"—meaning the "ghostly entities" of collectivism and the communal (xi). And Hans Blumenberg quotes Otto Neurath to the effect that humans trying to make sense of a language fraught with nonsense are like sailors reconstructing a ship at sea. In such critical context, "only metaphysics can disappear completely. The imprecise 'clusters' are always part of the ship" (77). But when Ophelia drowns and disappears, no luxury is expended, no metaphysics goes. On the contrary, the fact that her clusters (*Ballungen*), her garlands, tunes, and remembrances remain (here we are, evoking them) is proof that she is not ghostly in the ideological (ontological, metaphysical) sense. She is simply not real enough.[14] Metaphysical is no doubt the quality of much of what Hamlet cares to critically consider—human *haecceity*, the division of matter, cosmic spatio-temporality, postmortem life—but Ophelia appears to dwell, paradoxically, in the pastoral backyard of the prince's decrepit Southern mansion, surviving or surdying amidst the remains of *his* vanishing metaphysics. This sounds like Faulkner but is Hegel:

> and so this darkness, this colorless self-preoccupation of spirit bent upon itself, having been dispelled, existence shone transformed into the bright world of flowers—of which, as is well known, none is *black*.
> HEGEL, "Preface to the First Edition" to *The Science of Logic* 8

Did Hegel have *Hamlet* in mind? Probably not. Maybe something in Goethe. At any rate: how real are, for Hegel, those colored *flowers*, how much reality does he accord to the appearance lurking in the phrase "existence shone"? What intensity of *Realität,* what degree of *Wirklichkeit* can we grant appearance (*Schein*) in the Kant-Hegel-Nietzsche tradition? The irony of the above Hegel passage suggests he dismissed this blossoming as much as he deplored the anti-metaphysical lassitude of the scientific camp. I guess the Derrida of *Marges* and *Glas* could help us penetrate the arcana of Hegel's *botanics* and adjudge the exact degree of the existence of Ophelia, Notre Dame des Fleurs.[15]

---

14 Liberal suspicion of spectral communal entities is indeed widespread, but the hostility is also directed against the *naturalization* of the human subject and its appended rights. The birth of Ophelia is a routine natural occurrence. Her conversion into a subject is a cultural event, greeted both by liberals and rationalists. Two alternative configurations suggest themselves: 1) the natural being that fails to subjectivate and 2) the natural being that sidesteps subjectivation by being inflated—via ontological luxury and moralistic excess—into a turgid metaphysical persona.

15 In *De la grammatologie*, Derrida observes, apropos of a Rousseau passage, "Que la botanique devienne le supplément de la société, c'est là plus qu'une catastrophe" (212).

Hamlet's cruelty against her is aberrant, and is invariably premised upon her onto-phenomenal inanity, her uncreatureliness, often striking the bawdy note where nothing and vagina merge:

> HAMLET. Do you think I meant country matters?
> OPHELIA. I think nothing, my lord.
> HAMLET. That's a fair thought to lie between maids' legs.
> OPHELIA. What is, my lord?
> HAMLET. Nothing.
> OPHELIA. You are merry, my lord. (3.2.115–120)

The master plot of the liberal myth states that the survival of an individual human child is the worthiest—the most humane—of human goals. In his late romances, Shakespeare invested much in reconfiguring some versions of the myth. If the baby survives, it enjoys the opportunity of turning into a human *subject*, in the transcendental sense Badiou reserves for this complex term.[16] If the human subject survives enough to overcome her first critical interactions with other subjects, and to pull through the moral incandescence produced by such friction, then she is apt to leave experience behind, reprise her former coldness, and vanish into the social configuration. There is no shortage of Shakespearean adolescents and young women drawn to this momentous crisis. Some, like Juliet or Ophelia, flare up into spasm and voice, only to exit underground, underwater, inexorably offstage. But there is a difference between these girls: whereas Juliet is properly, affluently, subjectivated, Ophelia remains—ironically—on this side of the subject. Still, both show a parallel refractoriness to moralistic appropriation: they should be haunted by no *community* metaphysical spectre, tempted by no *identity* ontological luxury. Theirs is the liberal right par excellence, brilliantly formulated by a character in a William Gaddis novel: "the right to be let alone" (*A Frolic of His Own* 276).

Ned Lukacher has suggested that in *Hamlet* Shakespeare pointedly tried "to keep conscience unfettered, much more unfettered than the Puritans could ever have tolerated" (*Daemonic* 145). Could ever *tolerate*, I would add, for Puritanism has not completely subsided. Lukacher's argument is "that Shakespeare

---

Flowers abound, of course, in the essay "La mythologie blanche" in *Marges de la philosophie*, but also in *Glas*, where the Hegel texts are confronted to Genet's novel *Notre-Dame des Fleurs*.

16 Badiou: "We will call *subjective* those processes relative to the qualitative concentration of force." *Theory of the Subject*, 41; "Il faudra bien admettre que l'animal humaine peut ne pas être sujet." *Théorie axiomatique du sujet*, 22.

came to see the Puritan appropriation of the inwardness of conscience as so profound a danger that he began what I regard as a certain defense of conscience as poetry" (155). What would he have done, had he had the motive and the cue for passion that we have now, with Puritans going about their business in camouflage phenomenology?

4

Barely hinted at in the sources, Ophelia becomes an object of Shakespeare's—and Hamlet's—greatest concern. She grows into something rather unprecedented, is given strange voice and tune. But the sources are there. In Saxo Grammaticus' chronicle, she is just "a fair woman [*excellentis formae femina*]" cunningly placed in Hamlet's way in some "secluded place [*inter latebras*]," to "provoke his mind to the temptations of love [*ad amoris illecebras provocaret*]." If he ravishes her, this will prove his lethargy to be feigned. Hamlet manages however to "practice wantonness [*exercendae libidinis*]" with her without being overseen, and the secluded place turns, first into "a dark spot [*obscuro loco*]," and finally into "a distant and impenetrable fen [*ad palustre procul invium protrahit*]." She will keep it a secret, Hamlet knows, because "both of them had been under the same fostering in their childhood; and this early rearing in common had brought Amleth and the girl into great intimacy [*maximam familiaritatem*]." The pastoral-mythical resonance is very strong, reaching out to Paul et Virginie and Catherine and Heathcliff. And one can even discern Daisy Miller emerging from a Swiss lake only to fall back on a paludic Roman fen. Let us, at any rate, retain the figure of a woman of "excellent form" driven to a secluded place, a dark spot, an impenetrable fen, to be penetrated and sworn to silence by an intimate childhood friend. Belleforest adds little of essence to this basic sketch. Still, the way he laces the tale with a great deal of standard misogyny and a rather dreadful vitriol against female luxury helps deflect the figuration of the girl in the direction, eagerly exploited by Shakespeare's prince, of the fishmonger's daughter.

Out of this flimsy subtextual material, Ophelia breaks into the play as a discreet quantum of human energy, flares into voice, and disappears. Like Silvia in *The Two Gentlemen of Verona*, "her 'being', literally, is figurative. No wonder, then, that she ends up in the forest, voiceless" (Goldberg, *Shakespeare's Hand* 11). From the moment of her first appearance, her absence from stage and page torments the reader-spectator in the same way the exact position of an electron puzzles the physicist. According to biographical legend, Werner

Heisenberg first intuited the theory of quantum leaps while standing one night in a park behind the Copenhagen Institute of Physics:

> The young Werner walks about pensively in the park. It is really dark there; we are in 1925. There is only an occasional streetlamp, casting dim islands of light here and there. The pools of light are separated by large expanses of darkness. Suddenly, Heisenberg sees a figure pass by. Actually, he does not see him pass: he sees him appear beneath a lamp, then disappear into the dark before reappearing beneath another lamp, and then vanishing back into the dark again. And so on, from pool of light to pool of light, until he eventually disappears altogether into the night. Heisenberg thinks that, "evidently," the man does not actually vanish and reappear: in his mind, he can easily reconstruct the man's trajectory between one streetlamp and another. After all, a man is a substantial object, big and heavy—and big, heavy objects do not simply appear and vanish ...
> ROVELLI, *Reality* 90

But *dramatis personae*, like the electrons that are Heisenberg's true object of concern, are not substantial, big, and heavy objects.[17] No amount of naturalization and moralization, no added metaphysical ballast, will serve to turn a theatrical character into a "substantial object." Simon Palfrey has demonstrated, in an extraordinary book, that Edgar, the character in *King Lear*, is little more than a nagging disembodied voice.[18] And so is Ophelia, a vocal *quantum* (or sonic *quidam*) that manifests itself "only when it interacts, when it collides with something else [...] like a ghost in the dark, and then disappears into the night" (Rovelli, *Reality* 100). Her intermittence is particularly noticeable during her last stage apparition, in *Hamlet* 4.5, where she enters and exits twice. At that point of the play, the moment where she is more poignantly and memorably present, she is no longer there, she is already out and down, a *pièce de résistance* for "liberal shepherds" (*Hamlet* 4.7.141). Ophelia's recalcitrant non-presence poses an insurmountable obstacle to any "phenomenology of the work of art" ready to conduct itself as a "phenomenology of ghosts" (Garber 21): attention to the primal scene of writing—where Ophelia officiates as reader, writer, signer, singer, sign, song, unreadable *signans* and unreachable *signatum*—reminds us that the latter (the phenomenology of ghosts) is less a

---

17 Karen Barad offers a reading of Derrida's Hamlet from the philosophical perspectives opened by quantum physics. On the disappearance of the electron, see "Quantum Entanglements," 247.
18 The book is *Poor Tom: Living* King Lear.

possible science than a contradiction in terms. Phenomenology and hauntology are incompatible practices.

So Ophelia "disappears into the night," but her words and traces remain: her ephemeral trajectory leaves a trail that supplements the play as a fictional whole. Ophelia becomes Hamlet's primeval fiction, his necessary lie, in the same way as Marion supplemented Rousseau's mental life with an opportune fabrication. In the final essay of *Allegories of Reading*, Paul de Man tests his storytelling abilities by reprising a particular episode Rousseau narrates with special panache, opines de Man, an incident that constitutes "a central passage of the *Confessions*, [...] a truly primal scene of lie and deception," with the possible title of *The Episode of Marion and the Ribbon*, or, better, *Marion und der Zauberer*:

> The episode itself is one of a series of stories of petty larceny, but with an added twist. While employed as a servant in an aristocratic Turin household, Rousseau has stolen a "pink and silver colored ribbon." When the theft is discovered, he accuses a young maidservant of having given him the ribbon, the implication being that she was trying to seduce him. In public confrontation, he obstinately clings to the story, thus casting irreparable doubt on the honesty and the morality of an innocent girl who has never done him the slightest bit of harm and whose sublime good nature does not even flinch in the face of dastardly accusation: "Ah Rousseau! I took you to be a man of good character. You are making me very unhappy but I would hate to change places with you" (85). The story ends badly, with both characters being dismissed, thus allowing Rousseau to speculate at length, and with some relish, on the dreadful things that are bound to have happened in the subsequent career of the hapless girl.
>
> *Allegories of Reading* 279

The parallels with the Hamlet-Ophelia story are glaring. The dynamics of mutual moral exposure, with female honesty at stake, and near-public confrontation occasioned by redelivered remembrances, returned gifts, and a confiscated private letter, decisively informs Shakespeare's handling of the story. And so does the moral courage of the beautiful girl ("Marion était jolie"), her discretion, modesty and sweetness ("un air de modestie et de douceur qui faisait qu'on ne pouvait la voir sans l'aimer; d'ailleurs bonne fille, sage et d'une fidélité à toute épreuve"), her power to react with a display of pity for whom she takes to be the true victim of the calumny: "Ah Rousseau! I took you to be a good character!" "O, what a noble mind is here o'erthrown!." Both stories "end badly." In both cases, the girl is dismissed: "renvoyer" is the verb used by

Rousseau. But so are the young men—Rousseau is ousted "to speculate at length" and to throes of remorse and torments of guilt that prove so strong that he is compelled to write the *Confessions* in an attempt to free himself (*m'en délivrer*). Hamlet is discharged to his long speculation, his poem unlimited. And what about Ophelia? Well, if we stitch up the lexical shreds and tropes of the final sentence (*dreadful things, bound, happened, career, hapless girl*) we get a fairly accurate glimpse of her *figure in the carpet*, the poor wretch being pulled down to muddy death. An elegiac motif to bedizen a late-medieval tapestry, something for Gertrude to remember on rainy afternoons. Like Ophelia, Marion suddenly appears beneath the stage lamp, then briskly disappears into her original darkness. Rousseau names her and retells her case only to force her definite banishment, and thus achieve some kind of mental peace—"the closure of excuse: 'qu'il me soit permit de n'en reparler jamais'" (de Man 286). Translated into English: "the rest *be* silence."

De Man believed that the moral of Rousseau's inset tale is that Marion, initially a random name—"Marion"—dropped by the young Rousseau to escape the strait of accusation, obtains her significance retrospectively, by investing the free signifier of the name with a libidinal charge that was partly hidden to himself. We may say that the accident of his naming her rationalized his desire for possessing her, originally deflected towards (and disguised as) a craving to possess the ribbon. The performative excuse prompts an inscriptive event (the production of the name) whose *materiality* will change the past and compromise the future.[19] Similarly, Hamlet will learn of his love for Ophelia only after the "accidents" of her death (his *casus belli*) and of his naming her, his double *lapsus linguae*, from "Soft you, now, / The fair Ophelia" (3.1.91) to "What, the fair Ophelia!" (5.1.225). Again Claudius, of all people, holds the key to this *uncanny causality*, "as there are tongues, are hands, are accidents" (4.7.95.8).[20] The notion, then, that the girl's "entry into the discourse is a mere effect of chance," the idea that "she is a free signifier, metonymically related to the part she is made to play in the subsequent system of exchanges and substitutions" (de Man, *Allegories* 288–89) compounds further her liberal emptiness. And such kenosis parallels the hermeneutic reduction of Hamlet the person to Hamlet the character, and, further, of Hamlet the character to "Hamlet" the

---

19 See Derrida's careful rereading of de Man's analysis of Rousseau's passage in the extraordinary essay, "Typewriter Ribbon: Limited Ink (2)," especially 316–324.

20 Although *uncanny causality* is examined in depth in Marjorie Garber's study, *Shakespeare's Ghost Writers* (1987), this crucial motif is also the object of some brilliant speculation in Lukacher's earlier *Primal Scenes* (1986), where he exposes Shakespeare, with the help of Hegel, Freud and Althusser, to the "metaleptic logic of causality and the event" (181).

name, with the analytical proviso "that linguistic items that look like names but don't refer to objects of anyone's acquaintance are not genuine names at all but denoting phrases in disguise" (Cutrofello 118), and that therefore, Bertrand Russell concludes, "all statements about Hamlet are really about the *word* 'Hamlet'" (qtd. in Cutrofello, *All for Nothing* 119). *Denoting phrases in disguise*, like "Je me trouble, je balbutie, et enfin je dis, en rougissant, que c'est Marion qui me l'a donné" (Rousseau, *Les Confessions* 137), or "The fair Ophelia!." This second exclamation is uttered by a "guilty thing" (1.1.129) at the close of his first solo variation on the need to traduce thoughts into deeds, on the injunction, that is, never to "lose the name of action" (3.1.90), and it expresses joy at having found, suddenly, the very name of action, *the fair Ophelia*, used to very precariously denote the electron—the "nymph" or Eve or "little elf" (*The Scarlet Letter* 63)— that is about to cross the illumined (phenomenal) stage. The fact that Hamlet's initial course of action involves a labyrinth of non-referential calumnies and excuses around that very name "Ophelia," a labyrinth designed to gain or make, via retentions and protentions, phenomenal time—the time of his inaction— doesn't revoke the role that very name is called to play when, upon learning of her unphenomenal time—her suicide—, he decides to name her anew, *What, the fair Ophelia!*. Through this empty denomination he is finally moved to action, but more importantly, he confronts the fullness (the denotation, the *Bedeutung*) of his desire and his loss. No melancholy is required because he has had enough of it, because he has already mourned her in the first two acts of the play: in a sense, Ophelia dies to make retrospective sense of his original "obstinate condolement" (1.2.93). Her role, like that of Marion, is that of an "airy, weightless non-substance," an empty signifier, a supplementary fiction:

> Fiction has nothing to do with representation but is the absence of any link between utterance and a referent, regardless of whether this link be casual, encoded, or governed by any other conceivable relationship that could lend itself to systematization. In fiction thus conceived the 'necessary link' of the metaphor has been metonymized beyond the point of catachresis, and the fiction becomes the disruption of the narrative's referential illusion.
> DE MAN, *Allegories* 292

The operative precedence of the rhetorical machine—the slippage of names, traces, gifts, givens, remembrances, poems, flowers, tunes—institutes a use of language that is always *unphenomenal* because mechanical and formal, "no matter how deeply this aspect may be concealed by aesthetic, formalistic delusions" (294). Marjorie Garber argues that the way Laertes' describes "the scene of Ophelia's flower-giving, as 'a document in madness, thoughts and remembrance fitted' (4.5.175), identifies the documentary evidence, the displacement of the written and the writable, that Ophelia's subject position compels" (34), and she later construes such displacement, following de Man and Derrida, as taking place in the transition from *Erinnerung* (memory as interiorization) to *Gedächtnis* (mechanical memory). "Abruptly [...] wrenched from *Erinnerung* to *Gedächtnis*, from symbol to sign" (Garber 200), from the phenomenal to the written, Hamlet is doomed to traffic with signifiers, contingent words, and names: *the fair Ophelia!* The mechanical-anatomical implication of the term "remembrance" already juxtaposes both meanings in an impossible figure, that of an interior memory that is made of separate members or parts.[21] The transition from Ophelia figured to Ophelia disfigured threatens, we know, to desecrate the fulsome aesthetic splendor of the pre-Raphaelite icon and sets up the agenda of French symbolism in the direction of radical disappearance. Ophelia is neither a material fact nor an aesthetic *Jugendstil* essence: she is rather a language-incensed void.[22] This may explain why the inaesthetic choices of an anti-Puritan like Badiou appear to lead ineluctably to verbal scenarios of subtraction, isolation and vanishment, as in Mallarmé's poem "A la nu accablante tu," where the *sépulcral naufrage* is greeted by the "flanc enfant d'une sirène." Ophelia's non-referential and pre-subjective standing, what I am calling, with deliberate obfuscation, her liberal emptiness, is not to be confused with insignificance. It is rather marked by the overdetermination of arbitrary nominative significance, by the obligation first "to *treat* the trace, to remain faithful to it," and second, "*to name the name*, that is, to assert the name as an eventual naming" (Badiou, *Conditions* 51). Badiou's politics are far from liberal, but his habit of glancing askew at attempts to theorize ethics along moralistic lines into particularistic niches places him at one with liberals like Bertrand Russell or Jacques Derrida. To discover in Celan's apostrophic exhortation to the thrown disc (*Wurfscheibe*), "wirf dich / aus dir hinaus" (cast yourself / outside out of yourself), an instance of the *poetic naming* of an event, and to conclude that "to name a supplement, a chance, something incalculable, it

---

21   Apart from Garber, see also Lukacher, *Primal Scenes*, 227–229.
22   The "essentialist" connivance between phenomenological logicism and turn-of-the-century aestheticism was denounced by Adorno in terms reminiscent of *Hamlet*: "Husserl's concept of essence scintillates such ambiguity. Phenomenological purity, idiosyncratically against all contact with the factical, still remains perishable like a flower ornament. 'Essence' was the cherished Jugendstil expression for the consumptive soul whose metaphysical lustre springs only from nothingness and the renunciations of existence. This soul's sisters are the Husserlian essentialities, phantasmagoric reflections of a subjectivity which hopes to obliterate itself within them as their 'sense'" (*Against* 90).

is necessary to draw from the void of sense, in the absence of established significations, and to the peril of language" (*Conditions* 41–42) takes a great deal of unphenomenal tolerance, a rational-liberal capacity, that is, to resist the lures of aesthetic calculation. Ophelia means something, that much is clear. But we do not know what she means. All the same, we know that her semiotic force is not that of genuine denotation, as the meaning of a word (and Ophelia, for want of a better word, is a word) is just more words. The resulting referential uncertainty compromises the presentative and representative (the phenomenal) potency of a play *all* of whose signs (words) are, in point of fact, "denoting phrases without a denotation" (Cutrofello, *All for Nothing* 118). It is no accident that Merleau-Ponty, the arch-priest of the phenomenal religion, should find Saussure's notion of semiotic relationality untenable: "Idée difficile, car le bon sens répond que si le terme A et le terme B n'avaient pas du tout de sens, on ne voit pas comment il y aurait contraste de sens entre eux" (*Signes* 49). His *bon sens* fails or refuses to grasp that only differential interactions between these terms are likely to lend a semblance of phenomenal reality (*sens*) to otherwise meaningless entities. This *common sense*, also vindicated by Arendt—and Vickers, and Scruton—has today become the epistemic anesthesia used to defuse the critical power of Shakespeare's plays with a view to heightening, through calls to positivity and embodiment, their moral hyperesthesia. What gets lost in the surgery room is not only the not uncommon sense of the lying of language, already tested in Rousseau, but more specifically a sense of the lying of language "against 'sight'" (Fineman 16).

5

The fact that Shakespeare's biographical gossip labors to denote a Stratford girl, named Katherine Hamlett, perhaps more than Will's acquaintance, who drowned in mysterious circumstances in a local stream (Duncan-Jones 174–77), yields a factual *donnée* whose referential positivity, however, once taken up as sign within the playtext, goes under erasure: its exceptional status, like that of the linkage between Hamlet and Shakespeare's son Hamnet, aggravates rather than allays the emptiness of the resulting cipher. So *le terme A et le terme B*: Katherine Hamlett as Ophelia *et* Hamnet as Hamlet. Or is it Hamlett as *O filia*? It doesn't really make much difference, since once sutured by the relational (paratactic) conjunction (*et*) the play's immanence will take charge of significance, repudiating whatever strives to enter the playfield without shedding its historical and positive transcendence (its presence) and assuming the impresence of a trace. Ophelia, in short, is there to supplement her play with a cipher of nothingness, and to provide "un bon cavalier pâle / Un pauvre fou" (Rimbaud 30) with the one fiction that may set his case to rest. This pale night is Rimbaud's version of Hamlet in the sequence of three poems he wrote, mimicking rather than operating an aesthetics of subtraction, in tribute to Ophelia—"fantôme blanc" (29). Two features stand out in this elegiac triptych: her sexual innocence (*ton sein d'enfant*) and her liberty (*l'âpre liberté*). The latter motif reemerges, with uncanny weight, at the close of the second poem—"Ciel! Amour! Liberté!" (30). Who says that pictures only and false fair become a verse? Is Ophelia, Hamlet's fiction, not a symbol of freedom? And if she is, what kind of freedom are we dealing with, natural or socially instituted freedom? And, more importantly, of whose freedom are we talking about? Replace in the Derrida passage below Rousseau with Shakespeare, conceive of the existences of flesh and bone as Hamlett and Hamnet, Ophelia and *O filius*, and we shall have gone some way towards answering these questions:

> What we have tried to show by following the guiding line of the "dangerous supplement," is that in what one calls the real life of these existences "of flesh and bone," beyond and behind what one believes can be circumscribed as Rousseau's text, there has never been anything but writing; there have never been anything but supplements, substitutive significations which could only come forth in a chain of differential references, the "real" supervening, and being added only while taking on meaning from a trace and from an invocation of the supplement, etc. And thus to infinity, for we have read, in the text, that the absolute present, Nature, that which words like "real mother" name, have always already escaped, have never existed; that what opens meaning and language is writing as the disappearance of natural presence. Although it is not commentary, our reading must be intrinsic and remain within the text. That is why, in spite of certain appearances, the locating of the word supplement is here not at all psychoanalytical, if by that we understand an interpretation that takes us outside of the writing toward a psychobiographical signified, or even toward a general psychological structure that could rightly be separated from the signifier.
>
> *Of Grammatology* 159

Whence the crux of a meaning that is writing as the disappearance of natural presence, in an unphenomenal scenario restrained by the premise that Nature has never existed. By contrast, history, including natural history, exists: could it be otherwise? But the conjectural ligatures between *terme A* and its signified, between *terme B* and its signified, cannot stipulate an outside to the text where the deliverances of positive (phenomenal) meaning are miraculously expected to occur. This doesn't mean that there exists no transcendent outside to the text: therein lies a major anti-Derridean misrepresentation. Of course, this outside exists, it is *nearly* all that exists, but its bearing on immanent textual behaviour is not *only* governed by the order of the outside.[23] As Adorno sharply observed, "what makes existing artworks more than existence is not simply another existing thing [*nicht wiederum ein Daseiendes*], but their language [*aber ihre Sprache*]" (*Aesthetic Theory*, 104; *Ästhetische Theorie* 160).

And yet, no matter how quietly we name her, we can barely unsee her, barely, hard as we try, unburden Ophelia of her phenomenally embodied selfhood. Shakespeare, however, is certainly not to blame for this inauspicious burden— for the morbid rites of aesthetic iconophilia thickening around the empty signifier of her name. The poet discharged her with the same figural circularity— "Sweets to the sweet. Farewell!" (5.1.226)—that marked her inconspicuous life. Contra all mounting emblematic additions, she is, she should remain, "the invisible event" (4.4.9.40). Like all (no)things blessed with epistemic worth—"I think nothing, my lord" (3.2.106)—Ophelia revels in phenomenal negativity. If she "turns into positivity, [she] becomes untrue" (Adorno, *Against* 24).

6

The adjective "unphenomenal" also crops up in the Seminar on *Heraclitus* organized by Martin Heidegger and Eugen Fink in the Winter semester of 1966/67 at the University of Freiburg. Fink refers twice to *unphenomenal reality*. First in allusion to the gods mentioned by Heidegger during their conversation as an example of "what is" along with other phenomenal existents, like the sea, the earth or heaven (86). This problematic suggestion is made in the midst of an argument aimed at clarifying the enigmatic relationship that exists between ἕν (the one) and τὰ πάντα (all things)—a relation, to be sure, notoriously akin to the Heideggerian *ontologische Differenz* between beings and Being. And second, when Heraclitean fire is singled out as the trope that best expresses that mode of reality: "We have no language for the purpose of addressing the relatedness of ἕν to τὰ πάντα. The ἕν lights up to us only in lightning, in sun, in the seasons, in fire. Fire, however, is not the phenomenal, but the unphenomenal fire, in the shine of which τὰ πάντα come forth to appearance" (*Heraclitus* 103).

---

23 The first chapter of McDowell's important book, *Mind and World* (1996), deals precisely with this problem of external *causation* (Davidson)—of the logical space of nature *impacting* on the logical space of reasons and concepts.

Here the unphenomenal shuns the immediacy of presence and is contingent upon a totality whose unity and being it grounds and indirectly represents, not least by strategies of reflexive, albeit vision-enabling, visibility.[24] Like the Kantian sublime, or like the play of structure for Derrida, the unphenomenal presumes something that is unbound (*unbegrenzt*) and yet finitely total.[25]

Fink, Blanchot and Caputo use the term in overt oppositional allusion to—near-parodic echo of—the *phenomenal* apud Husserl. But only Fink manages to impart a sense of necessity—the necessity of an unbridgeable distance between the totality of what appears (the phenomenal) and its grounding condition of possibility (the unphenomenal). Fink's implicit reproach is that phenomenology was never sufficiently "transcendental," which translated into Heideggerian parlance means it wasn't sufficiently "ontological." But then, of course, a major problem arises, for when the drive to transcend doesn't reach all the way into the *transcendental*, it tends to satisfy itself with attaining the *transcendent*—i.e. the "external gifts" (*1 Henry VI* 5.7.3)—present-day phenomenologists wrongly take for *things themselves* (*die Sache selbst*). This remains a running predicament for phenomenology—whose initial Kantian zest and Cartesian impetus have gradually died out in an environment-friendly spree. Look around and seize whatever you see—"The cloud-capp'd towers, the gorgeous palaces, / The solemn temples, the great globe itself" (*The Tempest* 4.1.152–53). Thus runs the phenomenal mantra of world-avid Shakespeareans. To their thing-crowded minds thus to exercise the scopic faculties is tantamount to *doing Shakespeare* the wizard, the demiurge of the "present fancies" whose enactment, embodiment or (re)presentation is entrusted to friendly spirits. Fair enough, as reckoning with dissolution and the unsubstantial—going along, that is, solely with the *fancies* in the "present fancies" (*The Tempest* 4.1.122)—is likely to menace the ontic bacchanalia of *Phänomenologie als*

---

24   See Joel Fineman, 11. Heidegger's long exegesis of the episode of the Cave in Plato's *Republic* also emphasizes this motif of transcendental visibility: "In the 'allegory' the things that show themselves are the 'image' for the 'ideas'. But in the sun in the 'allegory' is the 'image' for that which makes all ideas visible. It is the 'image' for the idea of all ideas" (*Pathmarks* 165).

25   The fact that meaning gets started through difference doesn't completely annul the framing pressure of the transcendental and totality: *différance* becomes the new transcendental principle, and infinite difference plays itself out on a limited board (structure). The unphenomenal (as unrepresented possibility of meaning) depends on the "limite de la totalisation" (*L'écriture*, 423). I guess I am merely stressing the connection between the transcendental (Kant), the structural (Derrida), the total and dialectical (Hegel) and the unphenomenal. See Kant, *Critique of Judgment*, 116; de Man, "Phenomenality and Materiality in Kant" in *Aesthetic Ideology*, 75; and, of course, Jacques Derrida, "La structure, le signe, le jeu dans le discours des sciences humaines," *L'écriture et la différence*, 423.

(unstrict, lazy, hazy) *Wissenschaft*. But what if the unsubstantial—and also the unphenomenal—were always-already at work in Prospero's scripted "art" and doings (ποίησις, ἔργον, πρᾶγμα), long before he actually resolved to break his staff? Also brought home by the reproach is the guiltless longing for a "holistic ontology," a sentiment that appeals to thinkers as divergent as Badiou and Brandom, not to mention, of course, Fredric Jameson—our revisionist champion of totality.[26] Another related problem is phenomenology's inability to grasp real difference—at one with the lately refurbished neo-phenomenological tendency to celebrate insignificant, albeit sociologically apropos, diversity.[27] For there is, Deleuze demurs, no real phenomenology of real difference: "La différence n'est pas le phénomène, mais le plus proche noumène du phénomène" (*Différence et répétition* 287).[28] When Ophelia tells Laertes that he "must wear [his] rue with a difference" (4.5.177) she is wryly condemning him to epigonal dissolution. Unlike Hamlet's, his difference—the brisure or cadency he may manage to crack into his father's arms—will go unnoticed and leave no story behind. Only the fracture of a steadfast palisade—"Now cracks a noble heart" (5.2.302)—is likely to submit the difference requisite for unphenomenal meanings to get started, tropes to drift, and stories to go on being told. To risk the claim that "Shakespeare calls us to a universalism that is opposite to the 'simulacrum' of liberal universalism, one in which there are only differences, but 'there is nothing else'" (Wilson, *Worldly Shakespeare* 4) is no exigent task. It is much harder to abide the onrush of uncertainty to which such wager commits one: for the temptation to stop at some point along the chain of signifiers is well-nigh irresistible and yielding to such temptation will only be legitimate if the arrest is not induced by extratextual (phenomenal, particular) meanings. To stop at the name "Ophelia" and have other play-textual signs turn around it as if simultaneously attracted by and emerging from that "obliterated origin" is

---

26   The phrase "holistic ontology" can be found in Brandom's recent book on Hegel (185). For Badiou on the relevance of dialectic-idealistic totality, see his seminar on Plato.

27   When Jonathan Goldberg resignedly avows that at one point of his career he lost patience with "the indifference of difference" and that he began to believe that deconstruction should overcome "its inability to recognize the differences between the kinds of solidifications that one must resist and those that one must desire and further" (*Shakespeare's Hand* xviii), he was not necessarily yielding to phenomenological pressures, but rather contributing, by accepting this mode of "strategic essentialism" (Spivak), to the dismantling of dialectical thought as the ironic-sophistic celebration of the next difference.

28   Deleuze: "Le négatif, la négativité, ne capture même pas le phénomène de la différence, mais en reçoit seulement le fantôme ou l'epiphénomène, et toute la Phénoménologie est une épiphénoménologie" (*Différence* 74).

much more demanding, and surely more in keeping with (more tolerant with) the liberty of the play's immanent overdetermination.

Let me return to Heraclitan fire. Like any other *privative phenomenon* (Jameson *Valences* 27), an *unphenomenal fire* is, like Derrida's artificial light, something "giving more light than heat" (*Hamlet* 1.4.118). We may also liken it to the *uneffectual fire* (*Hamlet* 1.5.90) that preludes, in the tragedy, the ignitions of imperative memory—the mad admixture, in rues, of repentance and conscience, in daisies, of "thoughts and remembrance fitted" (4.5.175). And Hamlet remembers, of course, in an injured, damaged, and "damned light" (2.2.440). He will not be able to forget her name—*the fair Ophelia*!—because "everything that we know by heart and everything that strangely links memory as *Gedächtnis* to thought is of the order of the name" (Derrida, *Memories* 54).[29] Unphenomenal are too the flowers Ophelia shares with her brother, the Queen, and Claudius. Her bequest "gives nothing" (Sonnet 43.3) and her unused beauty is bound to disappear. The stage and figurative tradition depicting a pastoral Ophelia who literally dies *sub flore* shortly after presenting herbs and flowers is part of the (given) phenomenological *Myth of the Given*, soundly impeached by Wilfrid Sellars.[30] The actually vocal donation of invisible plants betokens rather Shakespeare's recalcitrantly unphenomenal dramaturgy. For Ophelia doesn't trade with real flowers: she gives words.[31] According to Ned Lukacher, the text Hamlet "reveals that the space of the feminine is the site of an epochal rift whose subject is not biological but linguistic" (*Primal* 216). In Hegelian terms adapted to the exigencies of psychoanalysis, "'the unconscious work' of the spirit is synonymous with the work of language" (*Primal* 212), and the botanical work, in the play, that Ophelia sets in motion is primarily a *work of language*. Despite her much-acclaimed madness, she delivers a paradigmatic case of "reason-drenched individuality, displayed in her dialectical richness" (Bloch, *Sujeto-Objeto* 31).[32] Lines in

---

29 Derrida here elaborates on the distinction, emphasized by de Man, between interior memory as *Erinnerung* and mechanical memory as *Gedächtnis*. See *Aesthetic Ideology*, 100–104.

30 Sellars famously attacked the immediacy of non-inferential knowledge: "The idea that observation 'strictly and properly so-called' is constituted by certain self-authenticating nonverbal episodes, the authority of which is transmitted to verbal and quasi-verbal performances when these performances are made 'in conformity with the semantical rules of the language,' is, of course, the heart of the Myth of the Given" ("Empiricism" 199).

31 Descartes often reiterates this central point of sensorial abstention: "ad mentes a sensibus abducendam" (*Meditationes* 96).

32 Ernst Bloch's book on Hegel (*Subjekt-Objekt: Erläuterungen zu Hegel*) was originally published in Spanish in 1949, in Wenceslao Roses' translation, and only later in the original German (1951). I am here translating from the Spanish version.

the play deliver one of the fittest accounts we may find in English literature of what Adorno called the unreduced experience in the medium of conceptual reflexion ("unreduzierte Erfahrung in Medium begrifflicher Reflexion," *Negative Dialektik* 25): the self-reflexivity produced by the transition from thing (pansy) to word (pansy) to concept (pansy)—"and there is pansies; that's for thoughts" (4.5.176)—hinges upon, or hangs from, the very word (*pansy*) whose buried etymology is to hang (*pendere*), just as Ophelia clambers to hang her coronet weeds on pendent boughs. For what hangs (*pendere*) is pensive, and so are the pendent boughs (the terminal thoughts) that strive to save Ophelia from drowning, to no avail. Think of Thomas Mann's construal of Castorp's introspective mood as that of one who "had barely settled to commune a little with his own thoughts, hands folded behind his head and eyes directed upon the ceiling" (*The Magic Mountain* 190). The German verb in the original—"und einem Gedanken nachgehangen" (*Der Zauberberg* 264)—is *nachhängen*, meaning to dwell on, to abandon oneself to, but literally, to after-hang or go on hanging.

7

After-hung to terminate her lover's mental abandonment, Ophelia is also the "un-naïve thinker [*unnaive Gedanker*]" who knows how far she remains from the object of her thinking, "and yet she must always talk as if she had it entirely [*und muss doch immer so reden, as hätte [sie] es ganz*]" (*Negative Dialectic* 14, *Negative Dialektik* 26). Even if such talk is just madness, or nothing. Again, the dialectical phantasm of totality, wavering between the unbound and the finite. This is, Adorno would add, Ophelia's *Clownerie*. And reason-drenched individuals (Iago, Rosalind, Falstaff, Beatrice, Portia, Juliet, Mercutio, Edgar) are in the habit of giving rich words. The donation of *what is not* is not simply no donation, but rather a prior-primeval mode of no-donation—an *Othing* rather than a *Nothing*, an *Ichts* rather than a *Nichts* (Žižek, *Less* 58), a *den* rather than an *ouden* or a *mêden* (Lacan *Les quatre* 74; Cassin 5)—"something that is even less than nothing, a 'decapitation of nothing'" (Comay & Ruda 60).[33] Marina called it—with Hegelian prescience—the "virgin knot" (*Pericles* 4.2.139). But the *othing* that best describes Ophelia's sharp evanescence and Hamlet's roomy emptiness is the symbol of "the white cold virgin snow" (*The Tempest* 4.1.61): the

---

33 See Jameson's emphasis on the "un- or non-intelligibility of the *Aufhebung* (and thereby also of mediation)" (*Valences* 107) and Ruda's reminder of the "peculiar non-being" of the idea (*For Badiou* 46) strike a similar note.

pure, white snow (*Hamlet* 3.3.50) that appears twice in Ophelia's mad songs. Laertes is right: her "nothing's more than matter." There is an Old English riddle, beautifully translated by Michael Alexander, that perfectly evokes the distinct dialectical force of the *unphenomenal* in *Hamlet*. The solution is snow:

> I was a pure girl and a grey-maned woman
> and, at the same time, a singular man.
> I flew with the birds, breasted the sea,
> sank beneath the wave, dissolved among the fish
> and alighted on land. I had a living soul. (80)

Sellars' noted injunction to avert *the foe of immediacy* was, we know, anticipated by other reluctant Hegelians like Adorno. As early as 1934–1937, the German philosopher was warning against "the most disastrous consequence of the assumption of immediacy" (*Against Epistemology* 20)—namely, the confusion between primitiveness and truth. But he screamed—alas—*in deserto*. The necessity of this collapse is so keenly felt today in some academic quarters that there seems to be no recollection of a time when the thing to do was certainly *not* to go to the thing itself or do the thing. But this—going to the things themselves, doing them—has today, in our *Leistungsgesellschaft* (Han) or society of positive achievement, become the phenomenal thing to do. So, if you are *Doing Shakespeare* (Palfrey) in the right way or *Thinking with Shakespeare* (Lupton) with minimal interference of rational (conceptual, textual) mediation, then you will attain to a *Phenomenal Shakespeare* (Smith) and become an assimilated celebrant in the mass of immediacy. Should you want to avoid such risks and grapple fitly with an *Unphenomenal Shakespeare*—an unpopular desire, I am aware—you would do well to recall Stanley Wells's passing observation that, in *A Midsummer Night's Dream* and in my opinion elsewhere too, "Shakespeare seems deliberately to draw attention to the discrepancies between what we see and what is described" ("Introduction" to *A Midsummer Night's Dream*, 19); to realize that whenever the aesthetic progresses into the meta-aesthetic (in Shakespeare, nearly always), the phenomenalism and referentiality of symbol and metaphor are rescinded by ironic distance or allegorical stringency;[34] one would do well to see less and read and listen more; well with Wells to mind the gap (the discrepancies), well to abstain, that is, from the commerce of sense—*mentemque a sensibus* [...] *abducere* (Descartes *Meditationes*

---

34 See Hugh Grady's useful commentary of Ophelia's allegorical bouquet in *Shakespeare and Impure Aesthetics*, 177–178.

84)—including the *trade* without a calling that is Pandar's in a play full of sweet sense (*Pericles* 4.5.71–75). Tellingly, an entreaty for abstention (ἐποχή, *Ausschaltung, Einklammerung*) informs Husserl's original project—one overly betrayed by followers who solely pine for the "material sap" (*King Lear* 4.2.36) forsaken with the natural attitude. This is not a Puritan recommendation to "refrain tonight" (*Hamlet* 3.4.151.5)—let alone an instruction to reject the flowers or "[abstain] from meat" (*Richard II* 2.1.76). This is just an invitation *not* to save the wrong appearances—to save only those *few* that dialectically hold the initial, apparently specious, truth (Žižek, *Plague* 158). Nor to save the totality of the appearances, in line with Hegel's requirement to conceive of the play of forces as salvaging all of them (Gadamer, *Hegel's Dialectic* 35–53). An invitation not to offhandedly take in so many useless givens.

This may be asking too much of those who cheerfully depend on the deliverances of sensibility—who see Banquo's dagger, feel the ghost, see the bear, smell Ophelia's flowers. Who discern, with Polonius, the shapes of the camel, the weasel, and the whale. Of those who trade in images and motions and emotions, who dwell in ambiences, engage in actor-networks, practice surface reading and face-to-face stupor, are touched by affects and affections and fondled by actions and reactions. Of those for whom Husserl's ante-predicative earth remains decidedly flat, untouched by the violence of thought.[35] Of those who, spirited enemies of cynical reason, are whole-heartedly swept by the *heftige antirationalistische Impuls* (Sloterdijk 12). Asking too much of critics whose privileged access to Shakespeare is through the *attente* and *jouissance* of "showings" that are—like those of Julian of Norwich—"*alive and vivid, horrifying and awe-inspiring, sweet and lovely*" (51). Of those who alone abide by, and force Shakespeare to submit to, the "tribunal of sense experience" (Quine, "Two Dogmas" 38). Of those, in short, for whom the *Pathos der Distanz* (Nietzsche, *Genealogie* 18) is an unfamiliar sentiment. They brush it off as defensive cynicism—or *chic ironic bitterness*.[36] They forget that Shakespeare was unremittingly ironic, bitter, and chic.

---

35 Badiou refers ironically to Husserl's anti-Platonic respect for doxastic and commonsensical impressions of and prejudices about the stillness of the earth (*Pour aujourd'hui: Platon!* 201–202).

36 Rita Felski (*Critique* 45) misrepresents the work of Peter Sloterdijk on cynicism as one of downright censure. Few books are more cynical and sarcastic than Sloterdijk's—in his case, emerging from a sheer combination of the critical talent to unmask and bad conscience in refusing to acknowledge the ascendancy of his real masters, thinkers like Horkheimer and Adorno. See Sloterdijk, *Kritik*, 17–26. Felski probably hasn't read Sloterdijk, whose work she mentions but fails to quote from. She has merely found information about the German thinker in Jay Magill's book. The exemption from source-reading and referencing is, I guess, one of the blessings of *postcritical* existence.

Today's Ophelias know better than the Danish girl. The revisions of gender, politically liberating, have also helped to rewrite some signal lines of the Hamlet script. Instead of Hamlet exhorting "Get thee to a nunnery" we have Ophelia protesting "Hit the road, Hamm, and don't you come back no more, no more, no more." And so we now have a host of elusive males hitting the road, escaping the domestic nightmare: from Huck and Jim, or Mason and Dixon, to Wyatt and Billy or the perturbed protagonists of Auster's and DeLillo's novels. But the old liberal plot is tenacious. Joyce recalls in *Ulysses* that "Jumbo, the elephant, loves Alice, the elephant" (433), and at the close of the second chapter of Agatha Christie's *They Came to Baghdad* (1951), we read that

> A remembrance of a rhyme once frequently recited by her old nurse came to her mind :
> Jumbo said to Alice I love you
> Alice said to Jumbo I don't believe you do,
> If you really loved me as you say you do
> You wouldn't go to America and leave me in the Zoo.

Less than a decade later, Sylvia Plath wrote "The Zoo-Keeper's Wife," where we read: "I can stay awake all night, if need be—/ Cold as an eel, without eyelids. / Like a dead lake the dark envelops me, / Blueblack, a spectacular plum fruit" (154). If we hope to auspiciously retrospect Ophelia, we must preserve a taste for this unphenomenal spectacle of cynicism and coldness, of perjured eyes, torn eyelids, and dead lakes, of darkness and insomnia and despair. We must tolerate it, and refrain from moralizing it too much. To recall a limpid phrase used by James in his reading of *The Scarlet Letter*, we must remain wary of "the obtrusion of a moral lesson" (*Literary Criticism I* 404). For nothing in *Hamlet*, least of all of Ophelia, prefigures "an agenda of potential liberation" (Grady 134) or "a template for a possible polity" (Lupton, *Thinking* 87). Adorno warned that "no message [*keine Aussage*] is to be squeezed out [*herauszupressen*] of *Hamlet*" (*Aesthetic Theory* 128). The truth content (*Wahrheitsgehalt*) of emancipation, once a reputable goal to which Adorno oriented some of his efforts, has now become an academic commodity (a message). The moralization of politics is no doubt to blame, but so is the phenomenalization of literary criticism.

CHAPTER 2

The Spectre of the Cartesian Subject

1

In the (early modernist) *beginning* (there) *was* (not) *Descartes*. Repeated enough times, the claim has swollen into an edict of expulsion. Early modern scholarship praises the self-sufficiency of a pre-Cartesian world where body and mind, far from being segregated from one another, engage in constant interaction. This world is supposed to be Shakespeare's. His new supremacy as the genie of mind-body synergies hinges on the banishment of Descartes, the commissary of separation. The coda is that Shakespeare is only accountable to his fulsome self—to his extended bodies, fluent humours, passionate affections, cordial pets. Therefore, *in the beginning was Shakespeare*. A particularly brisk formulation of this dogmatic view has been advanced by an influential scholar like Gabriel Egan:

> René Descartes was wrong, and Shakespeare could have told him so. Descartes' hard distinction between the inanimate and the merely living machine-matter, on the one hand, and the mind made of an immaterial essence, on the other, no longer convinces anyone.
> "Homeostasis" 77

Descartes was indeed *so* wrong, that contemporary neuroscientists like Antonio Damasio write books titled *Descartes' error*, where the error is described as "the abyssal separation between body and mind, between the sizable, dimensioned, mechanically operated, infinitely divisible body stuff, on the one hand, and the unsizable, undimensioned, un-pushpullable, non-divisible mind stuff" (250). Damasio reaches this conclusion after examining *one* single sentence by Descartes—*cogito ergo sum*—which he takes to suggest "that thinking, and awareness of thinking, are the real substrates of being" (148). That you can advertise in the title of your book the error of a philosopher and fail to read anything by that philosopher except one single sentence—and of course misrepresent the original meaning of the sentence—is a puzzling fact that serves merely to confirm the reach of a deep-seated anti-Cartesian prejudice to which Egan, of course, is not immune.¹ For, after all, Descartes' "error" is his "hard distinction"—an apt phrase, no doubt, for the distinction is indeed very strong in the writings of the French thinker, but Egan and the phenomenologists are bothered less about the distinction than about the mutual imperviousness of the things therein deemed distinct, a view best exemplified in the Rylean myth of "the ghost in the machine."² The inference from premiss to conclusion—since mind and body are different, the mind is like a floating ghost in the machine of the body—is simply bad logic, and therefore invalid. Oceans and atmosphere are distinct, but they are powerfully interrelated: Egan, fascinated with homeostasis, knows this well. He should also know that Descartes' description of reflex action, a notion connected to dynamic homeostatic self-regulation, remains central to the twentieth-century physiological study of neuromuscular function.³ Or that Hotspur's account of the eruptions in *1 Henry IV* III.1.25–33 remains—for all its evocative charm (the Gaia hypothesis) duly conjured by Egan—less valid than Descartes' comparable explanation of eruptive earth-cum-atmospheric phenomena in *Les Météors*—a treatise dedicated to the study of salt, wind, snow, thunder, the rainbow, vapours, exhalations, clouds, etc. The earth remains today a geological object *without* life, even if living things crawl, fly and swim about its surface: Descartes seeks to prove that its constant dynamism can be explained by describing, in a bottom-up fashion, from the smallest particles all the way up to the largest, without recourse to void, formal substances, real qualities or final causes, the fields of mechanical—yes, *mechanical*—interaction between its manifold components. Just like, according to Egan, Hotspur can tell Glyndwr that he is wrong, so Descartes—whose talents as empirical experimenter can easily be confirmed by anyone who bothers to read him—can tell Hotspur that he is also wrong. *Grandam* and *womb*, two of the terms used by Hotspur in his speech, are just tropes when applied to the earth. I am sure Shakespeare, who made no experiments that we know of, apart from the domestic ones he may have attempted in his garden, concurred with Descartes in this. Let me add

---

1   Interestingly, what Damasio takes the sentence to mean is much closer to the post-Hegelian appropriation of Descartes (Lacan, Žižek, Badiou) than what the French philosopher himself intended.
2   The myth is described and criticized in the first chapter of his 1949 book *The Concept of Mind*. Current interpreters tend to agree that Ryle's construal of what he calls "the official doctrine" of substance dualism, which, he argues, "hails chiefly from Descartes," is a ridiculous exaggeration (see Julia Tanney, "Rethinking Ryle" ix-x). It may be worth noting that Ryle, who titles this opening chapter "Descartes' Myth," never cites Descartes. Of course, there is no better way to mythologize somebody than by failing to read his work.
3   See F. Fearing, "René Descartes. A study in the history of the theories of reflex action".

that Descartes the rationalist probably performed more empirical experiments than Bacon, Locke, and Hume, all three put together, and that, unlike them, he effectively contributed to the empirical sciences.[4]

2

But the man is fatally unredeemable. Consider too Philippa Berry's essay on *Love's Labour's Lost*, where she laments the fact that a decade or so after the publication of this comedy, in the work of Descartes and Bacon, "a reassertion of the distinction between matter and human intellection was posited as the key to a new order of knowledge." To compensate for this epochal lapse, she decides to replace Descartes' "opposition between res extensa, raw matter, and res cogitans, thinking substance" with "Pascal's notion of the soul as a thing and the thing as soul-like" ("Salving" 97). It is not my intention to discuss the congruence of this replacement, but I wonder what Berry would say of Pascal's plea for separation and detachment in his *Prière*.[5] To speak of *distinction* is, as far as it goes, correct, but one is puzzled by her use later of the term "opposition." *Co-position* would indeed do more justice, as we will soon see, to the Cartesian conception of the relation between mind and body, and yet like "contiguity or proximity," rejected by Nancy, it fails to capture the specificity of a union of "two distinct things in a single indistinction" (Nancy, *Corpus* 140–41). Distinct, co-positional and indistinctly united: none of these predicates implies *opposition*. For where does Descartes speak of *opposition* between *res cogitans* and *res extensa*? Hard to say, for Perry doesn't quote a single word by the French philosopher. What is the point in reading and quoting Descartes if we all know he was wrong?

Cottingham, who had the bad taste to read him, rightly argued that Descartes "repudiated the kind of 'angelism' that took us to be merely incorporeal spirits

---

4   Bacon is regarded as the first great theorist of experimentalism, but he "made little first-hand contribution to science by means" of his method (Hesse 152). See also Paolo Rossi, *Francesco Bacone*, xxviii.

5   Pascal: "Car, Seigneur, comme à l'instant de ma mort je me trouverai séparé du monde, dénué de toutes choses, seul en votre présence, pour répondre à votre justice de tous les mouvements de mon cœur, faites que je me considère en cette maladie comme en une espèce de mort, séparé du monde, dénué de tous les objets de mes attachements, seul en votre présence, pour implorer de votre miséricorde la conversion de mon cœur; et qu'ainsi j'aie une extrême consolation de ce que vous m'envoyez maintenant une espèce de mort pour exercer votre miséricorde, avant que vous m'envoyiez effectivement la mort pour exercer votre jugement" (*Œuvres complètes* 447).

lodged in mechanical bodies" ("The Mind-Body Relation" 183). *The ghost in the machine, the angel in the body*: on close inspection, the trope fails to apply to the Cartesian corpus. Egan and Berry forget that the distinction was first, in the *Discourse on Method*, formulated as instrumental for other ends, most importantly, the epistemic assertion of indisputable truths (*scientia*), that it was greatly reformulated in the *Meditations*, and that, all in all, Descartes never questioned the mind-body union, which he described in private letters as an *ens per se* or *unio substantialis*.⁶ This of course doesn't mean that he believed that the two things (mind and body) converging in the *unio* were in fact the same or were made indistinct through it. The fact that he failed to explain the logic of such union (a third substance? God's intervention?) does not imply that he dismissed it as unreal.⁷ Many wide-ranging implications follow from this union, and early modern scholar Michael D. Slater has very elegantly singled out the most important:

> The Renaissance was no more without a conception of the *immaterial soul*—often thought to be infused directly by God into the body, since it could not be produced by the physical seed in generation—than Descartes was without a conception of the *embodied mind*. (594)

In fact, Descartes' last important book, *Passions of the Soul* (1649), betrays a constant fascination with the workings of the mind-body union, an obsession that can be traced back to the sixth Meditation. As Gary Hatfield notes, Descartes' theories of sensation and appetite are "manifestations of mind-body union and interaction" (*Meditations* 238). And John Cottingham reminds us that Descartes was intrigued by sensations that, being neither purely cognitive, volitional, or physiological, "straddle the world of spirit and matter" ("The Mind-Body Union" 182). The human being, in this view, comes forth as precisely "the bridge between the realms of mind and of matter" (182). Indeed, the existence of hunger, thirst, and, more crucially, pain, proves that the union is real. The essential difference between mind and body is that we tend to know

---

6   It is worth noting that Husserl did speculate with the possibility of an incorporeal, inanimate, and even non-personal consciousness: see *Ideas I* §54, 107.

7   Jean-Luc Nancy argues that the "substantial union" signifies, "first of all, that it is not a third substance: if that were so, given that a substance relates only to itself, it would be impossible for this one to have the slightest relation to the other two. Yet the union is precisely the relation between the two substances. But the union does not unite the two substances accidentally: it is, precisely, substantial. Or we could say that it enacts the substantiality of an accident" (*Corpus*, 140–41).

clearly and distinctly (the ideas of) our mind, whereas the sensations of our body are obscure. This doesn't mean that we do not have those sensations. On the contrary, *unknowing* (or knowing confusedly) our body is one of our most characteristic human experiences—and the experience is transcendentally apperceptive in that we know we unknow. In other words, *nescio* is as much of a conscious mental experience as *cogito*, and it is mostly prompted by external things—"bits of experiential intake" (McDowell, *Mind* 4–6)—impinging upon the senses, in particular our own body as our (inmost) external thing, obscene supplement, and grand *objet petit a*.[8] Lear's proviso, "we are not ourselves / When nature, being oppressed, commands the mind / To suffer with the body" (*King Lear* 2.4.101–103) shows how the body's afflictions elicit apperceptive unknowingness, and this in turn disrupts the certitudes of selfhood. Note the bones of the argument: when the mind is not in control, our (human) identity vanishes. Did Lear read Descartes? Did he read Lacan? King Real? How dare he? Let me get this straight. There is reason to agree with Cavell that the truth of skepticism—which he identifies with the truth of tragedy—is that "the human habitation of the world is not assured in what philosophy calls knowledge" (*Disowning* 25), but it is no less true that living through *the breakdown of knowledge*—"Who is it that can tell me who I am?" (*King Lear* 1.4.205)—spells a distinctly human way of inhabiting the world.

Evidence of Descartes' admission of a near-substantial integration between mind and body is abundant in Descartes' oeuvre. In the sixth Meditation, he proceeds to it tentatively, in the course of a demonstration of the existence of external things, which in turn leads him to examine the operations of the imaginative faculty. Our imagination is proof, Descartes suggests, that we have *cogitationes* that are not autonomously caused by our spirit but depend on the acceptance of an (to begin with, our) external body. The conditional mode betrays the prudence of the induction: "si quelque corps existe auquel mon esprit soit tellement conjoint (*sit ita conjuncta*) et uni qu'il se puisse appliquer à le considérer quand il lui plaît ..." (*Méditation* 6.VI, 211). Whereas in pure intellection the mind turns towards itself, in acts of imagination the mind turns to the body (*se tourne vers le corps, se convertat ad corpus*), and the very possibility of troping or turning is construed as evidence of a prior conjunction. The heights of self-reflexive intellection are always haunted by the original entanglement:

---

8   As Andrzej Warminski summarizes in his essay "Spectre Shapes: The Body of Descartes," "the example of the wax would demonstrate one more time that the mind knows itself, its own nature as thinking thing (*une chose qui pense, res cogitans*), more clearly and distinctly than it knows any body like, for example, a piece of wax" (*Material Inscriptions* 64).

> Et partant, de cela même que je connais avec certitude que j'existe, et que cependant je ne remarque point qu'il appartienne nécessairement aucune autre chose à ma nature ou à mon essence sinon que je suis une chose qui pense, je conclus fort bien que mon essence consiste en cela seul que je suis une chose qui pense, ou une substance dont toute l'essence ou la nature n'est que de penser. Et quoique peut-être, ou plutôt certainement, comme je le dirai tantôt, j'aie un corps auquel je suis très étroitement conjoint [*valde arcte conjunctum est*]; néanmoins ... (221)

Note the uneasiness of the concessions (*cependant, quoique, néanmoins*). This is a far cry from the triumphal acclamation of the disembodied *cogito*. And he indeed comes to it at once. There is truth in nature because God is to some (proto-Spinozian) extent nature, and

> par ma nature en particulier, je n'entends autre chose que la complexion ou l'assemblage [*complexionem*] de toutes les choses que Dieu m'a données. Or il n'y a rien que cette nature m'enseigne plus expressément, ni plus sensiblement, sinon que j'ai un corps [*habeam corpus*] qui est mal disposé quand je sens de la douleur, qui a besoin de manger ou de boire, quand j'ai les sentiments de la faim ou de la soif, etc. Et partant je ne dois aucunement douter qu'il n'y ait en cela quelque vérité. (225)

This way the existence of the human body, which is part of the assemblage mind-body, passes the taxing test of indubitable certitude. If Descartes has an *habeas corpus* privilege to elude local sheriffs and phenomenological bailiffs, it is because he admits to the possession of a body: *habeo corpus*. The mind's ownership and rule of the body is not, however, a matter of transcendent—i.e. external—regulation. Descartes' attempt to trope further the nature of the *conjuctio* or *complexionem* as unlike that of a pilot in his boat—cfr. *Romeo and Juliet* (1.4.112–113)—leads him to an assertion of partial immanence:

> La nature m'enseigne aussi par ces sentiments de douleur, de faim, de soif, etc., que je ne suis pas seulement logé dans mon corps, ainsi qu'un pilote en son navire, mais, outre cela, que je lui suis conjoint très étroitement, et tellement confondu et mêlé [*illi arctissime esse conjunctum et quasi permixtum*], que je compose comme un seul tout avec lui [*adeo et unum quid cum illo componam*]. Car si cela n'était, lorsque mon corps est blessé, je ne sentirais pas pour cela de la douleur, moi qui ne suis qu'une chose qui pense, mais j'apercevrais cette blessure par le seul

> entendement, comme un pilote aperçoit par la vue si quelque chose se rompt dans son vaisseau. Et lorsque mon corps a besoin de boire ou de manger, je connaîtrais simplement cela même, sans en être averti par des sentiments confus de faim et de soif: car en effet tous ces sentiments de faim, de soif, de douleur, etc., ne sont autre chose que de certaines façons confuses de penser, qui proviennent et dépendent de l'union et comme du mélange de l'esprit avec le corps [*ab unione et quasi permixtione mentis cum corpore*]. (225)

The mind-body distinction is, yes, harsh, but the bridges between both are not exactly burned. "What we so often designate Cartesian 'dualism'," Nancy argues, "can therefore be understood as entirely different from an ontological cut between body and soul" (*Corpus* 143). And concludes: "The soul can be touched by the body, and the body by the soul [...] Touch makes contact between two intacts" (141). As early as 1979 Nancy denounced the incessant anti-Cartesian vindication of a "*ré-incarnation*" which, considering Descartes' careful proposal of a "partage rigoureux" of mind and body in their "ajointement," could be said to proceed "directement de Descartes" (*Ego Sum* 131–132). He was obviously thinking of Merleau-Ponty's flesh-oriented stance. Descartes' concession that the feelings of hunger, thirst and pain are but confused or unclear modes of thinking could well serve as prelude to a posthumanist, animalist or ecocritical reflection in the field of early modern studies. I am surprised it doesn't. Maybe the derogation of "confuses" is too hard to swallow. Anyway, if what Gabriel Egan pines for is "a continuous spectrum (indeed, a chain) of complexity and sensitivity connecting the low-order life forms and the higher" ("Homeostasis" 77), a "continuous spectrum" along which lie "the mechanical and the organic," one, in short, that is "unencumbered by the sharp distinction of matter and mind that dominated Enlightenment science" he doesn't need to go all the way back to Shakespeare. Descartes may partly do. *Partly*, of course, as discontinuity occurs at some point in the alleged chain (*permixtione, conjunctio*), as a mode of ontological inconsistence (Badiou) or language-based excess (Derrida), allowing for the operational transcendence of a transcendental *rationality* that, *pace* Egan, is decidedly not "just a sophistication of simpler kinds of biological responsiveness" (77): Žižek quite rightly speaks of "a certain excessive moment of 'madness' inherent to *cogito*" (*Ticklish* 2). And yet, again, if what Egan is after is confirmation of Antonio Damasio's belief that "we think and feel with our bodies and not with disembodied minds" (77), then Descartes is a perfectly good place to start.

3

But this takes an intellectual generosity (perhaps curiosity is a better word) that is uncommon among impatient neo-materialists. Jonathan Dollimore, for instance, took Descartes for the quintessential representative—the founder, actually—of an "essentialism humanism" (*Radical Tragedy* 254). This attribution is performed as an ideological reflex, like the stock claim "that rationality is *biased* because it is a class-based or Western or whatever notion" (Nozick, *Rationality* xii). Dollimore observed that in Descartes we "can see a crucial stage in the history of metaphysics," for he put forth an argument to the effect that "the self was a pure, non-physical substance 'whose whole essence or nature ... is to think'" (*Radical Tragedy* 254). Well, not exactly. Descartes never spoke about the self as exclusively a mind. It is the mind or soul, not the self, that is a pure, non-physical substance:

> je connus de là que j'étais une substance dont toute l'essence ou la nature n'est que de penser, et qui pour être n'a besoin d'aucun lieu ni ne dépend d'aucune chose matérielle. En sorte que ce moi, c'est-à-dire l'âme, par laquelle je suis ce que je suis, est entièrement distincte du corps, et même qu'elle est plus aisée à connaître que lui, et qu'encore qu'il ne fût point, elle ne laisserait pas d'être tout ce qu'elle est.
> *Discours* IV 33; 103

Descartes is saying, yes, that he (as mind) is that substance, one "whose whole essence or nature is to think." But the self as mind is "*ce* moi" (my emphasis), that is, one among various ways of figuring selfhood. It is one way, one mode, one trope: *ce* moi. In fact, the figural nature of the argument is borne out in the appositional specification, "ce moi, c'est-à-dire l'âme," which suggest that the soul or mind is being compared to a kind of self: the mind is *like* a self, *as if* a self. But there is a more inclusive figuration of the self (self 1), one that encompasses both the mind as self (self 2) and the body, which cannot—and here lies the implied emphasis—be figured as a self.[9] The nature of this encompassing implies possession: self 1 *is* a mind (self 2) that *has* a body. The soul is the essential part of the self, that which allows it to be what it is, but it is just a part. The body (another substance?) is also there to cope with, no matter how hard it is

---

9 The oscillation between *moi* and *je* and the identification of the latter as soul (*âme*) instill an ambiguity which some English translations resolve by introducing scare-quotes: "Accordingly this 'I', that is to say, the Soul by which I am what I am, is entirely distinct from the body and is even easier to know than the body" (Ian Mclean's translation for the Oxford edition, 29).

to know both it and its (substantial?) rapport with the soul.[10] *Meum corpus* is also part of the *me totum* or self 1, and this composite self is "le vrai homme," an *ens per se* that happens to be, perhaps paradoxically, an outcome "*de composition*."[11] It is always salutary to see Descartes resort, albeit grudgingly, to shared common sense. Describing the plan of his *Meditations*, he points out:

> All the errors which proceed from the senses are then surveyed, while the means of avoiding them are demonstrated, and finally all the reasons from which we may deduce the existence of material things are set forth. Not that I judge them to be very useful in establishing that which they prove, to wit, that there is in truth a world, that men possess bodies, and other such things which never have been doubted by anyone of sense.
> Preface to *Meditations*

That men possess bodies: are the resulting selves (mind-selves + their bodies) also the infamous presumption of an essentialist humanism? Descartes, Gary Hatfield succinctly concludes, never lost interest in "the functional role of mind–body union in the economy of life" ("René Descartes").

In their "Introduction" to *Renaissance Posthumanism*, Joseph Campana and Scott Maisano pre-emptively, and quite rightly, observe that Descartes' "historical fate of late has been to embody all that is wrong with Enlightenment thought" (7). But they do little to revert this fate.[12] The very choice of verb—to embody—reveals their hostility to the "fantasies of disembodied and autonomy" Descartes would presumably have indulged. Indeed, *embodying Descartes* is the retaliatory dream of many an early modern scholar. Whilst the goal of

---

10   The problem, then, lies in the use of the term "substance" to denote the *je-moi* as exclusively soul. This rash denotation is greatly qualified in the *Meditations* (Rodis-Lewis, Notes to *Discourse* 643). The appositional reformulation, "*ce moi, c'est-à-dire l'âme*" (emphasis added), is used identically in *Discours* (103) and *Méditations* (221). The self has/is a mind than can think (*cogito*), but it also has/is a body, which can do other things. For "trialism," or the conception that "the mind-body complex is the bearer of distinctive and irreducible *properties*," see Cottingham, *Cartesian Reflections*, 33–34.

11   See notes 86 and 91 to *Méditations métaphysiques*, 1003–1004.

12   Scott Maisano rightly concedes a Cartesian anticipation in *Hamlet* and rejects Paster's exaggerated account of the importance of Galenic physiology of humors in early modern literary culture. Arguing in terms of continuity, he uses *The Passions of the Soul* as proof that Descartes gave importance to the passions. He discovers, taking his cue from Harold Bloom, that there is in *Hamlet* a defense of a *nondemonstrable subjectivity*. While he feels compelled to patronize "Descartes' eminently rational methodology" ("Infinite Gesture," 71), he fails to describe properly what, on Cartesian logic, gives a human being its sense of identity beyond the doubtful recognition of one's body.

the liberal-cum-essentialist humanist scholars has been construed as that of ensouling the deviant matters of literature, an operation that often involved much disembodying, the task of the neo-materialists and phenomenologists is, on the face of it, that of re-embodying the residual materials (spiritualized authors, incorporeal tropes, rarefied meanings, spectralized texts). This, however, they seldom achieve. For rather than remaining within the boundaries of the material text, they eschew heuristic immanence in favour of a positive transcendence of assorted things (objects, history, animals, affects). There is no need anyway to embody Descartes, for he himself saw to it that no res cogitans was *completely* insulated from corporeal extension. Two things can be undetached and yet remain incommensurable. The mind, for Descartes, is united and commensurable with the body when the self experiences pain or hunger, but when involved in intellectual action the mind becomes incommensurable with it. And yet, it is still united to the body. To cash out what Descartes is saying one should show some understanding of the singularity of intellectual work—of the harsh distinction or incommensurable difference, that is, between a *clear thought* and a *confused thought*. Take, for instance, Bruce Smith's brief consideration:

> Famously, what Descartes discovers in the course of this inventory are two clear and distinct thoughts: (1) I exist because I think ("my essence consists solely in the fact that I am a thinking thing" [VII.78]); and (2) I can think my body but my body can't think me ("I have a distinct idea of body, in so far as this is simply an extended, non-thinking being" [VII.78]).
> *Phenomenal* 16

A correctional principle is thereby suggested: my body *should* also be allowed to think me. In a Whitman book, or a skin-lotion add, the notion would be appealing, and we would all feel drawn to buy them. As a philosophical position, it demands more unpacking than the conceptual eloquence Merleau-Ponty, not to mention Smith, can provide. Descartes, we have seen, admits to the existence of confused thoughts that come from and depend (*qui proviennent et dependent*) of the union and kind of blend between mind and body— "l'union et comme du mélange de l'esprit avec le corps [*ab unione et quasi permixtione mentis cum corpore*]." But the body (alas) cannot think. It can do, Spinoza will later confirm, many things. But it cannot think.[13] If *the* singularity

---

13   Spinoza: "No one has yet determined what the body can do, that is, experience has not het taught anyone what the body can do from the laws of Nature alone" (*Ethics* III P2, 71).

of human thought (humans have other cognitive singularities which are not exactly thought) involves the capacity to use a system of arbitrary signs and to thereby draw logical or rhetorical inferences that lead to principles that are like "transmission devices for *probability* or *support*, which flow from data to cases, via the principle, to judgements and predictions about new observations or cases whose status otherwise is unknown or less certain" (Nozick, *Rationality* 5), then it is hard to grasp how the body can think. The body is not disconnected from the thing we call the mind. That much is clear. But if we refuse to admit that a capacity for a certain kind of thought is exclusive of the "mind"—a capacity that is at one with the use of natural language—and that therefore the logical space of reasons is *sui generis* (McDowell, *Mind* xx) then it is unlikely we may progress in an understanding of certain human accomplishments, including Shakespeare's work. Let me add in passing that my caveat on the virtual indistinguishability of thought and language is surely not something that many partisans of human-exceptional rationality—thinkers like Robert Nozick, Robert Brandom, or Graham Priest—would endorse.[14]

4

But let us probe a bit further the contours of this anti-Cartesian prejudice. Posthumanist scholar Karen Raber explains how "cognitive ecology" counters "the Cartesian dualism that divides a unitary, individuated 'mind' from the body and world it supposedly inhabits, as if reason occurred independently of and without reference to information gleaned by means of physical encounters" (*Shakespeare* 68). The issues are again misconstrued. The phrase "dualism that divides" is a *non sequitur*, as we explained above (hydrogen and oxygen are dual but undivided in water, for instance). Also problematic is the undecidable force of the "as if," for Raber does not intend the conjunction to be figurative. She implies that Descartes believed "reason occurred independently of and without reference to information gleaned by means of physical encounters." Anyway, whether tropical or not, the fact is that the comparative conjunction

---

14   Nozick argues that "language is a manifestation and vehicle of rationality" (*Rationality* 179). This is merely inadmissible in a certain radicalized Hegelian tradition that includes of course Derrida and de Man, but also, yes, Nietzsche and Adorno. For them, reason is language, and since language is deceptive and unstable, so is reason, and yet a deceptive and unstable reason is much more than the beast can afford. Recall, with Barbara Cassin, that "there's no such thing as animal speech, yes? You can't psychoanalyze a dog, or even a cat" (11).

(*as if*) introduces a false attribution of belief. In the *Discours de la méthode*, Descartes keeps a prudent distance from a dogmatic rehabilitation of the Scholastic dictum that "Nihil est in intellectu quod prius no fuerit in sensu"— which he translates as "qu'il n'y a rien dans l'entendement qui n'ait premièrement été dans le sens" (*Discours* 105–106)—but he never tires of reminding his readers, especially in the *Meditations*, that most of our liveliest ideas derive from input received via the senses: "facile mihi persuadebam nullam plane me habere in intellectu, quam non prius habuissem in sensu" ("je me persuadais aisément que je n'avais aucune idée dans mon esprit, qui n'eût passé auparavant par mes sens," 215). There is no incompatibility in rendering unto Caesar (knowing) the things that are Caesar's (God, the soul), and unto knowing through the senses only those, like insects and hands, that are not his.

Raber also contends that "prior to Descartes, the status of humans vs. animals was vexed; after Descartes, animals were 'beast-machines', inherently incapable of reason" (*Shakespeare* 91). She doesn't offer one single example of a relevant pre-Cartesian philosopher whose take on this allegedly "vexed status" is that animals are capable of reason. The questioning of human exceptionality—a philosophical position well documented before Descartes—does not entail the unequivocal attribution of reason, however tenuous, to the animal. To put it in Scholastic terms, the fact that a substance can use a lower-level substance as a constitutive matter to which it may on occasion relapse does not necessarily upgrade this constitutive matter into a higher-level substance. Porosity is no *de facto* evidence for a *de iure* replacement. Otherwise put, human-animal porosity is not a two-way road: the fact that we remain animals doesn't make animals any more human. Marx famously conceded that "human anatomy contains a key to the anatomy of the ape" but he readily added that "the intimations of higher development among the subordinate animal species, however, can be understood only after the higher development is already known" (*Grundrisse* 105), thus suggesting the dialectical "interim" of an incommensurable gap between the higher and the subordinate. Much of the "human density" (Gross, *Shylock* xi) we are likely to discover in characters like Shylock, Iago, Falstaff, Cordelia, Edmund, Edgar, Ophelia, or Hamlet is beholden to this gap. Descartes suggested something similar when he stated that "nous avons été enfants avant que d'être hommes."[15] But Raber is inflexible:

> Animals are their bodies for Descartes, mere objects put in motion by sense, and inferior motivating force [she refers to Fudge and Shannon].

---

15   Quoted by Jean-Marie Beyssade in the notes to *Méditations métaphysiques*, 996.

> Yet for posthumanist theory, that object-status is not the clear and resounding "truth" it was for Descartes. Ecomaterialists, for instance, would argue that in wearing and eating animals humans evidence their entanglement in their environments. (117)

But didn't Descartes—the author of tracts on the world, light, meteors, and the human body—also "evidence" his entanglement in his environment? Why did he begin *L'homme* with a study of the body, and why did he assert so forcefully at the beginning of that early tract that "ce deux natures," meaning the soul and the body, "doivent être jointes et unies" (*L'homme* 379)? Didn't he also know that humans eat and wear animals? How on earth could he construe the notion of reflex movement if not as evidence that we are also bodies in earth? Did he need eco-materialists to arrive in a time machine to teach him just that? Or maybe Shakespeare himself, reaching him from the past, to remind him that "nature needs not what thou gorgeous wear'st" (*King Lear* 2.4.264)? For recall that "René Descartes was wrong and Shakespeare could have told him so" (Egan, "Homeostasis" 77).

If some of these objections are merely ridiculous, some of the positive arguments employed by posthumanist scholars evince an odd disregard for philosophical sources. For instance, Raber's recourse to the automaton speculation in Descartes is symptomatic of the inconsistent and very narrow use posthumanists make of the Cartesian textual corpus. Arguably, the French thinker would have gladly subscribed to the supposedly posthumanist apercu that "what we call 'human' does not precede technology and machinery, but rather [...] the human is already inhuman" (145). Descartes was fascinated with technical instruments and military weapons, as a cursory look at the illustrations of his books can easily demonstrate. This Raber fails to note. Furthermore, his strong interest in the prosthetic condition of the human body turns Descartes, paradoxically, into a cutting-edge posthumanist (What is Tim Burton waiting for to shoot a steel-punk biopic of Descartes?). Especially because he didn't mobilize moral judgement to take stock of his findings, both scientific and speculative. For all her anti-Cartesian bile, Raber only quotes from Descartes once, the brief passage on artificial machines in *Discourse on Method*. Considering that Descartes is the Western philosopher most often mentioned in her book, this seems a rather scanty amount of text-based reference. Posthumanist theory is described in her book as a "codification of thought, particularly Western philosophical thought," enabling a position that "puts the premises and precepts of humanism into question" (8). One would expect the author to give these Cartesian premises and precepts more room to express themselves freely in their own textual terms. But such liberal largesse is ditched, I guess, as another outmoded humanist habit. What we get instead is a great deal of casual second-hand allusion and prejudiced hearsay.

Another instance of anti-Cartesianism fuelled by neglect of the Cartesian sources can be found in Kevin Curran's essay on *Macbeth*, first published in the special issue of *Criticism* titled "Shakespeare and Phenomenology," and later included in his book *Shakespeare's Legal Ecologies: Law and Distributed Selfhood* (2017). Curran quotes from the *Meditations on Prima Philosophia*, supposedly from the Hackett edition translated by Donald A. Cress (whom he misspells as Kress) of *Discourse on Method* and the *Meditations*, but page 21 doesn't correspond with the cited passage. The passage Curran is commenting appears on page 68 of the Hackett edition, in a translation (Cress's) that differs from the one he quotes:

> But then were I perchance to look out my window and observe men crossing the square, I would ordinarily say I see the men themselves just as I say I see the wax. But what do I see aside from hats and clothes, which could conceal automata? Yet I judge them to be men. Thus what I thought I had seen with my eyes, I actually grasped solely with the faculty of judgment, which is in my mind. (68)

Curran has probably lifted the passage from David Levin's book *The Opening of Vision*, where we can find several allusions to Descartes' text (pages 69, 96, 106, 125, and 139).[16] So you advertise your piece as an explicit critique of Cartesian "dualism" but fail to read and quote properly from Descartes. I find it strange, to say the least. But there is more. His use of a long quotation from the *Discourse on Method* to demonstrate that the self, according to Descartes, "has no need of any place nor depends on material things" (13), and that therefore "the *self* is its own place" (14) is simply preposterous. Descartes' entire reasoning depends on the operative and provisional *pretense* (*je pouvais feindre*) he has no body. Descartes knew he had/was a body more than any of his contemporaries, and his entire life research program was aimed at establishing the immanent mechanical laws of physical bodies. His philosophy of the mind is genetically a residual but radical spin-off of his physics of the body: *residual* because both the transcendence and transcendentality of the substance mind is only thrown into relief when the alternative substantial realm of bodies is immanently grasped as devoid of metaphysical-cum-spiritual adiposities,

---

16   The full reference is given in endnote 107, page 495 of Levin's book, as *Meditations on First Philosophy*, 155. The edition, listed in the bibliography, is *The Philosophical Works of Descartes*, ed. E. Haldane and G. Ross, New York, Dover Publications, 1955.

and *radical* because the resulting philosophy of the mind allows him to secure the transcendental regime of truths that makes the *true* knowledge of bodies possible in the first place. His is therefore a thought experiment—*hypotheses fingo*, "Je susi feignant"—leading him to the formulation of the autonomy of thought, not an axiomatic assertion of the isolation of the mind.[17] Let me recall what I noted above: when Descartes inserts the clarificatory apposition in "En sorte que *ce* moi, c'est-à-dire l'âme par la quelle je suis ce que je suis" (*Discours* 103), translated by Cress as "Thus this 'I', that is to say, the soul through which I am what I am" (19), and by Maclean as "Accordingly this 'I', that is to say, the Soul by which I am what I am" (29), he is very clearly using *ce moi*—apparently a neologism in the nominalization of the pronoun—in a figurative manner: there is *ce moi* (the soul) and *ce autre moi* (the body) which he has conjecturally disconnected in the *epoché* (*je pouvais feindre*) of my thought experiment. The fact that the former *moi* is more essentially defining of the human condition—among other things because it is the site of thought that allows for essences and definitions—does not rule out the fact that it is both "I"s that make up the human self. Descartes never proposed a complete disconnection between body and mind, he never defended—as his treatise on the passions shows—a life of the mind in complete abstraction from the body. He merely argued that the mind can do things that the body cannot do. If neo-phenomenological scholars find the resulting incommensurability—much boosted by Spinoza and Hegel—annoying, that is their problem, and they shouldn't mangle Descartes' work for it. Badiou reminds us that "Descartes oppose à la scolastique médiévale, servante de l'ordre dominante, Église et monarchie, une doctrine du libre Sujet pensant, compatible avec la science moderne" (*L'immanence* 84). The camps are clearly delineated: on the one side, Descartes' free thinking subject, on the other, the servitudes of church and metaphysical dogma—which echoes Deleuze's championing of Kant as the adversary of religious tribunals and empirical decisions. This delineation helps explain the metaphysical underpinning of neo-phenomenological anti-Cartesianism—with its new foundationalism of the body and its faddish essentialism of the affect.

---

17 For argumentative feigning in Descartes, see Nancy, *Ego Sum*, 116–117.

5

So, to return to the daily grind: *René Descartes was wrong, and Shakespeare could have told him so*. The anti-Cartesian prejudice is not new. In 1999 Slavoj Žižek opened *The Ticklish Subject: The Absent Centre of Political Ontology*, with a salutary display of confidence in the powers of the Cartesian subject. This bold tribute was preceded by the recognition, in the form of a satirical report, of the way in which "A Spectre is Haunting Western Academia ... the spectre of the Cartesian subject" (1). The recognition, in short, of the institutional resistance to the daemon, ghost or "thing" (*Hamlet* 1.1.19). Seventeen years earlier, let me recall, de Man was firmly denouncing *the resistance to theory*. The timely advent of the spectre, the Slovenian thinker lamented, needs to fight back "a holly alliance" of powers that have met to "exorcise" it:

> The New Age obscurantist (who wants to supersede the 'Cartesian paradigm' towards a new holistic approach) and the postmodern deconstructionist (for whom the Cartesian subject is a discursive fiction, an effect of decentred textual mechanisms); the Habermasian theorist of communication (who insists on a shift from Cartesian monological subjectivity to discursive intersubjectivity) and the Heideggerian proponent of the thought of Being (who stresses the need to 'traverse' the horizon of modern subjectivity culminating in current ravaging nihilism); the cognitive scientist (who endeavours to prove empirically that there is no unique scene of the Self, just a pandemonium of competing forces) and the Deep Ecologist (who blames Cartesian mechanicist materialism for providing the philosophical foundation for the ruthless exploitation of nature); the critical (post) Marxist (who insists that the illusory freedom of the bourgeois thinking subject is rooted in class division) and the feminist (who emphasizes that the allegedly sexless *cogito* is in fact a male patriarchal formation). Where is the academic orientation which has not been accused by its opponents of not yet properly disowning the Cartesian heritage? (1)

In the last twenty or so intervening years, neo-phenomenology springs forth as another academic orientation distinctively set up to dismantle the Cartesian heritage. The philosophical emphasis may be new, but their proponents draw on the agenda of some of the orientations lucidly inventoried by Žižek—in particular New Age obscurantism, cognitive science and Deep Ecologism. There are, in addition, some instances of retrograde updating: the stress on intersubjectivity, no longer discursive (Habermasian), harks back to Arendtian moral pragmatism. And some instances of broad-brush detraction: deconstruction is a late-modernist, not postmodernist, movement whose consanguinity with the Cartesian subject is incontrovertible. Still, despite these minor slips, Žižek's diagnosis retains validity. His essay "Plato, Descartes, Hegel: Three Philosophers of the Event" uses as epigraph a memorable remark by Lacan that sharply summarizes the point I am trying to make: "I don't much like hearing that we have gone beyond Hegel, the way one hears we have gone beyond Descartes. We go beyond everything and always end up in the same place."[18]

Once again, *In the (early modernist) beginning (there) was (not) Descartes*. The slogan may house a sensible rationale (Descartes is less *early* than Shakespeare), but those who most repeat it are driven by bad faith—for the former is certainly not any less *modern* for that. Understandably, coping with an *unphenomenal Shakespeare* proves taxing for those who condemn Descartes without having read much of his voluminous philosophical and scientific written production, have no idea of the continued interest this rationalist thinker had for "things outward" (*Antony and Cleopatra* 3.13.31), of his passion for "the world," that is, "and awkward casualties" (*Pericles* 5.1.84). If *Cartesian* designates, as is often implied, a solipsistic disinterest in the corporeal *Umwelt*—the accretive stretches of the *res extensa*—nobody less Cartesian than Descartes. If at some point, as some disapprovingly put it, he decided to turn inward, it was only the better to explain the variety and complexity of the outward. The *Discours de la méthode* and the *Meditationes de prima philosophia* are but methodological and only tendentially ontological digressions of a man whose chief aim was to grasp, like Wallace Stevens, "things as they are" ("The Man with the Blue Guitar," *Collected Poems* 165).[19] To determine the *objective* with criteria of certainty (clarity, distinction) he was drawn to the mental—not to the psychological, not to the spiritual. Only thus could he describe the external in a drastically unprejudiced manner—Husserl, we know, attempted the same Cartesian move (a sceptic reduction) three centuries later. The fact that Descartes reached quite far in trying to attain this goal—he was able to suggest, among other useful things, the law of momentum conservation—probably

---

18   See *The Palgrave Handbook of German Idealism*, 575. The Lacan quotation is taken from *Séminaire II: Le moi dans la théorie de Freud et dans la technique de la psychanalyse*. In the original, we read: "Et comme je l'ai souvent fait remarquer, je n'aime pas beaucoup qu'on dise 'qu'on a dépassé Hegel,' comme on dit 'dépasser Descartes,' etc. dépasser tout et toujours: on reste tout simplement à la même place" (91).

19   Attempts like Stephan Laqué's to rekindle without prejudice the latent possibilities in the Shakespeare-Descartes connection are very uncommon, and therefore all the more valuable. See "'Not Passion's Slave:' Hamlet, Descartes and the Passions."

bothers some furiously anti-Cartesian scholars: at bottom, they defraud their professed materialism by failing to recognise the thesis of the radical autonomy of the corporal. And this blindness originates in their unwitting reliance on extra-corporal forces (spiritual, moral) to explain the workings of the body. Descartes denied that the soul or mind was the animating principle of the living body, and this is scandal to pious materialists.

6

In *Theory of the Subject,* Badiou argued that there are three kinds of materialism, each adapted to the idealism it seeks to rebuke: religious idealism, humanist idealism and linguistic idealism (188). The kind of materialism he championed was a reaction against linguistic idealism, and this materialism posits a subject that is however informed by the idealist (structuralist) affordances of language—this is the case, for instance, of the Lacanian subject, constituted by language. The fact that Badiou did not rest content with the *decentred* and *subjugated subject* that resulted from the bargain and moved on to construct a *political subject* that remained compatible with materialism is something that need not concern us here. What is crucial is that he proceeded dialectically in his suggestion that "every materialism is [...] the *stiffening* of an old idealism" (187). And he added:

> Where did the materialists of the eighteenth century get their superflat machines, if not from Descartes? And Lenin brings Hegelian immanence to bear against the transcendental. And we, against Althusser's "process without subject," invoke Lacan. (187)

My contention is that very few self-dubbed materialist scholars working today in the field of early modern studies would be inclined to condone any of these three materialist outcomes—the Cartesian superflat machines, Hegelian immanence, or Althusser's process without a subject.[20] And their inability to

---

20   The ambivalent legacy of Descartes is borne out in Marx's and Engels' description, in *The Holy Family*, of the way in which both French metaphysics and French materialism of the late seventeenth and eighteenth century have their roots in Cartesianism. Interestingly, Marx and Engels lay the emphasis on the Cartesian descent of mechanistic materialism: "Descartes in his physics endowed matter with self-creative power and conceived mechanical motion as the manifestation of its life. He completely separated his physics from his metaphysics. Within his physics, matter is the sole substance, the sole basis of being and of knowledge. Mechanical French materialism adopted Descartes' physics in

tolerate these radical consequences of materialism derives from the fact that the "idealism" they dialectically sublate when they purport to endorse materialism (the body, the lifeworld, networks) is an archaic kind of idealism—neither the humanist nor the linguistic idealism identified by Badiou, but the *religious idealism* whose survival in modernity has taken various forms: modernist cabalism, fin-de-siècle spiritualism, hippy orientalism, New Age mystique, political theology. In July 1966 Althusser wrote that "la phénoménologie est la psychologie religieuse de notre temps" (*Écrits sur la psychanalyse* 67). His time is, alas, still ours. All of these spiritualist tendencies tend to rework materialist relations in terms of inter-subjective connectedness: again, *communities* and *networks*. We are thus thrown back to Madame Sosostris and the séance—back to the modernist Orientalism (the Buddhism in *Siddhartha*) that Adorno ridicules in the section of *Negative Dialectics* where he condemns the extravagant syntheses between modern science and philosophy promoted by those who, with the pretext of extolling the new liberties consequent on the shaking of a geocentrism and anthropocentrism, are actually reinvesting the new (infinite, empty) universe with subjective meaning. These people, Adorno argues,

> ignore the increasingly independent language of physical-mathematical formulas, a language that has long ceased to be retrievable into visuality or any other categories directly commensurable to the consciousness of man. And yet, the results of recent cosmology have radiated far and wide. All notions to make the universe resemble the subject, if not indeed to derive it as positing the subject, have been relegated to a naïveté comparable to that of Boeotians or paranoiacs who regard their hamlet as the center of the world.
>
> *Negative* 67

The problem with posthumanists is that, for all their protestations to the contrary, they never actually assume that the new arbitrary language of science (largely invented by Galileo and Descartes) *cannot* be retrieved to *visuality* or to categories *directly* (immediately) *commensurable* to the consciousness of man. Nor can it be co-opted by moralism or restrained by ideology.[21] Their

---

opposition to his metaphysics. His followers were by profession anti-metaphysicians, i.e., physicists" (169).

21 Žižek: "Science belongs to the Real and, as a mode of the Real of *jouissance*, it is indifferent to the modalities of its symbolization, to the way it will affect social life. Of course, although the concrete organization of the scientific apparatus, up to its most abstract conceptual schemes, is socially 'mediated', this game of discerning a patriarchal (Eurocentric, male-chauvinist, mechanistic and nature-exploiting ...) bias of modern science, in a way,

phenomenological prejudices prevent them from attaining to this truly non-correlationist or non-human-exceptionalist position. They are very happy inside their hamlets, by their neighbour Hamlet, irradiating moral-spiritual hospitality to the arch-different children of the earth.

In the "Introduction" to an edited collection titled *Spiritual Shakespeares*, Ewan Fernie propounds a "striking spiritual materialism, where spirituality is not so much an escape from material reality as an immanent chance for something better" (20), and praises John Joughin's chapter in the book for its "interplay between the material and spiritual as the inherent dialectic of dramatic form" (20). The attempt, moreover, to win Derrida over to the spiritualist camp is profoundly misguided, and rests mostly on a *disreading*—not misreading—of Derrida.[22] Happily, Descartes had no interest in chances for something better: he devoted his works and days to examining the things (the many things) that were before him. And, let me add, the "spiritual" was no relevant part of the wholes that mattered to him—the malicious demon being just a figural-imaginative means to a mental-transcendental, decidedly not spiritual, end. In Jane O. Newman's essay on Pascal included in Lupton's and Hammill's edited collection on *Political Theology and Early Modernity*, Descartes receives his due share of controlled aspersion for his decisive contribution to secularization, worldling, and self-consciousness, with the munitions of omnipotence (*Allmacht*) all packed up in the cogito as a way to warrant man's freedom in the world. Newman reads this de-sacralization as a nefarious "Schmittian political theology in reverse" (165) and pits it implicitly against Arendt's political-theological investment in St. Augustine. At bottom, Descartes is construed as the original historical opponent of "a world in which religious conviction motivates political action." Although Newman contends that she feels no nostalgia for such a world, she endeavors to excavate, we are told, "a clear narrative of the

---

  does not really concern science, the drive which effectuates itself in the run of the scientific machine [...] Heidegger is thus well aware that all fashionable 'critiques of science,' according to which science is a tool of Western capitalist domination, patriarchal oppression, and so forth, fall short of, and thus leave unquestioned, the 'hard kernel' of the scientific drive" (*Plague* 51–52).

22   Fernie speaks of a "poststructuralist spirituality" in allusion to Derrida's *Spectres de Marx*, but Derrida, for whom "Spiritualism is but a spiritism" (*Spiritual* 172) is far from promoting a spiritualist turn. He offers rather a critical analysis of philosophical discourse ridden with tropes of spirits and spectres. Colebrook points out that "Derrida's later work on Marx [...] insists that a return or retrieval of matter would always be haunted, doubled, spooked or ghosted by the sorts of immateriality the materialist had tried to exorcise" (*Jacques Derrida* 8). Spiritualism, in short, camouflages ideality or idealism behind the material mask of cultural, embodied, emotion.

importance of sacred logics in empowering Man to act" (177). Amen. No irony intended, for there is nothing essentially wrong in presenting Descartes as an echt-saboteur of sacred logics.

So, let me insist: card-carrying neo-materialist scholars are not, as we would expect, vexed by the autonomy of the *res cogitans*, but rather angered by the ineliminable separateness of the *res extensa*.[23] Since their materialism is a *spiritualized materialism*, they repudiate the self-explanatory rules of corporal immanence that Descartes strove to disclose in his more scientific tracts. The fact that we now read (if we do) the *Discours* and the *Meditations* texts and not these tracts would have probably shocked their author. I recommend, to the scandalized, a careful reading of *Dioptrique*, *Géométrie*, *Météores*, and *Traité du monde et de la lumière*. But, of course, copies of these texts, featuring a near-Goethean imagination enraptured by all earthly matters, are probably not in the bookshelves. For many early modernist scholars, Descartes is just one of the usual suspects—an incrimination solely based on hearsay. They unthinkingly pass on this prejudice to the next generation, and doctoral students are only too eager to obey a department-corridor injunction (do not read Descartes) which at that busy point in their professional careers comes as a blessing. Reading Bacon, they reckon, was taxing enough. These scholars own, at best, an old Pelican paperback of the *Discours*, falling apart on the edges, a relic that has managed to survive more than five moves, to be sure, but how many readings?

Descartes has been invariably singled out as a paper tiger in all belligerent theoretical preambles to phenomenological and posthumanist criticism in early modern studies.[24] The straw man is passed on from one generation of critics to another—from Latour now to a cheering crowd of posthumanist

---

23 Jean-Luc Nancy: "It's always an 'object,' a body ob-jected precisely *against the claim of being a body-subject*, or a subject-in-a-body. Here, again, Descartes is correct, and in the following way: I ob-ject my body against myself, as something foreign, something strange, the exteriority *to* my enunciation ("ego") from this enunciation it-self. Or, again, Hegel: 'the mind is a bone,' he says, referring to the conformation of the human skull, meaning that the bone eludes the mind, resists it, counters it with an impenetrable objection. (*Hoc est enim corpus meum*: it's an impossible appropriation, it's the very impossibility of appropriation in general.) Nothing of the 'me' is *extended*: as soon as *I* is extended, it's also delivered to others. Or again, I'm the extension that *I* am by being withdrawn, subtracted, removed, and ob-jected" (*Corpus* 29). Few neo-materialists would be willing to countenance this radical and ineliminable alienation of the internally distant body.

24 Perhaps exceptional is Steven Swarbrick's acknowledgement that "instead of solving Descartes' 'error,' it's high time we attempt to problematize it further: to think, along with Deleuze's theory of the event, of a strange 'materialism without matter'" ("Materialism without Matter").

mass-celebrants—with no time to stop and reconsider the grounds of the allegation. Stephen Thomson has rightly protested that "the disregard to which the father of modern philosophy succumbs is in itself quite familiar: it is the contempt that familiarity breeds, and which seeks and finds nothing in 'Descartes' that would resist compression into the tiny volume of the adjective 'Cartesian'" ("Jeu d'écarts" 192). This is very true, but it is not my intention to convoke an unfamiliar Descartes. In fact, Husserl's neo-Cartesian *Rückfrage* (*Cartesian Meditations* 1–25; *Crisis* 60–83) was in principle pertinent enough, and Jean-Luc Marion's attempts to render Descartes phenomenologically meaningful are always worthy of attention. The familiar Descartes I take up is a proto-Spinozian and therefore pre-Hegelian agent of intellectual curiosity who crosses—like Patrick White's Voss—the fields of experience and returns—unlike Voss—to the mind in a defensive gesture, striving to conciliate the apperceptive stability of consciousness with the combined forces of random empirical donation and verbal negativity. It is the Descartes ransomed by a current dialectical tradition that remains, against all odds and a great deal of uninformed aspersion, unashamed to return to "a seemingly obsolete moment of the past, namely to idealism" (Ruda, *For Badiou* 19).[25] It is the Descartes that folds back on Hamlet and Prospero. On Ophelia and Miranda too, facetiously advancing that "we know what we are" (*Hamlet* 4.5.42), and yet abandoned to a "bootless inquisition" around the mystery of "what I am" (*The Tempest* 1.2.34–35).

7

Shakespeare is an *earlier* modern thinker than Descartes. Granted. So what? On close inspection, in fact, their disagreements are far less relevant than their points of convergence. They share, for instance, a similar faith in separation (discrimination, distinction) as instrumental to grasping the *quid* of something. To reach the "thing inseparate" (*Troilus and Cressida* 5.2) is the aim of a noble epistemic pursuit, however doomed to recursive failure. Shakespeare and Descartes both rely on analytical powers of the intellect that are at bottom

---

25   It is, more specifically, the Descartes that Badiou consciously or unconsciously engages in a very productive fashion. Despite his Lacanian commitments, or perhaps precisely because of them, Badiou's admiration for Descartes runs through his entire production. See particularly his celebration, in the seminar *Théorie axiomatique du sujet* (1996–1998), of the figure of a subject who only finds its stability in close proximity to a truth (72–73).

linguistic-conceptual, and they refuse to be nothing if not critical. Both are content with the semiotic arbitrariness that simultaneously quickens and threatens epistemological *representation*. Both assume that the mind-body composition is inhabited by a gap—the void of excessive incommensurability—allowing for the operational autonomy of the cogito. This is what Hamlet possibly implies when he portends that "the body is with the King, but the King is not with the body" (*Hamlet* 4.2.25). If you replace King with mind, you may freely conclude that the mind—however formally extensional and contingent, however "a thing" in this precise sense—*is certainly not with the body*. A mind, in sum, flares verbal-conceptually into thought, and is thus able to separate, analyse, distinguish, criticize. The eventuality of this (human) conflagration doesn't warrant, however, a cognitively productive outcome. This is where Shakespeare, with his penchant for dialogue and dialectic, comes in to elaborate on possibilities of doubt and incertitude only partly dramatized by Descartes. Let us not forget that the breakdowns of ideationally monitored analysis bode the triumph of the dialectic, and that the wraiths of the sophist and the ironist (Descartes' demon included) have always haunted speculative-dialectic rationality as its enabling precondition. Let us recall too that "Hamlet, certainly an ironist, does not crave an ironical God, but Shakespeare allows him no other" (Bloom *Shakespeare* 386).[26] Or that Hamlet's freedom was, as Bloom suggested, the "*the freedom to infer*" (419). The art of drawing inferences and making explicit determinate-conceptual latencies is quintessentially analytic, critical, and dialectic. "Thought is free," Maria demurs in *Twelfth Night* (1.3.65), true enough, but the exertion of this freedom is—*pace* Kant—far from totally spontaneous: Hegel presents his *phenomenology of spirit* as the narrative of an exacting trial and arduous probation, not exactly "the fair adventure of tomorrow" (*King John* 5.5.23). The power of analysis—what Ezio Raimondi calls "razionalismo critico" in his reading of Tasso's dialogues ("La prigione" 13)—enjoys today bad press, but was integral to the constitution of a Renaissance author with neo-classical ambitions. If you believe Shakespeare doesn't fit the neo-classical type, please reread *The Rape of Lucrece, Venus and Adonis, Love's*

---

26   Bloom observes that "Everything in the play depends upon Hamlet's response to the Ghost, a response that is as highly *dialectical* as everything else about Hamlet" (*Shakespeare* 387; emphasis added). In the same vein: "Permit this dramatist a concourse of contraries, and he will show us everybody and nobody, all at once" (401). And also: "Shakespeare created Hamlet as a dialectic of antithetical qualities, unresolvable even by the hero's death" (406). Discussing the to-be-or-not-to-be soliloquy: "this soliloquy is the center of Hamlet, at once everything and nothing, a fullness and an emptiness playing off against each other" (409).

THE SPECTRE OF THE CARTESIAN SUBJECT 83

Labour's Lost and *Julius Caesar*. But the anti-rationalist prejudice is old and entrenched. Reliance on an undialectic scientific deployment of the analytic power was memorably captured by Wordsworth in four condemnatory lines:

> Sweet is the lore which nature brings;
> Our meddling intellect
> Misshapes the beauteous forms of things;
> —We murder to dissect.
> Poetical Works 377

Interestingly, irony was as unknown to the positivists despised by Wordsworth as to Wordsworth himself. Inspired by Gestalt psychology, unironic post-Husserlian phenomenologists believed that "the beauteous forms of things" could be grasped by a deeper form of perception, unsoiled by the piecemeal sensorial synthesis that is the flip side of rational analysis. Seeing, for Merleau-Ponty, is not patching together a something whose form was first patched together by a somebody (God, human artificer, Demiurg, Bard). Phenomenological seeing is a sweet commerce of beauteous forms that comes to pass outside the court of judgement or determining reflection: "the eye, left to itself, entirely ignores understanding; it only notices appearance (it is *Augenschein*) without any awareness of a dichotomy between illusion and reality" (de Man, *Aesthetic*, 127). *Dialectical seeing* is another matter: it is the *ex hypothesi* unfinished patching together of what was never fully patched together under the delusion that all the separate pieces could (might, must, shall) indeed fall under the guidance of a single form (*eidos*) whose apprehension is beholden to a conception of totality. Straddling the Analytical-Continental divide, but with the Continental leg—his left—bearing most of the weight, Wilfrid Sellars sharply observed that "the aim of philosophy is to understand how things in the broadest possible sense of the term hang together in the broadest possible sense of the term" (*Science* 1).[27] Dialectical seeing is presumed in a mode of understanding that owes much to the premises of generality and totality—what Heidegger called the thought of being (*das Seiende*) as such, in general (*im Allgemeinen*) and the thought of being as such, as a whole (*im Ganzen*) (*Identity and Difference* 58). And this mode of understanding was largely forged by Descartes.

Take the line "When yellow leaves, or none, or few, do hang" (Sonnet 73.2). Do you see anything? How can "none" (a quantifier pronoun) correct disjunctively

---

27 See also DeVries, 1–22.

"yellow" (a descriptive adjective)? What does "few" add to this imaginative embarrassment, beyond a puzzling rectification? What exactly "hangs"? How can you turn "none" into one of the terms of a choice without endangering the aesthetic solidity of the picture? How much of this mad—half-quantitative, half-qualitative—"typology" is based "on actual observation" and how much "on words" (de Man, *Aesthetic* 124)? Do you see the "beauteous form"? I don't. But I reread the line, I hear it, I sense something beautiful indeed, I am moved. Yet no distinct form, no clear *Bild*, comes to mind. Shakespeare—to me, anyway—has rashly sketched an imperfect early-winter *dialectical* vignette, hesitantly adding imaginative mending to conceptual revision. He has suggested the nothing of something. He has painted *unphenomenal* leaves.[28] William Carlos Williams repaints them in *The Descent of Winter* 10/28: "But there are / on second look / a few yellow leaves / still shaking // far apart." *On second look*, that is, with the intensity of vision only the (mediated, literary, intertextual) *eye of the mind* can afford. Williams doesn't see the yellow leaves. He remembers a sonnet.

Paul de Man argued that "literature involves the voiding, rather than the affirmation, of aesthetic categories" (*Resistance* 10). My book is designedly written in opposition to the belief that Shakespeare's playtexts are either not literature or bad literature in that they involve the *affirmation* of aesthetic categories. I hope it also gets around to showing, here and there, that the best of Shakespeare's playtexts—the *literary* highlights—transpires in the undoing (the voiding) of symbolic phenomenal figuration, symbolic representation, and the phenomenalization of reference:

> QUEEN GERTRUDE. To whom do you speak this?
> HAMLET. Do you see nothing there?
> QUEEN GERTRUDE. Nothing at all, yet all that is I see.
> HAMLET. Nor did you nothing hear?
> QUEEN GERTRUDE. No, nothing but ourselves. (3.4.122–124)

This is not Beckett. Not Paul Celan. Not Hemingway. Not even Eliot's *Quartets*. This is Hamlet, and his problems. Eliot argued that "we find Shakespeare's *Hamlet* not in the action, not in any quotations that we might select, so much as in an unmistakable tone which is unmistakably not in the earlier play"

---

28   For this mode and mood of dialectical atmosphere, see any of Nicholas Royle's brilliant Empson-like close-readings of terms, words and tropes in *How to Read Shakespeare*. In particular, his analysis of Antony's seven lines at *Antony and Cleopatra* (4.14.2–8): *How to Read*, 110–120.

(*Prose* 48): do you *see* the "unmistakable tone"? It may be worth noting that the dominant conjectural query informing neo-materialist, object-ontological and posthumanist research—"What would this assemblage of things look like without a human *look* or *like*?" or if you wish "What would the superposition and stratification of crude materials look like without Shakespeare to look and like?"—already involves a Cartesian subjectivity—a sort of Henry James goblin—dove-like brooding in the viewpoint's dark abyss, without necessarily making it pregnant.²⁹ One thing is to proceed, without the assistance of concepts, to the symbolic (concordant, harmonious) embodiment of non-human reality, and to fantasize with its "beltà, s'avesse corpo": this is a posthumanist hallucination barred to upholders of the noumenal sublime (Hegel, Lacan, Žižek). An entirely different thing is to dray-dream with the possibility of "aver occhio divino / per far [...] giudizio" (*Orlando Furioso* VI.69.6–8): this is the idealist hallucination whose excess and failure prompts occasions for critical literature. Because literature is either *critical* or nothing, and *nothing* if not critical—nothing meaning here metaphysics, ideology, religion or aesthetics. The failure of idealist internalization—the collapse of symbolic figuration—depends on the unphenomenal materiality of tropological inscription: awareness of the latter inflects the former with the critical detachment only literature and literary philosophy (Montaigne, Descartes, Pascal, Hegel, Emerson, Nietzsche, Derrida, Deleuze) are capable of obtaining. One of Hamlet's problems (there are others) is that he is unable to recollect his father: he can only *remember* him. For Hegel—and later for Proust too—recollection is an action of internalization (*Erinnergung*), an "inner gathering and preserving of experience" that is "also an integral part of the ideology of the symbol" (de Man, *Aesthetic* 101). By contrast, memory (*Gedächtnis*) resembles Proust's *mémoire volontaire*: "it is entirely devoid of images (*bildlos*) [...] but is not devoid of materiality altogether" (101) because it depends on the mechanical "inscription of names" (102) as mere signifiers. Memory, like memorization by rote, fosters imageless thought. Hegel reminds his readers of the observed fact that we remember best what we don't understand, when we don't need to internally recollect the meaning of what is registered. The resulting unlatching of signifier (form or formalized matter) from signified (ideal content) promotes the arbitrariness that is best realized, according to Hegel, in sign-dependent thought, as opposed to symbol-dependent beauty. Therefore thought, argues de Man, like the memory that makes it possible, is "entirely dependent on a mental faculty that is mechanical through and through, as remote as can be

---

29   Slavoj Žižek makes a similar point in his essay in *Reading Marx*.

from the sounds and images of the imagination or from the dark mine of recollection, which lies beyond the reach of words and of thought" (102). The move from *Erinnerung* to *Gedächtnis*, and the transcendental enabling and undoing of the former by the latter, anticipates the shift in structural linguistics "from the study of conscious linguistic phenomena to study of their *unconscious* infrastructure" (Levi-Strauss, *Structural Anthropology* 33), with *unconscious infrastructure* foreshadowing Derrida's material-transcendental *écriture*.[30] Indeed, the discarded (un-ingestible) materiality of writing in the metaphysical tradition paradoxically posits "ce *phénomène* externe" (*De la grammatologie* 51; emphasis added) as the paradigm of *unphenomenality*. Lukacher speaks of the cultural-historical process taking place in the wake of the Pauline internalization of *syneidesis* (*conscientia*) whereby "the daemon was demonized, since any un-interiorizable residue of language or thought pertaining to our self-certain sense of being had necessarily to be cast out into an unredeemable exteriority" (*Daemonic* 11). The moralistic repudiation of writing as bad nature (*mauvaise nature*) precludes its facile reduction to "un *phénomène* naturel" (53; emphasis added) among others.

Hamlet, in brief, may own and cherish "that within which passeth show" (*Hamlet* 1.2.85), an interiority, that is, closed off to words and thought, but this conjectural inside is ever undone by modes of "spiritual" restoration that are far from recollective or mnemic. "Remember me" (*Hamlet* 1.5.112), enjoins the ghost, and rather than treasuring his father's image in his dark mine of recollection, the prince decides to inscribe those very words in the tables of his memory. This way he makes himself an Oedipus, a demonized *conscientia*, whose hidden task is to reverse—through memory—the massive *refoulement* of writing: "Shakespeare's daemonic figures remember something that generally gets forgotten, which is that something has always been forgotten" (Lukacher, *Daemonic* 14).[31] We cannot discharge Prospero's and Hamlet's all-seeing but daemonic meta-consciousnesses, any more than we can *see* them *seeing*. In *Continental Philosophy*, Andrew Cutrofello closes the section on Heidegger with the question "whether Heidegger [...] manages to escape the Cartesian tradition, as he professes, or whether he simply radicalizes it by attempting to glimpse what it would be like to inhabit the elusive perspective of (cogito 4)"

---

30 In her "Introduction" to Derrida's *Of Grammatology*, Spivak examines the Levi-Strauss passage from which this quote is taken. See "Introduction," lvi–lviii.
31 Further down, Lukacher argues that "moral conscience is inseparable from the imperative function of language and [...] conscience operates by reactivating the memory of a moral imperative that has been forgotten or rendered passive during the act itself" (*Daemonic* 34).

(63). Cogito 4 is, in Cutrofello's elucidation, the highest possible level of reflective abstraction, sadly unaffordable to sub-lunar mortals and lesser spirits. But no feat of spiralling self-reflection is unattainable for Hamlet, Prospero, and their likes. This is their thing, this is what they do, to set off gathering layers of conscious reflexivity in full awareness that consciousness *is not*—is not the fullness, that is, of being, let alone Being. These people reign as supreme and gloriously miscarried as the light of Truth in Plato.[32] But it is John Ashbery who has best adumbrated the dialectical taste of Shakespeare's unphenomenal experience:

> Thus your only world is an inside one
> Ironically fashioned out of external phenomena
> Having no rhyme nor reason, and yet neither
> And existence independent of foreboding and sly grief.[33]

8

So, to sum up, although Descartes was wrong (Egan, Curran, Raber) the spectre of his nefarious subject is back (Žižek). But in what sense is it back? Can this return upset the firmness of the chronological assignation that has placed Shakespeare in an unassailable locus of pre-Cartesian antecedence. And would that disturbance compromise the rigidity of the ideological arbitration that ipso facto places any anti-Cartesian voice at the Left of the academic-political spectrum. Fortunately, some isolated voices, like that of Michael D. Slater, have been raised against the way overly simplifications of Cartesian philosophy disable in advance the likelihood of a smooth Shakespeare-Descartes rendezvous.[34] In order to identify *radical* ways of being a late-modernist Cartesian in these precarious times, we may retrace the lineage of reluctantly replicating mastery (paternity) that runs from Descartes to Kant, Heidegger, Levinas and Lacan (Derrida, *L'animal* 81). We could of course add Žižek to the

---

32 For a lucid explanation of the dialectic-speculative consequences to be drawn from the myth of the Cave, in particular from the images of the Sun and light, see Heidegger's analysis in *Holzwege* and Badiou's brilliant discussion in his seminar on Plato's *Republic* (*Pour aujourd'hui: Platon!* 147–173).

33 These lines are taken from the poem "Fragment," from the collection *The Double Dream of Spring*, included in *The Mooring of Starting Out*, 292–93.

34 Drawing on historians of philosophy, Slater brilliantly resists "the simplistic notion of the Cartesian self as irreparably fractured into two distinct substances: *res cogitans* (thinking thing) and *res extensa* (extended thing)" (595).

list of "re-pères exemplaires," but Alain Badiou seems better fit for the task. Indeed, Frank Ruda has recently contended that Badiou's philosophy presents a "*Cartesianism for the twenty-first century (to come)*" (84). In a 1996 essay titled "Descartes/Lacan," Badiou recalls Lacan's intimation that "the call for a return to Descartes would not be superfluous."[35] This call may be today less vociferous than the fight calls to phenomenology, but it is still resonant, and commands respect. Badiou has responded to it in a variety of rich ways, which seem to have deepened and expanded in the last two decades. In his Seminar *S'orienter dans la pensée, s'orienter dans l'existence* (2004–2007), he offers a succinct account of his growing Cartesian faith:

> Soit dit en passant, Descartes est quelqu'un avec qui je me sens de plus en plus en sympathie. Les thèmes que nous avons en commun sont finalement plus nombreux que je ne le croyais il y a quelques années. J'en énumère quelques-uns : l'anonymat de l'extériorité (dont le nom cartésien est: étendue), la maintenance de la catégorie de sujet, l'infini (l'idée qu'il s'agisse d'une notion bien plus simple et claire que celle de fini), la volonté comme catégorie majeure (je parlerais plutôt, quant à moi, de décision), la vérité comme terme non substantiel (i.e. distinct des deux substances que sont les corps et les idées), l'universalisme (le fait que la vérité soit transculturelle et translangagière; la transcription claire et intelligible de la pensée peut procéder dans n'importe quel dialecte, par exemple le bas-breton), enfin cette formidable invention qu'est la création des vérités éternelles (l'idée que même les vérités éternelles ont été créées, par Dieu en l'occurrence, mais Dieu est ici un opérateur historique; l'idée à retenir est que les vérités éternelles gardent leur caractère d'éternité en dépit du fait qu'elles ont surgi en un point du temps; elles sont éternelles parce qu'elles ont été créées, nullement parce qu'elles sont là depuis toujours.)[36]

Badiou's remarkably detailed self-clarification helps us to itemize five related theses: 1) the thesis of arbitrary representation; 2) the thesis of irrational rationality; 3) The thesis of the subject in the void of its subtraction; 4) The thesis of

---

35 Lacan drops this comment ("le mot d'ordre d'un retour à Descartes ne serait pas superflu") in his complex essay on psychic causality: *Écrits 1*, 162.
36 The comment is made in the lecture of October 25th, 2006. The seminar is due to be published on 2022 (Fayard, Paris). I use the version as it appears in the website: http://www.entretemps.asso.fr/Badiou/06-07.htm.

radical extensionality; and 5) the thesis of finitude violated by the infinite. Let us consider them in turn:

1)   The thesis of arbitrary representation

Descartes' epistemology marks a transition from a notion of iconic resemblance to that of arbitrary representation, where alone a faint remainder of global isomorphism is retained. It may not be completely useless to step back from the proximity of naturalized assumptions and reformulate, with Rorty, the old Cartesian question: "How do we know that anything which is mental represents anything which is not mental?" (*Philosophy* 46). Arbitrariness is primarily the arbitrariness of the linguistic signifier, because, as Descartes notes, "les paroles, n'ayant aucune ressemblance avec les choses qu'elles signifient, ne laissent pas de nous les faire concevoir" (*Le monde*, *Oeuvres philosophiques* 315–16). But this local finding dissolves in the broader arbitrariness that rules "the whole structures system of representings" (Brandom, *Tales* 26): "Car encore que chacun se persuade communément que les idées que nous avons en notre pensée sont entièrement semblables aux objets dont elles procèdent, je ne vois point toutefois de raison qui nous assure que cela soit" (*Le monde* 315). Robert Brandom, for whom Descartes remains an exemplary father (or *mighty dead*), highlights the structural potential of the French philosopher's idea that "one cannot determine the representational purport or potential of a representing item by considering just that item." Rather, "the first step in understanding the relation between a representing and what it represents is to consider the relations between that representing and other representings" (*Tales* 26). To translate this into Althusserian terms, these relations spell an order of structural causation or overdetermination. This, obviously, Brandom doesn't say, but is implied in his argument. As John Haugeland notes, Descartes' extraordinary contribution to analytic geometry, algebra and physics rested largely on his ability to fathom the different languages employed (numbers in algebra, lines, curves, and figures in geometry) as expressions of relational "proportions in general" (31). On this view, therefore, epistemological progress can only be obtained by keeping these proportions free from specific assumptions about the subject matter. This of course some naïve Heideggerians like Hannah Arendt construe as a retreat from the earth, as an "earth alienation" (*The Human Condition* 264).[37] They forget that we would never have started talking about the earth as a natural reality without retreating from its immediate positive riches into the flatlands of abstraction—there would be no Caliban, no

---

37   Arendt gives Descartes a prominent role in the creation of the modern scientific and rationalist mentality that brought the distinction between *vita contemplativa* and *vita activa* to a critical juncture (*The Human Condition* 267–291).

island, no sweet air, without Prospero's original reclusion in a distant Naples study (*The Tempest* 1.2.66–78). As Derrida has noted, the profound reliance of the Cartesian *method* on delegation, representation, memory, the imagination, and the (arbitrary) sign, was one of the reasons why Spinoza turned against Descartes ("Language" 74). Such denaturalized epistemology of representation marks the triumphal alliance between relationality and arbitrariness that we cursorily (and rightly) associate with Saussurean structuralism:

> But I had no intention on that account of attempting to master all the particular sciences commonly denominated mathematics: but observing that, however different their objects, they all agree in considering only the various relations or proportions subsisting among those objects, I thought it best for my purpose to consider these proportions in the most general form possible, without referring them to any objects in particular [*et sans les supposer que dans les sujets*], except such as would most facilitate the knowledge of them.
>
> *Discourse on Method* 52

The key gesture here is the reluctance to refer the "proportions" to any "objects [*sujets*] in particular." This anti-mimetic and anti-phenomenal reluctance may subtend too Descartes' penchant, in his philosophical prose, for an underground rhetoricity characterized by inscriptive materiality, errancy, and contingent arbitrariness (Warminski, "Spectre Shapes: The Body of Descartes?" in *Material Inscriptions*, 68–70). The neo-phenomenological dismantling of structuralism hinges, by contrast, on the constant and immediate presupposition of, assumption of, and reference to, particular subject matters, themes, and objects, taken in isolation of their relational configurations.

The thesis of arbitrary representation is best exemplified in Juliet's philosophical question: "What's in a name? That which we call a rose / By any other name would smell as sweet" (*Romeo and Juliet* 2.1.85–86).

2) The thesis of irrational rationality

Descartes' constitutive-foundational gesture—the assertion of the certitude of the cogito—is dialectically wound up with the containment of madness. Madness, *pace* Foucault, is not quarantined or excluded by the authority of Cartesian rationality. It is rather retained or sublated. As Lacan would put it, we should not forget that "la folie soit un phénomène de la pensée" (*Écrits I* 161), which translated into Cartesian terms means that

> the hyperbolical audacity of the Cartesian Cogito, its mad audacity, which we perhaps no longer perceive as such because, unlike Descartes'

> contemporary, we are too well assured of ourselves and too well accustomed to the framework of the Cogito, rather than to the critical experience of it-its mad audacity would consist in the return to an original point which no longer belongs to either a determined reason or a determined unreason, no longer belongs to them as opposition or alternative. Whether I am mad or not, Cogito, sum. Madness is therefore, in every sense of the word, only one case of thought (within thought).
>
> DERRIDA, *Writing* 56

This cohabitation of *raison* and *déraison* inside the citadel of cogito implies, among other things, that "total derangement is the possibility of a madness that is no longer a disorder of the body" (53), and that it remains legitimate, therefore, in Descartes' hypothetical argument, to "evoke madness from the interior of thought (and not only from within the body)" (54). Note that the body's lack of collaboration in the contractual production of madness is a rider that neo-phenomenologists would reject—being irrational has developed from a stigma into a (ontological) mark of distinction, when it should probably be neither. Nor would they acknowledge the resulting philosophical decisionism binding utterance to violence, law to force. To become a rational cogito involves, first and foremost, the irrational attempt to become it (61–62): "One does something, one counts oneself as (declares oneself) the one who did it, and, on the base of this declaration, one does something new—the proper moment of subjective transformation occurs at the moment of the declaration, not at the moment of the act" (Žižek, *How to Read Lacan* 16). So the weight falls less on the fact that we think (*cogito*) than on the fact that we declare that we do ("cogito ergo ..."). Adorno traced back this decisionist impetus or jolt, which he called the *addendum*, to Hamlet, and situated it before the consolidation of the split between *res cogitans* and *res extensa*, as a mental action as yet separated from thought (*Negative* 228). More importantly, "the addendum has an aspect which under rationalistic rules is irrational" (228). Hamlet's case is exemplary: "Bring me to the test, / And I the matter will reword, which madness / Would gambol from" (3.4.133–35). Derrida argues that "the-attempt-to-say-the-hyperbole" already involves a kind of madness: "But this crisis in which reason is madder than madness—for reason is nonmeaning and oblivion-and in which madness is more rational than reason, for it is closer to the wellspring of sense, however silent or murmuring—this crisis has always begun and is interminable" (62). The dialectical position founded by such "dire de l'excès" (*L'écriture* 94) places Descartes within a lineage of philosophical modernity leading to Schmitt, Badiou, and Laruelle. And to Žižek, who reworks the point as follows:

> again and again, the inherent logic of their philosophical project compelled the authentic philosophers of subjectivity to articulate a certain excessive moment of "madness" inherent to cogito, which they then immediately endeavored to "renormalize" (the diabolical Evil in Kant, the "night of the world" in Hegel, etc.).
>
> *The Ticklish Subject* 2

In the chapter devoted to Hegel in *The Ticklish Subject*, where both the constitution of subjectivity and the healing projection of a symbolic world are made to depend on a prior withdrawal into the nocturnal self, Žižek recalls that the thesis of the "passage through madness" was effectively rekindled by Derrida: "Was not this withdrawal-into-self accomplished by Descartes in his universal doubt and reduction to *cogito*, which, as Derrida pointed out in his 'Cogito and the History of Madness,' also involves a passage through the moment of radical madness?" (34). It was. And this way Derrida, and Žižek after him, withdrew towards the mighty-dead-father Descartes who kept summoning them to *remember* him. Although Adorno disobeyed this particular injunction, pretending *forisfamiliation*, cultivating oblivion, his brutal attack on Husserlian "common-sense" is cued by an admiration of Hegel that, on this particular count, should stretch back to include the discarded father:

> Never does he speak of Hegel otherwise than scornfully, even though the name of "phenomenology" may have been chosen in recollection of the one of spirit. He speaks the language of scientific rancour against a reason which does not capitulate before common sense.
>
> *Against* 49

Adorno quotes Husserl to the effect that "perhaps genius and madness are [...] allied, perhaps there are also lunatic rejectors of the laws of thought: these will certainly also have to count as men" (*Logical Investigations* I 93). So Shakespeare's characters are *Menschen*, after all. *Danke, Herr Professor.*

The thesis of irrational rationality is best exemplified in Troilus' exclamation "O madness of discourse" (*Troilus and Cressida* 5.2.142).

3) The thesis of the subject in the void of its subtraction

There are, we know, many kinds of subjectivity: there is the psychological subject, the anthropological subject, the biological subject, the religious subject, and the metaphysical subject, which quite often draws on the thematic dispositions of the other four. The original Cartesian move, later redeployed by Kant and, defectively, by Husserl, was to de-thematize or de-naturalize this overweight subject, rendering it both insubstantial and potentially void.

That post-Husserlian phenomenologists like Levinas and Merleau-Ponty tried escape routes from the cogito towards the Other or the body should not occlude the fact that Husserl's opening horizons were always the horizons of an evaporating transcendental subject.[38] That anti-Cartesianism is fueled by the recrudescence of the positivism of certain sciences (anthropology, biology, sociology) was something already pointed out by Jean-Luc Nancy in 1979. He proposed instead a genuine philosophical return to the problem of the *subject* (*Ego sum* 12). Badiou, the self-assigned pilot of such return, examined in his *Théorie du sujet* (1982) the double function of the operator "classical subject"—to assign an irreducible being of the existent, and to limit that which, from the 'remainder' of being, is accessible to knowledge. This way the classical subject "partitions that which is immediately given and that which is mediately refused to experience." If a logic of excess seizes the figure, two consequences follow: first, the "being of the subjective existent proves to be a being of nonbeing" (Sartre), and second, "the limit of knowledge proves to be an unlimitation" (Hegel). The inversion is however unreal, Badiou argues, because "consciousness is transparency of its transparency, consciousness (of) self, 'nonpositional in itself.' That such a being is nothing indicates from whence an ontology is possible, namely, from the cogito alone, which gives us the nothing, that is, existence in its essence" (*Theory* 278).[39] Badiou seeks thus to restore the potency of a Cartesian position—*cogito, ergo (nihil) sum*—that Sartre had partly obfuscated with his anti-dialectical proposal of a non-positional and pre-reflexive consciousness—"il y a un cogito préréflexif qui est la condition du cogito cartésien" (*L'être et le néant* 19)—that is rooted in phenomenology.

In his 1996 essay on Descartes and Lacan, Badiou emphasizes the Cartesian descent of psychoanalysis and locates Descartes' radical originality in the linkage between *being*—the being of cogito, subject or thought—and *place*, the necessity of which was confirmed by the Freudian and Lacanian insistence on

---

38   Derrida, in his deconstruction of Levinas' ethical metaphysics, observes that Husserl is more Cartesian than some phenomenologists would desire. Nothing revokes the abyssal positionality of the cogito: *"Mon monde est l'ouverture où se produit toute expérience, y compris celle qui, expérience par excellence, est transcendance vers autrui comme tel. Rien ne peut apparaître hors de l'appartenance à 'mon monde' pour un 'Je suis'"* (*L'écriture* 193). In addition, Derrida insists in *De l'hospitalité* on the autonomy of the language-speaking, language-carrying self. He contends that there is no hospitality without the ghost of such *auto-nomy* (121). The cogito emerges thus as *the* transcendental condition of an opening to the Other.

39   Badiou's argument has to be read against the background of section "Le cogito 'préréflexif' et l'être du 'percipere'" in Sartre's *L'être et le néant*, 16–23. For an excellent account of the Cartesian pedigree of Badiou's *"adventure of subtraction,"* see Ruda, *For Badiou*, 86–93.

a mode of displacement (*I am not where I think*) foreshadowed by the Italian teenager: "This is not Romeo; he's some other where" (*Romeo and Juliet* 1.1.191). The subject, then, is neither substance nor consciousness, but occurs exclusively "in the pure void of its subtraction" ("Descartes/Lacan"). The fact that Descartes had recourse to transcendence in order to secure the subject position as the locus of certainty would not diminish the originality of his finding, which Badiou rather wildly formulates as the "localization of the void." What remains moot in Badiou's reading is the pretermission of the role that language plays in the operations of placing and localization—a role that Lacan seldom failed to assert. Badiou, by contrast, bypasses the contingency of language on his way to the universal ideality of a truth that is described as "that indiscernible multiple a subject supports the finite approximation of," its ideality-to-come being "the truth from which one may legitimately designate" a subject as a "random figure." Cartesian remains, in this account, the sense of random and unpredictable approximation to a subject-constituting site of epistemic certitude. The topological abstractedness that warrants the subjective operation confirms the necessity of disembodiment. The sense of unpredictability and risk in the act of *cogito*'s self-foundation is aptly conveyed by Rodolphe Gasché in the introductory pages to his classical study on Derrida, where a clear effort is made to place him inside a tradition inaugurated by Descartes. Derrida, Gasché argues, is a philosopher of reflection, and reflection is—from Descartes to Kant—the gesture of a self-consciousness that posits itself as "the ground of deduction of the systems of knowledge." And this positing, the apodictic certainty of a self-reflexivity (*cogito me cogitare*) that aspires to become "the unshakable ground of philosophy itself" (17), represents, according to Gasché, "a still unanalyzed presupposition" (15). Just as in the mirror-stage is the image that provides the fragmentary set of members that is the body with a sense of unification and wholeness (the imaginary ego), the emerging subject is constituted as and through the resulting alienation. The subject is neither the fragmentary set (body) nor the unified image (ego), but rather the missing "gluon" (the gap) in the former that the latter labors to replace (fill in). So the subjective ground is shakable, and therefore ungrounded.[40] Descartes, in

---

40 The subject is primarily an empty word, a *name* without denotation, and as such it fulfills the implicit condition of "gluons." Only the *name* of the whole retrospectively projected onto the separate parts unifies them into the whole. Priest's failure to factor in the role names and words play in the metaphysics of the One (of parts, unities and wholes) he discusses in his book appears to me a serious drawback. If you describe, as Priest does, an "entity" as that which we can "talk about" then obviously anything can do, and your argument can take any conceivable direction. See Priest, *One*, 11–15.

short, before Lacan, teaches us that a localized void or ungrounded ground is a safe place to begin to think. And thinking—not owning bodies—is what makes us all powerfully, reliably, equal: "Descartes starts his investigation from a proper philosophical axiom, namely that we are all equal because we can all think" (Ruda, *For Badiou* 87). In *The Plague of Fantasies*, Žižek defends Descartes from charges of anthropocentrism by upholding the relevance of the Cartesian de-substantialization:

> Does not Cartesian subjectivity (as correlative to the universe of modern science) involve the "Copernican turn," does it not decenter man and reduce him to an insignificant creature on a small planet? In other words, what one should always bear in mind is how the Cartesian de-substantialization of the subject, its reduction to $, to the pure void of self-relating negativity is strictly correlative to the opposite reduction to a grain of dust in the infinity of the universe, to one among the endless objects in it. (13–14)[41]

Although the final phrases of this quotation are obviously bolstered by a time-honored Hamlet echo (*Hamlet* 2.2.289–300), the thesis of the *subject* (not the self, not the mind, not the spirit, not the soul, not the ego) in the void of its subtraction is best exemplified in the closing words of Edgar's soliloquy: "Poor Turlygod! poor Tom! / That's something yet: Edgar I nothing am" (*King Lear* 2.3.20–21).

4)   The thesis of radical extensionality

Finitude, that "basic fact of human existence" (Priest, *Beyond the Limits* 3), the metaphysical motif examined by Heidegger in his *Kantbuch*, is an ideologeme that can be of course traced back to medieval Christian philosophy, but Descartes—who insisted on the idea that we are finite beings, with finite bodies and finite intellects (*Meditations métaphysiques* 185)—gave the motif a new, unexpected spin. The finitude, moreover, of the body, is at one with its extension, and it is the Derridean conception of a *finite infinity* that best conjoins the "empiricité finie" (the extended body) and the "différance infinie" (the extended mind) under the banner of *extension* that transpires in the notion of "linéarité" (*De la grammatologie* 128) and "espacement" of arche- or transcendental writing:

---

41   After Descartes, and before Lacan, Kant speaks of "the deficiency which is in principle inseparable from the existence of a temporal being, [namely] never to be able to become quite fully what he has in mind" (*Religion* 100).

> Archi-écriture, première possibilité de la parole, puis de la 'graphie' au sens étroit, lieu natal de l'"usurpation" dénoncée depuis Platon jusqu'à Saussure, cette trace est l'ouverture de la première extériorité en général, l'énigmatique rapport du vivant à son autre et d'un dedans à un dehors: l'espacement. (103)

The differential spacing of writing thus inscribes the opening of a first exteriority that is far from figurative. Derrida makes a bold move when he adds that "le dehors, extériorité 'spatiale' et 'objective,'" which we believe to know as the most familiar thing in the world, "n'apparaîtrait pas sans le gramme, sans la différance comme temporalisation, sans la non-présence de l'autre inscrite dans le sens du présent" (103). And this move is unintelligible without considering the role Galileo and Descartes played in instituting the ontological validity (the objectivity) of spatial exteriority as extension. Harold Bloom, who also registered Shakespeare's cultural position "before the Cartesian engulfment, the flooding-out of a greater mode of consciousness" (*Anxiety* 72), identified this engulfment with the "continuity" of "extensiveness" (62), without realizing that Cartesian space is riddled with differential scansion and discontinuity. The fact that Derrida's notion of *espacement* is ultimately indebted to the Cartesian notion of extension doesn't of course mean that Descartes acquiesced to the notion of the divisibility of the mind.[42] But the emancipation of exteriority (*res extensa*) from the burden of supererogatory metaphysical categorization permitted a simplicity of description along lines of arbitrariness, relationality and difference that, because Descartes construed the *res extensa* as joined to the *res cogitans*, ended up contaminating the latter in an inexorable manner. The locus of this contamination was of course language, whence the correlation, constantly enjoined by Jean-Luc Nancy, between *corps* and *langage* (*Être singulier pluriel* 107–117). And because the verbal articulation or proffering of cogito occurs in a site as its very inscription (of site) then there is little sense in distinguishing between the ego and the locus:

> Not the body *of* the ego, but *corpus ego*, "ego" being "ego" only when articulated, articulating itself as spacing or flexion, even the inflection of a *site*. The enunciation of "ego" doesn't just *take* place. To the contrary, it *is place*.
> *Corpus* 25

---

42   Descartes: "en ce que le corps de sa nature et toujours divisible (*semper divisibile*), et que l'esprit est entièrement indivisible" (*Méditations* 235).

This way Nancy and Derrida culminate the chronicle of a contamination that is foreshadowed in Freud's posthumous note: "Psyche is extended; knows nothing about it [*Psyche ist ausgedehnt: weiss nichts davon*]."[43] All of which reinforces what Thomson has aptly called "the possibility of a deconstructive Descartes" (Thomson, "Jeu d'écarts" 193). If a subject is not given and must be found, then "Descartes thought he found it and located it (once and forever) as the empty and void (pre- and unworldly) place of any discursive (or structured symbolic) setting" (Ruda, *For Badiou* 89). Call this setting extension, or *différance*, or call it language.

The thesis of radical extensionality is best exemplified in the opening line of sonnet 110: "Alas, 'is true I have gone here and there."

5) The thesis of finitude violated by the infinite

One elusive but recalcitrant strand in Derrida's reading of Levinas is the former's resolve to pinpoint in the latter's oeuvre an uncompromising Cartesianism to which he could easily relate. This may come as a surprise to those who believe that Descartes is incompatible with advanced or deviant versions of phenomenology. From the opening pages of *Totalité et infini*, Levinas resorts constantly to Descartes' idea of the situated *advent of an infinity* understood in terms of radical transcendence : "Le rapport avec l'infini ne peut, certes pas, se dire en termes d'expérience, car l'infini déborde la pensée qui le pense" (*Totalité* 10). The resulting conflict (between finitude and infinity) recalls the *genetic* friction, detected by Husserl in *Krisis* and loudly denounced by Derrida, between the situated-contingent historicity of the scientist and the universal necessity of his transcendental-ideal discovery. But Levinas' argument is theologically colored. The notion of a thing (infinity) that overpowers its idea by a finite being—a notion that organizes Descartes' arguments in the third Meditation—is construed as the ground upon which Levinas' argument rests : "Ce livre se présente donc comme une défense de la subjectivité, mais il ne la saisira pas au niveau de sa protestation purement égoïste contre la totalité, ni dans un angoisse devant la morte, mais comme fondée dans l'idée de l'infini " (11).[44] Far from being confined to the "Preface," such defense of subjectivity founded upon an idea of infinity runs through the entire book as an organizing motif—with the constant proviso that such infinity must arrive from the outside and therefore

---

43 For a discussion of this enigmatic dictum, see Nancy, *Corpus*, 21–25. In *Ego Sum*, Nancy examines cogito as an *extrémité* or corporal "extreme" (115–116).

44 Levinas is implicitly scorning the existentialist philosophies of finitude that branch out from Heidegger's work, but he nonetheless acknowledges the role the presence of the infinite Other plays in the realization of human finitude: "à cause de la présence de l'infini dans cette pensée finie qui sans cette présence ignorerait sa finitude" (*Totalité* 232).

cannot be internally constituted.⁴⁵ And Derrida, who knows of the relation between Cartesian rationalism and the origins of phenomenology, delights in exposing the intensity of Levinas' indebtedness to Descartes: "Dehors absolu, extériorité qui déborde infiniment la monade de l'*ego cogito*. Ici encore, Descartes contre Husserl, le Descartes de la troisième des *Méditations* que Husserl aurait méconnu " (156). The charge is subtle: Derrida observes that Levinas' recourse to Descartes is aimed at correcting the Cartesian solipsism that plagues Husserl's phenomenology. In other words, Husserl, who sought to secure the idealist immanence of his project—what David W. Smith calls his "system" (*Husserl* 5)—would have failed to make the cogito vulnerable to the brutal violation of infinity. Without Descartes' philosophical move, the window would not open to the Other. Elsewhere, Derrida reminds the reader that—always according to Levinas—Husserl, Heidegger and Merleau-Ponty fail to go beyond a certain subordination of language to thought, characteristic of philosophies of finitude, towards the infinite irreducibility of the infinite Other.⁴⁶ According to Derrida, no matter how discreetly Merleau-Ponty was ready to acknowledge that "thought is *first* and irreducibly a relation to the other" (104), the thought-producing corporal intentionality he heralded fell short of enclosing (*se fermer*) the alterity of infinity. Once and again, the potential of Descartes' infinity is wielded against the founding fathers of phenomenology. Once and again, the admonishment is paradoxical because the original phenomenology (Husserl's) was explicitly crafted as a (re)set of *Cartesian Meditations*. This obviously runs counter to the depreciation of Cartesian thought encouraged by phenomenological scholars. But Derrida's genealogical tracing of the "Infini transcendant" to Levinas' hidden ancestors leaves no room for doubt: there is first the Greek *epekeina tēs ousias*, the excess beyond Being formulated in Plato's *Republic* (509b), and then comes

> the other ancestor, the Latin one, [which] will be Cartesian: the idea of Infinity announcing itself to thought as that which always overflows it [*ce qui la déborde toujours*]. We have just named the only two philosophical gestures-their authors aside-totally acquitted, judged innocent by Levinas,"
>
> *Writing* 312, n.12; *L'écriture* 127, n.1

---

45 Levinas: "Si Husserl voit dans le cogito une subjectivité sans aucun appui hors d'elle, il constitue l'idée de l'infini elle-même, et se la donne comme objet. La non-constitution de l'infini chez Descartes laisse une porte ouverte" (*Totalité* 232).

46 Derrida: "Est cette démonstration nous renverrait encore au Cogito cartésien de la troisième des *Méditations*, para delà Merleau-Ponty, Heidegger et Husserl" (*L'écriture* 154).

It is no accident that the trope of *débordement* or overflowing should be the one that organizes Juliet's erotic figuration: "My bounty is as boundless as the sea, / My love as deep. The more I give to thee / The more I have, for both are infinite" (*Romeo and Juliet* 2.1.175–77). Perhaps indirectly cued by Giordano Bruno's Italian dialogues, Shakespeare was keenly sensitive to the paralogisms ensuing from the recognition of an infinite desire or value that becomes, in execution, "slave to limit" (*Troilus and Cressida* 3.2.78). *Antony and Cleopatra* is after all a symphony that melodically elaborates the motif present in its two opening lines—the notion that a man's infatuation for a woman "o'erflows the measure" (1.1.1–2). This late play has the additional merit of turning the liquid overflow of the infinite Other into its unsettled setting (the Nile, the Mediterranean Sea). No such leakage is paradoxically felt in the maritime romances (*Pericles*, *The Tempest*, *The Winter's Tale*). But I don't want to press this point any further. Suffice it to say that the gist of Stanley Cavell's rehabilitation of Cartesian skepticism for hermeneutic purposes, and more particularly to the interpretation of Shakespeare's plays, is precisely located in the acknowledgement that for Descartes "the integrity of my (human, finite) existence may depend on the fact and on the idea of another being's existence" (*Disowning* 127), another being who is more complete, more perfect, and therefore (perhaps a tad) less finite, than me. It is very symptomatic that, while putting forward his argument about skepticism in his memorable "Introduction" to the book, Cavell fails to quote a single line from Descartes' texts, and that he only cites from the third Meditation when, in the opening of his reading of *Othello*, he feels the need to lend philosophical support to the notion of "a harrowing of the power of knowing the existence of another" (125) that is more perfect than the knower—which is not different from the process, first formulated by Descartes, and later evoked by Levinas and Derrida, of "the idea of Infinity announcing itself to thought as that which always overflows it" (Derrida, *Writing* 312). The fact that Cavell emphasizes less the ontological event of the overflowing irruption of the (more perfect) other in the finite and imperfect self than the epistemological consequences that thereupon ensue (the alleviation of unknowing) shouldn't blind us to the fact that his neo-Cartesian maneuver is analogous to Levinas'.[47]

---

47 It is worth mentioning that the only two allusions to Shakespeare to be found in *Totalité et infini* occur in the context of a discussion on the potential deceitfulness of phenomenal appearance and equivocal speech—in both cases connected to Macbeth's witches (92, 295)—that is related to Descartes' speculative conjecture of the evil demon. Shakespeare serves Levinas to illustrate a point about verbal prevarication and equivocation that shares ground with Cavell's focus in his book. For a revisionary approach to Cavell's take

T.S. Eliot wrote once that Henry James had "a mind so fine no idea could violate it" (*Selected* 151), and Ashbery transposed his precursor's irony to the mordant precept: "We should all be so lucky as to get hit by the meteor / of an idea once in our lives" ("Variations on 'La Folia,'" *Your Name Here* 49). Descartes' mind unironically aspired to be violated by the Idea of perfection and infinity. Respect for the eminence of this desire, this willingness, and the discovery that followed (the assertion of infinity as a thought) is something that both Badiou and Levinas, most unlikely bedfellows, share.[48] They also have in common, tellingly, their distaste for the Heideggerian exaltation of finitude. But Badiou's fidelity to Descartes runs much deeper than Levinas'. It inspires his entire philosophical output and emerges strategically at some crucial junctures. In the "Preface" to *Logiques de mondes*, for instance, his objection that apart from bodies and languages there are also truths is grounded on a celebration of Descartes' audacity to assert that apart from things endowed with some existence, there are also "truths that are nothing outside our thought" (*Principles of Philosophy*, qtd. in *Logics of Worlds*, 5). The stereotypical image of a dualist Descartes breaks under the pressure of a third participant: *there are* bodies, intellects, *and* truths.[49] And truths, in Badiou's latest magnus opus, are nothing if not eternal and infinite. Again the third Meditation provides the occasion for vital revelation, described by Badiou as the very "substance" of his book, "à savoir la dialectique du fini et de l'infini" conceived as the resort of a proof of God's existence (*L'immanence* 183):

---

on skepticism, see Palmer. In his essay on *Hamlet*, Budick also refers to Cavell's arguments in order to uphold a "picture of proto-Cartesian skepticism that can illuminate Shakespeare's plays" ("Hamlet's 'Now' of Inward Being," 135).

48 The notion of Infinity elaborated by Descartes in his third Meditation is perhaps the central motif in Levinas' *Totalité et infini*, 10, 40, 75–94, 214, 231–233. In his brief preface to the 1987 German edition of his book, the French thinker offers an ironic reflection on the compatibility of Descartes' infinity and Husserlian phenomenology: "Mais dans le discours de *Totalité et Infini* n'a pas été oublié le fait mémorable que, dans sa troisième Méditation de la première philosophie, Descartes rencontrait une pensée, une noèse, qui n'était pas à la mesure de son noème, de son *cogitatum*. Une idée qui donnait au philosophe des éblouissements au lieu de se loger dans l'évidence de l'intuition. Pensée pensant plus ou pensant mieux qu'elle ne pensait selon la vérité. Pensée qui répondait aussi avec adoration à l'Infini dont elle était la pensée. Pour l'auteur de *Totalité et Infini* ce fut là un grand étonnement après la leçon sur le parallélisme néotico-néomatique dans l'enseignement de son maître Husserl qui se disait, lui-même, disciple de Descartes!" (*Totalité* iv). Derrida insists on the importance of the Descartes-Levinas dialogue in *Adieu à Emmanuel Levinas*, 87–92.

49 Badiou wields the Cartesian claim to truths to combat what he calls culturalists and relativists. See also *Logic*, 513.

> La thèse de Descartes est que si rien ne vient excéder le fini, je n'aurais aucune raison de penser que quoi que ce soit existe en dehors de moi-même. Nous avons là une clôture possible de la finitude *dans la figure du sujet*, et non pas de façon purement abstraite, comme chez Spinoza. Par contre, si j'ai l'idée de l'infini, alors cette clôture ne tient pas et je dois avouer que Dieu existe, que l'extériorité absolue existe. (183)

Levinas called such absolute exteriority the Other and identified it with metaphysical transcendence. Derrida called it arche-writing and identified it with physical transcendentality. Two camps are thus delineated anew. You choose where to stand.

This thesis of finitude violated by the infinite, also at work in Shakespeare's lovers (Romeo, Juliet, Troilus, Cressida, Antony, Cleopatra), is best exemplified in Hamlet's eventful retort: "But I have that within which passeth show" (*Hamlet* 1.2.85).

CHAPTER 3

Misrepresentations

Shakespeare and the Phenomenologists

1

In this section I will briefly consider the retrospective glance at the theory wars cast by some influential early modern literary scholars whose work either inadvertently helped prompt the neo-phenomenological vogue (Jonathan Dollimore), or squarely epitomizes it (Bruce Smith). This cultural-historical consideration is intended to throw light on certain conditions of the academic scene that have facilitated the current phenomenological misrepresentation of the thing Shakespeare. I want to open with a reference to Bradshaw's brilliant study *Misrepresentations: Shakespeare and the Materialists* (1993), whose target was the "ideological critique" (6) practiced by neo-historicists and cultural materialists during the seventies and eighties. While some theoretical assumptions have, in the intervening decades, somehow shifted ground, the ideological arrogance identified by Bradshaw remains untouched among scholars working within some of the emerging sub-branches—the new -isms—of the discipline. Curiously, however, the archenemy remains the same. Essentialist humanism, often travestied into the nefarious liberal humanism, has astonishingly managed to stick around as the one opprobious "ideological fiction" (Bradshaw 2). Under the label "neo-phenomenologists" I bring together, with an inclusiveness my book works to justify, late practitioners of new historicism and cultural materialism, sympathisers of political theology, votaries of affect studies, aesthetic studies and performance studies, and devotees of new forms of materialism—posthumanism, object studies, ecocriticism and animal studies. These sub-groups share more than their phenomenological make-up. In fact, they are best identified by their antagonistic stance: their commitment to odds and ends of the reprogrammed phenomenological creed can hardly conceal their most reiterated and revealing doctrinal gesture: their sneer at—and very precarious grasp of—the *high theory* of the seventies and early eighties. The official name for this gesture was *the overcoming of formalism*, but behind it lurked an active indifference towards—possibly incompetence before—speculative-dialectic modes of criticism (Adorno, Althusser, Lacan, Derrida) with roots in German idealism. Such dismissal was bound up with the anti-Cartesian exorcism animating the whole enterprise, and it is no accident that the original historical meeting point of these four thinkers—Adorno, Althusser, Lacan and Derrida—was less Kant (or Hegel) than Descartes, the thinker who paved the way to *transcendental subjectivity*, and, ultimately, to off-balance *subject*-object dialectics, to the non-science of *ideology*, and to deconstruction as mediation-sensitive and ultra-sceptical *critique*. Another repeated rite connected to such dismissal was the celebratory sacrifice of Saussure—at bottom a wholesale amendment against systemic rationality, the logic of difference, and the triumph of contingency, relationality, and arbitrariness in language-based horizons of research.

So, if a new generation of Shakespeare scholars turns to the pre-reflexive, positive, empirical, and phenomenological methods that high theory left behind in the late sixties it is partly because of a constitutive (at bottom, formative) inability to engage in intellectual dialogue with theoretical postulates that, behind their structuralist or formalist appearance, were originally dialectical, and ultimately Cartesian. But also, of course, because dealing with things, cats and affections is in principle less daunting than understanding *King Lear*. There is a sublimely fatuous sense in which one becomes a phenomenological critic almost unconsciously, by accident or default, merely through the defective positioning of oneself as a breathing, touching and loving body inside a natural environment—under the sea wing, in a silent spring, with the sea around us, and a sense of wonder.[1] To do phenomenology is, in this delusive sense, a return to the paradise of the natural standpoint, the Eden of pre-theoretical *common-sense*. This holds only insofar as the activities of breathing, caring, touching, and loving, absorb the reader to the point of making her disregard the *winter and rough weather* running through the work of Descartes, Marx, or Derrida. Indeed, most soi-disant phenomenology-oriented early modern scholars have not only failed to read these thinkers, but also neglected to read and understand Husserl properly. There are many unmodern ways of becoming an early modern literary scholar, many ways, that is, of landing upon an unexpected past and sponsoring, innocently, unawares, "the restoration of pre-critical doctrines" (Adorno, *Against* 176). I know I myself revisit the past when I claim to try to labour under 1960s and 1970s conditions of thought—what I call, indistinctly, arrogantly, *high theory* or *strong theory*. But, believe me, their past is older than mine. Neo-phenomenological criticism bounces us back to the 1950s, and it is *reactive*—in the sense Badiou gives the term (*Logiques* 62–63)—and therefore potentially reactionary. The humanist,

---

1 These are all titles of Rachel Carson's extraordinary books, which pioneered modern environmental thinking. The Library of America has recently published them in one single handsome volume.

often Christian-existentialist Angst that characterized much post-war intellectual work was thick with moralistic assumptions through (and against) which scholars like Adorno, Lacan, Foucault, Althusser, and Derrida were forced to make their way.² In the US, some very gifted narrators like Truman Capote and Shirley Jackson managed miraculously to hold off from the pulpit. Neo-phenomenological criticism ignores the effort of these and other related writers and thinkers and return us *willy nilly* to the empiricist-cum-moralist mire. The displacement of valences—the salvation of the human has been replaced by the salvation of the non-human, the ordeal of the isolated self by the ethical trials of community, the existentialist vertigo of subjectivity by the claiming of the affective body, Ralph Ellison, say, by Toni Morrison—entails no discernible theoretical progress. We may feel ethically and aesthetically comforted by some responses to the challenges of the new moral dispensation, but this does not necessarily make them critically useful. The task, remember, is to understand Shakespeare's poems and playtexts, not to ingratiate you with your neighbour or make the earth a better place; to practice, that is, close reading from the vantage position of critical distance, and not telescopic or surface reading from the impaired position of ethical *overproximity*.³

When a moral compulsion rather than a rational necessity drives the project of reading Shakespeare's texts, the first visible effect is the need, felt by the morally interpellated, to defuse the potency of critique, and this is best achieved through the downright *naturalization of reason*: if we cannot beat reason, we force her to defect to our camp. This is where phenomenology came in handy. The risks were formidable, for "if philosophy becomes too naturalistic, hard-nosed positive disciplines will nudge it aside" (Rorty, *Philosophy* 168), and the ascent of phenomenology had precisely this particular effect—the comparative banalization of a discipline that presented itself as a rigorous science but was *not* a science—but also the side effect of attenuating its distinctively speculative strength.⁴ Once reason and its cohort of attending

---

2 See Judt, *Past Imperfect*, 13–98. Reading the early essays of Althusser, from 1946 to 1951, may prove instructive in this regard. See in particular the 1946 essay titled "L'internationale des bons sentiments " in *Écrits philosophiques et politiques*, 35–58. Also revealing are the essays Badiou dedicates to Kojève and Canguilhem in *L'aventure de la philosophie française*, 57–79.
3 Žižek detects in a letter by Schumann to Clara "the intrusive *overproximity*, the horrifying weight of the encounter of a neighbour in the Real of her presence? Love thy neighbour? No thanks!" (*Plague* 85).
4 Adorno soon denounced the scientific pretentiousness of Husserlian phenomenology: "Husserl's logical absolutism mirrors in its own foundation the fetishization of the sciences, which mistakes themselves and their hierarchy as an entity in itself" (*Against* 52). This caused, he argued, the replacing of "the transcendental" by "an ideal of knowledge derived from the empirically available sciences" (53).

conditions (mediation, difference, arbitrariness, universality, distance, discontinuity, abstraction, separateness, transcendentality) were properly deactivated and reassimilated into the *fluxus corporis et naturae* then anything could do as *casus belli*—Shakespeare's oeuvre could be assailed, or co-opted, from any position on offer in the rowdy market of the positive world. And this is exactly what happened. Today the Shakespeare thing can be effortlessly measured against other givens, other affections, embodiments, immediacies, other impromptu deliverances of the *Umwelt*. All amounts to a moral calculus in a restricted economy of moral redemption—alone reengaging things themselves, in our world, will save us, and Shakespeare is one of those things, if not *das Ding*. This explains the ongoing factionalism and fractionalisation of trends and sub-trends inside the field of Shakespeare studies, a tendency of ontic sectionalism and group-identity atomization consecrated, in a healthy spirit of pluralism (no irony intended), by prestigious publishing houses like Bloomsbury, in whose lists we find titles like *Shakespeare and Geek Culture*, *Shakespeare and Gender*, *Shakespeare and Posthumanism*, *Shakespeare and Postcolonial Theory*, *Shakespeare and Queer Theory*, *Eating Shakespeare*, *Shakespeare and Ecocritical Theory*, or *Shakespeare and Feminist Theory*.

2

I have nothing against the moral passions driving the members of academic sub-groups to *action*. But, as a left-from-centre liberal—a category I freely borrow from the great F.O. Matthiessen—I believe their passions are productive only when they ground effective *political action*. The *field work* of feminist, LGTB, civil-right, and ecological activists I find more necessary and meaningful than academic activity in the Humanities, including mine, and their work certainly makes the world a better place. When the *strategic essentialism* often attending their praxis is handled with speculative-dialectical gusto, as used to be the case in feminist and post-colonial studies, and is very often the case in gay studies, then the critical or interpretative gain is considerable. The critical lucidity of Sedgwick, Said, Bhabha, Belsey, or Butler is simply out of the question, but not all of their followers are aware of the dialectic-speculative exigence of critique that makes the work of their betters so distinct—and so distinctly a performance of *thought*. Sadly, what normally subtends the *intellectual action* of morally passionate scholars working in the above-mentioned sub-branches of Shakespeare studies is not so much an attenuated essentialism in the service of critical speculation as a crude naturalistic essentialism deployed in the interests of Puritan reprimand and moralist celebration.

Take Butler's definition of gender performativity:

> It is difficult to say precisely what performativity is not only because my own views on what "performativity" might mean have changed over time, most often in response to excellent criticisms, but because so many others have taken it up and given it their own formulations. I originally took my clue on how to read the performativity of gender from Jacques Derrida's reading of Kafka's "Before the Law." There the one who waits for the law, sits before the door of the law, attributes a certain force to the law for which one waits. The anticipation of an authoritative disclosure of meaning is the means by which that authority is attributed and installed: the anticipation conjures its object. I wondered whether we do not labor under a similar expectation concerning gender, that it operates as an interior essence that might be disclosed, an expectation that ends up producing the very phenomenon that it anticipates.
> *Gender Trouble* XIV

This is a nuanced description of a dialectical method. And note the comparative qualification ("as an interior essence"), which evokes Spivak's reliance on *strategic essentialism* (*In Other Worlds* 205). Indeed Butler concludes that "what we take to be an internal essence of gender is manufactured through a sustained set of acts" (XIV). In a figurative dialectic, these acts are the posing, positing, positioning, and setting (*Setzungen*) of tropes (de Man, *Allegories* 120–123). What Butler says above of "gender" can be extrapolated to the "human": here also the anticipation conjures the object. Identity politics denounces the essentialization of a trope (the human being) that is manifestly historical and constructed, but it tacitly assumes the existence of a stable unit of designation (an essentialized natural human being) over which the constructed ambiguities of gender or race can slide and disseminate. Yet this naturalized and anthropological human being—Marx soon realized, when swerving away from Feuerbach—is also a fabrication, another ideologeme (Althusser, *For Marx* 177–179). The genuine sliding is prior, the actual dissemination more originary. The elision of the simile and its conversion into an attributive marker brings about the miracle of the essentialist predication: *the human is* rather than *the human as*. It is like liberating the contingency of nonnormative sexualities over against the necessary essentialism of a normative sexuality whose ontic fixity had been paradoxically contested at the outset, a sleight of hand that fixes and sanctions the presupposition of a non-thematized and naturalized normality. And the problem with posthumanism and ecocritical thought is that in endeavoring to overpass the human they have ended up fixing the notion—"Man" as "the unique, primordial and fundamental concept, the *factotum*" (Althusser, "Marx's Relation to Hegel" 179)—essentializing the very thing whose historical arbitrariness the founders of these movements set out to denounce in the first place. There is no longer any sense of the dialectical anticipation, notional expectation, and contingent production that we find in Butler's incisive description of her mode of critical thought, a mode admittedly energized by the resources of what Hegel called the *speculative sentence*—where subjects are blind to the unfolding content of their predicates.

How distant this is from the standard mishandling of thought we find in current phenomenological criticism a brief glance at Bruce Smith's paper "Premodern Sexualities" (2000) may show. His first important remark is that "the fact that Darwin, tongue in cheek or not, can speak of plants as 'loving' suggests that sexuality as a concept was, by the late eighteenth century, beginning to include the affective, subjective qualities that interest us in the subject today" (318). *Us*? I will return to this abusive pronominal denotation—this typically phenomenological *claim to intersubjectivity*—in section 6. For now I want to focus exclusively on the phrase "sexuality as a concept," whose meaning he unpacks in the postulate that "sexuality" is "a time- and culture-specific formulation of a more general phenomenon that European culture has known as *eros*." But his argument doesn't live up to the claim. As it turns out, he grants the *phenomenon*—Husserl's *Seinsphänomenon*, translated by Levinas as *phénomène d'existence* (*Méditations*, 43)—a higher intensity of existence than the *formulation*, whence the aptness of adopting a *phenomenological* approach. Thus the phenomenon *eros* (always?) included the affective, and it was Darwin's merit to transfer this inclusion onto the conceptual-discursive plane. Nothing could be further from Butler's dialectical-constructivist take on gender-production. Moreover, confidence in the existence of the thing undergirds Smith's paradoxical resolution of the historical-phenomenological conflict: "If sexuality is not *there* [the premodern past], it must be *here* [our postmodern present]" (319). What is indisputable, for Smith, is that sexuality *is* somewhere—and that this somewhere is neither a transcendental empyrean nor a noematic cloud. I evoke these phenomenological tropes because the very gist of Husserl's *epoché* was to "inhibit the existential value of the objective world" (*Méditations cartésiennes* 53). We can impute a lot to Husserl, but not a naïve naturalistic faith. Anyway, no such ontological confidence transpires, as we have seen, in Butler's dialectical handling of gender. By contrast, Smith rather takes sexuality to be a pre-conceptual reality that is nearly always misrepresented in evolving historic conceptualizations. He suspects of over-cerebral (Lacanian) attempts "to put *eros* into discourse" (323) and aligns *discourse* with *rationality* (318). Note the spatio-temporal logic implicit in the syntax: eros is something that exists first in a place (nature?) as a kind of "unfettered pre-social libido" (Dollimore, "Wishful Theory" 23) and is next put (bundled off, misplaced) onto another site, that of discourse.[5] His handling of the problem of discourse is shot through with flamboyant anti-deconstructive asides whose incongruence I examine in section 12 of this book.

Smith professes to align himself with "critical readers since the 1960s" and mentions, as key movements shaping their shared mindset, the "sexual liberation of the 1960s, Feminism of the 1970s, and after queer radicalism and postcolonial revisionism of the 1990s" (319). This is fine. Let me simply recall that all of these movements are compatible—and were often so in a very explicit and creative manner—with the deconstructive and Foucaldian critique that Smith here pushes aside. It would appear that he retains the politics and throws away the theory, which is also fine, by the way, if his aim were *doing* politics. But we are analyzing an essay published in the *Proceedings of the Modern Language Association*, not in the opinion pages of *The Guardian*. I doubt anyway that the readers of this eminent newspaper would have condoned his philosophical coaching, even when tuned down to kindergarten levels: "The basic premise of phenomenology is simple: you cannot know anything apart of the way in which you come to know it" (325). Especially if they are informed readers, for this "basic premise," which is conceptually correct, is however wrongly ascribed to phenomenology. Indeed, the tautological conception of the problem of knowledge—"the problem that if everything that is known is basically nothing but a knowing reason, what we have is no real knowledge but only a kind of reflection of reason" (Adorno, *Kant's Critique* 69)—is but a slightly radicalized version of Smith's formulation of the premise, and Adorno's version displays the idealist credentials that are hidden in the latter. The "basic

---

5 Dollimore's disparagement of Butler's take on heterosexuality as a case of wishful theory betokens his anti-dialectical animus: see "Wishful Theory," 21–22. For all his defense of mechanisms of retroaction and re-inscription within binary oppositions, his take on desire both as a site of agency and as the object of repression is far from dialectical, and it relies both on the essentialism of a timeless, potentially transgressive, "agency" and on the "transhistorical essence" of the structure of the "perverse dynamic." See *Sexual Dissidence*, 33–34. And also Antony Easthope's subtle critique of his postulates in *Privileging Difference* (100–107), where he charges Dollimore with naturalizing (and essentializing?) "perversion" as a "real feel." I doubt very much Dollimore would be willing to countenance both the idea of life (and desire) fully constituted, suggested, cued by power, and—across the line—an alternative prospect of a life that is not different from death. Deleuze writes: "How can we 'cross the line'? And, if we must attain a life that is the power of the outside, what tells us that this outside is not a terrifying void and that this life, which seems to put up a resistance, is not just the simple distribution within the void of 'slow, partial and progressive' deaths?" (*Foucault* 95).

premise" is therefore a central idealist contention that we can trace back first to Greek rationalism (Parmenides, Plato) and next to German idealism (Kant, Hegel). The conviction that "method cannot precede formally or subjectively the being-known [*être-connu*] but constitutes the very act and content of a knowledge that is at the same knowing knowledge and known knowledge" is one that Derrida, for instance, ascribes to Hegel and Bergson, not to Husserl ("Language" 69). Phenomenology is precisely an attempt to unburden epistemology from the duty to recognize that there are *ways to go*—to be sure, the *routes*, *chemins*, and *voies* of Descartes' meth-*odo*-logical narrative, but also the "'longs détours' de Platon" lately hailed by Badiou (*L'immanence* 21). One such way is indeed Cartesian *méthode*; another is διαλεκτική or *Dialektik*. In upholding self-evidence and the intuition of essences as the gates to truth, phenomenology discards the meandering route of dialectics, and proposes instead a mediation-free—travel-free, way-free, concept-free—access to what "you come to know": something like a free-of-charge drive-thru vegan-roll. What you come to know you know because you already came to know it, you were already there, *in the beginning*—like Dylan's demiurgic Man, giving name to all the animals. Pledged to absolute beginnings, Husserlian phenomenology is an idealism without dialectical mediation:

> [The] phenomenological conception just rejects dialectical analysis and Hegel's negativity as the enemy. The doctrine that everything is mediated, even supporting immediacy, is irreconcilable with the urge to 'reduction' and is stigmatized as logical nonsense. Hegel's scepticism about the choice of an absolutely first (*absolut Ersten*), as the doubt-free and certain point of departure for philosophy, is supposed to amount to casting philosophy to the abyss. In the schools deriving from Husserl this theme quickly enough turned against all labour and effort of the concept, and thus bore the brunt of inhibiting thought in the middle of thinking.
> ADORNO, *Against* 4–5

What Smith calls "the way you come to know it" is what phenomenology inhibits as the "labour and effort of the concept." Smith would probably protest against this caricature of phenomenology as a *thinking without thought* arguing that Husserl took great pains to describe, in *Ideas*, the "scene of observation" that allows the onlooker to "know of" her "ambient world" (Smith, *Phenomenal Shakespeare* 20). It is likely that for Smith the ineliminable reciprocity that obtains between the positioning of the first-person onlooker and the knowledge she obtains of her ambient is enough to uphold the basic premise that "you cannot know anything apart of the way in which you come to know it."

But this would read like a routine concession to standard relativism, although of the most naturalistic kind. For he omits to specify two points. First, that this kind of knowledge, by Husserl's own admission, "involves no conceptual thinking [*ein Wissen dass nichts vom begrifflichen Denken hat*]," and boils down to "clear intuiting [*ein klares Anschauen*]" (*Ideen* 49). The fact that Husserl places the verb "know"—"ich gerade 'weiss'" (*Ideen* 49)—between inverted commas betokens the inferiority of this mode of perceptual intuition with respect to higher modes of knowledge that, in Husserl's phenomenology, enjoy the flashy bliss of primordial self-evidence: the intuition of essences (*Wesensschau*). As it happens, then, the caricature *thinking without thought* is not far off the mark, and it was in fact first sketched by Husserl himself. Second, and this important omission explains the rationale of the caricature, the fragment from *Ideas* that Smith quotes is Husserl's terse account of how "knowledge" of the factually existing actuality [*daseiende 'Wirklicheit'*], of the world-about-me [*meiner Umwelt*] (*Ideen* 51–53), is obtained from to "the natural standpoint" (*der natürlichen Einstellung*), a simplistic outlook the whole aim of phenomenological *epoché* is precisely to defeat. Phenomenology begins with the derogation of the natural standpoint, and this is first attained through the reduction. In conclusion, and I will return to this later, Smith completely distorts the meaning of *epoché*, misconstruing it for a basic procedure of perceptive *framing*. This doesn't mean, however, that higher (post-reductive) forms of phenomenological knowledge are good enough—dialectical enough—to elude Adorno's savvy caricature. But it suffices to show that Smith misunderstands phenomenology at its very root.

Smith's lapsed turn to phenomenology epitomizes the trials of the post-theoretical scholar who dreads the "formalist" excesses of the seventies and early eighties and yet aims to invest his moralistic and political criticism with a semblance of philosophical articulation.[6] Turning to some version of phenomenology would have been, who knows, a wise move if only the version had not been watered down past recognition. On his way to *historical phenomenology*, to whatever he understands for that, Smith keeps harping on deconstruction:

> Deconstruction shares, then, with New historicism-Cultural materialism a radical objectification of the subject of inquiry, a distrust of sense experience, of which erotic desire is surely an extreme exam [...] To name something is to turn it into an object, to position the analyst here and it

---

6 For the notion and possibilities of post-theory, see the essays gathered in the volume, *Post-Theory: New Directions in Criticism*, edited by Martin McQuillan *et al*.

over there so that it can be seen, known, mastered. *Eros* resists that kind of objectification. (325)

To be objective enough to become a subject of enquiry and at the same time to remain unobjectified by conceptual categories or structural subjection is a condition of being that poses a formidable challenge. Husserl faced it by positing the supra-psychological validity of logical absolutism, not by hatching ontic eggs somewhere at the far end of the spectrum. In either case the subject-object epistemological schema is ruthlessly undone. Smith's eros is one such ontic egg. Not only is it not objectified: it is not even an object. Indeed, "the attempt to assert objectivity"—the laws of logic, the pulls of eros—"outside the structures of mediation" (O'Connor, *Adorno's Negative Dialectic* 130) is a specific but widespread kind of phenomenal, and phenomenological, blunder: *phenomenological*, in Husserl's sense, when the outside is a logical absolute; *phenomenal*, in Smith's sense inherited from Merleau-Ponty's body-oriented revision of Husserlian phenomenology, when the outside is the body (yours or someone else's) close at hand.

Smith is not completely unaware of the risks he takes and is ready to confront some of the theoretical implications raised in taking them. He knows that at some point he is giving up mediation, but he justifies it by stigmatizing it as supervened: "In practice what a deconstructive critic finds in aporia is the need for more text, for the mediating text that is being provided by none other than the critic" ("Premodern" 325). This is simply untrue. Mediation is not a one-text hazard, a risk we may face or defuse at wish, simply by pressing a button or closing a book. To overlook the text-mediated nature of human (cultural, moral, ideological, political, affective, even sexual) experience is to ignore a basic Hegelian premise that subtends all branches of high theory. Of course one may pretend to do criticism as if Marcuse, Adorno, Althusser, Foucault, Derrida, Lacan or Žižek had not existed and call it a day. Or call it "historical phenomenology." But where does that land you? Well, it may leave you cataloguing Tudor sheets, examining extant 1593 quartos of *Venus and Adonis* for traces of dry semen, or blinking at the engravings of *I Modi*. Smith will not allow a *mediating text* (by Sapho, Ovid, Catullus, Cavalcanti, Aretino or Marlowe) to violate the ontic bliss of early modern eros. When discussing the merits of "historical phenomenology," conceived as "an attempt to reconstruct sense experience" (327), he anticipates the deconstructionist objection that this may involve a return to presence. But his response is that phenomenology only deals with "presence *effects*" (326). But what is a "presence effect"? Since Hans Ulrich Gumbrecht deployed it in a 2004 book called *Production of Presence: What Meaning Cannot Convey*, the concept has enjoyed good press among performance-studies scholars like J. Thomson, and it has made its way into Matthew James Smith's and Julia Lupton's "Introduction" to *Face-to-Face in Shakespearean Drama*. Bruce Smith may not have had in mind Ulrich's notion (he doesn't mention his book in the bibliographical references) but it is evident that he probably relishes the celebration of semiotic "materiality" and "non-hermeneutic" (sic) meaning the notion apparently entails (*Production of Presence* 16–20). It is not hard to see what these scholars *mean* or intend to *convey* when they speak of presence effects. Predictably, they amend Saussure by turning to the allegedly pre-semantic grounds of verse, rhythm, stanza, body, gesture, dance—by returning, that is, to the food and merry note under the greenwood tree. Our response is as you like it. It startles me, however, that phenomenology, historical or other, can be taken to deal with presence effects, for phenomenology is nothing if not a *metaphysics of presence*, and there needs no ghost, not even Derrida's, come from the grave to tell us this.[7] There is no room for effects—and no air for ghosts, no hauntology—in a metaphysics of *presence to being* (Fuchs 5), otherwise known as ontology. There is not even room for what Derrida would call "same-world-effects" (*On Touching* 192).[8] Husserlian phenomenology is—as Heidegger never tired of pointing out—an ontology, and Smith's phenomenal Shakespeare is a tendentially *ontic* not ontological Shakespeare. Attempting to do theory on ontic grounds is a risky venture—you may end up doing bad sociology, good journalism, or both. Smith's writing titillates on the verge of both, but his trained philological instincts nearly always come to his rescue. His essay closes with an invitation to adopt an "erotics of reading" that brings to mind Sontag's corny mid-sixties appeal: "In place of a hermeneutics we need an erotics of art" (*Against* 23). All of which reads like a James international tale adapted to the sixties, with the American ingenu withstanding the corrupt advances of French sophistication: "to take words not as symbols, signs with only an arbitrary relation to the thing toward which they point, but as indexes, signs with a natural or metonymic connection with

---

7   Many scholars who dissent from Derridean diagnoses on phenomenology are however in agreement with him about this: see for instance Fuchs, *Phenomenology and the Metaphysics of Presence*, 3–8. Zahavi, on his part, defends Husserl from charges of naivety, qualifying his beliefs with a resounding "but," and yet, at bottom, he acknowledges that "Husserl ascribes to a metaphysics of presence. The more immediate the object shows itself for the subject, the more it *is* present. And the more present it is, the more real it is. This idea ultimately culminates in Husserl's persistent emphasis on the fact that the existence of the object (its being) is correlated to its intuitive givenness for a subject" (*Husserl's Phenomenology* 95).

8   Derrida takes Merleau-Ponty to task for assuming, through a non-Husserlian appropriation of alterity, the existence of a shared "same world" capable of producing sharable "effects" and "senses of the world" (*On Touching* 193).

somatic experience" (Smith, "Premodern" 326). The reward of virtue is, in this Puritan fable, nothing less than somatic experience, phenomenal jouissance, sexual liberation: "Under the greenwood tree / Who loves to lie with me" (*As You Like It* 2.5.1–2). Nice, eh? Well, this relapse to Cratylean naturalism is of a piece with Smith's adoption elsewhere of the naturalist standpoint that even an anti-dialectical thinker like Husserl considered a burden to "scientific" philosophy. To camouflage this pre-critical naturalization of language under the label "erotics of reading" doesn't make it any more Platonic, let alone dialectical. This was probably not Smith's intention anyway, but it may not be totally irrelevant to recall that Socrates tended to side with the conventionalists in the dispute about language dramatized in *Cratylus*, and that this old conventionalist thesis underpins, of course, Saussure's defense of arbitrariness. Smith's reactive (and reactionary) argument in favor of a "natural connection" between signs and somatic experiences—Imogen's "corporal sign" (*Cymbeline* 2.4.119)—is at odds with his qualified defense elsewhere of deconstructionist reading practices for their power to identify absences and gaps in language— a "word" for one of those gaps, he concludes, "is eros" (327). Still, he enlists deconstruction in vain, for its task (Derrida would call it "travail") is not to fill in the gaps detected in language, but rather to detect them. We may give that (sensorial, referential, ontic) filling the name of *reconstruction*, following Smith's own usage (326, 327) when he alludes to the "reconstruction of sense experience" (desire, love, lust). And yet, let me insist: sealing textual fissures with bodily parts or leaves of grass, with reality bites or "bits of experiential intake" (McDowell, *Mind* 4) is *reconstruction* not deconstruction. Posthumus' and Othello's reconstruction and not Iachimo's and Iago's deconstruction. It is not even phenomenology, and certainly not phenomenal.

3

In an important 2009 book Hugh Grady deplored "the stagnating assumptions of post-Theory," that is, "the occlusion of the theoretical" (*Shakespeare and Impure Aesthetics*, 38) taking place in the aftermath of new historicism and cultural materialism. Similar complaints have been recently voiced by the late Catherine Belsey, ironizing over Greenblatt's actual familiarity with Foucault, stated that "poststructuralism played virtually no part in the composition of Renaissance Self-Fashioning" ("Historicizing New historicism" 29), and, more importantly, by Jonathan Goldberg, who lamented the "demise" of Theory's "promise, especially in early modern studies" and the fact that "Theory," in a deconstructive sense, "never did much of an impression on Shakespeare studies" (*Shakespeare's Hand* viii-x).⁹ This can be easily demonstrated. Suffice it to point out that the part the best Derrida (1954–1985) is asked to play in Richard Wilson's brilliant sociology-oriented *Shakespeare and French Theory* (2007) is disappointingly limited. The same can be said of Jonathan Gil Harris's narrative of the role deconstruction has played in the intersections between *Shakespeare and Literary Theory* (2009). To explain the expanding theoretical incompetence during the eighties and beyond one could search for strictly immanent reasons, but we should also attend to the sociological motivations that may have incited the *turn to phenomenology*. One of these motivations is what Richard Wilson himself has recently diagnosed as the "moralisation of politics" (Wilson, *Worldly Shakespeare* 18).

Jonathan Dollimore finds "a lot of so-called post-theory academic writing to be philosophically illiterate" ("Then and Now" 64). This is very true, and particularly apropos of post-theoretical—perhaps "post-philosophical" is the right word (Jameson, *Valences* 140)—writing on Shakespeare, even by scholars who would define their work in neither way. But it also applies to substantial sections of the corpus of influential scholars like Greenblatt, Sinfield, and Dollimore himself, who, under the spell of resounding catchwords like cultural materialism and new historicism, believed they promoted subversion by producing academic theory. It is worth noting that by the time they started producing their best work (the early 1980s) no less a thinker than Jean-François Lyotard was already complaining of "la lassitude à l'égard de 'la théorie', et le misérable relâchement qui l'accompagne (nouveau ceci, nouveau cela, post-ceci, post-cela, etc.)" (*Le différend* 11) and defensively imploring a return to real thought (*l'honneur de la pensée*) and philosophy (*l'heure de philosopher*). Six years later, Alain Badiou, author of a crucial *Manifesto for Philosophy*, described the end of the eighties as a time of "full intellectual regression" whose fashion was "moral philosophy disguised as political philosophy" (Badiou "Preface" to *Being and Event* xi), a time when "cultural relativism" remained fruitlessly stranded in "the trivial statement that different situations exist" without telling us "anything about what, among the differences, legitimately matters to subjects" (xii). An informed assessment of the liquidation of strong theory in the mid-to-late eighties remains still unwritten.¹⁰ If it ever comes into print it should start with a simple statement of fact: it happened. With hindsight, we now see the poverty—the flightiness and flummery—of much of the

---

9   Christopher Marlow echoes this complaint in *Shakespeare and Cultural Materialist Theory*, 4.
10 One major step in that direction can be found in Andrej Warminski's replies to Stuart Barnett in "Deconstruction at Yale," in *Material Inscriptions*, 214–232. For my chronology, which Warminski would alter, establishing the early eighties as *terminus ad quem*, see 221.

"philosophical" positioning adopted by some of the literary scholars mentioned above (Greenblatt, Dollimore) and most of their followers: Foucault came to Berkeley so I am, by the witchery of metonymic contiguity, a Foucaldian; I read some Marx and hate the middle-class bigotry of my formalist teachers so I am a materialist; I was at Yale during the reign of the gang of four, this was more than twenty years ago, so I am confidently post-deconstruction, etc.[11]

Karen Raber closes her recent *Shakespeare and Posthumanist Theory* with a recommendation to use a "slow, disabled, but environmentally aware posthumanism" to protect ourselves from the "minefields of Shakespearean, and Shakespeare's criticism's, idealism" (161). But what does she, and those within her context of utterance, understand by "idealism"? Have they gone through Plato and Hegel in order to unmask the thing (idealism) that supposedly poisons the man (Shakespeare) and thing (Shakespeare criticism as per August Schlegel, Coleridge, Bradley, Frye, Bloom, Nuttall, and their likes)? Like rationalism and humanism, "idealism" is a taboo catchword in posthumanist criticism—a paper-tiger abstraction. What would Raber do with Adorno's claim that "Hegel had returned to philosophy the right and capacity to think concretely [*inhaltlich zu denken*]" (*Negative Dialektik* 19)? When a scholar blesses us with a prefatory recollection of her training years this is often done to suggest that she is beyond graduate-school dogma—and that the *dépassement* was preceded by assimilation and overhauling. Such procedure is moot not only because it courts rigid modes of historicism we all thought were behind—the frantic, and stringently calendar-dependent, pre-and-post positioning of mindsets, ideologies and paradigms.[12] The procedure is problematic too because perhaps dishonest: did the assimilation of the overpassed theoretical paradigms (formalism, poststructuralism, deconstruction) actually take place? In what *place*? Was such superseding the balanced upshot of a dialectical absorption, or was it rather the hasty outcome of mechanical and tactical outflanking? Remember Lacan's super-subtle warning: "je n'aime pas

---

11 For Berkeley, see autobiographical information offered by Greenblatt in the "Introduction" to *Learning to Curse*, 1–21. The allusion to a Marxian education reflects on the standard life-story of the British cultural materialist. For Yale, listen to Karen Raber's college recollections in an interview with Neema Parvini. https://blogs.surrey.ac.uk/shakespeare/2016/09/30/shakespeare-and-contemporary-theory-28-shakespeare-and-posthumanist-theory-with-karen-raber/.

12 Recall that the most important historicist claim of my book, that dialectical critique (Adorno, Derrida) is not dated, is sustained by notions of non-simultaneity and incontemporaneity (*Ungleichzeitigkeit*) that Ernst Bloch first formulated in order to identify different layers of Renaissance thought. For Bloch's idea, see Remo Bodei's informed "Introduzione" to the Italian translation: *Filosofia del rinascimento*, 9–18.

beaucoup qu'on dise 'qu'on a dépassé Hegel', comme on dit 'dépasser Descartes', etc. dépasser tout et toujours: on reste tout simplement à la même place" (*Le moi* 91). There are probably people who say they have been in Kuala Lumpur simply because their flight to Australia from London included a 2-hour layover in the airport of the Malaysian capital. Where you ever *in* deconstruction, or was it just a 2-hour seminar layover perusing nervously a sibylline essay on Freud, inscription, and the scene of writing? Did the superseding take place in the mind of each critic involved, or was it rather a collective event registered in the Zeitgeist calendar of Anglo-American academia? Andrej Warminski warns against the facile dismissal of a deconstructive-sounding argument simply on grounds of presumption, "lest we think that this is familiar, all too familiar, and that that we have read, digested, and understood all of this before and can therefore relegate it to the past (and a shady, if not downright abject past at that)" ("Introduction" to de Man, *Aesthetic* 6). Of course, the headlines abjection that blocked the calm reception of de Man's four brilliant essays on Kant's and Hegel's aesthetic theory has very little to do with reading and digestion, let alone understanding. They have much more to do with cultivated ignorance and Puritan zealotry.

When Rita Felski asserts that she "was weaned in the Frankfurt School" in a very influential book titled *The Limits of Critique* (2015) where there are only two references to work by Adorno or Horkheimer (look again at the title!) the reader feels she has been taken for a ride. Something must have gone amiss in the weaning nursery. Or maybe Fredric Jameson and Martin Jay cried harder and were given all the milk.[13] Who knows? Terry Eagleton, a notorious faster on Frankfurt (School) diet, recently published a 250-page book on Marx where he is at pains to prove that he has read—ok, re-read—anything by this thinker beyond the *Communist Manifesto* and the Introduction to the *Critique of Political Economy*: we learn instead that he despises the *Daily Mail* and has a bear-stained teddy bear sleeping on his pillow (*Why Marx* 45–48). What is that—theory, pre-theory, or post-theory? I ignore it, but it is certainly devoid of the energy, intelligence and verve that informed his provocative 1986 book on *William Shakespeare*. On close examination, the declarations of the proponents of so-called post-theory serve to corroborate the very plain fact, already

---

13   The standards of Jameson's kindergarten education were indeed uncommonly high: "Now we need to see the whole process at work, by reading the famous opening section of the Doctrine of Being [in Hegel's *Science of Logic*] where, as every schoolchild knows, Being is declared to be 'the same' as Nothingness" (*Valences* 84). It may be worth noting that adult Coleridge, a notorious metaphysical mystificator, was scandalized by such identification—thus widening the then nascent Analytic-Continental Divide.

informing struggles over the Hegel legacy, that "it is easy for an unthinking person to think that the history of thought has reached its end" (Cutrofello, *Owl* 60). The problem may not be—was never, if you wish—the closing of the American mind, and yet the proliferation in departments of English of people ready to protest that thinking is not a relevant condition for personhood is hardly a controvertible fact. This view doesn't turn them into unthinking persons, but it doesn't exactly make them immune to the charge. John Brockman has remarked that "a 1950s education in Freud, Marx, and modernism is not a sufficient qualification for a thinking person today" (qtd. in Campana & Maisano 8). He is wrong: Shakespeare studies would become a much "better place" (*As You Like It* 2.4.13) if the people working in it proved they have proficiently covered two at least of the cultural fields of Marxism, psychoanalysis, and artistic modernism. When this is the case—I think of literary scholars like Margreta de Grazia, Stephen Orgel, Anthony Nuttall, Jonathan Goldberg, Andreas Höfele, Victoria Kahn, or Richard Halpern—their brilliant exegetic work on early modern literature effectively bears the imprint of that *Bildung*.

Interestingly, the intellectuals chosen by Brockman as representatives of the third culture are gurus of cognitive (Pinker) and artificial intelligence (Minsky), sectarian neo-rationalists moved by dreams of holistic explanation and consilience who would probably snub the pre-modernist nightmares of Freud, Marx, and Nietzsche.[14] Brockman's third culture euphoria is primarily a neo-cognitivist exaltation, and as such it can dispense, at its own risk, with the strong critical modernity that emerges in the Kant-Hegel dialogue running all the way up to modernism and modernism-inspired strong theory (Lacan, Adorno, Althusser, Szondi, Foucault, Deleuze, Derrida, Badiou, de Man, Miller, Bloom, Jameson, Hartman, Hamacher, Warminski, Brooks, Brandom, Pippin, Bersani, Chase, Attridge, Spivak, Said, Bhaba, Felman, Jacobs, Cixous, Butler, Jay, Žižek, Cutrofello, Comay, Lukacher, John Carlos Rowe, McKeon, Royle, Armstrong, Bersani, Sedgwick ...). What all of the above names share is a keen propensity to dialectical speculation, a respect for mediation: the conviction that there is more to perception and understanding than affection, and certainly more to consciousness—*pace* Husserl—than self-affection. The fact that neither Spinoza nor Sartre believed that in order to know you need to know that you know betrays the non-dialectical sides of their ultimately dialectical thought, the former too much of a rationalist, the latter (the early latter) too

---

14   Pinker characterizes Nietzsche's "ideas" as "repellent and incoherent" *Enlightenment Now* (446). His opinions and attitudes are, not his ideas. Pinker's patronizing attitude towards Marx (405) is part of the same strategy of occlusion of speculative thought.

much of a phenomenologist;[15] the conviction, then, that no meaning, including the self, can be immediately accessible (present) to consciousness in the form of a fulfilling self-givennes [*erfüllende Selbstgebung*] (Husserl *Cartesianische* 177)—or representation, or appresentation—and that human consciousness is precisely the exceptional site—"a mended stocking is better than a torn stocking: not so self-consciousness" wrote Hegel—of a non-identity gap caused by external pressures—writing, language, difference, the unconscious, ideology.[16] Still, it is the torn stocking that sets humans apart from everything else—*hyle, zoe, bios, gea, pathos*, the *sensible*—and such language-based exceptionalism is the *sine qua non* of dialectical modes of thought and critique—even for post-phenomenological thinkers like Derrida who affected, in his old age, to be chastened and subdued by staring cats. Incidentally, let me remind historical phenomenologists that Hegel's torn stocking doesn't exist, that it is just a metaphor, lest they feel tempted to track it, and—like a Jane Austen spinster—mend it. Hegel argued that

> the forms of thought are first set out and stored in human language, and one can hardly be reminded often enough nowadays that thought is what differentiates the human being from the beast. In everything that the human being has interiorized, in everything that in some way or other has become for him a representation, in whatever he has made his own, there has language penetrated, and everything that he transforms into language and expresses in it contains a category, whether concealed, mixed, or well defined. So much is logic natural to the human being, is indeed his very *nature*.
>
> *Science of Logic*, 12

Logic (language) is natural *to* the human being, yes, but it is not natural in itself, and it cannot be reduced to nature. It is not even—*pace* Pinker—an instinct. The same applies to the *unconscious*, which emerges in biological-psychological nature but is radically irreducible to it (Althusser, *Écrits sur la psychanalyse* 63). To be sure, Hegel is here implicitly relying on a Greek-philosophy-based extended meaning of logos, comprising logic, language, and reason. Derrida's *écriture* was coined to fill in an akin polysemous gap. There is no arrogance in that—all critical rationalists, including Nietzsche, assume

---

15 See Badiou, "Descartes/Lacan"; and Derrida, "Language," 75.
16 The English translation "fulfilling givenness of the sense itself" (151) misses the dimension of self-positing or self-donation. The Hegel dictum is drawn from *Aphorismen aus Wastebook* (*Werke* 2: 558). Heidegger misquotes it in his *Four seminars*.

that language may exert tropic seductions (*der Verführung der Sprache*), and that the petrified errors of/in reason (*der in ihr versteinerten Grundirrtümer der Vernunft*), which often enough signal unclaimed but significant experience, would not effectively exist (as meaningful actuality) without the transcendental frame warranted by discursive reason (Nietzsche, *Zur Genealogie* 35). To be sure, the complaint about the unreliability of language is a philosophical commonplace, but it takes on an unexpected anxiety in the tradition running Descartes to Husserl.

On this view, the significance of an arch-particular existent, what Robert Brandom would call an "individual"—say, Barnardine in *Measure for Measure*—cannot be calibrated outside the range of intelligibility provided by the *universality* of existence—and the latter is nothing if not a *discursive* phenomenon, which is to say an *unphenomenal phenomenon*.[17] Barnardine is, yes, a real graph standing for a putative voice, but his vocal aliveness is contingent upon an ability to express universality because "universality is not unrelated to particular identities; it is not their neutral container, but an antagonism that emerges from within each way of life" (Žižek, *Reading Marx* 37). To describe, for instance, a drunkard who is sentenced to death as "insensible of mortality, and desperately mortal" (*Measure for Measure* 4.2.134–35) takes a great deal of speculative genius. This limpid dialectical phrase, whose wavering between a reflective and a determining judgement affixes a doubtful universal or metaphysical phantasm (mortality) to the certain particular (mortal) it nonetheless determines, bears Shakespeare's unmistakable signature. In Shakespeare, the role of some potentially false abstract universals (mortality, honour, man) is not unlike that of Kant's transcendental concepts of reason:

> Although we must say of all transcendental concepts of reason that they are only ideas, they are not therefore to be considered as superfluous and useless. For although we cannot determine any object through them, they may nevertheless fundamentally, even if unobserved, serve the understanding as a canon for its extended and consistent use.
>
> *Critique of Pure Reason* 308

---

17 In an astute essay against object-oriented ontologies, Žižek argues: "This is why all the anti-Hegelian rhetoric which insists that Hegel's totality misses the details that stick out and ruin its balance misses the point: the space of the Hegelian totality is the very space of the interaction between the ('abstract') Whole and the details that elude its grasp, although they are generated by it" ("Marx Reads Object-Oriented Ontology," *Reading Marx*, 44).

Hegel took good note of that. The service here described is dialectical—inferential, conceptual, self-correcting. With "a bait of falsehood" (concepts, universals) the dialectical method "takes" a "carp of truth" (*Hamlet* 2.1.60). The potential falsity of ideas (Kant) or primitive terms (Pascal) doesn't invalidate their orienting and regulating function, their capacity to turn the mind (*portent la pensée*, argues Pascal) in a productive direction.[18] And the procedure is utterly negative in that critical-conceptual differentiation is the condition for dialectical penetration, even if "to allow for differentiation is to open the metaphysical door to phantasms and thus to let the Sophist get a foothold in being" (Cutrofello, *All for Nothing* 7). Thus to uphold linguistic-conceptual mediation—the deployment of transcendental concepts, universals, and other language-determined notional phantasms—as a precondition of significant human experience is not to be mistaken with a wholesale idealistic defence of "the appearance of a mediation which the actual Idea undertakes with itself and which goes on behind the scenes" (Marx, *Critique of Hegel's Philosophy of Right* 8): mortality is not an idea that goes on behind the scenes, mortality *is* a prisoner "many days entirely drunk" (*Measure for Measure* 4.2.138) that refuses to leave prison and patiently awaits his death. Nor is—alas—mediation to be construed as a thought-tool disclosing to us whatever goes on *before the scenes*. Nothing beyond incidental delusions (a dagger), insidious ghosts (a father), fleeting visions (a bear) and inset shows (a masque) is immediately decodable "as appearance, as phenomenon" (Marx, *Critique* 7) in the standard Shakespeare playtex. The performance histories of *Macbeth*, *Hamlet*, *The Winter's Tale* and *The Tempest* show that few things are more appealing to audience-flattering companies than showing the unphenomenal and staging the no-thing. Apart from that, little is phenomenally allowed to happen *before the scenes*. Like "psychoanalytic action," Shakespearean action exclusively "develops in and through verbal communication, that is, in a dialectical grasping of meaning [*saisie dialectique du sens*]" (Lacan, *Écrits* 83; *Écrits I* 101). Not even characters *de facto* happen in his plays. They are rather the aftermath of language. As Royle has discerningly noted, "wordplay precedes character" (*How to Read* 13).

---

18   Pascal's turn of phrase occurs in the opuscule *De l'esprit géométrique*, examined by Paul de Man in his essay "Pascal's Persuasion" in *Aesthetic Ideology*, 24–26.

4

Adorno argued that the work of philosophical self-reflection consists in unraveling the paradox of the dialectical anticipation of contradiction—between general and particular, concept and thing, identical and non-identical. "Everything else," he added, "is signification, secondhand construction, pre-philosophical activity, today as in Hegel's time" (*Negative Dialectic* 9). Many scholars in Shakespeare studies are right there, today as in Hegel's time, doing *Signifikation*, *Nachkonstruktion*, and *vorphilosophisch* work (*Negative* 21). They are doing anything but *critique*, whose limits, properly understood, remain unknown to us. Philosophical illiteracy per se is not a problem, as there are many eminences in the field who contribute extraordinary philological and hermeneutic work that is spectacularly bereft of philosophical considerations of even "explicit" theoretical assumptions. Stephen Orgel is an example. The problem lies in the hermeneutic consequences springing from allegedly innovative theoretical approaches whose post-theoretical implications betray philosophical confusion, if not ignorance. The post-theoretical in them is ultimately pre-theoretical, a modality of bliss enjoyed by scholars who never quite internalized the dialectical exigencies informing the poststructuralist speculation of thinkers like Althusser or Derrida. Let me recall that Dollimore not too long ago described the great critic Nicholas Royle as a "deco boy" ("Wishful theory"), an offhand dismissal that betrays the anti-intellectualist—at bottom illiberal—strand that is often latent in so-called academic subversion. It also reveals the way in which sometime between 1968 and 1988 the academic Left renounced the universalism—the "hunger for equality and social justice" also prioritized by Badiou and Žižek—that inspired the traditional Left and embraced instead the equivocal nirvana of identity politics, for much in Dollimore's comment, prompted by Royle's supposedly out-queering reading of Forster, depends—or so it seems to me—both on a wrongly patrimonial conception of gay hermeneutics and on the very narrow assumption, denounced by Royle himself, that *theory* is not informed by *desire*.[19] When the critical arguments of scholars besieged by theoretical innovation are replaced

---

19   Hobsbawm: "So what does identity politics have to do with the Left? Let me state firmly what should not need restating. The political project of the Left is universalist: it is for *all* human beings. However we interpret the words, it isn't liberty for shareholders or blacks, but for everybody. It isn't equality for all members of the Garrick Club or the handicapped, but for everybody. It is not fraternity only for old Etonians or gays, but for everybody. And identity politics is essentially not for everybody but for the members of a specific group only." According to Žižek, "today's postmodern politics of multiple subjectivities is precisely not political enough, in so far as it silently presupposes

by autobiographical declarations and confessional protestations crammed with egoic moral arrogance (my life, my eighties, my Shakespeare, my desire) this is a sign that all is not well.[20] And the problem is not so much that the critical ground becomes the lawn for anyone's picnic (that a was liberatory breakthrough): the problem arises when criticism becomes a personal description of the picnic. When I speak of "theoretical innovation" I do not mean the "post-theoretical" claims that Dollimore quite rightly shuns. I mean the dialectical theory (Foucault, Althusser) he himself brilliantly espoused in his early work (*Radical Tragedy*), and which appears to have defeated his own "materialist" (at bottom, political and moral) ends: if Althusser, Foucault, Lacan, Deleuze and Derrida do not allow my "spontaneous me" or "me myself" (Whitman) to do totally radical or dissident criticism, then I do radical autobiography instead.[21] Phenomenology—a stunted phenomenology tailored to petty ends and stuffed with egoic revelations—is the panacea that subsequent scholars have crafted with a view to mitigating the ailments of the resulting impasse. Dollimore's dig at Royle also betrays a small-minded esprit de corps, a pride in parochial-academic corporativism that often (not always) nourishes many of the sub-groups currently proliferating in early modern studies (cognitive ecology, object-oriented Feminism, queer phenomenology).[22] In 1998 Žižek argued that "there, in the strategy of culpabilizing the Other, also resides the limitation of 'postmodern' identity politics, in which the deprived minority indulges in ressentiment by blaming, and seeking retribution from, the Other" (*Plague* 45). Two years earlier, Hobsbawm had irritated many a sensible spirit by simply reminding that "collective identities are defined negatively; that is to say against others" ("Identity Politics" 41). And still earlier, in 1994, psychoanalysis theorist Joan Copjek declared that

a non-thematized, 'naturalized' framework of economic relations" ("Class Struggle or Postmodernism?" in *Contingency, Hegemony, Universality*, 108).

20 Jonathan Dollimore's late work is crammed with autobiographical evocations, See, for instance: "Wishful Theory and Sexual Politics" (2000), "Then and Now" (2014) and, of course, *Desire: A Memoir* (2021).

21 In his reply to Dollimore (see the chapter titled "Impossible Uncanniness" in *In Memory of Jacques Derrida*), Royle rightly imputes Dollimore's nervous response to his out-queering reading of Forster to Dollimore's realization that the writing off of deconstruction is easier said than done.

22 In Royle's elegant reply to Dollimore we read: "Insofar as it is a question of affirming one's identity (I am queer, or I am a queer, I will have been or I might be a queer, and so on), it is also one of attending to the secrecy and non-belonging that structure all movements of identification. As Derrida says in *A Taste for the Secret*: 'The desire to belong to any community whatsoever, the desire for belonging *tout court*, implies that one *does not belong* ...'" (qtd. in *In Memory*, 119).

the subject is not identical to itself and all attempts to think of the subject, or a group, or the human, as self-identical leads inevitably to establishing a boundary on the other side of which are those we do not like because they are not like us. The establishing of strong boundaries is what ego psychology recommends; it is also the protective gesture of identity politics. Establishing a politics on the basis of identity is not only reckless politically, it is also theoretically unfounded: identity is a fiction.
"Interview" 200[23]

The way the strong boundaries of identity politics are helping to un-dialectically remap recent theoretical trends and philosophical schools has recently become a critical target. A case in point is philosopher Ray Brassier's crude aspersion of the childish camaraderie generated around the movement of speculative realism—intellectually prompted by Quentin Meillassoux but soon arrogated by Graham Harman. His comment harbours an important critique of undialectical methods:

> The "speculative realist movement" exists only in the imaginations of a group of bloggers promoting an agenda for which I have no sympathy whatsoever: actor-network theory spiced with pan-psychist metaphysics and morsels of process philosophy. I don't believe the internet is an appropriate medium for serious philosophical debate; nor do I believe it is acceptable to try to concoct a philosophical movement online by using blogs to exploit the misguided enthusiasm of impressionable graduate students. I agree with Deleuze's remark that ultimately the most basic task of philosophy is to impede stupidity, so I see little philosophical merit in a 'movement' whose most signal achievement thus far is to have generated an online orgy of stupidity.
> "I am a nihilist"

Brassier's brilliant tirade reminds me of Samuel Johnson's bitter dissection of the Puritan bigotry of his time, "when any unsettled innovator who could hatch a half-formed notion produced it to the publick; when every man might become a preacher, and almost every preacher could collect a congregation" (*Lives of the Poets* 215). This kind of close fraternization over the grail of esoteric meaning used to be restricted to the decryption of eccentric opera by Melville, Joyce, Walser, Rand, Pynchon, and their likes. Now Shakespeare is also a victim,

---

23 For the failure of identity, see also Copjek, *Read My Desire*, 51–53.

yet not of *his* esoteric meaning, but rather of the specialized hermetic-technical jargon that is forced into his texts. Identity politics has not disappeared. On the one hand, it remains barely hidden in a certain strand of neo-phenomenological scholarship openly committed to religious at-homeness, worldhood, being-in-the-world, and rootedness in tradition;[24] on the other hand, it has merely been transmuted into a mode of *identity hermeneutics* based on an exclusive set of recognition tools like affection, eco-responsibility, network, immediacy, reciprocity, embodiment, interaction. The upshot is satisfactory enough—to unburden hermeneutics of the mediated textual opacity and lacunae that set it in motion in the first place, to reconstruct the deconstructed. The recipe for the phenomenological laxative required for this evacuation is deftly schematized by Brassier: "actor-network theory spiced with pan-psychist metaphysics and morsels of process philosophy." The only thing that the fraternity of corporate scholars needs to read is themselves in the recognitive effort of choreographing their collective *we*—something as playfully reassuring as what you see in Goya's oil *La gallinita ciega*. Doing Shakespeare is thus going—immediately—from the critic to the critic in a virtuoso turning "round about the cauldron" (*Macbeth* 4.1.4): "Indeed, we join in the conjuring, We join the round-dance. We revel the phenomenon. We like *it*; it likes *us*" (Bruce Smith, *Phenomenal* 5). Now slow down, sit, stretch your legs, listen:

> Have you felt so proud to get at the meaning of poems?
> Stop this day and night with me and you shall possess the origin of all poems,
> You shall possess the good of the earth and sun, (there are millions of suns left,)
> You shall no longer take things at second or third hand, nor look through the eyes of the dead, nor feed on the spectres in books,
> You shall not look through my eyes either, nor take things from me,
> You shall listen to all sides and filter them from your self.
>   *Complete* 54–55

O the comfort. The open or implicit appeal to the spirit and methods of phenomenology in current Shakespeare studies reverberates with this call to ignorance, this plea for immediate, first-hand, self-sufficient immediacy. What

---

24   Maybe we shouldn't overlook the role that Arendt's Jewishness may have played in her very conflictual, occasionally anti-universalist and anti-Enlightened, conception of identity. See Moran, 288–303. For a contrary view, that distinguishes carefully between Arendt's Jewish "identity" and "experience," see Jerome Kohn.

neo-phenomenology adds to Whitman's pastoral propaedeutics—"Twenty-eight young men bathe by the shore" (70)—is the invitation to be more yourself by joining hands, as in Matisse's painting *La Danse*. Whitman's are beautiful lines, among the best in the language. He wrote verse and spent whole days strolling about the beaches in Long Island, pleased with what he got. Doing criticism is another matter. It has little to do with holding hands, swimming, and singing. It brings into play other talents, shapes other ends.

CHAPTER 4

What Phenomenology? Kant to Levinas

A spectre is haunting early modern studies: the spectre of *phenomenology*. The name and its cognates (*phenomenological, phenomenal*) are dismally omnipresent. This usage is confusing, sometimes excessive, often unexplained, nearly always enforced to obtain cultural prestige. Few of its users are aware of the philosophical stakes involved and most seek to capitalize on the payoff of a fashionable label, especially when post-theory has confined you to the desert, it is very cold, and you feel the need to tell someone—your students, your readers, your scientific colleagues in campus—that you are actually doing something more than simply doing something, i.e. feeling, touching, networking, being affected by Shakespeare. "I am doing phenomenology" is oracular enough to silence skeptical others, including your mother-in-law. But it places you in an awkward position.

Defining phenomenology with any precision is a difficult task that lies beyond the scope of this book. However, since I often accuse others of misrepresenting the letter and spirit of Husserl's original version of phenomenology, I find it convenient to offer some theoretical clarifications. If I don't apologize for the technical density of what follows is precisely because, in avoiding this density, others have perpetrated, unwittingly or on purpose, some of the blunders I examine in this book. Very succinctly put, we can speak of five important versions of phenomenology: 1) critical: Kantian and Hegelian; 2) Husserlian 3) Heideggerian 4) Levinasian and 5) Merleau-Ponty's phenomenology of the flesh. What is known today as historical phenomenology draws mostly on the last of these versions. With the exception of Sartrean phenomenology, whose presence in early modern studies is negligible, I will try to describe what is central to each of these versions.

1

In the *Metaphysical Foundations of Natural Science* (1786), Kant spoke of *phenomenology* as "a part of physics concerned with the science of 'true motion' as opposed to only 'apparent motion,' and thus as having to do not with 'the transformation of mere appearance (*Schein*) into truth, but of appearance (*Erscheinung*) into experience (*Erfahrung*),' that is, into something from which we could learn" (Terry Pinkard, "Introduction" to Hegel, *The Phenomenology of Spirit* xviii).[1] But phenomenology also denoted the way "various theoretical formulations are to be related to experiment, that is, how the formulations and theoretical entities are to be related to the way they appear in our experience of them" (Pinkard xviii). Manifestly, for Kant phenomenology involves the significance of appearance in experience. Hegel picked up the second use of the term, and "focused on the way in which a theoretical term, 'Geist,' would be said to appear to us. 'Geist' would be the essence hidden behind experience, and the phenomenology would be the 'science' itself of how that essence makes its appearance, until at the end of the book, we supposedly would have comprehended just what 'Geist' really was" (Pinkard xviii). According to Cutrofello, who traces the philosophical origin of the term to Kant's contemporary Johann Heinrich Lambert, Hegel went further than Kant, "conceiving of his 'phenomenology of the spirit' as a reflection on the process whereby the Kantian doctrine of the transcendental ideality of appearances is first posited and then overcome by a subject who discovers that the concept of the thing in itself is untenable" (*Continental* 30). Hegel, moreover, took Fichte and Schelling to task "for thinking that Kantian dualisms can be overcome simply by taking the possibility of intellectual intuition for granted. Instead, he seeks to show how a sustained reflection on the difference between intuiting and thinking *culminates* in an identification of the two in absolute knowing" (30). Let us not lose sight of "the possibility of intellectual intuition," for Husserl's phenomenology plays itself out in perilous dependance on such possibility. Interestingly, the first title that Hegel considered for his book was *Science of the Experience of Consciousness*. So, for Hegel, initially, *phenomenology* was a *science*. Only later did it become the *experience* itself, whence the modification of the title: *The Phenomenology of Spirit*. This identificatory oscillation, prompted by the original enigma of appearance, between an experience (*Erfahrung*) and the science (*Wissenschaft*) that studies it spells an (idealist) ambivalence that will always accompany the notion of phenomenology. Pinker explains this oscillation:

> The book had started out as an inquiry into what was the true essence behind appearance, that is, into what Kant had already dubbed the thing in itself. Under the pressure of its own developmental logic, the book had instead metamorphosed into a larger enterprise, asking what the being-in-itself (Hegel's successor concept to the thing in itself) of spirit itself really was. (xxix)

---

1   The argumentative outlines of Chapter 4 of Kant's book, titled "Metaphysical Foundations of Phenomenology," foreshadow many of Husserl's analytical interrogations about the nature of perception in *Ideas 1*.

The *an-sich-Sein* of Spirit (*Geist*) turns out to be a turning-out, a developmental narrative of gradual unfolding:

> What had been an inquiry into the essence behind appearance has turned out as a "phenomenology" to show that Geist is in fact not the hidden essence behind appearance but actually is its series of appearances as it has shape-shifted itself in its history up to this point. A phenomenology itself thus turns out to be a way of examining the contingencies of Geist's appearances in history with an account of how its concept of itself has so shaped itself that in having completed this inquiry, it is now in a position to know that its self-certainty (its knowledge of what it is doing) is equal to its truth (what it is really doing).
> Pinkard xxxv

In Pinkard's account, Hegel's phenomenology is less the *experience* itself of Geist's successive configurations than the scientific *examination* of them. But Hegel remains ambivalent in this respect. When in the "Preface" he describes how "the phenomenology of spirit brings itself to its conclusion" he means the experience through which Being becomes "absolutely mediated" as "an object to itself:" "What spirit prepares for itself in its phenomenology is the element of knowing" ("Preface" 23). Thus, because the self-*examining* turn of *Geist* toward itself is the destination of *Geist's experience*, the confusion between experience and the science of experience appears inevitable. Heidegger insisted very much on this point. In one of the initial lectures of his 1930–1931 course on Hegel's *Phenomenology of Spirit*, he averred that "a clear differentiation is necessary in the interest of a real understanding of both [the Hegelian and Husserlian] phenomenologies—*particularly today, when everything is called 'phenomenology'*" (28; my emphasis). Ninety years have passed, but we remain somehow trapped in a "today" where nearly everything is called *phenomenology*. Heidegger described Hegelian phenomenology as "the manner in which spirit exists" (24), the mode of experiential appearing that is characterized by a moving-forward, a becoming-other-than-itself by coming to itself: "This movement is the self-verification of consciousness, of finite knowledge, as spirit. This self-verifying is nothing but the appearance of spirit, of phenomenology" (25). Hence the equivalence of phenomenology and experience as the "way in which absolute knowledge brings itself to itself" (25). To sum, *phenomenology* for Hegel is the *experience (Erfahrung)* of the *appearance (Erscheinung)* of Spirit to itself. This is not too far from what Kant had intimated.

This inaugural delineation of the meaning and scope of phenomenology delivers a first certainty: phenomenology has to do with the *appearing* in human experience of something to the human being. Although Hegel's parabolic lesson is that what appears is ultimately *Geist* to itself, appearing concerns in principle the appearing of something (first things, and only by extension other human beings) to the human self.

2

Let us now turn to Husserl. Influenced by Kant and Brentano, the early Husserl, the author of *Logical Investigations*, conceived of phenomenology in epistemological terms, as a "taxonomy of epistemic and cognitive acts which would serve 'empirical psychology'" (Moran 92). He first construed phenomenology as a *descriptive psychology*, but around 1913 he backed off and initiated a corrective crusade against psychologism.[2] His early misrepresentation placed phenomenology as a sub-domain of empirical psychology, "as a region containing 'immanent' descriptions of psychical events [*Erlebnisse*]" (*Ideas I*, "Introduction" 2). Husserl later bitterly protested that *pure* phenomenology is not psychology, but rather a regulating domain placed above psychology: "phenomenology is the court of appeal for methodologically basic questions of psychology" (*Ideas I*, Introduction 189). The juridical figure spells the transcendental stakes: "pure or transcendental phenomenology will be established not as a science of facts, but as a science of essential Being [...] a science which aims exclusively at establishing 'knowledge of essences' (*Wesenserkentnisse*) and absolutely no 'facts' [*Tatsachen*]" (*Ideas I*, "Introduction" 3–4). Dan Zahavi has rightly argued that Husserl soon came to realize that the specific and unique phenomenological question was transcendental and not psychological: "What are the conditions of possibility for appearance as such?" (*Husserl's Phenomenology* 54). The formulation of the question evinces its Kantian ancestry, and the tentative reply confirms it: "phenomenology is not a theory about the merely appearing, or to put it differently, appearances are not *mere* appearances. For how things appear is an integral part of what they really are" (*Husserl's Phenomenology* 55). The difference with Kant is that, for Husserl, the phenomenon-noumenon or appearance-reality distinctions are not absolute: the only distinctions that obtain in the external world are distinctions "internal to the realm of appearances" (*Husserl's Phenomenology* 56). He coincides with Kant however in the

---

2 See *Logical Investigations I*, 175–177. For the retreat from and critique of psychologism, see Zahavi, *Husserl's Phenomenology*, 11–13.

confidence with which he holds to the transcendental notion of *constitution*.³ But, since "how things appear" is our *experience* of *appearances*, phenomenology remains for Husserl a triangulation between appearance, experience, and knowledge. It remains, therefore, a transcendental, if not downright idealist, endeavor. But transcendental purification exacted reductions. The "eidetic Reduction" names the reduction from the psychological phenomena to pure essences, and from factual or empirical to essential universality. Thus, "the phenomena of transcendental phenomenology will be characterized as non-real (*irreal*)" (*Ideas I*, "Introduction" 4). The experiences phenomenology cares about are "transcendentally purified 'experiences.'" They are therefore "non-realities [*Irrealitäten*] and excluded from any connexion [*Einordnung*] within the 'real world [*wirkliche Welt*]'" (4). Section 50 of *Ideas I* keeps up the definitional momentum of the "Introduction." Reality (*Realität*), he insists, lacks independence (*Selbstandigkeit*). It is not something absolute and it binds itself to another reality, that of essences, in a secondary [*sekundär*] way. "It is," Husserl concludes, "absolutely speaking, nothing at all [*gar nichts*]" (*Ideas I* §50, 96), whence the pragmatic legitimacy of switching it off through *epoché*. On the phenomenological side of the cleavage (*der Scheidung*) validity is bestowed upon intentional and noematic meaning; on the far side languishes the real (*reel*) (§128, 267). The reduction places "out of action [*ausser Aktion*]" (§50, 96) the reflections ordered in accordance with the logic of experience.

Nothing at all, out of action: "O O O O that Shakespeherian Rag" (Eliot, *Collected* 67). Indeed, the fact that these analytic fragments echo both Hamlet and the grounds of its idealist appeal should make the "phenomenological" scholar interested in Shakespeare pause. "The basic field of Phenomenology," Husserl concludes, is the field of second-level acts of reflection directed towards the first-level acts of reflections we are ordinarily "living *in*" (*Ideas I* §50, 97). The *phenomenological standpoint* uses the reflections of the *natural standpoint* as its raw material and is safely separated from them by virtue of the reduction. By suspending all *transcendent* realities (*jederlei Transzendenten*), phenomenology becomes *transcendental* (*transzendentalen*) (§86, 180).⁴

---

3 In David Smith's words, "Husserl's phenomenology was presented in conjunction with a neo-Kantian doctrine of transcendental idealism, whereby the world is 'constituted' in a multiplicity of actual and possible acts of consciousness" (*Husserl* 20). See also Moran's discussion of the notion of *constitution* in his "Introduction" to *Phenomenology*, 164–175. Although committed to transcendentalist premises, Husserl never lost, according to Moran, sense of "the *transcendence* of being with regard to consciousness" (165).

4 This doesn't mean that the *transcendental* and the *transcendent* are unrelated. According to Zahavi, they are in fact essentially related: *Husserl's Legacy*, 24.

The key epistemological tool guiding the mind through this meta-sensorial, transcendental adventure is intuition: "Phenomenology, in point of fact, is a *pure descriptive* discipline which studies the whole field of pure transcendental consciousness in the light of pure intuition" (§59, 115). The disconnection (*Ausschaltung*), which so far has ousted psychology, external facts and even logic from the citadel of the mind, is a warrant of hygienic immanence: the standard (*der Norm*) that phenomenologists should follow is therefore "to claim nothing that we cannot make essentially transparent [*wesensmässig einsichtig*] to ourselves by reference to Consciousness and on purely immanent lines" (115). Phenomenology, he insists, is an eidetic science, "the theory of the essential natura of the transcendentally purified consciousness" (116). This accounts for its authority and primordiality: "phenomenology is bound by its essential nature to make the claim of being 'first' philosophy and to provide the means for all the rational criticism that needs to be performed" (126). Free from all assumptions and autonomous, phenomenology sets its own rules immanently.

The above definitional overview of Husserlian phenomenology should serve to emphasize a preeminent idea: phenomenology recoils from the *transcendent* (the empirical, the objective, the factual) into the *transcendental*—the realm of the conditions of possibility of knowledge. And good knowledge, for Husserl, is ideal knowledge or knowledge of essences. I stress this because neo-phenomenological scholars have crudely reversed the valences, prioritized the transcendent over the transcendental, and thus transformed phenomenology into a concept-free propaedeutic granting direct access to things. This reversal has been partly encouraged by Husserl's constant recourse to the notion of immediacy, but it is mostly motivated by the late swerve of his own philosophical project, increasingly open to the lure of embodiment and intersubjectivity. But this development doesn't shift an inch the transcendental stakes placed by Husserl early in his career. The attempt to cross the boundary and claim access to a transcendence made of bodies (Merleau-Ponty) and others (Levinas) is a major violation of phenomenology's original program.

3

A very close but critical disciple of Husserl, Heidegger always considered himself a "phenomenologist." In *Being and Time*, a book dedicated to Husserl, Heidegger follows a "phenomenological method of investigation" (*Being and Time* §7, 23) and subscribes to a conception of philosophy as "universal phenomenological ontology, taking its departure from the hermeneutic of Da-sein"

(34). He traces back phenomenology to Greek philosophy, where the call to *legein ta phainomena* is reset as "*apophainesthai ta phainomena*—to let what shows itself be seen from itself, just as it shows itself from itself" (30). Hence the transcendental nature of the thought operation involved in the attempt to "attain the 'things themselves'" (Letter to Eugen Fink, 1966, qtd. in Moran, *Introduction* 195), especially when the thing at issue is no other than Being:

> Being and its structure transcend every being and every possible existent determination of a being. *Being is the transcendens pure and simple.* And the transcendence of Dasein's Being is distinctive in that it implies the possibility and the necessity of the most radical *individuation.* Every disclosure of Being as the *transcendens* is *transcendental* knowledge. Phenomenological truth (*disclosedness of Being*) is *veritas transcendentalis.*
>
> *Being and Time* §7, 36⁵

Again, the *transcendental* vocation of phenomenology is most strenuously asserted. Indeed, because "ontology is only possible as phenomenology" (32), we may unambiguously state that, despite their gradual falling out, Heidegger the renovator of the ontological project always acknowledged his debt to Husserl. Still, he qualified his loyalty by defending a *heuristic* conception of phenomenology, more a possibility (of seeing better conceptual things) than an actuality (of seeing essences) (*Being and Time*, "Introduction" §7, 34). Heidegger's hermeneutic conception of the phenomenological *epoché* takes the reduction to be an act of verbal-conceptual *interpretation (Auslegung)*, a movement towards and away from its object that facilitates a possible transcendental-ontological thematization: "For us phenomenological reduction means leading phenomenological vision back from the apprehension of a being, whatever may be the character of that apprehension, to the understanding of the being of this being (projecting upon the way it is unconcealed)" (*Basic Problems* 21). This two-way process involves, moreover, a moment of phenomenological construction but also a *destruction,* even a *deconstruction (Abbau),* which Heidegger describes in terms very similar to those used by Husserl to characterize the reduction:

---

5   I use Stambaugh's translation, but I deviate from it in capitalizing the last "Being," as John Macquarrie & Edward Robinson do (*Being and Time* §7, 62). In the original we read: "*Phänomenologische Wahrheit (Erschlossenheit von Sein) ist* veritas transcendentalis" (*Sein und Zeit* §7, 38). For Heidegger's deviation from Husserl, see Annette Sell.

> It is for this reason that there necessarily belongs to the conceptual interpretation of being and its structures, that is, to the reductive construction of being, a *destruction*—a critical process in which the traditional concepts, which at first must necessarily be employed, are deconstructed down to the sources from which they were drawn. Only by means of this destruction can ontology fully assure itself in a phenomenological way of the genuine character of its concepts.
>
> Basic Problems 22–23

Thus, a *hermeneutical phenomenology* takes shape as the aspiration to decode the structures of Being as they "are revealed through the structures of human existence" (Moran 197), but with Heidegger this revelation is invariably a verbal-conceptual elucidation or interpretation (*Auslegung*). This is where Derrida connects with Heidegger, and what best explains the tendency to call the former a phenomenological thinker. We may do well in recoiling from Heidegger's resolve to curate the revelation and thought of Being but we should nonetheless assume that hermeneutic revelation names a transcendental operation that is philosophically less mystified than the attempts to intuit essences (Husserl) or to touch hands (Merleau-Ponty). Unlike these attempts, interpretation is a *mediation-sensitive operation*. Despite his impatience with Husserl's disownment of "factical" existence in *Logical Investigations* and the latter's consequent endorsement of *transcendental idealism*, Heidegger never gave up the *transcendental* dimension of philosophical thought. In fact, his examination of *being-in-the-world* in *Being and Time* reads like an exegetic exploitation of the conceptual—and figurative and etymological—resources of the German language. Moran insists on a *turning* in Heidegger's work from transcendental philosophy to modes of thought that could trace, in an undialectical and nearly immediate manner (that is, outside the subject-object correlation, beyond the reach of Dasein) the appearing or disclosure (*Unverborgenheit*) of Being. These modes of thought are poetry and art (painting and architecture), to which Heidegger paid growing attention from the 1930s onward, but especially in his late years. This supposedly detranscendentalizing *Kehre*—which is not total, for poetic exegesis remained a transcendental hermeneutic operation—was however notably invested with theological (apocalyptic and mystical) underpinnings. Heidegger thus returns to a theological preoccupation that marked his beginnings as a thinker interested in "the phenomenology of religion" (Moran 204). It is no accident that this theological Heidegger should be the one favored by neo-phenomenological early modern scholars.

There may be others, but two basic motifs of Heidegger's work have attracted the attention of these scholars: 1) his characterization of *Zuhandenheit* (handiness or readiness-to-hand, the kind of being that equipment possesses) in *Being and Time* §15, which has been invoked by Bruce Smith and Julia Lupton, the latter through the work of Graham Harman; and 2) his parallel conception of dwelling and building in the lecture "Bauen, Wohnen, Denken" (1951). Unsurprisingly, in both cases—human dealings with either tools or habitat—the ontological-transcendental dimension of thought is attenuated in favor of the mind-body permeation characteristic of *das In-der-Welt-sein* (Being-in-the-World, *Sein und Zeit* §12). Unsurprisingly, moreover, both modes of dealing appear immediate or unmediated, free, that is, from the mediations of written culture. Otherwise put, the Heidegger that neo-phenomenologists can make use of is the Heidegger that looks forward to Levinas's and Merleau-Ponty's transcendence-oriented and neo-spiritual phenomenologies of, respectively, the body and the Other. This means that their use of Heidegger completely overlooks a transcendental and hermeneutic dimension of phenomenology that is never completely absent from his thought and that would arguably deliver the best service to Shakespearean interpretation. In fact, what these scholars invariably overlook is the apperceptive thickness of *understanding* that ontologically—i.e. transcendentally—preempts and predetermines any possible interaction a *Dasein* may establish with her *Mitwelt*: "Dasein ist Seiendes, das sich in seinem Sein *verstehend* zu diesem Sein verhält" (*Sein und Zeit* §12, 52–53; emphasis added). And understanding (*Verstehen*), for Heidegger, is never the pre-reflexive or ante-predicative affair it was for Husserl, and later for Merleau-Ponty. Understanding is always verbal-conceptual understanding, Hamlet's verstehen of *Being*—"Seems, madam? Nay it is; I know not 'seems'" (*Hamlet* 1.2.76)—or Edmund's deconstruction of baseness—"Why brand they us / With base?" (*King Lear* 1.2.9–10). Note that in both cases their speech is literally mediated and dialectical, that is, ironic-echoic, responsive to prior speech. It is, in Bakthin's terms, an elaboration of *alien discourse*. More recently, Nicholas Royle comments on related processes of near-magical thinking and "mental contagion of words," whereby phrases are unknowingly repeated in instances of phantasmal "reenactment" (*How to Read* 67–68). Recall moreover that an ear for this dimension of speech and its ideological effects is, among other things, what places Shakespeare distinctively apart from precursors (Marlowe), contemporaries (Jonson, Lope de Vega) and posterior playwrights like Calderón, Dryden, even Racine.

4

Levinas's 1930 doctoral thesis was a study on Husserl's theory of intuition. Although informative and faithful to the spirit of Husserl's work, Levinas already shows dissatisfaction with the former's excessive reliance on ontology, where the sameness of being is privileged over the ethical relation to the other. Still, the fact that the phenomenological account of *intuition* (*Anschauung*) is discussed in an unproblematic way—as "vision directe de l'objet" (*Théorie de l'intuition* 126)—reveals the extent to which his subsequent apocalyptic move to the transcendent Other was largely sustained by an epistemology of *immediacy* (*Unmittelbarkeit*). The transcendence Levinas appointed as the terminus of a swerve away from the isolated mind—the lure that enabled consciousness to break through the transcendental immanence of phenomenological *Auslegung*—was *l'autre*, a dominant presence in Husserl's fifth Cartesian meditation. The *other* was the philosophical motif that drew Husserl to confront the problem of the "intersubjective constitution of the 'Objective'" (*Ideas I* §152, 365), and this confrontation was regarded as liberatory, because alert to the contingent situatedness of the ego in historical communities, by second-generation phenomenologists like Merleau-Ponty and Levinas. But the latter invested the other with supra-historical prerogatives, and its transcendence took on in his work a mystical-apocalyptic coloration (Moran 321–22). The relative *autre* (any other) was promoted to *L'Autre* (the non-personal other in general: language, culture, institutions) and further to *L'Autrui* (the absolute other person standing before me), thus gaining mythical traction. His resulting phenomenology of intersubjectivity and sociality, in principle compatible with Hegelian-phenomenological accounts of civil society, veered towards a hermetic phenomenology of the Other. This move away from orthodox phenomenology rested on a radical rejection of what he took to be ontology and on a non-heuristic (non-representational) conception of intentionality. The transcendental and properly hermeneutic underpinnings of phenomenology were abandoned in favor of a religious metaphysics of transcendence. The flight from ontology culminated in apocalyptic prophecy.

5

Maurice Merleau-Ponty's conversion to phenomenology is broadly determined by his lifelong association with Jean-Paul Sartre, who also turned to Husserl for inspiration to complete his *opus magnum, L'être et le néant. Essai d'ontologie phénoménologique* (1943). But whereas Sartre remained somewhat in the grip of a Cartesian rationalism that shaped both his solipsistic view of consciousness, cogito or *pour soi* and, more importantly, his respect for the transcendental stakes that characterize the Descartes-Kant-Heidegger tradition—note the phrase "phenomenological ontology" in the subtitle—Merleau Ponty pursued in *Phénoménologie de la perception* (1944) a path of radical detranscendentalization of phenomenology that was to determine the fate of this philosophical method. The French thinker turned to Husserl's late and unpublished work (the fifth and sixth of the *Cartesian Meditations, Crisis*, and *Ideas II*)—for the account of the *life-world* and the new attention to the body and intersubjectivity. Merleau-Ponty was resolved to resituate the mind in its body and the surrounding world—"Nous sommes pris dans le monde" (*Phénoménologie* 27)—to think through the insufficiently considered union of *res cogitans* and *res extensa*, and to that end he reactivated Gabriel Marcel's notion of the *être au monde* (being in the world) that was, like Heidegger's twin trope, invested with strong Catholic connotations. He adopted a tendentially naturalistic account of perception and thought that valorized, above anything else, the pre-reflexive and ante-predicative communion between mind and world characteristic of childhood: "Dans le silence de la conscience originaire, on voit apparaître non seulement ce que veulent dire les mots, mais encore ce que veulent dire les choses, le noyau de signification primaire autour duquel s'organisent les actes de dénomination et d'expression" (*Phénoménologie* 16). A religious-metaphysical nostalgia of origins underpins this flagrant naturalization of a language (a language of words, bodies, and things) that brings to mind Benjamin's parallel musings, but also the childhood nostalgia of Wordsworth, Dickens, or Proust. The whole project is moreover boosted by an unmediated conception of sensorial experience—the mind experiences the world "in one blow"—which marks it as radically anti-dialectical. Merleau-Ponty's overall aim was to uphold transcendence (the world, the others, my body) at the expense of the transcendental structures of consciousness, and this represents a radical inversion of Husserl's priorities. This inversion is particularly evident, as Moran sharply notes, in his misreading of the problem of intersubjectivity (*Introduction* 408). But the misreading extends to his determination to reverse too the transcendental chronology of the reduction: Merleau-Ponty aspires to make consciousness relapse to the natural standpoint that the *epoché* strategically disconnects. To call such aspiration *philosophy*, more particularly *phenomenology*, is absurd. Also preposterous is to claim that although phenomenology is the study of essences, phenomenology "is *also* a philosophy which puts essences back into existence [*replace les essences dans l'existence*], and does not expect to arrive at an understanding of man and the world from any starting point other than that of their 'facticity'" ("Preface" to *Phenomenology*, vi; "Avant-Propos," *Phénoménologie* 7; emphasis added). The elasticity of the term *phenomenology* reaches here a breaking point. Existential phenomenology remains phenomenology insofar as it doesn't give up the transcendental ambition: but as soon as facticity is hypostatized into a *transcendens pure and simple* (Heidegger) that stipulates its own mode of appearance, then we are left with the apotheosis of a de-transcendentalized ontology—typical of fetishistic empiricism, myth, metaphysics, and mysticism.

I have insisted on the denaturalization (adulteration) of the idea of phenomenology in Merleau-Ponty, for whom *the appearance (givenness, presentation) of things (to consciousness)* is less a matter of appearance than of things. To say the least. Indeed this denaturalization adopts the form of a detranscendentalizing re-naturalization (compensatory reduction to natural laws). This is also evident in his treatment of the problem of the body. The notion of embodiment emerges in Husserl's attempt to account for the problem of the mind-body duality within a phenomenological perspective inaugurated by the reduction or disconnection not only of the natural belief in the factual world but also of our first-level acts of reflection inside it. Since we are always-already enmeshed in a "concrete context of concernful dealings" (Zahavi, *Phenomenology* 78), the fate of original immersion in a practical lifeworld is obviously determined by our being not only a mind, but also a body. "Every world-experience is enabled by our embodiment": this is Zahavi's sharp summary of what Husserl has to say in the opening of section 18 of *Ideas II*, where "the experiencing subject-Body" emerges with full force for the first time: it will be fully fleshed out in the chapter titled "The Constitution of Psychic Reality Through the Body" (151–169). In *Ideas I* (1913) Husserl is less enthusiastic about the role of the body in knowledge. That the property of embodiment is something solely factored in from the natural standpoint, that is, from the view *des naïven Menschen* or "man in the street" (72)—the "consciousness of the embodied [*leibhaftigen*] self-presence of an individual object" which we (or Henry James) may upgrade to "perceiving consciousness"—is confirmed by Husserl's warning later that in the apperceptive interweavings with the corporeal, consciousness "forfeits nothing of its essential nature" (105). The notion that the mind is embodied but unbiased by the body loses some of its force in *Ideas II*, where scholars are agreed that Husserl makes room for "the legitimate theoretical version of the natural attitude" (Scanlon, "Foreword" to *Ideas II* xviii). This is, however, an overstatement. And, as Derrida demonstrates in a masterful exposé (*On Touching* 174–214), it is by virtue of a logic of overstatement and excess that Merleau-Ponty manufactured his phenomenology of the body (*corps*) or flesh (*chair*).

6

Once we have considered the most relevant conceptions of phenomenology, and examined their differences, let me briefly itemize the aspects of this layered historical-conceptual narrative that have lent themselves to misrepresentation in the hands of current early modern literary scholars:

1. Husserlian phenomenology is often wrongly taken to be a particularly focused way of describing *things themselves*, while it was actually (or attempted to be) a transcendental science of essences. This misreading, a running motif from Arendt to Kevin Curran and William West, is the object of section 13 "Doing Shakespeare: To the Things Themselves."
2. The scope and significance of the transcendental reduction in Husserlian phenomenology is often misinterpreted, the reduction revoked, and phenomenology returned to the very naturalistic standpoint the reduction sought in the first place to switch off. I examine this problem, with particular focus on the work of Bruce Smith and Sanford Budick, in section 11 "The Maladies of Abstinence: No More Cakes and Ale."
3. As a consequence of Merleau-Ponty's ascendancy in today's Renaissance studies, the role of the body and embodiment in phenomenology has been vastly overrated. This overestimation, whose impact is felt in the work of Bruce Smith, Jonathan Gil Harris, Julia Lupton and Simon Palfrey, among others, rests on a profound misunderstanding of the nature of phenomenology, no longer seen as a transcendental method.
4. The role of intersubjectivity in Husserl's phenomenology has been inflated beyond recognition. Husserl was a methodological solipsist, and his take on the experience of the other is far more discreet than is often represented. Hannah Arendt's impressionistic philosophical elaboration of political plurality, a major theoretical breakthrough for some Shakespeare scholars (Kottman, Lupton), can be seen as drawing on the overestimation of phenomenological intersubjectivity. Note however that neither the community Arendt discovers in Kant's *sensus communis* nor the interactive community these Shakespeare scholars favor is the plurality envisaged by Levinas, who warned that "to be *we* is not to 'jostle' one another or get together around a common task" (*Totality* 213).

To these nodes of theoretical friction, all of which spring from misconception or neglect of the Husserlian sources, we must add some genuine elements of Husserlian phenomenology that have been put into circulation among recent early modern literary scholars, either because they consciously strove to earn them or because they landed, unfiltered from the doxal tanks of the discipline, on their argument. These notions are *presence, presentation, immediacy, spontaneity*, and *fullfilment*. I consider some episodes of this appropriation of phenomenological categories in the final sections of my book. In what follows I offer some thoughts on the nature of the general appropriation of phenomenology in Shakespeare studies. By way of illustration, I will consider two specific cases—Paul Kottman's discreet approach to Hegelian phenomenology and Kevin Curran's misreading of Levinasian phenomenology. I will close this section with a reconsideration of some thoughts on Hannah Arendt's disputable status as a phenomenological philosopher.

7

Paul Kottman stands out among Shakespeare scholars on account of his familiarity with the Kant-Hegel philosophical tradition. He shares this distinctive position with Hugh Grady, Christopher Pye and Andrew Cutrofello. He can be credited with the attempt to provide a unified, coherent, account of Shakespeare's intellectual—philosophical—program. The ambition behind his work, occasionally informed by dialectical premises, is estimable and rare. Still, he hasn't exactly abstained from encouraging some of the phenomenological consolations that currently overburden the field of Shakespeare studies. True enough, his approach to phenomenology is particularly circumspect: he is aware, for instance, of the idealist pedigree of the term, and this is an uncommon form of awareness among scholars working in the field. Still, he may not be totally alert to what Heidegger called the "clear differentiation" between "[the Hegelian and Husserlian] phenomenologies" (*Hegel's* Phenomenology of Spirit 28). In the essay he contributed to the 2012 *Criticism* issue on "Shakespeare and Phenomenology," titled "No Greater Powers Than We Can Contradict," he begins by proclaiming Hegel the "inventor" of "phenomenology." This is not completely accurate (Kant preceded Hegel) but it contains much truth. Phenomenology shares, he argues, a "common procedure with tragedy, so much so that the dialectic employed in Hegel's *Phenomenology of Spirit* has been said to have a tragic structure" (445). In this same year of 2012 Kottman contributes an essay to an edited collection on *Political Theology and Early Modernity* where the same conception of "phenomenology" as a crisis-bound historical *experience* of recursively failed progress is used to explain Arendt's conception of revolutionary politics.[6] One can sense the tension between

---

6 Kottman argues that "Arendt offers something like a phenomenological retrospective of politics as the foundation of freedom [*constitutio libertatis*]" ("Novus ordum saeclorum" in *Political Theology*, 145) and implies that "the phenomenological form of On Revolution" is

Kottman's disinclination to adopt a steadfast phenomenological approach, and his need to respond to an invitation to contribute to a collection of articles on "Shakespeare and Phenomenology:" to bypass Merleau-Ponty and Husserl by harking back to Hegel is a wise bur risky move. Kottman compresses a triple equation into a single sentence: *phenomenology* is *Hegelian dialectic* is *tragic structure*. Not much can be objected to the second equation. Indeed, Kottman's determination to read the tragic structure of Shakespeare's plays via more or less effective analogies with dialectical experience is one of the signature characteristics of his critical work, and it commands respect. What is objectionable is to assimilate "phenomenology" to "Hegelian dialectic" without further explication or, rather, with a very crude explication:

> Very crudely stated, Hegel's phenomenological procedure involves, first, identifying and staging limit situations in which we find ourselves, pursuant to certain objective, worldly circumstances, and, second, showing how the experience of these limits invariably leads to particular kinds of crises, suffering, loss, or defeat in light of which the situation itself starts to look unlivable, unsustainable. (445)

The assumption is that Hegel follows a "phenomenological procedure" of *identification* and *staging* of liminal situations and of *showing* the resulting critical experience. Thus described, the procedure transpires as both heuristic or hermeneutical (identification) and demonstrative, performative or merely scenic (staging, showing). This is interesting as a suggestion, and indeed very apropos if your aim is, as is the case, to prove that Shakespeare contrived an alternative dramaturgy better fitted for the task of identifying, staging, and showing. But it does violence to Hegel's system insofar as it all too readily disambiguates the ambivalence of *phenomenology* as simultaneously the unfolding *experience* of *Geist* and the (its own) *examination* of it. Kottman reads Hegelian phenomenology as examination rather than experience. This is problematic because, insofar as it is the experience that is *ab origine* dialectical, the prioritization of the scientific moment of examination over experience inevitably relegates

---

"its movement from Rome to Machiavelli to Montesquieu to the American Revolution" (147). The phenomenological nature of Arendt's gesture could also be related, from Kottman's perspective, to a stress on experience that preempts formal-transcendental considerations. According to Derrida, "La synthèse a priori dont [Husserl] veut partir ne semble pas être celle d'un jugement et d'un concept formel, mais bien celle d'une expérience originairement concrète. Tout le développement futur de la phénoménologie est anticipé dans ce refus" (*Le problème de la genèse* 85).

dialectics to a marginal role in the retroactive process. Phenomenology, he concludes, "is the way in which we are brought to see the deep interrelation between that which had seemed, at least initially, indifferently related or even opposed: subjective experience and objective reality" (446). *We are brought to see*: phenomenology is not just an examen-based demonstration of a particular kind of liminal-critical experience, it is also, for Hegel, according to Kottman, a *monstration*, a showing, a show (a performance) of that experience. And since Shakespeare is, as common wisdom has it, the archdeviser of shows, then he may compete with Hegel on this count, whence the reasonableness, suggested by Kottman, of postulating an alternative phenomenology: "Shakespeare's phenomenology—or, what we typically call his dramaturgy—[which] signals a breakdown of the coincidence of dialectics with the tragic" (446). Kottman's position is open to the same criticism that Joan Copjek levelled against historicism:

> Historicism is faulted not because it is, in fact, not possible to recreate historical experience (that is, again, a psychologistic objection), but because this construction operates with the belief that it is *experience* that must be recreated, that the truthful and logical statements we make about a historical period are empirical generalizations about the ways in which people thought.
> Read 4

And hers is, of course, a psychoanalytical objection, hatched in the French hinterland of German idealism, a place where subjects think equivocally—if not pathologically—solely by virtue of their being *subjects*. Let me recall that four years before Kottman defended this concordance or "deep interrelation" between "subjective experience" and "objective reality," he had spoken in *A Politics of the Scene* (2008) of "the Shakespearean ontology" (5). Are *ontology* and *phenomenology*, for Kottman, the same thing? Whereas Hegel's "phenomenological procedure" aims to show that the tragic predicament expresses a conflict within the ethical order (the realm of the objective) that can be ultimately settled by reconciling subjective freedom with it, Shakespeare devises a "nondialectical conception of tragedy" that reveals an irreparable "split between the drama of human freedom and the rational, inheritable structure of our lives together" (450). Without reconciliation, Shakespearean dramaturgy exhibits experiences of subjective exorbitance characterized by the internalization of necessity (453). This is a fascinating thesis, and the instrumental deployment of a pre-Husserlian "phenomenology" (Hegel's) as a way to assess the singularity of Shakespearean tragedy is no doubt a provocative and original hermeneutic move. Still, the argument is vitiated by an inconsistency that remains *phenomenological* in the Husserlian sense, and the flaw becomes visible every time the term *dialectic* is used. I will leave aside the fact that Kottman's conception of Hegelian dialectic as invariably committed to the healing of diremption is intolerably flat and uncritical (447–48), and his view of Hegel's conception of tragedy is tendentiously simplified. I will focus rather on a plausible contradiction: Hegelian dialectic *is* phenomenology—Kottman's opening tacit presupposition—only if we assume the latter to be the effective experience of *Geist*. Because, for Hegel (and in my opinion for Shakespeare too) experience is originally configured in a dialectical manner. Since Kottman assumes instead that phenomenology is the examination (and demonstrative revelation) of experience, he finds no contradiction in moving on to describe Shakespeare's "nondialectical conception of tragedy" as a *phenomenology*—"Shakespeare's phenomenology" (446), "a Shakespearean phenomenology if you like" (452). The question immediately arises: what is a *nondialectical phenomenology*? Well, it is certainly not Hegel's, and if it exists it must resemble Husserl's and Merleau-Ponty's. It must be characterized by a distaste for mediation, a passion for immediacy, a knack for spontaneity, and a faith in the impromptu production of explosive transcendent (corporal, mystical, erotic) meaning beyond the incitement and reach "of the rational structures of our lives together" (450), including, of course, natural language. I am obviously delineating, following Kottman's cue, the romantic phenomenology of the *infinitely free subjective will* that is the target of Hegel's "Introduction" to his *Outlines of the Philosophy of Right*. The problem is that this phenomenology is less Shakespeare's than Kottman's, as the scholar is at pains to demonstrate that Romeo's and Juliet's aims are not dialectical, i.e. not mediated by the objective structures of the reality that has produced and inexorably determined them. Kottman cites Adorno's description of *Romeo and Juliet* to prove that the German philosopher has correctly grasped the uniqueness of Shakespeare's phenomenology, one where the tragic conflict is less "*within* the social world that is brought to light by the lovers' actions" than "*between* the social world and the concerns of individuals, a rift between worldly necessity and individual desires" (452). But if we read the Adorno passage

> Without the longing for a situation in which love would no longer be mutilated and condemned by patriarchal or any other powers, the presence of the two lost in one another would not have the sweetness—the wordless, imageless utopia—mover which, to this day, the centuries have been powerless.
>
> *Aesthetic Theory* 247

we realize that what is being stressed is precisely the *dialectical* dependence of the "presence" of the lovers and the "imageless utopia [*bilderlose Utopia*]" they evoke upon their "longing for a situation [*die Sehnsucht nach einem Zustand*]" untouched by the "patriarchal or any other powers" (*Ästhetische Theorie* 367). Since the latter (the longing) is inconceivable without the patriarchal power that brings it reactively into existence, the former (the presence and the utopia of the lovers) is by causal extension unthinkable without this regime, circumstance, or situation (*Zustand*). In other words, the presence and utopia of the lovers is dialectically beholden to their objective social world. Since there is, in sum, no outside to the objective social world, no exteriority to it, therefore no (external) interiority can be stipulated *between* itself (the subjective inside) and the outself (the objective outside). Everything happens *within* the boundaries of the social world, just as everything (meaningful) occurs within the limits of language. It takes of course an extended meaning of *Sittlichkeit*—ready to include, beyond institutions (Foucault), also ideologies (Althusser, Adorno, Žižek) and natural languages (Lacan), or all three at once (Derrida)—to authorize this analogy. Kottman's nondialectical phenomenology is, like Merleau-Ponty's—and not unlike Simon Palfrey's—a mystique of erotic-corporal transcendence, with volcanos of preverbal and antepredicative meaning exploding immediately, spontaneously, freely, in the evental interstices of our instrumental, prosaic, and taxonomized world. This is very mindblowing, groovy, even psychedelic, but is certainly not Shakespeare's phenomenology, not Shakespeare's experience, not Shakespeare's *phenomenology of experience*, which is nothing if not dialectical—nothing if not comprised in that "hybrid chain [*chaîne bâtarde*] which is made of fate and inertia, throws of the dice and astonishment, false successes and missed encounters, [...] which makes up the usual script [*le texte courant*] of a human life" (Lacan, *Écrits* 130; *Écrits I*, 159). Juliet and Romeo, the characters examined by Kottman in his essay, are certainly not partisans of an undialectical eros. Kottman suggests that their subjective love emerges in the objective social world and becomes readily opposed to it, thus creating a split *between* the subjective and the objective. This means it doesn't emerge *in opposition to* the objective world, *within* the preestablished coordinates of *Sittlichkeit*. But this undialectical view overlooks not only the socially assimilated quality of their erotic action—made of binding speech acts, legal compromises, and a rare profusion of conventional poetic diction—but also the deeply responsive and antagonistic nature of their language at its most original: their love is "boundless as the sea" (*Romeo and Juliet* 2.1.175) and occurs beyond titles, names (2.1.80–89) and "stony limits" (2.1.109). To sum up, their love—as it appears to us, as it phenomenologically unfolds before us—is not something that can pre-exist these *bounds, bonds, walls*, *names* and *limits*—just like "the will is not something complete and universal prior to its determining itself and prior to its superseding and idealizing this determination" (Hegel, *Outlines* 32)—but rather something that is asserted in defiance of them and therefore mediated by its own assertion: *their love is the determining and self-mediating assertion of such defiance*.[7] Their love is not their making love or having sex. Anybody can do that, today or in medieval Verona, and any couple can claim that their fusion (sexual, emotional) is wondrously unlike anyone else's, gloriously incompatible with the prose of the world—and be of course glaringly mistaken. The singularity of Romeo's and Juliet's love is the verbal articulation of their challenge to the objective repressive social world that has taught them the rudiments—and in their specific case, much more than the rudiments—of verbal articulation. It is therefore a *dialectical event* in a horizon of *dialectical experience*. So much for Kottman's case. I have singled it out as a brilliant attempt to enforce the hermeneutic rules of Hegelian phenomenology to the reading of Shakespearean tragedy that is ultimately defeated by the sweeping effect of post-Hegelian phenomenological assumptions of nondialectical immediacy. Only to prove that *phenomenology*, however productively applied to the reading of Renaissance playscripts, portends a very tricky rubric.

8

Let me now consider a different kind of misreading. In this case, my aim is to expose the risks of mechanically projecting the work of second-generation phenomenological thinkers like Emmanuel Levinas to Shakespearean interpretation. My case study is Kevin Curran's essay "Hospitality: Managing Otherness in the Sonnets and The Merchant of Venice," included in his book *Shakespeare's Legal Ecologies* (2017). With the exception of Deleuze, all of this book's presiding geniuses are *phenomenological* thinkers. The book's global thesis is that "Shakespeare's ethics of exteriority accrue from legally framed scenes of collective thought, interpersonal experience, and material embeddedness" (20). Predictably, the phenomenological motifs of inter-personality and embodiment recur in a creative recombination of more or less figurative lexemes. We hear a great deal about "interpersonal exchange" (3), "representational environments" (4), "Shakespeare's distinctly communitarian vision"

---

7 Since *determinacy* implies the willing or desire of "something" (Hegel, *Outlines* 30–34), and insofar as something is solely on offer in the social world outside the self, self-determinacy involves a mode of dialectical bondage to this inherited social and cultural world.

(4), "collectivity, otherness, and the external life of the senses" (4), "nonindividual selfhood" (11), "interconnectedness" (12), "self-as-ecology" (13), "distributed selfhood" (15), "community-making acts" (20). All of these ideologemes are marshalled by combinatory rules gleaned from the doctrinal archive of phenomenology—the works of Arendt, Merleau-Ponty, Ricoeur, object-oriented materialism, and Levinas. Bruce Smith's "relational way of knowing" ("Premodern" 325) is also duly acknowledged by a scholar very much aware of the tradition of though he works in—a neo-phenomenological trend that includes Julia Lupton, James Kearney, William West, and Paul Kottman.

What makes Curran's essay on Sonnets 34, 49, 87, and *The Merchant of Venice* stand out from the rest in his book is its strong reliance on Levinasian philosophy. This is odd, for the figurative lexemes I singled out above are hardly consonant with the very dubious Levinasian "phenomenology of sociality" (Moran 347). Curran argues that these four Shakespeare texts put forward a conception of hospitality as "radical selflessness" (51) that inasmuch as it troubles "liberal notions of individual agency and self-authorship" (50) demands a theoretical framework that is radically at variance with standard ontological accounts of selfhood. This is the case, he believes, of Levinas' "ethics of otherness" (55). What makes this ethics so appealing to a neo-phenomenological scholar like Curran is of course the "immédiateté" (Levinas, "Paix et Proximité" 345) of the unprincipled principle of responsibility that organizes the self-Other face-to-face relation. My brief gloss invites trouble, I am aware, but the trouble is not of my own making. What first catches our eye is the uncritical correlation between the liberal individual and the ontological self of the Western philosophical traditions. Curran's intermittent paraphrase of Levinas' philosophical intentions is beset by the constant tendency to reduce, first, the ontological Being to an ontological self, and, next, this ontological self to the possessive-individualist liberal self. Consider the following:

> In the broadest sense, Levinas's philosophy can be understood as an attempt to formulate a non-ontological account of Being. That is to say, an account of Being which is open and social rather than bounded and inward-looking. His most influential books [...] present a radical ethics of selfhood founded on the idea that subjectivity is relational, a property not of hermetic cognitive experience but of the self's encounter with, extension toward, and welcoming of an absolute other. Selfhood, to put it another way, is not a form of enclosed dwelling or sealed-off at-homeness, as Heidegger envisioned it, but a state of homelessness, a form of hospitality so complete that it calls into question what, if anything, is properly mine. (56–57)

The first error here is to suppose that in order to formulate a non-ontological account of Being, Levinas turns the Being of the philosophical tradition—which for the Lithuanian thinker is a blending of the Greek τὸ ὄν and Heidegger's *Sein*—into a *social* being. In the opening sections of *Totalité et infini*, Levinas distinguishes most clearly between "l'être" (sometimes capitalized as "l'Être") and personal "êtres" or "étants." The former is the Greek notion of Being, revitalized by Heidegger, which Levinas trustingly implements in one of the closing sections of the book, titled "L'être est extériorité"; the latter is the human individual or agent. When Levinas speaks of the Being of the ontological tradition he purports to dismantle he refers to the Being that Heidegger trilingually displays in *Being and Time* §1: "'Being' is the most 'universal' concept: τὸ ὄν ἐστὶ καθόλου μάλιστα πάντων. Illud quod primo cadit sub apprehension, est ens, cuius intellectus includitur in omnibus, quaecumque quis apprehendit" (2). The self that Curran wrongly scents behind that Being is what Heidegger calls *Dasein* and Levinas designates through a variety of phrases—*étant particulier, conscience, être particulier, être désirant, être séparé, être homme*, and *moi*. We could even tentatively include in this list "le Même," although Levinas makes it clear that "le Même et l'Autre" are but logical determinations of Being (*Totalité* 29). Curran's domestication of Being into your next-door neighbor waiting at the front door with a bottle of red wine reminds me of William West's attempt to lend a face to Hegelian *Geist* ("Afterword" 252). Properly speaking, not even Levinas' face owns a face, as it "escapes phenomenality altogether" (Moran 347). It is one thing to desacralize the solemnity of Continental thought: there is nothing wrong with that. It is another to turn its informing conceptual drama into a Netflix sitcom—or an Updike romance, or a Franzen potboiler. That is simply creepy. In other words, *Autrui* is no *relative* other (*Totalité* 211), even if our relatives sometimes appear to come directly from "th'other place" (*Hamlet* 4.3.34). Nothing in Curran's, Lupton's or Kottman's readings of Shakespeare prepares us for the "être infiniment distante" (*Totalité* 39) of the *absolute* Other. The alterity they identify is always a domesticated other—humanized, assimilated into the community, rendered guest in processes of controlled hospitality. Almost nothing in Shakespeare foreshadows Levinas' mode of sublime alterity—Shylock knocking at your door in pursuance of his due is almost there—and very few texts in English literature do—maybe Milton, Blake, Dickinson, E. Brontë, Melville, Geoffrey Hill. This doesn't mean, however, that personal opacity, subjective refractoriness to communal integration and extreme anti-social individuality are uncommon in Shakespeare. On the contrary, they abound. But radical Shakespearean individuals are not the survivors of an encounter with transcendent infinity, nor do they stand—more or less erect—for it.[8]

Let us assume *ex hypothesi* that Levinasian Being is both *Dasein*, the central character in *Sein und Zeit*, and the Moi, the reluctant leading figure in *Totalité et Infini*. The second error in Curran's passage is to pit Levinas' supposedly world-open and other-welcoming self against a Heidegger's allegedly "bounded and inward looking" self. Both suppositions are wrong. First, nothing in Heidegger's conception of *Dasein* is reminiscent of selfhood conceived as "a form of enclosed dwelling or sealed-off at-homeness." *Dasein*'s primary existential mode is that of *Geworfenheit*, the *thrownness* of being on its *there*, the facticity of its *being* delivered over (*Being and Time* §29, 132–133)—more Oliver Twist than Emma. Curran's copy of *Being and Time* must have been expurgated by Puritan censors and cut down to a fourth of its original size. The same must have happened with his copy of *Totalité et Infini*, for he is unmindful of section 2, "Rupture de la totalité," where Levinas conspicuously states that the radical and absolute violence posed by alterity can only be measured against the prior existence of an *also* absolute self-identical self:

> Être moi, c'est, par-delà toute individuation qu'on peut tenir d'un système de références, avoir l'identité comme contenu. Le moi, ce n'est pas un être qui reste toujours le même, mais l'être dont l'exister consiste à s'identifier, à retrouver son identité à travers tout ce qui lui arrive. Il est l'identité par excellence, l'œuvre originelle de l'identification. Le Moi est identique jusque dans ses altérations. Il se les représente et les pense. L'identité universelle où l'hétérogène peut être embrassé, a l'ossature d'un sujet, de la première personne. Pensée universelle, est un "je pensé."
> *Totalité* 25

And, in a typically Heideggerian gesture of existentialist-phenomenological analysis of the facticity of *Dasein*, Levinas moves on to itemize some modes or moments of Moi's existence: "séjourner," "*s'identifier* en y existent *chez soi*" (26) and "le corps, la maison, le travail, la possession, l'économie" (27). You get the idea: this list doesn't exactly spell a ravished ecology of homelessness. In the subsections of the part of his book titled "Intériorité et économie," under the headings "La Demeure," "L'habitation," "La Maison et la possession" and "Possession et travail," Levinas elucidates the compatibility between the

---

8 I believe Harold Bloom overestimates the heroic, sublime grandeur of characters like King Lear. Gloucester is much more a figure of pathetic sublimity than the King. The only true radical Others that I can discern in the Shakespeare canon are Julius Caesar and Coriolanus.

personal experience of a "jouissance extatique et immédiate" and the personal possession of goods, especially a house that is *first* described as "hospitalière à son propriétaire" (169). I am not forcing the Levinasian Moi into "a form of enclosed dwelling or sealed-off at-homeness" (Curran 57) in order to conjure something like a Trollope vicar, or a parson in Eliot's *Scenes of Clerical Life*, or even a comic-strip Lederhosen Heidegger sitting by the fireplace in his Black Forest hut. I am merely transcribing what Levinas says about the interior separateness of the Moi. To be sure, the Moi is also confronted by exteriority, by the infinity of an absolute Other or Autrui, but nothing in Levinas' narrative conveys the sense of radical self-alienation, genuine personal risk, and dispossession that Curran, possibly influenced by Derrida's existentialist (Bataillean) inflection of Levinas' thought, presumes.[9] Levinas' philosophy is, by his own account, a philosophy of subjectivity, and his most important book, *Totalité et infini* is described—let us not forget this—as a "défense de la subjectivité" (*Totalité* 11). This subjectivity is, to be sure, informed by a prior (pre-originary) constitutive experience of otherness—"car l'infini aura été pré-originairement accueilli" (Derrida, *Adieu* 51)—but so are all philosophies of subjectivity that in our Western culture deserve the name—those of Descartes, Kant, Hegel, or Sartre. Otherness in them (infinity, imagination, difference, nothingness) may lack a human face, but it preempts (predetermines, prepossesses) the scene of inception of a self-consciousness that is finite and empty (Kant) or infinitely negative (Hegel) or infinitely un-empty (Descartes) or all of these determinations at once (Sartre), enjoying "equiprimordiality" with the sameness of the self.[10] Levinas speaks of an "ethical relation" that "puts the I into question," that the "facing position" is like "a moral summons" (196), but there is no radical calling into question, as Curran assumes, of what is "properly mine" (*Shakespeare's Legal* 57). On the contrary, the presence of the radical Other "does not limit the freedom of the same" but rather calls it to responsibility, and this way "it founds it and justifies it" (Levinas, *Totality* 197). The other *threatens* the self, no doubt, but insofar as the self is already constituted by the experience of otherness, this threat can only materialize as the destruction of the self's separateness.[11]

---

9   For Derrida's rather profuse elaboration of Levinas' motif of the "hétérogéneité radicale de l'Autre" (*Totalité* 25), see *Adieu*, 95.
10 See Dieter Henrich, *The Unity of Reason*, 48–54. For the Kantian idea that self-consciousness is empty and finite, see 27–40.
11 This prior constitution of the self through otherness is not, for Levinas, a transcendental constitution, which would be necessarily contaminated, he believes, by objective representation. It is rather a sort of mystical, Benjaminian, constitution via vestigial images or anticipatory traces: I am, and in being I anticipate the other and am anticipated by

But if the abrogation of personal separateness materializes in the form of interpersonal "conversation," how can we speak of dispossession and "homelessness"?[12] Already in Heidegger, but mostly in the Marxian tradition of philosophy of language, conversation is little more than *Gerede*, an apotheosis of ideological at-homeness. And one of Shakespeare's most distinct lessons concerns the *unlikelihood of genuine dialogue*. The fact that my newly born ethical liberty doesn't allow me to possess the face of the Other—"le visage se refuse à la possession, à mes pouvoirs" (*Totalité* 214)—doesn't necessarily imply that I lose my possession in turn (as the cost for the gain of such liberty). It is not at all clear that the "accueil sans question" (Derrida, *De l'hospitalité* 31) leaves the host dispossessed, and very unclear that "la souveraineté du soi sur le chez soi" (53) is effectively threatened in Levinas' phenomenology of the self. Levinas speaks of a Moi that conserves and expresses itself in its confrontation with the Other (*Totalité* 340–41). The Other is not described, as in Hegel, as the negation of the Self: the relation between both (*Même-Autre*) is non-allergic, and therefore not mutually dispossessing (342). Moreover, Curran overlooks the *dialectical* dimension of Heidegger's phenomenological-existential outline of the shift from 1) an *Un-Zuhause-sein* (not-being-at-home) that is at one with being-in-the-world to 2) the momentary self-assurance of *Zuhause-sein* (being-at-home), followed by 3) the existential mode of not-being-at-home that is now informed by the sublated experience of "being-in" (*Being and Time* §40, 182–183). He also neglects the importance of "everyday lostness [*alltagliche Verlorenheit*]" (183) in Heiedegger's account of *Dasein*, a motif of *extraterritoriality* (*Heimatlosigkeit*) and *uncanniness* (*Unheimlichkeit*) that reappears as an organizing theme in his exegeses of Hölderlin's poetry. Curran's schematic and perfunctory reduction of Levinas' central theses is never properly applied to either the selected sonnets or *The Merchant of Venice*. Levinas' *Autrui* is never present in Shakespeare's world, which is a Christianized domain where ethical demands have been policed and subdued, adapted to civil and increasingly secular conditions of existence. I doubt that Curran and other scholars who turn to Levinas for trendy terminology and a couple of resounding moral claims are actually ready to assume the trail of allegorical, scriptural, and mythical implications that are built into the latter's micro-social, vaguely tribal, and deeply mythological ecology of the family-bound face-to-face.[13] There is no

---

the other; so when I confront the other, I merely experience a direct abolition of my separateness.

12 Although Levinas stresses the hierarchical relation that rules all conversations, he assumes that understanding occurs (*Totalité* 103–104).

13 See Moran's severe judgement on the philosophical incapacity that Levinas shows in his discussion of the face-to-face, "hardly a philosophy of the face at all" (350).

clean exteriority in Levinas, but a limited field-force stretching around an asphyxiating *Familenroman* made of one transcendent God and may God-fearing and discombulated selves.

Curran's readings of these sonnets and of *The Merchant of Venice* fails to produce convincing textual evidence and exegetic perspicuity. He cannot demonstrate that the sonnets are not self-centered texts about an abyssal cogito, likely to be analyzed in Cartesian-Lacanian ways. And he doesn't prove that radical hospitality in *Merchant* is a motif we relate to Shylock, for he is actually presented by Shakespeare as an agent who pragmatically enforces—through an exorbitant *parodic performance*—the normative civil laws of Venice. The extreme munificence of hospitality is Antonio's, and Curran is at pains to reconcile the two positions, unable to save the Jew from the comedic derision, aspersion, and abjection that he is exposed to. But there are other shaky moments in his argument which reveal Curran's dubious grasp of Levinas' work. For instance, when he examines the question of the limits of personhood in the sonnets, he could have supplemented his claims with the idea, developed in *Totality and Infinity*, that thanks to the time of generations, an ego surpasses itself through its children—"I do not have my child. I am my child" (177). He also fails to establish the evident parallel between Athens and Venice—"à Athens, l'étranger avait des droits. Il se voyait reconnaître le droit d'avoir accès aux tribunaux" (*Totalité* 25)—and the related analogy between the apologies of Socrates and Shylock. An additional problem is Curran's very limited grasp of the Derrida-Levinas dialogue, whose focus on hospitality is not restricted to the former's explicit essay on that topic. Curran resorts exclusively to this essay and cites neither his early and very important essay on Levinas, included in *L'écriture et la différence*, nor, perhaps more apropos because it also thematizes hospitality, *Adieu à Emmanuel Levinas*.

Still, the most alarming problem in this instrumentalization of Levinasian thought for Shakespearean exegesis rests on a misunderstanding—a scholastic simplification—of the nature and significance of the French philosopher's work. In the opening sections of *Totalité et Infini*, Levinas makes it very clear that for self-identity to emerge as an ontological coordinate, for the Moi to constitute itself, there must already exist a range of alterities ready to be reassimilated into it (26–27). Everything Curran, Lupton and other scholars take to be the radical other is actually not the radical *Autre* (or *Autrui*) that Levinas elsewhere discusses, but rather the supplementary alterity that exists solely to confirm selfhood. The Shakespeare scholar is thinking of a *relative other*, gentrified, domesticated, and cut down to Hegelian civil-social proportions, and yet capable of irrationally sublimating itself to the trans-social height of an infinite demand: it's like children playing doctors and nurses when suddenly one of them turns into a really wounded and bleeding adult, crying desperately for help. This is not exactly what Levinas envisages as the social space.[14] His prophetic *communitas* is no space at all. Since the "epiphany" of the Other's face "breaks with the world that can be common to us [*qui peut nous être commun*]" (*Totality* 194; *Totalité* 211), the "community of genus" can only exist to "nullify alterity" (194). Levinas obviously found it inadequate to retain certain phenomenological parameters to characterize sociality: we are no longer dealing with configurations of corporeal agents spontaneously engaging in respectful, recognitive and recreative interactions with the capacity to either objectify the Spirit or to cradle the dove of a better communal future. This social vision is a phenomenological redescription of Hegel's civil society, and Levinas' violates it through constant appeals to the passionate overflowing (*débordement*) of an ethical *surplus* (Hayat 132–133): he delineates an interruptive field of violent bilateral rapports, with each self destined to the ultimately non-relational transcendence of its own other-spurred Infinity. This fact gets shrouded, in his work, in a vapid enveloping argument about language as the field of "social" (hierarchical, master-pupil, Other-self) relationality secreted by the Other's visage (*Totalité* 94–104; 224–232). There follows an addressee-oriented conception of language that betrays the narrow trust on the situational positivity of *parole* that Saussure (and modern linguistics) sought to overpass. The resulting moral epistemology, whose central motto is "vivre est une sincérité" (*De l'existance à l'existant* 67), would have met the derisive opposition of Hamlet, Rosalind, Portia, and Edgar. If life is a sincerity that unfolds in the other-revealing medium of language, what is the point of using language in theatrical fiction to denounce life experienced as theatrical fiction, the point of using a lie to denounce the lie of life? Life, in Shakespeare, is always the doing and undoing of human beings by verbal equivocations that no card can chart, predict, or police. And no Other with a face impose on. Perhaps a big Other. But that is another story, one whose authors (Marx, Lacan, Žižek) alone can tell in profoundly anti-phenomenological terms.

The phenomenological construal of the social space is by contrast characterized by recognitive relationality, by a mutuality that draws part of its strength from negativity (from *not* being the other, while acknowledging her presence).

---

14   It is very unclear what exactly Levinas thinks of the social space. At one point, in *Totalité et Infini*, he suggests that all social relations derive from "la presentation de l'Autre au Même," without representative intermediary. And adds, quite significantly, that "L'essence de la société échappe, si on la pose semblable au genre qui unit les individus semblables" (235). So what he understands for society is a rhapsodic field of isolated tensions and unrelated (same-to-other, face-to-face) intensities.

But Levinas rejects negativity (*Totalité* 32–33), vaguely identified with Hegelian dialectic and Saussurean structuralism, as much as he rejected the Same-based ontological totality, which he identified with war, and implicitly with Heidegger. Levinas thinks at the border where phenomenology subsides, and theology opens. He was obviously mindful of Husserl's inviting nod: "Our immediate aim concerns not theology but phenomenology, however important the bearing of the latter on the former may indirectly be" (Husserl, *Ideas I* 99). Levinas feels that phenomenology is insufficient—insufficiently open to the transcendence he craves—and leaves it behind: "la phénoménologie est une méthode philosophique, mais la phénoménologie—compréhension de par la mise en lumière—ne constitue pas l'événement ultime de l'être lui-même"(13). According to Derrida, because Levinas "had to appeal to phenomenological self-evidences against phenomenology" (*Writing* 141), Husserl's philosophical method became for him a useless tool when it came to matters of ethics, language and justice. In point of fact, no phenomenology, not even a reprogrammed phenomenology, can do in the face of the exigency—the infinite demand—stipulated by Levinas.[15]

Since its inception, phenomenology has been paradoxically beyond itself, outsmarted by internal deviations, developments, recusations, overcomings, reductions, abrogations, interruptions; and not only in Heidegger, Merleau-Ponty, Sartre or Levinas, but also in the unfolding work of Husserl himself. At a certain point, however, the internal recusation of phenomenology takes a rather suicidal turn—whether toward the over-presence of positive transcendence or into the abyss of ironic immanence. Whereas Merleau-Ponty and Levinas represent the first kind—the metaphysical kind—of suicide, Adorno and Derrida epitomize the critical liquidation of phenomenology from within.[16] With the latter, the necessary distance from the philosophical vocabularies is finally reached. Their critique of phenomenology is that of liberal ironists (the late Adorno would despise this category, but it matches many attitudes of his early self) questioning the validity of a terminal vocabulary that has reified the presences to which it presumably gives immediate access. They are also able to identify the wrongness of the phenomenological claim, first made by Husserl, to have initiated a radically new method or science, shorn of metaphysical presuppositions. In fact, as Derrida soon pointed out, it is the very presupposition

---

15 According to Derrida, "aucune phénoménologie ne peut donc rendre compte de l'éthique, de la parole et de la justice" (*L'écriture* 157).

16 For a discussion of the role that the novel conception of *ethical necessity* plays in phenomenology's *interruption* of itself, see Derrida, *Adieu*, 94–97. Derrida speaks of an "*épokhé* de la phénoménologie elle-même" (95).

of presence that makes it prevent phenomenology from enduring with its growing penchant for a *relative other*.[17]

Theoretical interest in the other in Shakespeare studies is of course not exactly new. Initially post-colonial, this interest is now—in our post-theoretical now—window-dressed in Levinas' moral-eschatological concepts. The outcome of this development is the gradual transformation of Arden Forest into the desert plains of Jericho, and of Shakespearean textuality into belated Scripture—protruding rather awkwardly out from a horizon of Greek political philosophy. The citizen-saint championed by Lupton has become the saint (Derrida, *Adieu* 14): "Dans sa position éthique, le moi est distinct et du citoyen issu de la Cité, et de l'individu qui précède dans son égoïsme naturel tout ordre" (Levinas, "La souffrance inutile" 338). What goes missing in this deeply unalert espousal of Levinasian terminology is of course the relational immanence of the *transcendental*, which has been rapidly traded for prophetic *transcendence*, but also the dialectical correction implicit in two parallel statements by Hegel and Derrida: "the identity of identity and non-identity [*die Identität von Identität und Nichtidentität*]" (*Science of Logic* 51) and "une identité de l'identité et l'altérité" (*Le problème de la genèse* 8). This notion, which organizes Adorno's indefatigable responses to Hegel, portends that for phenomenology to unfold it is necessary to work through the negativity and the sublation of difference. Only this way can alterity become a moral asset in civil society. The operation, of course, never attains to pure reconciliation—to the reconciliation (*Versöhnung*) that the Hegelian dialectic serves (Adorno, *Negative* 18)—and a trail of unintegrated alterity and unincorporated particularity (the leaks and remains of otherness) is always bound to follow. Here Adorno and Derrida also concur, even if they construe this (material) residual alterity in different ways.

9

I want to close this section with a consideration of Hannah Arendt's role in the rise and consolidation of neo-phenomenological approaches to Shakespeare. Her importance is most keenly felt in the work of Paul Kottman and Julia Lupton. In both cases, however, a great deal of confusion burdens the assessment of the genuinely "phenomenological" standing of her work. In *A Politics of the Scene*

---

17 Derrida: "Que les thèmes de la non-présence (temporalisation et altérité) soient contradictoires avec ce qui fait de la phénoménologie une métaphysique de la présence, la travaillent sans cesse, cela nous parait n'ailleurs incontestable et nous y insistons ailleurs" (*L'écriture* 178).

(2008), Kottman describes Arendt's approach to political philosophy—the fact that she rejected this category is irrelevant here—as framed within an "antimetaphysical ontology," an "embodied, contextual, relational ontology" (16), i.e. an ontology of plurality. By arguing that Hobbes discontinues the tradition that saw in the "phenomenological perception of human interaction [...] the theoretical starting point for political philosophy" (60), Kottman implies that Arendt's attempt to recontinue this tradition by reconnecting with Aristotle involves a redeployment of the *phenomenological perception*. In *Thinking with Shakespeare* (2011), a book much indebted to Kottman, Julia Lupton explains that the subtitle, "Essays on Politics and Life," is "executed in partial homage to Arendt," and argues that she takes "life as that which names the existential and phenomenological interests of the plays" (8). Lupton states she will follow "those strong phenomenological elements in Arendt's thought that emphasize the polis as a recurrent possibility for human action" (11), a claim she later rephrases as a resolve to follow "the existential and phenomenological redistricting projects modeled by Arendt" (16). In conclusion, Arendt's example moves Lupton to have recourse to "phenomenological interests," "phenomenological elements," and "phenomenological projects." What exactly these are we don't know. We are told, instead, that the neglected strains in social and political theory that these interests, elements, and projects, open a new window to are those of hospitality, consent, and virtue. The adjective "phenomenological" is here but an echo, a word as resoundingly empty as "ontological" in Kottman's "Introduction" to *A Politics of the Scene*. Lupton is probably aware that the term is technical and specific enough to demand elucidation. Citing Arendt and Kottman is not enough, and she widens the arc of reference to Bruce Smith's *Phenomenal Shakespeare*, to the work of Gail Kern Paster, because the latter "calls her work on Renaissance humoral psychology 'historical phenomenology'" (29 note 5), and finally, in the last note of the "Introduction," we read not only that "there is a phenomenological dimension in Derrida's late work on animals, *The Animal Therefore I Am*"—a bizarre characterization, since the phenomenological dimension runs through Derrida's whole production, and because *The Animal Therefore I Am* is not a work *on animals*, but a critical, tendentially deconstructive, analysis of philosophical texts dealing with the animal-human division—but also the following invitation: "On Shakespeare and phenomenology, see Witmore, *Shakespearean Metaphysics*" (23 note 43). This is enigmatic, for although Witmore's book portends to disclose "a new and different kind of materialism, one that is grounded in bodies but emphatic in asserting the reality of their dynamic interrelations" (*Shakespearean Metaphysics* 2), a goal Lupton surely finds congenial, his book contains no single reference to Husserl, Heidegger, Levinas or Merleau-Ponty, and no mention of the term "phenomenology." But, again, who's counting: one basic rule of this reprogrammed phenomenology is that you do it without noticing it, without proclaiming it, without quoting texts, without even thinking. It is as undeliberate and simple as breathing. It is phenomenal. But Lupton is a systematic and careful scholar. On pages 14–15 something of a clarification is offered. Like Kottman, she purports to "read Arendt" not only as "an existentialist," but also as "a phenomenologist" (14). She explains:

> By *phenomenology* I mean inquiry into the conditions of human appearing; phenomenology concerns not "thing in themselves" (*noumena*) but rather how things take shape in consciousness (*phenomena*). Phenomenology always concerns the subject as a point of reference, but often within an arena constituted by the attentive presence of other people as well as the draw of things. Arendt's phenomenology addresses what Dermot Moran identifies as "'*die Öffentlichkeit*' (publicity, publicness), that is the 'public space' (*der öffentliche Raum*), the public realm, *res publica*, the 'space of appearances.'" (15)

Very briefly, "the conditions of human appearing" is an equivocal phrase, for "appearing" is *always* "human" insofar as—in the Kantian sense whereby the mind constitutes phenomenal appearance—it is necessarily an appearing *to* humans. Lupton should have spoken of the conditions of the appearance of things (including objects, animals, and other humans) to humans. But this is not what she has in mind. She is thinking, exclusively, of the appearing of humans to humans, following Kottman's invitation to escape, with Arendt and Shakespeare, from the Hobbesian closure or "circumscription of what can appear and what cannot appear in the light of day," from a "field of visibility"—we could also call it, with Rancière, a *distribution of the sensible*—that "is *not a fully human sphere* of appearance" (*A Politics* 84–86). To be sure, Kottman, following Arendt, investigates "the conditions of human appearing," understood as the co-appearing of humans in a shared political space of action. And since Arendt can be loosely called a phenomenologist, and Kottman is, on Lupton's account, a phenomenology-oriented scholar, then it follows that "by phenomenology" she means "inquiry into the conditions of human appearing."[18] In the

---

18 In her "Response" to Kottman's piece on *Romeo and Juliet*, Lupton argues "Kottman calls his approach 'philosophical dramaturgy,' understood as the ongoing and engaged phenomenological inquiry into the performative origins of our key concepts and experiences of action, life, love, and thought" ("Response" 41). And further down: "Although Kottman's work might seem very far from performance studies, his writing contributes to a certain

book's first chapter, phenomenology is described as an account "of the conditions under which animate and inanimate things appear as such to human consciousness," and Lupton reiterates her indebtedness to Arendt's delineation of "politics as the arena of a specifically human appearing." In Arendt's "political phenomenology" (30), polis becomes "the space of appearance in the widest sense of the word, namely, the space where I appear to others as others appear to me" (*The Human Condition*, 198–99).

This in, in short, what Arendt, Kottman, and Lupton *mean*, but not what phenomenology is about. The logic of such theoretical determinations, pressed through claims of affiliation and professions of debt, is as narrowly circular as a local *Privatsprache* equipped with one single "bare presence," to which all fingers ostensibly point to: Shakespeare's hologrammatic community of pragmatic political actors. It is only in his late period, in *Ideas II*, in the fifth Cartesian meditation, and in his texts on the phenomenology of intersubjectivity that Husserl faces the problem of otherness and the interpersonal, but his focus on notions like *apperception* and *appresentation* proves that he was less interested in the unpredictable political creativity of subjects interacting in a given world-space than in the transcendental intersubjectivity whose predictable power constitutes both that world and that space.[19]

In Lupton's brief theoretical sketch we read that "things take shape in consciousness": this is a strong and genuine phenomenological claim, though somewhat at odds with Lupton's constant interests in what she aptly calls "the draw of things." What are the things that draw? The things as they take shape in consciousness or the non-correlated things as they stand twice before consciousness—before as in front of consciousness, before as prior to the action of consciousness? No answer is given. The "Introduction" is followed by specific essays—not on Shakespeare, recall, but on "Politics and Life"—where we hope to see the phenomenological interests, elements and projects take hermeneutic shape. In the first chapter, Lupton contends that the distinctive nature of her approach to *The Taming of the Shrew* is "my interest in phenomenological and existential fruits of animal husbandry in Shakespeare," further described as "features of human-animal cohabitation broached in Shakespeare's play" and "the modes by which Shakespeare makes them appear in the space of theatre." By examining these phenomenological fruits, features and modes, Lupton seeks "to probe the possibilities of experience, cognition, interaction, imagination, and subjective disclosure what we continue to share

---

theatrical discourse, thanks to his nonmimetic, dramaturgical, and phenomenological account of drama and its scenes" (44).

19   See Zahavi, *Husserl's Phenomenology*, 109–125.

with Shakespeare" (27). Phenomenology is here understood as a loose method of sharpened attention to themes as they are conceptually inferred from words in a text. A sharpened attention dismisses the sedimented, predictable, meaning of terms and aspires to the hermeneutic liberation of unexpected significance. This mode of phenomenology as *Auslegung*, which we often encounter in Heidegger, in Jean-Luc Marion, Nancy, Agamben, and Derrida, is of course inspired in Husserl's call to find new—unburdened by metaphysical prejudice—routes of access to old concepts, the genuine call, that is, to go to the things themselves. This is in a sense the only kind of phenomenology that Arendt can be said to practice, and here Lupton closely follows her mentor. The problem is that this method is only effective when the *Auslegung*, the interpretation, occurs *ad pedem litterae*, across the contingent materiality of a text, and not in the stratosphere of de-textualized, merely thematic, speculation, as is very often the case with Arendt. Heidegger, Derrida, Nancy, Agamben and Marion, by contrast, are always *reading a text* even when they appear to be doing something else (reflecting, speculating, divagating). A paradigmatic example can be found in Heidegger's *Die Grundprobleme der Phänomenologie* (1927), where texts of Greek and Christian-Medieval philosophy are carefully scanned for fresh meaning. In the case of Lupton, the presentist resolve to use a Shakespeare text in order to probe contemporary possibilities of experience, cognition, and interaction places her in principle exegetic stance on the verge of a thematic precipice, over which she might float successfully in beautiful reconsiderations of life, or fall into the banality of "intellectual journalism," the phrase used by Moran to characterize the work of Arendt (Moran 290). In neither case, moreover, will she be doing phenomenology, nor, I am afraid, thinking with Shakespeare. She will rather be *thinking with Arendt* on life apropos of Shakespeare. This doesn't detract much from the book's extraordinary value: as in the case of Bruce Smith, her best readings tend to be sustained by fine exegetic-philological intelligence.

The term phenomenology keeps reappearing in the rest of the chapters, not always consistently. All in all, five meanings of the term can be detected: 1) phenomenology as the study of features of human pragmatic relationality, a meditation on the *ex post facto* resourcefulness of inter-personal action and human-nonhuman interaction, and on the way this performative resourcefulness informs the conceptuality of everyday life (phenomenology is here linked to performance studies) (46); 2) phenomenology as a mode of attentive analysis of a given thematic-conceptual field (phenomenology as thematic *Auslegung*, admittedly Arendt's forte) likely to produce insightful conceptual redefinitions (5, 48, 73); 3) phenomenology as the narrative of a mind awakening to itself (this meaning draws on the Hegelian mythos of the temporality of consciousness) (114); 4) the "phenomenology of embodiment and temporality" (240), a meaning that lodges a nod to Merleau-Ponty and admittedly blends meanings 1 and 3;[20] and 5) a more specific allusion to Agamben's "invitation to think phenomenologically about Paul's account of temporality" (236), where thinking phenomenologically includes assuming Derrida's critique of Husserl (Agamben, *The Time that Remains* 102–104), a condition that Lupton predictably waives.

Let me finish by merely registering Kottman's decision to link Arendt's ethical-political views on action to phenomenology, and Lupton's subsequent resolve to call Arendt a phenomenologist, to conceive of Kottman as a scholar doing phenomenology, and to place her own work under that very banner, however vaguely understood. But is Arendt really a philosopher connected to phenomenology? Dermot Moran, a scholar whose extraordinary book on phenomenology is cited by Lupton, is reluctant to call Arendt not simply a phenomenologist but also a philosopher proper.[21] Isaiah Berlin famously

---

20 Merleau-Ponty's *Phenomenology of Perception* is cited in the Bibliography, but I wasn't able to find any actual reference to this work in Lupton's text.

21 She practiced, he argues, phenomenology in an "original and idiosyncratic manner," but "exhibited no particular interest in the phenomenological method and contributed nothing to the theory of phenomenology." Moran adds that "she was suspicious of all methods and systems" (289). This anti-systematic suspicion may explain her disinterest in Adorno and Sartre, which she cloaked in grounds of personal dislike. The fact that "she had come rather late to Marx" (Moran 291) may be a much better explanation for such disinclination. In a sense, she could be inserted in the loose tradition of thought that Althusser described as "une Phénoménologie de la 'praxis'" and described as a set of idealist interpretations of Marxism as a philosophy of work, based on the themes of the 1844 Manuscripts ("La querelle de l'humanisme" in *Écrits philosophiques et politiques II*, 511). This anti-philosophical dimension of her thought has a lot to do with her intolerance of rationality and dialectical systematicity. But we all know that disinterest, suspicion, and intolerance are often euphemistic ways of naming ignorance. The fact that she conducted repeatedly anthropological, impressionistic, psychological, and emotional readings of Heidegger, raising petty objections to matters of sociological exactitude rather than confronting the rationale of his ontological vision and the often phenomenological method of his arguments reveals the precariousness of her position vis-à-vis the mainstream of German contemporary thought (Husserl, Heidegger, Jaspers). The fact that Heidegger invariably ignored her as a thinker is also proof of her uncertain position in that tradition. Habermas argued that in *The Human Condition* Arendt "does not rely on an exegesis of classical texts; she drafts an anthropology of communicative action" ("Hannah Arendt's Communications Concept of Power" 7). He further accuses her of stylizing "the image she has of the Greek polis to the essence of politics as such" (14): this has a bearing on Lupton's "hologrammatic" conception of communitarian utopia, which I examine in the last sections of this book. In particular, Habermas rejects Arendt's narrow conception of politics, blind to the "insoluble social question" (15). He also faults her for screening "all strategic elements, as force, out of politics," and, more particularly, for being

opined that "she produces no arguments, no evidence of serious philosophical or historical thought. It is all a stream of metaphysical free association. She moves from one sentence to another without logical connection, without either rational or imaginative links between them" (*Conversations* 82). And he maliciously evoked Scholem's private communication to the effect that Arendt was not respected by serious thinkers in Germany, only by "littérateurs" unused to ideas, and that "for Americans she represented Continental thought" (84). Berlin is a bit harsh, and like many other "serious" intellectuals—perhaps *male* intellectuals, including Heidegger—he was very probably jealous of Arendt's growing popularity with American readers. But his criticism is not completely unfounded. What he says about her style is very true, and recalls Dermont Moran's lucid appraisal of Levinas' philosophical diction:

> His style is to make assertions, followed by further assertions, without any attempt to justify them, other than through some king of appeal to deeply human, perhaps even mystical, intuitions, or, alternatively, to phenomenological insight, though such notions are never systematically explicated by him [...] He introduces distinctions which later on are forgotten or transgressed [...] he produces extraordinary metaphorical assertions which are difficult to unpack and hence to grasp critically (321–322).

Arendt's style is not as obscure as Levinas. Her English is enviably exact, supple, and clear. Her conceptual distinctions and tropes are firmly controlled. Still, the concatenation of unwarranted assertions, shorn of sufficient textual illustration—whether of historical evidence or philosophical support—turns many stretches of her prose into a distinctively non-exegetical, undialectical, exercise in divagation. To be sure, when her digression consistently pursues one single topic, she approaches the kind of phenomenological interpretation we find in Heidegger or Derrida. But she is not a close reader, and the lack of exegetical penetration often leaves her conceptual findings sadly unmoored. The risk therefore of professing to do phenomenology and using Arendt as your entry point to the phenomenological nexus is considerable, especially when no side glance at Husserl is attempted. Scholem was probably right, and Berlin rejoiced in repeating it: "for Americans she represented Continental

---

"unable to grasp structural violence" (16). This evokes Levinas obsessive "philosophical," not "biographical," blindness to the pervasiveness of "war," and explains the banality of projecting Arendt's communicative-pragmatic paradise onto Shakespearean experience, which is nothing if not the experience of grasping structural violence.

thought." In the times of post-theory, when the French high-theory dinosaurs are at last proved extinct, and nothing but a heap of broken Benjamin images remains from the Frankfurt School archives, it is Arendt that has come to represent Continental thought. It is, yes, Continental. It is for Americans. For some Americans. But is it *thought*?

Thinking is no thematic surfing, no gliding over the surface of the presumed *transcendens*—the body (Merleau-Ponty), the Other (Levinas), the polis (Arendt). Thinking is no *raisonnement*. Thinking begins in the empty decision to become an empty subject and to assume the transcendental constitution of whatever is thereby posited as transcendent, which is a rather oblique way of saying that, in modern times, it begins with Descartes and Kant. In this precise sense, and despite the fact that he failed to internalize Hegel's dialectical lesson, Husserl remains a thinker. In this sense, too, phenomenology is a terminal—undialectical—version of idealism or high thought. The fact that Arendt sought to break the transcendental immanence of Kant's critical system by postulating the historical, if not existential, transcendence of the *sensus communis*, shows how tempting it is to put an end to thought. Levinas did something similar when he criticized Kant's intimation of a society "whose members would only be reasons" and suggested instead a conception of the self both informed and surpassed by its own *affective* drive to transcendent *happiness* (*bonheur*) (*Totality* 119; *Totalité* 124). And Merleau-Ponty strove to break the spell of immanence in Kant's system by arguing that the refrain "if a world is to be possible" expresses the dependence of "the intrinsic possibility of the world as a thought upon the fact that I can see the world" (*The Visible* 34).

So I can see a world, I can see a common world, I can see a common world of happy human beings—and I am happy. How tempting to put an end to thought. How happily easy. "My mind presageth happy gain and conquest" (*3 Henry VI* 5.1.71). How phenomenal.

CHAPTER 5

Spontaneous Me

1

In an important essay, Nicholas Royle courteously took the trouble to remind Jonathan Dollimore that "deconstruction, if there is any, is first of all a deconstruction of the spontaneous, or what is supposedly immediate, or of one's own free will" ("Impossible Uncanniness," *In Memory* 118). I take this forewarning to be the sum and substance of my book. Walt Whitman, we know, was in love with his "Spontaneous Me, Nature" (*Complete Leaves of Grass* 194). Spontaneity—another term for unmediatedness or immediacy—is a romantic trope whose phenomenological afterlife makes it very amenable to the new schools of Shakespeare criticism. Posthumanist scholars like Scott Maisano and Joseph Campana speak, for instance, of the "spontaneity, freedom and mutual respect" of a pastoral inter-species sharing of the open ("Introduction" to *Renaissance Posthumanism* 14). The uncertain and unexpected political creativity (futurity) of spontaneous interpersonal (collective) action is also an Arendtian motif that recurs in the critical work of Paul Kottman and Julia Lupton. The former, for instance, describes the actual enactment of tragedy—including Shakespearean tragedy, and particularly *Hamlet*—as "an ulterior attempt to close the diremption of nature from sociality—an attempt to let the latter derive from the former, through *spontaneous* affect" (*Tragic Conditions* 77; emphasis added). Most of the scholars who openly or implicitly put the ideologeme of *spontaneity* to "critical" use seem oblivious of the fact that *critique* is contingent on the reduction of spontaneity, i.e. that the very *raison d'être* of criticism is to forestall the explanatory seduction of spontaneous action. In Marx, Lenin, and Brecht we find a constant assault on the revolutionary-socialist worship of spontaneity, on spontaneous ideologies, and Althusser and Žižek have tirelessly called attention to the argumental centrality of this motif in materialist dialectics.[1] In *Misère de la philosophie*, for instance, Marx recursively berates the insanity of construing production in terms of spontaneity.

---

1 On Lenin's critique of the effect *the ideology of spontaneity* has in the revolutionary movements of the working classes, see Žižek, *Repeating Lenin*, and also "Afterword: Lenin's Choice," 183–189. See also Althusser's discussion of this problem, and his related commentary on Brecht's critique of *spontaneous ideologies* in *For Marx*, 95–116 and 133–135. And Jameson, *Valences*, 28.

The notion of the Prometheic production of an integrated collective of workers (*la société personne*) that leads to *spontaneous* surpluses of goods and of ideas is a theoretical aberration that occludes the ideological mediations of class conflict and social antagonism (*Misère* 84, 148–51). Marx makes this point very clear:

> Mais du moment qu'on ne poursuit pas le mouvement historique des rapports de la production, dont les catégories ne sont que l'expression théorique, du moment que l'on ne veut plus voir dans ces catégories que des idées, des pensées spontanées, indépendantes des rapports réels, on est bien forcé d'assigner comme origine à ces pensées le mouvement de la raison pure.
> *Misère* 157

Mutatis mutandis, when Arendt, Nussbaum, Kottman, and Lupton, mobilize the ethical vocabulary of capabilities, virtues and affects to extoll the thrills of spontaneous interpersonal praxis they are themselves investing in a spontaneous surplus of meaning a theoretical force that could go, alternatively, into the recognition of the dialectical mediation of superstructural ideas and the real antagonism of infrastructural relations. They rather content themselves with spontaneous ideas (praxis, affect, virtue, capability) that falsify mediated realities—including, of course, the very human reality of "concurrence" (201), which evokes Hobbes's "competition" and "contention" (*Leviathan* 161)—as seamlessly spontaneous processes. The notion that nature, as an unmediated necessity, can be pitted against the contingencies of the social sphere, and that there is always the possibility of a clean social restart from nature, from the coming together of the human faculties and capabilities stored therein, is a naive romantic ideologeme, as mystified as the moral desire "to close the diremption of nature from sociality," articulated as "the attempt to let the latter derive from the former" (Kottman, *Tragic Conditions* 77). We know that Marx and Engels held ambivalent beliefs about the *generatio aequivoca* or spontaneous generation of life, but they were adamant about the irrecoverability, for socialized humans, of a spontaneously productive natural realm.[2] Refuting Feuerbach, they comment:

---

[2] As John Bellamy Foster argues, Marx did believe in the spontaneous generation of life, which means that he and Engels endorsed a self-sufficiently materialist account of the emergence of life in earth, based on chemical reactions rather than on an act of divine creation: *Marx's Ecology: Materialism and Nature*, 116–121. That was arguably the only *spontaneism* he allowed his system to be contaminated with.

> Of course, in all this the priority of external nature remains unassailed, and all this had no application to the original men produced by *generatio aequivoca*; but this differentiation has meaning only insofar as man is considered to be distinct from nature. For that matter, nature, the nature that preceded human history, is not by any means the nature in which Feuerbach lives, it is nature which today no longer exists anywhere ....
> *German Ideology* 63

Can Hamlet derive a novel sociality from a nature that "no longer exists" and is for him but "the quintessence of dust"? In phenomenological terms, Hamlet has always-already given up the natural standpoint that secured him a *spontaneous* access to nature (*Ideas I* §28). This is in keeping, of course, with standard phenomenological prudence. The problem is that the Hamlet that has disconnected the natural standpoint also lacks the access to "spontaneous actionality" that Husserl reserves for the abstemious and abstaining phenomenological consciousness. His contact with the spontaneous (affect, virtue, capability) is always compromised. If "free spontaneity and activity consists in positing, positing on the strength of this or that" a number of theses that "radiate"— like a "fiat"—from the indweller, then Hamlet is certainly not a champion of a "*spontaneity modus of a so-to-spear creative beginning*" (Husserl, *Ideas* §122 253). If the "thesis" of the natural attitude "c'est l'histoire veçu spontanément" (Derrida, *Le problème* 183), then this thesis is certainly not Hamlet's. His theses are rather tied to the unimaginative finitude of an always-already created world—a time and space that will never be "set [...] right" (*Hamlet* 1.5.190) and that is therefore beyond recreation. And he delivers them dialectically, circuitously, in recursive gestures of self-cancellation. *Hamlet* is less a Renaissance play of spontaneous beginnings than a Baroque play of retarded ends.

But the romantic inducements of spontaneity are hard to give up. Let me recall the beautiful sentence where Lupton attempts to capture the singularity of Viola's felicitous pragmatic resolve: "Viola is candle, match, and flame" ("Virtue in *Twelfth Night*" 1). This is the same scholar, let me note, that in 1993 upheld "Lacan's genealogy of the object of desire," arguing that desire designates "neither the immediacy of an affect nor its cutting off by meaning, but the allegorical mood and mode produced by that scission" (*After Oedipus* 70). I see no contradiction in this, just a development from mediation to immediacy, from the conceptual to the corporal, from obscure allegory to transparent symbol, from theory to post-theory, a recoil, in short, to the frictional inflammable Given. And I take this recoil to imply a demonization of the daemon, the exorcism of the essential ghost that "haunts every notion of spirit, *esprit, spiritus, pneuma,* breath, exhalation, ghost, *Geist*, gas, and flame" (Lukacher, *Daemonic*

5). With three simple words—candle, match and flame— Lupton, who is conversant with Arendt's analysis of St Augustine's "view of the human will as the origin of spontaneity and creativity" (Moran 295), places us at "the point of the mysterious emergence of transcendental 'spontaneity'" (Žižek, *Ticklisch* 61). But is her account "transcendental" enough? Did Viola's noumenal freedom allow her to traverse the abyssal nightmare of abstraction, did she consider the "ontological gap" and "traumatic excess," before moving on to dance her life away, at the beat of the tabour, in the shores of Illyria? Traversing—to use a Žižek verb—like reading, takes time. I am defending the retarding temporalities of reading in opposition to the sham instantaneousness of phenomenological intuition, evidence, immediacy, and givenness. Viola's reading of reality takes time, her time, the time of her experience—and she will end becoming her non-self, her own deferred temporality, when she is "ready," like Sebastian, "to distrust [her] eyes" (*Twelfth Night* 4.3.13). And this happens because she uses the match to light the candle and read—to read, that is, herself against the backdrop of experiences she both instigates and endures. There is, in short, freedom and freedom—spontaneous freedom and responsible freedom—and what tells them apart is the agent's assumption, in the latter case, of inescapable constrains to the extent and reach to which her freedom can push her.[3] Like Hamlet, Viola is bound to the "primo-secondarité" of *deferred obedience* (Derrida, *Mal d'Archive* 91). Responsible freedom is a limited freedom because its assignee is bound to respond to the (ideological) script of external determinants in order to negotiate the exact terms of use. I am talking about the time of response, deciphering, negotiation, and responsibility. This is certainly not the time, predicted by Arendt, of continuous ontological beginnings (*Origins* 478–79).[4] Nor is it the time, adumbrated by Lupton, for the spontaneous combustion of flames. In *The Politics of Friendship*, Derrida writes:

---

3 Viola's "romance" environment connects to the green-world aestheticized creatures that Hugh Grady invests with moral-political *possibility*. Commenting on Böcklin's expressionistic paintings "Isle of the Dead," "Naiads at play" and "A Faun playing the flute," Adorno writes: "Something naturalistic belongs to all these creatures. They appear as unreal and yet as graphic copies of something practically real, as tractable imitations of alleged fauns or elementary creatures, not as the expression of thought for which its part determines the possible as something new, and distinct from every existing thing. They are not 'free'" (*Against* 198–199). For an excellent (Althusserian) analysis of the ideological construction of the "free subject" during the early modernity, with a special focus on Spanish literature, see Juan Carlos Rodríguez, *Theory and History of Ideological Production*.

4 Most beginnings are but repetitions (Marx, Nietzsche, Derrida), just as most promises are parodies of earlier performatives (Derrida). Arendt's reluctance to confront these basic facts may explain her "disinterest" in Heidegger's course on Nietzsche.

> Elsewhere, as we know—in the *Timaeus*, for example, the value of constancy is quite simply tied to that of the true or the veritable, in particular where it is a question of opinion or belief in its sheer stability, this assured certainty is not natural, in the late and current sense of the term; it does not characterize spontaneous behaviour because it qualifies a belief or an act of faith, a testimony and an act of responsible freedom. Only primary friendship is stable (*bébaios*), for it implies decision and reflection: that which always takes time. Only those decisions that do not spring up quickly (*me takhu*) or easily (*mede radíos*) remit in correct judgement (*ten krísin orthen*). This non-given, non-"natural," non-spontaneous stability thus amounts to a stabilization. (15)[5]

The notion of friendship grounded on a non-spontaneous act of responsible freedom that "implies decision and reflection" is much closer to Schmittian than to the Arendtian conceptions of friendship—as an intimate "distribution of affect" between equals leading to the constitution of a "nascent polity"—that we encounter in Kottman's and Lupton's interpretations of *Hamlet* (Kottman, *Politics* 147; Lupton, *Thinking* 84). Schmitt's dialectical conception infiltrates the tragedy of *Hamlet* at all levels, forcing the permanent proviso that, since "the poor advanced makes friends of enemies," one is ultimately bound, in all games, to "draw both friend and foe" (*Hamlet* 4.5.139). To use Lupton's astute categories against her very claim, I would say that the "civic latitudinals" of comradeship and friendship are necessarily sidetracked and rectified by "the play's awful longitudinals," especially "parent-child" and "sovereign-subject" (Lupton, *Thinking* 81). Rectification here is also re-Oedipalization. In the last scene, Horatio is never addressed by Hamlet as friend, only as man—"as thou'rt a man" (*Hamlet* 5.2.284)—and his dying voice is exhaled to consecrate a new vertical sovereign, Hamlet's father's desired son.

2

I have briefly considered, from a critical stance borrowed from Marx and Derrida, the pitfalls of spontaneity in relation to *material production* and the revolutionary production of sociality, and tried to reorient the resulting critique to spontaneist readings of Shakespearean experience. It is now the

---

5 For an interesting application of Derrida's take on friendship to Shakespearean reading, see Rothleder, *Fraught Decisions*, 29–61.

turn to consider in some detail the spontaneity of *ideational production*. In *Ideas I* §23, Husserl argues that "'conceptual construction' certainly takes place spontaneously, and free fancy likewise, and what is spontaneously produced is of course a product of mind" (42). Here Husserl overly relies on Kant, and it is to his first *Critique* we shall turn. I have already quoted from Cutrofello's *Continental Philosophy*, a provocatively mistitled book that is diffusely about Shakespeare and profusely about Kant. This original book outlines a counterintuitive narrative of the history of contemporary philosophy, making its most visible conflicts—notably the Continental-Analytical Divide—originate in unresolved tensions in Kant's philosophical system—receptivity versus spontaneity, heteronomy versus autonomy, transcendence versus immanence, and empirical versus transcendental. This is original because standard accounts of contemporary philosophy, especially on the Continental side, would choose between Descartes and Hegel in order to establish the rightful beginning of modern thought. Quite often, however, the claim that Descartes triggered the whole affair is made compatible with the surmise of a Hegelian restart. Kant is there relegated to the role of the industrious engineer arbitrating between two genial architects. In fact, in his more explicit book on Shakespeare, *All for Nothing: Hamlet's Negativity* (2014), Cutrofello opts for the Descartes-Hegel partnership in order to go about his critical business, and he shrewdly allows Descartes to play the role of "Prologue." Subjecting the notion Hamlet's selfhood to critical scrutiny, "from Kant and Deleuze to Hegel and Žižek," Cutrofello contends "that the capacity for self-affection is rooted in a more fundamental power of negativity, and that it is this power that Hamlet personifies" (*All for Nothing* 2). I fully subscribe to the tenor of this contention, and add that if the harmonization of negativity and self-affection is a desirable challenge, likely to submit the figure of modern self-alienation—"je ne nie pas que moi, qui pense, sois distinct de ma pensée" (Descartes *Meditations* 349), "so kann Ich nicht sagen was ich nur meine" (Hegel), "je est un autre" (Rimbaud); "wo Es war soll Ich werden" (Freud)—the reconciliation of other-affection and thing-affection with negativity is a far more taxing demand, especially in times, like ours, where the third-person has become the object of an organized man-hunt. Choosing Kant, in his earlier book, as the beginning goes against the grain—especially today, when the Hegel revival (Žižek, Badiou, Malabou, Ruda) holds the Continental field—but it certainly conforms to a historicist construal of the consequence of Kantian criticism that has inspired the work of thinkers like Adorno, Nancy, Lyotard, Blumenberg and, in some ways, Derrida. It has the additional effect of allowing Cutrofello to synchronize the clocks at both sides of the Atlantic, as Kant is probably the one and only name the House of Continental and the House of Analytic share.

The first dichotomy considered by Cutrofello is that between *receptivity* and *spontaneity*, and the thinkers he examines in this section are Kant, Nietzsche, Bergson, Husserl, Heidegger, Bachelard, Sartre, Merleau-Ponty, Foucault, Derrida and Deleuze. This way he maps out a territory of primarily epistemological speculation with grounds in the allowances of ontology and consequences for the rational compossibility of the aesthetic. This latter goal places his effort on a par with de Man's late-life project of exposing the theoretical impossibility of the aesthetic—a discursive discipline whose epistemological ambition (since Kant) is undone by irrepressible material impeachments and plenteous ideological aberrations. The inclusion here of three thinkers (Foucault, Derrida and Deleuze) also commonly aligned in the ranks of theory serves to defamiliarize the equivocal label of *poststructuralist theory*, and restore a sense of genuine horizons: what Lacan, Althusser, Foucault, Derrida and Deleuze all shared was a speculative-dialectical passion, with roots in the Kant-Hegel conjunction.[6] The fact that this dialectic-speculative drive infiltrated literary studies and complemented—and blasted—an already existing formalism (Russian formalism, New Criticism) under the name of structuralism and poststructuralism is accidental and irrelevant to the afterlives of German Idealism. For that's where we are—after-living and pre-dying in Kantian prose and pose.

The original Kantian distinction articulating the dichotomy is that between the intellectual *spontaneity* of concepts and sensorial *receptivity* of intuitions: "concepts are therefore grounded on the spontaneity of thinking, as sensible intuitions are grounded on the receptivity of impressions" (*Critique of Pure Reason* B93).[7] Otherwise put: "*receptivity* can make cognitions possible only if combined with *spontaneity*" (A97). Needless to say, as we have seen, Husserl held steadfastly to the idea of the spontaneity of concepts, arguing that "a *primordial dator* consciousness of an essence (Ideation)—we are here clearly concerned with essential relations—is in itself and necessarily spontaneous [*ein spontanes*]" (*Ideas I* 42). This neat distinction raises the question of the possibility of *intellectual intuition*, to which Kant turns in the third *Critique*

---

6 The fact that Deleuze opted for a *transcendental empiricism* doesn't detract an inch from his constant reliance on dialectical procedure, both in his transformation of negativity into difference and in his reliance on an "initial formalism" to set off the train of nomadic subversion. For a contrary view, see Alain Badiou, "Une anti-dialectique" in *Deleuze: 'La clameur de l'être'*, 49–54. Deleuze's very early work on Kant proves that the forces of vitalism (Bergson, Nietzsche) were always internally resisted, in his thought, from a critical-idealist barricade. Cutrofello's section on Deleuze in *Continental Philosophy* (98–110) offers a sharp and precise account of these tensions.

7 I here follow Guyer's and Wood's edition of Kant's *Critique of Pure Reason*.

(§77). Much of what we call phenomenology is staked on this possibility: as Cutrofello has observed, Husserl "suggests that intuitions without judgements are not as blind as Kant had thought" (41). The evolution of phenomenology is informed by a paradoxical reversal: whereas the early Husserl held fast to an absorption in the logical space of pure concepts that represented "the operations of spontaneity as a frictionless spinning in the void" (McDowell, *Mind* 11), second-generation phenomenologists like Merleau-Ponty and present-day historical phenomenologists allocate the operations of spontaneity in what we could contrastively call a frictional ebbing in the flood. Such reversal betrays the need to reinstate the Myth of the Given, possibly a pantheist version of Bardolatry—*William in rebus*. Anyway, though Kant is adamant about the impossibility of exchanging the functions of the faculties of sensibility and understanding (B75), his analysis leaves two hypothetical faculties in the air: *sensorial spontaneity* and *conceptual receptivity*.

Sensorial spontaneity would refer to an active involvement of the sensorial faculties, immediately prompted to seize a sensible content (the Given) that is however anticipated by the world-directedness intentional drive. This runs against the drift of Kant's argument in the first *Critique*, where the *actus* of spontaneity "cannot be regarded as belonging to sensibility" (B132), but it does capture something of the "spontaneous affect" (de Man, *Aesthetic* 123) he theorizes in the third. Thus this new construal of intentional perception would allow "the spontaneity of the power of representation" not to depend on the faculty of the understanding; the senses, in their new capacity to experience "pure intuitions" (B75), would suffice to bring about the *conjuctio* of a manifold (B130). The notion of a pure *and* spontaneous intuition doesn't necessarily rule out the givenness (and therefore the receptivity) of sensorial contents: it merely stresses the unmediated or impromptu exertion of the intention that foresees, prepares for and compossibilizes whatever is given. Although the incompatibility between sensibility and spontaneity is firmly asserted by Kant, the attempt to reconcile the two faculties lies *in nuce* in Husserl's work, and Merleau-Ponty brought it to fruition with his defense of a primordial, ante-predicative vision, and his championing of the "extase de l'expérience" (*Phénoménologie* 99).[8] Lacan, let me recall, quickly saw through this delusion, and cavalierly chastised it in his 1961 essay "Merleau-Ponty, in memoriam." Undoubtedly, the combined facts that for Kant "the imagination is spontaneity" and that the Romantic aesthetic tradition enthroned his

---

8   Kant: "In human beings this consciousness requires inner perception of the manifold that is antecedently given in the subject, and the manner in which this is given in the mind without spontaneity must be called sensibility on account of this difference" (*Critique PR* B68, 189).

productive imagination (B152) as the concept-indifferent and immediate faculty of the creative artist, greatly fostered the phenomenological apotheosis of inner vision. It took ages to reattach *Bildung* to *Begreifen* and *Wortung*. Thus the significance of a notion like *sensorial spontaneity* is primarily adversarial: it draws its strength from the repudiation of conceptual mediation in the construction of an object. And this notion is always implied in phenomenological uses of the term *intuition*, from Husserl to Levinas and Merleau-Ponty. Much phenomenological criticism of Shakespeare hinges on an overestimation of the self-sustaining power of the noematic projection of intentional content, which renders the dependencies of receptivity utterly negligible. This fosters the absurd view that, in the case of the Shakespeare thing (performance, show, representation), we externally see what we already intuitively, spontaneously, internally have seen—whence, of course, the *irrelevance of reading*, readily discarded as a mode of defective seeing.[9]

Conceptual receptivity is bound up with the question of conceptual acquisition, to which the rationalist tradition up to Kant failed to find an answer.[10] It names the epistemological *sine qua non* stipulated by linguistic determinists, linguistic behaviorists, language-turned thinkers, deconstructionists, and materialist-dialectical critics generally. The notion they all share is that for knowledge—as both *denken* and *erkennen*—to get started, a prior reception of Kantian concepts and schemes must take place in the human mind, and that this reception depends on random linguistic input. No ideas but in words, and no knowledge but in ideas.[11] The implication is that neither ideas nor words are innate—and so cognitivism, and its conjecture of a language instinct or organ, is rejected as an intellectual aberration or a "minching *malhecho*" (*Hamlet* 3.2.124). This deterministic take on language is compatible with the post-metaphysical suggestion of tropological materiality, "the materiality of language itself, which remains utterly external to cognition and sensation even as it makes possible the translation from one to the other" (Lukacher, *Daemonic* 74). Another scandalous implication is that since the outside is per definition normatively unparsed, and the outside is yet invited to constitute interiority, "the unintelligible repressed returns as the condition of intelligibility" (Rorty, "Deconstruction and Circumvention" in *Essays on Heidegger and Others* 93) To be sure, Kant would cringe at the notion that the concepts and

---

9   For the tensions between an ideology of transparent sight and the opacities of materialist reading, see Althusser, *Lire le Capital*, 8–15.
10 See Brandom, *Tales of the Mighty Dead*, 30–31.
11 I am obviously playing a variation on William Carlos William's memorable prescription: "No ideas but in things" (*Paterson*).

schemes of the understanding are contingently received through the input of verbal experience, but there is a sense in which the correction initiated by Marx's *Ideologiekritk* impinges just on this reversal, and this productive correction is implied in the work of dialectical (antithetical) critics like Blumenberg, Derrida or de Man, all of them Kant-leaning scholars, pledged to critique, who refuse to forsake the necessity of concepts. De Man's astute observation that *The Critique of Judgement* has at its center a deep, fatal discontinuity—that "it depends on a linguistic structure (language as performative as well as cognitive system) that is not itself accessible to the powers of transcendental philosophy" (*Aesthetic* 79) captures the strain that linguisticity puts on the cogency of Kant's transcendental project. But language and rhetorical turns also tax metaphysical postulates. The reduction, suggested by Brentano, Aubenque and Wieland, of Aristotle's modes of being to simple modes of saying, is a parallel exercise in critical disenchantment. So if being is said in many ways (τὸ δὲ ὂν λέγεται μὲν πολλαχῶς, *Ens autem multis quidem dicitur modis*, Metaphysics 1003b33), the many ways of truth are *heard* before they can be *said*. Nothing truthful, no friend, and much less a society, can be spontaneously (naturally, affectively) produced in abstraction of prior scripts guiding—*determining in the last instance*—such production. Phenomenological criticism of Shakespeare thrives in the neglect or ignorance of this radical view.

3

I consider these two extreme positions because I believe their radical rendition of the theoretical stakes helps unearth and organize what all too frequently remains unstated in prefatorial theoretical footwork of phenomenology-oriented scholars when they discuss Shakespeare. It also gives a sense of historicist direction and sociological intelligibility to the hermeneutic magma that has sedimented, in the last four decades, over and around Shakespeare's words. This is one possible version of the story, clad in familiar taxonomy to inhibit obscurity: at some point in the early eighties, literary criticism in Anglo-American departments abandoned the rigors of poststructuralist hermeneutics (Marxism, psychoanalysis, deconstruction) and embraced modes of reading that were less textual, less dialectical, and allegedly more politically and sociologically sensitive (feminism, race studies, new historicism, cultural materialism, performance studies, postcolonialism). Instrumental for this dismantling of strong theory was the incendiary and cantankerous reaction of traditional philologists like Brian Vickers who wrongly placed Derrida and de Man alongside sociological and political scholars, thus encouraging an erroneous version of the Shakespeare-studies wars as one of owners (the philologists) versus the usurpers or appropriators (the rest). In Shakespeare studies, to Vickers' dismay, the sociological and political critical modes held the field for a good three decades, and they are still kicking and very much alive in their own terms and in those of their related sub-disciplines. The "Parisian nonsense machine," to use Scruton's charming phrase (*Fools* 159), took the floor. The degree of survival of poststructuralist acumen in the work of some prominent scholars contributing to the second theoretical wave, academics like Catherine Belsey, Terry Eagleton, Jonathan Dollimore, Alan Sinfield or John Drakakis was far from homogeneous. Belsey, for instance, never quite forsook close-text-oriented speculative insight, while the rest waived dialectical duress to embrace the living thrills of contextual immediacy. The case of Stephen Greenblatt is ambiguous: his aestheticist-cum-representational *poetics of culture* was not bad as a *sociology* but was hardly a *poetics* at all—let alone a dialectic. The work of some notables like Frank Kermode, A.D. Nuttall, Stephen Orgel, John Kerrigan, James Shapiro, David Scott Kastan, Jonathan Bate, Colin Burrow, Michael D. Bristol, and Graham Bradshaw, reveals broad familiarity with theory, even while their primary interest lies elsewhere—close philological reading, Performance studies, ideological contextualization, book history, even biography. For good or bad (consistently for good, in their case), theory was not a priority.[12] In the last twenty-five years or so true theoretical innovation in the field is uncommon. And among the *rarae aves* who have managed to adopt a consistently original theoretical stance there are very few whom I would describe as dialectical (speculative, antithetical, ironic) critics: they are Marjorie Garber, Harold Bloom, Jonathan Goldberg, Margreta de Grazia, Richard Halpern, Andrew Cutrofello, Ned Lukacher and Nicholas Royle.[13] While these and other scholars were producing their best work on Shakespeare—from the 1990s up to the present—a third wave of theoretical approaches broke on the strand, trying to wash away whatever residual memory lingered of the dialectical name. Most of those who surfed the third tsunami proudly trusted they were doing good theory, and they called it *post-theory*: ecocriticism, phenomenology, neo-materialism, object-oriented studies, posthumanism, affect studies. Two notable pioneers of this third wave are Bruce Smith and Jonathan Gil Harris to whose work I turn in several places in this book.

---

12   Perhaps Kastan and Bradshaw are exceptions. See Kastan's *Shakespeare after Theory* and Bradshaw's *Misrepresentations: Shakespeare and the Materialists*.
13   I have not included Allan Bloom because his best work on Shakespeare dates back to the 1970s.

The cases of Richard Wilson, Simon Palfrey, Julia Reinhard Lupton, and Paul Kottman pose a different kind of problem. They can be warmly receptive to dialectical criticism, they can brilliantly practice it, but they have lately succumbed to the lure of phenomenological aestheticism, immediacy, spontaneity, and presentism. Their articles, essays and books make up the best organized, most dedicated, and most consistently sophisticated body of critical work that is today being produced on Shakespeare. This is of course a personal—broadly indemonstrable—opinion and based on it I single their work out as the object of some local commentaries, designed to illustrate my general thesis: phenomenological criticism of Shakespeare is wrong because methodologically mistaken about its object. I read them reading—or what I take to be misreading or failing to read—Shakespeare and take them to task—figuratively, for argumentative purposes—wherever I find their arguments foundering on the shallow waters of phenomenology. If I address their work rather than that of less talented critics it is not only because their refined scholarship has a greater authority to sanction error, but also because discussing it proves a most rewarding endeavor. My impression is that they take too many risks—especially Wilson and Lupton—by espousing trendy critical rapprochements (Shakespeare side by side ecocriticism, posthumanism, presentism, object-oriented studies) that dilute their insight in a sloppy pool of eclecticism and ecumenism: the more theoretically inclusive, the weaker. Besides, these post-theoretical tendencies work all, as I will try to show in this book, against their best hermeneutical and dialectical instincts: scriptural and comparative text-hermeneutics (Lupton), and dialectical-materialist sociology (Wilson). In the cases of Simon Palfrey and Paul Kottman, their critical output describes a different kind of trajectory. Their work is theoretically more focused, idiosyncratic, and self-contained—Romantic expressionism (Palfrey) and aesthetic idealism (Kottman) prove uncongenial to expansiveness and fashion—and they rarely surrender to the glimmerings of the post-. Conceivably, therefore, the blindness of their very powerful insight is more severe for that.

Despite this broad focus, I also consider in some detail the work of other scholars (Jonathan Gil Harris, Scott Maisano, Karen Raber, Kevin Curran) whose uses of theory—of phenomenology-oriented theory—is more mechanical, derivative, and, on occasion, uninspiringly crude; but also the work of critics whose resort to philosophy is either very lucid and provocative (Christopher Pye) or very distracting (Sanford Budick).

CHAPTER 6

The Harm That Good Men and Women Do

1

In a 1927 essay titled "The Harm that Good Men Do," Bertrand Russell suggested "that the standards of virtue now prevalent are incompatible with the production of good poetry" (*Sceptical Essays* 94). To illustrate this point, he argued that "Shakespeare, to judge by the Sonnets, would not have been allowed by American immigration officers to land in New York" (93). Indeed, the troubled reception of *Shake-speares Sonnets* in literature departments of the English-speaking world during the 1920s and 1930s proves that Russell's instinct was right.[1] It is a blessing that, by way of ironic compensation, some very bad men (Eliot and Pound, especially) were at the same time very busy producing remarkably good poetry. In 1996, South-African novelist and critic J.M. Coetzee complained that "the Puritan project of legislating moral standards has not died out in America" (*Giving Offence* 25): I don't cite this as a particularly original judgement, but rather as an authoritative piece of sociological opinion. Today, almost a century after Russell voiced out his point, one can safely state that the standards of virtue now prevalent remain incompatible with the production of good poetry. In fact, they have occasionally turned remarkable poets into bad ones. These standards remain untouched by Badiou's caveat that thought, including poetic thought, "doesn't obey injunctions of a moral kind" (*Pour Aujourd'hui* 178). They are also incompatible with the interpretation of good poetry, including Will's. There are too many good men (and women) around for his "figures of delight" (Sonnet 98.11) to flourish.

These good men and women are what Althusser called "professionals of ideology, people of religion and morality" (*Machiavel et Nous*, in *Écrits II* 72). Let me give some examples. Kevin Curran closes his Introduction to *Shakespeare's Legal Ecologies* with a reformulation of the "core assumption of Shakespeare's ethics of exteriority," to wit, "that there is no self prior to or separate from the world" (21). I have already examined the unsuitableness of talking of *ethics of exteriority* in Shakespeare and about the incorrectness of Curran's rendition of this Levinasian trope. Here I am only interested in the coda: "The insight is simple but important, and perhaps especially so at a time when the greatest threats

---

1 See Katherine Duncan-Jones, "Introduction" to *Sonnets*, 80–85.

to *our* social and ecological well-being come shrouded in languages of absolute liberty and the claims of extreme individualism" (21; emphasis added). I will not probe either the possible inconsistency in pitching your scholarly argument at such a level of moral-political indignation—the moral wrath of a selfless ecological persona apparently bothered by liberal calls to individual freedom—inside an industrially produced, largely unsustainable, Illinois-printed book where the most visibly repeated thing is the name of the individual author, subject both to authorship-based copyright laws and individual-career-oriented professional promotion. It is very easy to sneer at the excesses of liberty and individualism when both middle-class ease and the unbound latitudes of freedom of speech, including the freedom to criticize sneeringly, are taken for granted as *the* indisputable, unnegotiable, horizon of existence—that of most Anglo-American, and many European, university scholars.[2] Curran construes Shakespeare's vision of personal and political experience as "distinctly communitarian" (4), and argues that the poet "regarded living, thinking, and acting in the world as materially and social embedded practices" (4). Since his vision of selfhood can be legitimately redescribed "in communal, embedded and intersubjective terms," then he can no longer be described, as Peter Holbrook does, as "an author for a liberal individualistic culture" (10). So, in conclusion, Shakespeare was an anti-Cartesian, anti-liberal thinker.[3] At one point, Curran presses on the readers *our* supposedly shared obligation to "find a way to imagine, and even defend, a version of the good that runs counter to self-interest" (62). A *version of the good*? Can the Platonic ἀγαθός sustain the calvary of mutable versions, finite diversions, and perversions? No need to panic, for this is probably a decaf—openly communitarian, covertly Utilitarian—version of the good. And we are invited to find a way to imagine, and even defend, it. This is a difficult challenge, particularly if the finding is expected to occur

---

2   The natural "environment" identified by big ecological thinking is the perfect "elsewhere" of present-day philanthropic scholarship. Žižek: "Many Western academics cling to some humanitarian ritual (helping to educate poor children, etc.) as the proof that, at the core of their being, they are not just cynical career-oriented individuals but human beings naively and sincerely trying to help others. However, again, what if this humanitarian activity is a fetish, a false distance that allows them to pursue their power struggles and ambitions with the clear conscience that they are not really 'that', that their heart is 'elsewhere'?" (*Organs Without Bodies* 159). Of course, many scholars manage to cultivate their own set of moral-humanitarian fetishes without broadcasting or wielding them during their daily teaching and research.

3   There are many references throughout the book to "liberal" individuality as a site of possessive autonomy (*Shakespeare's Legal Ecologies* 37, 46–47, 50, 53–54) challenged by visions of selfhood dependent on inter-subjective collaboration, communal participation, human-nonhuman-distribution, etc.

in the Shakespeare excavation site. At the end of the book, in the Coda titled "Shakespeare's Ethics of Exteriority," Curran recognises that at a number of points during his work on the project, he found himself "wishing there was a place in the canon where Shakespeare pushed harder on these ethical insights [those of a political practice based on collaboration, acknowledgment, and responsibility], a place in which they were explored in a more concentrated and sustained manner" (133). His despondency proves however temporary, for he believes he had found a brief passage that reveals eloquently this ethics of exteriority, this assertion of selfhood partaking in creaturely life, construed as a "singular moment of appearing" to which we respond by knowing, "unmistakably, that we're supposed to *care*" (133). Italicized, the term *care* is aimed at exceeding its Heideggerian conceptual limit (*Sorge*) to reach a notion of otheroriented Levinasian *curation* that inheres in Curran's very common use of the term *curate*: the permeable boundaries between *care*, *cure* and *curation* are also variously exploited by Paul Kottman and Julia Lupton, most recently in the latter's "Introduction" to *Entertaining the Idea*. It is also aimed, of course, at striking a key of extra moral urgency. Well, interestingly, the passage in question is Shylock's plaidoyer of Jewishness (*The Merchant of Venice* 3.1.59–67). But, honestly, if this eloquent explosion of resentful interiority is the best doctrinal precis of Shakespeare's putative ethics of exteriority, then we must conclude that Jessica, Shylock's daughter, is no part of the creaturely life he—and, by extension, we—are being invited to care for. The man that cares so much about the hands and affections of the generic Jew responds this way to the news that his daughter cannot be found:

> Why, there, there, there, there! a diamond gone, cost me two thousand ducats in Frankfurt. The curse never fell upon our nation till now; I never felt it till now: two thousand ducats in that; and other precious, precious jewels. I would my daughter were dead at my foot, and the jewels in her ear! would she were hearsed at my foot, and the ducats in her coffin! No news of them? Why, so: and I know not what's spent in the search: why, thou loss upon loss! the thief gone with so much, and so much to find the thief; and no satisfaction, no revenge: nor no in luck stirring but what lights on my shoulders; no sighs but of my breathing; no tears but of my shedding.
>
> *The Merchant of Venice* 3.1.76–88

The same persona speaks both speeches, with an interval of seconds and less than ten lines. If this man called Shylock who prizes diamonds and ducats higher than his own daughter is the best illustration Curran can find of

Shakespeare's investment in an ethics of distributed selfhood that rules out in advance the ethics of possessive individualism, then his argument is hopeless. Few Shakespearean personae are more tightly egotistical, verbally idiosyncratic, so uniquely self-centred. Few are, for that very reason, so fascinating. His speech is very moving, but only if we abstract it from a brutal, grotesque, comedic context onto which it is grafted, a context that is quick to undo it—just as Hamlet's *Oration on the Dignity of Man*, "What a piece of work is a man!," is swiftly cancelled by the coda, "And yet to me what is this quintessence of dust?" (*Hamlet* 2.2.294–298). Similarly, Shylock's "Hath not a Jew eyes?" (*The Merchant of Venice* 3.1.50) is followed, without solution of continuity, by "I shall never see my gold again" (3.1.93), which may help explain why having eyes is so important for him. The best precis of the whole anti-Semitism affair in *The Merchant of Venice* remains, to my mind, Lukacher's:

> It is as though Shakespeare were saying, "We must have done with these Puritans and their canting conscience, and since they rely so heavily on the patriarchal law of the Jews, there is no harm in having done with them as well." Shakespeare must take responsibility for writing a text that could be so easily appropriated by hatemongers, and he must be blamed for masking the bitter and politically risky pill of anti-Puritanism beneath the glib humor and theatrical effect afforded by a facile anti-Semitism.
> *Daemonic* 117

But note that thus to conclusively apportion blame doesn't cancel the validity of the first premiss: that Shakespeare "knew all he needed to know about [the Jews] through the Puritans" (110). And yet, although he knew his Puritans well, one cannot help but wonder how he would have reacted to the moralistic rage of present-day phenomenological neo-Puritans. It harrows me with fear and wonder.

Following an entrenched habit among literary academics, Curran collapses the Cartesian cogito and the Lockean self into a liberal figure of insulated legal autonomy that is supposedly asserted in abstraction, constituted prior to the "webs of interlocution" (Taylor) facilitated by "the societal bond" (Ricoeur), by the self's "sustained relationship with human life" (Arendt) (*Legal Ecologies* 132). And Curran has felt the need to prove that Shakespeare anticipates Arendt, Ricoeur, and Taylor—and Husserl, Merleau-Ponty, and Levinas—because he purports to curate, via the deployment of the legal resources of his tradition or through other means, "spaces of encounter and [to] knit discrete persons into the social and material fabric of the world" (131). He appears to ignore that this encounter and this knitting were precisely the horizon of sociality—what Marx called "the various *cul-de-sacs* of feudal society" ("On the Jewish Question," *Early Political Writings* 48)—Shakespeare's contemporary existents were born into; that there was a surplus, not a deficit, of spaces of encounter, distributed selfhoods, corporate personae, professional guilds, organic communities, that this densely integrated world—"this land of such dear souls" (*Richard II* 2.1.58)—was the (medieval-feudal) *given* of Shakespeare's existential and creative venture; and that what he made of it, or added to it, was precisely a choir of *disembodied* voices producing distinctly individual and autonomous lines of flight—Timon's, Edgard's, Coriolanus's, and Hamlet's.[4] Let me recall that Ernst Bloch begins his *Lectures on the Philosophy of the Renaissance* with a reminder that the apex of Renaissance individualism is to be found in Shakespeare, "where the interesting, unchangeable, irreplaceable [*unverwechselbare*] person, the *Multiversum* of human beings, appears" in opposition to high-class and citizenship homogeneity (*Vorlesungen* 9). If you smell a fault, and feel this reeks of essentialist humanism, you may want to know that Bloch was a Marxian materialist philosopher, and one of the best. When in *Untimely Matter in the Time of Shakespeare*, Jonathan Gil Harris discusses the notion of the "out-of-time" and resorts the Nietzschean notion of the untimely (*unzeitgemässe*), what he is really after is Bloch's notion of the *Ungleichzeitig* (non-simultaneity, non-synchronicity). It is strange that a book like Harris' so committed to "the possibility of a new future" (*Untimely Matter* 11) should fail to refer to Bloch, the thinker of the *Hoffnung* principle.

2

The possibility of *our* better *future* is the moral desideratum of scholars like Lupton, Kottman, Curran, Harris, and others, and they seldom fail to instil their readings of Shakespeare with the force of their moralistic wish. We even find it in Simon Palfrey, who believes Pericles' "pre-civility anticipates a new political dispensation" (*Late Shakespeare* 78). Or in Hugh Grady, who understands "the fundamental possibilities of aesthetic representation," and in particular of the representation in *A Midsummer Night's Dream*, to "lead *us* into imagining other modes of living and loving" (*Impure Aesthetics* 69). It is not *moralistic* to wish the advent of a communal world—an "other Eden, demi-paradise" (*Richard II* 2.1.42)—that may overcome the shortcomings of noxious

---

4 See Peter Laslett, *The World We Have Lost*, 1–80. For "social embeddedness" see Charles Taylor, *Modern Social Imaginaries*, 50–60.

individualism, unnatural statism, and inauthentic socialization. That is a common enough moral wish—I myself do not particularly nurse it, or not in those particular terms, but we all have wishes, and terms. What is moralistic is precisely to obviate the fact that *we*—the readers of Shakespeare and of essays on Shakespeare—all have different wishes, that we are different individuals redescribing our more or less efficient, and more or less shared, vocabularies, within a social field where sharing is not always, or not necessarily, wished. It may be worth recalling that Derrida, asked about Nancy's recent theoretical intervention on the problem of community, stated: "I don't much like the word community, I am not even sure I like the thing" (*Points* 355). And it is moralistic too, and very, to turn your wish into the driving force of your public activity, including of course your professional activity, letting others constantly know about the nature of your social-political desires. Not only because it may betoken a certain strand of puritanical exhibitionism—I will talk about *Macbeth* in a minute, but let me first tell you what a good (socially motivated, environmentally aware, community caring) person I am—but also because wishing and understanding, wishful thinking and critical thinking, may not be compatible actions.[5] The most politically penetrating thinkers of our modernity (Machiavelli, Hobbes, Locke, Spinoza) put forward radically para-moral— often plainly immoral— explanations of the polity. No convincing argument has been yet raised against the placing of Shakespeare in this very select group of sceptical-critical thinkers of the saeculum. There is a sense, in fact, in which the work of Lupton and Kottman (perhaps also Victoria Kahn) can be read as the strongest attempt to date to produce such oppositional argument.

Jane Bennett and Michael Shapiro have recently denounced the *politics of moralizing* that is visible in academic work produced both on the Right and on the Left sides of the political spectrum, and that is characterized by "its urge to purity, to present the world as if its contingent parts could be reconciled, its paradoxes solved, its tragic dimensions erased" ("Introduction" to *The Politics of Moralizing*, 2). In Shakespeare studies, the erasure of the tragic dimension leads quite often to a *comedification* of the tragedies realized from the standpoint of

---

5 In the late eighteenth century, moral exhibitionism was linked to a sensibility for nature that is not wholly unlike the professed sensibility of eco-caring scholars. Adorno: "Natural beauty is ideology where it serves to disguise mediatedness as immediacy. Even adequate experience of natural beauty obeys the complementary ideology of the unconscious. If in keeping with bourgeois standards it is chalked up as a special merit that someone has feeling for nature-which is for the most part a moralistic-narcissistic posturing as if to say: What a fine person I must be to enjoy myself with such gratitude-then the very next step is a ready response to such testimonies of impoverished experience as appear in ads in the personal column that claim 'sensitivity to everything beautiful'" (*Aesthetic Theory*, 68–69).

a shared drive to reconciliation. The moral prospect of our better communal future is articulated, inside readings of Shakespeare's plays and poems, through the active deployment of pronominal markers like *our* and *we*, which are more than instances of *pluralis auctoris* (or *modestiae*) or rhetorical signposts of *captatio benevolentiae*. The *we* of these scholars is a standard presence in phenomenological utterance (the case of Husserl's *Cartesian Meditations* §49–50 is paradigmatic) and is therefore bound up with the *claim to intersubjectivity* that lies at the core of the revised phenomenological program. Husserl could only evade charges of solipsism by invoking the transcendental sharing by everyone of the phenomenological experience proper (the experience of disconnection), thus bequeathing an equivocal legacy to followers like Merleau-Ponty, who spoke of "le ridicule d'un solipsisme à plusieurs" (*Phénoménologie* 417)—something like the absurdity of sharing our private masturbation. The solution the French philosopher devised in order to avert ridicule, and secure the egoic passage to *autrui*, was a phenomenology of shared affective corporality that, because of its reliance on the notion of the *same world*, was likely to attract the illiberal liabilities attendant on what Mill called the *tyranny of the majority* and *public opinion*. He argued that "the only freedom which deserves the name, is that of pursuing our own good in our own way, so long as we do not attempt to deprive others of theirs" (*On Liberty* 16). This strong premise leads the Victorian thinker to contend that "there is a limit to the legitimate interference of collective opinion with individual independence" (8–9), this limit being the right to intervene when the safety of others is at stake. But "his own good, either physical or moral, is not a sufficient warrant." If I insist on the occasionally conservative—whether illiberal or plainly anti-liberal—stance of the scholarship produced by progressive academics like Kottman, Lupton, and Curran it is because they keep pressing on the reader, both through deictic-pronominal means (*us, our, we*) and through the tacit assumption of shared ideological views, the naturalized ideologeme of affiliated plurality— affiliated, of course, to *bürgerliche Gesellschaft*, to integrated *ecclesia*, to operative *communitas*. Such eagerness to secure a plural hearing and co-opt moral complicity is no doubt related to the assumption, standard in performance studies, of enlarged empathetic identification between Shakespearean actor and plural spectators, but also on the reconfigured communicative role that Hannah Arendt assigned to the position of plural spectatorship in her lectures on Kant's third *Critique*: "Spectators," she argued, "exist only in the plural" (63). This way the reader of an academic study on Shakespeare is presumed to be also a spectator or witness to the Shakespeare thing itself, and likely therefore to issue aesthetic judgements of taste. It was in these lectures that Arendt pressed the correlation between *sensus communis* and *sensus communitatis*.

"One judges always as a member of a community, guided by one's community sense, one's *sensus communis*" (75). At the end of the fourth lecture, she sketches a similar thought:

> Men = earthbound creatures, living in communities, endowed with common sense, *sensus communis*, a community sense; not autonomous, needing each other's company even for thinking ("freedom of the pen") = first part of the *Critique of Judgement*: aesthetic judgement. (27)

This rests on two possible misrepresentations: 1) she violates the immanence of Kant's transcendental analysis by forcing the entrance, into the aesthetic-cum-axiological activity of consciousness, of the metaphysical *transcendens* of the community; and 2) she relies on a naïve communicative conception of language, for "the notion that critical thinking implies communicability" (40) does not necessarily mean that communication is effective. The fact that she is lecturing on a text proves, first and foremost, that this text is permanently open to misconstruction. Is a community of mis-communicators still a community? Ask Nadine Gordimer and J.M Coetzee. Anyway. Assuming infallibility, feeling sure of their doctrine, the aforementioned Shakespeare academics and "subsequent teachers of virtue" undertake to decide the question of the *good life* "for others" (Mill, *On Liberty* 26–27). Moralistic cajoling would not be that irksome in books titled *Tragic Conditions in Humans, Human Dwellings*, or *Human Legal Ecologies*, for we would assume that a certain measure of doctrine and, indirectly, of indoctrination, is due, but it becomes incomprehensible in books titled *Tragic Conditions in Shakespeare, Shakespeare Dwelling*, and *Shakespeare's Legal Ecologies*. Why should their idea of the *good life* have anything to do with the Shakespeare experience? Why shouldn't, they would reply. Why should we, the readers, be forced to assume that idea? Why not, they would reply. I leave these questions open, as I understand that many readers, who very possibly partake in this idea of the good life, would grant these scholars their right to be right and reply. I am glad to discover, nonetheless, that someone like Louis Menand holds in contempt the academic pretense to know what the *good life* is, and to use the "great books" of the miscalled "liberal culture" to facilitate the undergraduate's access to it.[6] I am merely trying to

---

[6] The present-day illiberal appropriation of this originally liberal trope constitutes a fascinating ideological phenomenon. For the trope of the *good life*, see Kymlicka, *Liberalism, Community and Culture*, 11–15, 33–37, 56–80. Menand: "What qualifies a man like Arnold Weinstein, who has spent his entire life in the literature departments of Ivy League universities, to guide eighteen-year-old in ruminations on the state of their souls and the nature of the good life?

delineate the terms of a problem, and to bring into the open what is often left unstated; but also suggesting it would do no one no harm if everyone stopped "running after everybody else to preach to 'em, i'stead o'bringing up their families and laying by against a bad harvest" (*Adam Bede* 122)—or instead of quietly reading Shakespeare by firelight, moonlight, or environment-friendly led light.

3

In his remarkable book *Politics of the Scene*, Kottman describes his overall goal as an attempt "to recuperate from the dramatic canon, specifically from three plays by William Shakespeare, a different theoretical articulation of politics," that is openly anti-Hobbesian and that "forgoes a comprehensive theoretical account of what constitutes a polity in order to articulate political existence more contingently, in terms of the singular webs of scenes and relations from which political life is spun" (6). The latter assumption—that political life is spun of contingent and singular webs of scenes and relations— is indebted to Arendt's anthropological construal of ethics and politics, and this non-dialectical construal, which strongly invests in myth and attitude, is *ontological* through and through. It is very strange that Kottman should try to persuade the reader, halfway through his book—when the terms *ontology* and *ontological* have already been used *ad nauseam*, quite beyond their conceivable meanings—that the theoretical-philosophical determination of his (and Shakespeare's) *politics of the scene*, in the tradition of Heidegger and Nancy, is after all useless (105–106). Kottman opens his book with an implicit adhesion to the phenomenological resourcefulness of these terms, and then seeks to waive them in favor of "the significance and value of *undefined* relationships for politics" (106). But his temporary reliance on an ontological and phenomenological approach to the conditions of political togetherness cannot be easily foregone, and this approach gives a sense of theoretical direction to moral passions committed to "relationships" that are undefined, unpredictable, uncertain. The moral passions drive Kottman to restore what he takes to be the authentic sense of politics, and this causes some pronominal dancing: "It seems (to me, at least) that we ought not pretend that we can comprehend what exactly we are talking about when we say 'that polity' or 'this community'"

[...] And if, as these authors [Roosevelt Montás and Arnold Weinstein] insist, education is about self-knowledge and the nature of the good, what are those things supposed to look like? How do we know them when we get there? What does it mean to be human? What exactly is the good life?" (66–68).

(8). The difference between this "we" and the *pluralis auctoris* that I myself for instance use often in this book is that I refuse to include Shakespeare under the pronominal rubric: I may sometimes imply what I believe are his political views, but I never assume that we all share them.[7] Nor do I assume the reader assumes mine.

Kottman wants us to share in the political idea, articulated by Arendt and Cavarero, that "politics becomes the name for the valuation or redemption of human uniqueness-in-plurality insofar as politics confers meaning on the human condition itself" (20). Thus, a secular religion of *moral anthropolitics* replaces the old faiths: but the *redemption* remains, and so do other sacred figures like *haecceitas* and *miracle*.[8] In Marx's astute terms, "religion becomes *unfinished politics*" ("On the Jewish Question," *Early Political Writings* 39). To consider that the unique individual is the political asset par excellence, that the first political gesture is to scenically declare (silently show, pragmatically perform) your uniqueness before others, forcing them to recognize it, seems to me an inadmissible thesis. I do not discuss the opportunity of attributing to Shakespeare an interest in human singularity: I think Kottman is very right in doing so. What I challenge is the propriety of considering that individual uniqueness is a political resource, and that the individual person's "demand for acknowledgement" must be taken as the founding "*political* question" (Lupton, *Thinking* 1): "If you prick us, do we not bleed?" (*The Merchant of Venice* 3.1.54).[9] I believe rather that individual uniqueness is both a natural fact *and* a moral value, with the proviso that morality is not premised upon "nature"—Locke being the last rational-liberal thinker to indulge such terminological fantasy. Then, of course, came Rousseau and other romantic "teachers of virtue," including Arendt, whose bid for the moralization of politics has radically changed the face of political theory. But not irreparably. No politics can be built around the individual flagging of unique, particularized "agony, pleasure, suffering or rage" (Kottman, *Politics* 102). Making a personal scene, forcing others to share your singular affects, is, I believe, no way of "being with and toward others"

---

7   Furthermore, one starting premise of my book is that I assume that my views are decidedly not going to be shared by most readers. When I use the pronoun "we," or more importantly the "we ought to" formula, the reader is invited to turn the irony switch on. I insist: I am not trying to persuade the Shakespeare student or scholar to agree with what I say. I am aware the battle is lost. I am just trying to show her the extent and depth—*the gross and scope*—of a semi-buried disagreement (a pending critical quarrel) she may not be fully aware of.
8   For the *miracle*, see Arendt, *The Human Condition*, 178, 247; Kottman, *Tragic Conditions*, 118; Lupton, *Citizen-Saints*, 6, 23; and *Thinking with Shakespeare*, 24.
9   Lupton opens her book with Shylock's question, significantly without quotation marks, assuming that it is also *our* question.

(102), and if Kottman's politics of the scene demands the sacrifice or rational exchange—his critique of Habermas-leaning Arendtians is telling—then I fail to grasp how the resulting polity can be operative at all. Politics demands of individual human beings that they give up their uniqueness and accept their general resemblance to others, their universality—the "universality," that is, "that no politics can do without" (Butler, "Restating the Universal," *Contingency, Hegemony, Universality* 32). Only by asserting your provisional and conventional equality to others, never your constant natural difference, can politics begin—this is a basic tenet in radical Left politics (Žižek, Badiou) that most well-behaved liberals happen to accept.[10] You are not your neighbor, granted, but when you both stop at a light, you become rigorously equal—and equal too to the guy that drives his car before the two of you. Kottman's political valorization of contingency, which tends to identify it with accidental particularity, overlooks the dialectic-materialist entente between *contingency* and *universality*: the (conventional, arbitrary, temporary, fragile, riven, contradictory, antagonistic) scene of our empty—and at bottom impossible, but who's counting—equality, universality and indifference may well be more contingently political than the scenes examined by Kottman. This of course doesn't mean that your uniqueness vanishes—private life has its own stages, scenes, plots, and dramas, where uniqueness may morally and emotionally shine. To extrapolate the moral exigencies of your extended *domus* to the political sphere is, I believe, a very dangerous theoretical and practical move. As Montaigne, Descartes and Badiou have suggested, in cases of necessary public extrapolation the best thing one can offer is a *provisional morality*—never a *moralized* or *moralistic politics*.[11] At any rate, the extrapolation is exegetically useless, if not downright catastrophic, when the scholar aims at recuperating the resulting moral *anthropolitics* from a canon of Shakespeare plays. Let me recall that the framing thesis of Kottman's book rests on an overinterpretation of Jaques' lines in *As You Like It*: "All the world's a stage / And all the men and women merely players / They have their exits and their entrances" (2.7.139–41). To build from these lines an ontology—"the Shakespearean ontology" (*Politics* 5)—"that reveals

---

10 See the very productive exchange between Judith Butler, Ernesto Laclau and Slavoj Žižek in *Contingency, Hegemony, Universality: Contemporary Dialogues on the Left* (2000).

11 To fight back the current moralization of Shakespeare scholarship it may not be enough to propose a *provisional morality*—something like Spivak's *strategic essentialism*—but it is not a bad start. Badiou speaks of "une moral provisoire" in his seminar *S'orienter dans la pensée, s'orienter dans l'existence*: see Ruda, *For Badiou* 27. Badiou finds inspiration in Descartes, who spoke of a "moral par provision" (*Discours* 96). The Latin text says "ad tempus" (temporary), although Descartes elsewhere calls it "imparfaite": see note 211, pages 634–535 of the same edition.

the world as stage, and that orients itself from the start toward an interactive horizon of words and deeds among unique actors and witnesses" (4)—takes a great deal of moral imagination. Can we really describe the "horizon of words and deeds," say, in *Hamlet*, as one of "interaction"? Do ironic remarks, direct insults, loud threats, prudish warnings, torturing questions, equivocal songs, duplicitous replies, and haywire soliloquies make up an "interactive horizon of words"? And does the invariably violent elbowing of characters out of stage—towards a nunnery, England, or death—make up an "interactive horizon of deeds"? I find it euphemistic, to say the least. *Prima facie*, Shakespeare probably intended Jaques' lines to mean that human beings are like billiard balls, with their entrances and exits, and that they expend whatever momentum they had on their entrance in moral delusions and corporal collisions, pretending and wrangling, lying, and dying. Hobbes would agree.

Kottman is not unaware that his arguments may appear inflected by moral desire and wishful thinking, rather than by reason and critical thinking:

> I again wish to emphasize that the following pages do not represent an attempt to outline a new political theory in the traditional sense. I am not a political scientist and do not wish to propose or advocate a particular organization or model of political organization, utopian or other. Instead, by developing and deepening theoretical observations made by Arendt and others, I wish to imagine or speculate on how drama—not as a unified concept but as a limitless collection of singular scenes of interaction—might provide an essential resource through which to more fundamentally redefine politics as emerging out of the ontological plurality, reciprocal vulnerability, and interdependence of the human condition. (101)

So: I *wish to imagine* politics as emerging out of *ontological plurality*. Desire and Imagination at the service of beings (*Seienden*) incorporated (and redeemed) in communal Being (*Sein*). If Kottman's figural stance is not Utopian, it looks very much so. And it is certainly prophetic. The plural address of his critical stance is more openly at work in his next book, *Tragic Conditions in Shakespeare* (2009), where he argues, for instance, that Hamlet's words—he refers to "the heartache and the thousand natural shocks / That flesh is heir to" (3.1.64–65)—"are not unfamiliar to *us*. His words still speak to *us*." And adds: "But it may be that the drama of such suffering and endurance—*our* experiences and their attendant affects—correspond less and less to inherited ways of making sense of what *we* actually do and say with one another." And concludes: "can Shakespeare's play be said to yield insights into the significance of *our* actions?"

(*Tragic* 1; emphases added). So this is not a study of Shakespearean experience, but rather an invitation to reconsider our experiences, our words, our deeds, our actions, premised upon the conviction that *Hamlet is like us*. This admission takes a great deal of confidence. I certainly don't have it. There are still people, I hope, who read and watch *Hamlet* to confront an incommensurable difference, and to savor the sublime comforts of the very unfamiliar.[12]

Kottman's two readings of *Hamlet*, in *Politics of the Scene* and *Tragic Conditions in Shakespeare*, identify a similar primeval position of face-to-face intimacy of witnesses (*Politics*) and affective bodies (*Tragic Conditions*) that supposedly holds the key to Shakespearean (phenomenological) ontology. This primeval position he derives from Arendt's theoretical work, but he could have resorted to Merleau-Ponty:

> The reason why I am able to understand the other person's body and existence "beginning with" the body proper, the reason why the compresence of my "consciousness" and my "body" is prolonged into the compresence of myself and the other person, is that the "I am able to" and the "the other person exists" belong here and now to the same world [*le même monde*], that the body proper is a premonition of the other person [*premonition d'autrui*], the *Einfühlung* an echo of my incarnation, and that a flash of meaning [*éclair de sens*] makes them substitutable in the absolute presence of origins.
>
> *Signs* 175; *Signes* 174

So, my somatic empathy with the corporality of the other (say, Hamlet) prompts a flash of meaning that renders my consciousness of myself and my consciousness of the existence of Hamlet substitutable in the absolute

---

12 If I myself reread *Hamlet* and do my best to continue teaching it to my students it is not because I think it can help me or them to understand ourselves better, but rather because it helps us to understand something or somebody very different from most of us, whose words and deeds—whose experience—is and remains disturbingly alien. Defamiliarizing *Hamlet* is the real task of a teacher of literature today. To attempt the understanding of Hamlet's experience—especially of his verbal experience—on the basis of the play's call for empathetic identification (2.2.488–528) is deeply misguided. We can hardly be struck by *him* so to our soul, hardly force our soul to *his* conceit such that we may become him: maybe Goethe, Coleridge and T.S. Eliot could. But neither are we them. Hamlet's verbal experience cannot be naturalistically retranslated into the ordinary middle-class terms—even if the play putatively chronicles the dawn of the cultural horizon that makes those terms meaningful, and even if our uncles are still today killing our fathers and marrying our mothers. McEwan's enjoyable failure in *Nutshell* bears witness to this fact.

presence of origins, which is a rather complicated way of suggesting that our compresence renders me and Hamlet mutually replaceable. *Flash of meaning*? *Absolute presence of origins*? These are the very metaphysical fireworks that Adorno detected in in the sky of Husserl's phenomenology. Needless to say, he drew the curtain and corked the room-walls. Not only Adorno. In *On Touching*, Derrida expressed some obvious reservations to this mystical-metaphysical radicalization of phenomenological analysis.[13] If you are so committedly the affectionate witness (Kottman) and friend (Lupton) of Hamlet that you end up nearly becoming him, and if your world is his very same world (*le même monde*), then why study *Hamlet* at all? This silly tendency to turn Hamlet into your loving neighbor reminds me of Žižek's jocular dismissal of the New Age attitude—at bottom one more episode in the petty-bourgeois plot of moralistic self-gratification—"that ultimately reduces my neighbors to my mirror-images, or the means to the end of my self-realization" (*How to Read Lacan* 43).[14] The phenomenological knack for assessing the value of Shakespeare's "ideas" according to their susceptibility of "application in the immediate vicinity" (McDowell, *Mind* 62) is immensely, depressingly, banal. Confronting students with what they already are—our lovely neighbor Ophelia and her lugubrious boyfriend Hamlet —remains a popular solution to the challenge of teaching a Shakespeare play, and it probably makes the teacher very popular. Confronting students with what they *are not*—and this rebus need not necessarily be "the unfathomable abyss of radical Otherness" (43)—must be, I am aware, a very outdated requirement of liberal education. This is a very old book indeed.

The new moral criticism of neo-phenomenological scholars appeals constantly to this *same world*, the shared horizon of addressed plurality. In the "Introduction" to *Tragic Conditions*, Kottman points out that "there seems to be a gap between what *we* feel ourselves go through—both the events themselves

---

13   Derrida: "And so, must we not think, and think otherwise (without objecting to it frontally and integrally), that the said 'same world' (if there is some such world, and if it is indeed necessary to account for it, and account for its 'effect,' as 'sense of the world') is not and will never be the 'same world'? The fact that this proposition is intelligible and even convincing for 'every man,' throughout more than one possible world, does not contradict its content. When I take into account a whole history, from hominization to socialization connected to verbal language and its pragmatic conditions, and so forth, I can convey to 'every man's' ear that the world of each person is untranslatable and that finally there will never be any 'same world.' These two possibilities are not incompatible; they even condition, and call for, one another, as paradoxical as this may sound" (*On Touching* 193–194).
14   For Žižek on the nightmare of neighbors see "Love Thy Neighbor? No Thanks!" in *The Plague of Fantasies*, 55–106.

and *our* affective response to them—and *our* inherited social activities; whatever *we* routinely, or on special occasions, do and say with one another" (2; emphases added). Feelings and affections circulate between us and us in a small, splashy, inflatable pool of *Einfühlung*. *Routinely* for whom? For us. *Special occasions* for whom? For us. Can we relate our middle-class twenty-first centuries *routines* and *special occasions* with those of Hamlet and Edgar and Rosalind? Kottman believes we can, and "like Edgar and Gloucester, we grasp one another's hands on foggy terrain that we cannot even see" (3). This is beautifully rendered, and perhaps true, but it comes too close to Anglican catechizing—both to Donne's homiletic prose and to the Victorian tradition of Shakespeare sermons—to be of much critical use. Edgar's and Albany's final plight, the prospect of an "individual or collective fate" unattended by the experience of their elders, is described as "*our* predicament" (3; emphasis added). The dramas of Hamlet and Edgar are seen to "offer us insights into the inheritable conditions of *our* lives together" (4; emphasis added), and more specifically, Kottman raises the question "Do Shakespeare's protagonists undergo transformations or experiences from which, or through which, *we* might learn about our lives together?" (5; emphasis in the original). Interestingly, the critic here both italicizes the pronoun and settles the disjunction between the individual and collective fate in favor of the latter, of "our lives together." This way the plural deictic (we) becomes increasingly transtemporal and unspecific, all the way to the climactic vaporization of

> How we are *moved*, therefore, becomes an essential measure of the extent to which any given sociality—any 'we'—can learn from and about itself and devolve from past to future. Our affective response is a manifestation that we care, individually and collectively, about our bonds to one another ... (8)

But note how the unspecific plurality—"any 'we'"—ends up collapsing, once and again, into the "we" of Kottman's personal sociality, whose reciprocal "bonds" are partly described in the acknowledgement section of the book as "conversations," "exchanges," "camaraderie." What is here being constantly taken for granted is, first, that togetherness, reciprocity, and mutuality are more meaningful than individuality, which is a moral assumption (the rational assumption is that they are more convenient), and second, that sociality can only be secured through emotional not rational means, which is another moral assumption. Karl Marx, we know, also "wanted reciprocity, but not via moral exhortation" (Claeys, *Marx* 69). Both assumptions in turn owe much to the ethical reprogramming of phenomenology as per Levinas, Merleau-Ponty and

Arendt. "Does the play [*Hamlet*] *move* us; and if so why and how"? wonders Kottman, "What is the relation, if any, between Hamlet's fate and our collective self-conception?" (44). Note that no reference is made to *understanding*: only *caring* matters. No allusion is made to *personal* relevance: only the *collective* bearing counts. The chapters in Kottman's book close with a parallel appeal to pluralized significance, to a relevance that is less transcendental (rational) than empirically emotional:

> There is no transcendental or categorical ground for recognizing *ourselves* in the fate of Hamlet—no ground for *our* sociality, that is, beyond the contingency of Hamlet revealing to *us* something of *ourselves*.
> 77; emphases added

> In testing *if*—not *how*—we are still moved by what *we* can do to and with one another, Shakespeare forces *us* to make sense of the actions *we* have witnessed [in *King Lear*] by confronting the inadequacy of *our* inherited ways of responding to misdeeds and suffering. If what *we* have seen *ourselves* perform leaves *us* bereft of insight and affective comprehension into those deeds, how are we now to see *ourselves*?
> 131; emphases added

> But *we ourselves* are not yet released from the island. *We* may have believed that *we* left Prospero behind; however *we* find that he has followed *us* beyond the confines of the "play." Nothing is sacred in the play, it turns out; not even its (artistic) separation from *us*. We find *ourselves* implicated; evasion is not to be countenanced. We are not yet 'released' from what has transpired and cannot claim to be. At least, not until *we* undergo an as yet unscripted, self-induced transformation in *our* recognition of ourselves and one another.
> 165; emphases added

Let me focus on this third paragraph on *The Tempest*, which closes the book. Kottman is adamant: no distance, no aesthetic, *artisti*c or intellectual distance, no defamiliarization, no estrangement, no *separation*, remain when the play comes to its end. We are inseparate from, integrated with, assimilated into the play, invited to participate in an *unscripted* and spontaneous (*self-induced*) metamorphosis—a recognitive transformation that awakens us to the significance of our collective fate. Remember Whitman: "Twenty-eight young men bathe by the shore, / Twenty-eight young men and all so friendly." *Unscripted* and *self-induced*: these two adjectives lodge the thrust of Kottman's undialectical and phenomenological critical methodology. The combination of the adverbial "as yet" and the noun "transformation" delineate the Utopian future-gazing coordinates of his moral program. In his earlier book, Kottman closed a piece on Arendt's conception of the revolutionary spirit with a paean to "the earthly happiness intrinsic to freedom" which is not "separable from its renewed worldly pursuit as politics—from the experience and inheritance of crushed dreams, lost hopes, and thwarted chances for a sharable happiness into which newcomers are born" (*Politics* 155). Such pastoral vagary crystallizes in a sharp formulation—politics as the pursuit of sharable happiness—that neither liberals nor socialists would endorse, *sharing* being anathema for the former and *happiness* striking the latter as a Utilitarian entelechy.

4

I have examined in some detail Kevin Curran's and Paul Kottman's moralistic appeals to the reconsideration (renovation, reinvention) of plurality and community. Let me now turn to Julia Lupton's similar calls. In *Citizen-Saints: Shakespeare and Political Theology* (2005) she adopted the Hegelian notion of civil society and redescribed it, with Marx's help, "as the arena in which new forms of human interaction and emancipation can be fashioned" (7). The sleight of hand is the accommodation of Marx's critique of Hegel's conception of civil society to her own communitarian interests. Lupton has the courage to confront Marx's arguments in the *Critique of Hegel's 'Philosophy of Right'* and in "The Jewish Question," and boldly records his claim that the state is "a fantasmatic projection and and false harmonization of social conflict on a plane of illusory commonality" (Lupton, *Citizen-Saints* 7). So far so good. What is arguable is her construal of the Marxian redescription of civil society as an arena for *new forms* of human interaction and emancipation, for Marx only stipulates *one* form:

> Only when the actual individual man absorbs the abstract citizen of the state into himself and has become in his empirical life, in his individual labour, in his individual relationships a *species-being*; only when he has recognized and organized his "own forces" as *social* forces, and therefore no longer separates the social force from himself in the form of *political* force; only then is human emancipation completed.
> "On the Jewish Question," *Early Political Writings* 50

I am not sure Lupton would be ready to accept the de-naturalization of civil-social distinctive and differentiating communal rituals (including of course those of religion, property, education, occupation) that this unique form of emancipation entails. Marx is thinking less of a productive experiment in life and identity forms than of a radical dismantling of the naturalized bourgeois prerogatives that very often sustain those forms. Rather than regarding society, as Lupton does, as a "field" or "matrix" of "multiple memberships" (8–10), Marx saw it as a realm of multiple de-affiliation, the place where membership to the *Gattungswesen* (species-being) of an essentially productive human nature is universally offered to human beings. Lupton reads Shakespearean drama "as an extended midrash of citizenship, that is, as a poetic, exegetical, and narrative exploration of the dilemmas of community-formation that take their orientation from biblical topoi and mythoi" (15). This "neo-exegetical" approach should not be mistaken, Lupton avers, with "reactionary criticism that would take religion as either content or context, dogma or history" (15), but the fact is that both her readings and the "Humanifesto" she places at the end of her book do take religion as content, context and history, let alone as pretext, and are strongly sustained by the belief that community-formation—in Shakespeare or elsewhere—is a rewarding object of study because communities are good, because communities must be formed, and because the "literature of citizenship," which Shakespeare's plays supposedly epitomize, "offers means of gathering together" diverse genres, modes and skills, "means of linking the kinds of materials" animating interdisciplinarity; "assembles its readers as a body of listeners gathered together in a space (virtual or real) that implies a public, even ritual, dimension;" and provides a "covenant [...] constituting a people through an act of agreement on shared principles," and "[epistles] addressed to a community of listeners" (215). *Gathering, linking, assembling*—these are but the operations of *religatio* advanced by the institutions of *ecclesia*, the workings of a religion complete with a body, rituals, a covenant, shared principles, and epistles addressed to the members of the community. Again and again, in Lupton, religion becomes—as Marx anticipated—*unfinished politics*. If religion is not overtly "taken," as Lupton remonstrates, it is because it is so intimately presupposed that there is no need to make the adhesion explicit. Of the three central ideas pursued in her book—virtue, hospitality, consent—the first two are political only in a morally puffed and religiously tumescent sense of the word—a sense at work, for instance, in the work of George Eliot. There is nothing intentionally "reactionary" in the creative and ingenious work of Julia Lupton, but in the wrong hands her implicit endorsement of operative communities could lead to illiberal and conservative positions. At an exegetic level, however, it no doubt contributes to gentrify, bourgeoisify, and domesticate Shakespeare in brazenly rightist directions.

The particularly moralistic and religious tonality of *Citizens-Saints* is passed over to the collection of essays edited by Graham Hammill and Julia Lupton, titled *Political Theology and Early Modernity*. Here the program is again less to understand something (early modern cultural products) than to facilitate a new future of harmonious commonality. According to Hammill and Lupton, political theology is instrumental in furnishing "imaginative formulations with the power to reveal and constitute new norms, communities and forms of life" (7), and they openly rely on "*our* expectations of coherence and community" (6; emphasis added) to reorient "the promise of a new future" (9). Like Kottman, Lupton finds in Arendt's work inspiration to interrogate the separation between private and public spaces, domus and polis, life and politics, and like Kottman she uses Arendt to read Shakespeare as much as she uses

> Shakespeare to read Arendt [...] in order to disclose [...] the many places in both her writing and Shakespeare's plays in which divergent forms of life—the lives of men in their political plurality, of humans in their domestic multiplicity, of animals in their biodiversity, and of objects in both their durability and their decay—enter into world-building and future-founding relations with each other. (9)

From a theoretical point of view, this adds little to Kottman's moral-political program, but her willingness to grant communitarian membership to animals and objects spells no doubt a momentous decision, one that forces her "to develop strains in political and social theory that tend to be neglected or undervalued in postcolonial, materialist, and Neo-Marxist approaches to literature and culture" (16). In other words, if she deviates from progressive critical dogma, it is only to become still more progressive. The notation is relevant because it helps to mark a turning point towards a field of research—present in the work of Martin Heidegger, Walter Benjamin, Merleau-Ponty, Jean-Luc Marion, the late Jacques Derrida, Giorgio Agamben, Roberto Esposito, Gail Kern Paster, Erica Fudge, Donna Haraway, Laurie Shannon, Jonathan Gil Harris, Scott Maisano, Michael Witmore—that could be loosely described as environmentalist, animalist, object-oriented, neo-materialist, and historical-phenomenological. If I am right, this is the first time Lupton states her explicit adherence to *phenomenological* protocols of analysis (*Thinking* 14–15). Her search for thought-fragments and *Urphänomene* that may emerge into what Arendt calls *the world of living* (Arendt)—investing it with "divergent forms of life"—betokens a moral inflection towards *vita activa*, also extolled by Simon

Palfrey in his reading of Pericles (*Late Shakespeare* 63–65), and this bias blurs beyond recognition the liberal trope of the *good life*. All in all, she concludes,

> *Thinking with Shakespeare* is ultimately in search of ways to live with Shakespeare, as one might learn to live with AIDS, with cats, or with children. This means acknowledging the sources and the scope as well as the limits of Shakespeare's several discourses on virtue, not in order to declare *our* greater wisdom concerning human arrangements, but in order to recover their potentialities for the project of living well.
> 24; emphasis added

The project of living well, the phrase that closes the "Introduction" to her book, is the kind of prophetic slogan we expect to see upheld in Anglican homilies or denounced in anti-totalitarian dystopia. Do we read and study Shakespeare in order to discover or reform *our* project of living well? I don't think so. Many people have turned to Shakespeare to find inspiration in their project of "living in thrall" (*The Passionate Pilgrim* 17.16), "living on the common road" (*As You Like It* 2.3.34), "living in posterity" (Sonnet 6.12), "living idly" (*1 Henry VI* 1.1.142), "living low" (*3 Henry VI* 4.7.20), or merely living dangerously. Furthermore, I find it very hard to see how *thinking with Shakespeare* (an attractive prospect) should necessarily slip into *living with Shakespeare* (a very dubious venture), let alone whether and how *living with Shakespeare* can be compared to learning to live with cats or with children. Accepting the rationale of Lupton's invitation demands an intensity of scriptural sagacity and mystical wisdom that I personally cannot afford. I am sure, nonetheless, that most students are delighted to hear that Shakespeare is like cats and children. The problem is they might want to know why.

Since the project of living well is after all *our* project, the plural address surfaces and resurfaces in Lupton's book as a constant reminder of moral affiliation. She proclaims her disinterest in theoretical debates and in the afterlife of Shakespeare "in later instances of thought." Rather, she has made a more practical than theoretical—I would call it *post-theoretical*—decision

> to use the orienting scenarios, compelling subjectivities, and object world of the plays—Petrucchio's animals, Kate's laundry, Timon's rage, Hamlet's friends, Helena's recipes, Caliban's constraints, Hermione's reticence—to stage the philosophical and political questions that continue to engage Shakespeare's audiences. To think with Shakespeare is, ideally, not to instrumentalize the plays in the service of an ideological

> program [...], but rather to think alongside Shakespeare about matters of shared concern (as one speaks "with" a friend). (23)

If Lupton doesn't realize the considerable "ideological" implications encased in her nonchalant and apparently commonsensical confidence in the very possibility of "thinking alongside Shakespeare" about matters of "shared concern" with readers and with Shakespeare himself, then of course her claim stands to reason. But failing to see those implications strikes me as a problem. *Shared concern*? This demands an assumption of trans-temporality—the *nunc stans* of human essence—that may explain why Lupton invariably dismisses historicism (17, 27, 71, 198). Existentialism is described as a "philosophy oriented around human being in the trembling vulnerability of *our* multiple dependencies on each other and *our* permanent exposure to the scars, mutations, and new births delivered by the slings and arrows of *our* own signifying practices" (14; my emphases). This program of sanitary attention and moral reparation, focused on *vulnerability* and *exposure*, may be *existentialist* in a Arendtian sense, but not in the original sense of the term. Before existentialism became a distinct philosophical tendency, Nietzsche was already berating the ethics of weakness Lupton's description invokes. I am not implying that Nietzsche is right. I am simply redescribing Lupton's description in order to gain some perspective. The third chapter of the book tries to respond to the presentist question "What continuum obtains between consent and coercion in the early modern period and in *our* own?" (21; my emphasis), and in the first chapter, Gremio's collection of household goods, "caught between the play's Italian setting and its English performance space, invites *our* own creative curation of objects culled from several worlds" (69; my emphasis). In the fourth chapter on *Timon of Athens* we learn that "What Timon reveals [...] is *our* terrifying incompleteness with respect to other people, the world, and *our* own vitality, as well as *our* shaping and scarring by the signifying practices through which we manage as well as avoid *our* connectivity" (151; my emphases). Our *curation*, our *consent*, our *incompleteness*—these are moral figures in a scripted life of mandatory connectivity. Kant held that the truths of religion are important but *problematic* things. That they are by their very nature problematic is, according to Hilary Putnam, a good thing, not a bad one: "This is where Kant's break with the medieval is total" (*The Many Faces* 50). Consider Putnam's coda:

> What Kant is saying, to put it positively, is that we have to think for ourselves without the kind of guide that Alasdair MacIntyre wants to restore for us, and that fact is itself the most valuable fact about our lives. *That* is the characteristic with respect to which we are all equals. We are all in the

same predicament, and we all have the potential of thinking for ourselves with respect to the question of How to Live. (50)

What makes us equal to other human beings is *our* capacity to think for ourselves without guide (about virtue, or other moral values), and not *our* proclivity to slip into someone else's arrogated *we*, into her solution to the question of the form and meaning of life. Early modern studies would do well in breaking totally with lingering medieval assumptions. If only because not all Aristotelian revivals (Arendt, Nussbaum) are necessarily emancipatory.

5

In their "Introduction" to *Entertaining the Idea: Shakespeare, Philosophy and Performance* (2021), Lowell Gallagher, James Kearney, and Julia Lupton make it clear that their commitment to philosophy is premised upon philosophy's prior "commitment to the formation and transformation of persons through spiritual exercise and the ethical and cognitive work of trust, care, and courage / encouragement" (13). This obviously rules out philosophy understood as a search for truth or critical analysis. It would take much mending to make Descartes, Spinoza, Kant, or Hegel endorse such commitment. Not even Brandom's study on Hegel's *Spirit of Trust* would be able to accommodate the moralist gleam of the phrase "spiritual exercise." Yet many other current monographs or edited collections would surely welcome "the glittering extremes of affect" (9) the editors of this book examine. They are interested less on Shakespearean performance proper than on the "inherently enactive character of core ethical concepts such as acknowledgement, virtue, habit, love, judgement, and care" (6), a declaration that rather dramatically narrows down their understanding of philosophy to *moral philosophy*. In fact, the only philosopher they mention in the "Introduction" is the undialectical thinker Walter Benjamin, whom they accost for grip on notions like "natural history, in which the consequences of human action metabolize with the physical world" (7). So much so that, by their own account, in Shakespearean drama, "sublunar beings seek, avoid, or respond to the idea traces impressed in their souls, secreted by their somatic processes" (7). It goes without saying that as soon as ideas are held to be *secreted by somatic processes*, we step out of serious philosophy into some other place—call it salad paradise, nirvana, or the heaven of "affective comprehension" (Kottman, *Tragic Conditions* 131). Earlier in the "Introduction," the same scholars state that Shakespeare's plays supply "readers, listeners, viewers, and performers of diverse backgrounds with equipment for living" (4). *Spiritual exercise? Equipment for living?* What is this? The Globe or Little Gidding?

In a recent lecture on "Shakespeare's Virtues," Julia Lupton states that she aspires "to keep this work [on virtues in Shakespeare] as real and relevant and responsive as possible to actual virtue-work in the world."[15] Although her speech is focused on *Twelfth Night*, she confesses that in her work she is "not just looking for new meanings or interpretations of the plays. Instead, I'm looking for new tools and templates, tools and templates for learning and also for living." The result is a rash exercise in presentist extrapolation, with Shakespeare's comedy singled out as the site where the virtues of capacity building and placement delineate a virtue ecology brimming with gay activists, foster children, unemployed graduates, immigrants, and refugees. The lecture highlights one single passage in the play where virtues are mentioned as existential assets not to be concealed (*Twelfth Night* 1.3.110), but she interestingly silences several other references in the play to genuine virtue as something perilously inseparable from feigned virtue, that is, vice. The same omission blunts the force of her argument in the related essay "Virtue in Twelfth Night: A Humanifesto," where she does refer to Feste's disturbing correlation between virtue and sin, but only because he emphasizes, like Aristotle, argues Lupton, the "patched" condition of virtue. All in all, the new essay is a celebration of virtue construed as "participation: the movement of several persons into a scenario that invites the actualization of capacity and affirms their mutual ensoulment" (16). This celebration presupposes rather than demonstrates Shakespeare's contribution to the very loose sense of virtue whose roots she discovers in Aristotle. She recommends de-freezing the dormant concepts of virtue, which implies "reading them in their original context" (18). But does *Twelfth Night* and other Shakespearean texts really constitute one of those original contexts? Is the "wisdom" of virtue truly "manifested" in the Shakespeare play? If, as Lupton submits, these Shakespeare texts have been "entrusted to our care" shouldn't we express that care by abstaining from reading more into them than they permit and restraining the reach of our anachronic extrapolations? In accordance with Lupton's criteria of virtuous behavior, abstention

---

15   The transcript of this lecture can be accessed through https://spotlight.folger.edu/2021/01/22/encores-shakespeares-virtues-lecture-by-julia-reinhard-lupton-2018/ In the parallel essay, titled "Virtue in *Twelfth Night*: A Humanifesto," we read "that testing Shakespeare's virtues in the multivalent matrix provided by ethical philosophy, performance studies, organizational and design studies, and theories of pedagogy and enskillment will allow me to reframe the virtuous dynamics of Shakespearean drama in a manner responsive to the value and import, the powers and offices, of the humanities today" (3–4).

and restraint hardly count as virtues, but they seem to me virtuous exercises in critical responsibility. There are many ways, I think, of reconciling scholarly criticism with teaching and social activism. Keeping these *practices* separate may not be an unwise decision: it was Alasdair McIntyre, after all, who described virtue as an acquired human quality the possession and exercise of which tends to enable us to achieve those goods which are "internal to practices" (*After Virtue* 218–219).

Let us briefly reconsider the question of *virtue* in *Twelfth Night*. Virtues in Sir Toby's speech carries an ironic implication, for the dominant sense of the term in the play is set by Olivia being described by the Captain as a "virtuous maid," a notion later developed by the clown when he calls her a "mouse of virtue" (1.5.61). To Olivia's near-Puritan standards of moral excellence, Prince Orsino's nobility fails to warrant his virtue: "Yet I suppose him virtuous, know him noble" (1.5.27). Virtue here is mark of restraint—what the Duke calls "retention" (2.4.94) and Olivia "delay" (1.5.90) and works as a moral quality in opposition to the liberal prodigality commonly associated with nobility (the Duke resembles Antonio in *Merchant*). A sense of resistance to action-promoting liberality underpins the use of the term in Sir Toby's protestation to the clown: "Dost thou think, because thou art virtuous, there shall be no more cakes and ale?." Finally, the term reappears in Antonio's angry retort, "Virtue is beauty, but the beauteous evil / Are empty trunks o'er-flourished by the devil" (*Twelfth Night* 3.4.333–34), a couplet that resonates with the built-in ambiguity of this moral concept. Not only is virtue correlated in the play with the historical-Christian sense of life-blocking restraint (Puritan passivity), but also with immorality and epistemic sham (Platonic appearance).[16] In Shakespeare's comedies and romances, the sense of what is being repressed (experience as antagonism) is always stronger than the achieved harmonies and reconciliations whose basic function is to chloroform life and decommission experience. This is why Levinas' description of violence accounts much better for the genuine Shakespearean experience of dis-communication, discontinuity, disguise, and inaction:

> But violence does not consist so much in injuring and annihilating persons as in interrupting their continuity [*interrompre la continuité des personnes*], making them play roles [*jouer des rôles*] in which they no longer recognize themselves, making them betray not only commitments but

---

16   It is not uncommon to find the term *virtues* in uneasy correlation to *traitors* in *All's well that Ends Well* and *As You Like It*.

their own substance, making the carry out actions that will destroy every possibility for action.

Totality 21; *Totalité* 6

Lupton relies strongly on Nussbaum's talk of virtue inflected by moral luck rests on a brutal abstraction of the human game from societal-ideological determinants. The fact that Aristotle's take on ethics is hampered by this abstracted view is of course predictable, but the notion that Nussbaum, in her critical gloss, should restrict "the more ungovernable part of the human being's internal makeup" to the so-called "irrational parts of the soul," namely "appetites, feelings, emotions" (*Fragility* 7), without taking stock of the many ways in which "external contingency" (7), in the form of ideology, quite literally *makes up* the internal makeup, and *constitutes* it as an unconscious subject, is less forgivable. Nussbaum reads Greek literature and philosophy from the anthropological standpoint—from the *nunc stans* of human essence—of a positivist tradition whose assumptions are metaphysical: the human being has a body and a mind, and then there is a world outside, and a language for the mind to communicate with other minds. This is a nice picture, but also, as Habermas pointed out in his critique of Arendt, nicely untrue—for Sophocles and Shakespeare, anyway.[17] Like Aristotle's Being, external contingency is said (and occurs) in more than one way, and the opposition agent-versus-world fails to capture the complexity of internalized exteriority lurking inside a "conflicted cultural field."[18]

---

17   As I have already pointed out, in his essay, "Hannah Arendt's Communication Concept of Power," Habermas criticizes Arendt's coercion-free conception of power, and brilliantly exposes her stylization of Greek political life and culture.

18   Nussbaum's open hostility towards Butler evinces a reluctance to accept the force of structural determinants: she finds herself "unsettled" by "[Butler's] narrow vision of the possibilities for change" and disturbed by the "exaggerated denial of pre-cultural agency." Indeed what Butler calls "ironic hopefulness" seems not enough for earnest Nussbaum. And she quotes with some anxiety Butler's powerful remark that "there is no self that is prior to the convergence or who maintains 'integrity' prior to its entrance into this conflicted cultural field. There is only a taking up of the tools where they lie, where the very 'taking up' is enabled by the tool lying there" ("The Professor of Parody"). For the Nussbaum-Butler debate, and its overspill to Derrida, see Alfano, *Derrida Reads Shakespeare*, 41–45.

6

American philosopher Robert Nozick noted once that "standards of rationality are a means whereby we rise above, or check, our own particular hopes, wishes, and biases" (*Rationality*, xiii). This opinion is not exactly popular, and neither was Nozick, whose defense of the minimal state in *Anarchy, State and Utopia* won him lifelong enemies among the academic Left. Yet his ultraliberal stance in favor of the *underdetermination of moral theory* (*Anarchy* 45–47) effectively contributes to strip the "good life" from its moral-ideological inducements and to remind us that "the meaning of life" is an "elusive and difficult notion" (50). What are after all "*our* expectations of coherence and community"? Do we all aspire to live in *coherent communities*?[19] Is language *good* (coherent) enough for our *good life*, good enough, that is, to correct a bad life? But what is a *bad life*? Do language and goodness stand, as Levinas ridiculously portended, side by side, face to face, hand to hand (*Totalité* 38)? And if that is the case, why do we keep expecting people to remember they should "speak by the card" (*Hamlet* 5.1.126)? Moral philosophy is the only placebo—the anti-philosophy, Badiou would call it—capable of deactivating the possible relevance of these questions. According to Levinas, "la morale n'est pas une branche de la philosophie, mais la philosophie première" (*Totalité* 146). Husserlian phenomenology is not to blame for this radical position, but it is indisputable that the undialectical tendency of phenomenology lodged a potential for the moral-ethical deviation, endorsed by Arendt, that Levinas' radical statement proclaims. The priority of morality and ethics over nearly anything else is one of the causes of the current *défaillance* of critical reason. Moralist exasperation infiltrates the fashionable drive to combine Biblical tropes of *ecclesia*, republican-revolutionary motifs of the *vivere civile*, neo-humanist calls to *vita activa*, and post-sixties inklings of authentic community in readings of early modern literature, particularly Shakespeare. And Levinas, Derrida rightly pointed out, was actively involved in prompting this combination: "toutes les pensées classiques interrogées par Levinas sont ainsi trainées vers l'*agora*, sommées de s'expliquer dans un langage éthico-politique qu'elles n'ont pas toujours voulu ou cru vouloir parler"(*L'écriture* 145). Indeed, resistance to this *ethical-political language* is not only a defensive prerogative of the classical (ontological) philosophemes (self, other, one,

---

19   For an interesting critique of the metaphysical underpinnings of community, see Derrida, *Points*, 355. Derrida is here partly responding to the new vogue of critical reflection on the problem of community prompted by the publication of Jean-Luc Nancy's very influential long essay, *La communauté desouvrée* (1986). See also Caputo, "Community without a Community".

many, being, infinity), but also a foundational gesture of liberal thought, from Hobbes, who was particularly hostile to seventeenth-century Romans, to John Locke, whose silence about Hobbes can be read, among many other things, as a way of assuming the latter's suspicion of neo-classical resuscitations. The precarious allegorical chain of transferential figures—the Temple of Jerusalem is like the Athenian polis like the Roman forum like the Venetian assembly like Arden forest like the picnic across my lawn in Rutherford—shows too many fault-lines and breaking points to be scholarly efficient.

Moralism disfigures the task of philosophy by forcing its agenda to attend to the present. The urge to register the contemporary occurrence and adjudicate its moral valence reveals a presentist-moralist compulsion to celebrate immediacy and propinquity. No *khorís*, no gap, no distance, no difference, survives the moralist flooding. Jean-Luc Nancy's critique of philosophical 'novelty' as it was coined by the *nouveaux philosophes* in the mid-1970s throws light on our problem here. The correlation between *philosophie* and *nouveauté*, the replacement of an old-fashioned philosophical style conceived as the work of the uncontemporary (*inactuel*), a style best exemplified by Heidegger, by a philosophical discourse conceived as the proclamation of an original contemporaneity (*une actualité inédite*) implies the substitution of an anthropological subject for the genuine philosophical cogito. Philosophy becomes *presentist prophecy*. In whose name? asks Nancy. The answer is conclusive: "Comme par hasard, au nom du même sujet, du sujet anthropologique, qui devient, dans la prophétie et pour qu'il puisse y avoir prophétie, sujet moral, ou moralisant" (*Ego sum* 16). In the name, he replies, of the moral or moralistic subject. The arrival of this subject was foreseen by Paul de Man in 1973. The Belgian critic detected and ironically described the moral urgency driving the supposedly epistemological ambition to overcome formalism:

> We speak as if, with the problems of literary form resolved once and forever, and with the techniques of structural analysis refined to near-perfection, we could now move "beyond formalism" towards the questions that really interest us and reap, at last, the fruits of the ascetic concentration on techniques that prepared us for this decisive step. With the internal law and order of literature well policed, we can now confidently devote ourselves to the foreign affairs, the external politics of literature. Not only do we feel able to do so, but we owe it to ourselves to take this step: *our moral conscience* would not allow us to do otherwise. Behind the assurance that valid interpretation is possible, behind the recent interest in writing and reading as potentially effective public speech acts, stands a highly respectable *moral imperative* that strives to reconcile the internal,

formal, private structures of literary language with their external, referential, and public effects.

Allegories 3; emphases added

Our moral conscience, our highly respectable moral imperative, the public effects. Prevail upon it, if the doors of academia were cleansed, everything would appear to the post grad student as it is, Infinite. For the scholar has closed herself up, till she sees all things through narrow chinks of his cavern. William Blake and Aldous Huxley are fine as stylists, visionary artists, and existential provocateurs—I personally love both—but their prophetic-moral arrogance may be unsuited for literary research. Of course, I may be wrong, for the truth is they have been heard, and the foreign affairs department has never been so busy—in the arch-American manner, of course, of separating good from evil. The proliferation of the figure of the *sujet moralisant*—the good men and good women—in English departments all round the world, but especially in the English-speaking world, has resulted in an inevitable moralization of literary studies. The moralistic attitude, let me recall, has nothing to do with the moral law, which is empty and potentially uncanny. In fact, what Lukacher describes as "the late modern or postmodern return to the daemonic figures of conscience that cannot be internalized and that are prior to and irreducible to the moral law as it has been traditionally understood" (*Daemonic* 33) presumes an institutionalized internalization—actually, a demonization— of the *daimon* that is still today operative in the *aesthetic phenomenalization* of a world (Shakespeare's) that has, they tell us, inexorably sided with the *good*. But the contingent *daimon* of conscience is prior to the moral distinction—"the daemon is neither good or evil" (*Daemonic* 14)—and both Shakespeare and some exceptional voices of the present (Derrida, Lyotard, Deleuze, Žižek) are here to remind us of the irreducibility of the daemonic figures to a moralized, phenomenalized, and depleted moral law. Lukacher makes the convenience of such return and reminder rest upon the speculative perception that "deep within the silent voice of conscience Shakespeare discerns not the moral law, not a realm of values, but the silent play of the letter" (*Daemonic* 135).

Kant said that there was only nature (the set of phenomena objectified by the understanding) and freedom (the empty, noumenal site of morality), and his critique of judgement very uncertainly broke a middle-ground where phenomenological scouts have laid their tents and tepees. The best way to undo Kant's distinctions was to lessen the expectations of human freedom by exposing the human will's dependence on superstructural (ideological, verbal) determination, and to recall that the givenness of nature to concepts is also mediated by these superstructural determinants. But moralist scholars with a phenomenological inclination decided to pursue, and further blur, the middle path opened by Kant. By disfiguring (detranscendentalizing, repsychologizing) the faculties (senses, imagination, judgement, reason) and blending them up to the point of their utter mutual indiscernibility, what they give us under the guise of a new critique of (ultra-affective) taste is a *tribute to the morality of nature*. Interestingly, the critique of the moralistic aestheticization of pure nature is a running and possibly constitutive motif in Adorno's *Aesthetic Theory*:

> *khorís* [distance] from the empirically existing, takes up a position to it in accord with Hegel's argument against Kant: The moment a limit is posited, it is overstepped and that against which the limit was established is absorbed. Only this, not moralizing, is the critique of the principle of *l'art pour l'art*, which by abstract negation posits the *khorismós* of art as absolute. (6)

What I want to highlight in this comment is Adorno's instinctive rejection of moralizing critiques of the autonomy of art. The immanent formalism of radical aestheticism may be flawed—especially ideologically flawed. There is no question about that, especially in a field—Shakespeare studies—that was momentously altered in the eighties by anti-formalist (also anti-aestheticist) tendencies. But the question about the legitimate grounds of the anti-formalist offensive remain, for there are many ways of saying that Mallarmé's art is *wrong* or *untrue*—and not all of them hold the same value. Adorno, in particular, fiercely scorned the moralistic tendencies that tried, in the aftermath of two world wars, to revoke the autonomy of art in favor of its relation to its other (real things). In short, the non-conceptual relation of the artwork to its object is not to be naively mended by immediately reintroducing the object into the artwork: "The crisis of the pure artwork in the wake of the European catastrophes cannot be solved by breaking out of the pure work into an extra-aesthetic materiality whose moralistic pathos is pitched to obscure the fact that it is the easy way out" (Adorno, *Aesthetic* 182). The idea that Shakespeare is here with us, inside our homes and kitchens, and that if we wish to reinforce our moral commitments to our communal lives we can simply open the fridge and defreeze some of his ideas is wrong on three counts: wrong to Shakespeare's ideas, because they are not portions of transcendent materiality that have been given to us, but rather mediated by a formal work that forestalls the immediacy of givenness; wrong to our right to remain uncommitted to certain figurations of community or to anything else; wrong to the lives of many people who never de-freeze because they have no homes, let alone kitchen refrigerators.[20]

The moralist scholar has given up reading Shakespeare's playtexts in favour of intuitions (seeing, feeling) of the plays that work, imaginatively, as so many *paysages moralisés*. By de-antagonizing, naturalizing, and harmonizing the communal configurations whose fragments are scattered through *The Merchant of Venice, Hamlet, King Lear, The Tempest*, and *Twelfth Night*, scholars like Curran, Kottman and Lupton mix up *sollen* (moral duty) and *seien* (ontic reality), *virtue* and what they take to be *natural innocence*. This operation gives a blank cheque to animalist and posthumanist scholars. Coetzee, now invoked less as an informed witness than as a shrewd critic, pointed out that whereas

> innocence is a state in which we try to maintain our children, dignity is a state that we claim for ourselves. Affronts to the innocence of our children or to the dignity of our persons are attacks not upon our essential being but upon constructs—constructs by which we live, but constructs nevertheless.

Dignity, virtue—metaphors we live by. Coetzee further calls dignity "a fiction that may well be indispensable for a just society, namely, that human beings have a dignity that sets them apart from animals and consequently protect them from being treated like animals" (*Giving Offence* 14). This echoes Richard Rorty's insistence on the avoidance of *cruelty*, "the humiliation of human beings by other human beings" as a central prerequisite of a liberal society (*Contingency* XV). Two ideas can be drawn from this: 1) neither virtue nor dignity are natural realities—they are, unlike innocence, cultural constructs (innocence is natural because it is a lack—of knowledge in the first place) in

---

20 See Julia Lupton's description in *Thinking with Shakespeare* (253–254) of her kitchen as studio—where *thinking with Shakespeare* becomes *living with Shakespeare* and eventually *cooking with Shakespeare*. One may compare it to Arendt's passing remark in her book on Kant: "You must be alone in order to think; you need company to enjoy a meal" (*Lectures* 67). One could also compare Lupton's defiant and imaginative domesticity with Levinas' less emancipatory correlation of feminity and frailty ("Phénoménologie de l'éros," *Totalité* 286–298) and with his discussion of "L'habitation et le féminin" (*Totalité* 164–67), where we read that "La femme est la condition du recueillement, de l'intériorité de la Maison et de l'habitation"(*Totalité* 165–66). Dermot Moran rightly invites us to confront Levinas' speculation on feminity and domesticity, which understandably drew the ire of first-generation feminists, with Hannah Arendt's thoughts on the problem of the depoliticization of household experience.

liberal societies that value shared culture and 2) we remain socially dignified as humans inasmuch as we refuse to be treated like animals.[21] When we naturalize human virtue as innocence, or, worse even, when we naturalize animal dignity as innocence, then we perilously blur a constructed (not natural) distinction and disable the means of protecting ourselves from ourselves. What about a world in which animals are no longer "treated like animals," where it is not humans but animals that (who?) perform the human distinction, a world where it is temple-haunting martlets, and not Scottish barons, who do the labour of dwelling, nurture, and care? Would we then need the distinction? More than ever, I think.[22]

Our current Puritan censors and moral deputies, our ecocritical Angelos and posthumanist Malvolios, would probably say no—blind to the fact that "it is a feature of the paranoid logic of the censoring mentality that virtue, *qua* virtue, must be innocent, and therefore, unless protected, vulnerable to the wiles of vice" (Coetzee 6). Any reader of Marivaux, Richardson, Diderot, Rousseau, Sade or Austen knows not only that "for each virtue there are [....] two corresponding vices" (McIntyre, *After Virtue* 154) and that professions of virtue are commonly infelicitous (as speech acts) and hypocritical (as social

---

21 Discussing the projection of babies and "the more attractive sorts of animals," Rorty comments: "This view of the attribution of pre-linguistic awareness—as a courtesy extended potential or imagined fellow-speakers of our language—has a corollary that moral prohibitions against hurting babies and the better looking sorts of animals are not 'ontologically grounded' in the possession of feeling. It is, if anything, the other way around. The moral prohibitions are expressions of a sense of community based on the imagined possibility of conversation, and the attribution of feelings is little more than a reminder of these prohibitions" (*Philosophy* 190). Indeed, as Rorty goes on to argue, too many facts (about apparently border cases and "quasi-people") remain undiscoverable independently of moral sentiment.

22 I would personally refuse to live in a world where animals are treated like humans—inside a Beatrix Potter tale, a Walt Disney fantasy, or a posthumanist ecoscape, which amount basically to the same thing. When Deleuze and Guattari quite rightly ridiculed the sentimentalized animal in the form of the "little house dogs" owned by old ladies, they could hardly imagine the lash of Puritan rage their comment would awaken among academic Angelos. Haraway responded that she was not sure she could "find in philosophy a clearer display of misogyny, fear of aging, incuriosity about animals, and horror at the ordinariness of the flesh" (2008: 30). This proves little beyond the fact that Haraway has read very little Western philosophy, Deleuze and Guattari included, for misogyny is there galore, and that she probably dislikes *Moby Dick* and other related megalomaniac dick-centred literature like D.H. Lawrence's. In footnote, Deleuze and Guattari quote from D.H. Lawrence's letters: "I am tired of being told there is no such animal .... If I am a giraffe, and the ordinary Englishmen who write about me and say they know me are nice well-behaved dogs, there it is, the animals are different .... You don't love me. The animal that I am you instinctively dislike." *The animal that I am: L'animal que donc je suis.*

acts), but also that virtue itself—our honouring the commitment to such cultural construct—can be profoundly un-innocent. This truth is lost on the contemporary, phenomenology-oriented, critics who attempt to salvage remnants of innocent life, glimmerings of virtuous *Umwelt* interaction, the flotsam and jetsam of meaningful objectality, the thriving rumour of the antepredicative experience, from the ruinous battlefield landscape (Folio 1623) left behind by a bad man (William Shakespeare) who decided to inflict a viciously exceptional-humanity on the thingy and creaturely body of sacrality of his pre-modern and post-secular play-worlds. These critics are like early Waterloo tourists, scavenging for odd trophies with their Baedekers (Agamben, Latour, DeLanda) the hills where battle took place. *Thinging with Shakespeare*, they are shockingly unmindful of the human waste. But they admire the lily that grows amid the human bones, and whistle to the strayed dog that has been scoffed at by the human who believes it "has no more pity in him than a dog" (*The Two Gentlemen of Verona* 2.3.9). The bad human. The bad man.

CHAPTER 7

Affective styles

1

Derrida opened his first essay on Levinas with an epigraph from Matthew Arnold's *Culture and Anarchy* stressing the historical importance of the tension between Hebraism and Hellenism. The relevance of this moot point comes to surface in the final sections of the essay, when Levinas' overall project is described as "an interpellation of the Greek by the non-Greek at the heart of a silence, an ultralogical affect of speech, a question which can be stated only by being forgotten in the language of the Greeks" (*Writing* 133; *L'écriture* 196). I am interested in this *affect ultra-logic de la parole*, as it brings the non-rational exactions of affect fully into the open. This exposure also spells the eschatological opening of the question of history, ontologically construed—"in the language of the Greeks," repeats Derrida—as logos, finitude, and violence. The fact that the religious revival in Shakespearean studies, often cloaked in the conceptual garments of *political theology*, relies on occasion on scriptural traditions with a stake in ethical reconfigurations of the political community—on the constitution of "new norms, communities, and forms of life" (Hammill and Lupton, "Introduction" to *Political Theology*, 7) may not be totally disconnected from the determination to circumvent Greek-based ontology and epistemology. Nor is Levinas' effort dissimilar from Arendt's attempt to domesticate Heidegger in an ethical direction, and to force Greek philosophy to speak the language of the Book. Behind the revival of Aristotelian ethics—visible, as we have seen, in the philosophical work of Arendt and Nussbaum, and in the critical work of Julia Lupton—breathes indeed an interest in religious modes of ritualized (non-logical, non-finite, non-violent) communitarianism—in the "part played by myth, fantasy and affect in the founding and sustaining of collectives" (Hammill and Lupton, 5). Such transcendent drive towards the infinite absolution of the communal is at odds with other readings of Hebraic scripture—like Freud's—which emphasize *radical finitude* (Derrida, *Mal d'Archive* 38). Before these transcendent efforts to place the infinite amnesty of *political theology* at the service of a *biopolitics* understood as "commensal entertainment in the form of communicative action" (Lupton, "Pauline Edifications" 214)—one is tempted to reformulate the words uttered by a French observer during the Charge of the Light Brigade, *C'est magnifique, mais ce n'est pas la guerre*, as

"Very cool, but this is not Shakespeare."[1] Thus Aristotle gets interpellated by the non-Greek, ontology by ethics, or better, political ethics by theological ethics, and the result is not only a resurgence of organic socialization but a comeback of affect—the affect whose *waning* Jameson diagnosed as consequent upon the "poststructuralist critique" of the hermeneutic of depth (*Postmodernism* 61). The problem of an *ethical Shakespeare*, which is also that of an *affective Shakespeare*, turns therefore around the question whether the English of his putative interpellation is underwritten by the language of the Greeks or by the language of the Hebrews. Derrida rightly spoke of an interminable "dialogue between phenomenology and eschatology" (*Writing* 133). Vickers believed that preventing Shakespeare from speaking French any longer and having him return to "English purposes" (*Henry V* 2. Chorus 15) was enough. He was wrong.

In his "Introduction" to *Against Epistemology*, written in New York in 1955–56, some twenty years after he had completed a first version of his critique of phenomenology, Theodor Adorno already cautioned against the emotional arbitrariness guiding many of Husserl's "scientific" or, by his own admission, "ontological" moves. Something volatile and very much unprincipled was posited as *origin* before his transcendental deduction of principles could unfold—later Levinas would place as origin, as primitive notion, the "fundamental event" ("The Paradox of Morality" 168) of the face-to-face relation.[2] Adorno was particularly alert to the ideological and political effect the appropriation of this flippant *attitudinal motif* could cause, ranging from existentialism to fascism. This is intriguing, as Husserl himself regretted the de-transcendentalizing of phenomenology in the hands of recusant existentialist disciples, like Heidegger. Husserl was possibly blind to the existentialist impulsion secretly driving his whole enterprise. At any rate, what stands out in this evocation is Adorno's detection of a puerile "attitude" that swells at the expense of dialectical reflection: "Today the more total the claim of ontology, which stretches out to mythos over all reflective thought, the more dependent it becomes on mere 'attitude' (*Einstellung*), which in Husserl functions as practically an existential of cognition" (*Against* 22). We are, of course, aware of the role the praise of existence at the expense of essence was asked to play in academic circles during the early 1960s, when a post-existentialist horizon was giving way to the rise of structuralism and poststructuralism. The

---

[1] Quoted by Thomas Pynchon in *Gravity's Rainbow*, 10. Lupton's essay is about Renaissance tapestries but the conceptual and tonal context of her discussion is the same we find in her readings of Shakespeare.

[2] For a similar attack on metaphysical-religious suggestions of *origine* rather than *surgissement*, see Althusser, *Écrits sur la psychanalyse*, 66–68.

work of Fredric Jameson uniquely testifies to this transition, which in some quarters (California, for instance) took place very much under the influence of an ethical-existentialist construal of *Kritik* (Marcuse, Huxley, Bloch, Fromm). During this transition, faith in existence as opposed to essence remained a group-identity sign, not always distinguishable from nods of adhesion to post-war neo-humanism—including Arendt's. Today, and this is not Adorno's today, memory of the dialectical entanglement of existence and essence has been completely obliterated: what we are offered is *existential attitude* as a crude emotional explosion, as an outlet for individual *authenticity*. In the mid-1990s art historian Robert Hughes berated the growing narcissistic emotionalism of American culture. He deplored "the emphasis" on "the subjective: how we feel about things, rather than what we think or can know" (*Culture* 13). He was chronicling the effects of a growth of neo-Puritan exhibitionist, confessional enthusiasm with roots in the post-war past. We have many astute chronicles of the immediate and delayed effects of the arrival of *Eigentlichkeit* to USA, especially California, in the sociological essays of Aldous Huxley, Theodor Adorno and Charles Taylor, in Joan Didion's journalism, Michelangelo Antonioni's movies, the novels by Nathaniel West (*The Day of the Locust*), Evelyn Waugh (*The Loved One*), or Thomas Pynchon (*The Crying of Lot 49*), among others. But the impact the "existential of cognition" (Adorno) has had in literary studies is not exactly uplifting. Nothing suits a teacher of literature better that the discharge of reflection, followed by a turn—or return—to attitude. *Equal affections*, the title of David Leavitt's second novel, largely set in California, turns out the precise coordinates of the new critical atmosphere. Many things will prosper in this relaxed ambience, from LSD psychotherapy to pet funeral services, from *The Courier's Tragedy* to *Phenomenal Shakespeare*. This is again Robert Hughes on the destructive effects the lowering of college educational standards had in American universities during the decades of the 1970s and 1980s, not least due to "the sixties' dioxins accumulating more each time":

> Education [...] is downscaled to their [the students'] reduced ability to read texts, sift information and analyse ideas. Thus it becomes an impoverished coda to the intensive learning students were once offered, and to the expectations that were made of them; geared to the students' limited experience of life an ideas as though this were some kind of educational absolute (whereas, of course, it is the thing the real education seeks to challenge and expand), mushy with superficial social-studies courses that inculcate only buzzwords and are designed, as far as possible, to avoid hard questions of historical context, it is short on analysis and critical scrutiny but long on attitude and feeling. The full results of this

emasculation will appear in the nineties, and the political-correctness flurry—which is all about feelings, and more common, it seems, among teachers than among students themselves—is merely one of their premonitory symptoms. For when the 1960s animus against elitism entered American education, it brought in its train an enormous and cynical tolerance of student ignorance, rationalized as a regard for "personal expression" and "self-esteem." Rather than "stress" the kids by asking them to read too much or think too closely, which might cause their fragile personalities to implode on contact with college-level demands, schools reduced their reading assignments, thus automatically reducing their command of language. Untrained in logical analysis, ill-equipped to develop and construct formal arguments about issues, unused to mining texts for deposits of factual material, the students fell back to the only position they could truly call their own: what they *felt* about things. When feelings and attitudes are the main referents of argument, to attack a position is automatically to insult its holder, or even to assail his or her perceived "rights;" every *argumentum* becomes *ad hominem*, approaching the condition of harassment, if not quire rape. (59)

This is a long quote, I know. But I believe the point is well argued and remains valid. Dismissing the point as a sour rant typical of traditional humanist scholars—say, the two Blooms—serves merely to confirm how helpful the defensive recourse to ad hominem argument becomes when one is unable to refute the point immanently, that is, on its own terms. Hughes is not always right: his disregard for French structuralism—what he calls "Derrideanism" alongside Althusser and Foucault—reveals sublime ignorance and suffers from the same ad hominem aloofness he imputes to PC progressist academics. But his diagnosis of excessive attitude in educational and academic environments remains sadly accurate, both in the US and in many other Western countries.

2

Rita Felski's *The Limits of Critique* (2015) is a case in point. With postcritical exultation, she questions the "inherent rigor" of reading practices affiliated to *critique*, the obduracy of methods whose practitioners describe as "consisting simply of a series of propositions and intellectual arguments" (3). She finds much fault in this rationalist astringence and pines for the greenness *des Lebens goldner Baum* (Goethe 64). Her remedial formula is a novel implementation of "affective styles." As William Pfaff said of Kissinger, hers is also "a striking case of style over substance. It is an American success story."³ The fact that the discoverers of opaque (barbarous) mediation behind and under the documents of culture, the so-called hermeneuts of suspicion (Marx, Freud, Nietzsche), were both motivated by and driven to "affective" states of vigilance and wariness, often of sceptical despair, was not a matter of choice. Nor is being very affective, affectionate, or affected—or simply mad—a matter of choice either.⁴ Believing otherwise may lead people to recommend other people to complete a marathon without perspiring. I am not suggesting that we should all sweat our way through Shakespeare's texts in a state of paranoid gloom. I am just intimating three things. First, with Barthes, that "the *epoché* of vigilance," the abstention from rational vigilance is doomed to be "desired as something impossible" (*The Neutral* 102). Second, that a change in "affective styles" won't make an unperceptive critic any wiser—or, to use Felski's phrase, any more politically "radical." And third, that the stock Shakespearean situation doles out, to use a Morrison quibble, "more affliction than affection" (*Song of Solomon* 127). Felski's advocacy of new modes of *hermeneutic affection* is attuned to posthumanist calls to put an end to "the supremacy of reason over emotion" (Raber, *Shakespeare* 3) and is of a piece with an erotics of reading that, greatly boosted now by phenomenological methods, finds support in Sontag's fatuous call for an experience of art in its "pure, untranslatable, sensuous immediacy" (*Against* 14).⁵ The appeal to *immediacy*—a tendentially conservative call already brandished by royalist apologists in 1642 (Skinner, *Liberty Before Liberalism* 2)—is often couched in the jargon of embodied mediation.

---

3 Quoted by William Gaddis in *The Rush for Second Place*, 59.
4 Psychoanalysis teaches us, among other things, that one doesn't decide to go mad. Nor can we choose to have the best affections. T.S Eliot tended to be rightly un-inclusive in this respect: "The intense feeling, ecstatic or terrible, without an object or exceeding its object, is something which every person of sensibility has known" ("Hamlet," *Selected Prose* 49); "Poetry is not a turning loose of emotion, but an escape from emotion; it is not the expression of personality, but an escape from personality. But, of course, only those who have personality and emotions know what it means to want to escape from these things." ("Tradition and the Individual Talent," *Selected Prose* 43). So was de Man in his ironic comment on Kant: "Moral nobility is the best ego booster available—though Kant is not so blind as not to know of its cost in hidden error" (*Aesthetic* 84–85). Let me also quote Donald Greene to the effect that we find in Samuel Johnson "a great deal of the habit of complex irony that one associates with most sensitive minds" (18).
5 Felski closes the Introduction to her latest book with a recommendation not to be "so excruciatingly tongue-tied about our loves (sic)" (Limits 13). In her critique of "symptomatic reading," Anne Anlin Cheng advocates a "mutual pedagogy of erotics" between critic and work. Qtd. in Best & Marcus 9.

Raber closes the section "Minds" of his book on *Shakespeare and Posthumanist Theory* with the following consideration:

> I would add that humans never actually quite speak for themselves in any case: the meaning of speech is always mediated, delegated, alienated, whether through blushes, gestures, books, writing, the shape of tongue and teeth, by the memory of words, of grammar, of literary sources or by any other factor that influences the process. And ultimately communication is itself a process of bringing one part of the body, the hand or mouth, into relation to other bodies, and of expressing a figment of the imagination—the "mind"—through all the available material instruments the body can muster. (74)

Raber is trying to elucidate some of her unspoken premises, and this is laudable. As it turns out, her theory of communication turns out to be—like that of Bruce Smith in *Phenomenal Shakespeare*—plainly pre-Saussurean: she advocates an ebulliently Romantic, draconianly object-oriented (she forgot the cell-phone!), very expressionistic and routinely based on body-oriented immediacy. And it has the added charm of imputing to disembodied *écriture* the immediacy that only the mediation of the body supposedly overcomes. We are all aware that signifiers are embodied—that airy nothing is something, that saws of books are copied in the table of memory—but that doesn't mean that arbitrary sounds and graphs organized within a formalized system do not enjoy an exceptional competency to remain efficient (i.e. communicative) in abstracted, tendentially disembodied, decidedly trans-bodied contexts: "L'itérabilitié idéale qui forme la structure de toute marque, c'est ce qui lui permet sand doute de se soustraire à un context, de s'émanciper de tout lien déterminé avec son origine, son sens ou son référent, d'émigrer pour jouer ailleurs, en totalité ou en partie, un autre role" (Derrida, "Mes chances," *Psyché* 368). This potential for iterative re-emergence in different communicative contexts grants the mark a (rational) universality which we would do wrong to deride, for only such formal, semiotic, trans-temporal, trans-spatial, and medium-indifferent continuity allows us to go on discussing the thing Shakespeare in the first place. Raber doesn't bother to distinguish primitive communicative tools like blushes or the shape of the tongue from sophisticated instruments like human natural languages. The phenomenological drive to fix the Shakespeare thing in the *hic et nunc* of embodied representation reveals its mistrust of modes of discontinuous continuity that are unlikely to be bound in the nutshell of phenomenal performance. If no exceptionality is attributed to the abstract arbitrariness of signifiers and the semiotic economy of natural languages—the potential to exponentially mean a lot with very few elements—then there is no point, I guess, in reading Shakespeare. One would do better studying painting or dance. If you are planning to see Juliet blush (she gives us hope in 2.1.128), be patient, take your time, get yourself a couple of beers, and make yourself very, very comfortable. I prefer to listen to what she has to say. Surely, Raber's claim about *the mediation of blushes* doesn't deserve much attention. Nor should we be much troubled by the fact that Ewan Fernie, claiming to write "less from a committed critical position than from direct engagement with Shakespeare's text" and describing his book as "a polemical intervention in favour of the new turn in criticism towards empiricism and the aesthetic" (*Shame in Shakespeare* 4), devotes many pages to blushing in *Hamlet* (63–65). When I first read the formulation of his intentions—that "direct engagement with Shakespeare's text"—I was a bit startled (can we engage directly with a text?), but then I understood that the *being there* of the blush as an *empirical* and *aesthetic* thing perfectly explained the *directness* of his *textual engagement*. How foolish of me to have been taken aback.[6]

The fact, however, that a philosophically informed scholar like Paul Kottman should have authored a more complex version of a similar argument is reason enough to stop and reconsider. In *Tragic Conditions in Shakespeare* (2009), Kottman suggests that Hamlet epitomizes the conditions of tragedy in the way it compels us "to gauge the relationship between individual action and a collective, affective response without any prior, prescriptive criteria with which to make the judgement" (77). Three things stand out: 1) the centrality of the antepredicative affective and collective (interpersonal) response, and its superiority to individual modes of reaction, 2) the neglect of the role prescriptive or institutive performatives in organizing the social field and 3) the resistance to assume that some degree of prescriptive performative (tropological) institution (or constitution) precedes and predetermines the creativity of interpersonal affective praxis. Admittedly, Kottman dabbles in romantic-phenomenological lore. To prove his point, he analyses Hamlet's conversations with his mother (*Hamlet* 3.3) and with Rosencrantz and Guildenstern (*Hamlet* 2.2). In the first one he focuses on the prince's desire to force Gertrude to a "non-verbal confession," to reveal her "blush" (3.3.81). In the second, Hamlet is intent on disclosing "confession in your looks" (2.2.279). In both cases, Kottman argues, the non-verbal disclosure of a meaningful emotion betokens, for Hamlet, the revealment of the "authentic; it appears (if it does) as the uprising of the body's

---

6   What Lukacher argues about guilt in Shakespeare could be applied verbatim to the problem of shame: "Guilt is a linguistic as well as a temporal problem" (*Daemonic* 34).

nature from within, and out of, social artificiality. We know Rosencrantz and Guildenstern were lying; and we know their bodily affects to be truer than their words" (74). The correlation between the authentic, the natural and the bodily affective gets further supplemented with the trope of the common:

> Moreover, where that natural affect—the blush or tears—is observable, and therefore shared, it might immediately make of itself a (potential) ground for commonality. Indeed, where the *social* dimension of theatricality turns out, as we have seen, to be the emptiness of the performative—the self-alienation of every subject from herself and others—the *affective* dimension of the theatre reveals itself capable of instituting its own nascent sociality; namely, the sharing of a natural "affect." (76)

I don't doubt that *shared* affections may help institute a nascent sociality. But are the embarrassment of Gertrude's erotic betrayal and the shame of deception in Rosencrantz and Guildenstern, affections that Hamlet, the emotional tormentor and moral inquisitor, can or ought to share? They are most certainly not shared: they (embarrassment, shame) are emotions wrenched out for the sake of momentary punition. What the inquisitor and the victim *share* after the trial is the confirmation of a *common understanding*: each one knows the other knows. In both cases, what Hamlet enjoys is an intellectual victory—he enjoins others to recognize his transcendental consciousness. Hamlet: "I *know* the good king and queen have sent for you" (2.2.274), I want you to know that I know, and want you acknowledge that I am right. Hamlet: "it is not *madness* / That I have uttered: bring me to the test," I am fully in my senses, what I say is true, you know it, and I want you to tell me so. Can a nascent sociality emerge in a community ruled by a philosopher-King who exacts common truth at the price of enforced unidirectional shame? Where are the coercion-free conditions of communication that Arendt stipulated for political action to be able to emerge? Kottman would protest that Hamlet is no detached critical prince, that he is one of us, part of the "plurality" to which we, as readers and spectators, belong, "each of whose members can speak as one witness to another" (*Politics* 165). Ask Ophelia what she thinks about that.

In an early sentence of Dürrenmatt's last novel, the narrator opposes doing something *im Affekt* (in a passionate state) to doing it *bewusst* (in a conscious manner) (*Justiz* 14). While Dürrenmatt was always intrigued by overconscious characters, and drawn to their perversion, we are now plunging into unconscious depths of passion. To expostulate that Shakespeare deeply mistrusted affective actions, and much preferred conscious actions, would lead us nowhere, as his authority is no longer a ground for arguments. Hegel sensed that Kant's "reduction of the sublime" implied "a return to the triviality of subjective moods, affects and faculties of the mind, which he, Kant, fails to inscribe within the dialectical progression of cognition" (de Man, *Aesthetic* 121). The aftershocks of this aberrant retrogression are still strongly felt. Take, again, the blush in *Romeo and Juliet* 2.2. Neo-affected critics would contend that because Juliet cannot conceptually argue the terms of her plight, she blushes: when (incorporeal) judgement and reason founder, (embodied, physiological, somatic) affection takes over—and the empirical scholar is there to record and diagnose through "direct engagement." But is this really what happens or matters in this extraordinary conversation? Or is it rather the triumph of Juliet's preternatural dialectical gifts that should solicit our critical attention? Appeals to immediacy, which today enjoy an unwonted resurgence, conflict with the necessary retardation that is presumed in the reading protocols of the best structuralist-cum-poststructuralist critique—Barthes argued that *critique* consists in "dire avec retard, mais en se plaçant tout entire dans ce retard" (*Essais* 265). The erotics of *retardement* should not be underestimated—even at a time when delay, especially Hamlet's, was supposedly "simply not an issue" (de Grazia, Hamlet *without Hamlet* 171). Neither *trop vite*, pointed out Paul de Man quoting Pascal, nor *trop doucement*, but with the right velocity, with a speed that has fully sublated delay: only this way can the symptomatic reading proceed to the work of detection.[7] In Victorian studies—a field that flourishes well beyond "the horizon of 'critical thinking'" and is therefore in no need of Felski's loving guidance—the combined pressure of undialectical positivism and quaint affectivism is now happily meeting some organized resistance. In the Manifesto of the V21 Collective we read: "At its worst, positivist historicism devolves into show-and-tell epistemologies and bland antiquarianism. Its primary affective mode is the amused chuckle. Its primary institutional mode is the instrumentalist evisceration of humanistic ways of knowing." Did they say "humanistic"? The nerve.

The writer's ability to creatively affect (*poiein*) no longer matters. What counts is just the reader's disposition to be affected (*pathein*) (Plato *Sophist* 147d; Aristotle *Categories* 2a3–4). Everything now turns around the existential-emotional immediate experience of the reader, now finally liberated from the burden of factoring in holistic considerations, structural conditions, and the detours of conceptual inference. Not to mention the liberation from having to confront the intellectual iciness of characters like Edmund, Iago, and, in some

---

7   Paul de Man chose for opening epigraph in *Allegories of Reading* the following Pascal sentence: "Quand on lit trop vite ou trop doucement on n'entend rien" (*Pensées*).

cases, Hamlet: their affectless nature is the perfect alibi for a hermeneutic abdication that in giving them up forsakes Shakespeare.[8] This lowering of the rational defences is a common enough contingence, detectable even in Kant:

> This language of the affections is what gives Kant's discourse [on the sublime] some of the triviality of the particular, which often becomes audible in the ostensible silliness of some of his examples and illustrations, though never of his arguments. This blandness is hard to interpret, though it is possible, and even necessary, to develop a taste for it.
> DE MAN, *Aesthetic* 123

Many in Shakespeare's studies are making of than necessity their virtue. The related attempt to give up symptomatic reading along with the hermeneutic of suspicion is as ridiculous as the analytical responses to Marx's *Capital* by critics whose "existential requirement" was "that whatever is attributed to the system or totality of capital have its equivalent or foundation in individual experience." This pretence, Fredric Jameson rightly argues, is vitiated by undialectical habits of thought:

> This is tantamount to effacing the Hegelian dialectic of essence and appearance (of which Marx observed that if they coincided in real life, "science would be unnecessary"). This particular argument (which can also be used against psychoanalysis and Freud's doctrine of the Unconscious) has, intentionally or not, the result of abolishing the distinction between value and prices, central to much of the work of *Capital*.
> JAMESON, *Representing* 128

Extrapolating to the real of the text, if essence and appearance, value and price, coincide in the textual surface, what is the point of reading? If surface begets *surfeit* it is because there is no real starving in the first place, no need to eat the text: reading Shakespeare, this should be pressed, is not prescriptive. Immediate hermeneutic apprehension—let's call it textual surfing—is not exactly reading. It is indeed as banal and deceptive as face reading—let's call it textual facing—in Levinas. Such a wonderful life: surfing, facing, surfacing, interfacing. Others may want to recall, with Ulysses, that "the fool slides o'er the ice that you should break" (*Troilus and Cressida* 3.3.208), and that, if we decide to skate over playtext ice we may end up precluding access less to fabulous

---

8   Bloom argues that Edmund is "amazingly free of all connection, all affect" (*Shakespeare* 502).

depths than to more significant surfaces. "Therefore, *paucas palabras*; let the world slide. Sessa!" (*The Taming of the Shrew* Induction 1.4–5).

3

I have singled out Felski's book *The Limits of Critique* because I believe it epitomizes an important tendency in current literary studies—the attempt to articulate a space of critical arguments that remains ethical beyond the theoretical complexities of the so-called ethical turn, committed without forthright political assignation, and freshly affectionate or affective in response to the rationalist-structural dryness of criticism produced in the age of high theory (1960–1985). The specificity of phenomenological criticism, a modal—and modish—expression of this tendency, originates in its pretence to remain philosophically rooted and therefore *theoretical*. I maintain that it fails on both counts: the affection-driven ethos is simply affected, and the theory is bad theory. I believe it is about time to defend the Shakespeare textual corpus from the hermeneutic distortions begotten by this mode of critique. I hold, with Hobbes, that in critical work—he would speak of "scientific" work—the establishment of ethos is unnecessary, since "in the very shadows of doubt a thread of reason (so to speak) begins, by whose guidance we shall escape to the clearest light" ("Epistle Dedicatory" to *De Cive* 5).[9] Hobbes, often wrongly ditched with the insular empiricists, was rationally reacting against moral philosophers inebriated by the humanist promises of the *vivere civile* and *vita activa* and misled by "attractive and emotive language to superficial opinions" (5). The cycle of reaction remains open: I take Hobbes's and Descartes' related appeal to the *filum rationis* showing us the way *in lucem clarissimam*—again the unphenomenal fire—as a corrective answer to the questions left open by over-moralistic, loosely emotive, randomly empiricist and imperfectly skepticist—let alone materialist—philosophical doctrines: Badiou's burlesque decision to tag his *dialectique matérialiste* as little more than an "atmosphère idéologique" (*Loqique* 11) and Jameson's ironic notation of the circumstance that today—he was writing in 2009—"everyone likes to talk about materialism" (*Valences* 82) is oxygen to the unconverted.[10] Perhaps the best corrective

---

9   I take the phrase "the establishment of ethos" from Skinner (*Reason* 259).
10 Copjek comments on the relation between the return to affect and neo-materialism: "Affect is not a separate thing beyond language, but a dimension of it. Much of the current interest in affect is associated with the new 'materialist' trend, which pines for the 'great outdoors,' for that which is beyond language, beyond representation. New materialists and affect theorist (of a certain stripe) want to escape what Jameson once dubbed the 'prison

to worked-up neo-materialists is Valéry's condensed thought "Doubt leads to form."[11] I see this correction as resonating vigorously with the discursive-ironic rationalist stance in Shakespeare textual work. And I see the modern (rationalist) reaction against moralism and poor empiricism—the reaction that retains and safeguards something essential in Shakespeare—as inscribing an antidotal gesture that is cyclically to be repeated, as a principle of recurrence, several times in the history of Western philosophy, most notably in Hegel's refutation of naturalism and romantic emotionalism, and next in Derrida's and Adorno's critique—yes, good old *unlimited critique*—of phenomenology. The fact, moreover, that important Badiou interpreters like Frank Ruda have openly reassessed the opportunity of a *Descartes revival*—intermittently adumbrated in his *For Badiou: Idealism without Idealism*—as a direction to thought *in dürftiger Zeit* testifies to the relevance of this rationalist gesture. To protect the Shakespeare text from phenomenological misreading involves, therefore, the determination to withhold, and eventually sustain, this text by the thread of reason—and to let it glow in unphenomenal light. The fact that pure reason and the *lux clarissima* may not exist (they obviously don't) doesn't detract from the value of the *decision* to abide by the guidance of both. We may thus help protect the Shakespeare text from high-minded moralist critics who promote "the obfuscation of its constitutive antagonism" (Žižek, *Reading Marx* 46). No better solution can be found for this than the appeal to Hegel, whose *Phenomenology of Spirit*—a text where phenomenology is presented as the "*absolute self-presentation of reason* (ratio—logos)" (Heidegger, *Hegel's Phenomenology* 30) and not posited as a managerial concern—chronicles a self-movement on the part of the concept that can be referred and reduced, at bottom, to "the stages of antagonistic society." Furiously reading Hegel against Husserl with the aid of incisive Marxian lenses, early Adorno portended that "what is antithetically developed, however, is not, as one would no doubt currently have it, the structure of being in itself, but rather antagonistic society" (*Against Epistemology* 4). Laclau and Žižek would have profited, in their analyses, from this original emphasis on societal antagonism, which dates back to 1955–56. But Adorno's book has been sadly neglected. In the same way as de Man's deconstructive exposure of the failure of the aesthetic was accompanied by a propitious relocation of "truly productive political thought" (de Man *Aesthetic* 107), now seen to rise at the juncture where aesthetic theory undergoes the test of epistemological speculation, Adorno's critical exposure

---

house of language.' Lacan teaches, however, that language is an unlimited prison from which it is impossible to escape." ("Interview" 196).

11   Paul de Man quotes Valéry in his essay on Montaigne: *Critical Writings*, 10.

of the failure of the phenomenological foundationalism is indissociable from his recourse to Marx's critique of ideology as an adept political tool.[12] Although their appreciation of "antagonism" may widely differ—what Adorno takes to be a "debit structure" (*Against Epistemology* 13) of societal debt relations de Man construes as "tropological structure" of language exchange relations—in both cases they pit the mediating materiality of an infrastructure against the effacement of mediation procured by the (ideological, metaphysical) superstructure. In both cases, an illusion is shattered: whereas Adorno dispels the "illusion of the natural" (4), de Man chases away the illusion of the phenomenal. Phenomenological criticism systematically effaces and obfuscates the inner contradictions, symptoms, and inconsistencies that ripple through the Shakespeare text, thus defusing an antagonism that is the mark both of its finitude and its totality, of its being particular haunted—surged, inflamed, ravaged—by the airy nothing of figurative universals. What is needed is a mode of critique that restores the speculative-dialectic tension that was not exactly uncommon in the much-maligned "liberal-humanist" tradition, a style of thought where a sound judgement—a statement like "the parallel concepts of 'nothing' and 'soul' [...] are, indeed, almost interchangeable in Shakespeare" (Wilson Knight, *Wheel* 293)—can be made, sustained, and ungrudgingly understood.

The V21 Manifesto mentioned "the amused chuckle." Many in Shakespeare studies are still there, chuckling and choking. To believe that thinkers like Merleau-Ponty, Arendt or Latour are worth reading is not itself a sign of what Dollimore called "philosophical illiteracy." On the contrary. It bespeaks intellectual gusto. But to set such reading as the priority for a theoretical renovation of Shakespearean critique, at the expense of other philosophical trends and voices, is a tricky endeavour. It places the scholar in very uncertain terrain—it leads, for instance, to a ludicrous reliance in the modish work of controversialists like Graham Harman, himself a convert to Latour, who considers that Heidegger's tool-analysis in *Sein und Zeit* "still represents the high-water mark of recent philosophy" (96).[13] This is very amusing, chucklingly amusing in fact,

---

12   It is symptomatic that de Man mentions twice the name of Adorno in his essays on Kant and Hegel collected in *Aesthetic Ideology*, always favorably. In the essay "Hegel on the sublime," he refers to him, alongside Benjamin, Lukács and Althusser, as one of the "aesthetic thinkers" that have manages to produce "the most incisive contributions to political thought and political action" (107). De Man traces back this seemingly paradoxical collapse of the political into the aesthetic "to Marx himself [sic], whose *German Ideology* is a model of critical procedure along the lines of Kant's third *Critique*" (107).

13   The work of Harman, relevant to postcritical gurus like Felski (see *Limits*, note 4, 195–96), is obligingly cited by early modern scholars like Julian Yates and Julia Lupton. Emphasis

since such analysis takes less than half an hour on our first day at the *phenomenological kindergarten* (Heidegger, *Four Seminars* 12–13). Whenever phenomenal critics refuse to see beyond a mere mode of feeling, an intuition, or even a mere representation (*bloße Gefühlsbestimmung, Anschauung oder auch bloße Vorstellung*) (Hegel, *Science of Logic* 515), the affective chuckle ripples across the pre-K phenomenological classroom.

4

Let me consider one final example, Drew Daniel's *The Melancholy Assemblage: Affect and Epistemology in the English Renaissance* (2013). The book opens with John Ashbery and closes with Lars von Trier. By winking at these postmodernist masters, Daniel flags his presentist refusal to remain within the chronological boundaries of his subtitle. At times, indeed, the chronological specification appears merely anecdotal, as the book is driven by the theoretical ambition to redefine melancholy in ways that seal its cultural validity across time. Dollimore would quickly smell the fault of "essentialist" scholarship. In this particular sense of theoretical instigation, the book is ambitiously innovative. The theory is, however, simple enough: melancholy has never been a thing, but rather the studied pretence of a (black, intestinal) thing; nor has it ever been an idea, but rather the protracted inquest on an (elusive, mental) idea. Put otherwise, melancholy is the epistemological *effect* of a doubtful *affect*. In an attempt to overcome the Scylla and Charybdis of Galenic materialism and Aristotelian spiritualism, two traditional takes on melancholy enjoyed by their essentialist compulsion, Daniel resorts to the Deleuzian notions of assemblage and deterritorialization and fabricates a new heuristic concept, the *melancholy assemblage*: "Treating melancholy as an assemblage rather than a type or substance or a type of subject breaks its conceptual unity into an extended, provisional, and modular set of relations between and across material elements, and relationships between and across individual subjects, with no particular local expression enjoying any particular ontological priority over any other" (*Melancholy* 12). The central theoretical support is found in Deleuze and Guattari, but tactical links are also established with Benjamin, Althusser and DeLanda. Despite the tendency to self-congratulatory over-gloss, the theoretical parts of the book are rewarding.

---

on knowledge-how at the expense of knowledge-what—the idea that our knowledge about things, facts and events is beholden to our practical skills—is already prominent in Dreyfus' 1991 reading of *Sein und Zeit*.

Problems arise when the theory is put to test in readings of *Love's Labour's Lost*, *The Merchant of Venice*, *Hamlet*, *The Anatomy of Melancholy* and *Samson Agonistes*. In these readings, Daniel combines ennui with the existing criticism of these works (by Eliot, Dover Wilson, Fish, and other lesser wits) with an exhilarating display of confidence in the novelty of his approach. Thus, regrettably, the meaning of the works recedes under the weight of methodological digression and meta-theoretical bravado. Of course, one suspects that Daniel is not searching for the meaning of these works, but rather tracing the specific way in which the melancholy assemblage is contingently articulated within them. But even in this reductive view, the readings fail to stand up to the requirements of the theoretical model. To take an example, Chapter 3 on *The Merchant of Venice*, opens with the *petitio-principii* verdict that Antonio is melancholy. Surprisingly, no diagnostic resource is deployed: there is no retrieval of verbal, ideational, postural, or somatic traces to back the conjecture that a melancholy assemblage actually takes shape as the plays unfolds. Daniel furtively relies on an equivocal textual cue—Graziano's allusion to a "melancholy bait" (1.1.101)—and on a critical tradition he elsewhere ridicules. The reader is unreservedly forced to admit that *The Merchant of Venice* is a (melancholy?) play casting, among other wonders, a "melancholy mind" (95), a "melancholy subject" (96), a "melancholy trope" (98) and a "melancholy body" (99). I fear this definitional frenzy or attributive compulsion flatly violates the anti-essentialist nominalism presiding over the Deleuzian idea of assemblage, according to which only the set is melancholy, never its components. This is a problem of theoretical oversight, typical of undialectical modes of scholarship that are *immediately* engrossed in particulars or "things themselves." A different problem arises when the model is projected over the text with celebratory nearsightedness, leading to hermeneutic extenuation. This happens in Daniel's circular reading of *The Anatomy of Melancholy*, where Burton's "magpie hoard of scholarship" (156) is not only viewed as a melancholy performance per se, but also recommended as "an original and forward-thinking model for how to perform scholarly work which is both slyer and more generative than either Fish or his respondents let on" (165). This sounds misguided: Fish's essays did not perform the self-consumption they described, nor was Foucault on madness necessarily mad. On the contrary, both displayed an exemplary analytical capacity for discrimination and hierarchy squarely at odds with the postmodern logic of collage and parataxis that underpins Daniel's book. In the final sections of this book, I will have more to say on the negative effect that eclectic phenomenological empiricism has on critical methodologies. Given Daniel's sustained comparison between Burton's and Benjamin's methods, it may be worth recalling Adorno's fierce epistolary attack on Benjamin's non-dialectical drive in the *Passagen-Werk*. Another objection: melancholy and its twin-passion madness were not the only affects that invited unstoppable epistemological examination, shuttling between the inner-personal and the outer-social. Many moral imponderables like honesty, virtue, sin or shame were also subject to this categorical indeterminacy. Finally, Daniel's book shows a deficit of literary-contextual awareness. *Comparaison n'est pas raison*, granted. But additional Shakespearean evidence would have done no harm. For instance, the combined reading of Hamlet's opening asides and the line "For I have that within which passeth show" as showily announcing "the very antisocial withdrawal that it violates, transmitting inner affect outward, drawing eavesdropping auditors inward" (137) applies word for word to Cordelia, for all we know a decidedly non-melancholy character. Dialectical attention to totalities and ensembles is the first step in comparative analysis, and formal comparison of objective (mediated, textualized) realities is the only way out of an affective scholarship of affects.

The current phenomenological criticism of Shakespeare is, to use a Hegel phrase, "the quintessence of shallow thinking" because it "bases philosophical science not on the development of thought and the concept but on immediate perception and contingent imagination" ("Preface" to *Philosophy of Right* 9). By contingent imagination Hegel meant a moral sense exposed to shifting ethical affiliations that respond first and foremost to sociological-historical oscillations. Hegel's criticism targeted the conviction that a human being exists "immediately to [itself] as the ego of affection and action" (Husserl, *Crisis* 107). The pale cast of thought is of little avail when the native hue of resolution is so immediately present to itself. Something of the "sophistry of wilfulness" that Hegel spotted among romantic pseudo-revolutionaries intoxicated with anti-philosophical celebrations of "free infinite personality" (Preface to *Philosophy of Right* 10–13) remains the standard neo-historicist recantation: *Will in the World*, *Will Power*, *Free Will*.[14] And the immediate-to-itself ego of affection and action compels different modes of loyalty: while Lupton and Kottman set their hopes in the ethic-political affordances of action, Bruce Smith digs mostly in the "fond affectif" (Merleau-Ponty, *Phénoménologie* 123). All three would surely endorse Nussbaum's call to consider emotions as laden with "rich intentionality or cognitive content" ("Preface to the Revised Edition," *Fragility* xviii). Emotions, intentionality, cognitive content: these are all phenomenological coordinates.

---

14 These are titles of books by Greenblatt (*Will in the World*) and Richard Wilson (*Will Power*, *Free Will*). Who spoke of the death of the author?

CHAPTER 8

A Pastoral Philosophy

1

Let me tell you a story. Once upon a time there was a community of fellow humans (also animals) who fluidly engaged in respectful interactions: they shared their words, their emotions, their thoughts, and their natural sense of civic entitlement. Their togetherness occurred under conditions of immediacy—what they thought and felt was readily and transparently conveyed to others—and phenomenal embodiment—what they thought and felt was conveyed to others and to themselves in material actions that made visible, without conceptual gaps, tropological leftover or material leaks, the symbolic-metaphorical substance of *the communal*, what Marx called *das Gemeinswesen*.[1] Kant has duly summarized this mythical view: "All allow that the world began with something good: with the Golden Age, with life in Paradise, or an even happier life in communion with heavenly beings" (*Religion* 53). This desirable time, this something good, is, alas, no more. It was already past time in Shakespeare's time. What is outstanding about Shakespeare, so the story runs, is that he managed, in his poems and plays, to call back that past time and its attending social configuration—the immediate *communitas*. The task of the critic is to scan the presence of that vestigial hologram—that intentional content, that rational idea, that ethical trope—to examine the traces, that is, of the bygone community as they appear in Shakespeare's theatrical world. But the critic shouldn't stop there, for the critical act involves too a committed interaction with that theatrical world—it is assumed that only by engaging immediately with the manifold embodiments of that theatrical world can the critic immediately relieve the intentional content of the embodied community. Otherwise put, only by entering the buried community in Shakespeare's plays are we in a position to discover it—to turn up, that is, "a better world than this" (*As You Like It* 1.2.251). The rest is not silence, but rather the moralist attempts to model *our* new future with evidence collected through deficient exegetical work.

With Marxian verve and Hegelian prescience, Francis Bacon observed in *Thoughts and Conclusions* that

---

[1] Marx uses this concept in some early texts, including the *Critique of Hegel's Philosophy of Right*. For a clarification of its exact meaning, see O'Malley's "Introduction" to the *Critique*, especially 43–44.

the traditional philosophy of things might be accepted as a probable account, if man himself did not exist nor any of the mechanical arts by which he transforms nature, and if we could be content simply to regard nature as a spectacle. As things are, this placid and leisurely contemplation of the universe deserves only the name of pastoral philosophy.

    qtd. in Farrington 13

This wasn't the first time Bacon spoke of a "pastoral philosophy." In *The Advancement of Learning* he had described Telesius' work as just that, "pastoral philosophy, full of sense but of no great depth." All too evidently, my above story draws on the undialectical immediacy of this pastoral philosophy, and invokes what one may style the *Youkali utopia*, a wondrous place (Illyria, Arden, Tarsus, Bohemia …) reached by a young woman afield in the woods, adrift in the waves, the grove, shore, or island inhabited by fairies more amiable than Sycorax or Alcina: "C'est presque au bout du monde / Ma barque vagabonde / Errante au gré de l'onde / M'y conduisit un jour / L'île est toute petite / Mais la fée qui l'habite / Gentiment nous invite / A en faire le tour." Roger Fernay, the author of the lyrics, probably had in mind Shakespeare's "romantic" seascapes (*Twelfth Night*, *Pericles*, *The Tempest* and *The Winter's Tale*) when he wrote the following lines:

> le pays de nos désirs [...] le bonheur, c'est le Plaisir [...]
> C'est la terre où l'on quitte tous les soucis [...]
> Youkali, c'est le respect de tous les vœux échangés
> Youkali, c'est le pays des beaux amours partagés
> C'est l'espérance
> Qui est au coeur de tous les humains
> La délivrance
> Que nous attendons tous pour demain

The land of exchanged vows and shared loves, the future-gazing, hope-laden isle of natural, affectionate interactions. The locus of deliverance. Phenomenological critics would probably, at a conscious level, refrain from identifying this island with the England of Richard II's soliloquy. But their ultimately conservative unconscious pines for an archaic utopia not unlike the one sketched by the Duke of Lancaster—"This blessed plot, this earth, this realm / [...] / This land of such dear souls, this dear dear land" (*Richard II* 2.1.50–57). Indeed, the ways of ideological continuity are far less inscrutable than God's. In an ironic response to Hugo Grotius' arguments, Robert Filmer asks rhetorically how God Almighty could "ordain a community which could not continue" (*Patriarcha* 218).² This sharp warning about the *ubiquity of discontinuity* in our mythical-political master narratives should not be easily shelved as a piece of reactionary cynicism. Locke, who was anything but a reactionary, was also bothered by this sense of interruption: how and why did we move out of the "state of nature" to a "political society" or "community of government"? The motivation for such discontinuity is so evident, the grounds for its occurrence so robust, that Locke is left wondering about the valences of the dialectic (nature-culture) in a way that prefigures Levi-Strauss and Derrida:

> *History* gives us but a very little account of men, *that lived together in the State of Nature*. The inconveniences of that condition, and the love, and want of society, no sooner brought any number of them together, but they presently united and incorporated, if they designed to continue together. And if we may not suppose *Men* ever to have been *in the State of Nature*, because we hear not much of them in such a State, we may as well suppose the armies of *Salmanasser* or *Xerxes* were never children, because we hear little of them, till they were Men, and imbodied in Armies. Government is every where antecedent to records, and letters seldome come in amongst a people, till a long continuation of Civil Society has, by other more necessary arts, provided for their Safety, Ease, and Plenty: and then they begin to look after the history of their *Founders*, and search into their *original*, when they have out-lived the memory of it: for it is with *Common-wealths* as with particular persons, they are commonly *ignorant of their own Births and Infancies*: and if they know any thing of their *Original*, they are beholden for it, to the accidental records that others have kept of it. And those that we have, of the beginning of any Polities in the world, excepting that of the *Jews*, where God himself immediately interposed, and which favours not at all Paternal Dominion, are all either plain instances of such a beginning as I have mentioned, or at least have manifest footsteps of it.
>
> Second Treatise of Government, in *Treatises* 334

This powerful passage delivers several signposts for critical thought: 1) that the state of nature was no picnic: it may have existed, but the natural "condition" was manifestly *inconvenient*; 2) that "safety, ease, and plenty" are the original provisions (not givens) of the political condition; 3) that the cultural construction of the natural state depends on written records, and since government

---

2 See John Dunn's discussion of this point in *The Political Thought of John Locke*, 59–60.

and civil society are antecedent to records, the memory of the natural state is per definition mystified; as Royle has sharply urged, "it's not a question of spontaneity but of reckoning with the argument (already explicit and fundamental in *Of Grammatology*, that 'immediacy is derived' (OG, p. 157)" (*In Memory* 119); and 4) that reconstructions of the natural condition are never natural, but cultural, and therefore open to ideological distortion: the analogy employed foreshadows our *cultural* realization that infancy is itself a *cultural* construct. If you condemn this diagnosis as an ultra-liberal précis, you may want to know that Derrida rehearsed it, nearly verbatim, in 1967. There is little doubt that our *own births and infancies* are a reality—a natural reality, a genuine event—but to turn natality into an unscripted bio-a-political horizon of free unexpected eventality adapted to the institution of new political foundations—*constitutio libertatis*—is an undialectical move, insofar as it overlooks the force of ideological mediations: birth is domestically scripted—ideologically domesticated, if you wish—before it can count as asset in higher-order realms of political calculus.[3] And the *Familienroman* is not the only pre-determined narrative into which the naked baby falls: an equivocal natural language, class tensions and incomprehensible biopolitical norms will greet the crawling infant in the remotest recesses of the *Menschenpark*.[4]

The only objection that Derrida and de Man would add to Locke's lucid synthetical account of the dialectical entanglement attending the human aspiration to grasp political origins is that governments or civil societies are not "everywhere antecedent to records," as they are predicated upon consent and agreement, and these performatives demand a certain degree, however tenuous or repressed, of inscription—of *écriture* breaking through as *force de loi*. Origins, whether political or moral, are always-already bound up with grammatological perversion. As Kant argued, "no matter how far back we direct our attention to our moral state, we find that this state is no longer *res integra*" (*Religion* 92). Neither *res integra* nor *tabula rasa*. Derrida astutely noted that Saussure honored a deep-seated fidelity to a tradition "qui toujours a fait communiquer l'écriture avec la violence fatale de l'institution politique. Il s'agirait

---

3 I am alluding, of course, to Hannah Arendt's claims about the political significance of natality, made in *The Human Condition*, to which Kottman and Lupton constantly refer. Recall Peter Laslett's observation that in the early seventeenth-century "the family was thought not as one society only, but as three societies fused together. There was the society of man and wife, that of parents and children, and that of master and servant" (*The World We Have Lost* 2).

4 Louis Althusser called attention to "l'extraordinaire aventure qui, de la naissance à la liquidation de l'Oedipe, transforme un petit animal engendré par un homme et une femme, en petit enfant humain" (*Écrits sur la psychanalise* 34–35).

bien, comme pour Rousseau par example, d'une rupture avec la nature" (*De la grammatologie* 53–54). This is the very rupture—or diremption—around which Paul Kottman's Hegelian theory of tragedy hinges. The assumption, rare for two citizens of Calvinist Genève, is that such fatal violence effectively desecrates a prior natural arcadia, and the contemporary American scholar appears to agree. The metaphysical assumption that the *bon nature* is ravaged by political graphs owes much of its force to the aesthetic persuasion of *simplicity*, a pastoral trope that attends most appeals to *prima philosophia*.[5] Kottman's view of the Hamletian attempt "to close the diremption of nature from sociality" and "to make the latter derive from the former" (*Tragic Conditions* 67) was based, we saw, on belief in the emptiness of the social performatives, but this view occludes the inscriptive priority of performatives, regardless of their worth and moral valence. The materiality of tropical inscription and figurative repetition bears witness to the core of Kantian ethics, where "the empty form of the Law functions as the promise of an absent content [never] to come" (Žižek, *Plague* 292).[6] Conversely, for romantic phenomenologists there is no question that the gap can be closed, and the content made present. The absolutely first (*Allerersten*) is posited as a reserve of simplicity, purity, primitiveness, and persistence that supports—through figures like πρώτως, εἰν, εἶδος, ἀλεθεία, ὑποκείμενον—the metaphysical workings of romantic ideology, from late Toryism (Coleridge) and ultra-Catholicism (Chateaubriand) to fascism (D'Annunzio). Adorno identifies this primitivistic drive not only in Heidegger's antiquarian strain but also, and this is less predictable, in Husserl's modernist primitivism, and exposes the logical vice subtending it in ways that anticipate deconstruction: "The philosophy of origins, which as method first matured the very idea of truth, was also, originally a ψεῦδος" (*Against Epistemology* 12). Adorno's denunciation obviously draws on reserves of standard Marxian critique: in *The German Ideology*, Marx and Engels scorn the German philosophical tendency to resort to pre-history without actually explaining "how we proceed from this nonsensical 'prehistory' to history proper." In their opinion, German thinkers "seize upon this 'prehistory' with especial eagerness because they imagine themselves safe there from interference on the part of 'crude facts'" (*German Ideology* 49) and able to indulge aimless speculative fantasy. What they call "crude facts" are those of infrastructural history, and not the *données* spontaneously delivered to phenomenological sensibilities. Admittedly,

---

5 For William Empson's discussion of *simplicity* in pastoral literature, see *Some Versions*, 21—ff.
6 Lukacher writes about "the strangely irreducible retroactivity of the law 'before the law', which is utterly without content and whose only trace is to be found in daemonic figures" (*Daemonic* 36).

the tendency in phenomenological criticism, very visible in the work of Julia Lupton, to engage with Shakespearean comedic "romances"—plays whose action largely unfolds in a kind of prehistoric site, what Northrop Frye called the *green world*—evinces how intensely and damagingly the inscriptive, performative, facts of history interfere with romantic-phenomenological *alegoresis*. When history turns up, it is immediately reduced to scriptural (Hebraic, early Christian) myth—a figurative version of natural pre-history. This reduction is, moreover, a typically ideological operation, "ideology at its purest, that is, the direct embodiment of the ideological function of providing a neutral all-encompassing space in which social antagonism is obliterated, in which all members of society can recognize themselves" (Žižek, "Class Struggle or Postmodernism" in *Contingency, Hegemony, Universality*, 113). Kottman's Shakespearean readings are also singularized by their drive to obliterate social antagonism and camouflage—de-thematize and naturalize—the infrastructure of economic relations (Žižek, "Class Struggle" 108). For instance, his "apotropaic" recourse to Hegel's "phenomenological" motif of the duel comes through as a magical means to expel the threat of antagonism or dissent. Kottman is courageous enough to want to traverse Shakespeare's primeval tragic phantasy, but the problem is that he actually traverses it and manages to decamp it nearly unscathed—reflectively glancing at Shakespeare's characters as beings that manage, after some temporary struggle, to reach their humanity or manhood ("Duel" 413–414).

2

I suggested in the "Introduction" that Shakespeare's textual world is one of finitude, war, and logos—the very (ontological) realm of conflict that Levinas wished to leave behind. It is sustained by a notion of history as deranged temporality or *sad time* (*King Lear* 5.3.322) than no strong prophecy is likely to amend. To pit, as many do, the consolations of pastoral comedy and romance against this tragic horizon is futile, as the constrains of genre, along with their attending ideological deceptions, are much more strongly felt in the former. Everything is of course illusion in Shakespeare's play-textual realm, but some illusions are, I believe, more delusive than others. Delusive is, for instance, to conceive of a theatrically tended *original position* (John Rawls, *Theory of Justice* 11) where humans may produce a political community through spontaneous interaction. Shakespeare never indulges such fantasy: the final communities he manufactures in his comedies and romances are chiefly familial, scripted in accordance with inherited rules, and tend to be circumscribed to the noble rank. To invest much moral energy in the hermeneutic exaltation of conventional comedic-romantic motifs like deliverance, resolution, familial hope, island renascence, social magic, ritual interaction, common sharing, recognitive happiness, and shared futurity, betrays, in my opinion, no small amount of what a leftist intellectual like Fredric Jameson has rightly called "left infantilism" (*Valences* 236). Kottman and Lupton share this strong fascination with the restorative and redemptive social-moral inducements of the comedic convention, but whereas the latter has repeatedly confronted them head-on in direct readings of comedies and late romances, Kottman's special consists in the *comedification*—the aesthetic-romantic reduction—of the great tragedies.

To imply, as Lupton does in several essays, that Shakespeare's romantic-comedic reunited families and newly-wed couples are exponents of a polis-to-be or promissory figures of communal civility seems to me farfetched. The *original position* of Shakespearean characters is never *original* enough, and the pragmatic spontaneity they supposedly deploy to attain their very reactionary ends (nostos, family reconciliation, marriage) is anything but spontaneous. How free is Viola to perform her social tricks and attain the bliss of wedlock? How free to walk, and talk, and sing, the graceful and expeditive way she does? As it happens, not very. As a member of a noble family, she has received the best education. So her participation in the social game doesn't take place on a basis of equality with others—including the Captain and Olivia, to mention only two characters. Her freedom is a function of her unfreedom, of superstructural determinants, and this ideological conditioning allows her a range of expectations that are culturally scripted, coded, and therefore mediated. Let me recall at this point Habermas' strongest objection to Arendt's concept of power based on spontaneous praxis emerging from unconstrained communication and unimpaired intersubjectivity:

> Structural violence does not manifest itself as *force*; rather, unperceived, it blocks those communications in which convictions effective for legitimation are formed and passed on. Such an hypothesis about inconspicuously working communication blocks can explain, perhaps, the formation of ideologies; with it one can give a plausible account of how convictions are formed in which subjects deceives themselves about themselves and their situations. Ideologies are after all illusions that are outfitted with the power of common convictions. This proposal is an attempt to render the communicative production of power in a more realistic version.
> "HANNAH ARENDT'S Communications" 21–22

Systemic pragmatic violence (Machiavelli, Hobbes, Nietzsche, Schmitt), rampant ideological obfuscation (Bacon, Marx, Adorno, Althusser, Žižek) and intrinsic linguistic error (Hegel, Nietzsche, Lacan, Derrida): all these determinants preempt—and ultimately preclude—the spontaneous power-generating dance of interpersonal communicative socialization. But since Habermas is boring, and Viola, the musical instrument, is our food of love, play on. Greenblatt praises the girl's "improvisational boldness [...] eloquent tongue and [...] keen wit" and concludes: "Viola seems to draw on an inward principle of hope" ("Introduction" to *Twelfth Night*, 1688). And more recently Julia Lupton, drawing on the candle image used by McIntyre in his discussion of virtues as "the qualities which sustain a free man" (*After Virtue* 122), describes her, as we have already seen, as "candle, match, and flame" ("Virtue in *Twelfth Night*" 1). But Viola is far less *inward* and *free* than these remarks suggest. We may well translate Lupton's description into the chimeric notion of *spontaneous human combustion* and bear in mind not only Marx's hostility to these pre-scientific tropes, which tended to camouflage the work of structural determination, but also his critique of Proudhon's belief in *libre arbiter*. Marx rejects the notion of freedom constructed by Utopian socialists, whom he scorns as "chevaliers du libre arbiter" (*Misère* 90) stupefied by the "étiquette d'une langage humanitaire" (98). I believe Greenblatt's and Lupton's language is also informed by a humanitarian etiquette, perhaps not Socialist, but certainly Utopian. The moral shaping of critical language may appear today as an asset, but it was certainly not for Marx. To read, in sum, *Twelfth Night* as a romance of personal self-reliance aimed either at a transgender paradise of emotional intimacy and bonding (Greenblatt) or at the good life of virtuous social participation (Lupton) is, in my opinion, erroneous, largely because the implicit interpersonal egalitarianism—anyone can be Viola because Viola is simply herself, i.e. her own rich resource of selfhood—upon which these readings rest wipes out from the text nearly all traces of social antagonism and ideological heteroglossia.[7] In the hands of Utopian reformers, Marx construed equality as an ideological misconception: "En résumé, l'égalité est l'*intention*

---

[7] I have already lamented the illiberal stakes implicit in the coaxing of the reader into a shared view of the *good life*. Even Nussbaum shied away from this risk: "In a deliberate departure from Aristotle, who surely believed that politics ought to foster functioning in accordance with a single comprehensive conception of the good human life, I argue that politics should restrict itself to promoting capabilities, not actual functionings, in order to make room for choices about whether to pursue a given function or not to pursue it" ("Preface" to the Revised Edition of *Fragility* ix). This is fine, but Nussbaum's positivist-analytic reliance on the separability of moral and volitional faculties like capability and choice bespeaks a certain anthropological naivety, obviously inherited from Kant: we promote your *natural* capability,

primitive, la *tendance mystique*, le *but providentiel* que le génie social a constamment devant les yeux" (*Misère* 172). And the social genius responsible for this figment is that of a pacified bourgeoisie: "L'école philantrope est l'école humanitaire perfectionné. Elle nie la nécessité de l'antagonisme; elle veut faire de tous les hommes des bourgeois" (*Misère* 179). There is no room, in Marx's critical analysis, for a "réalité idealisé" (179), and we should learn to keep our distance, as Shakespeare did, from the prescriptive idealizations of comedy, among which social homogeneity is perhaps the most equivocal. The risk of remoralizing *Twelfth Night* is certainly built into Shakespeare's *ironic* composition of the play, but I guess we should all know better—and learn to recognize how moral delivery is always-already preemptively—apotropaically—defused by a castrating ironic cacophony.

No action is ideologically unscripted, immediate, unmotivated. To a certain extent, the work of phenomenology attempts precisely to erase this realization, and to produce a version of pragmatic action that is utterly spontaneous and free from the pressure of ideological determinants and infrastructural conditioning. There is a great deal of pre-Marxian liberal fantasizing in Arendt's neo-Aristotelian ethic-politics, and it is no surprise that neo-phenomenological scholarship should feel attracted to it, for phenomenology is animated by what Luc Ferry and Alain Renault called "la tentative pour inscrire l'historicité (ou, si l'on préfère l'historialité) dans le régistre de 'sans-pourquoi'" (*La pensée 68* 111). The situationist coordinates delivered by this phenomenological erasure of what has been thus inscribed postulate a notion of action as unpredictable event, as "initiation/inauguration absolue" (111). The possibility of a radically new political life hinges upon the "startling unexpectedness [...] inherent in all beginnings and all origins" (Arendt, *The Human Condition* 313). As I have already pointed out, Lupton's recourse to Nussbaum's idea of *moral luck* evinces a fascination with unconditioned unpredictability or merely *fortuna* that tends to blur the critical discriminations brilliantly enforced by Marx and Engels. Before them, Pascal was already reluctant to throw reason overboard in moral contemplations of the future: "quand on travaille pour demain, et pour l'incertain, on agit avec raison: car on doit travailler pour l'incertain" (*Pensées* 229). The phrase (*avec raison*) is idiomatic, but the implications are not. *Agir* or *travailler avec raison* for the uncertain is a far cry from spontaneously joining hands in the dance of future sociality. Marx and Engels believed (perhaps wrongly, whence the risk of their *Utopia*) that the conditions of the free

---

now you *freely* choose. This would work beautifully if we didn't have to factor in ideology and the unconscious.

development and movement of individuals could be placed under the control of revolutionary proletarians. Such conditions were judged (perhaps rightly, whence the force of their *critique*) to be

> previously abandoned to chance and had own an independent existence over against the separate individuals just because if their separation as individuals, and because of the necessity of their combination which had been determined by the division of labour, and though their separation had become a bond alien to them. Combination up till now (by no means an arbitrary one, such as is expounded for example in the *Contrat social*, but a necessary one) was an agreement upon these conditions, within which the individuals were free to enjoy the freaks of fortune [...] This right to the undisturbed enjoyment, within certain conditions, of fortuity and chance has up till now been called personal freedom. These conditions of existence are, of course, only the productive forces and forms of intercourse at any particular time.
>
> *German Ideology*, 85–86

To the assertion of Viola's spontaneous freedom we could thus reply that "with money, every form of intercourse, and intercourse itself, is considered fortuitous for the individuals" (*German Ideology*, 91). "It is clear," Marx and Engels argue earlier in the same book, "that individuals make one another, physically and mentally, but do not make themselves" (*German* 55–56), yet this reciprocal making is less spontaneous, less impromptu, more scripted—by infrastructural overdetermination, by ideology, by discursive mediation—than Lupton or Kottman are ready to admit. Acknowledgement of the necessity and precedence of loosely scripted normativity—whether based on statute or precedent—is not only a basic tenet of open liberal societies, but also an implicit consequence of the grammatological take on the nature/society divide. The neglect of such conventional (and arbitrary) normativity leads to a bizarre, neo-romantic, reliance on transrational, mystical, criteria.

Thus, for instance, *consent* is either tutored by the law or inexistent: it cannot be freely, spontaneously, invented by someone—someone other than the consenting subject—operating outside the previsions of the law.[8] To be sure, the moral provision of a "twilight zone" where the arbitrary fictions of the law

---

8   See Julia Lupton, "Epilogue: The Literature of Citizenship: A Humanifesto" in *Citizens-Saints*, 205–206. Lupton uses Pedro Almodóvar's film *Hable con ella* (2002) to try to prove the utility of "sublimating" the problem of legal consent. In the movie, Benigno, a male nurse, rapes a comatose patient. Almodóvar's attempt to redeem through sentimental claptrap (he loved

are exposed is a salutary exercise, but to expect, as Lupton appears to do, that social origination necessarily taps the irrationally uncertain, and that the twilight zone should therefore be that "between the citizen and the saint" is a stretch. Why not between the citizen and the philosopher, or rather, between the citizen and the human being? To force the citizen to keep company with the saint is like forcing Kant's pure reason to remain tied to metaphysical and theological aberrations, which can only deliver—think of Georges Bataille—a crude re-ontologization of the critical project. Paul Kottman seeks to restore and set anew "an ontology that reveals the world as stage, and that orients itself from the start toward an interactive horizon of words and deeds among unique actors and witnesses" (*A Politics of the Scene*, 4). This interactive horizon of spontaneous verbal and pragmatic encounters is precisely what Lupton pines for—the marshalling of institutional and collective energies "in innovative collaborations that can help each of us articulate our individual and collective goals and values within a new civic space" (206). Illiberally, consent in this new space is not something requested and given: it "is evoked, elicited, invented" (*Citizen-Saints* 205). By whom? By the community?

Lupton's neo-ontological program of social action, conveyed in Manifesto format, closes her second book on Shakespeare. This is intriguing. Adorno reminds us "that the wish is a poor father to the thought (*Dass der Wunsch ein schlechter Vater des Gedankens*) has been one of the general theses of European enlightenment ever since Xenophanes, and the thesis applies undiminished to the attempts to restore ontology" (*Negative Dialectics* 408). There is, in short, wishful thinking and critical thinking.[9] They are not the same, and Shakespeare is best served by deploying the latter. The confusion, in Shakespeare's studies today, between the life experiences of the scholar and the Shakespeare experience is best illustrated by looking at the acknowledgement sections of the standard monograph, where special emphasis is placed on the virtues of collaboration, community, interaction, ecclesia, what have you. These tropes, in turn, become the object of study in the monograph proper, because Shakespeare supposedly put them in performative circulation in order to

---

her, they have a stillborn baby, she awakens from coma) the brutal fact of the rape is simply embarrassing.

9 In *Truth and Justification*, Habermas discusses the underlying paradox of a "morally self-regarding action": "Is there something like a metamorality of action whose goal is to fulfill the necessary institutional conditions for moral judgement formation and moral action?" (46). The problem with moral critics is not so much that they do not seek such institutionalization of the conditions for moral judgement formation—Habermas' standards are too highly placed—but rather that they should take them for granted, as being those, that is, they particularly cherish.

ontologically (morally) articulate his phenomenal experiences. The resulting circularity leads inevitably to the confessional coloring of the critical work, which, as I have already noted, characterizes the late work of Dollimore. "It may seem unusual to specify in such detail the context and culture from which an article emerged," he argues in the Introduction to a reedition of his article "The Cultural Politics of Perversion: Augustine, Shakespeare, Freud, Foucault," after describing this context in lavish detail. And adds: "But the recognition of the importance of context to intellectual work is precisely one aspect of the cultural materialist project, as is the emphasis on that work as the result of a collectivity, rather than the scholar isolated in his or her tower."

To be sure, this *collectivity* is a materialist avatar of Husserl's transcendental subjectivity, the same one we encounter—filtered through Hegel's civil society and Arendt's nascent sociality—in the work by Lupton and Kottman I am looking at. But the phenomenological stakes implicit in this vision of togetherness may have reached these scholars, and others like Curran or Kearney, from the work of other heirs of Husserl. Thus, for instance, the eschatological conception of the collective as a flame to be lit in the future belongs too in the prophetic-apocalyptic logic of Levinas' metaphysics. "Le désir métaphysique," he argues in *Totalité et infini*, "n'aspire pas au retour, car il est désir d'un pays où nous ne naquîmes point" (22). The name of this land is Canaan, Athens, Venice, Youkali. In *Totalité et infini* he states that "de la paix, il ne peut y avoir qu'eschatologie" and describes his philosophical program as a retreat from the (ontological) objectivism of war to the (ethical) subjectivism of peace: "Nous opposons à l'objectivisme de la guerre une subjectivité issue de la vision eschatologique" (9–11). Furthermore, the first chapter of *Totalité et infini* opens with Rimbaud's famous maxim "La vraie vie est absente." Levinas corrects the coda: "Mais nous sommes au monde." Merleau-Ponty would further specify: *au même monde*. Real life is absent, but we are in the world, in the same world—in the *Umwelt* of *Mitwelt*. *La vraie vie*? What is that? Make peace not war? I have no idea, but don't worry, the Shakespeare scholar knows. To be sure, the ghost of *das eingentliche Leben* has haunted human experience in German post-romantic narratives, from Kleist to Musil, Walser, and Hesse, all the way down to Peter Weiss, but they give us fictions, and we tolerate their interruptive moral instigation because it is ragged, deformed, and wrapped up in self-conscious contradiction. To instrumentalize Shakespearean exegesis in order to enforce an idea of the *authentic life* is a hopeless and illiberal measure. While Shakespeare would have recognized his own voice in the protests and demurrals of Koolhas and Törless, I doubt he would have easily related with the vision of the good life proposed by some of his new exegetes.

3

Dollimore, we have seen, prefers collective intellectual action to "the work of the scholar isolated in his or her own tower." To the work, say, of Hamlet or Prospero—not to mention Caesar, Timon, Coriolanus and Edgar, all of them isolated in their dark tower, all of them scholars in their own way, all of them lavishly realized by Shakespeare.[10] Dollimore's preference may not be Shakespeare's (I think it is not) but it is surely coincidental with that of many neo-phenomenological academics. The new Youkali experience involves the mystified extrapolation of the desired scenario (the hologram of spontaneous togetherness) from its scholastic scene of formation: the Shakespeare experience is no longer that of a lonely man reading a playtext (Dryden reading Shakespeare, Johnson reading Shakespeare, Malone reading Shakespeare, Lewis reading Shakespeare, Coleridge reading Shakespeare, Bradley reading Shakespeare, Frye reading Shakespeare), but rather that of many participants sharing and exchanging fleshed-out meanings. I stress the scheme of the reviled scenario not only because it may reveal something to young scholars who are unaware of the adversarial instinct of their teachers, but also because its intellectual payoff is never quite lost on serious scholars of an older generation: I think, for instance, of James Shapiro, who opens *Shakespeare and the Jews* with a sympathetic excursus into a note by Coleridge on Donne (2–3). Coleridge's scandalized response to a flagrant anti-Semitic passage in Donne's Sermons provokes in Shapiro a complicitous emotional response that helps largely to make up for the jarring anti-communal dissonances that shall spring in his analysis of the cultural-historical contexts and performative effects of *The Merchant of Venice*—admittedly, a comedy *without* communal resolution. *Sans délivrance.*

The small Youkali commune can be an actors-audience network of "copresence," and nothing—no distance, no difference, no verbal mediation—shall "challenge the immediacy of co-presence by insisting, say, on the prison house of language and subjectivity" (Lupton & Smith, "Introduction" to *Face-to-Face* 6). A great deal is being thrown overboard here—Descartes, Derrida, even Jameson, who remains in full shape in the prison-house of language and dialectics. The disembodied Cartesian centaurs deciphering graphs are replaced by a community-event—an ecology of humans and

---

10   Levinas defends that society antedates the apparition of the impersonal structures of reason : "Ce n'est pas l'impersonnel en moi que la Raison instaurerait mais un Moi-même capable de société" (*Totalité* 229). Shakespeare's worlds run contrary to this thesis. Prospero's, for instance, is the story of a *moi-même* disqualified for society.

environmental actants (things, animals, weather) sharing their ceaseless flow. This community is moreover polarized around the moral emotions of pity and commiseration—unbeknownst, according to Rousseau, to the isolated philosopher, in thrall to rational reflection, *replié sur lui-même* (*Discours* 97). For the French thinker, remember, "l'homme seul est sujet à devenir imbécile" (80). No room therefore any longer for the secluded and lonesome and potentially imbecile savant (Descartes, Hobbes, Locke, Spinoza), immortalized in Antonello da Messina's painting of St Jerome in his study, and whose apologetic swan-song was intoned by Sybille Lewitsharoff in *Blumenberg*. This spells not solely a dissatisfaction with the hegemonic practices of disembodied cognition in our rationalist—allegedly, Cartesian—tradition: it also spells a sociopolitical reaction against liberal possessive individualism: the white middle-class proprietor (of goods, money, knowledge, and professional position) presuming to own Shakespeare. One wonders whether the new generation of pastoral-collaborative scholars has ever intended to give up this institutional possession. But anyway. The contestation of the abhorred scenario—a white man reads a book at home and then goes to a seminar room to tell students what he has read—has taken, we know, many forms. Most of the elements in the above sentence have been duly confronted: 1) the exclusivity of the white man has been replaced by a variety of racialized and gendered agency (this was a major breakthrough, with extraordinary liberating effects); but, 2) the book has been replaced by more visual sources and interactive tools; and 3) the classroom has been changed from a space of unidirectional telling into a high-tech field of collective synergy. The last two replacements are hardly improvements. The popularity of phenomenological criticism owes a great deal, I believe, to the undiminished sway of a critical-pedagogic turn that draws its force paradoxically from the moral embarrassments consequent upon the depoliticization of academic departments, and upon the resulting yearning, amongst its members, to seek for compensatory alternative scenarios in unexpected—and yet supposedly radical—directions: since we cannot do things out there (the broad social space), we will do them here (in the classroom), thus remaining *activists*. This shift of priorities can be attributed to what Lentricchia called the "occupational alienation" of the American Cultural Left (qtd. in Rorty, *Essays on Heidegger* 133). The teaching of literature—a brutally open liberal program, to be sure, premised by mandatory readings—is replaced by the social-moral magic of *literary education*, whatever that is.[11] The

---

11 Julia Lupton styles herself as a "literary educator." As early as 2005, she ranked Shakespeare's plays, together with Almodóvar's film, among what she called "the literature of citizenship," which she conceived as "a field of scholarly inquiry but also of artistic

original scenario was criminalized as an exercise in Cartesian "lone-wolf auto-phenomenology" (Dennett 20), typical of the standard *Steppenwölfe* readers in the Shakespeare tradition, like Coleridge, Bradley, Wilson Knight, Empson, or Bloom. Racializing or gendering the teacher of *Othello* is not enough, nor does it suffice to racialize and gender further a play that is—after all, of course—all about gender and race. One should not rest content either with teaching the play in an embodied format (with no copy of the playtext around) and an interactive methodology (with little or no room for the author's voice). The thing to do, the radical and political thing to do, is to turn the play itself into a radical polis, a site of embodied interaction, which, for lack of anything better, can be represented by, say, a classroom production of the play, or better, a classroom discussion of the production of the play. The playtext, both the pretext for and the pretextual extrapolation of the multicultural, dialogical, citizenized seminar community, exits the classroom. The playtext students are given what they already are—or believe to be. "The purchase is to make men glorious" (*Pericles* 1.0.9): the magic of teaching is accomplished. Which explains, of course, why nobody wants to teach *Othello*, not to mention *The Merchant of Venice*, *Titus Andronicus*, or *The Taming of the Shrew*. How do you teach, for instance, *Titus Andronicus* or *The Rape of Lucrece* from the fluid civic standpoint of revisited consent?

In a powerful indirect reading of *King Lear*, Derrida reminds us that there is chance and chance, actually, *chance*, *non-chance*, and *méchance*, and that to pit the contingencies of society against the necessity of nature, in order to secure a sanctum of potential-natural capabilities, affections and virtues, occludes the fact that natural necessity is not unlike the mediated *necessity* of a productive

---

capacity that might draw humanists towards matters of public interest and consequence without diluting the integrity of what we do" (*Citizen-Saints* 206). If an *education in literature* implies forcing students to read and understand the meaning of literary texts for their own sake, a *literary education* instrumentalizes the literary text as a means to learn something else. What is that something else? The good life, the better life, the best life, community. The fact that politics in America has always been invested with the religious (apocalyptic-revolutionary) aura of a moral obligation, and that American political history furnishes, globally, lessons in emancipation one *must learn* (is actually taught) to live by, may help explain the distinctive moralism of some American scholars. I guess in Europe citizenship is seen by most cultivated people more as a contingent legal right than as a necessary second skin. This doesn't make the European attitude any better, but it may prevent its constant overspill to areas of life traditionally considered non-political. I know that the belief in non-political spheres of human life reeks of conservative liberalism, but I am also aware that there are greatly illiberal ways of misinterpreting and tightening the Marxian-Foucaldian knot that lies at the core of the thought of Rancière, Badiou, and others.

contingency (Althusser, *Lire* 46)—and that to be born a bastard is as much an accident in the order of nature as it is in the "order of law" (*King Lear* 1.1.18).[12] The fact that the outcome (the bastard) is also called a *natural* is part of the necessary irony controlling this logic. There is, in short, no way to tell these two orders apart, because "the art of our necessities is strange" (*King Lear* 3.2.67). A profound natural necessity determines the *bastard course*—what Derrida calls the "démarche bâtard" and "chemin bâtard" (*Glas* 12) of all human experience, and the *détournement* (the deviation, the clinamen) that "bâtardise" inserts in genealogical flows is proof both of our constitutive finitude, of our limitation, and of our scripted *destinerrance* (Derrida, "Mes chances," *Psyché* 360–384). To assert—with Christian philosophers, with Kant and Heidegger—that we humans are finite, is to venture an ontological delineation. To assert that we are vulnerable, precarious, and in need of recognitive curation and communal repair, is to overstep the critical-rational boundaries of a certain ontology and to enter moral territory. Have a safe journey.

---

12 See Chiara Alfano careful analysis of this Derrida essay in Chapter 5 of her book *Derrida Reads Shakespeare*, 135–172.

CHAPTER 9

What Matters in Shakespeare?

1

What matters today in Shakespeare? The answer to this question is, to a large extent, *matter*, under four distinct guises: 1) the matters of Shakespeare's characters' putative bodies: the humors and fluids of *physiological materialism*, a sub-branch of the discipline much boosted by the so-called "affective turn" (Cummings & Sierhius, "Introduction" to *Passions and Subjectivity* 1); 2) the matters of the original performance: the stage props of a *theatrical materialism* that performance studies and historical phenomenology purport to give us access to; 3) the matters of the objectal world the play supposedly invokes: the things of *object-oriented* and *ecological materialism*; 4) the matters of writing and publication: the hand, quill, ink and printed paper of *writing-and-print materialism*. In the four cases, the rights of materialism are reclaimed by phenomenology, especially *historical phenomenology*. Elsewhere in this book I comment on the first three modes of materiality. Here I want to focus only on the last, that of *writing-and-print materiality*. I will examine two very influential essays, Margreta de Grazia's "The essential Shakespeare and the material book" (1988) and the one she wrote in collaboration with Peter Stallybrass five years later, "The Materiality of the Shakespearean Text" (1993), but also some of the arguments and claims put forward by Jonathan Gil Harris in his also influential book *Untimely Matter in the Time of Shakespeare* (2009). Let me fix atop the gate to this section Althusser's old warning to the effect that we should "stop confusing the *materialist proclamations* of certain 'materialists' [...] with *materialism itself*" (*For Marx* 30). Vale.

While the romantics sought to retrieve an archaic voice (*Ursprache*) buried inside an archival mass of written documents, the phenomenologists now seek to release a primeval life-event taken hostage by sclerotic philologists, undaring humanists and musty archive-guardians. Both the romantics and the phenomenologists come to Ariel's rescue. This life-event is a Bild or hologram in action, a dynamized *aesthetic idea* (Kant), the motion tableau of a lost social experience which, in the case of Shakespeare's art, the playtext only defectively transmits. This is manifestly an introjected fractal version of the ethnographic pastoral allegory that pits the oral accents of the *sauvage* against the writing practices of Western culture.¹ The purpose of phenomenology is therefore ethnographical or, better, archeological, i.e. to resuscitate a *Lebenswelt* pragmatic-aesthetic occasion that Shakespeare's written art only imperfectly preserved. Historical phenomenology strives to rescue the material odds and ends involved the play's involved world. Performance studies strives to rescue the material infrastructure underpinning the play's performance's involved world. Aesthetic critics seek to restore the play as (if) it imaginatively happened before Shakespeare took the trouble to transcribe its latent script. And when none of these dealings pays off, when the manifold operation of restoration falls short of furnishing the raw materials (*le cru*) of Shakespeare's culinary art (*le cuit*), then the workaround is to fall back on the last bastion of extant primeval materiality: the materiality of composition (ink, quill, papers) and publication (quartos, folios). In the first case we have a metaphorical substitution: since the play *stands for* the primeval occurrence of a life-event, we proceed to track down the latter's traces. The workaround offers a metonymical escape: since the play *stands by* its medium of composition and publication, we can always, *faute de mieux*, turn to this medium and upgrade it to the material key to Shakespeare's art. The scene of representing experience (the *scene of writing*) is the soteriological scenario of the community of phenomenological-materialist scholars that set out to dig up, in the first place, the scene of represented experience, and came back home empty-handed. But this is, we will see, a hopeless solution. The original expectation was based on a delusion: the credence in the existence of a material-sensorial reality prior to or consequent on the playtext that alone the printed version seeks to represent. Failure to retrieve such reality leads to the sacralization of material writing-cum-publication relics. But the underlying belief, I insist, is specious. The playtext seeks to represent nothing. When Wittgenstein censured Shakespeare for not being "naturwahr" (*Culture and Value* 84), he forgot to add that no actual text is true to nature or life: it is very easy to say that a writer is "the mirror of life" when one's view of life is itself a mirror-induced delusion. What Samuel Johnson understood for life is indissociable from his literary education and textual ideology, and did he know it: "Our grandfathers knew the picture from life; we judge of the life by contemplating the picture" (*Lives of the Poets* 9). As Rorty lucidly pointed out,

> justification is not a matter of a special relation between ideas (or words) and objects, but of conversation, of social practice [...] we understand

---

1 See Jonathan Goldbert, *Writing Matter*, 15–16.

knowledge when we understand the social justification of belief, and thus have no need to view it as accuracy of representation.
Philosophy 170

Every teenager that has gone through *The Metamorphosis* recalls the moment when she put down the novel and discovered, suddenly, at last, that she too, of course, was a beetle. Is that *naturwahr*? "We live in the mind," wrote Wallace Stevens (*The Necessary Angel* 140), which translated into structuralist terms means that we are in the prison house of languages, or, better, that since our life is indistinguishable from (mediated by) our *pictures of life*, one may conceivably say that we live in (through) our pictures. This doesn't mean that the positive-empirical materiality of our pictures and tropes is the primary condition—the material cause—of our existence. It is rather the instrumental condition of another materiality, a *transcendental* or *formal materiality* of differential trace-inscription, that alone explains the durability and universality of its grip on human life. I use *transcendental* in the specific Kantian sense, but also in the broader Derridean sense evoked by Jonathan Goldberg in a lucid gloss: "Because the opening is not foreclosed, because the system is not static and at rest but in movement from the start, these relaying structures are not 'there' all at once except within the possibility of a structure that is never there all at once" (*Writing Matter* 25). The non-static system of relaying structures that are not there all at once within an ever-excessive structure that is never totally given and never totally closed off is what I call—playing a variation on a Deleuze motif—a *transcendental materiality*.[2] It is transcendental because—like a ghost—it is at the same time determinant and in excess of the evental meanings contingently produced at local—Badiou would say *situational*—level.[3] *Transcendental* is here the mark of an abject collusion, described by Colebrook as "the imbrication, if not the indistinction, of matter and ideality" ("Matter without bodies" 7). Transcendental causation is of course, no one-to-one mechanical transaction, but an eminently structural affair of multilateral overdetermination (Althusser). And this materiality explains, among other things, the intimate relationship between, on the one hand, the fact that a Sicilian boy feels today, simply by browsing a brand-new printed paperback titled *La metamorfosi*, that he has always been treated by relatives as "un enorme insetto" and, on the other hand, the fact that a man called Franz

---

2 Deleuze famously spoke of a *transcendental empiricism* in *Différence et répétition*, 79.
3 The spectral nature of this transcendental materiality is somehow evoked by Claire Colebrook in her astute analysis of Derrida's take on the problem of matter. The ghost would here stand for the very impossibility of materialism. See *Matter without Bodies*, p. 3.

Kafka used a pen in 1912 to scribble the phrase "ungeheuren Ungeziefer" in a notebook. Or that Balzac and Turgenev could dress, address, and redress Lear in, respectively, French and Russian robes. What can be left out as positively negligible in this powerful transfer is precisely both the original matter (ink, notebook, folio) and the final matter (printed volume or paperback). What makes the transfer possible is a transcendental transaction that occurs in the "relaying structures" (ideological, tropological, grammatical, logical) of natural language(s). Only through the arbitrary and formal *instance of the letter* can this brutal attribution come into excessive utterance—"I am a beetle," "Pelican daughters," "Detested kite"—and this interpellation is less medium-dependent than mediation-sensitive. It is, I am afraid, an unphenomenal interpellation.[4]

2

In 1990, Jonathan Goldberg published a book titled *Writing Matter: From the Hands of the English Renaissance,* which he described as "a study of handwriting in the Renaissance" with a focus "on manuals of instruction, the materials and the materiality of a practice that extends from the manuals to the hand of the writer, and on the social and historical positions that these instructions and those instructed come to occupy" (1). The reader is soon accosted by three cognate lexemes: *matter, materials, materiality.* The iteration is daunting. This is a book, we are led to expect, about the materiality of writing in the English Renaissance. But this is not exactly so. The study is presided by a strong Derridean vigilance against the facile gratifications of empirical facticity and historical positivism. And, although he never here cites Althusser and Foucault, Goldberg is too immersed in a dialectical understanding of ideology and institutionalized discursivity to give in to the banalities of unmediated phenomenological embodiment. The strictures of Derridean vigilance he often finds exasperating and seeks to bridge the gap between a sufficiently demystified, transcendental understanding of writing as *archi-écriture* and a "cultural graphology" that accommodates historical difference. His strong political bias, moreover, forces him to dismiss the correlation between literacy and rationality that is, in my opinion, a bit more than dormant in Derrida's early texts. And yet, his deconstructive alertness saves him on the whole from fetishizing the hand or naturalizing writing.

---

4 The *instance of the letter* is of course Lacan's phrase: "D'où l'on peut dire que c'est dans la chaîne du signifiant que le sens *insiste,* mais qu'aucun des éléments de la chaîne ne *consiste* dans la signification dont il est capable au moment même" (*Écrits I* 499).

It was broadly felt by conscientious Derridean scholars like Goldberg that the celebration of certain matters, materials and materialities had a structural limit. This did not prevent some of them, including Goldberg himself, from joining the new textualist church, and laying out on the altar all the textual variations—including the so-called bad quartos—of the once-revered isolated plays. The ceremony of the mass was to become more democratic and, according to some, more materialist as well. In 1988, Margreta de Grazia publishes in *Textual Practice* the essay titled "The essential Shakespeare and the material book," where the scholarly idealization of the Shakespeare work is explicitly resisted. The title flags a running opposition, materialism versus essentialism, and the essay, more specifically, celebrates the mystique of playhouse versions and scribal copies, the new "emphasis upon the material processes of book production" (69). *Material processes* is the phrase that carries the weight of theoretical—ultimately Marxian—prestige. De Grazia argues that the new editorial revolution is not that new because its practitioners apply an "'anti-materialist' or 'idealist'" technique of purification already used by earlier editors: "In both cases the essential manuscript must be extricated from the accidental printed matter within which it is imagined to be located" (71). The essay's goal is therefore to expose this "fundamental anti-materialist strain" (80). This is clear enough. More doubtful is her use of the terms "matter" and "materialist." We encounter phrases like "the physical properties of the book" (69), "the physical phenomena of the Shakespearean text" (69), "the physical making and make-up of the book" (70), "the physical elements of the book" (70), but it is never totally clear what these *phenomena* are, let alone why they are not characterized as *formal* rather than *material*. De Grazia speaks of physical properties "even in their most ready form," referring to "the precise letter and words on a page" (70) and correlates the discarded "physicality" (the term is used twice on page 72) with the "compositor's mark on the page" (70). But *marks*, *words*, and *letters* are all *formal* configurations, and if you want to make these signifiers significant at all, then you must strip off their materiality (density, ink). What does a trained paleographist do if not extricate a limpid form out of an abstruse (deformed or excessively formed) form or out the garbled matter of a presumptive graph (That stain there is an "r"!)? But the tenor of her argument forces de Grazia to dismiss the Saussurean caveat about the inherently formal nature of language and focus on the *physicality* of the signifiers, whatever she means by that. The dismissal is carried out at no small cost. These resilient and lingering and very enigmatic *physical phenomena*, moreover, are sharply opposed to the "abstract and metaphysical plane" (69) of scholarly abstract rarefaction. Thus the polarity materiality-ideality and/or materialism-essentialism (idealist and essential are frequent adjectives in the essay) is now recast as physical-metaphysical, all the way down to the article's resounding close: "Devoted to what may be termed an 'incarnational' text— material in form, immaterial in essence—the study of book as physical object thus remains metaphysically mystified" (82). I will leave aside the phenomenological echo in the theological trope of *incarnation,* which smacks of *embodiment,* not without noting that the idealist metaphysics that sustains the trope remains at work in the critical practice of those who profess to restrict their faith to the worshipping of (material) relics. Derrida already warned in his essay on Nancy against Merleau-Ponty's "discourse of flesh and incarnation" (*On Touching* 188), a mode of discourse much admired by Hannah Arendt (*The Life of the Mind* 33). Indeed more mystified still, and certainly metaphysical, is the phrase "material in form," anticipated in an earlier sentence: "In theory at least, the *material form* to which Shakespeare was consigned, in order be produced as performance and as book, must be cast away to reveal the underlying manuscript" (80; my emphasis). What is a *material form*?

Five years later, her arguments are revised and rehearsed in another important piece written with Peter Stallybrass, titled "The Materiality of the Shakespearean Text." In this new essay, essentialism remains the target of an argument that questions editorial practices driven by illusions of permanence and transparency and calls attention to the "inert and obsolete matter" that has been sacrificed in the process. The focus of the essay, the authors declare, are features that editorial "modernization and emendation smooth away," namely "old typefaces and spellings, irregular line and scene divisions, title pages and other paratextual matter, and textual cruxes." These "constitute," they argue, "the 'materiality of the text'" (256). One could be tempted, in principle, to style the materialism implicit in this argument as a *textual materialism* in de Derridean sense, but this is an unduly excessive concession. To be sure, their notion of matter or materiality is shaky and non-specific, and one is at pains to tell, in the circumvolutions of their reasoning, form and matter apart, not only because "typefaces," "spellings," and "divisions" are all terms that designate *formal* not *material* arrangements, but also because the authors insist on blurring the distinction—central, one would expect, in an essay purporting to deal with *materiality*—between form and matter. At one point they contend that "attention to these earlier material traces is no exercise in antiquarianism. These older forms return as active agents calling our own forms into question" (257). And they close their introductory section by warning that "past forms [...] return to try present standards" (257). So, the presupposition is that *earlier material traces* are *older forms* or *past forms,* and an essay titled "The materiality of the Shakespearean text" deals, we are told, with the latter—with the older and past forms. The material and the formal are thus nonchalantly invited to intermix—which is either a straight blunder or a sublime intellectual proposition. It is intriguing, to say the least. Arguably, the fact that such collapse occurs in the presence of the term "trace" could be taken as evidence of a Derridean construal of materialism staked on the indifference or undecidability of the matter/form difference. But this would entail a formalist (textualist) conception of matter, rather than the materialist—historicizing, empiricist, fetishizing—conception of form that Stallybrass and de Grazia unwittingly make provision for. More on this later.

De Grazia and Stallybras frame their critique of dated editorial practices as an anti-essentialist, anti-metaphysical, philosophical argument. This is not necessary, I believe, for the congruence of the case they advance, but they obviously seek to finesse their claims with a poststructuralist edge. And this, of course, is not devoid of risk. Their first important claim is that the recent discovery that there are "many *Lears* instead of one" has cast into doubt "the self-identity of the work" (255), "identity and difference" being, they argue, in likely allusion to a Heidegger title, "the basis of perception itself" (255). What they probably mean is "the identity of the work." Self-identity, a concept designed for discussions of personal identity, is a meaningless tool in a discussion of things (works, texts). If what they mean is *auto-identity*, then the concept is simply redundant, for identity is always the identity of something with itself. What they probably have in mind is equality, not identity. As Heidegger noted in the essay mentioned above, it is not the identity of something that is normally in question in discussions of identity, but rather the equality of something with another thing. Thus, for instance, the statement or formula *Lear* = *Lear* expresses a relationship of equality, not sameness or (real) identity.[5] These distinctions may appear fastidiously distracting, if not utterly banal, but the fact is that, according to the Hegel logic embraced by the poststructuralist intelligentsia (Lacan, Althusser, Derrida, even Deleuze) *nothing* is ever identical to itself—the equal or unequal being a predicational attribution we apply to the *non-identical*.[6] Gabriel Egan was right to show exasperation with new textualist shibboleths like the *self-differing* text, which turned *King Lear* into a rebus defined by *non-identity with itself*.[7] In fact, the question of "the fundamental

---

5 The underlying philosophical crux is not so much that of self-identity and difference, as that originally formulated in the principle of non-contradiction, in its most original (Parmenidean) formulation—"that what is not is"—*what is not* being the contaminated *Lears* that threaten to suppress what is, that is, the original *Lear*.
6 See, for instance, Deleuze, *Différence et répétition*, 385–387.
7 The latter phrase he quotes from de Grazia's and Stallybrass' essay (258). Still, Egan's grasp of "structuralist," Saussurean and Derridean ideas, is far from firm. See the section on Saussure in his book.

status of the textual object before us" that De Grazia and Stallybrass describe as an oscillation between "one or more," between "identity and difference," is not exactly a *question*. True enough, the one-many dialectics runs through de Grazia's scholarly output, marked by titles like "What is a work? What is a document?," where the indefinite article ("a") is also a cardinal quantifier ("one"), and "The Question of the One and the Many?" There exist, however, many ways of construing *what the one is not*, and even if we reach out for poststructuralist conceptions of difference (Derrida, Deleuze, Lyotard), this must be done tactfully, for these conceptions differ. Thus, merely to replace a mystified "getting back to 'the thing itself'" (256)—meaning Shakespeare *the one* author or *King Lear* the *one* play—with an upbeat worship of alternative *things themselves* (playhouse transcripts, acting companies' promptbooks, scribal copies, print-shop's versions) is hardly a poststructuralist gesture per se. If a textual object is before us, it is *one* and remains *one*, even if a particled one, and it is in principle (phenomenally, in the logic of appearance and representation) *equal* to itself—and note, again, that equality often screens non-identity, in a broadly Hegelian sense. It may not be equal to another object that we have in mind or by our elbow, and that we tend, rightly or wrongly, to designate with the same name. But that is a different kind of problem—a Platonic debate on universals and particulars that Bertrand Russell partly rekindled with his descriptive theory of proper names, with "Hamlet" and "Napoleon" as distinguished examples. It is not, I insist, a problem of identity. According to Frege, one, the number, is merely a concept we apply to another concept—"one cat" concerns the concept cat and not the/a particular cat which the phrase may also contextually refer to—but so are two, and three, and four. To speak of four *Lears* presupposes, therefore, the single (one) concept *Lear*.[8] We do not enumerate the particular objects of things (the play manuscripts, playbooks, playscripts, play quartos ...) but the concept that, supposedly standing behind them, or inside them, or before them, allows them to enter the regime of computation. This is just to show how hard it is to relinquish what de Grazia and Stallybrass would call "metaphysical phenomena": in discerning the different, multiple *Lears* we always-already inevitably assume they repeat an abstraction—less the "ideal representation" or "ideal text" (de Grazia & Stallybrass 261) than "the writer's relatively stable *ideal*" (Egan 224; my emphasis) that new editorial and critical work (Erne, Cheney, Gurr) are beginning to open our eyes to. In addition, the oneness of an extant printed play is compatible both with its constitutive

---

8   See Frege, *The Foundations of Arithmetic*. The relevant sections can be found in *The Frege Reader*, 84–129.

emptiness and with the multiplicity of the field to which it belongs. This is a structuralist lesson that runs from proto-structuralist linguists like Saussure to para-consistent logicians like Graham Priest: "For something to be one thing is for it to have its being by relating to other things: something could not be a one thing unless it was located in a field of relations" (*One* 202). I am not sure that neo-materialists and phenomenologists would tolerate the local sacrifice of empirical riches this structuralist view entails. Surely the new textualist fetishization of early, supposedly theatrical, quartos, is largely incompatible with such emphasis on arbitrariness and relationality, and this throws into light the potential misuse of poststructuralist catchwords that is so common among its practitioners and followers. Worse still is, of course, their overuse of materialist refrains.

3

Still, the minor conceptual slip in their use of "self-identity" (the phrase is after all a poststructuralist catchword) anticipates their discussion, in the fourth section of the essay, of the problem of unified authorship. Their attempt to rouse us from the "hypnotic fascination of the isolated author" (the phrase is Jerome McGann's) leads through a very extravagant argument about the slipperiness of the "Shakespeare" signed and printed signifier to the conclusion that "the name of the playwright is itself a variable material sign inscribed in books, not a fixed essence that lies imperceptibly behind the text" (275). I do not know of any scholar that has argued that Shakespeare's *name* is a *fixed essence*. What has been often implied is that the same person Shakespeare stands always perceptibly—therefore essentially—*behind* a text as its genetic source, and *genetic* and *behind* can be jointly construed—by the way—to suggest a wayward scene of sodomitical inception akin the one depicted in the Plato-behind-Socrates-writing postcard so memorably scrutinized by Derrida (*La carte postale* 15–30). The alternative postcard proposed by new textualists is that of a band of invidious authors, undiscerning actors, meddling scribes, careless printers, fatigued compositors, and unscrupulous publishers, standing behind Shakespeare, who sits at his desk, struggling unsuccessfully to keep his foul papers and sugared lines away from the reach of the medusa-spreading hands of his intrusive, and yet brilliantly creative, collaborators. This allegorical elaboration screens the deeper paraphrase implied in Derrida's transcript of the postcard—that of "a tale of the will's [and Will's] not belonging to itself, a tale of its fundamental otherness, a tale of the possibility of its belonging to language" (*Daemonic* 139).

The name of a person then was a slippery as it is now. Otherwise US Immigration officers or airlines forms would not ask you to type your name "as it appears in your passport," implying that we all are safely identified by names that are routinely expected to be variable. To construe the carelessness of authors, scribes, and printers in spelling names as evidence of the unfixity and vagrancy of authorial identity is absurd. The fact, after all, that the authors of this essay misquote the title of Margreta de Grazia's (de Grazia? deGrazia? Margreta? You mean Margaret? Ok, Margie, how do you spell that?) essay "The Essential Shakespeare and the Material Book" as "The Essential Author and the Material Book" (see note 4, page 256) is no further proof of Shakespeare's essential inessentiality, but rather a confirmation that editorial work has always been—is still today—inherently exposed to error.

Their argument is flawed in another central respect. Following new textualist dogma, de Grazia and Stallybrass seem to legitimate whatever alteration, modification, variation that the more or less contemporary early theatrical and printing industry inflicted on malleable and permeable texts that were allegedly composed to be recomposed, but they condemn a similar operation—for instance, textual conflation—when it is done by later editors. Whereas editorial conflation is blamed with "ideal representation," the textual commixtures perpetrated at stage or hack-printer stage are celebrated as demotic, liberatory and antimetaphysically subversive. This is silly. As preposterous, or more, as exalting the prehistory of textual repressions behind *David Copperfield*, and celebrating the errors of the Cheap edition (1858), while condemning Robert Graves' rewriting of the novel in 1933.[9] The irrationality of such asymmetrical valorization exhibits a moralistic bias—"the material production of letters has been moralized; spiritualized; placed, in short, within a regime of value that appears to take its source from some transcendent realm" (Goldberg, *Shakespeare's Hand* 117). To pretend that no assumption of originality, authenticity or identity, no illusion of ideal representation or ideal reading, drove the endeavors of actors and publishing agents of Shakespeare theatrical texts is manifestly absurd. Also unreasonable, of course, is to believe, in accordance with phenomenological prejudice, that the ideal illusion—the intentional content—is sufficiently strong to keep the text under control. Still, the unquestionable rule of material contingency cannot simply efface

---

9   The three texts (Dickens' autobiographical fragment that made its way into Forster's *Life of Charles Dickens* in 1872, the Cheap edition of *David Copperfield*, and Graves' *The Real David Copperfield*) are *errors* (errata, errancies) in a non-axiological sense of the term. And we may favor (we often do) one of these errors over the rest. For the notion of Shakespeare's playtexts as "composite texts" see also Goldberg, *Shakespeare's Hand*, 9.

the effective determination of idealist or intentional drives—of a form, whatever that is, that sets other forms in motion, with the material implications such formal dissemination entails. The authors of this essay drink to D.F. McKenzie's motto "the normality of non-uniformity," coined to express "the confusion of titles and texts in multiple *Lears* and *Hamlets*" that was "typical in the early modern printing houses" (259). And "non-uniformity" overspills this local determination, becoming a powerful catchphrase in their discussion. The question is: how do you know that the non-uniform variant was not produced by agents aiming at uniformity? Admittedly, uniformizing forces and tendencies may underwrite the very field of nonuniformity, just like a field of permanent errancy may be bolstered by constant corrective efforts. Just like a thrown stone would surely think it is completely free, and that it continues in motion for no other reason than that it so wishes (Spinoza), a swerving atom would believe to be always moving in a permanently straight direction.

A related problem in their argument is the narrow understanding of notions linked to that of non-uniformity, like difference, multiplicity, or heterogeneity. The field of instability does not open when and where the author sits to write an authorial text. The field of textual instability or clinamen is always-already open, and the authorial manuscript must be construed as composite patchwork performed on an unstable field of overlapping textual sources. The One, in short, doesn't need the playhouse and printshop Many to fall into unstoppable proliferation, to become, that is, normally nonuniform: the One is already deconstructed by the antecedent Many it contributes more or less successfully to propagate.[10] Put otherwise, the One doesn't need the subsequent Many to become non-identical. The differential, multiple and nonuniform are not introduced solely at the rehearsal, compositorial, or printing process—to be identified and recorded through the local operation of critique. It is in fact the local scope of such operation—the fact, that is, that the critical decision is to study Shakespeare, and not a wider trans-authorial segment of disseminating textuality, or *King Lear*, rather than more comprehensive chains of subtextual

---

10   The ghost-like retro-positioning to transcendental condition of possibility (of the One) of the differential caesura marking the delay and *afterwardness* (*Nachträglichkeit*) of disseminative meaning (of the Many) is the deconstructive gesture par excellence: to be one is *ab origine* to have the possibility to be other and many, and only such possibility (difference, otherness, multiplicity) secures the oneness (identity, unity, singleness) of the one. Lacan and Derrida, following in Hegel's footsteps, introjected the overdetermining contingent effect of transcendental (linguistic, symbolic) conditions and made it coincide with the earliness of Aristotelian potentiality (δύναμις): thus the reciprocal co-determining of subject and substance occurs without a clear assignation of origin or cause. This ambivalence or unfixedness threatens the identity of the One.

play-scripture—that determines both the contention of the One (the one author, the one text) and the preposterous decision to undercut this very contention through an appeal to the different many. It is the One (Shakespeare) that pays, of course, at all institutional levels (Chairs of *Shakespeare studies*, collections of *Shakespeare studies*, editions of *Shakespeare* plays, Conferences of *Shakespeare* associations), and one should make no bones about this. But do you smell a fault? Multiplicity, let me insist, was there way before the putative *auctor* set out to stabilize it by producing his version: there were many *Hamlets* before *Hamlet*, some *King Lears* before *King Lear*, various *Romeo and Juliets* before *Romeo and Juliet*. The author inserts his piece in a virtually unstoppable chain of ever-differing versions, and the piece will be meaningful if it manages to alter, pre-determine, and prepossess the chain such that, say, even if *King Lear* is never, *ex definitione* identical to *King Lear*, the *King Lears* that follow a certain *King Lear* shall remain nearly *equal* to the brutal, inscriptive accident that we tend to call *King Lear*. Note my phrasing: the versions are relationally ever-differing between themselves, not in themselves. In themselves they are simply non-identical, which spells a more primordial sense of difference, one, by the way, that we can describe as the transcendental effect that rapports established between the differing versions has on the most inscriptive of them: the strongest One is the version that is the likeliest to be retroactively haunted by whatever deviations result from it, and sources lead to it. And the ever-differing process that occurs between texts at all levels is but confirmation of the *différance* informing the arche-writing that brings them forth. But each version, this is important, seeks to remain identical with itself—even as it may ironically celebrate its membership in an ongoing series (this is quite evident in *Romeo and Juliet* and *Hamlet*).[11] In fact, the Spinozian *conatus*, the thing's drive to persevere in itself (in its identity) is certainly not incompatible with a will to power that forces a body, to secure such aim, "to grow, spread, seize, become predominant" (*Beyond Good and Evil* 203): *I grow, I prosper*, says a bastard aiming to become legitimate (the one, the earlier, the older). Ned Lukacher's discussion of the Freudian *Trieb*, which takes "the subject back to an earlier state of things," places the uncanny under the deconstructive logic of subtextual earliness and serial repetition: "the uncanny is another term for this temporal phenomenon, for the experience of feeling the call of what is absolutely earlier" (*Daemonic* 58–59). Materialist scholars, who are fascinated by the somewhat minor (material) differences between versions, ignore the

---

11   This is a central, but often neglected, claim in Derrida's essay on *Romeo and Juliet*, titled "Aphorism Countertime" in *Acts of Literature*, 414–434.

compulsion towards inscriptive earliness and declare a state of general indifference. Bawcutt rightly ridiculed a "modern veneration of printing errors" (Egan, *The Struggle* 216) that would have shocked early modern dramatists. Modern worshippers should be puzzled instead by the massive proportion of formal repetition surviving such errors and potential cuts, by the fact that one at least of the *King Lears* produced within Shakespeare's circle possessed sufficient inscriptive, constitutive force to warrant its *formal* survival in whatever material version was afterwards concocted by actors, scribes, compositors, printers or publishers.

There is nothing wrong, or metaphysically mystified, both in assuming the existence of one contingent inscription (one of the *Lears*) that Shakespeare favored more than others or in trying to ascertain which of the extant versions is closer to it. When de Grazia opens a sentence with the allusive clause "As base contagious clouds" (78), she takes recourse to an inscribed trope that we all assume, perhaps rightly, that was coined by a man called Shakespeare, for confirmation of which we may rummage the seven extant quartos of *1 Henry IV* that offer the "complete" play as well as the Folio edition, only to corroborate that in fact that formal configuration ("base contagious clouds," *1 Henry IV* 1.2.176) survives as *textual matter* (that is to say, as form) in abstraction of ink, hand, quill, paper and compositor's sweat. De Grazia's ability to relocate in her essay this formal configuration renders the scholar more complicit with the redemptive purity of the prince than she would consciously allow. De Grazia opines that it is ideologically impure, and therefore mystified, to pine after "a conjectural and immaterial authorial manuscript" (81), but I guess no scholar has ever in fact assumed the existence of an *immaterial manuscript*. Manuscripts are *ex definitione* material things. What some scholars have assumed is the *existence* of an *inexistent manuscript*. This is an obfuscated assumption if it rests on belief in a pure immaterial semantic intention that the inexistent manuscript would merely (materially) reproduce. The search for an ideal *Lear* beyond or before its textual configurations is indeed an idealist chimera. But the conjecture makes sense if it limits itself to strategically assuming the existence of an unfound manuscript or printed version that could contain most if not all the formal traces of Shakespeare's decisive intervention into the chain of running versions—and note that his intervention could have often involved the inclusion of playhouse additions. Andrew Gurr's suggestion that this object *is* the licensed playscript is extremely imaginative. Shakespeare was composi(ti)ng after all, and he was indubitably open to what de Grazia calls "non-authorial meaning" (82). Actually, de Grazia rightly observes that, in the idealist camp, the difference holds between the "authorial manuscript" and the "authorial meaning" (82). What she doesn't say is that *this* difference, and not the difference between an authorial manuscript and other materials, is the real conundrum. There is nothing idealist or metaphysical in the postulation, as a starting hypothesis in a critical experiment, of the occurrence of a textual accident—call it authorial manuscript, licensed book, or call it otherwise, the document favored by Shakespeare—that is more lasting (more inscriptive, more constitutive, more determinant) than other accidents. And it may not be excessively far-fetched to assume that of all the participants in the collaborative project behind the global production of a play, Shakespeare was the best-trained mind to decide which of the textual accidents—which of the playscripts—was the best suited for performance or publication. He was neither a stage-oblivious literary dramatist nor a book-indifferent agent in an acting company. The unexpected become inevitable is a sufficiently common incident in the life and times of contingency as a philosophical concept. We may therefore talk of *the necessity of contingency* without incurring much metaphysical expense, for necessity here is not construed as ideality, but as particularly strong contingency. True enough, "every repetition introduces difference" (de Grazia & Stallybrass 260), but there is difference and difference, and to find out which difference makes real difference is the task of a critic. Patrick Brontë had a son and three daughters, who differed from him and his wife but also deferred them, and yet only Emily wrote *Wuthering Heights*, only one of his offspring propitiated an accident still regarded today as a (necessary) sport of nature. Cervantes wrote twelve exemplary novels, but only the impossible thirteenth became *Don Quijote de la Mancha*. This novel was an accident that made a difference, and the first to realize it was Cervantes himself, who allowed it wildly to defer, and the next to realize it were Shakespeare and Fletcher, who wrote *Cardenio*. Let me recall that *differ* and *defer* are etymologically connected, something not lost on Hamlet, the boy who differed from a father who kept asking him not to defer. As Marjorie Garber has shown, the (transcendental) hauntology of accidents is after all one of Shakespeare's dominant concerns. To title a book "*Hamlet* without Hamlet" and not, say, "*Hamlets* without *Hamlet*" betrays no doubt a more than pragmatic trust in the necessity of one of the *Hamlets*, in the profound if repressed credence, that is, in the One over the Many.

To argue that "photo-reproduction arrests the textual drift characteristic of both the mechanics and semantics of the early quartos" (261) is odd. Textual drift may be characteristic of the mechanics of the early quartos in that printing-house practices unintentionally favored textual instability. One (printing-house practice) is the cause of the other (textual drift). But the arresting of a textual drift is already built into the very fabric of the quarto: like

Mallarmé's *coup de dés*, to print is to stabilize the unstable, and far from abolishing chance, it merely enthrones it. Printing both provokes the drift and arrests it, thus sanctioning the power of chance. Each printed quarto becomes in turn unstable when compared with other printed quartos of the same play, but that doesn't mean that the semantics of each of the resulting plays is unstable: it is stable within its contingently produced stability, like the ping-pong ball in the water jet in Ashbery's poem. The problem with this line of argument lies, as is common in neo-materialist scholarship, in its phenomenally undialectical short-sightedness, in its inability, that is, to take stock of the wider horizon of instability (the genus) of which this printing-house episode of "textual drift" is but one simple instantiation (the species). What they call "textual drift" is the very condition of writing, and Shakespeare's mind is the stage of a textual drift that includes pretextual currents, intertextual streams, and subtextual intensities that are wider and broader and surely more meaningful than the so-called "mechanics [...] of the early quartos."

De Grazia and Stallybrass—and Orgel, and Harris, and many others—believe that there is critical infraction in trying to arrest a chain of material multiplicity with the violence of an ideal-essential one (Shakespeare, *King Lear*). They are wrong. The real lapse is the attempt to halt a chain of formal dissemination through the intimidating ostentation of a "real presence" of transcendent matter—ink stains, goatskins, and the allegedly multiplicity of textual others and subtextual material "traces." Harris has gone as far as to claim, in his "polytemporal" reading of early modern texts, that "the apparition if the 'old' text shatters the integrity of the 'new' by introducing into it a radical alterity that punctures the illusion of its wholeness or finality" (15). *Radical alterity*? Openness to transcendence takes many forms, and it is always sweet to see how the once-underground tropes of cultural materialism take on the sublime pathos of Levinasian piety. Predictably, phenomenology becomes the backyard depot where these transfigurations can occur.

4

The poststructuralist scaffolding of the article was, I noted above, both unnecessary and risky. "'The thing itself,'" De Grazia and Stallybrass argue, "the authentic Shakespeare, is itself a problematic category, based on a metaphysics of origin and presence that poststructuralism has taught us to suspect" (256). More problematic, I have suggested, is to substitute a phenomenological veneration of the things themselves for the speculation over the thing itself.

This substitution entails a transit from a bashful *metaphysics of presence* to a sanguine *metaphysics of presences*. Derrida's critique of a metaphysics of origin and presence—especially in *Limited Inc* (1990) and "Qual Quelle: Les sources de Valéry" (1971) (*Marges* 325–263)—identifies the temporal precedence of an identical ideal content or theme conceived as presence prior to all potential derivations. This doesn't mean that Derrida eschews the possibility of original texts, or even of original intentions. The "crise de l'origine" (*Marges* 346) he examines in his essay on Valéry names a perplexity before a *source* that opens itself, like time, "as the delay of origin (*retard de l'origine*) in relation to itself" (*Margins* 290; *Marges* 345). The delay is produced by the non-coincidence, noted by Valéry, of *presence* with an *initial event* (*Marges* 345). Whereas the initial event may stand for the contingent tropical-textual inscription—an inscription that eventuates materially and historically but is tendentially formal in its effects—the presence is the presence of the speaker to itself, of the meaning or content to itself, and of the phonic-graphic substance to itself. The three cases share a similar pattern of presumptive autocratic constitution, whereby a putative *causa sui* substance claims (or is by philosophical delegation held) to be present to itself. The deconstruction of the metaphysics of presence is just an attempt to disqualify this pretense, not a blanket rejection of presences and origins. There are presences, but they are neither real (Steiner) nor ideal (Husserl): they are simply shaky and impugnable. And there are origins, effects of origin, situated miracles, inscribed sites (*Marges* 341–42). And authorship, including Shakespeare's, is bound up with presence and origin in the same bid for philosophical legitimacy, reclaiming the same restricted economy: "the source is produced only in being cut off from itself" (*Marges* 285 n12). Think of the Edmund, the bastard. And yet, however denied a presence and blocked from itself, the origin remains an origin. We may describe this beginning, following Hegel, as a result rather than a cause—*Der Anfang ist das Resultat*—and extend the definitional attribution to Shakespeare himself, an absent-to-itself source that is also the outcome (the river mouth) of preexisting affluents and sources (Ovid, Plutarch, Chaucer, Belleforest, Bandello, Marlowe, Spenser), as well as to his works, things that do not (cannot) mark a "départ comme ab-solu," a "surgissement délié de toute détermination" (*Marges* 333). *Lear, Hamlet, Othello*: although relative and predetermined, these plays are still departures, sources, origins. One need only to lower the volume of exigency and tune the editorial and textual argument about these plays to "a certain heterogeneity of the source" (*Margins* 309). Cut off from itself, the source lets itself be.

Derrida has never rejected the possibility of tropological or textual sites of contingent origination: what he admired in Husserl was precisely his courage in confronting the historical origin of transtemporal meanings.[12] What he rejects is that they constitute—or they can constitute themselves into—a *pure* origin. His chief philosophical gesture is to discover bastardy, hybridization, contamination, where stabilizing forces (consciousness, ideology, institutionalized narratives) posit a pure, absolute origin. He rejects too the possibility of the effective control an original intention may exert over the text: an author may set out with a formal conception in mind and end up with a work that differs markedly from it. A formal conception is, by the way, little more than a remembered configuration. The (provisionally completed) work is the result of a blending of accidents and choices. As such, the meaning of the resulting text is not the original intention, but rather the text itself as *objet trouvé*. Thus an original text can be said to *exist* as the best accidental finding the author is able to fashion by subjecting a host of verbal (subtextual, intertextual) materials to the driving force of an intention (a formal conception) that is constantly being modified in the contingent process of creation, encroached upon by alternative formal solutions that press in from a variety of determining material sources. It is ridiculous to suppose, as Orgell, Stallybrass and de Grazia appear nonchalantly to do, that Shakespeare wouldn't have wanted to choose—and actually chose whenever he could—between the different versions of his plays (manuscripts, transcripts, promptbooks) that cropped up in the playhouse upon rehearsal. If there is a sense in which he could choose and did choose, then it is legitimate—*pace* Orgel—to talk of an *authentic Shakespeare*. One who probably preferred Hamlet's to-be-or-not-to-be soliloquy in the Q2 or Folio version to the Q1 solution. And it's not just a question of line-cutting forced by the economies of performance. It is also a matter of technical felicity. Derrida, like Nietzsche and de Man, believed that certain textual (rhetorical) solutions have more inscriptive force than others. To be

---

12   In "The Origin of Geometry," Husserl examines the paradoxical fact that geometry, a science which supposedly deals with eternal truths, makes one day its factual entrance into human history. Husserl's courage in refusing to avert his eyes from that temporal truth—the truth of the historical (*historisch*) origination of timeless meanings—leads him no doubt to descriptive obfuscation (he speaks, for instance, of a "spiritual genesis"), but his resolve to confront what Derrida calls "l'historicité des objectités idéales" is bracing and cannot be questioned. Husserl's evolving commitment to various versions of genesis (psychological, transcendental, phenomenological) and his final attestation, in *Krisis*, of the irruption of the historical within the phenomenological, make up a courageous narrative of restless recognition. Derrida's protracted reading of this narrative includes his long "Introduction" to "The Origin of Geometry" and his "Mémoire pour le diplôme des études supérieures," titled *Le problème de la genèse dans la philosophie de Husserl* written in 1953–54 and published in 1990.

sure, this force may often depend on political coercion, but political coercion is chiefly a function of ideological persuasion, and ideology is also made of tropes. So (nearly) everything amounts to a *matter* of tropological inscription, of what Derrida, in "White Mythology: Metaphor in the Text of Philosophy" called *tropes 'instituteurs'* (*Marges* 261). A trope's inscriptive force is proportional to its potential iterability, which in turn is determined by a will power, *conatus*, or tendency to survive that is paradoxically at one with the death drive—with the proviso that the trope doesn't kill itself (a strong trope never dies). Only the organic-phenomenal-aesthetic life-effect that flourishes in its scriptural wake is likely to vanish. The institutive inscription of a strong trope (or a strong text, or a strong author) presupposes neither a metaphysics of origin nor a metaphysics of presence. On the other hand, Derrida never discusses the authenticity of Valéry's "original" texts—he solely interrogates the extent to which these texts are in fact determined by their more or less conscious elaboration on (thematic) sources.

The fetishism of textual variety—the idea that the search for an *original text* is metaphysically burdened, that there are only versions determined by "historical, theatrical, and editorial contingencies" (de Grazia and Stallybrass 256, n3) which is the task of the critic to mind, collect, and celebrate—overlooks the very plain fact that Shakespeare would undoubtedly have favored one of the versions: this doesn't turn it into a necessary original, but rather into the best of the (contingent) derivatives. De Grazia and Stallybrass argue that "'The thing itself,' the authentic Shakespeare, is itself a problematic category, based on a metaphysics of origin and presence that poststructuralism has taught us to suspect" (256). Granted. So let us replace the thing itself (the original text) with the things themselves (the many versions). Now what? Let us not forget that the empirical craze that draws these scholars to salvage the material traces erased by eighteenth-century editorial manipulation of the earlier texts is also metaphysically burdened, for an "empirical moment characterizes the metaphysical dimensions of the mind" (de Man, *Aesthetic* 85). Recall too that the opposite of the empirical-material is not the metaphysical, that the empirical-material is, alongside most ideological contingencies, an expression of metaphysical (transcendent) exteriority, and that this exteriority conflicts alone with the transcendental realm.[13]

The real challenge, it would appear, is not to replace an idealist or essentialist transcendence with an empirical transcendence, for the terms and logic of

---

13   The profound, uninterrupted complicity between *empiricism* and *metaphysics* is one of Derrida's most imperative, albeit often secret, running motifs. It reaches a peak of rare articulacy at the close of his first essay on Levinas: *L'écriture*, 224–225.

this transaction remain eminently metaphysical. The challenge is to allow for a materiality to result within the boundaries of a transcendental immanence, and this transcendental—not transcendent and surely not transcendentalist—materiality is either formal or nothing, or both simultaneously formal and nothing, actually a *nothing* that *is more than matter*. Paul de Man, we know, spoke of a materialism that took the form, in Kant, of a "radical formalism" (*Aesthetic* 128), but this is certainly not what de Grazia and Stallybrass have in mind. Or is it? On the face of it, they appeal to a new attention to the "materiality of the text," meaning the features of the early texts, obliterated in modern editorial emendation: "old typefaces and spellings, irregular line and scene divisions, title pages and other paratextual matter, and textual cruxes." They speak of "inert, obsolete matter," of "material traces" (257). Despite their fascination with these rejected debris, they argue that they "have no desire to perpetuate the illusion that we are presenting "original" or "unedited" text, in either its worn archival or fresh simulacral form" (257). So what is then the point in celebrating these "traces"? To remind us of "our own historical situatedness"? To remind us that our belief in the notion of an "original" or "unedited" text relies on "the persistence of the epistemological categories that make us believe in its existence"? This is circularly correct, and also (alas) correctly circular. But antiquarians, including Ezra Pound and Walter Benjamin, may also be very aware of the gap, of their situatedness, and even, ironically, of the productive deception that drives them to search the holy grail. They are no more deluded, therefore, than Jackson Pollock protesting "I am nature." De Grazia's and Stallybrass's claim, therefore, proves nothing. It certainly doesn't prove that restoring primitive textual features is *not* an exercise in editorial paleontology. I guess we are basically dealing with the credibility of a claim. Just as one doesn't become a materialist merely by claiming she is a materialist—or, for that matter, by screaming "I am nature"—so a thing doesn't become material simply by calling it material. None of these allegedly material traces exhibit the actual "materiality of the letter" (Goldberg, *Shakespeare's Hand* xi) whose repression Paul de Man denounced in the early 1980s. The Belgian thinker criticized "Jauss' lack of interest, bordering in outright dismissal, in any considerations derived from what has, somewhat misleadingly, come to be known as the 'play' of the signifier, semantic effects produced on the level of the letter rather than of the word or sentence and which therefore escape from the network of hermeneutic questions and answers" (*Resistance* 65). In his two essays on Kant's materiality, de Man mentions effects of morphological disarticulation and homophony (89–90) as "factors and functions of language that resist being phenomenalized" (Warminski, "Introduction" to *Aesthetic Ideology* 3), instances of the wild materiality that subtends, and eventually undoes, the very possibility of the aesthetic, whose most adept executor is the representative content-form congruence of the symbolic (more on this in the closing sections of this book). Recall that such congruence—at the aesthetic level—is but an instantiation of the broader phenomenological fulfillment or *Erfüllung*, and that both (congruence and fulfilment) metaphysically presuppose matter's transcendent arrogation of the (transcendental) scene of writing. Derrida once called attention to the fact that Lambert's original understanding of phenomenology is closer to Peirce's semiotic theory than to Husserl's philosophy. In fact, the latter's delusive reliance on a metaphysics of presence, and the resulting reduction of the sign to the thing signified "pour laisser ainsi la chose signifiée briller dans l'éclat de sa presence" is incompatible with Lambert's and Peirce's construal of "phénoménalité" (Derrida, *De la grammatologie* 72) as the semiotically, transcendental-materially, *unphenomenal*.

Let me insist: to call attention to the variability of printing-house production practices, to the diversity of an author's printed name and of play's titles, and to the non-uniformity of editorial conventions as a means to assert the materiality of the Shakespearean text is a very dubious undertaking. The gesture betrays a blend of anti-enlightened antiquarianism and fluency craze—the passion for variability, unfixedness, fluidity ("the fluidly variable," "the textual drift," 261)—which in turn is more redolent of 68 situationism than of anti-metaphysical critique. The undertaking is dubious not only because materiality may be asserted in safer ways, but also because one of these ways is reluctantly—inchoately and confusedly—implied in their argument. De Grazia and Stallybrass argue that the very notion of an "'ideal representation' bears witness to the unattainable goal of achieving an exact reproduction of a text that never possessed a single or fixed form" (261). The implication here is that ideal elaborations (representations, simulations, reproductions, copies) of the diverse texts run afoul of the *formal unfixedness* of the play at hand. So what is then unfixed and subject to mutability—the *matter* or the *form* of the Shakespeare text? Idealization is pitted against formal unfixedness, not material variability. So what we have is the ideal (formal) *one* versus the ideal (formal) *many*. Thus de Grazia and Stallybrass talk about the materiality of the text when they are actually dealing with editorial variations (title, authorial attribution) and with (copy-right) property status. The first is a formal concern, the second a legal one—and therefore a formal one too, however material its consequences. Let me resume, to conclude, the charge of inconsistency I have interruptedly leveled against de Grazia and Stallybrass, not without reformulating it: the essay titled "The Materiality of the Shakespearean Text" is less about materiality than about form. As an essay on materiality, it fails; as an essay on form, it is reasonably correct.

5

A similar inconsistency mines Harris's take on matter in his book *Untimely Matter in the Time of Shakespeare*. Harris is very aware that the revival of materialism among object-turned scholars working in early modern studies may betray "an insufficiently Marxist understanding of materialism" (5). He knows, with Douglas Bruster, that the new scholarship on early modern things models a materialism that "neither Karl Marx nor Fredric Jameson would be likely to recognize," and that it therefore runs the risk of degenerating into "tchotchke criticism" (qtd. in Harris, *Untimely Matter* 5–6). Such awareness of the dialectical strictures of Marxist materialism, and the willingness to confront them, no doubt honors Harris. This theoretical boldness is very rare among phenomenology-oriented scholars. Still, the solution he devises to meet the potential objections dialectical materialism may raise against his own kind of scholarship—one openly committed to the "property of things" (7), to the "cultural biography of things" (8)—is anything but un-contradictory. This solution is a conception of objects as "polychronic assemblages" (10) that bring to light "the multiple traces of time embedded in things" (9). Textiles, for instance, are seen as objects "multiply inscribed by corporeality and memory" (10). On this view, partly derived from Latour, objects are also construed as agents placed within larger networks (12). One such object, manifestly linked to the textile, is the palimpsest. In the section titled "The Temporalities of the Palimpsest," Harris illustrates his theoretical position through a speculative commentary of an extant medieval manuscript he calls the "Archimedes Palimpsest." The commentary is a spiraling reflection on "the logic of supersession" prompted by the agency of multitemporal and polychronic sub-traces and traces as they become legible—through a "temporality of explosion"—in the text "matter" (13–15). The focus on the legibility and replaceability of different traces reveals Harris' determination to meet the dialectical objection, but the choice of a palimpsest as the "thing" or "object" that best illustrates his theorems is either provocatively self-defeating (palimpsests are too obviously things endowed with cultural thickness) or silly. As it happens, it is silly, for Harris is determined to demonstrate that the palimpsest (the object) is a palimpsest (an active and open site of textual significance) *because* it is a goatskin (a dry slice of animal matter). Harris implicitly attributes both the logic of supersession and the temporality of explosion to the affordances of a matter that is specifically extolled for being "obstinately antisequential" (16). This is odd and misleading. It doesn't take much speculative attention to realize that the subtextual or intertextual logic of the palimpsest—what he calls the logic of supersession—is exclusively a *dialectic of forms*: the material properties—the material provision, the physical availability and affordances—of the palimpsest are irrelevant to the play of signification that the traces as formal signifiers concert on the surface of the matter used to inscribe them. This matter sets no doubt contingent limits on the possibility of inscription, but what gets inscribed is a formal value that, due to its readiness to engage in multidirectional (and no doubt polychronic) relations, transcends its subservience to positive materiality. It is, in short, medium-indifferent. In a certain tradition of aleatory materialism (Democritus, Bruno, Marx, Nietzsche, Althusser) pure matter could be said to enjoy a kind of eternal, cyclical, present. Only forms (formalized matters) come and go. Harris' entire argument about written inscriptions (signs, traces) in palimpsests is an argument *about forms*. In a palimpsest, it is no doubt the resilience of a given matter (ink) that secures the survival of an apparently buried form (signifier), but it is the form, and its relational permanence, that turns the mere goatskin into an agent of differential signification. The fact that Harris can evoke the fraught meaning of that medieval manuscript in a printed book and that I can resume his discussion, now, in the screen of my laptop proves that meaning is not medium-dependent. The undialectical nature of Harris' argument is best exposed contrastively, by raising the question: is the real, material, palimpsest the only example of a textual meaning that originates through the transformative displacement of prior inscriptions? Obviously not: this is what writing generally does because writing is made of words, phrases, tropes, narrative swerves, that are historically dense in their accumulation of sedimented meaning. But this density, and the polychronicity it courts, is formal and relational, not obtusely material. What Harris tends to overlook is that writing is per definition palimpsestal, that all meaning is palimpsestal meaning, and that the palimpsestal condition of writing is exclusively dependent on the relational permanence of forms (traces, inscriptions, signs). We don't need to scratch the printed word melancholy to know that the textually-scripted physiological implications of black vile breath under it. Just like the concept "dog" doesn't bark (Spinoza) so the "rotten" signifier of the state of Denmark doesn't stink. The cultural agency of the word does not originate in the material dimension of its signifier. Agency is a formal pulsion that originates in a formalized body and runs through another formalized body, informing it, reforming it, or deforming it further.

Aware that there is what he would take to be figurative uses of the term palimpsest in poststructuralist thought, Harris reminds the reader that "the palimpsest is [...] not just a metaphor for untimely matter: it *is* untimely matter" (17). This oracular assertion means that, unlike Genette, he refuses to use the "palimpsest as a metaphor for an array of paratextual effects whereby past texts are echoed, parodied, and rewritten" (16–17). The palimpsest, for him, is "also [this adverbial is telling] a complex of polychronic assemblage of material *agents*" (17). Our question is: what is the agency of the "writing surface," of the "parchment or vellum"? Harris gives no answer beyond asserting that this material surface "enables [...] the writing on it" (17), thus subscribing to an Aristotelian, and later Marxist, notion of matter as "potentiality [*dynameos*]" (7). To say that the agency of parchment is its susceptibility or potentiality to be written on is like suggesting that the active liberation of women depends on their ability to be inscribed (tutored, repressed, abused, scripted, inscribed) by men: it is no accident that patriarchal narratives—including Aristotle's distinction between matter and form—have very often resorted to the male-female difference. Readiness to be written on is a very dubious and unlikely mode of agency. Let us consider Harris' gloss of Marx's first thesis on Feuerbach:

> In the "Theses on Feuerbach," he argues that understanding matter "only in the form of the object" ignores the dynamic dimension of praxis. Matter, he insists, should be conceived of less as a physical actuality than as a sensuous, workable potentiality that implies pasts, presents, and futures. (7)

The second sentence is an overinterpretation of the Marx passage, but this is not the problem. The real problem lies in a denigration of an "actuality" that is, in accordance with the Aristotelian echo, correctly assimilated to form. What turns matter into a "workable potential" is not its raw sensuousness or crude physicality. Harris misrepresents Marx. It is rather the always-already actuated and actual, formalized, and formal, side of matter that makes it potentially useful: matter is workable because it is always already not only matter, but also form, it is already worked, already inscribed, already actuated and formalized. It is therefore the palimpsestal condition of matter as the open locus of relational formalization that turns it into the perfect site for a productive practice, praxis, agency. Commenting on this and other related Marx passages, Louis Althusser stresses the German thinker's resolve to have "any process of scientific knowledge" begin "from the abstract, from a generality, and not from the real concrete":

> When Marx declares that the raw material of a science always exists in the form of a given generality (Generality 1), in this thesis with the simplicity of a fact he is putting before us a new model which no longer has any relation to the empiricist model of the production of a concept by good abstraction, starting from the real fruits and disengaging their essence by abstracting from their individuality.
>
> *For Marx* 155

For Marx, Althusser argues, this thesis is part of "an empiricist and sensualist ideology" and is therefore no "organic part of dialectical materialism." The latter demands to have as starting-points Generalities I rather than "concrete subjects":

> This is the thesis Marx rejects when he condemns Feuerbach for conceiving "sensuousness ... only in the form of the object," that is, only in the form of an intuition without practice. Generality 1, for example, the concept of "fruit," is not the product of an "operation of abstraction" performed by a "subject" (consciousness, or even that mythological subject "practice")—but the result of a complex process of elaboration which involves several distinct concrete practices on different levels, empirical, technical and ideological (To return to our rudimentary example, the concept of fruit is itself the product of distinct practices, dietary, agricultural or even magical, religious and ideological practices—in its origins.) (156)

Harris could protest arguing that the kind of production he has in mind is not the production of scientific knowledge involved in theoretical practices, but rather the natural or artificial production of things tout court, where raw material and human labor may intermingle. But what he has in mind is irrelevant: what matters is what Marx says. And Althusser clearly explains that the critique of Feuerbach should be understood in the context of a debate over the dialectic of theoretical practices, where concrete subjects and objects yield the floor to "generalities," that is, to conceptual and ideological constellations that have always-already inexorably scripted the object in advance. Undialectically, Harris refuses to see the fruit preempted by the concept, the fruit on the grip of the signifier, the fruit arrogated by a conceptual-ideological network that Althusser describes as "a complex process of elaboration" and that is both formal and a practice (an instantiation of agency). This process is as multi-level and polychronic as the palimpsestic sheaf of goatskin pages envisaged by Harris, and its procedural, multitemporal, dynamic, and agentive condition also depends on the field of negative relationality produced through the multi-directional rapport of forms (signs, traces, words) inscribed in its equivocal surface. To prove that a palimpsest is no metaphor for untimely matter, but is itself untimely matter, Harris adduces the case of some copies of the Book of Hours "which were repeatedly annotated by their many readers in the fifteenth and sixteenth centuries" (17). The result is a "collation of materials" where the "books' original texts" made of "Catholic collections of psalms, prayers and other devotional manuscripts" are overlaid "with biographical jottings, personal reflections, and pious alterations." At work in this collation is what Derrida calls "le pouvoir de *consignation*" (*Mal d'Archive* 14), but Harris rather surprisingly doesn't consider this important 1995 essay on archives.[14] This multitemporal "annotative reworking," Harris argues, curates a scene of post-Reformation spiritual-hermeneutic reparation, for the "old textual matter" of these materials "could also get to work on the reader, prompting edification, nostalgia, or religious dismay" (17). Is Harris really suggesting that what prompts edification, nostalgia and dismay are the matters (dust, vellum, cloth, leather, gesso, red clay, shell gold, pigments, ink) and not the formal contents (words, words, words) of the Book of Hours? If so, then the meaning of "edification" has been narrowed down beyond recognition: on this logic, dogs are "edified" when given a toy ball. Most of us, compulsive readers, love handling books and even smelling the pages, but we are also in the crazy habit of relapsing into the silent ocular-internal-aural unscrambling of forms we call reading. If there is, as Harris suggests, "reworking" in an object that gets "to work on the reader," if there is, that is, effort, labor, and practice, then there is this decoding of forms that is reading—"a complex process of elaboration which involves several distinct concrete practices on different levels, empirical, technical and ideological" (Althusser, *For Marx* 156). That reading is the most relevant thing you may do with a book is, I know, a very unphenomenal presumption. My apologies for even mentioning it.

Untimely Matter in the Time of Shakespeare is a book about untimely *forms*, the textual forms in goatskins but also the actors' bodies in performances, whose movements and gestures Harris wrongly reads as avatars of matter. Harris' attempt to make us believe that his constant reference to the word "matter" and his invocation of goatskins and actor's bodies perform the necessary magical trick of turning form into matter is futile. He talks about rather conventional mechanisms of hermeneutic inter-textual dialogue, and this

---

14 In *Mal d'Archive*, Derrida underscores the precedence of *formal* or *hauntological agency* (a mental inscription, a historical truth) over both the matters of writing and printing—what Freud itemizes as paper, ink and the printer's work and material—and the "material truth" of Biblical episodes (*Mal* 21, 95). Derrida recalls his earlier confrontation with the Freudian tropology of impression, and the way he noted that "Freud does not explicitly examine the status of the 'materialized' supplement which is necessary to the alleged spontaneity of memory" (*Mal* 30; *L'écriture* 336). Indeed the materiality of the external substrate seems always in excess of the deadly play of formal iteration that constitutes memory. The substrate, in short, is reduced to another "figure," another "concept," in dialectical parlance, and it is no accident that it is often the Bible, or Book of Books, for every book is a book of books.

dialogue is a formal and tendentially transcendental dialectic. If, with Yeats, we are unable to "know the dancer from the dance" ("Among School Children," *Collected Poems* 222) it is not so much because the dance risks relapsing into the material body of the dancer, but rather because the matter of this body is always-already "swayed to music."[15] And this doesn't entail the complete subordination of material nature to a "ghostly paradigm of things"—it merely suggests that there are no things without ghosts (concepts), and that if the Book of Hours conveys edification, nostalgia, or dismay it is because it is ab initio *ghosted* by writing. This dialectic is no doubt facilitated by the medium, by material surfaces and bodies, but the bearing these surfaces and bodies have on the significance of the encryption is not properly assessed by Harris. Like Rilke and Yeats, Shakespeare knew that "the children learn to cipher and to sing / To study reading-books and history," and that the cultural recurrence of the scene of writing-and-reading—the scene to which Jonathan Goldberg gives pride of place—testifies to the fact that there is no singing without the study of formal ciphers—without grammatological discipline—as well as to the fact that the world, alas, does not speak or sing: only we do (Rorty, *Contingency* 6).

6

Adorno, who wanted to rid the nonidentical from "spiritualized coercion [*vergeistigten Zwanges*]" (*Negative Dialectic* 6; *Negative Dialektik* 18), examined different versions of dialectic and judged them according to the degree and quality of the subject-object "reconcilement" they managed to achieve. The value of this "reconcilement" was, of course, a function of their ability to erase antagonism, whence Adorno's constant tendency to judge it invalid. Therefore, more pervasive still, more dangerous, and yet more literally *necessary*—for the materialist Adorno—is the unreconcilable coercion of things:

> We have to answer that the object of a mental experience is an antagonistic system in itself—antagonistic in reality, not just in its conveyance to the knowing subject that rediscovers itself therein. The coercive state of reality [*zwangshafte Verfassung der Realität*], which idealism had projected into the region of the subject and the mind, must be retranslated [*zurückzuübsersetzen*] from that region. (10)

---

15   The closing line of Yeats' poem was famously scrutinized by de Man, *Allegories*, 11–12.

In a related fashion, I have argued that Shakespeare's formal-textual materiality must be constantly retranslated from the sphere of transcendent and spiritualist mystifications that seek to appropriate it. Shakespeare's texts are "antagonistic in reality," and so are the textual things that they supply—things like Macbeth's *dagger* or Desdemona's *handkerchief*. As textual tropes, both the dagger and the handkerchief come through first and foremost as "antagonistic systems" or, to put it in Althusserian terms, as "the result of a complex process of elaboration which involves several distinct concrete practices on different levels." They are, in other words, chunks of "sedimented *Geist*" (Adorno, *Zu einer Theorie* 245). When we confront a Shakespeare poem or playtext, we should not look for the reality bites (textiles, goatskins) that presumably await us in an empirical "coercive state," begging us to be re-transposed into the region of subjective morality or spirituality. We should rather respect the coercive state of their dialectical, unreconciled, and antagonistic materiality, and seek merely to parse it with the help of philology, hermeneutics or *Auslegung*.

The neo-phenomenological retranslation from the material into the spiritual is characterized by the claim that the material is originally agentive. Thus, while, for instance, Harris assumes that Desdemona's handkerchief is blessed with material *agency*, Curran maintains that Richard II's selfhood is constituted through the *agencement* his body establishes with the objects of his immediate and distant environment. In both cases the point is both overstated and lacking in philosophical support. While Harris seeks, at his own risk, to rise above Marx's supposedly limited "understanding of matter" by locating agency not only "on the pole of the subject," as the German thinker did when discussing fetishism, but also on the pole of the object, Curran misrepresents Spinoza, Deleuze and Guattari by putting forward a vitalist monism that is nowhere to be found in Spinoza's mechanistic-dualist universe and only partly retrievable from the authors of *Mille Plateaux*.[16] Let me consider the case of Desdemona's

---

16   There are many problems with Curran's allegedly Deleuzian approach to Shakespearean materiality and selfhood. His reliance on Bennett's *Vibrant Matter* makes him co-opt and misconstrue the thought of Spinoza, Deleuze and Guattari. His use of the notion of *agencement* (assemblage) is problematic because it leaves behind the mechanistic dimension that is always alive in Deleuze's thought. Vitalism is of course a Deleuzian concern, but the kind of vitalism Curran describes is not fully alive in the Deleuzian concept of *agencement*, which is more informed with notions of mechanical code, arrangement, and *dispositif* (See, for instance, Thomas Nail's essay, "What is Assemblage?"). Curran's effective acquaintance with Deleuze and Guattari's ideas is questionable. It is strange that in a discussion on selfhood and property in *Richard II* that is supposedly framed in theoretical coordinates gleaned from Chapter 4 of *Mille Plateaux*, Curran should miss the opportunity to refer to the treatment of "l'agencement féodal": "Taking the feudal assemblage as an example, we would have to consider the interminglings of bodies defining

handkerchief. Harris argues that in the logic of the play "the handkerchief emerges less as a fetish than as a palimpsest, a writing surface upon which multiple signs and narratives are inscribed and erased" (179), a claim that manifestly locates agency less in the writing surface than in the subjects of the verbs "inscribe" and "erase." This is not the only contradiction, for also inconsistent is to centre your analysis of untimely *matter* on the effectiveness of "signs" and "narratives," which are *formal* means of meaning-production. Harris appears to believe that inviting the reader to "[expand] our understanding of agency, and [move] beyond binaries of agentic subject and passive object" (*Untimely Matter* 189) and invoking "Bruno Latour's theory of mediation and the actor network" (181) is enough to get him out of trouble. It is not. Harris never gets to demonstrating that the handkerchief "too is an actor, contributing to the collective agency of its mediation" (181). Collective agency is described as follows:

> *Othellos*'s handkerchief enters into a diverse array of actor networks: Desdemona and handkerchief is, if only for Othello, a network performing matrimonial chastity and honor; Iago and handkerchief is a network that induces a seizure in Othello; Bianca and handkerchief, spied by Othello and egged by Iago, is a network performing "ocular proof" of Desdemona's guild (3.3.365). There are other, more mundane networks into which the handkerchief enters: it is used to bandage an aching head (3.3.289–90) and "wile [a] beard" (3.4.440), or blow a nose, clean an ear, and wipe a mouth ("nose, ears, and lips") ([4.1.39–40]). (181)

Harris adds that, given the diverse array of actor networks into which the handkerchief enters, we must "be wary [...] of subordinating what is *done* with the handkerchief to the question of what it ultimately *means*." The reason: "there are too many networks within which it acts for its meaning to settle" (181). The point is clearly made. But is he right? I think not. For one, as Colebrook has observed, the renovation of materialism is not necessarily predicated upon political notions of collective agency. Derrida's, for instance, is decidedly "not a matter of collective labour or social praxis" ("Matter without bodies" 13),

---

feudalism: the body of the earth and the social body; the body of the overlord, vassal, and serf; the body of the knight and the horse and their new relation to the stirrup; the weapons and tools assuring a symbiosis of bodies—a whole machinic assemblage" (*A Thousand Plateaus* 89; *Mille Plateaux* 112). Also incomprehensible is his failure to engage in a productive dialogue with Deleuze's and Guattari's treatment of Shakespeare's kings in "historical dramas," and more particularly of Richard III's engagement with the "war machines" and the "State apparatus" (*A Thousand* 125–126).

or only indirectly (mediatedly) so. Second, we must distinguish between the functional "meaning" of the object when used to bandage a head, wile a beard, blow a nose, clean a beard, and wipe a mouth, and its allegorical "meaning," correctly identified by Harris as "matrimonial chastity and honor." I guess we all agree that the networks obtained around the functional meaning are in principle irrelevant to the meaning of the play. Unless told otherwise. As it happens, Harris praises Peter Stallybrass' determination to remain "attentive to how the meaning of the handkerchief cannot be extricated from the bodily actions it performs" and illustrates his point by adducing that "it is a powerful signifier of dirtiness and promiscuity precisely because of its close association with the body's apertures and their effluvia" (181). This functional meaning of dirtiness and promiscuity is submitted then as an instance of "what is *done* with the handkerchief" that cannot be subordinated to "what it ultimately *means*" (181). But is this really the case? Obviously not: the meaning "dirtiness and promiscuity" belongs in the semantic range of the meaning "matrimonial chastity and honor," expressing merely a modulation of degree. This means that the master allegorical meaning controls the functional meanings produced in the "more mundane networks." But the "transcendental" control of the archi-trope (the allegorical meaning "matrimonial chastity and honor") is also firmly felt in the rest of the "actor networks." This is Harris's second error. All of the networks he stipulates (Iago and the handkerchief, Bianca and the Handkerchief) draw their functional rationale (inducing a seizure in Othello, performing "ocular proof" on Desdemona's guilt) from the allegorical meaning that organizes the first network (Desdemona and handkerchief): Othello falls into seizure because Iago prevaricates with a word *handkerchief* that allegorizes matrimonial honor and chastity, and the ocular proof is proof, for Othello, of the degrading alienation of matrimonial honor and chastity. In conclusion, nothing in the play is *done* with or *meant* by the "handkerchief" that is not predetermined and preempted by its master allegorical *meaning*. The agency of *Othello*'s handkerchief is therefore exclusively a function of its tropological force, and this force depends upon (is mediated by) a literary and cultural tradition—especially medieval and Christian: the Veronica, Laura's *fazzoletto*—that has hegemonized a potentially empty signifier, investing it with an ineliminable allegorical significance.

7

The materiality of the Shakespearean text undoubtedly has to do with the material realities surrounding the author who wrote it—his surrounding physical world, his own body, his clothing, his clotted ink, his quill pen, his tables. But these things are completely lost to us, and they were lost to the play the minute Shakespeare completed the playtext. This doesn't mean that they don't determine the sense of what is written therein. The problem is that such determination (or, if you wish, overdetermination) has to be ascertained through dialectical methods sensible to the immanence of meaning-production within structural totalities. The transcendence of the material-real with respect to the written text doesn't entitle us to neglect the importance of immanence at three levels: a) the structural immanence of the text (first totality) as a semiotic whole; b) the structural immanence of the ideology or the ideologies (second totality) that, in their figural, narrative or mythical articulation, produce the text; and c) the structural immanence of the socio-economic system of forces of production and relations of production (third totality) from which the ideology emerges that produces the text. The capacity to establish connections between these three levels is what is at stake in materialist-hermeneutic work, and this is certainly more than simply fantasizing about London weather in 1601 or about ink stains in bad quartos.

Indeed, the safest way to assert the materiality of the Shakespearean text is, I believe, through the heuristic deployment of a *transcendental materiality*, which we may dub indistinctly as formal or textual. Let me recall, with Dan Zahavi, that the adversary of transcendental idealism is not materialism, but objectivism (*Husserl's Legacy* 101–102). We could even include here the *institutional materiality of statements* proposed by Foucault in *L'archéologie du savoir*, and described as a "repeatable materiality" that is independent from the ordinary materials of writing and printing (paper, ink ...) and can only be identified by its capacity of defining "*possibilities of reinscription and transcription*" (*Archeology* 102–103). This materiality hinges exclusively on the text as an instantiation of writing conceived as the transcendental locus of iterable inscriptions: this is, I believe, the only reality that *matters*. What we imaginatively see when we read the play, in whichever version of reading we wish to consider—us alone reading the first folio under the greenwood tree, the production director reading quietly at home and re-reading the actors' lips during performance, or the playgoers listening to what the actors are internally reading across themselves and the audience—owns whatever phenomenal reality we decide to grant to it to our inward eye and ear, and since we are many, and inner sight and hearing is a free as thought (*Twelfth Night* 1.3.57), then we may say that this has an inherently *unphenomenal* reality. Otherwise put, we don't see what we see. When Polonius tells the King that Hamlet has requested the troupe "this night to play before him" and beseeched him "to entreat your majesties / To *hear and see the matter*" (3.1.22–23; emphasis added), he refers to a written matter. It is perhaps interesting to remark that Claudius doesn't react at the dumbshow which conspicuously performs, before his very eyes, a murder like that of his brother's: he only jumps at Hamlet's verbal anticipation of what the actor playing Lucianus is about to do.[17] Let me formulate this more slowly: the man who interrupts the show at *Hamlet* 3.2.261—"Give me some light, away"—right after *hearing* Hamlet's words—"'A poisons him in the garden for his estate" (3.2.224)—is the same person who only a hundred lines earlier fails to react after *seeing* a player take off the crown of another player who sleeps upon a bank of flowers and pours poison in his ears. Wasn't that enough for Claudius to abort the show? The precedence of the verbal-aural over the figurative-visual in a play signally riddled with "auricular figurations" should give us pause.[18] We can find another example in the Prologue to *Romeo and Juliet*, where the Chorus asks the audience to attend "with patient ears" (*Romeo and Juliet* "Prologue" 13), not with their eyes. The playtext is a written document whose reading produces conspicuous aural effects, but very unclear and indistinct visual effects beyond the careful ocular registering of printed signs (mostly words) in irregularly regular lines. To entrust the significance of a Shakespeare playtext to the visual reception of a theatrical performance based on that playtext is profoundly delusive. Maybe it is about time we all awake "from the pleasure of performance intoxication" (Cheney, *Shakespeare's* 10).

A new materialism is either a *transcendental materialism*—in any of its versions: transcendental empiricism (Deleuze), dialectical materialism (Žižek), idealist materialism (Badiou)—or is nothing, more metaphysical deception. Conjoining Derridean and Deleuzian insights, the phrase *transcendental materialism* could be summarily described as an understanding of matter as *form differing through the discontinued repetition* of mechanical inscription.[19] I guess

---

17 This seldom noted fact was first observed by Walter Wilson Greg. See John Dover Wilson, *What Happens* 5.
18 Ned Lukacher follows Joel Fineman's suggestion to the effect that "Shakespeare's fascination with the ear may function like 'an instrument of delay and deferral' that somehow inserts a kind of spacing and timing, a certain 'dilation', within the essentially visual apparatuses underlying the ideology of Elizabethan power" (*Daemonic* 131).
19 This tentative definition finds support in a deManian conception of "materiality without matter" or "materiality of inscription." According to Tom Cohen, J. Hillis Miller and Barbara Cohen, "in referencing an *other* 'materiality' to inscription, we are left with one that inverts the usual promise of the term that includes in its genealogy the promise of reference, the irreducible real, the prefigural and nonlinguistic. Whatever *inscription* designates, it conjures sheer anteriority. It does not deliver us to any immediacy of reference, to any historical narrative that presumes to encode such, but to mnemonic programs that appear to precede and legislate these—together, necessarily, with reading models, the 'senses' for that matter, the 'human' as fiction or category, perhaps the humanities as an

Jonathan Gil Harris was trying to say something similar when he argued, in the "Introduction" to *Untimely Matter in the Time of Shakespeare*, that matter "is rather a site of inscription and of *différance*. Matter is a surface that can be written on; but it is itself a species of 'arche-writing' in Derrida's sense, inasmuch as it is characterized by an ontological and temporal self-differentiation and hence deferral" (8). As much as one may appreciate the stammering staccato (*rather, but, inasmuch*) of this brave and proviso-laden speculative moment, I cannot help registering several inconsistencies: 1) if matter is *différance*, matter cannot be a site or a surface, but rather the arche-writing on the site or surface; 2) matter does not exist prior to the inscription, but is rather constituted differentially through the very operation of the inscription; 3) Harris ontologizes matter when he should rather dialecticize it, and the dialecticization of matter can only take place (i.e. constitute extensionality) via the framing of transcendental coordinates, as Derrida did by resorting to Husserl, in the passage from *De la grammatologie* that Harris is quoting from. It is the suppression, in Harris' tentatively Derridean determination of "matter," of dialectical and transcendental parameters that disables in advance his claim. Harris is on the verge of saying that matter is constituted transcendentally through the inscriptive operation of difference, both as difference and as the site where difference occurs, but he pulls back from that edge. The upshot is an undialectical construal of matter that overlooks the virtual recursiveness of the temporal regression: just as matter is not prior to writing, writing cannot get started without a minimal spatial (site, surface) horizon, but this minimal horizon is dialectically synthesized—Derrida speaks of a "synthèse originaire" (*De la grammatologie* 91)—by the original (transcendental) inscription of the trace. Thus, "la difference est donc la formation de la forme" (92) and it is precisely the operational dynamism that inheres in the term "formation" that spells out the materiality of form, or, as I put it, the *becoming-matter of form—form differing through discontinued repetition* after a first mechanical inscription.[20] Matter-form is not

---

      institution situated over (and against) a disturbance he finds within the 'aesthetic' as routinely defined" ("A 'Materiality without Matter'?," viii).

20   Form is *eidos*, and the idea is the *mark* (trace) of an absence or void, the not-being that signals the Being of a being. Manifestly, a thing that is defined by its not-being is a no-thing, a nothing. So a form is a nothing. A trace marks (is) the emergence of a form, and this emergence is always-already characterized by the attestation of its own derivativeness, as the mark/trace retroactively designates the absence (the form) which it significantly, differentially, doubles. The problem arises, then, when a nothing or absence is repeated. The repetition of a nothing is inscriptive or presentative. It is the condition of possibility of the trace as well as of the ghost. But a form repeated spells both formalization repeating itself and difference formalizing itself—and this formalization institutes matter: what we call unformalized matter is just matter in a lower-order stage of formalization, because

just a binarism open to deconstruction, but manifestly the provisional notional balance of a dialectical process. Harris' claim is also ontological because it freezes the locus of differential inscription into a site or surface—the whole point rests on the being-there of "things"—and openly attributes an *ontological* status to the dynamics of temporal-cum-spatial self-differentiation. The word Derrida consistently uses is *transcendental*, not ontological, and this terminological choice is in keeping with the explicit dependence of his argument on Kant (transcendental synthesis, ideality of time) and Husserl (the retention-and-protention-sensitive phenomenology of time).

Transcendental matter (all matter, at bottom) gets consistently *phenomenalized* when its subjective reception fails to go beyond a basic level, characteristic of judgements of taste and aesthetic judgements, of corresponding formalization—unable to resist the "spiritual coercion" (Adorno) of symbolic concordance—into an arbitrary and contingent realm of conceptual generalization which (paradoxically) alone affords the existential shine of the particular and singular. As Tom Cohen, Hillis Miller and Barbara Cohen argue, "the term materiality in de Man's recitation conjures a locus through which sheer anteriority is in transit, both accessed and preceded as the facticity of inscription out of which human perception forgetfully is staged" ("A 'Materiality without Matter'?" X–XI). As soon as we forget the anteriority of this facticity, the earliness of this inscription, and set up the stage for perception, we phenomenalize matter (as noumenal substance or sensorial aesthesis) and impede understanding. To put this dialectical conception in familiar Rortean terms, the phenomenalization of matter thrives in minds reluctant to—critically, ironically—either forgo or redescribe their original—tendentially simplistic

---

radically unformalized matter is a *contradictio in termini*. Higher-order formalization is obviously contingent on the prior existence of matter. But original matter emerged solely from tensions in a field of formal interactions (a field of forces, of energy, a domain of clinamen, from Democritus to Marx and Nietzsche). If matter is per definition what belongs in the order of presentation, of what is present, then matter is always inscriptive and repetitive, that is, formal. Colebrook recalls Deleuze's conception of a transcendental empiricism. "In the beginning would be the relations among forces, from which known stable bodies or matters would emerge" (13). A force is a non-being that seeks to formalize itself into a being and that, short of an unformed matter it can apply itself to, it ends up informing itself (via differential repetition) into matter. The impossibility of separating form and matter is implicitly clear even to a Deleuzian scholar like Colebrook, who argues that according to Derrida, "a concept would be both material—always traced and articulated—and ideal (always bearing the potential to open an actual context to a not-yet)" (15). Note the explicit and for her unproblematic assimilation of "material" to "traced" and "articulated," two adjectival past participles that we would in principle attribute to the "formal".

and pictorial—vocabularies, whence the necessary link (the identity) between phenomenality and ideology, and the complicity, so often celebrated by the late de Man, between the transcendental, materialism, and critique. *And* literature. Badiou's intricate reading of Mallarmé's poetry in *Conditions* submits an analogous view of cancelling, of the crossing-out of evental vanishing, the constitutive undecidability, and the atony and void of place, as distinctive signposts of evental materiality (53). Badiou's aims and methods differ from those of Derrida and Deleuze, but his decidedly *unphenomenal* conception of aesthetics—the choice of Mallarmé as arch-poet is telling—places his materialism alongside that of his forerunners. Foucault's description of Raymond Roussel's language submits a telling refutation of the romantic tropes of origin, nature, and materiality. Beholden to the transcendental horizon of formal reiteration, the vision of literature that emerges from such refutation is much closer to Derrida's vision of literature than Foucault would have probably acknowledged:

> Le langage de Roussel est opposé—par le sens de sens de ses flèches plus encore que par le bois dont il est fait—à la parole initiatique [...] En sa lecture, rien ne nous est promis. Seule est prescrit intérieurement la conscience qu'en lisant tous ces mots alignés et lisses nous sommes exposés au danger hors repères d'en lire d'autres, qui sont autres et les mêmes. L'œuvre, en sa totalité [...] impose systématiquement une inquiétude informe, divergente, centrifuge, orienté non pas vers le plus réticent des secrets, mais vers le dédoublement et la transmutation des formes plus visible : chaque mot est à la fois animé et ruiné, rempli et vidé par la possibilité qu'il y en ait un second—celui-ci ou celui-là, ou ni l'un ni l'autre, mais un troisième, ou rien.
>
> *Raymond Roussel* 19–20

Obviously, this kind of language demands a mode of reading attuned to a dialectical complexity made of directions and not matters, semiotic linearity and not objectal protuberance, the identity of identity and non-identity, and formal duplication and transmutation. Such exigency would rule out neo-phenomenological scholars—like Harris, Curran, Lupton, and Kottman—with stakes in materialism or aesthetics, for they rely too strongly on non-inferential knowledge. Consciously or unconsciously following Merleau-Ponty's reliance on primordial perception, they root knowledge in the (non-inferential) ability to *sense contents*, without even considering the possibility that cognitive growth may rest on the process of subsuming signifiers in chains of differential repetition or, more orthodoxically stated, in subsuming particular under universals, a process that involves "learning, concept formation, even the use of symbols" (Sellars, "Empiricism" 258). In other words, the attestation of non-cognitive facts—asking the reader to see, with Macbeth, the dagger, and, with Othello, the handkerchief—does not add up to criticism. We may call it names, like empathetic-intersubjective phenomenological object-oriented identification. But such a celebration of fusion and propinquity is not criticism. Criticism is analysis, not synthesis, and is therefore based on separation and distance. Not because—or not only because—like Machiavelli and Hobbes, we may fancy it that way, but rather because the objects of criticism (things made of words, words, words) are constituted through difference and scansion, separation, and distance, *celui-ci ou celui-là, ou ni l'un ni l'autre, mais un troisième, ou rien*. And the nothing thus conjugated is certainly more significant than matter.

8

So what is the *matter* with/in Shakespeare? What is, then, the Shakespeare *thing*? What is the thing to do when we claim to be *doing Shakespeare*? Well, in my opinion, the thing to do is to read a Shakespeare playtext. To read, that is, a text written by a man—William Shakespeare—particularly attuned to "the language's speculative spirit [*spekulativer Geist der Sprache*]" (Hegel, *Science of Logic* 12); by a man, that is, unusually gifted with "the skill to conjure the speculative content hidden in the logical instinct of language" (Gadamer, *Dialectic* 45); by a man who is, like all true subjects, "ce qui du réel pâtit du significant" (Lacan, *L'éthique* 142)—yet alone so in an abnormally enhanced fashion: a man more in the Real than other subjects, and certainly more sensitive and vulnerable to the work of the signifier. It is a text written by this man and read by actors and readers, learnt by heart by actors and some readers, and its performance is the text mentally read aloud—some call that recited—by actors on stage. The Elizabethan audience attended the playhouse to "hear" a play, not to see it. It is a text that we compulsively revisit because we don't understand, and that we fail to neutralize because it capitalizes, much more than the standard Shakespeare scholar or the average Hegel interpreter is ready to admit, on *the essential discursivity of thought*.[21] Nothing but words happen in the production of a Shakespeare play: all relevant actions are speech act(ion)s.[22]

---

21 The phrase is Pippin's (*Hegel's Realm of Shadows* 185) and it is repeatedly used in a brilliant book that fails however to draw its many implications.
22 Harold Bloom rightly observed that Hamlet's rhetoric and "aggressivity of high language" is "itself [...] a mode of action" (*Shakespeare* 416).

All the relevant input is verbal input. To believe that "Shakespeare's characters encounter their worlds through sensory inputs, often confusing or confused synaesthetic experiences, and are constructed through their relation to those inputs" (Raber, *Shakespeare* 65) is a plain phenomenological delusion. Neither characters nor actors (all of them *personae*, after all) care much about the world outside them: they care about the language spoken by people around them. They care about what is being said, largely because it cues them to proffer their own speech actions. Educated playgoers anticipating the lines of a Shakespeare character played by a dull actor during a flat production find themselves in the same situation as those attending William Gaddis' uncertain reading of William Gass' fiction: "Wouldn't you rather have been alone at home, reading this lovely page?" (Gaddis, *The Rush* 129). Reading alone—just like Bernhard read Novalis, Kafka read Kleist, Gordimer read Lawrence, Blake read Milton, Morrison read Faulkner, Proust read Racine. "[*A trunk and arras. A*] *bed* [*is thrust for with*] INNOGEN [*in it, reading a book.*]" (*Cymbeline* 2.2): what shall we do, phenomenologically, with that vortex? What shall we do with the *othings* of reading when all then scholars have rushed out to rehearse Giacomo's phenomenological prospection, and carefully stopped—in Ruskinian fashion—"to note the chamber" (2.2.23–24)?[23]

Actors, I surmised, don't listen. But neither do real people in real life—nothing disproves Habermas' theory of communicative action more sharply than the rise of the divorce rate, or the rise of pet keeping. Katherine Hayles' conception of "the posthuman" as being "seamlessly articulated with intelligent machines" (34) takes a very free—positively non-marital and rigorously first-world (If you cannot afford to pay a wifi connection you are not post-human?)—understanding of the phrase "seamless articulation." The bad joke, again: alas, the times when marital discord behind divorce used to be a privileged subject-matter in Shakespeare criticism (what's wrong with the Macbeths? Did the former queen cheat on Lear? When did Calpurnia lose *l'antica fiamma*?) are positively gone! Ours is not even "the Age of Caliban" (Bloom, *Caliban* 1). We've entered the era of pets. The time is past for Kates to scrutinize Petrucchios. It is the time for cats to glance, questioningly, at Shakespeare, "stark naked" (*Antony and Cleopatra* 5.2.58). A time for hospitable ecologies, domestic polities, posthuman cooperation, trans-anthropic passions. Remember Black? *It's a wonderful, wonderful life.*

---

23 It is as if representation-oriented or phenomenological readers would try to translate the dialogical dynamism of the play into its very painterly suspensions (see Jameson, *Antinomies of Realism*, 8). For the recurrence of *scenes of reading* in Shakespeare, see Royle, *How to Read*, 29.

Derrida's transcendental conception of matter is indebted to his early interpretations of Husserl, who "called the irreducibly egoic essence of experience 'archi-factuality' (*Urtatsache*), nonempirical factuality, transcendental factuality (a notion to which attention has never been paid, perhaps)" (*Writing* 131; 192). This fascinating parenthetical notation is registered in Derrida's 1964 essay on Levinas. Of course, Derrida's take on transcendental materiality is not exactly bound to the *Urgrund* of the egoic experience, but this parenthesis inscribes the symptom of a need to save the material phenomena (facts, things) under non-factual and non-empirical conditions. According to Colebrook, Derrida's early construal of materialism

> was hailed as "the materiality of the signifier," as though one would not be lured into imagining any unmediated contact with the real, as though we recognized not only the conditioning structures of signification, but that the *materiality* of those systems would prevent us from grounding them into something organic (such as life, speech or meaning).
> "Matter without Bodies" 2

Similarly, Foucault relied on the *materiality* of institutions to secure the non-factic materiality of statements. *Institution, structure, system*: these terms imply a pattern of transcendental self-regulating *formalization* oriented not simply to the inscriptive (Derrida) or eventual (Foucault) production of significance in the form of tropes (Derrida) or statements (Foucault), but more importantly to their mechanical repetition. We are dealing, I insist, with a *formalist materiality* whose roots we may trace back to Democritus, but also to Kant. Recall that for the moral law to exist, we need to be able to apply a categorical imperative which looks at the (universal) form of a maxim rather than at its specific content. The ineliminable arbitrariness implicit in that form, and in the mechanical iteration of the *prima facie* empty imperative's application, prefigures the transcendental principle of arbitrariness as it reemerges in Saussure and Derrida. In an excellent essay, Claire Colebrook has warned against the attempts to naturalize, along cognitivist or evolutionary lines, the textual materialism proposed by Derrida. She also reminds us of Derrida's constant warning against Marxist materialism as another expression of metaphysical foundationalism:

> So the Derridean materialism we might be left with would be amenable neither to the discourse of naturalism—and so the idea of a naturalized phenomenology, returning meaning to the organism's capacity to make sense of its work would have to be abandoned—nor a discourse of ethics

or politics, if these were to be grounded in conceptions of the polity, or the habits and ways of life of ethos. (14)

The idea of *naturalized phenomenology* must be discarded. That much is clear. But what is, or how can we describe, Derrida's textual or textualized materialism?[24] This is Colebrook's precise answer to a question without a precise answer:

> Concepts therefore have the force of an essential impossibility, for their meaning or repeatability gestures to an ideality that exceeds any context, any actual material instance; and yet concepts—because of their materiality—are marked, scarred, deflected and contaminated by their singular conditions of emergence. (15)

---

24 Apart from Colebrook's essay, see: Crockett, *Derrida and the End of Writing*; Michael Nass, *Miracle and Machine*; Karen Barad, "Quantum Entanglements"; Deborah Goldgaber, *Speculative Grammatology*.

CHAPTER 10

Undialing the Dialectic

1

Hostile to appreciations of experience in terms of negativity, relationality, and totality, phenomenology is first and foremost, we have seen, an anti-dialectical method. Levinas identified *totality* as the arch-enemy of the ethical system and rejected it because it was, he believed, inextricably bound up with the ontological project (*Totalité* 7). He held that eschatology could connect with Being outside the range of totality or ontology. Being, in short, named an exteriority situated beyond the immanence of totality, whence the possibility of a "rupture de la totalité, la possibilité d'une signification sans context" (8). The crowning phrase in this statement—*signification without context*—encapsulates the anti-structuralist and anti-dialectical animus of Levinas' whole project and lays the ground for phenomenological interrogations of Shakespearean meaning in decontextualized, de-textualized, embodied, local, or presentist terms. Saussurean structuralism, we know, relies on a notion of signification emerging from arrangements of formal relationality within a context that is regarded as both immanent and total. This is the context brandished by David Scott Kastan when he argued, in a 1997 essay significantly titled "Shakespeare After Theory," that "writing, understood as an imaginative act, is inevitably less an invention that an intervention, a motivated entrance into a preexisting set of linguistic and discursive possibilities" (*Shakespeare After Theory* 39). Any departure from this notion runs formidable risks. Not even a life-oriented philosopher like Deleuze could conceive of novelty and creation without placing *immanent* activity, as Badiou shrewdly noted, "sur fond de totalité" (*L'aventure* 42). It is no accident he styled himself a *transcendental empiricist*, with the adjective *transcendental* registering a nod of recognition to the dialectical horizon that Deleuze always strove to keep at a distance. Two materialist thinkers like Fredric Jameson and Slavoj Žižek have repeatedly pointed out that much worse than dogmatic foundationalism is flippant, relativistic, postmodernist anti-foundationalism, and worse than dogmatic advocacies of totality are uncritical rebuttals of totality (*Valences of the Dialectic* 201–222; *Reading Marx*, 43–44). They lay the ground for the cognitive and empiricist fallacies that await the Shakespeare scholar around every corner.

The (transcendental) anticipation of an ungraspable totality—the totality of writing, of ideology, of the unconscious realm, of the broad intertextual field, of the Shakespeare canon, of the play under consideration—helps among other things to contain the *manifold* (Kant's *Mannigfaltige*) of empirical experience which assaults the scholar confronted with a textual crux. Relevance, discrimination, and focus can only spring from the presumption of totalized signification. But phenomenologists, alas, have other ways of processing the many. What the standard academic article on Shakespeare offers by way of policing the avalanche of particulars that is the specialty of late neo-historicist, posthumanist and phenomenology-oriented readings is the application of *one* single concept. This concept the carefree post-theoretical scholar normally shoplifts from the nearest delicatessen in town—paperback copies of Benjamin, Arendt, Merleau-Ponty, Levinas, Serres, Agamben, Landa, or Esposito. There follows a routine deployment of *the one* concept, artificially swelled to phony allegorical conformity to a Shakespeare play cut down to exiguous and unrepresentative proportions. Two concepts, and the ensuing dialectical relations—between the concepts, between each concept and its "thing," between each concept and the totality of concepts—would endanger the neat logicism of the "conceptual net" that "gives Husserl's phenomenology its peculiar hermetic character, a masturbatory quality, a powerful effort to lift India rubber weights" (Adorno, *Against Epistemology* 108). Let me illustrate this by way of a parody. Imagine the circulation of the leaflet titled "How to write an academic paper on early modern literature" among very young scholars and doctoral candidates during a conference on Shakespeare:

> Dear graduate student
>
> Privilege the dynamic over the static, the unfixed over the fixed. Repudiate categorical determination. Straddle clefts. Overpass boundaries. Navigate fringes. Bridge the abysses and ruptures. And, oh, don't forget to elide the divides. Traverse all coercive delineations, all proscriptive linearizations. "Force upon all limitations and cut across all boundaries" (Arendt). Shun essentialism. Pretend that humans have been stupid in trying to determine their being human. Believe your pretense. Use terms like interface, network, archive. Verbs like restage, rezone, reshape, refigure, reconfigure, rework, rethink, redescribe. Go re. Repeat, in the same order, the repeated quotes from Aristotle, Hobbes, Descartes, Kant, Heidegger in order to unmask the futility of definitional attempts at chasing the human. Nag at the fact that they are all men. Revile, particularly, Hobbes, in passing: that always works. Call attention to the multiple natural-object landscape surrounding the putative victim of the man hunt. Establish the logical dependence of that empty nothing (human) on the rich something around it (non-human). Deconstruct the polarity.

Yes! You're doing fine. Allow for some mutual interpenetration, interaction, interrelation. Go inter. Turn horizontal. Call it cross-fertilization, co-imbrication, collaboration. Drop, here and there, words like osmosis, permeation, homeostasis, don't forget the fuzzy contours, the porous boundaries and, ah, the fissured categories. Salute the inclusive cosmopolities, expansive bioethics, zoe-centered egalitarianisms. Gaze at the future: insist on the need of alternate polities. On the need, why not, of rezoned academic departments, reconfigured lives. Stress the idea of risk, of openness. Use, if only sparingly, terms like partnership and hospitality: no implication of duality should be assumed. All scenarios of encounter, response, call. Introduce comments about everyday connectivity with your technological gadgets (refrigerator, watches, cell phones, computers). Humble yourself in their likeness: go tech. Crack a couple of jokes about your earlier, happily-defeated techno-clumsiness. Or, better, don't: such jesting is the province of unfunny humanist critics of an older generation. Still, let some occasional quirkiness outdo the dependencies of academic etiquette. Keep cool, don't overdo it. Resume technical jargon. Use the adjective ontological—three or four times: any noun will do. Deploy the plurals: ecologies, sovereignties, theologies: any adjective will do. Quote from Latour, Agamben, Merleau-Ponty, Serres. Mention late Derrida and any Deleuze. Relish your erudition. Treasure your eco-awareness. Don't forget to sneer at Schmitt. Call him supremacist and Nazi. Extend the insult to de Man. Not to Heidegger: we have brought him into line. You have already used 7.500 words. You need to come to an end. If your personal readings reach somewhere beyond comics, Asimov, and Beatrix Potter, then give it a try and produce some nice six lines from, say, Shakespeare or Milton, where flies or buttons are mentioned. Fungus will also do. No need to explain the passage. Pep it all up with a dash of bewildering—apparently Socratic—unwisdom, in the form of an augural question. Two interrelated questions are even better. For example: "What if monkeys and apes both had a renaissance?" (Maisano, "Rise" 65) "Was Shakespeare really capable of imagining anthropoid and autobiographical nonhuman apes?" (Maisano 70) What if dung beetles were not merely the convex animal mirrors of human sovereignty but rather creatures that embody alternative polities and bodies politic? But, then, what if dung balls were not merely the objectal refractions of beetle exceptionalism but rather things that embody inclusive cosmopolities where prosthetic coleopters may be disciplined, redefined, and absolved from their default zo(l)o(g)o-graphic arrogance? Don't spoil your adorable acumen with an answer. Don't tell anyone, not even your cat, you actually ignore the answer.

Game over. You did fine. Welcome to academia.

This is, of course, a caricature, but the originals exist, as the quoted material proves, and are often in excess of my excess. Hegel rightly despised the "unthinking inertia [*gedankenloser Trägheit*]" (*Phenomenology* 51) that informs this kind of criticism as a pernicious avatar of empty formalism, here also instanced in the sophomoric mishandling of a supposedly deconstructive undoing of binarism. Hegel's description of the routine formalist procedure—"the shapeless repetition of one and the same formula [*die gestaltlose Wiederholung des Einen und Desselben*], only externally applied to diverse materials" (8)—perfectly evokes this sense of triviality and hermeneutic exhaustion, conducive to the serialization of formulaic research. As Althusser cautions, one single concept won't do the trick—it is not *binding* enough because it overlooks the heuristic bearing of a truly structural and tendentially holistic—necessary—*problematic*.[1] This is an arch-dialectical monition also rehearsed by Heidegger in his essay on Hegel's concept of experience: "The normal activities of the usual criticisms in regard to philosophical knowledge are equivalent to the procedure of someone who intends to represent an oak but takes no notice that it is a tree" (*Off the Beaten Track* 104). The moral is not only that Shakespeare belongs to the genus Western Renaissance author and that anyone intent on studying his work would do well to become acquainted with Spenser, Marlowe, Ronsard, Ariosto, Tasso, and Cervantes. But that particular battle is sadly lost. The moral is also that in order to get started, one needs at least two concepts—say, an oak and a tree (and when I say a tree I mean a real tree, and not—*pace* phenomenologists—a noema tree or a stage greenwood tree).[2] For instance, determining whether and why *The Merchant of Venice* and *Othello* are *comedies*—before committing oneself to the absolution of any of its blistering particulars (the Jew, the Moor) is no ludicrous decision, and it may save much trouble: it is never ill-advised to examine the constraining literary conventions of late-medieval anti-Semitism and Islamophobia before moving on to the circuitous vertigo of local

---

1 In his "Introduction" to what he called "Feuerbach's Manifestoes," Althusser writes: "For borrowing a concept in isolation may only be of accidental and secondary significance. Borrowing a concept in isolation (from its context) does not bind the borrower *vis-à-vis* the context from which he extracted it (for example, the borrowings from Smith, Ricardo and Hegel in *Capital*). But borrowing a systematically interrelated set of concepts, borrowing a real *problematic*, cannot be accidental, it binds the borrower" (*For Marx* 6).

2 For the "noema tree," see Husserl, *Ideas I* §88. And also Adorno, *Against Epistemology*, 173–79.

denunciations and foolhardy exculpations. This is no invitation to monastic political quietism or black-forest speculation off the beaten track. It is just a reminder that reaching immediately after whatever immediately comes by—be it twenty particulars or one concept—is the original thoughtless gesture of what Hegel called "natural knowledge." "Come forth into the light of things / Let nature be your teacher": never was this Wordsworth injunction (*Poetical Works* 377) more religiously observed. This is Heidegger's description of a gesture that smacks of the rapacity of self-worship:

> Natural knowledge holds to its own. Everything that occurs to it can be expressed as follows: it is and remains mine [*das Meine*] and is a being as this thing that I meant [*als dieses Ge-meinte*]. In understanding representation as opinion [*Meinen*], Hegel detects in 'opinion [*meinen*]' several related meanings: 'meinen' as being directed, without mediation, toward …; 'meinen' as the trusting acceptance of what is given; and 'meinen' in the sense of keeping and claiming something as one's own. This *meinen*, opinion, is the fundamental state of all representing in which natural consciousness moves. For this reason, Hegel is able to say in the paragraph that natural consciousness "sticks to a system of opinion."
> *Off the Beaten Track* 112

Thus, for instance, the natural consciousness moving inside credulous Leonato is apt to bring about the radical fusion between his opinion, his property, and his defamed daughter: "But mine and mine I loved and mine I praised / And mine that I was proud of, mine so much / That I myself was to myself not mine" (*Much Ado About Nothing* 4.1.131–33). Likewise, Shakespeare's natural critic is apt to succumb to the doxal *ignis fatuus* of her phenomenal sensorium, absorbed in the mute recreation of her intuited manifold of appropriated particulars. A prereflexive arrogance informs the resulting empiricist figure of passive affluence: "L'empiriste ne veut jamais anticiper, il prétend procéder passivement, fidèlement, raconter, réciter (*erzählen*) ce qu'il croit voir, énumérer un certain nombre de prédicats qui viennent à sa rencontre" (Derrida, *Glas* 113). Despite the strict program of embargos and reductions that characterized Husserl's philosophy, second-wave phenomenologists quite often relapsed into such porous naturalism. In fact, however forcefully Merleau-Ponty strove to observe the strictures of human finitude—an attitude he constantly opposed to the infinite ambitions of *intellectualisme*—his phenomenological program inevitably harbors an infinitist drive, already latent in Husserl's claim that phenomenological reductions allow us "to set aside the limitations of knowledge essentially involved in any nature-directed form of investigation" ("Introduction," *Ideas I* 3).

What the resulting short-circuit bypasses is precisely the dialectical mediation of the concept. In a crucial letter, Adorno reproached Benjamin for refusing to accept that appearances—not only the game—can also be dialectic, and he urged him to employ "a bit more of dialectic" (*Complete Correspondence* 136). He never tired of reminding Benjamin, even at the risk of falling out with him, that positive things at the base could not be randomly redeemed by ideas tactically chosen from the superstructure; that if we decide to overlook in materialist-hermeneutic work the mediation of the global conceptual process (schemata, categories, determinations, tropes) we risk either slipping into "immediate materialism" (272), an outcome Husserl's proud offspring—bound to *their* things themselves—seldom dreads, or, as Hegel argued in a note against Jacobi, relapsing into "metaphysical understanding" (*Encyclopedia* 171). When Stanley Wells says apropos of *A Midsummer Night's Dream* that "the illusory has its part in the *total* experience of reality" (34; emphasis added) he is, perhaps inadvertently, endorsing both Plato and Hegel in their resolve to welcome shards of conceptuality into the fabric of the real. Well's sharp comment applies to all of Shakespeare's plays.

Gadamer has rightly characterized Hegelian dialectic as a rejection of *raisonnement*—a repudiation of the fruitless and vain discoursing over the glassy externalities of things (*Hegel's Dialectic* 27). Speculative thought, by contrast, is conceptual thought—a sophisticated game through which the mind rediscovers in reality, not without a vengeance, the determinations it posited there in the first place: "Two truths are told" (*Macbeth* 1.3.26), says Macbeth, shortly after helping himself to a vatic speech only his mind has placed in the mouths of three vagrant ladies. Hegel clearly observed that "the movement of the Notion (the concept) is development: by which that only is explicit which is already implicitly present" (*Encyclopedia* 161). Wherefore, the vengeance: a cognitive surplus (an excess) that, while exposing the aboriginal lack of the mind (a gap), manages to expand the self-reflective compass of reality, and keeps the game going. The game involves the *interim* that, "like a phantasma" (*Julius Caesar* 2.1.65), cuts in between the apperceptive ego and its *cogitata*, a sort of delay of the source in relation to itself (Derrida, *Marges* 345). If no *retard* is due, we may well expect a pastoral saturnalia of presences:

> What is love? 'tis not hereafter;
> Present mirth hath present laughter;
> What's to come is still unsure:
> In delay there lies no plenty;

> Then come kiss me, sweet and twenty,
> Youth's a stuff will not endure.
> *Twelfth Night* 2.3.43–48

Dialectics, by contrast, ordains the ceaseless procrastination of *plenty*, the deferment of presence—*present* mirth and *present* laughter. Dialectics bodes the acme of *delay*, the triumph of the *unsure hereafter*. It is more a *coming* than a *stuff*, and it *endures*.[3] This is not a Viagra commercial, but the very game of dialectics, defined by Polonius as a method of delay whereby "your bait of falsehood takes this carp of truth" (*Hamlet* 2.1.62). The dialectical critic first overlays the textual reality at hand with "what forgeries you please" (*Hamlet* 2.1.20) the better to receive discriminated slices of "wisdom" (*Hamlet* 2.1.63). Critical forgeries, known in modern hermeneutics as *Vorurteile* (prejudices), are notional devices that help organize the reality under study—in our case, the Shakespeare text— into some intelligible shape, a step only accomplished by placing it under conceptual umbrellas alongside other presumably related texts. If criticism seeks to remain progressive and avoid the conservative "overtenderness toward all that exists" that characteristically sacrifices the *all* for an "inclination towards the concrete" (*Wollen des Konkreten*), then conceptual scanning requires both comparison and a sense of "more comprehensive totalities" (Mannheim 95–102). To read, for instance, *Hamlet* speculatively and dialectically involves, first of all, allowing the play to be tempted by genre-related conceptual baits like "tragedy," or "revenge tragedy," or "Senecan tragedy," and seeing how it reacts to this inducement.[4] It also entails, of course, engaging aspects of the play to conform to pre-established heuristic concepts like plot, myth, character, source, period, the normative paraphernalia characteristic of what Rancière unadvisedly dismisses as a bygone mimetic regime. The nonconceptual confrontation with *Hamlet* that so much attracts aesthetic-cum-phenomenological readers is as preposterous as Hamlet's Heathcliffean attempt to "be buried quick" (*Hamlet* 5.1.264) with Ophelia. Hamlet only becomes significant by situating its "contents in a 'space of implications'" (Brandom, *Trust* 114). This search for horizontally connected contexts of intelligibility must also be extended to include the way in which an allegedly authorial text negotiates its way into

---

3 Lukacher argues that Hamlet returns to England "with a new 'readiness' to wait for what will come, knowing now, as he had not known before, that what is to come may be something from very much earlier" (*Daemonic* 151).

4 For a bold and original attempt to read the tragedies as textual practices that dialectically internalize their own opposing expectations of genre, see Dianne Rothledder's *Fraught Decisions in Plato and Shakespeare*.

a book. The replacement of vertical literary analysis bent on decoding deep intention or meaning with horizontal modes of reading alert to networked semiotic-material production was seen by Kastan as a post-theoretical step (*Shakespeare After Theory* 40), but the resolve with which he avers that "both reading and writing are *not unmediated* activities" (31; my emphasis) is in itself an echt-theoretical determination. If we waive critical protocols that hinge on the disclosure of mediation, we are likely to usher the reader into a *paysage moralisé* or to ensnare him towards the deadly quick sands of facticity. Nothing, no situationist glamour (Rancière) and no deviant multiplicity (Foucault) will be able to save her in that deadlock.[5] This is one the risks of dabbling in "picture-book phenomenology."[6] The reader is likely to freeze into an emblem or suffocate by empirical fumes, all the while rejoicing in what Hegel called "ignorance of the nature of mediation [*der Unbekanntschaft mit der Natur der Vermittlung*]" (*Phenomenology of Spirit* 11). Critics like Nuttall, Bloom, Frye, or Kermode seldom failed to overlook these multidirectional, and often hierarchical, networks of literary conventions. Today, critics like Kastan, Goldberg, de Grazia and Orgel represent a critical tradition that, for all its investment in theoretical innovation, never loosens its grip on dialectical considerations of genre. Orgel's short piece on *Othello* as a comedy as well as his extremely balanced edition of *The Tempest* are characterized by a strong dialectical impetus. His only, rather obtrusive, disregard of mediation—"My use of the term gay is anachronistic only in the sense that the term is modern; there have always been men who fell in love with other men" (*Spectacular Performances* 94)— opens up an enticing abyss of trans-textual and trans-historical immediacy in an argument carefully stayed with guide and climbing ropes. Such tempting point of fugue is the kind of luxury only a dialectical argument can afford. Dialectical arguments are not uncommon in the work of Margreta de Grazia, Richard Wilson, Julia Lupton, and Paul Kottman, but they are often abandoned in favor of positive riches (Wilson, de Grazia) or ideal vistas (Kottman, Lupton). In a more restricted sense, then, there are very few truly dialectical readers of Shakespeare. I can only think of Joel Fineman, Stanley Cavell, Catherine Belsey, Harold Bloom, Agnes Heller, Marjorie Garber, Jonathan Goldberg, Ned Lukacher, Nicholas Royle, and Andrew Cutrofello. Still, unyielding dialectical pressure is often deflected through calls to positivist pragmatism. It was Cavell who in the "Introduction" to *Disowning Knowledge* argued, with an astuteness partly derived from Emerson, that his "aim in reading is to follow out in each

---

5 For the idea of the odd or deviant multiplicity, see Deleuze, *Foucault*, 15–18.
6 For the satirical dismissal of *picture-book phenomenology*, see Zahavi, *Husserl's legacy*, 28.

case the complete tuition for a given intuition" (5). But this sharp Hegelian insight was soon reversed in the parenthetical closing of the sentence, when he readjusts with positivist assurance: "tuition comes to an end somewhere." Plato's dialogues abundantly prove that the end to exercises in the connected arts of tuition as paideia and tuition as money-making comes about exclusively through the (physical and spiritual, often both) exhaustion of those involved. But the open-endedness of experience does not end in (one) life. In a recent book, Dianne Rothleder reminds us that the motifs of *pleonexia* (unbound desire) and *hysteresis* (the historical inertia of objects) also inform the tragi-comic expectations of Shakespearean characters mediated by "interpretive choices" ("Introduction" to *Fraught Decisions*, xix). Cavell's corrected dialectic is akin to Simon Palfrey's confidence in the comprehensive exhaustion of semantic possibility within the standard Shakespeare trope. But, and this Palfrey's strong precursor, William Empson, abundantly proved in his philological action, just as there is no assurance for the beginning (givenness) of intuition, there is no end (revocation) for always-already-started tuition.

2

Discussing Kant's and Hegel's dialectical-transcendental penchant for "exalted categorial and speculative-logical philosophical concepts," Robert Brandom has recently argued that

> the best way to understand what they are saying about their preferred topic of concepts operating in a pure, still stratosphere above the busy jostling and haggling of street-level judging and doing is precisely to focus on what those metaconcepts lets us say about what is going on below: the clarifying perspective they provide on that messy, noisy spectacle.
>
> *Trust* 5

It is therefore not enough to record the "busy jostling and haggling of street-level judging and doing" that articulates the "messy, noisy spectacle" implied in Shakespearean drama. In order to perform a dialectical operation we must allow this spectacle to be unabashedly informed by speculative metaconcepts. This is why James Shapiro's naïve assumption that Shakespeare's was an "aural culture," its back turned on "printed books," and that the poet therefore found his real sources in the street "sounds reverberating around him" (*1599* 93) can be characterized as hopelessly undialectical.

A dialectical procedure involves therefore a great deal of speculative footwork, the constant reworking of premises in view of faulty logic or inadequate conclusion, and —*quod erat remonstrandum*— the open-ended retraction of retraction. Rinaldo's claim to the king encapsulates this sense of necessary error: "ma quel medesmo error che 'l suo germane / a morir trasse, a lui pon l'arme in mano" (*Orlando Furioso* v.84.5–6). This seeming aberration, which Hegel radicalized into an open-ended "positing of presuppositions" (Žižek, *Less* 98), became for Shakespeare an object of permanent fascination. According to A.D. Nuttall, he put it to good service in the three parts of *Henry VI*.[7] Portly English common-sense had a name for this abuse in Elizabethan time: Popish casuistry, or, more specifically, Jesuit equivocation. But Shakespeare use of it was never totally uncomplimentary: let me recall that Edgar is probably Shakespeare's most intelligent character. Cardinal Pandulph's precis of the dialectical procedure in *King John* reveals a virtuoso meta-mastery of near-Socratic diarrhesis. Doubtlessly, the Shakespeare eiron (the cynical smiling dog) pulls the strings of an argument that reads in retrospect like a Derridean parody of Searle's advocacy of speech-act intentionality:

> What since thou swor'st is sworn against thyself,
> And may not be performèd by thyself;
> For that which thou hast sworn to do amiss
> Is not amiss when it is truly done;
> And being not done where doing tends to ill,
> The truth is then most done not doing it.
> The better act of purposes mistook
> Is to mistake again; though indirect,
> Yet indirection thereby grows direct,
> And falsehood falsehood cures, as fire cools fire.
>   KING JOHN 3.1.194–203

Cavell's suggestion that "freedom for speculation" (20) was not quite available in Shakespeare's English histories is inaccurate. The above rhetorical delivery is, to be sure, a far cry from the ultra-subtle and arch-dense tropic undercurrents in *Antony and Cleopatra*, but it proves nothing if not freedom for wild—clammed and clumsy—speculation. To rank out *King John* as a premature exercise in Marlovian bombast is to ignore the limits of Marlowe's nondialectical

---

7   Nuttall argues, apropos of the rose-plucking contest in *1 Henry VI*, that "the apparent clarity of the event is involved in a spider's web of indefinite presuppositions that drain away the promised explanatory power" (30).

drama. The author of *Doctor Faustus* never reached Shakespeare's taste for original meta-reflective parody—the opening speeches of the German doctor are a rash schoolbook explosion of anti-doctrinal *refutatio*—nor was he ever capable of saving particular phenomena in the safely indirect way Shakespeare often resorts to. The author of *Love's Labour's Lost* is alive to this dialectic structure of knowledge, to the conception that nothing except the *undergoer*—the bedraggled *Untergeher* that boasts of having "gone here and there" (Sonnet 110.1)—gets actually lost in Sophia's labors, Venus's labors (*Venus and Adonis* 981), Hercules's labors (*Much Ado About Nothing* 2.1.736), or the Muse's labors (*Othello* 2.1.916); to the speculative notion that "truth kills truth" (*Midsummer* 3.2.129); and to the Marxian idea, also upheld by Derrida, that meaning is something *produced* (*Grundrisse* 81–93), the outcome of a certain "travail textuel" (Derrida, *Positions* 88–100). The rest (the manifold remainder) is always retained and found in the more or less piercing dignity of its insignificance. Only Prospero appears to believe his *labors* will come to an end (*The Tempest* 4.1.260), but this is just his closing delusion: his final plea to be relieved by prayer proves, among other things, the inability of the aesthetic to infuse redemptive closure into an ongoing dialectical circuit. David Bevington's claim that Shakespeare appears to "work his way through a dialectic of thesis and antithesis toward synthesis" (*Shakespeare's Ideas* 177) reveals a combination of hermeneutic impatience and inattention to irony. If Caliban remains in the island, a new Prospero will come to try, ineffectively, to absolve himself through him. If they all leave for Milan, the urb will soon be stormed into an island, and torment recommence. Shakespeare was not blind to the Platonic fact that, by piling transitory concepts (error) upon dispensable tropes (error), the eroticized ignorant in search of wisdom often forgets "to demand that truly which [he would] truly know" (*1 Henry IV* 1.2.4). Prospero and Hal stand therefore for the absolute statesman who is bound to look after "le *katholou*, la totalité, l'ensemble des affaires de la cité" (Castoriadis 61). They are cognizant, that is, of the sustaining force of the "totality of (surface) show [*Ganzes des Scheins*]" (Hegel, *Phenomenology* 87), of the dialectical "primacy of totality over phenomenality" (Adorno, *Negative* 303): in the truth-logic of the plays' plot the all-seeing sun (the unphenomenal fire) defeats the base contagious and curled clouds (*1 Henry IV*; 1.2.176; *The Tempest* 1.2.193).[8] And yet, this final sublation

---

8   It is important to note that Husserl's emphasis on totality, sometimes identified with infinity but often with indeterminacy (see the second Cartesian meditation), an emphasis that runs parallel to his interest in the notions of structure and horizon, is invariably neglected by a certain trend of French phenomenology (Levinas, Merleau-Ponty), more interested in intuition and immediate evidence.

does not invalidate the particular victory of food-and-drink-measured temporality over the icy rigor of mechanical time: Hal's necessity does not (cannot) overrule Falstaff's contingency and Prospero's "purpose" fails to wipe out "the particular accidents" of island life. Adorno rightly pointed out that Hegel destroyed the very mythology of "something first," that while nothing is given immediately, conceptual mediation (the Cardinal's "mistake") is there exclusively to allow experience to be grasped: good mediation does not predate bad immediacy. Both come into action (not being) simultaneously in the process of *Erfahrung* (experience): empirical observing, hearing, feeling, comes always within the territory of the concept, and this territory gets remapped as the process of experience pulls ahead. Thus, again the Cardinal, *indirection grows direct*. Likewise, the mere attested existence of "irrational actuality [*unvernünftigen Wirklichkeit*]" (Marx, *Critique* 64), admittedly the quarry for much phenomenology-inspired critical extravagation, doesn't completely rule out Hegel's claim that the rational is actual—*das Vernünftige wirklich ist* (Marx, *Critique* 64).[9] Only a discernible quota of rationality—Žižek and Badiou would say of "universality"—can turn contingent action into significant (polis-oriented) action. We may all agree that Hal's sun is but a deficient and unsavory symbolic resolution or reconciliation (*Versöhnung*) of the differential antagonisms that run through the conceptual tissue of the play, that it emerges as a makeshift unified concretization of dispersed meaning, a siphoning of beings into ersatz Being, as an instance, in short, of sham onto-theological modelling. And yet the ideas—the ideas, to be sure, of national union—of this mock-ruler will win battles, will win, that is, "the king's whole battle" (*1 Henry IV* 4.1.130). And these ideas are predicated upon totality. His world is the "whole state" (4.3.94) that troubles Hotspur's dreams of jointure: "Yet all goes well, yet all our joints are whole" (4.1.84). Yet this whole—that of the soldiers' bodies' and that of the nation's body—is never totally *given* in a play instigated and thwarted by perilous gashes (4.1.43), never fully available to actants for pragmatic engagement and virtual disposal, or to democratic citizens for sensible relocation. It is only given in an apperceptive, self-conscious, speculative-conceptual gesture (Pippin, *Hegel's Realm of Shadows* 101–138). The sun of this *Roi Soleil* may not be fully unphenomenal—as it betrays with moral-symbolic obscenity its allegorical cathexis—but his professed abstention from phenomenality helps to secure his position as a Shakespearean Ur-subject. We may dislike Hal's

---

9   Marx obviously alludes to the axiomatic statement in the "Preface" to the *Outlines of the Philosophy of Right*: "What is rational is actual and what is actual is rational" (14). Marx underestimates the potency of Hegel's working conjecture. No piece-meal irrational actuality can be detected without prior assumptions of totalizing rationality.

politics, even revile them as reactionary, but "what is at stake in emancipatory thought is almost always an overcoming of a mythical kind of thought and practice—combatting the myth(s) of the (unquestionably) given" (Ruda, "Marx in the Cave" 64). Hal's growing abstention from the men, women and things to which he was once, like the vile Bardolph, "altogether given over" (3.3.31), may not pave the way towards England's freedom, but it goes some way towards explaining *his* emancipation. Politics—Althusser and Foucault remind us—begins at home.

Shakespeare's comedies make room for a great deal of experience that is only partly, and only sometimes, atoned through the ceremonies of indirection. Some of his problem plays and tragedies are dialectically articulated as failed sublations of direct—deeply comic—experience: *Othello* and *King Lear* are rich comedies that get out of hand and degenerate into Christian erotic-sacrificial drama. Without discernible tragic conflict or absolving resolution, they are stories of disillusion and delayed revelation that culminate in the certitude of frailty, moral limitation, and finite knowledge. Some very perfect plays like *1 Henry IV* achieve near-complete "redemption" through the rather forced strategy of repressing comedy in the interests of political drama. Still, despite the transitory lapse into local gratification some of his history plays afford, the category "history play" is the one that best suits the totality of Shakespeare's plays—historical because no other rubric would do, or better, because *nothing else is*. Historical because, as Samuel Johnson noted, as they have no plans, they have no limits (*Selected* 269), whence the apt but implicit self-description of *Hamlet* as a "poem unlimited" (*Hamlet* 2.2.382).[10] Historical because, in the last instance, unbending to transcendence, even if locally possessed by the transcendental and prepossessed by totality: "I know you all" (*1 Henry IV* 1.3.173). Historical because although marked by tragic pathos in its subservience to heroic ideology and violent inscriptive eventuality—*the first time as high tragedy*—the relapse into grotesque bathos is never far off—*the second time as low farce* (Marx, *The Eighteenth Brumaire of Louis Bonaparte, Later Political Writings* 31). Historical because total, moving back and forth between the deliverances of the particular and the overarching rule of the general. According to Lukács

---

10 In the *Preface to Shakespeare* we read: "History was a series of actions, with no other than chronological succession, independent of each other, and without any tendency to introduce or regulate the conclusion. It is not always very nicely distinguished from tragedy. There is not much nearer approach to unity of action in the tragedy of *Antony and Cleopatra*, than in the history of *Richard the Second*. But a history might be continued through many plays; as it had no plan, it had no limits" (*Selected* 268).

only in this context which sees the isolated facts of social life as aspects of the historical process and integrates them in a *totality*, can knowledge of the facts hope to become knowledge of *reality*. This knowledge starts from the simple (and to the capitalist world), pure, immediate, natural determinants described above. It progresses from them to the knowledge of the concrete totality, i.e. to the conceptual reproduction of reality. This concrete totality is by no means an unmediated datum for thought.
        History and Class Consciousness 8

But although it may not be immediately given, the spell of totality enjoys a transcendental precedence over the field of particulars that unsettles Lukács' inferential schema. This precedence signals a dialectical caesura—the gap extending between the (ungiven) total and the (totally given) partial: *I know you all*. Adorno's spectacular effort at salvaging Hegelian *Erfahrung* (experience) from facile charges of idealism is not at odds with his famous pronouncement *Das Ganze ist das Unwahre*—"the whole is the false" (Adorno, *Minima Moralia* 50)—a variation of which is "the whole is the spell [*der Bann*]" (*Negative* 158; *Negative* 161). In his 1967 lecture on Goethe's *Iphigenia*, Adorno held that the dictum that art must again become nature is at the same time true and untrue. True because it reminds us that art must speak [*sprechen*] in the name of the repressed by any mode of dominium, including rational dominium. Untrue because such speech [*Sprache*] can only conceive itself in a rational manner [*rationale*], mediated by the totality of culture [*durch die Totalität von Kultur vermittelt*] (*Noten zur Literatur* IV, 10). *I know you all*. Awareness, however, of totality is no visa for saying anything or everything. It is rather a warning about the extent and intricacy of what we cannot say. One should not be afraid of resuscitating an old idealist ghost: the prince's boasting—"I know you all"—registers a level of cognitive attainment only conceivable within the context of what Jameson has aptly called "the persistence of the dialectic," and such mastery confirms Adorno's disclaimer that the totality is the lie. What the standard Shakespeare transcendental cogito—his official apperceptive center of consciousness (Hal, Iago, Hamlet, Prospero)—shows us is that in order to disown knowledge and give the lie to totality one must first hold and traverse—, however incompletely, *thas, thas, thas* (2 *Henry IV* 3.2.249)—the cognitive fantasy of totality.

    Derrida, who found it very hard to keep his pivotal notions—*différance, pharmakon, supplément, hymen*—away from the contamination of Hegel's "speculation dialectique" (*Positions* 56), described deconstructive renversement in terms strikingly similar to those commonly associated with Hegelian *Aufhebung*—as an *écart* which, via the prior deconstructive inversion of a sublimating or idealizing genealogy, facilitates the advent of precisely such excursive surplus, "l'émergence irruptive d'un nouveau 'concept,' concept de ce qui ne se laisse plus, ne s'est jamais laisse comprendre dans le régime antérieur" (*Positions* 57). The underlying logic here is akin to that of Badiou's construal of the event, but it is crucial to bear in mind that Derrida speaks solely of a conceptual—not ontic, and certainly not ontological—irruption. Humans are not vermin, but the minute Gloucester, prompted by Edgar's abject presence, is led "to think a man a worm" (*King Lear* 4.1.34) there is no return from such new conceptual breakthrough to the old familiar dispensation. We should never forget, however, that Gloucester's domestic regulation is fault-lined from the outset by Edgar, the "son by order of law" (*King Lear* 1.1.16), who is "no dearer" than the Bastard in the father's account and endeavors "to prevent the fiend, and to kill vermin" (*King Lear* 3.4.146). In his end (a king) is his beginning (a thing), the task of learning which is incumbent on the father.

3

Dialectic, Adorno recalls in an important essay on Hegel, is "the effort to conjoin reason's *critical* consciousness of itself and the *critical* experience of objects" ("Aspects of Hegel's Philosophy" in *Hegel: Three Studies*, 9–10; my emphases). The binding role of dialectical criticism emerges through a dual restriction whose ultimate unity is found in conceptual mediation. Dialectic preserves the distinct moments of the subjective and the objective while "grasping them as mediated by one another" (7). Mediation, in sum, "takes place in and through the extremes, in the extreme themselves" (9). Because beholden as an open method to the procurements of mediation, dialectic is not a closed ontology. Adorno speaks of a Kantian concept of mediation where a balance is sought between the priority of the subject and the otherness of a thing-in-itself standing behind the object (*Negative* 184). In *King Lear* it is Edgar, we are told, who is "the thing itself" (*King Lear* 3.4.97), and blind Gloucester stands at the opposite extreme of critical consciousness, seeing things "feelingly" (*King Lear* 4.6.145), that is to say, through the tentacular mediation of Q&A interlocution.

Hegel, we saw, rejected *raisonnement* as a vain discoursing over the glassy externality of things. Deprived of his glassy eyes, Gloucester is in no position to glide across externals. He must either work through his experience inferentially, conceptually, dialectically, or die. It is bad luck that his brief stage life should have compelled him to confer with two demons—one of them an equivocal monster (Edmund) and the other a genuine foul fiend (Edgar). He could also have died dialectically, which is what Lear, probably Kent, maybe the fool, will do. Following Hegel, Sartre sardonically enjoined that "il ne faut pas confondre le papillotement des idées avec la dialectique" (*Critique* 47). Unassisted by the conceptual light that only structured wholes and complex processes can cast on the historical thing, unaided by the hierarchical totalization of determinations and of hierarchical realities (*Critique* 48), ideological practices either slip into the butterfly *raisonnement* of thaumaturgic-mythic speculation—important sections of work by Heidegger, Benjamin, Arendt and Agamben are exactly that—or collapse in the dazzling witchery of one-to-one (concept-to-thing) reflection. The renunciation, conscious or not, to place critique under the sway of dialectical totality transforms the external concept into a (mystical, magical) idea. But neither ideas nor things are concrete enough grist to the mill wheel of theoretical work. Recall Sartre's irked behest: "les faits particuliers ne signifient rien, ne sont ni vrais ni faux tant qu'ils ne sont pas rapportés par la médiation de différentes totalités partielles à la totalisation en cours"(*Critique* 30). By virtue, however, of the phenomenological embargo, ideas and things find in this new scholarly work the means to complete their voyage to empirical-sensual immediacy and idealistic transparency. Still, what phenomenological scholars believe to see "as clear as is the summer's sun" (*Henry V* 1.2.86) is but an illusion of immediacy. Mediation only comes off under the rule of a dialectical totality, to the gaze, that is, of the "all-seeing sun" (*Romeo and Juliet* 1.2.92).

It is sight, more than any other sense, that makes us cognizant of what (where) we are not, of the factual existence and virtual complexity of what lies beyond the bound of our perceptual consciousness. If *toute conscience* is, with Merleau Ponty, *conscience perceptive* (*Phénoménologie* 452), then it is our eyes that keep reminding us of how limited and poor this *toute* may turn out to be—how insignificant, that is, in the face of the ever pre-given complex whole or "structure toujours-dejà-donnée" (Althusser, *Pour Marx* 172).[11] Indeed, as Macbeth one day discovers, "nothing is / But what is not" (*Macbeth* 1.3.140–41). And Helena growls at a power "that makes me see and cannot feed mine eye" (*All's Well That Ends Well* 1.1.204). Small wonder then that phenomenological critics should be particularly impatient with the ocular compulsion of structuralist and post-structuralist thought, for scopophilic circumspection both affords and evinces the drive to systemic totality they seem to have anxiously renounced in favor of "more urgent touches" (*Antony and Cleopatra* 1.2.164)

---

11   Jameson rightly accuses Merleau-Ponty's version of phenomenology of falling prey to non-reflexive strategies that favor either the uncritical monism of the *corps propre* (*Valences* 231; *Marxism and Form* 347–48) or a bland aesthetics of the Imaginary (*Ideologies* 104).

and "diversity of sounds" (*The Tempest* 5.1.237).¹² Deleuze's characterization of Foucault's special gift—"une puissance de voir qui était en rapport avec sa puissance d'écrire" (*Deux régimes de fous* 256)—duly recaps the worthiness of a theoretical outlook—the poststructuralist outlook—that remained faithful to the etymology of *theory* through its very compulsion to look out. By contrast, the phenomenological critic finds herself in the position of the *precise* and opportunist Angelo, who makes a big fuss over the first thing that comes his way while committing to darkness whatever he fails to see:

> The jewel that we find, we stoop and take't
> Because we see it, but what we do not see
> We tread upon and never think of it.
> *Measure for Measure* 2.1.24–26

But at least Angelo is not blind to his Puritan dissembling. The phenomenological scholar, by contrast, abandons herself ingenuously to the random discharges of contingency—"give it a plum, a cherry and a fig" (*King John* 2.1.162)—thus becoming "a feather for each wind that blows" (*The Winter's Tale* 2.3.154). What the arch-ocular critic—which I here identify to the very expert reader (Empson, Frye, Kermode, Bloom, Orgel, Goldberg, de Grazia) likely to hand over a fit *explication du texte*—can alternately boast of is, like Jacques, a maximal aptitude to register experience: "ROSALIND. Then to have seen much and to have nothing is to have rich eyes and poor hands. JACQUES. Yes, I have gained my experience" (*As You Like It* 4.1.23). These critics possess what Hegel called "the instinct of Reason" (*Phenomenology* 149). However elastic and self-conflicting, Hegel's reason also stands by the rule stipulated by Russell: "reason may be a small force, but it is constant, and works always in one direction" (*Sceptical Essays* 100). Perhaps it is relevant to point out that none of the critics I have mentioned is exclusively a Shakespeare scholar: their concept of experience—of reading experience—extends well beyond poaching in Arden forest, spitting in Rialto, fornicating in Vienna, dying in Egypt. Their readings of these Shakespearean experiences are mediated by other exegetic inroads and by the conceptual elaborations—the determinate negations— attendant therein. No doubt the resulting surplus in textual experience would render any appeal to totality, if they ever were tempted to make it, all the less embarrassing. They might "the globe [not] compass soon" (*A Midsummer Night's Dream*

---

12 For a discussion of the way in which eminent phenomenologists like Sartre and Merleau-Ponty resisted Husserl's qualified *ocularcentrism*, see Martin Jay, *Downcast Eyes*, 160–227.

4.1), but they do stand a chance of outdistancing the undiscerning. "There's more in him than shallow eyes can see" (*Hamlet* 11.165), says the Danish King, referring to his nephew, only in Q1.[13] But what, if anything, can *shallow eyes* see? Maybe they can skate the "surface of separation" between the self and the other that is, in Merleau-Ponty's estimate, also the place of their reciprocating union (*The Visible and the Invisible* 266), but the prince-with-the-eye-in-the-mind, and Lacan with him, would dismiss this solution to the problem of mind-reading and solipsism as a flagrant evasion: there is always more in him than bi-directional perceptual union may nose out, and that more is the gap *within*—Lyotard's *sublime*, Žižek's *abyss*—which *passes* phenomenal *show*. It is this gap that turns the coveted totality into what Sartre called a *detotalized totality* (*Critique* 78). The discredit of the concept of *totality* among contemporary literary scholars remains an obstacle to elementary understanding. Hugh Grady's contention that Adorno rejected Lukács' concept of totality in *Negative Dialectic* (*Shakespeare and Impure Aesthetics* 25) is a mistaken inference in an important book that, however, systematically occludes the power of rational conceptuality in favor of an aesthetic utopia. To enlist Benjamin for the advancement of such goal is a reasonable move. But Grady's persistent appeals to Adorno, and his construal of the Adorno-Benjamin rapport as a seamless intellectual partnership, strike me as strained and misguided. "Truth," Benjamin proudly stated, "does not enter into relationships [*tritt nie in eine Relation*]" (*Origin* 35; *Ursprung* 18). And this bid at epistemic absolution conceals a moral drive for daily, hourly, messianic atonement that in *Measure for Measure* receives the name of *foul redemption* (*Measure for Measure* 2.4.114). But Shakespeare never accepts this throwaway solution to the problem of experience. To court deliverance through unrelated truths is to throw the baby out with the bathwater. The thing Shakespeare in conjunction with his idea, whatever that is, get lost in the bankrupt assertion of immediate truths. Many Third Series Arden Introductions to Shakespeare plays, and many of the brief introductory essays in the Norton Shakespeare (Maus's are an important exception) are exactly that: a toxic blending of drab factual opulence (bad facts) and moral correction (affable ideas) with no effort at dialectical mediation, i.e. at placing concepts or texts under the transitory jurisdiction of relational totalities.

---

13   I use Ann Thomson's and Neil Taylor edition of Q1.

4

Not all the mannerisms of phenomenology—its crazed attempt to reconcile object donation and logical essentialism, its shopworn epistemology of evidence, its veneration of immediacy, its craving for the sensorial—are imputable to Husserl. Still, he is to blame for much of the smoke. Gadamer and Habermas remind us, for one, that it was Heidegger who managed to replace the phenomenological model of description of perceptions with a hermeneutic model of interpretation (*Auslegung*) of texts ("Foreword to the second edition," *Truth and Method* 32–33; *Wahrheit und Rechtfertigung* 83)—and it is this perfected model that seems to have vanished in neo-phenomenological work.[14] Julia Lupton's recent book, *Shakespeare Dwelling* is a case in point. Not only does she implicitly embrace a grassroots version of phenomenological description—the author describes lavishly all sorts of things (temple-haunting martlets, Warden pies, fishing nets) but she makes explicit phenomenological commitments at the very outset: "I build the concept of dwelling from mixed materials that include phenomenology, modern design theory, Renaissance husbandry and housekeeping, and scripture and theology" (5). Obviously, phenomenology and modern design theory, the only two non-period "materials" included in the list, take some sort of precedence over the rest as higher-order methodological-theoretical frames. In the hands of Lupton, moreover, phenomenology ultimately becomes little more than design theory, what Zahavi calls "picture-book phenomenology." She professes to draw on Heidegger's "phenomenological attention to the continuum of building and dwelling" (7), and supplements this philosophical legacy with Arendt's attempt "to restore action as the domain proper to both politics and drama" (7). The book thus "addresses [...] moments in which [Shakespeare's] plays frame the condition of action in object worlds and built environments" (7–8). One is reminded of Kant's architectonic conception of space in the third *Critique*: "Space, in Kant as in Aristotle, is a house in which we dwell more or less safely, or more or less poetically, on this earth" (de Man, *Aesthetic* 81). But this Kantian *Augenschein*, de Man rightly implies, is hindered by its own materiality to apportion a sense of human-nature interpenetration and dwelling: the vast all-embracing vault (*ein weites Gewölbe*) (*Critique of Judgement* 130), for instance, meant little to

---

14 See also in Gadamer, *Truth and Method*, 271–272. The Heideggerian transformation of the sense of the phenomenological method has already been mentioned in the previous section, but remember that "der methodische Sinn der phänomenologischen Deskription ist Auslegung" (*Sein und Zeit* 37).

Hamlet. But neo-phenomenological scholars seldom turn to the Danish prince for arguments of authority. Don't blame them.

The Husserlian resonance of Lupton's argument is clear: from *Dingwelt* to *Umwelt*. She conceives of dwelling as Merleau-Ponty of the human body, as a "champ de presence primordial" (121) or an "horizont latent de notre expérience, présent sans cesse [...] avant toute pensée déterminante" (122). Yet despite a declarative positioning laden with overt *phenomenological* implications, the scholar neither mentions Husserl nor cites any of his works. Lupton only mentions Merleau-Ponty, and quotes only twice from the "Introduction" to *Phénoménologie de la perception*. Are these two allusions and the brief reference to Heidegger's short essay "Bauen Wohnen Denken" sufficient motive to place your book under the credit of "phenomenological attention"? Well, in the economy of prodigal name-dropping and frugal philosophical debit that organizes the field, it is more than enough. To be sure, quoting philosophers is no evidence that you have read them and understood them. But it is very difficult to understand them if you don't read them, and you can only show you have done so if you either 1) internalize their thought so powerfully that it shows in whatever you do or say or 2) you actually take the trouble to quote them. Neither option transpires in this book with respect to phenomenology. The same occurs with deconstruction. Many card-carrying deconstructive critics know very little about Derrida's work, and it is very rare to find deconstructive work where the author's internalization of the theoretical sources is so keen that it can dispense with even mentioning it. The only such case that I know of is Sedgwick's extraordinary *Between Men*, written by "a deconstructive and very writerly close reader" (xvii) who doesn't even care to type the name of the French philosopher.

To return to Lupton, the problem with her "phenomenological" approach is that it is indeed, like all phenomenological work, disturbingly undialectical. Žižek exemplarily marked out this problem when he argued, in overt rebuttal of object-oriented ontologies and assemblage theory, that "the vision of 'democracy of objects' where all objects occupy the same ontological standing, or the 'inhuman' view of an assemblage deployed by Jane Bennett, are only possible from the standpoint of an (empty) subject" (*Reading Marx* 58). The phenomenological refusal, in short, to take stock of the "cuts and inconsistencies in the field of phenomena" (59) reflects a deeper unwillingness to welcome a *sujet barré* (Lacan), a (barred) subject driven to inscribe itself in the sites marked by the cuts and inconsistencies: recall that an *empty subject* is not exactly an *emptied subject*. For phenomenological readers, Lupton included, nothing appears to *inconsist* in the all-seeing plenitude of Shakespeare's phenomenal dramaturgy: the empty subject called "Shakespeare" image-thinks an embodied world that is, in turn, *given* (*gegeben*) to us, spectators as the object—the very tangible *Ding*—of our thought-imagination.[15] Never was the idiom *food for thought* so fittingly deployed. There would be nothing wrong, in principle, in proclaiming that ontological plenitude ought to be the conjectural starting point for phenomenological-hermeneutic work in the Shakespeare corpus, in assuming, for instance, that "nature (or being) is as full as an egg" (Jameson *Valences* 37) and in moving on to prove such claim on the evidence, say, of *King Lear* 1.4.125–149:

FOOL   [...] Give me an egg, nuncle, and I'll give thee two crowns.
KING LEAR. What two crowns shall they be?
FOOL.   Why, after I have cut the egg i' the middle, and eat up the meat, the two crowns of the egg. When thou clovest thy crown i' the middle, and gavest away both parts, thou borest thy ass on thy back o'er the dirt: thou hadst little wit in thy bald crown, when thou gavest thy golden one away. If I speak like myself in this, let him be whipped that first finds it so.

Singing

Fools had ne'er less wit in a year;
For wise men are grown foppish,
They know not how their wits to wear,
Their manners are so apish.
    King Lear 1.4.136–147

But none of Shakespeare's undialectical critics seems fit for the job. They overlook the arbitrary autonomy of the signifier-container—Lacan's *instance de la lettre*—the allegorical destination, the figural force. They are all too busy eating up the meat they have been prodigally *given* by the bard's delegate—foppish,

---

15   But Lupton is a scholar of diversified talents and multiple resources. The dialectical reader of *After Oedipus* and typological reader and text-bound hermeneut of *Citizens-Saints* was much more aware of—or simply more interested in—scriptural inconsistency. In the former book, written with Kenneth Reinhard, the reader bumps into a description of a mode of "criticism of the residual" to which my book fully subscribes: "a criticism that tracks the obdurate remainders of dialectical symbolization in the structures of culture, history, and tradition, and criticism as precisely the remainder of those literary and linguistic operations" (*After Oedipus* 4).

apish Lear—to pay due attention to the empty cloven shell. The phenomenal positivity they strive to retrieve from Shakespeare's dramatic worlds (the white, the yolk) is *without* "dialectical intensity" (Jameson, *Valences* 39). What we witness in this Lear passage, and in so many others that could be chosen at random in scenes where the Fool or Edgar are present, is "a reduction from symbolic feeling to mere words, [...] a loss of pathos, of theatricality" (de Man, *Aesthetic* 123), along with an upsurge of verbal-speculative energy. Failure to register it, or reluctance to valorise it, is a critical shortcoming. This flaw may also be common in flat Deleuzian readings of Shakespearean dramaturgy, but at least Deleuze and Guattari, who were rarely un-intense, would not have recoiled from celebrating, with the Fool, that apes (not only certain men) are also apish (*King Lear* 1.4.147), i.e. "stupid, imitative" according to the Norton edition annotation. The fact that this platitude is anathema to posthumanist positivism makes it all the more amenable to dialectical appropriation (more on apes and chimpanzees in section 15). The constant animalist derogation of Lear is significant because it is pitted against Stoic-sceptical meta-humanist divagations like the following "When we are born, we cry that we are come / To this great stage of fools" (*King Lear* 4.6.176–177). That the person who is able to argue in this way can be described as being less than a fool, and little more than a beast (an ass or snail), betrays an ironic intensity only Socratic dialectics and its literary progeny (Menippean satire, Medieval carnival, Christian comedy) can afford.

CHAPTER 11

The Maladies of Abstinence

No More Cakes and Ale

1

In *Différance et repetition* Deleuze argues that the phenomenon of difference is never captured in phenomenology because this science deals exclusively with phantoms: "toute la Phénoménologie est une épiphénoménologie" (74). For other thinkers, phenomenology is little more than Platonic mysticism in disguise.[1] True enough, "le tournant théologique de la phénoménologie," piloted by thinkers like Levinas and Ricoeur, only confirmed a strain that was there from the beginning, waiting to be actualized.[2] Thus, for instance, when Husserl writes *reduction* Benjamin reads *redemption*: "phenomena (*die Phänomene*) do not, however, enter into the realm of ideas whole, in their crude empirical state (*in ihrem rohen empirischen Bestande*), adulterated by appearances, but only in their basic elements, redeemed (*gerettet*)" (*The Origin of German Tragic Drama* 33). Redemption, we know, is a strong motif in Adorno's writing, and he probably drew it from his older friend. But even if he granted that "the need to lend a voice to suffering is the condition of all truth" (*Negative* 17), he never actually went down the path of irrational asceticism often taken by Benjamin. The *Einklammerung* (bracketing) or *Auschaltung* (disconnection) Benjamin redescribed is not unlike the "foul redemption" (*Measure for Measure* 2.4.114) Angelo proposes to Isabella, a bargain that certainly leaves no one (Angello, Isabella, Claudio) any "[freer] from touch or soil" (*Measure for Measure* 5.1.140). Benjamin hoped to have it both ways, to flutter between the nunnery (the constellated ideas) and the brothel (empirical reality), the better to bring about "the salvation (*Bergung*) of phenomena in ideas" (*Origin* 32). Marina's doubtful *salvation*—"save poor me, the weaker" (*Pericles* 4.1.86)—from the material comforts of "profit" (4.2.110) rehearses a parallel confusion. In his early article on "Husserl and the Problem of Idealism," Adorno characterizes Husserl's equivalent

---

1 Fredric Jameson has some intelligent things to say about Adorno's indebtedness to Benjamin's notion of *constellation*, a notion that is overdetermined with mystical overtones: *Late Marxism*, 53.
2 In his essay on Ricoeur, Alain Badiou evokes this apt phrase by Dominique Janicaud: *L'aventure*, 81.

scheme to "reduce the world to either the factual or the essence" to the position of Baron Münchhausen, "who tried to drag himself out of the swamp by his own pigtail" (11)—but even the ass knows "when the cart draws the horse" (*King Lear* 1.4.215). Something similar, and similarly impractical, is what phenomenological readers of Shakespeare now intend. To put it in the Marxian jargon of base and superstructure that Shakespeare would have endorsed, these critics are "too noble to conserve a life / in base appliances" (*Measure for Measure* 3.1.86–87). Let me insist: their Shakespeare things are neither things nor concepts. For one, their unseemly call *to the things themselves* hides a squeamish withdrawal from the bog, the quagmire (*King Lear* 3.4.53), and the standing pool (*King Lear* 3.4.123). A latent prudishness directs their compensatory efforts at footloose material feasting: let us *touch* and *soil* the *thing Shakespeare* (his bodies, food, furniture, garments) now that the ban is lifted, and yet let us at the same time save this "thing enskied and sainted" (*Measure for Measure* 1.4.33) from the adulterating appearance of concepts. Let us save him, in short, from *theory*. Let us celebrate the "flat ontology" of his worlds.[3] And yet let us do it as if rationally and through the right (empirical) concepts. The sweeping avidity of the phenomenological critic bespeaks an epistemic-critical insolvency whose lemma is "More particulars / Must justify my knowledge" (*Cymbeline* 2.4.77–78). But as McDowell has astutely urged, "calling something to which spontaneity does not extend 'a concept,' and calling the linkage 'rational,' is fraudulent labelling: in effect, labelling a mere *exculpation* a *justification*, in the vain hope that it could make it be one" (*Mind* 20; emphases added). Thus exculpating Shakespeare means taking complete stock of his empirical cargo—spontaneously earning his Given. Including the victuals. And this way we are treated, for example, to a *Culinary Shakespeare*, whose bourgeois distance from real thought was mutatis mutandis evoked by Brecht:[4]

> The bourgeoisie was obliged to liquidate its purely intellectual exertions in a period when the pleasures of thinking were likely to involve immediate risks for its economic interests. Where thought was not completely turned off, it became even more culinary [*immer kulinarisches*]. Use was still made of the classics, but an ever more culinary use [*nur mehr kulinarischen Gebrauch*].
> qtd. in JAMESON, *Brecht and Method* 37

---

3 In his pointed critique of assemblage theory, Žižek accuses its practitioners of advocating a flat ontology (*Reading Marx* 46).
4 See *Culinary Shakespeare: Staging Food and Drink in Early Modern England*, an edited collection that contains essays by Karen Raber and Julia Reinhard Lupton.

One is also reminded of the radical Wilhelm Weitling's advocacy of uniform clothing and communal eating, dismissed by Marx as "barrack's communism" (qtd. by Claeys, *Marx and Marxism*, 36). A gentrified version of this communism pops up in Lupton's essay on the role dessert plays in the Shakespearean dramaturgy of dwelling:

> What engages me, however, are not castles of sugar but, rather, the way in which dessert constitutes a final act in the sequence of the meal, opening a space in which renewed forms of social, gustatory, and environmental encounter can take place. Although I am interested in the politics of sugar, my focus is not on sugar's racial and imperial history but, rather, on the role of dessert in crafting spaces of disclosure, encounter, and digestive reflection.
> *Shakespeare Dwelling* 200

This flashy appeal to *digestive reflection* is of a piece with the deeply anti-dialectical drive to construe the scene of thought as one of contained empirical assimilation. To style this scene *phenomenological* is only partly accurate, as we will see in a moment. What is undeniable is that the mere postulation of a digestive mode of reflection, of sugar or any other substance, a possibility writ large upon the academic archives of early modern physiological materialists (Gail Kern Pastern to Drew Daniel), suggests "an instinctive self-repression of real thought, on an all-too-knowing turning away from anything that might lead you to unpleasant truths" (Jameson, *Brecht* 37). The unpleasant truths, that is, of dialectical antagonism. Indeed nothing illustrates better "the stagnating assumptions of 'Post-theory'" (Grady 38) than this appeal to digestive reflection.

So much of what passes today for cutting-edge Shakespeare criticism is driven by the ornamental impulse that made the sentimental Victorians contrive things like *A Choice of Shakespeare's Verse for Bird-Watchers*, or *The Food of Love: Morsels from Shakespeare*. These are indeed forms of doing and dwelling with Shakespeare. By contrast, knowing Shakespeare has been discarded as a profitless venture in the economy of current academic production. After all, anyone—including toddlers—can boast of a "politics of sugar" or of "knowledge by acquaintance" (Sellars, "Empiricism" 256): who doesn't *know* Shakespeare?[5]

---

5 For anyone interested in a real "politics of sugar," I strongly recommend Fernando Ortiz's extraordinary essay, *Contrapunto cubano del tabaco y el azúcar* (1940).

The task of knowing his works has been replaced by the call to sense him—to touch and taste his sugared sonnets—to feel and collect his things. And this, let me insist, is a reactionary call. As early as 1929, Heidegger critiqued those who "invoke a turn to the Object—a turn which is praised again today all too noisily and with all too little understanding of the problem" (*Kant and the Problem of Metaphysics* 51). Indeed, so "little" is today's understating of the problem that the scholars who all too noisily respond to the invocation no longer speak of *objects*: they have reverted to the sensible, to affects, to empirical *things*. Let me recall, in passing, that Adorno's utopian redemption of particulars was always presided by the dialectical proviso that the particular is either an *object* to a subject or *is not*.[6] Nothing else is. What is amiss in the critical display of such fastidious miscellany of creaturely exotica (bodies, food, furniture, garments) is the scorn of structural totality that alone makes it possible. But "no philosophy can paste the particulars into the text (*die Einzeldige in die Texte kleben*), as seductive paintings would hoodwink it into believing" (Adorno, *Negative* 11). A compulsive reader of Wittgenstein, Ingeborg Bachmann was well aware that "injections of reality [*Injektionen von Wirklichkeit*]" (*Malina* 76) were useless without a conceptual prescription anticipating and predetermining *all* of reality—the totality of facts (*die Gesamtheit der Tatsachen*) unfolding in logical space (*im logischen Raum*) (*Tractatus* 1.1 and 1.13). Roland Barthes believed he was quoting Nietzsche to the effect that "one must lose respect for the whole" (*The Neutral* 64), but he was actually, via Deleuze, misrepresenting the source. What Deleuze cited in his Nietzsche book was: "Il faut émietter l'univers, perdre le respect du tout" (*Nietzsche* 26), and this loss of respect is coterminous, if not identical, with the eagerness to understand it, because, at bottom, Deleuze avers, "rien n'existe en dehors du tout" (26). Therefore, abstinence of the world of facts is not phenomenology's grossest offense. The real crime is to suspend a presumption of the whole, and this presumption is nothing if not conceptual. What is bracketed in the *epoché* is also, then, a dialectical conception of totality whose specificity Žižek never overlooks:

---

6 Schweppenhäuser glosses Adorno's despair as follows: "even natural things, lacking both thought and subjectivity, must be judged according to the criteria of moral truth and falsity. In the total insanity of unfolding public events, not only objectified humans but even objects themselves are robbed of their right to exist, reduced to mere material for an alien project" (*Theodor W. Adorno* 19). I want to retain the gesture that puts the abrogation of objectivity in favor of non-dialectical claims to materiality at the service of the new courts of moral truth and falsity, for this gesture remains very much at work in current Shakespeare studies.

THE MALADIES OF ABSTINENCE 301

> Totality is not a seamless Whole (...) it is by definition stitched or (...) sutured (...) it is not just that totality is split, traversed by antagonism; antagonism is what holds totality together (...) 'totality' is not an ideal of an organic Whole, but a critical notion—to 'locate a phenomenon in its totality' does not mean seeing the hidden harmony of the Whole, but includes in a system all its distortions ("symptoms," antagonisms, inconsistencies) as its integral part.
>
> Reading Marx 43–44

It is this *critical notion* of an antagonistic totality that serves my purpose in this book, as a memory of what gets lost in phenomenological *raisonnement*. The corresponding gain, the phenomenological scholar would expostulate, lies in the power to "locate a phenomenon in its totality." And the origin of this power they trace back to the phenomenological reduction or *epoché*—where, to their minds, a supposedly contained and harmonious totality is placed at hand for engaged spectatorship or critical inspection. But this is a misconstruction. In what follows I am going to examine three related misrepresentations: first, Bruce Smith's erroneous retroactive reading of Heideggerian *Zuhandenheit* into Husserlian *Vorhandenheit*, which allegedly paves the way to phenomenological bracketing; second, Bruce Smith's wrong interpretation of *epoché* as framing; and third, Sanford Budick's misreading of the Husserlian conception of what remains of the *now* in the wake of *epoché*. Finally, let me recall that these three episodes of misreading occur in essays intended to understand Shakespeare.

2

In *Phenomenal Shakespeare*, Bruce Smith argues that Husserl speaks of the "world-at-hand" and quotes from sections 27 and 28 of Husserl's *Ideas*. "The world 'at hand,' the world of things and people," Smith glosses, "is always present in its teeming plenitude. It is the always-present ground out of which figures emerge, the ground against which figures come to be known" (22). Note that he uses quotation marks for the prepositional phrase "at hand," implying that it is Husserl's own expression. As it turns out, if we check the edition of *Ideas I* used by Smith, which features Kersten's translation, we never find the phrase "at hand." What we find, in a passage where Husserl shifts the argument from spatial to temporal horizons, is the phrase "on hand":

> What is the case with the world as existing in the order of the spatial present, which I have just been tracing, is also the case with respect to its *order in the sequence of time*. This world, *on hand* for me now and manifestly in every waking Now, has its two-sidedly infinite temporal horizon, its known and unknown, immediately living and lifeless past and future.
>
>   *Ideas I* 52; emphasis added

Later, fusing both horizons in a sort of continuum for the waking consciousness:

> In my waking consciousness I find myself in this manner at all times, and without ever being able to alter the fact, in relation to the world which remains one and the same, though changing with respect to the composition of its contents. It is continually "on hand" for me and I myself am a member of it. Moreover, this world is there for me not only as a world of mere things, but also with the same immediacy as a world of objects with values, a *world of goods, a practical world*. (53)

The *world on hand* in both cases translates the same German phrases "für mich vorhandene Welt," "für mich 'vorhanden'" (*Ideen* 49–50). Boyce Gibson's translation gives us "this world now present to me" and "'present' for me" (*Ideas I* 52, 53). Evidently, Husserl here paves the way to Heidegger's more radical distinction between the handiness (*Zuhandenheit*) of things-to-hand and the presence (*Vorhandenheit*) of things-on-hand, coupled with the path-breaking conception of the *zuhanden* as the useful and instrumental (*Being and Time* 69–74). Thus in Husserl's work the *vorhanden*, which should always be translated as *on-hand*, is subordinated to a distant, contemplative, theoretical and ultimately proprietorial-acquisitive—note the terms "goods" and "values"—attitude of the witness-position (the seer-knower). This is the very contemplative attitude that Heidegger will later re-determine contrastively.

The first reference to *Vorhandenheit* (presence-at-hand) in Heidegger's *Sein und Zeit* occurs in the second chapter of the Introduction, when he describes λέγειν (and νοεῖν) as "the simple apprehension of something objectively present in its sheer objective presence [*Vorhandenheit*]" (24). The objectivity of this presence rests on its amenableness to a mode of distant ocular perception akin to the aseptic grasping of theoretical apprehension (*theorein*) or commercial acquisition. By contrast, *Zuhandenheit*, translated as *handiness* (Stambough) or *readiness-to-hand* (Macquarrie & Robinson), names the mode of being of things that are useful, that is, instrumentally liable to human dealing (*Umgang*): "We shall call the useful thing's kind of being in which it reveals itself by itself handiness (readiness-to-hand) [*Die Seinsart von Zeug, in der es sich von ihm selbst her offenbart, nennen wir die Zuhandenheit*]" (*Sein und Zeit* 69). To grasp better the difference between *Vorhandenheit* and *Zuhandenheit*, let me quote this brief passage from the second translation:

> Only because equipment has this 'Being-in itself' and does not merely occur, is it manipulable in the broadest sense and at our disposal. No matter how sharply we just look [*Nur-noch-hinsehen*] at the "outward appearance" ["*Aussehen*"] of Things in whatever form this takes, we cannot discover anything ready-to-hand. If we look at Things just "theoretically," we can get along without understanding readiness-to-hand. (98)

Thus the theoretical outlook reifies the *vorhanden* into an objectivity that cannot properly account for Dasein's knowledge of his own being as being-already-alongside-the-world (*Schon-sein-bei-der-Welt, Sein und Zeit* 61), as being *in* the world, concerned about the world, interested in the world, willing to interact with it. It is very unlikely that Smith's construal of the man-world interaction or entwining should go all the way to accommodating functional or technical instrumentalization—Adorno's and Horkheimer's stigmatization of functional reason (*Verstand*) met little obstacles in the California of the sixties. But Heidegger's backwoods jargon of hammers, nails, and wood may have appealed to the haptic turn of Smith's phenomenal imagination, where hands and handy objects play a prominent role. This may explain his readiness to wrongly conflate Husserl's plain spectatorial presence (*Vorhandenheit*) with Heidegger's pragmatic handiness (*Zuhandenheit*).

Thus through misquotation Smith underhandedly reads Heidegger's contrastive analytical development into Husserl's early formulation. To update Husserl in a de-transcendentalizing direction is no easy task, but Smith is resolved: "In Husserl's mind (and in the minds of Martin Heidegger, Maurice Merleau-Ponty, and later phenomenologists) the natural world presents itself in the here-and-now" (22). Smith would be sad to know that Husserl cared intellectually very little about the here-and-now natural world. Actually, he even suggested that, to maximize the true thinking of the true, we would do well in feigning the downright inexistence of the natural world. Anyway, the concept of the "world-at-hand" becomes the pivotal notion in Smith's book. He proposes "three basic paradigms" for "experiments in historical phenomenology" and argues that each of them involves a psychological subject set within what Husserl calls "the world at hand":

The physical dimensions, temporal reach, and content of these worlds at hand will vary, of course, according to the main variable, the psychological subject, to wit:
  author ↔ world-at-hand (phenomenology of transcription)
  characters ↔ world-at-hand (phenomenology of representation)
  reader/sensor ↔ world-at-hand (phenomenology of reception) (31)

The notion is later taken up, and conveniently activated, in each of the three hermeneutic exercises that make up the practical section of the book. I will not dispute the elegance of this conceptual pattern, placed in a book that is distinguished by philological acuity, expository gracefulness, and a constant sense of balance. What I dispute is the pertinency of the theoretical framework. I am now considering the erratic use of notion "world-at-hand," but something could also be said about "psychological subject" as a very inadequate choice of phrase, considering that Husserl sought to adapt his meditations to Cartesian parameters, and that in neither case (Descartes, Husserl) is the psychological subject an operative variable. The most salient attitude that Descartes and Husserl share is their animus against psychological realities and psychological explanations. Obviously, the reader may protest, my criticism concerns minor terminological objections: if we see through them, then the hermeneutic proposal makes good sense. Well, I beg to differ. Smith presents his book as a kind of manifesto—it is actually published in the "Blackwell Manifestos" series—and it is therefore to be read as one in a set of "timely interventions" designed to "address important concepts and questions" for "readers interested in ongoing debates and controversies in the humanities and social sciences." Maybe the generic pressure of the manifesto format drove Smith to theoretical negotiations for which he was not fit, but this explanation ignores the polemical theoretical verve that characterizes his work elsewhere. All in all, his controversies come down to a primeval strife: Smith *morally* wishes to uphold the purchase that the body-body continuum—as opposed to the body-mind discontinuum—had on Renaissance art, including Shakespeare's poems and playtexts. The strife results in the antagonistic impulse to disown epistemologies and ontologies intent on keeping the mind-body divide open. If I italicize *morally* it is because his opposition to rationalism rests less on argumentative evidence (speculative or empirical) than on implicit grounds of moral superiority: it is better for the reader to read Shakespeare his way, he presumes, not so much because Shakespeare meant it to be read that way or because his reading strategy is theoretically better grounded in sound philosophical principles but rather because his way is, well, the best way—the way that takes into account the value of feeling and experience. It is, therefore, the moral authority of the scholar clad as *the man of feeling* (Mackenzie) that legitimates his hermeneutic task. Let me insist: I have no objection to that. In fact, Smith's remarkable philological and aesthetic sensibility leads him to a number of interesting apercus, some of which obtain a temporary theoretical shimmer—I am thinking of the fascinating near-neo-historicist, tendentially Foucaldian, comparison between Coke's legal determination of penetration in cases of rape and the figuration of penetration in Shakespeare's *Venus and Adonis*, and the brilliant analysis of gender fluidity in this same poem. Smith could have simply proceeded, in both cases, in the predictable theoretical direction, in a mode of analysis congenial to Greenblatt or Sedgwick. But, even when he momentarily goes down the trodden path, he always returns to his framing "phenomenological" argument: the "entwining" of human subjects with plants and animals (128), the idea that "carnal knowledge [of the material world-at-hand] is located, not *in* the body or *on* the body or inside the body, but *between* the body and the world-at-hand" (131). And this return to the framing argument is done in a deliberate spirit of opposition to alternative rationalist suggestions of reading that could possibly crop up at each step. One example of this is his observation that "William Shakespeare as Author's Venus does not need Lacan to tell her about the interchangeability among orifices and between orifices and wounds" (113). Well, the fact is that Smith's reading would have greatly profited from an enhanced attention to the correlation between the Freudian concern with castration and the figuration of female genitalia as absence (nothing) and the Lacanian connected investment on the loss of the phallus, the emptiness of the subject, and the floating signifier. The fact that he describes a detail in Jacob Matham's painting *Venus and Adonis* (1600), as a "discreet but curiously stiff fold that covers her vagina" (95) brings home the complexity of the issue, as what the fold covers is the vulva, not the vagina, the former being the female sex organs that are outside the body, and the latter, the vagina, being a canal that leads from the uterus to the external opening of the genital canal. A vagina is an empty canal "covered" by the inside flesh of the female body. It can be penetrated, but not *covered* anew. My point may seem as ridiculously superfluous as the prude fold that ignites the discussion. But Smith is at his best when reminding us of the (etymological) significance of the seemingly superfluous words (*like, cod, wound, bower, penetrate*) within a figurative economy that, while it fails to oppose inward to outward, emptiness to plenitude, mind to body, owes its existence to the structural nothingness of words. The coda is a rationalist-dialectical lesson that was never lost on Lacan. Nor on Shakespeare, for whom one could simply never do (let alone ado) much about *nothing*—with "'nothing' [suggesting] the female genitals (often linked to the shape of a zero)" (Greenblatt's note to *Hamlet* 3.2.105).[7]

3

Let me remind the reader of what is left out (suspended, bracketed, disconnected) when the *epoché* is accomplished:

> In the first place, it goes without saying that with the suspending of the natural world, physical and psychological, all individual objectivities which are constituted through the functional activities of consciousness are suspended—all varieties of cultural expression, works of the technical and of the fine arts, of the sciences also (so far as we accept them as cultural facts and not as validity-systems), aesthetic and practical values of every shape and form. Natural in the same sense are also realities of such kinds as state, moral custom, law, religion.
> *Ideas I* §56, 110–111

This reads like a modernist rerun of Hobbes' account of the "condition" of war, a memorable passage ending with the notation that there would be "no society."[8] Husserl wraps up his consideration with a very similar exclusion: "Human being as natural being and as person in personal association, in that of 'society,' is excluded; likewise every other animate being" (*Ideas I* 132). This strict ablution is the *epoché*. Is Smith ready to let the cogito forgo all of those things—the natural world, the psychophysical world, and society? I think not. But why does he turn then to Husserl's idea of reduction or bracketing? Very simple: because he misunderstands it, wrongly reading into it a notion (visual framing) that suits his interpretive interests.

Let me insist: *Phenomenal Shakespeare* is credited to be the most solid attempt at readdressing the stakes implied in reading a Shakespeare text along theoretical lines freshly drawn from pure phenomenological sources like Husserl and Merleau-Ponty. The first two chapters of the book, devoted to *As*

---

7 For Os and zeros in *Hamlet*, see Royle, *Hélène Cixous*, 169–170.
8 Hobbes: "In such condition there is no place for Industry; because the fruit thereof is uncertain: and consequently no Culture of the earth; no Navigation, nor use of the commodities that may be imported by Sea; no commodious Building; no Instruments of moving and removing such things as require much force; no Knowledge of the face of the Earth; no account of Time; no Arts; no Letters; no Society" (*Leviathan* 186).

You Like It and the Sonnets, make use of Husserl's ideas. Unfortunately, as we have already noted, this use is characteristically heedless and superficial. The frisky ambiguity of the title is therefore undercut by his misrepresentation of what Husserlian phenomenology actually is about, and this misreading is particularly notorious when it comes to putting to use the notion of the phenomenological reduction (*epoché*), which Smith understands as the *framing* of a particular section of a human being's experience of the ambient world—be it really perceived or simply imagined. By framing he means, like defamiliarization in Shklovksy's theory, a kind of "attention-giving" (22) technique that allows us to see better a determinate portion of our experienced reality. The Husserl passage he cites to instantiate his view of *epoché* is taken from *Ideas I* §27, in F. Kersten's translation. I reproduce below the section of the passage he quotes, but use Boyce Gibson's translation instead:

> I am aware of the world, spread out in space endlessly, and in time becoming and become, without end. I am aware of it, that means, first of all, I discover it immediately, intuitively. I experience it [...] I can let my attention wander from the writing-table I have just seen and observed, through the unseen portions of the room behind my back to the verandah, into the garden, to the children in the summer-house, and so forth, to all the objects concerning which I precisely "know" that they are there and yonder in my immediate surroundings—a knowledge which has nothing of conceptual thinking in it, and first changes into clear intuiting with the bestowing of attention, and even then only partially and for the most part very imperfectly. (51–52)

According to Smith, "what Husserl attempts here is a step-by-step *framing* of experience that begins with himself as a first-person observer and moves outward by degrees into the ambient world" (20; emphasis added). This gradual framing, he adds, marks the difference between Husserl and his nefarious precursor: "Where Descartes looks inward, Husserl looks outward" (20). This oracular statement is merely hilarious, considering the outward-looking experimental drive of Descartes' research of light, body movement, meteors and earth phenomena, and Husserl's sedentary study-room habits. But my concern here is with Smith's decision to call "framing" what Husserl calls the "Zuwendung der Aufmerksamkeit"—"the advertence of attention" (Kersten) or "bestowing of attention" (Gibson). The equivalence is reiterated: "By *turning attention* to this or that aspect, Husserl *frames* the ambient world" (22; emphases added). So far, with the exception of the undue allusion to Descartes, Smith's gloss is impeccable. The problem—and this is no small problem—begins when he goes on to identify the act of attention-giving, which Smith calls framing, with Husserlian *epoché*:

> "Bracketing," "reduction," "putting in parentheses," and "epoché" (suspending judgement) are other terms that Husserl uses for this act of *attention-giving*. In such acts of *framing*, all actions, presuppositions, theories, and hypotheses are set aside. Instead, the observer attends to objects as they present themselves to him and, no less important, he attends to himself as he is present to objects.
>
> 22; my emphases

It is very true that *epoché* brings about the setting aside of presuppositions, and basically correct that its basic aim is to focus correctly on what really matters, but what matters (what should be "framed") for Husserl is the eidetic structure of experience. But it is wrong to assume that through the reduction of *epoché* we step *into* a natural frame ("I can let my attention wander …"). In fact, we "step *out* of the natural attitude" (William Casement 234; emphasis added).[9] It is unacceptable to suppose that the "attention-giving" scene described by Husserl in the above passage is, as Smith implies, a scene of bracketing or *epoché*. It is not. It is actually a description of the *natural standpoint* whose metaphysical confidence—the belief in the existence of a factual world out there—the *epoché* does not exactly invalidate, but simply sets aside, disconnects or brackets (see *Ideas I* §30 and §31). The thesis of the

---

9   What Smith describes here is but one initial stage in the (gradual) process of reduction, which we could designate with the prepositional phrase *framing out*. To frame *out* spurious, supervened, intellectual garbage (presuppositions, theories, hypotheses) is indeed a necessary task within the sanitation agenda of pure (*reine*) phenomenology. But this doesn't mean that Husserl moves on to readily embrace the *things* supposedly made available by such decontamination process. The reduction doesn't purify things by removing their concepts: the "knowledge which has nothing of conceptual thinking in it" is characteristic of the natural standpoint, and the "eidetic cognition" characteristic of Husserlian phenomenology is predicated precisely upon its overcoming. Husserl never forsakes his innermost ambition—"the rationalization of the empirical [*der Rationalisierung des Empirischen*]" (*Ideas I* 21). It is simply impossible to silence the Descartes breathing inside Husserl. The "abstention" from passing judgement on "the theorical content of all previous philosophy" Husserl calls the philosophic *epoché*. In fact, Adorno's rendition of the phrase "auf die Sachen selbst," and the concomitant explication, concern this mode of philosophic reduction. The problem arises when we move from the ejection implied in *framing out* to the inclusive composition that the nude form of the verb *frame* (as *framing in*) suggests. Smith wrongly extrapolates from the semantic resources of the verb, believing that the bestowing of attention in the natural standpoint—"I am aware of a world"—constitutes the *framing in* of *epoché*.

natural standpoint—"the thesis according to which the real world about me is at all times known not merely in a general way as something apprehended, but as a fact-world that *has its being out there*" (*Ideas I* §31, 56) is not abandoned, but it undergoes a modification: "we set it as it were 'out of action,' we disconnect it,' 'bracket it'" (*Ideas I* §31, 57). "The thesis," Husserl concludes, "is experience as lived [*Erlebnis*], but we make 'no use' of it" (57). In other words: phenomenology makes no use (*keinen Gebrauch*) of the world of the natural-standpoint experience (*die Welt der natürlichen Einstellung*) Husserl so lavishly describes in the passage quoted by Smith. What Smith understands as *epoché* and calls framing is exactly what *epoché* correctly understood as disconnection brackets out of consideration. As we will see in section "Doing Shakespeare," the *things themselves* that *epoché* is bound to frame as a consequence of the reduction are not exactly the verandah, the garden, and the children. But it is not hard to see why Smith, whose devotion for Merleau-Ponty is not exactly a secret, should indulge such misconstruction—and pass it on to his followers. In the "Introduction" to *Entertaining the Idea*, Lowell Gallagher, Hames Kearney and Julia Lupton close their Introduction to the collection of essays titled *Entertaining the Idea: Shakespeare, Philosophy, and Performance* urging that

> Shakespeare's eclectic philosophy of theatre convenes various forms of performance, including Aristotelian habit, sceptical exercise, Socratic dialogue and role playing, and experiments in phenomenological bracketing that continually restage occasions to welcome the arrival of new forms, new ideas, of how to live together. (14)

The first important modern philosophical notion that Smith inserts in a book programmatically titled *Phenomenal Shakespeare* is that of Husserlian *epoché*. And it is both wrongly construed and flagrantly misapplied. The last important modern philosophical notion that Gallagher, Kearney, and Lupton drop in the closing sentence of their programmatic "Introduction" to a book on Shakespeare and philosophy is the same notion, that of Husserl's phenomenological bracketing. And it is, likewise, improperly determined and incorrectly enforced, both by them and by the scholar (Sanford Budick) in charge of realizing this determination. I ignore the moral of this, but I am certain it is no coincidence.

In conclusion, what is suspended, in the case of the *phenomenological reduction*—carefully described by Husserl in *Ideas I* §31–32—is the need to pass judgement on epistemic matters of evidence and certitude inherently raised by the natural standpoint. So, to *reduce* is not to stage or *frame* what is naturally given for the purposes of a better examination, as Smith argues, but rather to suspend (frame out) the existential concerns stemming from the natural standpoint so as to better disclose the *essential* structure of the experience (*cogitationes*) at hand. When the disclosure of this essential structure is hindered by the interference of sedimented conceptual prejudice, then a further reduction is needed. In fact, the latter technique of ascetic idealism was indeed approved, and also called *reduction*, by no other than the empiricist Francis Bacon:

> Is not the ground, which Machiavel wisely and largely discourseth concerning governments, that the way to establish and preserve them, is to reduce them *ad principia*, a rule in religion and nature, as well as in civil administration? Was not the Persian magic a reduction or correspondence of the principles and architectures of nature to the rules and policy of governments?.
>
> The Advancement of Learning 87

The fittest Latin rendering of *auf die Sachen selbst* is *ad principia*: "reduction or correspondence." Smith, who begins his philosophical narrative with Bacon, should have known better.

Make no mistake: Husserlian *epoché* is a transcendental move that has *everything* of "conceptual thinking [*vom begrifflichen Denken*]" (*Ideas I* §27, 52) in it. Although it is hard to see how playtexts may accommodate the primeval phenomenological scene of *epoché*, the violent undoing of phenomenal excess (the erasure of the verandah, the garden, and the children) may convey the idea. There are many ironic moments in Shakespeare's plays where a similar unphenomenal abstention is both recommended and excoriated. For instance, Hamlet's to-be-or-not-to-be soliloquy examines the pros and cons of a disconnection (death as sleep) that puts to "end the thousand natural shocks" (*Hamlet* 3.1.61). And an eloquent dramatization of bracketing as "abstinence" from the worldly natural attitude is of course to be found in *Love's Labour's Lost*. Also informed by a radical *reductive* determination are paradigmatic theatrical moments like Faustus' opening soliloquy— "Then read no more" (*Dr Faustus* 1.1.10)—and Hamlet's parallel gesture in the remember-me speech: "I'll wipe away all trivial fond records, /All saws of books, all forms, all pressures past, / That youth and observation copied there" (*Hamlet* 1.5.99–101).

4

In an interesting essay titled "Hamlet's 'Now' of Inward Being" (2018) Sanford Budick conducts an analysis of the "now" in *Hamlet* that also misrepresents the meaning of *epoché*. The misrepresentation is transferred to another essay, titled "Shakespeare's Now: Some Philosophical Perspectives on *King Lear* and *The Winter's Tale*" (2020), where the theoretical sections of the earlier piece are literally reproduced. Budick places the phenomenological reduction at the end of a sequence of philosophical gestures, like Cartesian skepticism and the Kantian transcendental deduction, supposedly designed to facilitate *the disclosure of an inward self*. Shakespeare's similar gesture in *Hamlet* would provide the first link to the sequence. Budick devotes a great deal of attention to Husserl, and the *epoché* features in his essay as a sort of optimal paradigm of the process he has in mind as constitutive of Hamlet's mind:

> According to the broad outlines of this model the meditative mind goes (1) from suspension—often called a "reduction"—of consciousness of the external world to (2) a residual consciousness of self that is independent of experience of the world—often, in this sense, called "transcendental"—and even to a special temporality or 'now' to (3) reclaiming consciousness of the external world and its temporality. (131–32)

The first thing that calls our attention is the appeal he discovers in *Hamlet* to a "consciousness of the external world." The entire model is aimed at this phenomenal reclamation. Nearing the close of his essay, Budick resumes the claim: "the now of inward being that emerges, in silence, from Shakespeare's chiasmus of theatricalization, as from Husserl's reduction, finally turns [...] toward rejoining the world" (151). Reclaiming consciousness of the external world and rejoining the world are identical activities, and both ultimately intend a return to *the things themselves*. The maladies of abstinence are over. If reading *Hamlet* as an invitation to reengage with non-transcendental reality looks to you as a stretch, reading Husserl as sending the same invitation is even more preposterous. I discuss this particular misreading in the section 13 titled "Doing Shakespeare: To the Things Themselves." Let us for now consider the rest of the passage quoted above.

Despite the broadly phenomenological outline of the model, Budick's constant resort to the Kantian sublime, and his never fully fleshed-out proposal of a correlation between sensorial-aesthetic inhibition and transcendental deduction, implicitly redescribes the Husserlian *epoché* as inhibition, to wit, as the "momentary condition" whereby "the mind experiences a suspension of the world's spatio-temporality, in effect, a negativity in which the residual self abides in its own temporality" (136). This new *temporality* the essay systematically construes as downright atemporal—"an atemporality where inward being is disclosed" (137). The essay then moves on to reading *Hamlet* as a play where the pervasive use the rhetorical figure of chiasmus helps the character "constitute a meditative action that furthers the mind's deepest aims, such as, say, the realization of a Cartesian or Kantian or Husserlian reduction" (136). But this reduction is obviously not an end in itself: it serves the more radical aim of constituting and "inward being."

The essay is conventional in that it aims to demonstrate that Hamlet has a special interiority. This is a traditional thesis that the play itself sustains with abundant textual evidence, like the infinitely quotable "but I have that within which passeth show" (*Hamlet* 1.2.85). A favorite site for romantic celebration and liberal-humanist memory, Hamlet's interiority is also however dogma amongst neo-historicists like Stephen Greenblatt, whose opinions are mentioned by Budick in a footnote (136, n.9). The dullness of these conformist confirmations is aggravated by the rather surprising fact that Budick takes no distance from the related conceits "inward self" (131), "inward now of subjectivity" (134), "inner being" (140, 147), "innermost being" (150), "inward being" (134, 142, 144, 145, 146). When he insists on "the actuality" of Hamlet's "inward being" (140) he does it without precautionary marking, thus suggesting the endorsement characteristic of indirect free thought. Is he quoting Hamlet the character, or citing those critics, including Greenblatt, who assume the play constitutes such thing as an "inward being"? And if it is indeed free indirect thought, is the echoic mention ironically intended? I am afraid not. He is both quoting and failing to acknowledge the source, which means that he takes full responsibility for the meaning of the trope "inward being." The seriousness of his intentional commitment to the meaning of the trope is borne out in the following justification: "Of course it is possible to contend that there is no need to demonstrate the grounds of experience of inward being because it is universally available and self-evident" (14). Wow. Read again the end: "universally available and self-evident." Feel the pride—and the prejudice. The resort to self-evidence reveals glimmerings of Cartesian epistemology filtered through Husserl vocabulary, and the overarching phenomenological schema becomes apparent in his formulation of a "*now* of immediate self-presence" (148). In the light both of Budick's careful acknowledgement, in footnotes, of Derrida's dismantling of phenomenology's core philosophical assumptions (intuition, evidence, immediacy, presence) and of his arguably deconstructive treatment of the trope of chiasmus in the second part of the essay, where de Man is not exactly hidden under the carpet, the uncritical acceptance of "inward being" on grounds of *experience, self-evidence* and *immediate self-presence* is to say the least perplexing. In short, the unconventional and original dimension of his tropological reading is undone by his conventional confirmation of the traditional trope of inward being along phenomenological lines. But this is not what troubles the attentive reader most in this complex essay.

The argument is glaringly flawed in two theoretical respects—the conception of *epoché* and the conception of time in Husserl. First, the strategy of wholesale assimilation—Cartesian doubt (is like) the Kantian transcendental deduction (which is like) Kantian aesthetic before-the-sublime inhibition (which is like) Husserlian reduction *and* all are anticipated in Hamlet's chiasmus of theatricalization (AB:BA)—leads to an unacceptable conclusion: that "the mind's inability to grasp" the totality of the exchange curated by the chiasmus "produces a powerful *epoché*" (139). This is wrong because the mind's difficulty in grasping the virtually unstoppable speculation prompted by a line like "What's Hecuba to him or he to her," which Budick glosses as "*play-acting* (experiencing Hecuba in fiction) to *would-be non-play-acting* ("him," the live actor, in real existence) // *would-be non-play-acting* ("he" the live actor) to *play-acting* ("her" in the fiction)" (139), does not produce a disconnection or bracketing. *Epoché*, let me get this clear, is not a suspension of thought before a difficulty, not the mind's momentary holding back in argumental bewilderment, not the standstill of dialectical impasse. Husserl is no doubt interested in what Budick calls the "interminability" of chiastic exchanges, in the *ad infinitum* "layering" of conflicting or incompatible possibilities clashing within the framework of a putatively rational argument. In section 138 of *Ideas I*, titled "Adequate and inadequate evidence," he argues that

> the phenomenology of the Reason in the sphere of the types of Being which can on principle be only inadequately given (the sphere of *transcendents* in the sense of realities, *Realitäten*) has therefore to study the different occurrences within this sphere which have been indicated *a priori* and in advance. It has to make clear how the inadequate consciousness of givenness, the partial appearing, is related to one and the same determinable x, whilst only passing over into one another, and also to indicate the essential possibilities which here present themselves; how, on the one hand, a sequence of experiences is possible here and constantly motivated on rational lines through the rational placements [*positings*] that are continuously at one's disposal, namely the course of experience in which the empty places of the appearances that have preceded get filled again, the indeterminacies more closely determined,

moving forward all the time towards *a thoroughgoing harmonious filling out, with the steadily increased rational power that goes with it*. (289)

But Husserl astutely cautions that we have to make clear the opposite possibilities, "the cases of *fusions or polythetic syntheses where there is disagreement or determination otherwise* of that x which we are constantly aware as one and the same" (290). Thus the oscillation between pure and impure evidential vision, and between purely formal (analytic) and purely material (synthetic-a priori) evidential vision is further rehearsed in a vacillatory tension between adequate and inadequate self-evidence that accounts for cognitive undecidability before potentially *ad infinitum* sequences (of sensorial and/or conceptual determinable givens), before what Priest calls "contradiction at the limit of the iterable" (*Beyond* 26). But this epistemic undecidability is not *epoché*.

In a section titled "The Now of the Spectator or Onlooker," Budick devises a three-stage model of meditative experience that travels from the suspension of consciousness of the external world to the intentional consciousness of it and its temporality via the "residual consciousness of a self in an atemporal now that is independent of the world" (136). It is hard to know what exactly he means by this, let alone its connection with specific Husserl texts. He claims that it is the application of bracketing, reduction or *epoché* that "produces the 'now' of the 'onlooker'" and alludes to Husserl's *Cartesian Meditations*. In the corresponding footnote, however, he doesn't quote from that book, and refers to the pages in *Ideas I* that cover the fourth section of Part 2, titled "The Phenomenological Reductions." But neither the problem of the now nor the function of the onlooker is discussed there. The disinterested onlooker is discussed in *Cartesian Meditations*, and the structure of temporality characteristic of the now is discussed in the section titled "General Structures of Consciousness" of Part III of *Ideas I*, more particularly in §81 "Phenomenological Time and Consciousness of Time." Here we read about "phenomenological time" as a unity, "one endless stream of mental processes":

> I take heed, in the particular case, of the mode of "Now" and accordingly of the fact that a new and continually new follows upon this Now and, of essential necessity, upon every "Now" in necessary continuity, of the fact that in unity therewith every actually present Now is changed into a Just Now, the Just Now once more and continuously into an always new Just Now of the Just Now; and so forth. This holds for every new ensuing Now. The actually present *Now* is necessarily and remains something punctual, *a persisting form for every new material*. It is likewise with the continuity of "just now"; it is a continuity of forms of always new contents. At the

same time this signifies: the enduring mental process of joy is given "in the manner peculiar to consciousness" in a consciousness-continuum of constant *form*: A phase, impression, as the limit-phase of a continuity of retentions which, however, are not on an equal footing; they are instead *to be related to one another continuously-intentively*—a continuous complexity of retentions of retentions. The form always contains a new content, thus continuously "attaches" to each impression in which the Now of the mental process is given, a new corresponding continuously to a new point of the duration; an impression continuously changes into a retention; this retention continuously changes into a modified retention; and so forth.

Ideas I, KERSTEN's translation 194

Budick incorrectly urges that, according to Husserl, "the momentary bracketing of external reality transforms our sense of time into an internal, atemporal 'now'" ("Hamlet's 'Now'" 136). This is wrong. Our sense of time is not *transformed*. Our "sense" of time is the only thing we gain phenomenologically when we decide to exclude what Husserl calls "objective" or "cosmic" time along with the near-animal "perception" of it. The *Ausschaltung* or exclusion of objective time is required precisely to permit the emergence of a temporality—Levinas will call it *"temps immanent"* (*Théorie de l'intuition* 65)—that no further reduction can eliminate.[10] So what we have is the reduction of external time that permits the full emergence of an internal time that has been there all along, not the *transformation* of the former into the latter. Husserl clearly holds that whereas a "'sensed' temporal datum" contributes to the constitution of phenomenological time, a "perceived temporal datum" signifies "objective time" (*Phenomenology of Internal Time-Consciousness* 25).

---

10 In *The Phenomenology of Internal Time-Consciousness*, Husserl assumes the existence of an immanent time: "To be sure, we also assume existing time; this however is not the time of experience, but the *immanent time* of the flow of consciousness" (23). Experience (*Erfahrung*) may seem an odd lexical choice here, but it must be contrasted with the *Erlebnis* (also translated by Churchill as "experience") of "the perception and representation of time itself" (22; *Zur phänomenologie des inneren Zeitbewusstseins*, 4–5). Husserl reserves *Erfahrung* to objective time *Erlebnis* to phenomenological temporality. The latter, the immanent time of consciousness is a constitutive temporalization made of retentions and protentions, not an atemporal *now*. Husserl sharply begins with the exclusion of objective time as a transcendent existent closed to phenomenological analysis: "The lived and experienced [*erlebte*] now, taken in itself, is not a point of Objective time" (24). Like objective space, objective time would demand an experience *Transzendenz* (transcendency). The lived experience (*Erlebnis*) of temporality is by contrast immanent.

As Derrida shrewdly suggested in his first important text on Husserl, what is suspended or reduced in phenomenological time is the very possibility of a genesis (*Le problème de la genèse* 108). Only through this *reduction of genesis* can the *vécu constituent* enjoy a temporality of its own, untouched by the constituted events of History (108). Husserl needs to escape the circularity of a subjectivity that is at the same time intemporal (originary and constituting) and temporal (historical and psychological) (109). Derrida's formulation of the crux takes on the chiastic sharpness of the Hamlet passage analyzed by Budick. Compare:

> There's a special providence in the fall of a sparrow. If it be now, 'tis not to come. If it be not to come, it will be now. If it be not now, yet it will come. The readiness is all.
> *Hamlet* 5.2.156–160

> *There is a certain providence in the fall of an "ideal sphere."* If it is atemporal and originary, subjectivity can no longer be simultaneously constituting and temporal: if it is temporal, then it is purely historical and psychological; if it is constituting, then it must be reduced to the ideality of a formal "I think." *The readiness is all.* (54)[11]

Unlike Budick, though, Derrida doesn't make the emergence of the inward *atemporality* of the now depend on the phenomenological reduction. First, because he doesn't acknowledge the relevance to phenomenology of such *atemporal* now;[12] and second, because what the reduction or exclusion of objective or cosmic time (*Weltzeit*) facilitates is precisely the emergence of a *temporal* flow that, although made of *nows*, is never fixed, rarefied, abstracted, or sublated into one *atemporal now*, as Budick argues. According to Derrida, "what remains after this putting out of circulation [the *Ausschaltung* or *mise*

---

11 In this third quotation, the first sentence is my version of the immediate context; the last one I have inserted.

12 Indeed, Derrida's careful redescription of Husserl's *now* foreshadows the transcendental-formal extensionality, made or retention and protention, of his own notion of *différance*: "La ponctualité du 'maintenant' implique donc, en tant que telle, une antériorité; elle comporte une rétention puis une rétention de rétention, etc. Elle a une densité continue. Elle est concrète. La forme pure ou le moi pur sont donc impossibles sans une histoire génétique où la création de 'maintenants' toujours nouveaux se continue par une rétention incessante et nécessaire" (*Le probème de la genèse* 168). The resulting retentional auto-affection, and the threat it poses to self-presence, are brilliantly analyzed by Martin Hägglund in the chapter on Husserl and Derrida in *Radical Atheism*, 50–75.

hors circuit of objective time] is thus phenomenological duration [*durée*], immediate apperception of time that constitutes the only possible and valid beginning, the only originary certainty of a reflection of time" (55; *Le problème* 110). In a brief but incisive account of *epoché*, Christian Beyer has rightly argued that "there is still something left at this point, though, which must not, and cannot, be bracketed: the temporal flow of one's "present" experience, constituted by current retentions and original impressions."[13] In conclusion, what the local reduction of objective time fosters is the emergence of phenomenological time as duration. If what Budick means by "atemporal now" is this duration—an unlikely but not inconceivable possibility—he should express himself more clearly and ground his point on the relevant sources.[14]

To Budick's construal of the atemporal now I would oppose Nicholas Royle's alternative reading of the *Hamlet* passage on readiness, augury and falling sparrows. The "now," for Royle, names an "uncertain time" that inscribes, echoically, in the play, "a dislocated, eerie series" inaugurated by Barnardo's "'Tis now struck twelve" (1.1.7):

> "Now to my word" (I, v, 111), "Now could I drink hot blood" (III, ii, 373), "Now might I do it pat, now he is praying" (III, iii, 73), "Where be your gibes now, your gambols, your songs, your flashes of merriment that were wont to set the table on a roar" (V, I, 180–2), so many "nows" that are "not nows"—so long as we mark a disjunction here with the presupposition, still monolithically prevalent in Shakespeare criticism, that *Hamlet* is about forms of deferral, delay or afterwardness to be thought *on the basis of the present*.
>
> *In Memory* 31

5

I have paid separate attention to three related philosophical misconstructions. In the three cases, a modern early modern scholar (Smith, Budick) misrepresents a theoretical Husserl notion—*presence, epoché,* the *now*—in the course of an argument which aims to formulate a similar aspiration: "to reach the world-at-hand, the world of things and people" (Smith, *Phenomenal* 22), to

---

13 See her entry "Husserl" in the *Stanford Encyclopedia of Philosophy*.
14 For the temporality of the *now* in Husserl, see Olbromski.

achieve a "*framing* of experience that [...] moves outward by degrees into the ambient world" (Smith 20), and to "turn toward rejoining the world" (Budick, "Hamlet's 'Now'" 151). Noble as it is, this endeavor is decidedly not Husserl's. It can only be called *phenomenological* in an adulterated and epigonal sense of the word. Neo-phenomenological scholars use the *epoché* as a device of summary framing and transitory containment of the virtually infinite particulars (the things themselves) that make up the Shakespearean *Faktwelt*. But this operation is flawed on two basic counts. First, it is not, as I have argued, a genuinely Husserlian *epoché*—it has more affinities with Merleau Ponty's attention to the sensorial and corporal. And second, it is not a critical operation or an operation of thought. It is rather a mechanism to regulate gluttony or abstinence, depending on the position you take.

So, *I can let my attention wander* ... Adorno discerned in the Heideggerian call to Being a mode of anti-subjective fervor bound to relapse in the bondage to Being: "Feeling face to face with the cosmos, the believer clings [*hestet*] without much ado [*ohne viel Umstände*] to any kind of particular [*an jegliches Partikulare*], if only it is forceful enough in convicting the subject of its weakness" (Adorno, *Negative* 67; *Negative* 76). Since so many Shakespeare scholars are bent on reminding all *subjects*—especially Descartes—of their weakness, this neo-ontological slogan can be redirected for neo-phenomenological uses. Everywhere we look, we find the scholar clinging without much ado to any kind of particular—the verandah, the garden, the children, or the summerhouse. To characterize the resulting set of phenomenological parodies of ontology we may reserve the term Francis Bacon used to describe the work of Telesius: "pastoral philosophy, full of sense [of *common sense*, we would add], but of no great depth" (*Advancement* 105). One senses the reverential awe with which posthumanist pastoral early-modernists psalmody the Whitmanesque versicule of Latour's new gospel: "The tiniest maggot, the smallest rodent, the scantest river, the farthest star ..." (*Politics of Nature* 216). Richard Wilson's frantic search for the hidden recusant testament or Edmund Campion's cut thumb (*Secret Shakespeare* 55; *Worldly Shakespeare* 132) in the Shakespeare canon is another telling instance of critical mystification around a particular framed *donnée*—in this case, an irretrievable and yet *immediately* available given of history, immediately made to bear on whichever textual pass the critic deems opportune. Kastan has rightly observed that "Shakespeare's faith cannot be recovered" (*Will* 30). And more recovered particulars—Shakespeare's cats and cakes and Kates—will atone nobody's unwisdom. When the critic runs out of particulars because there are "no more cakes and ale" (*Twelfth Night* 2.3.115) a deadly vacuum sets in the pre-reflexive ground. What follows is facticity for facticity's sake, a dead-end haunted still by the warble of many an old new-historicist. What most flashy supporters of object-phenomenologist, speculative realist and posthumanist Shakespeare are currently performing is actually a relapse into the undialectized anthropological humanism that Marx managed to leave behind but Feuerbach never abandoned. The grounding prescript of this flat (essentialist, anthropological) humanism was aptly parodied by Althusser : "Si vous voulez connaître l'essence de l'Homme, cherchez-la où elle est: dans ses Objets, dans son monde" ("La querelle de l'humanisme" 460). The notional seedbed of this phenomenological-environmentalist trope could be vaguely traced back to Heidegger or Arendt, but the genealogical prospection should reach further up along the inverted tree: the belief that "l'Essence de l'Homme est *le monde de ses objets*" (Althusser 460) is a much older delusion, a pre-dialectical postulate beholden to essentialist—Derrida would call them metaphysical—assumptions about nature, the subject and alienation. In fact, further down in the tree, Husserl's appeal to what Levinas translated as "une espèce de réflexion" (*Méditations cartésiennes* 81) by means of which the human body relates to itself—admittedly, a kind of *corporal reflection*— foreshadows Lupton's idea of a *digestive reflection*. But there is one major difference: Husserl speaks in figurative terms, and one is never sure whether Merleau-Ponty and his contemporary followers are careful enough to keep the tropological distance.[15] At stake in that distance is the possibility of genuine thought. "The point," Cutrofello has rightly advanced, "is not to be either like Kant or like Sade, but to be more than a lamp, a towel, or a plate" ("On the Idea of a Critique," 101). Or an assimilating body, or a digestive tract.

No doubt a reinvigorated petit-bourgeois humanism lurks too behind the mock-radical posturing of soi-disant posthumanists. One should always caution against returns to theology and ontology that seek to circumvent the critical powers of a critically subdued reason, lest one should become, when dealing with Shakespearean criticism, like Pascal, "grand theologian en peu de temps" (*Les provinciales* 43). Adorno complained that "left to its own devices, "the unreflective immediacy [*reflexionslose Unmittelbarkeit*] of the method" lends itself "to any kind of license" (*Negative Dialectic* 62). The ontological spell (*Bann*) lying behind unreflective phenomenological methods is therefore

---

15   In *Phénoménologie de la perception* (116–17) Merleau-Ponty speaks rightly of a *distance* between the human animal and the nature to which it is sensorially exposed, and of a related loss of *spontanéité* in the human-animal reaction to sensorial stimuli, but he systematically fails to carry the implications of this idea through. The idea of a kind of corporeal "reflexion" he traces back to Husserl's *Cartesian Mediations* (*Phénoménologie* 122) is not enough as an attestation of mediation. Curiously, Merleau-Ponty misquotes Levinas' translation ("une espèce de") for "une sorte de".

> perpetuated in whatever would be the subject's downright otherness, just as the *deus absconditus* always carried some of the irrational features of mythical deities. The corny exoticism of such decorative world views as the astonishingly consumable Zen Buddhist one casts light upon today's restorative philosophies. Like Zen, they simulate a thinking posture [*eine Stellung des Gedankens*] which the history stored in the subjects makes impossible to assume. Restricting the mind to thoughts open and attainable at the historical stage of its experience is an element of freedom; non-conceptual vagary represents the opposite of freedom.
>
> Negative 69

Non-conceptual vagary (*das begriffslos Schweifende*), what Hegel called *raisonnement* and Sartre *papillotement des idées*, remains in fact the thinking posture of many early modernists in academic meetings: *I can let my attention wander.* We might not be able to spot "Zen Shakespeare" listed in Conference seminars of Shakespeare professional associations—actually a "Shakespeare Yoga" was announced in the 2018 SAA Conference held in LA—but one cannot get too much of the corny exoticism denounced by Adorno. Non-conceptual vagary addicted to decorative particulars is a perfect way of describing much of what passes today for Shakespeare criticism. When Robert Brandom speaks of "the conceptual inexhaustibility of sensuous immediacy" (qtd. by Pippin, *Hegel's Realm of Shadows* 167) he is already presuming the (conceptual) mediation that renders immediacy altogether ineffective as spontaneous donation. For Hegel, only Being (whatever that is) is spontaneously given. But Shakespeare critics believe in the phenomenal (concept-free) inexhaustibility of sensuous immediacy—and there's the rub. The penchant for embodied mythemes is one more episode in the narrative celebration of (mimetic-aesthetic) mythos at the expense of (rational-dialectical) logos. Szlezák has clearly stated that the widespread hermeneutic assumption according to which "the myths have a greater capacity for truth derives from the perception of modern irrationalist trends and cannot be supported by any arguments of Plato's" (*Reading Plato* 74). Interestingly, it is in the work of an arch-expert on myths, French ethnologist Claude Levi-Strauss, that we find the most adroit critique of phenomenology. His target is French phenomenology:

> La phénoménologie me heurtait, dans la mesure où elle postule une continuité entre le vécu et le réel. D'accord pour reconnaître que celui-ci enveloppe et explique celui-là, j'avais appris de mes trois maîtresses [Saussure, Freud, Marx] que le passage entre les deux ordres est discontinu : que pour atteindre le réel il faut d'abord répudier le vécu, quitte à le

> réintégrer para la suite dans une synthèse objective dépouillée de toute sentimentalisme.
>
> Tristes tropiques 61

It is one thing to understand the fatigue that bad theory—the effects of inept schoolbook bowdlerizing, short-lived academic-fashion craze and crude scholastic indoctrination—must have produced in the generation of Anglo-American Shakespeare scholars who started writing in the 1980s and 1990s; it is quite another to sympathize with their apparent disinterest in settling the account straight. The upshot of this indifference is that the scholar quite often relapses *post festum* into what Althusser calls "ideological practice," as opposed to the "theoretical practice" ("On the Materialist Dialectic," *For Marx*, 131), thus causing the reader to pause, like the old Duke, and puzzle: "Did he not moralize this spectacle?" (*As You Like It* 2.1.46). Reacting to the dangers of moralism already present in the Utopian socialism of thinkers like Proudhon, Marx wrote: "Il n'y a plus de la dialectique, il y a tout au plus de la morale toute pure" (*Misère* 167). His complaint remains valid. But of course this may only prove questionable if one is willing—discreet enough or fool enough—to grant the arch-dialectical authority of someone like Althusser in the first place. If we opt for conceding it—I do—then we must stand by the injunction that "the external application of a concept is never equivalent to a *theoretical practice*" (*For Marx* 134). To the unconcerned by the prattle of over-determination and infrastructure, to the spotless, to the un-interpellated, let me recall that "the mathematics and the metaphysics / Fall to them as you find your stomach serves you" (*The Taming of the Shrew* 1.1.37–38); that the (Feuerbachian) gastro-intestine and the (Hegelian) Spirit are communicating organs; that they feed us also idols of the cave when they presume to deliver "reality sandwiches" (Grady, *Shakespeare* 39). Sensualist hyper-empiricism betrays, Derrida noted in the 1970s, profound metaphysical underpinnings: "Le réalisme ou le sensualisme, l'"empirisme," sont des modifications du logocentrisme" (Derrida, *Positions* 87). In *De la grammatologie*, he also berated the scientificist objectivism as another unperceived or unconfessed metaphysics. This "objectivisme naïf" (90), which fosters the deadly coincidence of the pre-critical and the ultra-transcendental, is only to be countered, Derrida believes, through a prudent return to the transcendental. This Kantian move reveals Derrida's complicity with dialectic.

Recall Descartes: "De plus il me tombe encore en l'esprit, qu'on ne doit pas considérer une seule créature [*unam aliquam creaturam*] séparément [*separatim*], lorsqu'on recherche si les ouvrages de Dieu sont parfaits, mais généralement toutes les créatures ensemble [*omnem rerum universitatem*]" (*Méditations* 179). Replace Dieu with Shakespeare and you're almost there.

You wanna write your thesis on Shakespeare? Fine. Become a comparatist first. Choose your creature, say, the snail. Subject your scanning of the totality of Shakespeare's plays to a contrastive analysis of the work of other playwrights and writers of his time and you will have progressed quite a bit. Broaden further the focus and welcome writers of other periods into the comparison. Allow, finally, other writers from other linguistic traditions to enrich the picture. Next, spend at least three years reading literature of non-Renaissance periods. Next, read philosophy, the originals if possible. Once you're done with that, let your attention wander, return to the verandah, the garden, the children, and the summer-house. You will probably lose, along the way, a teaching position, a house, some weight, and a couple of girlfriends. But you will certainly end up—like Lear—equipped with rich confusion and a snail shell. Good luck.

CHAPTER 12

The Naturalization of Reason

Who Is Afraid of Ferdinand Derrida?

1

In his first essay on Levinas, Derrida concedes that through "the restitution of metaphysics" prepared by the previous "reductions of phenomenology and ontology," the author of *Totalité et infini* would have managed to avoid a specific pre-metaphysical pitfall, the possibility that "reason would be nature [*la raison serait nature*]" (*Writing* 96). Althusser and Adorno would have been appalled by this slippage, the last generationally in a line of thinkers running all the way down from Kant and Hegel, and including Feuerbach, Marx, and Lenin. Also dismayed is Derrida, here the sympathetic chronicler of the relapse, but elsewhere a furious anti-metaphysical detractor of "empirical freedom" (*Writing* 96). A temporary disciple of Althusser, from whom he learnt to distrust the lures of "rationalist empiricism" (*Lire* 32), Derrida furtively quotes from his *maître à penser*'s edition of Feuerbach in the footnotes to this memorable essay.[1] *Reason would be nature*? In what possible world? In what *La La Land* of Western academia?

In the Hegelian tradition, reason originates in nature, but it immediately becomes *incommensurable* with it and *irreducible* to it. The gap, in the transit from nature to linguistic reason, is particularly dramatic, and no ethical leap from self to Other, no political shift from selves to polis, compares to it. To account for Shakespeare's daemonic disjunctions, Lukacher correctly refers to the "fundamental relation of language to self-consciousness which exceeds the very limits of the self-relation" (*Daemonic* 2). Deciding, say, that a human life is equal to any other human life and superior to that of an animal does not outline an ethical exorbitance: it registers rather a rational *decision* to become exorbitant. Call it decision or call it excision (Lacan), or even, at limit, speak of the circumcision of the heart (St Paul). Whatever the prefix (*ex-*, *de-*, *circum-*), the truth is that, for a human to arise, something must go (*caedere*). And this fall—whose remainder tarries as a grotesque and obscene supplement—is

---

1 The English version cites an original German edition of Feuerbach's writings. See *Writing*, 314, note 33; *L'écriture*, 149, n.2.

contingently cued by, and hardly distinguishable from, the necessary *daemon*, a creature sadly ignored by sanctimonious animalists. But note that it is not such reason-based human exorbitance or exceptionalism—some specimens of some animal species kill one another, but we humans should not—that makes us superfluously unnatural (Lear's late realization). It is rather the game of self-differing sameness in totality. Without the brutal assumption—the ontologically violent premise—that we humans are all equivalent finite beings dwelling in the limited habitat of a finite planet—since, on rational inspection, this reduction obtains—there would be no sense of ethical equality.[2] If we are not first rationally divested of our face and name, and turned into—alas—a number, then no ethics begins. This is no enlightened-capitalist-administrative inhuman rationalization: this is rather emancipation through the genericity of the universal, or *liberation through the unparticular*.

Conversely, the current recourse to phenomenology is driven, we have seen, by a nostalgia for the natural particular. When it engages matters of reason or language, this phenomenology becomes *cognitivism by other means*, as it betokens a "cognitivist" inability to grapple with the dialectical tradition—visible in the ridiculous cognitivist resolve to *place* language in the particular brain, as a region or an instinct—not openly for the sake of an omni-explanatory universal rationality—although, let me insist, cognitivist-new-age phantasies loom large in gadget-crazed posthumanism, object-oriented neo-materialism and aestheticist-phenomenological scholarship—but rather in the interests of a *new immediacy*, that is, the impromptu interaction between a re-world human and the de-humanized environment. Something of the new spiritualist agendas is also visible in this cult of the immediate. In a recent collection of essays titled *Face-to-Face in Shakespearean Drama: Ethics, Performance, Philosophy* (2019), cognitive prejudice—in short, reliance in the near-somatic naturalization of reason and language—is redoubled by an agenda of recognition and reciprocity derived directly from Levinas and indirectly from Hegel.[3] *Cognitive, recognitive*: anything will do to prevent the old adversaries—rationality,

---

2 Arendt's disregard for the problem of equality (Moran 318) is symptomatic. And recall that equality is a *problem* because 1) we are obviously *not* equal; and 2) we must pretend we are if a political space can open. This political space will open only if the actions conducive to it are specifically described. Arendt's vagueness in that regard invites the kind of criticism Popper's levelled against Utopian (Marxian) engineering, in favor of piecemeal engineering (*The Poverty of Historicism* 58–65). Left to its own devices, the political space opened by random human interaction will very likely become a space of inequality, hierarchy, fear, and repression. See Habermas' criticism of "Arendt's Communications Concept of Power."

3 The editors, Matthew James Smith and Julia Lupton, write in the "Introduction": "The forms of intimacy, conflict, cognition and re-cognition that animate the choreography of co-presence

reason, logos—from gaining ground.[4] From embodied cognition to face-to-face recognition: such vicious circle allows for a refunding of meanings immediately earned from sensible motives and visible intentions (arguments of the book are sometimes illustrated with pictures) that makes scant room for textual cruxes, the multiple opacities and indeterminacies of unphenomenal dramatic-poetic language. It is surprising, for instance, how little attention, if any, is given to the trope of prosopopoeia in a book explicitly dealing with the meaning-conferring powers of the face and the face-conferring powers of meaning: the neglect of prosopopoeia is also alarmingly visible in the chapter on "Faces" in Raber's *Shakespeare and Posthumanist Theory* (74–88).[5] The reason for this pretermission is clear. To attest to the role of prosopopoeia is to acknowledge the vigour of figurative mediation, and this liberal-dialectical concession is, remember, passé. Figurative aberration, moreover, turns the face-giving power of ethical politics into an anti-social landscape of recursive *defacement* (de Man, *The Rhetoric* 81). But the chirpiest moment in the "Introduction" to the *Face-to-Face* book comes when the editors cite a colleague citing a "Husserlian psychoanalyst" (sic) who comments, apropos of "the contact improvisations of Rosalind and Orlando," on the mutual shaping of "inferred intentions" (Lupton & Smith, "Introduction" to *Face-to-Face* 10). The problem here lies not in the fact that inferring intentions is, among rational bipeds, more a matter of conceptual explicitation than of facial gesture reading: one need to be Robert Brandom to corroborate that; the problem is not even that you should place yourself in a position such that the flamboyant label "Husserlian psychoanalyst" makes sense—Daniel Stern is a prestigious therapist whose appropriation of the phenomenological notion of the "interpersonal" proved fruitful for the study of the psychic life of the infant; not even the fact that such position precludes the most basic understanding of the argument advanced by Derrida in *Limited Inc.*: this may be a desirable effect, for not

---

are the matter of this collection" (7). These "forms" are obviously not verbal forms, nor is the matter anywhere near the verbal matter of a playtext. The field of analysis of the collection's essays is then an imaginary "choreography of co-presence" the authors have constructed in their minds with the help of their playhouse, photograph, movie and television memories: the "Introduction" is illustrated with pictures of contemporary rehearsals of productions of Shakespeare's plays. I am at a loss to decipher what do those pictures tell us about a Shakespeare playtext. Only Matthew James Smith, assisted here by Paul Kottman (see notes 18 and 19), bothers to acknowledge the Hegelian weight of the concept of recognition.

4   The term "cognitive" occurs often in the essays of *Face-to-Face*.
5   For a classic deconstructionist reading of the trope of *prosopopoeia*, see De Man, *The Rhetoric of Romanticism* (76–81) and *Allegories of Reading* (110–118). See also Michel Riffaterre, "Prosopopeia" (1985).

even Searle understood it, and it would reduce the odds that you may end up yourself needing a therapist (the *cordon sanitaire* erected around preverbal or nonverbal intentions, whether authorial of those of character, remains however a sound hermeneutic measure in the literary-studies field); the real problem is that you believe that what works for the pre-linguistic infant works *best* for Shakespeare's cagey meta-verbal juveniles (from Juliet to the first-quarto Hamlet). What is the point in inferring intentions when the task in question is to scan playtexts interwoven with verbal retention and protention? Unless, of course, we discount the playtexts from the outset and "work from the performances outward" (Lupton & Smith, "Introduction" to *Face-to-Face* 11). This is in fact the operation involved, and the operators have at least the honesty to acknowledge it: they "work from the performances outward, testing explanations from Wittgenstein, Arendt, Levinas and Hegel as Shakespeare's plays create amenable conditions for them" (11); Matthew James Smith insists that the aim of the essays "is to bring some of the offerings of performance studies to bear on matters of ethics in Shakespearean drama" (77); and Kevin Curran explains that his analysis of judgement in *Measure for Measure* rests upon a counter-intuitive premise: "rather than using a concept to give a reading of the play, I have tried to use a play to give a reading of the concept" (173). So, in brief, their goal is not to read the plays, not even to elucidate their performance logic or history, but rather to test philosophical concepts on matters of ethics, and to "use" the "offerings of performance studies." Shakespeare, and the Shakespeare playtext more particularly, is an excuse. This is fine: great speculative work has been done (by Hegel, Marx, Freud, Derrida) using Shakespeare's plays as a pretext. But then the merit of this kind of work is a measure of the authors' ability to make the philosophical debate move forward in a productive, innovative, or unexpected direction. Thus, assessing the merits of the essays in a book like *Face-to-Face in Shakespearean Drama* would imply: 1) examining their contribution to a better understanding of Shakespearean drama, a goal they themselves openly disavow; 2) determining the range and novelty of their conceptual discussion on ethical matters; in this case, and with all due respect, I doubt their discussion will change the course of ethics studies; and 3) determining the degree of their contribution to performance studies: maybe this they do accomplish. Trained as a literary scholar, and mindful and respectful of the methodological specificity of performance studies, on this count I prefer to shelter in Tractarian *Schweigen*.

The neo-phenomenological craze attending the work of many of the critics swept by the tendencies mentioned above (posthumanism, object studies, new materialism, performance studies, affect studies, ecological studies) often leads to a naïve reliance on a mishmash of trendsetting chichi technology and cognitive science. Much in this work is characterized by the same scientific flimsiness that Heidegger restlessly denounced in the fifties: "hence there is nothing but mischief in all the makeshift ties and asses' bridges by which men today would set up a comfortable commerce between thinking and the sciences" (*What is Called Thinking?* 8). The same was denounced by his nemesis, Adorno, who opined that "extravagant syntheses between developments in philosophy and in the natural science are odious, of course" (*Negative* 67). And we may add Žižek's allergy to spiritualized neo-materialists and new-age cognitive gurus. So if Hegel, Adorno and Žižek can be seen as jointly subscribing to Heidegger's dictum—"We stand outside of science" (41)—it is fundamentally because the four (Hegel, Heidegger, Adorno, Žižek) show a salutary respect for the restriction of scope, confined success, pragmatic efficiency and autonomy of real science. The four would share, in addition, an aversion to scientific co-optations of speculative thought, especially by media-haunting cognitivists and big-cheese neuroscientists, to the pseudo-scientific meandering of the critical spirit, to the flat naturalization, in short, of logos (Heidegger) or dialectical reason (Hegel, Adorno, Žižek). The four have, alas, decidedly lost the swing, or never had it. Others—let's call them post-dialectical thinkers—have managed to overcome the block, and their charming flow, their awesome interaction—Merleau-Ponty glissading along Husserl's "concepts 'fluents'" or *Flieszende* (*Phénoménologie* 76)—is not to be spoiled by the mediation of language, the signifier-bound, negative-cum-differential (no)structures of the literary tradition, ideology, the unconscious, or culture at large. It is always salutary to recall Lacan's honourable profession of distance from the appeals to scopic unity made by Merleau-Ponty in his phenomenological work, even if these were (or seemed to be) released from "physiological assignation."[6] The return to physiology and humors in early modern studies has become a narrow-sighted field of historicist research, testifying solely to the fact that the *desire* to practice materialist criticism is hardly a guarantee of success.

There is a difference between a thing (*die Dinge*) and the fact (*Sache*) as "concept of the thing [*der Begriff der Dinge*]." For Hegel, only the latter matters—only the latter "becomes the subject matter [*Gegenstand*]" (*Science of Logic* 19). But the incompatibility between mediation-sensitive or dialectical (reflective, speculative) methods and phenomenological methods is not the

---

6 Lacan: "C'est cette présupposition qu'il y ait quelque part un lieu de l'unité, qui est bien faite pour suspendre notre assentiment. Non qu'il ne soit manifeste que ce lieu soit écarté de toute assignation physiologique, et que nous ne soyons satisfaits de suivre en son détail une subjectivité constituante là où elle se tisse fil à fil, mais non pas réduite à être son envers, avec ce qu'on appelle ici l'objectivité totale" ("Maurice Merleau-Ponty" 250).

only reason why practitioners of the latter systematically ignore the findings of the former.[7] There is also an important sociological factor of sheer intellectual indolence, if not stolidity. The successful implementation of a hermeneutic of mediation—be it ideological, literary, linguistic, scriptural, psychoanalytic or cultural in a large sense—involves not solely a theoretical familiarity with negative and differential dialectics (reading the central work of Kant, Hegel, Nietzsche, Marx, Freud, Adorno and Derrida), but also an extensive knowledge of the field whose inscriptions constellate, in each case, the mediated figures.[8] As Žižek argues, "totality is differential structure thought to the end—that is, a differential structure that includes subjectivity and a constitutive antagonism" (Žižek, *Reading Marx* 18). In an essay on Hamlet, Goldberg aptly described subjectivity as little more than a "scene of writing" (*Shakespeare's Hand*, 111). On paper, Greenblatt's cultural poetics stands out as a remarkable instance of a hermeneutic of mediation, and he managed to put forward some very brilliant interpretations of key texts of the English Renaissance. But aesthetic prejudice, empiricist mania, and the gradual narrowing of contexts, combined to dedialecticize the standard neo-historicist piece to an intolerable degree.

It is in the phenomenological incapacity or reluctance to come to terms with *the Hegelian moment* (I here adapt a Pocock formula) that most of the problems in current post-theoretical interpretive practice originate. It was Hegel who first denounced that "the primary vice of Understanding consists in the effacement of mediation" (Jameson, *Valences* 98). If good old theory

---

7   Husserl's refractoriness to genuine *mediation* is the theme of Derrida's early hermeneutic engagement with the work of the German philosopher. In *Ideas I*, Husserl speaks of "essential contents" that are "mediated [*mittelbaren*]," emerging as "data in and through the mediating insight of thought [*die im mittelbar einsichtigen Denken*] and indeed on principles that are throughout immediately transparent [*durchaus unmittelbar einsichtige*]" (18). The incompatibility between mediation and insight is borne out precisely in the provident recourse to the "immediately transparent." Husserl shows no real interest in "the mediated mental steps [*mittelbaren Denkschritte*]" (19) which he identifies with stages in the insightful labor of inference: he speaks of "mediated positions" and "mediate reasoning [*mittelbare Begründungen von Urteilen*]" (19). He is engrossed with the possibility that the eidetically valid meaning be "brought without mediation to primordial givenness [*unmittelbar zu originärer Gegebenheit gebracht werden könne*] (as being immediately [*unmittelbar*] grounded in essences of which we have primordial insight [*in originär erschauten Wesen*])" (19).
8   I am far from assuming a simplified or fully amenable construal of mediation, but I certainly favor a linguistic or discourse-based conception of it. The conceptual infiltration of material-cum-objectal reality I take to be, at bottom, a tropological—and narrative insofar as figurative sequences spawn narratives— infiltration. According to Fredric Jameson, "in thought, mediation is nothing but a word subject to all the most damaging anti-dialectical objections; in reality it is a mystery that blocks thinking altogether. We must handle it with the greatest caution and virtuosity" (*Representing* Capital 8).

was, as Jameson problematically suggests, already post-philosophical, then today's jumpy post-theoretical outmanoeuvring can rightly be seen to stand at two removes from philosophical correction—yes, I said correction, implying *critical-anamnestic* fidelity to the complex literalness of philosophical textuality.[9] And, I would suggest, such correction can only be tendentially restored once a dialectical critique "aimed at confusing prejudice" (Gadamer *Dialectic* 32) has managed to clear up the field. Derrida rightly spoke of Husserl's strong dislike of the term "dialectics."[10] Indeed he despised the reality behind the word. Husserl's penchant for a necessary and absolute detachability "in principle of the whole natural world from the domain of consciousness" (*Ideas* 89) can be seen as rehearsing the sceptical drive to an "absolute dialectical unrest" (Hegel *Phenomenology* 124), a medley of confuse sensations and chaotic thoughts, that Hegel believed to be genuinely undialectic. Hegel had no patience with self-proclaimed new philosophies that refused to acknowledge the conceptual texture and relational condition—the cultural-ideological density, so to say—of things, let alone thoughts. His impatience is a lesson in resistance to our neo-phenomenological times. When Merleau-Ponty conceded something on the Hegelian question of textual-conceptual mediation—the recognition, for instance, that we think "avec les instruments culturels que m'ont préparé mon éducation"—it was only to have it sponged up in the immediate absorption of the *monde vécu*—"mes efforts précédents, mon histoire" (*Phénoménologie* 89). We return to the kind of confessional self-vindicating narrative I criticized in an earlier section apropos of Dollimore and others: this is *mon histoire*, my life, my Shakespeare. The absolutization of the eidetic in Husserlian phenomenology was counter-balanced, by followers like Merleau-Ponty, by a mysterious absolutization of empirical reality, and both absolutes were left to wander in their own respective structureless mediums—their immediate mediums or *immediums*—without conceptual-relational assistance.[11] This undialectical outcome was strongly feared by Adorno, who condemned Benjamin's unreflective short circuit between positivism (empiricism) and magic (bad idealism), and requested from his friend "more *dialectics*" (Letter 18 March 1936, *The Complete Correspondence* 131). But at least Husserl was alive to the true

---

9   I don't think Ruda's concept of "meta-critical anamnesis" (*For Badiou* 44–47) is either sufficiently clear or particularly effective. Without an elucidation of what exactly is meant by critique and, especially, by dialectic, there is no way we can assess the benefits of modal renovations of either practice.
10 Jacques Derrida, "Introduction" to Husserl, *L'origine de la géométrie*, 46.
11 Derrida notes in several places the complicity between Platonism and empiricism that phenomenology is at pains to elude: see *L'origine*, 51.

dimension of the project he was up to. He knew he was doing *transcendental* philosophy, not *transcending* philosophy. By contrast, card-carrying neo-phenomenological scholars see themselves as Joan of Arc upon the battle-scene, visited by supernatural *infusion* (*1 Henry VI* 1.2.85) and boasting of their prescience: "Ask me what question thou canst possible / And I will answer unpremeditated" (1.2.87–88); or as Harvey Keitel in *Pulp Fiction*, showing up at the metaphysical crime scene, carrying their *vitaactivactor-network* toolkit and announcing: "I solve problems." But this is sadly no fiction, it's real, and not even speculatively real. Husserl knew, with Kant, that let to its own devices, the factual world is axiologically and semantically tight-fisted: "from facts [*Tatsachen*] follow always nothing but facts" (§19). But this basic recognition—what Jameson very early designated as the priority of "the fact of sheer inter-relationship" (*Marxism* 6) not only over facts themselves but also over conceptual categorization—is not registered in the syllabus of the phenomenological kindergarten.

So, to return to the original question, what are the effects of this undialectical tendency in discussions of reason and language? The most visible are, in this order, the exaltation of speech and the revival of cognitivist assumptions. The first is built into the history of the decay and fall of phenomenology, where the glorification of parole (of a somatic, embodied, direct, living, interactive, pragmatic speech) runs through the work of Merleau-Ponty, Levinas, and even Arendt, who argued that "action and speech are so closely related because the primordial and specifically human act must at the same time contain the answer to the question asked of every newcomer: 'Who are you?'" (*The Human Condition* 178). Shakespeare's characters, incidentally, could always reply, "How can I know? If you are interested in identifies [Arendt was, very], check the 'Names of the Actors' or 'The Persons of the Play' in a printed copy of this play." To grasp the relevance of the second effect one must remember that cognitivism began as a radicalization of an ultra-rationalist conception of language (Chomsky's generative-transformational grammar, inspired in what he called Cartesian linguistics) and developed into a multidisciplinary position whose stock-in-trade is the naturalization of reason. From the notion that language is a universal rational competence (Chomsky) we have moved to the lesson that language is an instinct (Pinker). This only apparently contradictory development betokens the undialectical need *to shrink from mediation*, to sway, that is, from the extreme of spontaneous (innate, immediate) reason to the other extreme of proximal (co-given, immediate) nature—without letting the pendulum get caught in the middle of mediation. In disciplinary terms, this oscillation translates as an exigency, readily met by early modern literary scholars, to turn away from Saussure, and this deflection is attained either by overlooking his contribution to linguistics or (more commonly) by misreading his work.

2

To illustrate this point, I will now examine what two important early modern scholars, Brian Vickers and Bruce Smith, have to say about Saussure. It may appear pointless to devote much space to discuss Saussure in a book about Shakespeare, but the fact that Bruce Smith is drawn to the puerile endeavor of refuting Saussurean linguistics in a book titled *Phenomenal Shakespeare* seventeen years after Brian Vickers published another manifesto-like book titled *Appropriating Shakespeare* where he devotes the opening seventy pages to what he believed was setting the record of Saussurean linguistics right, gives me the motive and cue for this revision. Since Smith and Vickers often refer to other scholars and linguists (Roy Harris, Simon Clarke, Vincent Descombes, Michael Halliday) for arguments of authority, I will also appraise, here and there, the correctness of the their claims. Not unlike anti-Cartesianism, anti-Saussureanism is plagued by bigoted hear-say, third-hand reference, neglect of primary sources, and sloppy scholarship generally. In a final section, I will briefly explain how all the important notions used by Saussure—*negativity, difference, relationality, arbitrariness, totality*—betray a rational-transcendental standing that harks back to Descartes, Kant, and the dialectical tradition, and looks forward to the linguistic materialism upheld by deconstruction, where language is conceived, in Ned Lukacher's sharp formulation, as a "radically material but nonempirical medium" (*Daemonic* 6). Whereas Brian Vickers's misreading of Saussure is sustained by two phenomenological prejudices—the prejudice of intention and the prejudice of intersubjectivity—Bruce Smith's is informed by the phenomenological illusions of embodiedness and proximity. All four notions (intention, intersubjectivity, embodiedness and proximity) draw their significance from the metaphysical resources of *positive presence*—what George Steiner called *real presence*. Vickers and Smith rightly, if implicitly, read Saussure as discommending positive presence in favor of *negative relationality* or *differential absence*, but in the course of arguing against his work they disfigure it past recognition.

Let me begin with what Bruce Smith has to say about Saussure. In the chapter titled "How Should One Read a Shakespeare Sonnet" of his book *Phenomenal Shakespeare*, he premises his demonstration of how to read sonnet 29 as it appears in the 1609 with a reconsideration of Classical and Renaissance rhetoric. The standard expectation "first words, then gesture" is reversed, he argues, by the realization that "gesture comes *first*" (*Phenomenal* 49). The proposition is, Smith realizes, counter-intuitive, and he embarks on a metatheoretical disquisition to elucidate it:

> We need to distinguish two fundamentally different models of language. The first is the one that has held sway—in academic circles at least—since the linguistic turn of the late 1960s. In the transcribed lectures that comprise Ferdinand de Saussure's *Course in general linguistics* the professor distinguishes between two ways of framing the study of language. The more influential of these two frames in the late twentieth century was *langue*: a critical interest in the structures that make the marking of meaning possible, a synchronic framing of language in which particular utterance are less important than the deep structure that makes all utterances possible. In our fascination with these structural principles and the deconstruction they enable, we have forgotten the other framing of language described in Saussure's linguistics: *parole*, the diachronic consideration of language as it operates in time, language as particular utterances, language as process, language as dramatic event, language as speech-acts. (49)

The above passage contains four major errors:
1. The distinction between *langue* and *parole* is not, as Smith argues, a distinction between two "*frames*" or "*two ways of framing* the study of language" (emphases added), but rather a distinction between two *object*s of study: an individual *act* or *practice* (*parole*) and a *social product* or *object* (*langue*) (23).[12] True enough, Saussure opens Chapter 3 of his *Course* with a reflection on the difficulty of determining the "object" of study of the discipline called linguistics, and on the variety of approaches (*points de vue*) that the multi-faceted phenomena of language (syllables, words) call for (23–24). Depending on how we view it, the vast reality of *language* (which he also calls a *faculty*) shows different faces: an individual face, and a social face; or a present face (system, institution) and a past face (history, past product); the object of study is slippery. Its study has "plusieurs côtés à la fois" (24) and can be marshalled along many "dualités" (25), but he soon proceeds to make out a distinct object, *langue*, which he first characterizes as the "*norme* de toutes les autres manifestations

---

12   Saussure: "En séparant la langue de la parole, on sépare du même coup: 1 ce qui est social de ce qui est individuel; 2 ce qui est essentiel de ce qui est accessoire et plus ou moins accidentel" (*Cours* 30).

du language" (25; my emphasis).[13] Note the opposition between norm (rule, system) and manifestation (appearance, phenomenon). Unlike *langage*, which is "multiforme et heteroclite," *langue* is "a tout en soi et un principe de classification" (25). *Langue* is variously described as a code, a social tie, an interior treasure, a storehouse, a deposit or a sum (of treasures, deposited verbal images, of coinages), an average (13), even a trace.[14] The object of study called *parole* is outlined contrastively through this meticulous determination of *langue*:

> La *langue* est un ensemble de conventions nécessaires adoptées par le corps social pour permettre l'usage de la faculté du langage chez les individus. La faculté du langage est un fait distinct the la langue, mais qui ne peut s'exercer sans elle. Par la *parole* on désigne l'acte de l'individu réalisant sa faculté au moyen de la convention sociales qui est la langue.[15]

Parole is therefore a distinct and separate object of study: the individual *act* of the faculty of language realized within the social conventions of the *langue*. The act of *parole* is shaped as a "speaking circuit" (*circuit de la parole*) with two persons conversing with each other. What *parole* amounts to in this complex process, which implies the existence of a "social crystallization" of language (i.e. the existence of a *langue*), is only the "executive side [*le côté éxecutif*]" of the circuit, what we call *speaking*. The identification of *langue* as a distinct, autonomous, object of study marks the originality of Saussure's approach and is the foundational gesture of all modern linguistics. This identification is reiterated at the close of his unpublished manuscript, "De l'essence double du language:" "Un état de langue n'offre à l'étude du linguiste qu'un seul *objet* central: rapport des forms et des idées qui s'y incarnent" (*Écrits* 86; emphasis

---

13   Saussure's disinterest in the material (vocal, phonic) nature of language when dissociated from its contribution, as parole, to a sign that is already an immanent, interior, object of consciousness, is also a constant point in his discussion of the double essence of language: see "De l'essence double du langage" in *Écrits de linguistique générale*, 17–88.

14   *Langue* is a *determined part* of language: "C'est à la fois un produit social de la faculté de langage et un ensemble de conventions nécessaires, adoptées par le corps social pour permettre l'exercice de cette faculté chez les individus" (24). One of the best definitions of *langue* is the following: "C'est un trésor déposé par la pratique de la parole dans les sujets appartenant à une même communauté, un système grammatical existant virtuellement dans chaque cerveau, ou plus exactement dans les cerveaux d'un ensemble d'individus; car la langue n'est complète dans aucun, elle n'existe parfaitement que dans la masse." Mounin offers an excellent survey of the different definitions of langue both in the sources and in the *Cours* proper (*Saussure* 35–37).

15   In note 63, p.419 of the French edition of the *Cours*, Tullio de Mauro rescues this definitional passage present in the manuscript and not included in the first edition.

added). By saying that *langue* and *parole* are not two different objects of study, but the same object approached in two different ways, Smith seeks to level them, turning the choice of approach into some kind of non-hierarchical, democratic game. He is wrong. If you believe that by studying *parole* you are examining *the whole* reality of language in *a* particular way, you are profoundly mistaken. You are only looking at a part of the reality of language (the individual executive side of the speaking-circuit) and omitting the most important part, the social code that Saussure calls *langue*.[16] In brief, *langue* is decidedly not just a "framing way" or a "a critical interest." The two realities (*langue, parole*) may determine or dictate two incompatible paths (*routes*) for the study of language—Saussure admits that much—but they are certainly not *ways of framing* or *frames*. They are not two different approaches to the same object: they are, epistemologically speaking, two different objects demanding two different approaches.[17] From an ontological standpoint, however, we are forced to acknowledge that *langue* and *parole* are like two attributes of the same substance (language), with the proviso that their relation is *dialectical* (Mauro, *Cours* 422, n65). The originality of this distinction—which is ultimately the distinction between message (*parole*) and code (*langue*)—is indisputable, and the pitfalls one may encounter when giving up, in a study of Shakespeare, the formal, transcendental, systemic productivity of the code are quite phenomenal.

2. The distinction between *langue* and *parole* is not, as Smith implies, predicated upon the distinction between the synchronic and the diachronic. The latter distinction originates in and exclusively applies to the study of *langue*, which may be conducted *statiquement* (synchronically) or *historiquement* (diachronically) (*Cours* 140). A synchronic study of *langue* focuses on *language states* (*états de langue*) in a given moment of time: it

---

16 On the fallibility and irrelevance of some "approaches" or "points of view" on language, Saussure argues: "Celui qui se place devant l'objet complexe qu'est le langage pour en faire son étude abordera nécessairement cet objet par tel ou tel côté, qui ne sera jamais tout le langage en le supposant très bien choisi, et qui peut s'il est moins bien choisi n'être plus même de l'ordre linguistique ou représenter une confusion de points de vue inadmissible para la suite" (*Écrits* 22).

17 Saussure often reiterates that *langue* is a distinct object: "Elle est un object bien défini dans l'ensemble héteroclite des faits de langage [...] La langue, distincte de la parole, est un objet qu'on peut étudier séparément" (*Cours* 31). This is the passage where Saussure speaks of ways as *routes*: "Pour toutes ces raisons, il serait chimérique de réunir sous un même point de vue la langue et la parole. Le tout global du langage est inconnaissable, parce qu'il n'est pas homogène, tandis que la distinction et la subordination proposées éclairent tout. Telle est la première bifurcation qu'on rencontre dès qu'on cherche à faire la théorie du langage. Il faut choisir entre deux routes qu'il est impossible de prendre en même temps; elles doivent être suivies séparément" (*Cours* 38).

examines the balances or states achieved by "logical and psychological relations that bind together coexisting terms and form a system in the collective mind of speakers" (*Course* 100). A diachronic study of langue examines the evolutionary change and transformation of the different "termes" of *langue* across time: "Diachronic linguistics, on the contrary, will study relations that bind together successive terms not perceived by the collective mind but substituted for each other without forming a system" (100). Just as many acts of *parole* may occur in a given synchronic moment, so many acts of *parole* may follow one another in the diachronic course of the *langue*. In short, the fact that *parole* favors the dynamism and transformation of the terms (sounds, syllables, words) of the system doesn't necessarily turn it into the object of diachronic or evolutionary linguistics, which remains the system of *langue*. It may also be worth recalling that Saussure stresses the synchronic nature of *parole*: "La première chose qui frappe quand on étudie les faits de langue, c'est que pour le sujet parlant leur succession dans le temps est inexistante" (*Cours* 117). In conclusion, Smith has fatally misinterpreted Saussure's forceful point about the contribution of *parole* to diachronic change—"tout ce qui est diachronique dans la langue ne l'est que par la parole" (138)—wrongly assuming that *parole* becomes therefore "the diachronic consideration of language as it operates in time" (*Phenomenal Shakespeare* 49). *Parole* is not a *consideration*: it is the individual, executive side of language. The diachronic consideration of language as it operates on time is a consideration that presumes of course the operations of *parole*, but its relevance applies exclusively to *langue*, as it is the system of *langue* that may be thereby readjusted and transformed. Let me reproduce the table that Saussure used in his lectures to explain "the rational form that linguistic study should take" (*Course* 98; *Cours* 139):

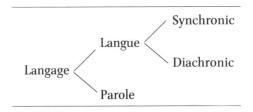

3. To describe deconstruction as a critical-discursive practice "enabled" by the "structural principles" discovered in langue is doubly inaccurate. First, because *every* single verbal act is enabled by them, from Lear's repudiation of Cordelia to the menu in the diner across the street. Second, because deconstruction is largely spurred by the critical recognition of the importance of some of these

principles (arbitrariness, difference, relationality, negativity), which in turn have roots in the rational, speculative-dialectical tradition, from Descartes to Hegel. Without ever reading Saussure, Derrida could have coined the term *différance* and fleshed out the many implications of this concept along similar lines to those we find in *L'écriture et la différence* and *De la grammatologie*. To be sure, the *Cours* worked as an extremely productive catalyst, and Derrida was niggard in his recognition of indebtedness: he never fully and openly acknowledged that Saussure's dialectical-transcendental conception of the system of *langue* was informed by the principles of the dialectical tradition (reflexivity, speculation, negativity, relationality, arbitrariness, difference) that he was already deploying in order to fight back phenomenology.[18]

4. The phrase "deep structure" is doubly incorrect. First, Saussure only describes *langue* as a *structure* once: the term he uses repeatedly is *système*. Second, there is nothing inherently "deep" in the Saussurean construal of *langue* as a *système*. Saussure reserves the adjective (*profonde*) and the adverbial (*profondément*) to what is very marked or very conspicuous. Although he speaks twice of the *depth* of certain linguistic phenomena, and once of the *profound* unity of the diversity of languages, he construes *langue* as a transcendental (not deep) system that permits the effective (not superficial) realizations of *parole*. "Deep structure" is not a Saussurean notion, but a Chomsky coinage, indebted to Hockett, which applies exclusively to grammatical and syntactical analysis. Hockett, by the way, only spoke of "deep grammar."

One may object that these are minor errors, the detection of which reveals a fastidious mind. Well, what is fastidious, in my opinion, is Smith's very unnecessary recourse to Saussurean linguistic arguments—complete with reproduced figures and brief quotations from the *Course*—in order to sustain his interpretive claims. To prelude his hermeneutic remarks on a sonnet by Shakespeare with a putative demolition of Saussurean linguistics is a risky endeavor, especially if one is not sufficiently acquainted with the target. But he is undaunted: "Before *langue*, before *parole*, Saussure recognizes a primordial chaos of thoughts and sounds" (49). This is also untrue: nothing precedes *langue*, not even anxiety. The system of language, however rudimentary its diachronic stage, is the *transcendental* condition—Saussure doesn't use this

---

18   With hindsight, the reading of the two sections titled "Négativité et différence" in the unpublished manuscript "De l'essence double du langage" (*Écrits de linguistique générale*, 64–66) serves to reinforce still more the affinities between deconstruction and Saussure's theoretical discovery, and gives the lie to those who argue that the radical philosophical implications of Saussure's concepts of negativity and difference have been exaggerated past recognition.

Kantian phrase, but his argument implies it—of everything that we may come by in the way of verbal creation, linguistic change, or individual verbal utterance. Historically, of course, Saussure concedes, there is *parole*—and change and readjustment—*prior to* (as a determining cause of) given stages in the systemic consolidation of *langue*, but he is very much aware that no occurrence of *parole* can take place in isolation from the transcendental (formal, systemic) frame of *langue* that enables it. As Mounin avers, for Saussure the "processus générateur" is always conditioned by the possibilities contained in the system that is *langue* (*Saussure* 99).[19] In Althusserian terms, *langue* is the structural cause of every single instance of *parole*, including those that alter *langue* beyond recognition: "Toute création doit être précédée d'une comparaison inconsciente des matériaux déposés dans le trésor de la langue où les formes génératrices sont rangées selon leurs rapports syntagmatiques et associatifs" (*Cours* 227).[20]

Smith's mistake is to read genetically (in terms of diachronic genesis) what in Saussure is just speculatively conjectured as a synchronic abstraction. Saussure argues that

> Psychologiquement, abstraction faite de son expression par les mots, notre pensée n'est qu'une masse amorphe et indistincte. Philosophes et linguistes se sont toujours accordés à reconnaître que, sans le secours des signes, nous serions incapables de distinguer deux idées d'une façon claire et constante. Prise en elle-même, la pensée est comme une nébuleuse où rien n'est nécessairement délimité. Il n'y a pas d'idées préétablies, et rien n'est distinct avant l'apparition de la langue. (155)

---

19 To put it simply, the rudimentary acts that set the *contingent*—yes, *contingent*: this is what soi-disant "anti-essentialist" scholars fail to understand—system of langue going were similar to but not yet acts of *parole*: only the "transcendental" retroaction of the embryonic language system over subsequent acts of phonation or inscription lent them the character of *parole*. That certain (meaning-and-knowledge-producing) transcendental orders are the contingent outcome of a historical inscription is what puzzled both Husserl and Derrida, eliciting responses from each that make up one of the most fascinating dialogues in recent philosophy.

20 The translation reads: "Any creation must be preceded by an unconscious comparison of the materials deposited in the storehouse of language, where productive forms are arranged according to their syntagmatic and associative relations" (*Course* 165). In this particular sense, it is erroneous to conclude that something like a "primordial chaos of thoughts and sounds" prescribes its inevitable anteriority.

Note the two caveats : *psychologiquement* and *prise en elle-même*. This is manifestly, as Hjemslev rightly noted, the beginning of a *Gedankenexperiment* or thought-experiment, for since we never effectively encounter the shapeless continuum of thought, we can only conjecture it retrospectively and figuratively as an uncharted nebula once the constitution of language has already occurred. And just as thought cannot be effectively conceived of as something preexisting language, so the plastic matter making up the phonic substance is also a conjectural medium conceptually retro-posited in order to conduct the thought-experiment (Mauro, *Cours* 461, n225). Therefore, ultimately, we are always-already inhabitated by a *langue* that is constituted differentially as a series of vertical cuts connecting two horizontal planes: "Nous pouvons donc représenter le fait linguistique dans son ensemble, c'est-à-dire la langue, comme une série de subdivisions contiguës dessinées à la fois sur le plan indéfini des idées confuses (A) et sur celui non moins indéterminé des sons (B)" (*Cours* 156). Thus, Smith's sentence, "Before *langue*, before *parole*, Saussure recognizes a primordial chaos of thoughts and sounds" (*Phenomenal* 49)—an observation no doubt congenial to certain cognitive-phenomenological readings of *Hamlet* (chaos of thought) and *The Tempest* (chaos of sound)—is a meaningless sentence. The only primordial chaos Saussure recognizes is that of historical linguistics. The chaos of thoughts and sounds Smith alludes to Saussure merely postulates *ex hypothesi* with a view to explaining the dual nature of *langue*. More ludicrous still is Smith's following remark: "Vertical lines indicate the cuts, the difference-markings that speakers make amid the chaos of thoughts and the plenitude of sounds" (49). The speakers don't make the cuts, the cuts are already made available for them by a preexisting langue that is both a collective transcendental realm of semantic possibility and a historically contingent reality. The cuts are not genetically introduced in both wave-planes at once by the individual speaker, thus constituting a sequence of differences. The differential sequencing transcendentally (generically, collectively) preexists the individual act of *parole*. Anyone repelled by Heidegger's dictum that "die Sprache spricht" (*Unterwegs* 10) or Lacan's intimation that "l'inconscient est structuré comme un langage" (*D'un discours* 152) will be insensitive to the originality and richness of implication of Saussure's notion.[21] But recall that ignorance breeds mistrust. Smith's most outrageous comment is: "Saussure himself attended to the waves as well as to the lines, but most of his disciples since the linguistic turn have not done so" (49–50). First, Saussure attended neither to the wave of thought—he was not interested, like William

---

21   For Lacan's notion see Sean Homer, 65–70; and Paul Ricoeur, *De l'interpretation*, 385–425.

James or Henri Bergson, in epistemology or mental states—nor to the isolated wave of sound—he was not interested in phonetics or acoustics, only in phonology. Second, the linguistic turn is not a philosophical movement that depended exclusively on Saussurean linguistics to get started. In analytical philosophy (Frege, Russell, Wittgenstein, Quine), the linguistic turn took place independently of the *Cours*.

3

It is now the moment to consider Brian Vickers's criticism of Saussurean linguistics. His approval of the phenomenological emphasis on intention, expression and meaning suffuses the totality of his book. It is explicitly borne out when he endorses Simon Clarke's dissatisfaction with the way the linguists of the Prague School, who "started from Husserlian phenomenology, seeing language as 'an intentional object whose structure is an expression of its function as an instrument of human communication,'" broke with this tradition of thought and turned their research "into a formalism that ignored questions of communication and meaning" (*Appropriating* 15).[22] He also shares Harris' focus on the centrality, in studies of language, of communicative interaction. Such commitment to "interactive social activity" (Harris, *Reading Saussure* 204) betrays the kind of pragmatic penchant for interactive polis-making that prevails amongst Arendt-inspired early modern scholars. Let me say that this view is at least more developed than the outdated stance, still held by Scruton, that "the primary purpose of language is to describe reality" (*Fools* 9). So, with our souls teeming with *intention, expression, communication, meaning*—this is how to do things with words. This is how we do things here, or did, before Saussure. And down this path, Austin and Husserl pragmatically hold hands. Vickers was correctly aware that the path was that of *phenomenology*:

> While semiology has faded, its limitations all too evident, phenomenology and hermeneutics continue to develop, and remain of great value to anyone concerned with literature since they also take as axiomatic the existence of author, text, and reader in a communication cycle, with language as essentially a medium for the expression of meaning.
> *Appropriating* 117

---

22   The inside quotation is from Simon Clarke, *The Foundations of Structuralism*, 146.

So this is how we do things here. Before Saussure, before the arrival of those French-speaking thugs from across the Channel, from Switzerland, France, and Belgium, that were obviously looking for trouble and trying to confound our good old English common sense. Now that they are gone, now that semiology has faded, we may return to the happy verdure of our English hills, to the honest prelapsarian world where "words [are] made of breath" (*Hamlet* 3.4.181).[23]

Let me start with what I take to be Vickers' errors of interpretation, and I do so in fear and trembling, very much aware that his censure of Saussure was widely acclaimed by reviewers.[24] The first error is to consider that "while emphasizing that *langue* and *parole* are interdependent, Saussure gives priority to parole" (*Appropriating* 5). This is manifestly wrong. Georges Mounin, who knew something about the Belgian linguist, says the exact opposite (*Saussure* 41), and grounds his opinion on the very basic fact that Saussure never developed, in the *Cours* or elsewhere, a linguistics of *parole*: his basic groundbreaking contribution is the isolation of *langue* as an autonomous object of study, and the set of analytical determinations that he managed to bring forth within the immanent boundaries of this newly discovered domain. The second error is Vickers' construal of the act of parole as an "intentional" act, "since whoever wishes to communicate his ideas must have an intention" (6). Well, if you "wish" to communicate them, you obviously have that "intention," but you may well "communicate" ideas without the intention to do so, or without any discernible intention. Vickers is tacitly adopting the phenomenological thesis to the effect that every act of language presupposes the intention to communicate: Husserl spoke, in *Logical Investigations*, of an intimating function (*die*

---

23 For the blessed corporal proximity of communicative *breathing* (*respiration*), see Levinas, *Autrement qu'être*, 276–78.

24 Some reviewers of Vickers' book praise the acumen of his reading of Saussure. Bevington spoke of "a lucid and partly admiring analysis of the great linguist Ferdinand de Saussure, along with a useful critique of Saussure's reductive approach to the functioning of the linguistic sign" (355). This is funny, considering that Saussure invented the conceptual object we call "the linguistic sign." This is like accusing Bell of reductionism for not foreseeing cell phones. Miola speaks of "the rigor of his mind and method," and mentions the "devastating critiques" contributed by scholars like Clark (sic.), Timpanaro, Harris and Holdcroft, on which Vickers draws (285). Miola concurs with Vickers in the countertheoretical claim that "language is intentional and communicates meaning" and agrees that deconstruction occludes a sense of "drama as interaction between characters with clear goals and values; it cannot address performance, neither the actor's art nor the audience's reaction" (286). Grace Tiffany argues that Vickers "heroically disentangles key passages in the writings of Saussure" and praises his capacity to retrieve Saussure's "own acknowledgement that linguistic signs derived meaning from their reference to concepts and things" (253).

kundgebende Funktion) of the sign, which permits a hearer assume that the speaker is trying to communicate something.[25] But maybe what he is trying to do is something else, as we can *do* many *things with words* other than convey knowledge or information to someone else. We cannot presume that the occurrence of an utterance or act of *parole* is always motivated by the speaker's desire to communicate ideas. What are the *ideas* Edgar *wishes* to *communicate* to other characters in *King Lear*? This might take more than five acts to figure out. There is speech without intention, speech without communication, and speech without ideas. There are effects of ventriloquism without origin, without emission, without addressee: "des effets de ventriloquie sans origine, sans émission et sans destinataire" (Derrida, *La carte postale* 363). Take Beckett: "The expression that there is nothing to express, nothing with which to express, nothing from which to express, no power to express, no desire to express, together with the obligation to express" ("Three Dialogues" 103). Or take Foucault's non-grammatical and non-psychological conception of statements (*énoncés*) in *L'archéologie du savoir* (105–115). Of course, Beckett and Foucault may be wrong about language, and Edgar may not be the best informant, but if you give up Edgar, Beckett, and Foucault, you might as well give up Shakespeare. Pick Dryden instead, or Shaw. You will have a ball.

Further, and this is the third related error, Vickers stresses the genetic or "initiating role" played in communicative acts of parole by "thought." He quotes Harris to the effect that "concepts" are "the prime movers in the activity which occupies the speech circuit" (*Reading Saussure* 213) and endorses this scholar's use of the expression "cognitive system" (199). This is doubly problematic. First, Saussure didn't see language as a *cognitive* system. He sought to insulate the system of *langue* both from the unreality of nonverbal thought and from the unthinkability of reality. Vickers finds it hard to swallow that "Saussure kept his distance from all theories of reality as far as he possibly could" (9). But the truth is that only this way he protected a real reality (as unknown as Lacan's Real) from the categorial grasp of language: what Vickers and so many others staunch common-sensical realists call reality or reference is actually

---

25 See *Logical Investigations 1*: "all expressions in communicative speech function as indications. They serve the hearer as signs of the 'thoughts' of the speaker, i.e. of his sense-giving inner experiences, as well as of the other inner experiences which are part of his communicative intention. This function of verbal expressions we shall call their intimating function" (189). Levinas' conception of the self-Other interaction is largely grounded in this assumption: "La presence d'Autrui ou expression, source de toute signification, ne se contemple pas comme une essence intelligible, mais s'entend comme langage ... " (*Totalité* 331).

little more than what the language they humor and speak leads them to construe as reality and reference, and the same applies to thought.[26] Putnam has rightly argued that "one can be both a realist and a conceptual relativist" (*The Many Faces* 17). In my opinion, this perfectly applies to Saussure and Derrida, whose evident cultural relativism originates in their moral respect for an enigmatic reality they feel they must keep, epistemologically speaking, at bay (The regardful distance Hegel, Heidegger, Adorno, and Žižek show towards genuine science stems from the same rule of ontic politeness: respect the real!). Many anti-idealist academics forget that if Kant and Hegel turned away from the *empiricist faith in sensible reality* it was the better to *protect reality from sensible faiths*. There is more *amor mundi* in Descartes, Kant, Hegel, Saussure, Adorno, and Derrida than in most self-proclaimed world-wooers. It may appear odd to see Saussure listed in such company, but this is his place. In a remarkable essay, Robin M. Muller has rightly spoken of a "linguistic idealism" (133) in Saussure that shows an affinity with Kantian transcendental idealism. Thus, Saussure's gesture is not unlike Husserl's Cartesian move: let us give up the natural attitude, let us forget about the nature, structure, consistency and even existence of reality, and focus on the structured formalizations and schemata that orient our apprehension of such reality. Although Saussure often has recourse to the category of the psychological, his "dominant view" is not, as Simon Clarke opines and Vickers repeats, a mentalist one (Clarke 120–126). Like Husserl, Saussure aimed to rule out psychological considerations from the study of language. His apparent residual mentalism or psychologicism is always geared towards a transcendentalist formalism akin to Husserl's pure pan-logicism. In this sense, both the early Husserl and Saussure conduct themselves in a Kantian manner. As Muller points out, *langue*, for Saussure, "is a hermetically sealed system of the Kantian sort: Kantian in the sense that the sealing off of the world in itself in favor of attention to purely psychological processes constitutes a foundational move of Kant's *Critique of Pure Reason*" (132). Replace *psychological* with *transcendental* and we will have gone a long way towards reaccommodating Saussure into his dialectical-idealist family.[27]

---

26   Muller: "One famous and well-rehearsed consequence of Kant's new transcendental idealism is the realization that, rather than thought conforming to the world *as it is*, the world *in so far as I can understand it* conforms to the forms of thought" (133).

27   Muller quotes from a Kant letter: "I noticed that I still lacked something essential, something that in my long metaphysical studies, I, as well as others had failed to pay attention to and that, in fact, constitutes the key to the whole secret of hitherto still obscure metaphysics. I asked myself: What is the ground of the relation of that in us which we call 'representation' to the object." And then she goes on to quote Longenesse: "this shift from causality to conditions of possibility is only a manifestation of a more fundamental

This re-accommodation takes, of course, some bumping and pushing. Note, for instance, that whereas for Husserl logic is an eternal a priori, for Saussure, the a priori of the system of *langue* as a transcendental frame is the outcome of a contingent, historical, collective production, which is thereby constantly open to readjustment, revision, and change. It is, in short, an *a posteriori* promoted to *a priori*. And note too that the gesture whereby you contingently posit your own necessary presuppositions is, as Žižek has observed, a prototypical idealist gesture, already at work in Fichte (*Less than Nothing* 168–171). Derrida also recognized this gesture—the erasure of the contradiction in an ideal necessity that is historically produced—as a constant motif in the work of Husserl. The gesture is of course dialectical, and Mounin has stressed the "profoundly dialectical character of Saussure's thought," which he characterizes as "dialectical realism" (*Saussure* 45, 58).[28] The historical change of language, however, is never the outcome of an intentional or cognitively-directed drive on the part of the collective of speaking individuals: it is rather the result of random alterations that enter the system policed into regularities. Languages, for Saussure, do not develop in a goal-oriented, teleological manner, but, as in Darwinism, they rely on the inscriptive force of propitious accident: they are "constantly and irrepressibly transforming one into one another along a continuum through the unconscious adaptation of minute changes that over very long periods of time had cumulative effects" (Bouissac 136). Citing Roy Harris, Vickers takes offense at the fact that "Saussure never shows what 'collective ratification amounts to' (225)" (12). Well, anyone acquainted with a gradualist or catastrophist conception of tradition, be it the legal tradition of the common law, the English constitution, or the literary canon, that is to say, anyone familiarized with the writings of Edward Coke, Edmund Burke, Walter Bagehot, or T. S. Eliot will not be alarmed at the notion of an internal, self-contained system that remains however open to transformative readjustment from the pressure of outside input. If Vickers has a problem with this notion, it is his problem, not Saussure's. As in the Darwinian paradigm, collective ratification is a largely unconscious business whose occurrence and dynamics are structural, i.e. beholden to differential relations between the formal elements of the system, and whose outcome—the self-organizing but ever-changing system—is likely not only to operate as a transcendental frame but to accommodate

---

shift: Kant is no longer examining the relation of two heterogeneous elements (one 'within' and the other 'outside' representation), but the relation of two elements both internal to representation."

28   In the passage I quote from, Mounin chides Marxian interpreters for failing to appraise the dialectical dimension of Saussure's work, and of accusing him of idealist.

the semblance, in expressive intentions, of a situated teleology. There always have existed, of course, institutional ways to secure the invariance of what is exposed to variation, from newspapers and dictionaries to school instruction, from pulpit preaching to fire-side reading of novels borrowed from circulating libraries. Let me add that this historicist-pragmatist conception of the transcendental is not totally incompatible with what Rorty called "epistemological behaviorism" and made depend on a "conversational justification" that is "naturally holistic" (*Philosophy* 170). At any rate, Vickers' tactical interest in Harris' objections sets us on an interesting track, as the latter's conscientious discussion of the question of collective ratification is one among a number of problems singled out by this lucid interpreter that supposedly reveal the shaky and seemingly paradoxical quality of Saussure's theoretical proposal. Another is that of communication:

> The root of the problem with Saussurean linguistics is that it has not worked out the connection between language and communication in any theoretically satisfactory way. Although it couples language with communication in an intimate partnership, the two partners are condemned to dancing in perpetuity to the tune of what one linguist has called Saussure's "hesitation waltz" (Gagnepain 1981: 149). This odd composition is the result of starting linguistic theory from the wrong end. Saussurean linguistics begins by focusing upon the properties of the individual linguistic sign in the abstract, and hoping that somehow at the social end, where signs are put to everyday use, everything will work out satisfactorily in terms of communicational corollaries. Unfortunately, it does not work out at all.
>
> *Reading Saussure* 230

Ok. So let us focus rather on the social end—on the transcendent horizon of the bodies of the speakers interacting in the open space of the polis. Will the waltz between language and communication work at all if we begin there? Do Elizabeth and Darcy communicate satisfactorily while they dance in Chapter 18 of *Pride and Prejudice*? Will they go on communicating satisfactorily after their wedding? What about Ivanhoe and Rowena? What would Thackeray say? And Balzac, Dickens, Fontane? Do we know of any human being, let alone any Shakespeare character, for whom signs "work out satisfactorily in terms of communicational corollaries"? The assumption is ridiculous. If we assume that the primary function of language is communication, and that in local speech acts communication indeed works, then, of course, "everything," any linguistic theory you devise, "will work out" for you. If your assumptions are different—and you believe that even in ordinary communicative situations "equivocation will undo us" (*Hamlet* 5.1.126)—then you will need a toolbox. No normative conception of satisfaction or fulfilment can be made to depend on the vanishing contingency of situated acts of *parole*. The best we can say is that *all of them* are satisfactory insofar as they take place. But this pragmatist ruse is not what Harris and Vickers imply.

Another moot point in Vickers' reading of Saussure is his assessment of the relationship between linguistics and semiology. For one, Vickers relies strongly on Chapter 3 of Vincent Descombes' book titled *Le même et l'autre*, where the author's exposé of semiology is carried out without a single reference to Saussure's *Cours*—which is like offering an overview of atomic physics without mentioning the name of Ernest Rutherford. Descombes is a serious thinker, but his grasp of the indebtedness of French structuralist thought to linguistics is not exactly firm. To assess the meaning of Saussure exclusively through the work of Serres, Levi-Strauss and Lacan is an unsound venture. As Roy Harris has abundantly demonstrated, even Saussure's most sympathetic interpreters are not immune to misrepresentation. It is Harris, Vickers' authority elsewhere, who stresses that Saussurean "linguistics will occupy a privileged position within semiology, by providing a model (patron general) for all semiological investigation" (*Reading* 28). And this genetic subordination should not make anyone panic. But Descombes is dismayed by it, and so is Vickers, who explains that as the former has shown, "semiology took over several assumptions which are alien to natural languages [....] First, by preceding the message, the code defines all the situations in which it can be used" (Vickers, *Appropriating* 28). To be sure, Descombes argues that, in structuralism, a linguistic message is not the expression of an experience, but rather the expression of the possibility (*il exprime plutôt les possibilités*) and limits of the code employed in relation to the experience (*Le même et l'autre* 115). More specifically,

> Le code est indépendant du message, le sens du message émis, quel qu'il soit, est déjà capitalisé dans la langue. Mais, s'il en est ainsi, la conversation ne va-t-elle pas se réduire à un échange de signaux déjà enregistrés et répertoriés dans un code des usages, des bonnes manières? Jusqu'où la vie sera-t-elle opprimée par la convention? (115)

The final question is the very one Romeo, Juliet, Hamlet and Edmund raised, and there is no need to recall the answer their Shakespeare plays, and Derridean exegesis, gave to it. But I will: *until death, until early death*. At any rate, to return to the letter of Descombes' claim, possibilities are not *expressed*: they are *materialized*. An act of *parole* materializes indeed the finite possibilities contemplated in the code, but the possibilities of such materialization, contrary to what Descombes and Vickers suppose, are contingent and potentially infinite. This doesn't mean that they are registered and inventoried, as Descombes holds. This is like assuming that $E=mc^2$ was registered and inventoried in the mathematical apparatus of the physics paradigm describing, at Einstein's time, the laws of inertia, gravitation, and thermodynamics. It wasn't: Einstein had to produce (to materialize) his equation, to actualize one of the latent—but yet unproduced, unfound, unregistered and non-inventoried—possibilities afforded by the "transcendental" *field* of the more or less mathematized physics of his time. Similarly, the act of *parole* "bare ruined choirs" (Sonnet 73.4) actualizes a possibility of the system (*langue*) of the English language in the late sixteenth century, and someone had to produce the phrase—and this production we call finding, *inventio*. This is the case not only due to the inherently large breath and scope of the elements making up all the subsystems of language (phonological, morphological, lexical, syntactical, textual), which allow for virtually uncountable combinations, but also by virtue of the pressure of other systematized realities (biological, sociological) that impinge on the speaker's verbal creativity. The unpredictable can happen, and does happen, in concrete linguistic situations, and the very unpredictable we call literature, or wit: "How absolute the knave is!" (*Hamlet* 5.1.126). This doesn't mean that individual verbal action can do away with convention. On the contrary, *parole* is a contingent and more or less creative application of necessary and conventional rules— of rules, let me add, that are constantly violated and altered in (e)very creative application(s). This is a basic tenet of transcendental (haunto)logy: one may step into the unlimited by simply playing within a "system of limits" (De Mauro, *Cours* 420 n65). At bottom, what is stake is Descombes' and Vickers' refusal to countenance the *equiprimordiality* of the transcendental and the actual, the formal and the empirical. They hold that the notion that *langue* always precedes *parole*, or the signifier always comes before the signified, is a perverse radicalization, initiated by Levi-Strauss, of an originally Saussurean idea (Descombes 115; Vickers 27–28). But in what sense is *precedence* being construed? There is always formal precedence in any empirically realization of the formal (transcendental) possibility, but since the realization is what actually occurs in a sensible manner, we necessarily deem it anterior to the *variable* law of its occurrence. The problem of variability brings us back to the rapport between *langue* and *parole*, which is of necessity marked by the problem of linguist change. Recall Eliot's dialectical—transcendental and hauntological—view of the literary tradition

> The existing monuments form an ideal order among themselves, which is modified by the introduction of the new (the really new) work of art among them. The existing order is complete before the new work arrives; for order to persist after the supervention of novelty, the *whole* existing order must be, if ever so slightly, altered; and so the relations, proportions, values of each work of art toward the whole are readjusted; and this is conformity between the old and the new. Whoever has approved this idea of order, of the form of European, of English literature will not find it preposterous that the past should be altered by the present as much as the present is directed by the past.
> "Tradition and the Individual Talent," *Selected Prose*, 38

The essay to which this passage belongs was published in 1919, only three years after the publication of Saussure's *Cours*. The insight, never fully fleshed out by Saussure in these precise terms, is nevertheless the same. Eliot is also talking about an "ideal order," about "relations," "values," "alterations," about the "form" of Literature and about the "supervention of novelty," and he could alternatively have concluded, in Saussurean jargon, that no one should find it preposterous that *langue* should be altered by *parole* as much as *parole* is directed by *langue*. Crucial here is that "the supervention of novelty" (the expressive creativity of an act of parole) is for Eliot coterminous with and simultaneous to the alteration of "the *whole* existing order" (the system of langue), which remains an *order* in spite of this *alteration*. Can a formal-ideal-transcendental order originate in time (in historical, contingent time), and be altered in time, and still remain a transcendental order? Kant would obviously take exception. But we can remain Kantians in a latitudinarian sense and respond affirmatively. So both *langue* and *parole* are, in this sense, equally precedent. As Nicholas Stang argues, "transcendental idealism is the view that objects in space are "outer" in the empirical sense but not in the transcendental sense" ("Kant's Transcendental idealism"). Similarly, *parole* is prior to *langue* in an empirical sense, but not in a transcendental sense.

The precedence of signifiers over signifieds or vice versa is an entirely different issue, as this distinction can only be made within the immanent boundaries of the system of *langue*. Here, signifier and signified are also equiprimordial because they originate together, as the recto and verso of a sheet of paper (*Cours* 157), through an articulation that is like the pattern of decomposition that punctuates the surface where two nonsolid substances meet (156): "Le signe linguistique est donc une entité psychique à deux faces," namely "concept" (signified) and "acoustic image" (signifier). "Ces deux éléments," adds Saussure, "sont intimement unis et s'appellent l'un à l'autre"

(*Cours* 99). So whose is the precedence? The much proclaimed autonomy of the signifier is a logical inference drawn from what Saussure postulates and it does not *per force* contradict the principle of equiprimordiality, nor the idea of an intimate union between signifier and signified. The fact that my body parts are subject to a physiological system doesn't prevent them from enjoying a certain "expressive" autonomy: I can use my ears as a jewelry-holder or move skin from one part of my body to another. There is a limit to the expressivity that my body can bear (I can die if I fool around too much altering functions of my limbs or exposing parts of my body to external functions) but the physiological system (the order) does not die with me. My neighbor's is the same, and it will work for him.

Vickers is proud to oppose the view of language put forward by the great English linguist Michael Halliday to the linguistic speculations of Saussure's alleged followers. But he seems to forget to what extraordinary degree Halliday's outstanding view of language is indebted to Saussure. Halliday's neat separation between theoretical and descriptive linguistics is Saussurean through and through. His creative reconsideration of the related meanings of system and structure, the theoretical basis of his Systemic Functional Grammar, would have been inconceivable without a Saussurean legacy he imbibed through the work of John Firth. Halliday's basic theoretical contribution, to prioritize the paradigmatic choice within a systemic conception of language, depends upon a distinction—paradigmatic-syntagmatic—originally introduced by Saussure. When Halliday speaks about the relation between a "code" and the culture that creates and transmits it to the next generation, he is already operating with Saussurean parameters. When he argues that "vocabulary only 'reflects' culture by courtesy of its internal organization as a whole" (xxxi) he wields a principle of structural immanence that the *Cours* rendered popular. When he points out that the structures that are the output of the system networks in English grammar "collectively realize the sets of features that can be chosen" (xxvii) he is unmistakably, if unwittingly, recognizing *a* certain priority of social structure (*langue*) over individual system choice (*parole*). To say that "a systemic grammar is not syntagmatic but paradigmatic" inside a book that omits the name of Saussure (Worf, Hjemslev, and Firth are mentioned) is at best strange. And so on, and so forth.[29]

---

29 In *An Introduction to Functional Grammar*, Halliday acknowledges his debt to Firth's system-structure theory and more broadly to Hjemslev and the Prague School, and he doesn't mention that the "abstract principles" and "ideas" (xxvi) he draws from them are chiefly rooted in the *Cours*.

Curiously, Vickers never mentions Saussure in his exposition of Halliday's views on language. His joy at being flanked by such brilliant (healthy-minded, common-sensical, function-oriented and English!) linguists as Halliday depends much more on the purely theoretical speculations of a depressed Swiss linguist interested in science and philosophy and steeped in German linguistic culture than he would be willing to acknowledge. Calling a grammar *functional*, as Halliday does, does not automatically render *functional* the language it depicts and theorizes. Halliday confidently asserts that "language has evolved to satisfy human needs" (xiii). The sentence, which betrays positivist practicality and analytical good sense, speaks to the philosophical assumptions of Russell, Ayer, Quine, Strawson, Davidson, and their likes, including Rorty. In a sense, the sentence is correct. Still, a different but no less authorized philosophical tradition would rephrase it as "The human being has evolved to satisfy linguistic needs." Humboldt, Nietzsche, Wittgenstein, Heidegger, Lacan, Derrida, de Man, and even Rorty, would all more or less concur that such rephrasing captures a neglected aspect in the study of the relationship between humans and language. This aspect is no other than the feedback dynamics whereby we use language as much as—perhaps less than—language uses us. On this view, language is functional because it is used to solve the practical challenges it induces its speakers to face. No doubt the underlying objective of nearly all functions of language—the goal of survival—is genuinely natural, but many of the derived goals and aims that we use language for are linguistically induced in an ongoing feedback process that distinctly overruns, and eventually leaves behind, the original natural objective. Is Hamlet's logorrheic *stoliditas* a sound survival strategy? Well, yes and no, and the *no* inscribes the spectacular unmotivation (the arbitrariness?) of a self-contained speech (five soliloquies and a set of Socratic dialogues) around which we still gravitate. We want to communicate largely because we have a language that offers us the possibility of communicating and thereby of satisfying a need that probably didn't preexist the language that induces us to communicate. Would we want to squeeze fruit if we didn't have squeezers? Or open locks if we didn't have keys? De Man suggested once that the human Self resembles a lock devised to respond to the existence of a key that is rhetorical language: we later indulge in the fantasy that we are the key that opens all locks.[30] Lear started begging nearly everyone around him

---

30   De Man: "In all these instances, rhetoric functions as a key to the discovery of the self, and it functions with such ease that one may well begin to wonder whether the lock indeed shapes the key or whether it is not the other way round, that a lock (and a secret room or box behind it) had to be invented in order to give a function to the key. For what could be more distressing than a bunch of highly refined keys just lying around without any

"to reason not the need" (*King Lear* 2.4.259), but the superfluousness of most cultural-social needs soon dawned on him. The brutal irrelevance of social additions, including language, was by contrast no news to the young nihilist who could use it (or be used by it) to say meaningfully meaningless things like "Why brand they us / With base? with baseness? bastardy? base, base?" (*King Lear* 1.1.9–10). Is that line and a half an instance of normal, interpersonal communication? What is the intention? What is the content? What is the reality alluded to? Is that reality (bastardy) alien (and prior) to the language that denotes it? Is the speaking subject (the bastard) alien (and prior) to the language he impishly, playfully, appears to denigrate? Obviously not. Both the subject and the reality are constituted by linguistic *branding*, and the logic that operates in the language used for this and other acts of stigmatization is as wildly arbitrary as the homophony deployed by Gloucester's illegitimate son. The idea that language is a historical-accidentally constituted structural field of transcendental possibility whose largely contingent and random functionality has helped to passively shape the human subject as a flawed, finite, libidinal machine predetermined by language-based conceptions and expectations is intolerable to the staunch English intellectual who is convinced that language functions because we make it function—and fails to see that the needs, conceptions, desires and intentions that presumably prompt us to make language function are most in the first place a function of the language that we speak. But then, are virtues (Lupton) and capabilities (Nussbaum) also a function of our arbitrary, cultural, language? I think so. It was always comforting to see seasoned scholars like the late Catherine Belsey acknowledge Saussure's immense contribution to the dialectical conception of the human being that emerges from Lacan's writings and seminars, a conception that is based on the same principles of negativity, relationality and difference that rule deconstructive work (*Shakespeare in Theory and Practice* 29). In the field, awareness of this dialectical conception—memory, in sum, of the "homo dialecticus" (Foucault, "La folie" 442)—is gradually fading out.

Thus far we have considered the positions of some of Vickers' sources of authority on Saussure—Roy Harris, Vincent Descombes, Michael Halliday. Let us now examine more carefully some of the ideas advanced by the British sociologist Simon Clarke. He holds that the application of three central

---

corresponding locks worthy of being opened? Perhaps there are none, and perhaps the most refined key of all, the key of keys, is the one that gives access to the Pandora's box in which this darkest secret is kept hidden. This would imply the existence of at least one lock worthy of being raped, the Self as the relentless undoer of selfhood" (*Allegories of Reading*, 173).

contrasts—between *langue* and *parole*, form and substance, synchrony and diachrony—"defines a closed corpus of scientific facts, an objective system of language supposedly divorced from any particular application of the system or from any particular interpretation of it" (*Foundations* 120). This is gloriously inexact. It is like saying that the endocrine (physiological) system is divorced from the growth of a teenager's limbs. Rather than being divorced from the situated applications of it, language *rules* them:

> un tel système gouverne la *parole*, existe au-dessus d'elle; et c'est là que réside son unique raison d'être (ses limites, c'est-à-dire la distinction entre un signifié et un autre, entre une entité signifiante et une autre, ne dépendent d'aucune cause déterminante inhérente à la nature du monde et de l'esprit, ou à celle des sons) ; si bien que l'on peut dire que la *langue* ne vit que pour gouverner la *parole*.
>
> DE MAURO, *Cours* 420 n65

Granted: to live above your spouse, governing him/her, is a deplorable modality of marriage. But we call it marriage, not divorce. *Langue* is decidedly not "divorced" from *parole*. Clarke's next irrelevance is: "*Langue* is, therefore, strictly comparable with Durkheim's collective conscience as an objective system that is external to the individual and resistant to the individual will" (120). The notion that *langue* is resistant to the individual would be very appealing if: 1) the individual will were not an imaginary faculty whose (un)reality corresponds to an unconscious that is, as Lacan argued, already structured as a language; and 2) the objective system of *langue* were not also internal to the individual. True enough, Saussure argues at one point that langue as a social system is "extérieure à l'individu" (*Cours* 31), but he constantly reiterates that this system is like a treasure deposited in the mind of every individual: "L'object concret de notre étude est donc le produit social deposé dans le cerveau de chacun, c'est-à-dire la langue" (*Cours* 44). The notion of an internalized exteriority, of an outside that is inscribed, deposited, and stored in the brains of individuals is not hard to swallow for anyone familiar with the concept of *ideology* in Marxian dialectics—in Marx, Engels, Freud, Lukács, Gramsci, Lacan, Ricoeur, Althusser, Adorno, Marcuse, Derrida, Jameson, or Žižek. Let me return to my refrain: if Clarke has a problem with this, it is his problem, not Saussure's. It is obvious that Clarke cannot tolerate the idea of a *traumatic internalization of exteriority*—we call that trauma a *subject*—for he moves on to rationalize the resulting paradoxical position in the following manner:

> Saussure believed that langue was a specific reality which has its "seat in the brain." Saussure, therefore, retained the mentalism of his contemporaries, seeking "to explain the facts of language by facts of thought, taken as established." Hence, for Saussure, the linguistic sign is a "psychological entity," uniting a "concept" and a "sound-image," and linguistics is a specialized branch of psychology. (120)

This is not so. Clarke's failure to see it reveals his inability to understand that Saussure's psychologicism is but a misnamed transcendentalism.[31] Saussure's "mentalism" and "psychologicism" are pragmatic, strategic, accommodating. For Saussure, linguistics is certainly not a specialized branch of psychology. He says that linguistics is a part of a science of *social* or *general psychology*, as opposed to individual or particular psychology, and he calls the former *semiology*. That is very different. What Saussure calls general psychology is a *transcendental* psychology, and therefore a realm of studies with no room for the kind of elements (sensations, feelings, emotions, passions) that we commonly label *psychological* and that have always been the object of rationalist abstention or *epoché*, from Descartes to Husserl. Otherwise, Clarke's later formulation—"By abstracting altogether from substance linguistics acquires its autonomy from physiology and psychology" (*Foundations* 121)—would be meaningless. Linguistics cannot be at the same time a part of psychology and autonomous from psychology. In conclusion, Saussure's use of the term reveals a terminological constraint, the effect of a cultural limitation he greatly contributed to revoke. It is perhaps useful to recall that Husserl, in *Ideas I* (1901), still described phenomenology as a descriptive psychology, or, perhaps more significantly, that Freud believed he was doing psychology.[32]

So, summing up, the system of langue is not, as Clarke contends and Vickers repeats, *divorced* from parole, completely *external* to the speaker's mind, or *psychological*. Nor is it *ideal*—and this adds another wrong determination—in any conventional sense of the word. According to Clarke, "although langue is an ideal-object, constructed by the analyst by abstraction from the actual

---

31   Firstly, Saussure offers a mentalist argument. His psychologism means that he is interested essentially in establishing "logical and psychological relations" (*Course* 99–100). The synchronic viewpoint, therefore, "predominates, for it is the true and only reality to the community of speakers" (*Course* 90), while the historical connections have no psychological reality. This argument clearly depends on the mentalist assumption that linguistics is a branch of psychology (Clarke 122).

32   For this mild paradox, see Žižek, *The Sublime Object of Ideology*, 32; and Ricoeur, *Freud and Philosophy*, 5, 9.

THE NATURALIZATION OF REASON   353

sentences used by native speakers, Saussure believed that *langue* was a specific reality which has its 'seat in the brain'" (120). Undoubtedly, Saussure uses various ways, some openly figurative, to describe what langue is—he was after all describing this epistemological object—*producing* it, Althusser would say—for the first time. And astute interpreters like Hjemslev or De Mauro have collated all these expressions and definitions and concluded that the most adequate technical terms to denote what Saussure understood by *langue* are those of *schema, pure form, norm of realization* and even *material form* (De Mauro, *Cours* 416 n45). Not *idea. Langue* is not, for Saussure, as Clarke contends, an "ideal object." The Swiss linguist uses very sparingly the adjective *ideal*—he speaks twice of an *ideal form* (of geographical diversity and lexical forms)—but never to the effect intended by Clarke. *Langue* may be—it is—*transcendentally ideal* in the corrected sense I have sketched above, one that renders possible the inside dialectical corrections of contingency, time, change, externality, and matter. Whether and how Kant's transcendental idealism may bear such pressure is something I examine in other sections of this book.

But there is more. Predictably, Clarke also bumps into the stumbling block of arbitrariness. He accuses Saussure's system of being contradictory in trying to reconcile psychological and linguistic assumptions about language. He bases this claim on the fact that whereas from a linguistic viewpoint language as a social system may be characterized by the arbitrariness of its signs, the psychological perspective renders such arbitrariness inoperative, since, he argues

> the meaning of the sound "tree" for a particular individual is not determined only by its relations with other linguistic sounds: its contrasts with "bush," "house," "sky," "pole," etc. It is also determined by all the previous uses of the sign that the individual has encountered: the trees to which it has been applied, the contexts within which it has been uttered. (123)

The first sentence is correct. The second isn't. The additional significance that determines the sound "tree," which may be accounted for through terms like *Sinn* (Frege) or connotation, has nothing to do with the *value* of the linguistic sign "tree." Nowhere in the *Cours* do we find, in the analysis of the value of the sign where arbitrariness emerges as *the* normative standard, a concession to this kind of individual psychological considerations. Saussure's entire project is an attempt to quarantine the systematic logic of language both from the physiology of historically changing sounds and from the emotional, associative vagaries of individual psychology. If there is a mentalism in his project, it is, let me insist, a *transcendental mentalism*. I don't deny that the "previous uses of the sign that the individual has encountered" may, as Clarke points out, determine the significance the user attaches to the sign. What I deny is that Saussure makes that claim, that he inserts that claim in a characterization of the value of the sign, and that therefore he falls into a "contradiction" that endangers the coherence of his postulate of arbitrariness.

4

To sum, the basic problem in Brian Vickers' and Bruce Smith's critical attitude towards Saussure is that they fail to grasp what is truly original in the *Cours*. Due to this failure of assessment, they attach an epistemological relevance to some developments in post-Saussurean linguistics—functionalism and body-oriented cognitivism, respectively—that is disputable, inasmuch as these developments glean much of their force from the interested occlusion (functionalism, generativism) or ignorance (cognitivism) of the truly meaningful theoretical findings in the *Cours*. Bloomfield's and Chomsky's very equivocal stance before Saussure's work epitomizes an attitude of niggard responsiveness and distrust that is probably also informed by cultural prejudice against a Continental *speculative* product.[33]

Vickers and Smith are reluctant to concede what was clear to Hjemslev and is today accepted by anyone conversant with the history of modern

---

33 See Harris' overview of Bloomfield's and Chomsky's reception of Saussure in *Reading Saussure*, 59–75; 152–170. Although the defense of arbitrariness offered an important point of convergence between Bloomfield and Saussure, Harris identifies serious "blind spots" and "oversights in Bloomfield's grasp of the central notions like *langue* and *sign*" (62–68), or the "wholistic character of Saussurean synchronicity" (67). Harris concludes that, aside from the fact that Bloomfield "manufactured a 'Saussure' whom he could manipulate for his own purposes," he also, "whether through a cursory reading of the CLG or a lack of intellectual penetration, or both, never succeeded in getting to grips with the originality and subtlety of Saussure's thinking, and merely read his own theoretical assumptions into the text" (75). Harris' appraisal of Chomsky's interpretation of Saussure is similar: Chomsky "misunderstood or misrepresented" central aspects of Saussurean theory, like the distinction langue-parole, while at the same time he tried to "see Saussure as a possible Chomskyan" (153). But this assimilation is problematic. Harris clarifies, for instance, that Chomsky's concept of "competence" or "normal mastery" of a language is not "*langue* in the Saussurean sense," but it rather "combines or conflates *langue* with *parole*" (158). Another important misrepresentation concerns the notion of the sign in Saussure, which "pairs an acoustic image with a concept" and "*not*," as Chomsky would have it, "a description of an acoustic image with a description of a concept" (163). Harris concludes that "Chomsky had evidently not read the CLG (or Baskin's translation) carefully enough to see that Saussurean linguistics" (165) to ascertain the actual points of convergence and divergence between his and Saussure's vision of language.

linguistics—that Saussure's "theoretical iconoclasm went far beyond his editor's perceptions or the linguistics of his contemporaries" (Harris, *Saussure and his Interpreters* 93), and that Saussure's is, therefore, the most important contribution to the creation of a modern discipline of *general linguistics* where the sheer notion of the *linguistic sign* becomes operative. Drawing on diverse sociological and linguistic sources (Durkheim, Whitney, Comte, Tarde, Courtenay, Marty), driven by a nostalgia to return to pre-romantic philosophical conceptions of grammar (Port-Royal, Leibniz), trained in scientific methodologies (chemistry, mathematics), Saussure soon realized the limitations and contradictions of the school of the *Junggrammatiker* who, with their focus on historical grammar, held the field when he started doing research. His new attention to *langue* as an immanent and self-organizing system whose positive elements (signs) engage synchronically in a logic of differential relations that can be deciphered without recourse to historical change, external reality or the mental life of the speaking subject was a momentous breakthrough. His notion of the exclusively *formal* value of the linguistic sign as an arbitrary dialectical interplay between signifier and signified is an extraordinary theoretical construction.

Failure to grasp the relevance of these contributions, and to see what is truly original in Saussure, originates in ignorance of the state of "linguistics" at his time, in inability to engage in a dialectical mode of thought beholden to transcendental sufficiency and logical autonomy, and in sheer prejudice against the very name Saussure. What Vickers, Smith and others refuse to see is that neither Saussure nor his presumed heirs (Levi-Strauss, Barthes, Derrida) deny that language is an instrument of communication where real speakers, in real and changing historical conditions, *seek* to express intentional meaning *presumably* connected to personal thought and social reality (my italics add a skeptical inflection that is latent in Saussure and open in Derrida). This is what language is, has been, will be. This expressive and communicative dimension of language was obviously taken for granted inside a *new theoretical paradigm* that strove merely to deflect attention from what had hitherto commanded the linguist's and philosopher's interest—linguistic change, intentional psychology, physical sound, empirical reference—towards the watertight immanence of the system (*langue*) organizing the different elements of the language supposedly implied in the contingent transactions of—often communicative, sometimes expressive—*parole*. As all good philosophers—and recall that Mounin, for one, treats him as a philosopher—Saussure created, through redefinition, new concepts—*langue, synchrony, value, linguistic sign*—by ingenuously overdetermining conceptual resources stored in the dialectical tradition (negativity, relationality, arbitrariness) and he put forward a conception of language that remains still largely hegemonic—even unconsciously by those who deprecate it.[34] One may of course regret that Saussure didn't pay more attention to diachronic change or the creative possibility of *parole*. But the fact is that he never denied their role in the erection of a new general linguistics, and if he didn't devote more time in his courses to these aspects of language it is because the other aspects (arbitrariness, formality, systematicity, synchrony, relationality) had been neglected by his contemporaries, and demanded more attention.

The originality of Saussure's ideas was best appreciated by his direct disciples. Albert Séchehaye, one of the students whose notes served as the basis of the first edition of the *Cours*, argued in 1917 that the many particular contributions to the thriving field of comparative grammar in a historical perspective was sadly never accompanied by theoretical reflections on the general nature and structure of language. What they offered, at best, was undialectical *raissonement*—a hoard of "singulières divagations" ("Les problems de la langue" 2). The situation wasn't better in the Oxbridge academic ecosystem. This deficit must be factored in if we wish to assess the extent of Saussure's innovativeness. His combination of analytical concentration, taste for intense theoretical speculation and conceptual reinvention, and sheer iconoclastic attitude towards received dogma reminds us of Einstein's similar breakthrough in physics research in 1905. Linguistics and physics were never the same after their intervention. In both cases, moreover, the intervention was less experimental than theoretical.

In 1950, the great English linguist John Firth pointed out "nowadays professional linguists can almost be classified by using the name of de Saussure. There are various possible groupings: Saussureans, anti-Saussureans, post-Saussureans, and non-Saussureans" ("Personality and Language," 179). This is perhaps the most precise compliment ever paid to the originality and impact of Saussure's ideas on language. The exact affiliation to these grouping of phenomenology-inclined literary scholars is unclear, for whereas Vickers comes through as a staunch anti-Saussurean, Smith performs the one miracle—he exits the roster and becomes a pre-Saussurean. To become a non-Saussurean or an anti-Saussurean demands more critical energy than he exhibits. Roy Harris, an authority on Saussure who keeps a considerable

---

34   The first chapter in Mounin's excellent book on Saussure is significantly titled "Saussure et la philosophie." The idea that philosophy is a discursive practice that involves the creation of concepts is of course Deleuze's and Guattari's: *Qu'est-ce que la philosophie*: "La philosophie, plus rigouresement, est la discipline qui consiste à créer des concepts" (10).

distance from his subject of study, has called the *Cours* the "Magna Carta of modern linguistics" (*Reading* x), observes that "Saussure on linguistic theory is far more worth reading today [1987] than many of his 'advanced' successors" (xi). He later avers that "Saussure's status as the founder of modern linguistics is unproblematic" (26) and observes that "by formulating the antithesis between these two principles—one [system of cognition] denying and the other [mechanism of activity] admitting an involvement of linguistic structure with the structure of the external world—the *Cours* makes the most profound revolution in grammatical theory since Port Royal" (77). But Smith, finding support in William James, Lev S. Vygotsky, David McNeill, and Michael Spivey, makes a new revolution by expunging systematic cognition from the purview of language, and reducing it to a body-oriented circuit of interpersonal communication. His revolution is a return to groovy continuity and phenomenal "flow," not "chain" (*Phenomenal* 53), a return to "thought without speech," a return, that is, to the flowing mind and the thinking body, complete with "quantum-mechanics models of perception" and "the circulations of *spiritus*" (53). This sounds like Allen Ginsberg saluting Carlos Castaneda. Involutionary revolutions are not, we know, uncommon accidents.

Bruce Smith and Brian Vickers share a view of language as primarily an instrument of communication of meanings that are intentionally projected by speakers in specific situations of speech. The key notions are those of intention, meaningfulness, communication, and speech, and all of them are regarded as *naturally* produced elements in a whole (language) whose rationale is ultimately, in the final instance, made to depend on the *natural* needs and constitutions of speakers. This partly phenomenological view necessarily tends to occlude the systemic factors of distance, relationality, negativity and, especially, arbitrariness, that Saussure identified in language. And it openly sets out to reverse the valence of Saussure's radical critique of *naturalization*: "No one has proved," he argues, for instance, "that speech, as it manifests itself when we speak, is entirely natural [*entièrement naturelle*], i.e. that our vocal apparatus was designed for speaking just as our legs were designed for walking" (*Course* 10; *Cours* 25). Saussure sharply distinguishes, in his theory of the linguistic sign, between natural relations and arbitrary relations. This distinction, inspired in Whitney, marks a turning point in modern linguistics and philosophy of language. But Smith is determined to reduce the latter to the former and thereby to return to 1910. Let me be totally clear: anti-Saussurean linguistics can easily slip into pre-Saussurean linguistics, and nothing really innovative can come from the derogation of the structural principles of arbitrariness, relationality, and negativity in language.³⁵ Saussure's conclusion is unbending: "En linguistique les données naturelles n'ont aucune place" (*Cours* 116). Once again, now in the language of the bard, "natural data have no place in linguistics" (*Course* 80).³⁶

Saussure's basic lesson is, like Derrida's, procedural—and it involves the differential manner of conducting analysis of linguistic material:

> It was more a way of construing whatever level of analysis one chooses as systems of distinctive elements whose identities depended on their mutual relations and systematic interdependence. The fundamental thesis was that no element can be a purely positive entity but has an identity and a value that are determined more by what it is not than by what it is.
> BOUISSAC 128

So no purely positive entity, no natural remnant. Never had language been so separated from nature, never so forcefully asserted as convention. Descombes indignantly requested to know for how long life would be repressed by convention. Vickers and Smith replied that a limit had been reached and worked to re-naturalize language (and by extension reason) along lines partly laid out by second-generation "phenomenologists" like Merleau-Ponty and Levinas, but also Arendt. This re-naturalization was conducted as a basic search for the *transcendens* that could anchor language back in natural motivation—this *transcendens* was the body (Merleau-Ponty), the speaker (Levinas),

---

35 If somebody intends, as Smith does, to tell you that a mode of natural (symbolic, motivated) body-oriented or nonverbal-thought communication is somehow better than arbitrary linguistic communication, the simple act of telling you that—through written sentences in a modern vernacular language in a printed book about Shakespeare, the author of texts written in a modern vernacular language—constitutes a not negligible disclaimer of his claim. To expose this *performativer Widerspruch* (Habermas) and call his claim self-refuting is of course a standard anti-deconstructive gesture—to stress, for instance, that it is impossible to talk within the rationalist parameters of an acculturated natural language against reason. This was, for instance, Habermas' standard antithetical gesture in his very influential *The Philosophical Discourse of Modernity* (119, 127, 185–193). Vincent Descombes called this a ruse, a stratagem, and he sought to deploy it against Derrida's own philosophical language (*Le même et l'autre* 162–165), without realizing that Derrida's official claim is never the metaphysical one that presence is present in determinations of identity or sameness. Vickers, we will see in a moment, also tried to catch Derrida with his pants down. He forgot that Derrida wrote naked, with electric light and an impudent cat staring at him.

36 Tullio de Mauro observes in his note to the paragraph to which this sentence belongs that "le passage montre avec une grande claret le lien entre l'arbitraire du signe et la méthode d'analyse synchronique" and he dismisses as erroneous Trubetzkoy's claim that Saussure's insistence on synchronicity is motivated by a contingent polemic.

interpersonal action (Arendt). Only Merleau-Ponty tried to engage directly with Saussure's ideas with a determination that honors him. Still, he failed to grasp the transcendental value of the notion of a systemic totality, and prejudicially dismissed Saussure's views in favor of a body-prompted, speech-located and world-oriented conception of language.[37] Levinas instead digressed, in a rhapsodic romantic-mystical way reminiscent of Walter Benjamin, about a "Dire pré-originel" that is "antérieur aux signes verbaux qu'il conjuge, antérieur aux systems linguistiques et aux chatoiements sémantiques [...] il est proximité de l'un à l'autre, engagement de l'approche, l'un pour l'autre, signifiance même de la signification" (*Autrement qu'être* 17). And limited himself to reinterpreting the Saussurean notion of the *signifiant* (signifier) as "the speaker in the first person singular subjectivity of its me" (Llewelyn 120), the *signifié* (signified) being nothing but its saying.[38] This nonsensical recycling of Saussurean terminology evinces his anxiety to abolish arbitrariness—the central tenet of modern linguistics—while keeping a façade of linguistic knowingness. To this distinction he adds the idea, anticipated in Husserl's *Logical Investigations*, of *significance*—no longer the semantic signification of the message, but the signification of the sense-giving implicit the message, of the speaker's intention, that is, to communicate meaning. In all three cases, the hidden goal of

---

37 The essays included in *Signes* contain relevant moments of his dialogue with Saussure. I have already commented on his obstinate refusal to take in the originality of the ideas put forward in the *Cours*. Consider the following paragraph, full of calls to transcendence as expressive *dépassement* towards *sens*, evocative of the calls to ostensive presence made to settle the *Privatsprache* dispute: "C'est que l'énoncé prétend dévoiler la chose même, c'est qu'il se dépasse vers ce qu'il signifie. Chaque parole a beau tirer son sens de toutes les autres, comme l'explique Saussure, encore est-il qu'au moment où elle se produit, la tâche d'exprimer n'est plus différée, renvoyée à d'autres paroles, elle est accomplie et nous comprenons quelque chose. Saussure peut bien montrer que chaque acte d'expression ne devient signifiant que comme modulation d'un système général d'expression et en tant qu'il se différencie des autres gestes linguistiques—la merveille est qu'avant lui nous n'en savions rien, et que nous l'oublions encore chaque fois que nous parlons, et pour commencer quand nous parlons des idées de Saussure. Cela prouve que chaque acte partiel d'expression, comme acte commun du tout de la langue, ne se borne pas à dépenser un pouvoir expressif accumulé en elle, mais le recrée et la recrée, en nous faisant vérifier, dans l'évidence du sens donné et reçu, le pouvoir qu'ont les sujets parlants de dépasser les signes vers le sens" (*Signes* 79). He also alludes to Saussure, critically, in his defense of the "sujet parlant" as subject of a "praxis" (*Le visible et l'invisible* 251–52). A brilliant overview of Merleau-Ponty's systematic misuse of Saussurean categories can be found in Mounin's *Saussure*, 80–81.

38 For Levinas on language it is important to consider the section "Le Dire et le Dit" and the last chapter of *Autrement qu'être ou au-delà de l'essence*, entitled "Au dehors," 16–20, 269–284.

the terminological redescription is to render *positive* what in Saussure is *negative*: the signified becomes the actual (present) positive utterance, the signifier becomes the actual (present) positive speaker, and significance "testifies to the positivity of my being accosted by another human being" (Llewelyn 120). Levinas' specific take on language hypostatizes the Saussurean "circuit de la parole" (*Cours* 27), famously illustrated with the image introduced by the caption, "Soient donc deux personnes, A et B, qui s'entretiennent" (*Cours* 27), into a face-to-face encounter, with real meaning evicted from the immanent, relational, bilateral, flow—Einstein would call it the *field*—of the circuit. Levinas' hostility against the Saussurean position is more generally visible in his running critique, especially in *Totalité et infini*, of systematicity, negativity, totality, and relationality. Derrida observes that in Levinas' world "le moi et l'autre ne se laissent pas surplomber, ne se laissent pas totaliser par un concept de relation" (*L'écriture* 141). Another important ground of dissent would be Saussure's implicit recognition of the systemic finitude of langue. As Derrida pointed out, "totalité veut dire, pour Levinas, totalité finie" (*L'écriture* 158), and Saussure sees the system of langue as a totality of finite elements and definite rules that paradoxically license an *indefinite* number of possible variations. Again Derrida, whose own conception of the *jeu* was also informed by the notion of a *finite infinity*, points out in this 1964 essay on Levinas that "un *système* n'est ni fini ni infini. Une totalité structurale échappe en son jeu à cette alternative" (*L'écriture* 180).[39]

The idea of a structural totality sends us back to the Kantian notion of the *transcendental* that I have often invoked as being appropriate to designate the distinctive quality of the Saussurean take on *langue*. Both in the "Introduction" and in the notes to his extraordinary critical edition of the *Cours*, Tullio de Mauro has emphasized this "transcendental" dimension of Saussure's conception of *langue*, and he has not recoiled from mentioning Kantism or Kant by name.[40] This dimension is obviously beholden to the distinction between *langue* and *parole*. This distinction is openly characterized by de Mauro as "dialectique" (420, n65), an adjective also used by Georges Mounin to the same effect, as we have already seen, and Jakobson described the Swiss linguist as the great revelator of "linguistic antinomies."[41] The use of terms like *dialectic* and

---

39   Derrida's lecture "La structure, le signe et le jeu dans le discours des sciences humaines" was delivered in 1966, two years after the publication of his essay on Levinas.
40   Discussing the derogatory connotations of the term "abstraction" in the philosophical culture of the turn of the twentieth-century, de Mauro notes that "Les analysis de Saussure se placent sur l'arrière-plan de l'epistémologie kantienne, idéaliste, positiviste" (426, n70).
41   De Mauro notes that Saussure had read Victor Henry's *Antinomies linguistiques* (Paris, 1896).

antinomy helps place Saussure's philosophical attitude within unmistakable Kantian coordinates, whence the pertinence of using the additional notion of *transcendental*. To further confirm the suitability of this co-optation—of Saussure's linguistics by Kantian critical-idealist rationalism—we may also consider Hjemslev's early use of the term "schema" to designate what in Saussure remained shrouded in vague, tentative categories like *psychological* or *abstract*. Indeed Saussure's very brave decision to describe the signifier and the signified as formal, not material, entities, and to conceive langue as a relational, formal system, gestures toward the kind of *transcendental schematism* that Kant developed in his first *Critique*. One must also bear in mind that the grounding of Saussurean formalism upon an inexorable logic of repetition— two unrepeatable sounds may convey the same *repeatable* signifier and the same *repeatable* signified—determines the *hauntological* potential of his conception of *langue*. Frege's suggestion that a number is a conceptual determination we apply to a concept, not a thing, expresses a similar rule of transcendental apriorism, one that lethally preempts any appeal to exceptional thinghood or evental singularity—one that, in short, forestalls any attempt at the naturalization of reason. The possibility that the death drive inhering in the formal repetition of an invisible same may also be an invitation for an inscriptive materiality to produce new modes of self-differing meaning should not be too readily discounted. Paul de Man suggested that Kant's third *Critique* already contained the seeds of this anomalous materialism, which we could certainly assimilate to Althusser's *matérialisme aléatoire* or *matérialisme de la rencontre* (*Écrits philosophiques I*, 553–591) And this materialism can already be identified in Saussure, as de Mauro's consideration of the central notion of *arbitrariness* shockingly demonstrates:

> La linguistique se trouve, dans leur description, devant des phénomènes contingents, temporellement et spatialement circonscrits, produits par le résultat imprévisible de la rencontre, dans le système, d'événements hétérogènes, internes et externes par rapport à l'équilibre du système linguistique en une certaine phase. (XIII)

To put it bluntly, far from being teleologically binding, the transcendental formalism proposed by Saussure is genetically compatible with contingency, heterogeneity, undecidability and unpredictability. This condition seals its radical historicism: if the forms of language spring from a negotiation of systemic limits, this negotiation is forced by the historical co-occurrence and simultaneous pressure of numberless material forces—some natural, most social. De Mauro also mentioned the notion of the *forme matérielle* as a suitable conceptual candidate to capture the singularity of the Saussurean proposal apropos of the *langue*. And this material form contains *in nuce* the thrust of Derrida's textual materialism.

5

In 2012, Bruce Smith contributed a short piece titled "Phenomophobia, or Who's Afraid of Merleau-Ponty?" to the *Criticism* issue on "Shakespeare and Phenomenology" edited by Kevin Curran and David Kearney. There he complained about what he took to be a "neglect" (479), an "avoidance" (480), a "phobia" (480) even a "fear" (483) of phenomenology among first-class literary scholars who, in the midst of the post-theoretical apathy of the first decade of the twenty-first century, embarked in novel critical returns or innovative theoretical directions. Smith was disheartened by the fact that, while some of them employed distinctly phenomenological concepts and methods to examine overly phenomenological concerns, they refused to employ the term *phenomenology* or cite Husserl, Heidegger or Merleau-Ponty. The time had come, Smith proclaimed, to put an end to dissimulation and mistrust. The essay closed with the supplication: "Fear not Merleau-Ponty" (483).

Ten years later, I would like to raise an alternative question: "Who is Afraid of Ferdinand Derrida?" Smith's question was, in my opinion, irrelevant, because one may reject and avoid the philosophical writings of Merleau-Ponty, but nobody, I think, hates him or is afraid of him. You can only be afraid of an author if you feel that her ideas are either horrible or incomprehensible, or horribly incomprehensible. There is fear of understanding and strongly disliking, fear of not understanding, fear of misunderstanding. The fact, moreover, that Smith reduces the choice between, on the one hand, formalist critical tendencies and phenomenologies that do not speak their name and, on the other hand, explicit phenomenology, to a question of emotional-affective *attitude*—don't be afraid of "affects" and "powerful […] feelings" (480), fear not the "objects that occasion emotions" (482)—a fact no doubt aggravated by his rather tasteless coinage of *phenomophobia* (an unlikely reality) in imitation of *homophobia* (a very real reality), invalidates the rational congruency of his supposedly meta-theoretical claims. The latent correlation between enhanced affection and homosexuality couldn't be more inexact, passé, and stereotypical, and the claim for attention to difference-based identity that his argument betrays—you are doing phenomenology, be proud, proclaim it and demand recognition—is suffused with the punctiliousness of the moralist censor.

Fears of not understanding and of misunderstanding are what the works of Ferdinand de Saussure and Jacques Derrida very often awaken, whence the relevance of my alternative question. I take these two thinkers in tandem under the name of Ferdinand Derrida. The chances of misinterpreting them are so high that even in their particular case, where Derrida's indebtedness to Saussure is very considerable, the former misrepresented the latter in a number of places. For one, he very unfairly spoke of Saussure's "accents de moraliste et de prédicateur" (*De la grammatologie* 52; 56), when there is actually no trace whatsoever of moralism in the prose of a linguist whose only discernible passion was the perfect objectivity of science (mathematics, botanic, chemistry). Derrida wildly overinterprets as a mark of *moral* graphophobia Saussure's praise of a linguistics liberated from the tyranny of the "signes graphiques" (55): the motivation for Saussure's appreciation is exclusively scientific, for a differential and relational study of writing intended as the prelude to real linguistics would have misled the field into a mire of inconsequence, and eventually prevented someone like Derrida from enthroning *écriture* as language's "inconscience" (*De la grammatologie* 55). He also overrates the philosophical implications that follow from Saussure's use of categories such as *monstruosité*, *pathologique*, or *tératologique*, which the Swiss linguist derives as technicisms from contemporary biology. Derrida apparently assumes Jakobson's rendering of structuralist thought as holding that "le langage est un système de signes" (*De la grammatologie* 24–25), when it is the *langue* that is the system of signs. He misconstrued "lien naturel [...] du son" (*Cours* 46; *De la grammatologie* 53) to mean the bond between sound and sense, when Saussure meant the continuity of sound (speech) across temporal periods: this way he read into the *Cours* a *naturalized phonocentrism* that was not there in such a way, if at all. To contend that Saussure's sought to save the "*vie naturelle* de la langue" (*De la grammatologie* 57) is manifestly absurd, as it both contradicts Saussurean terminology (he probably meant "du langage") and the strong anti-naturalist strand that runs through the *Cours*.[42]

---

42 For some of these misreadings, and others that I have not mentioned, it is essential to read Roy Harris' chapter "Derrida's Saussure" in *Saussure and his Interpreters*, 171–188; and also Russell Daylight's book, *What if Derrida Was Wrong About Saussure?* Roy Harris has a lot to object to Derrida's reading of Saussure, but the fact is that in his earlier book, *Reading Saussure*, he makes observations about the arguments' unconscious dependency on writing that are notably akin to Derrida's. "It is ironic," he comments parenthetically, "given Saussure's views on writing, that the *Cours* here employs conventions of written symbolism to express linguistic distinctions for which *la langue* apparently has no structurally articulated counterparts" (*Reading* 35). Harris' overall response to Saussure's remarks on writing are presided by this sense of mild ironic surprise: "in somewhat curious terms"

Not only did Derrida misrepresent Saussure through overreading or decontextualizing in a number of places for his own purposes. He was also niggard in his recognition of his indebtedness to the *Cours*. As I have already suggested, Derrida probably didn't need Saussure's lessons in order to engage productively in a dismantling of the metaphysical presuppositions that underwrote the phenomenological views of intention, expression, and communication. But it would be silly to overlook the impact that Saussure's emphasis on systematicity, arbitrariness, negativity and difference had in the way he engaged in the different avatars (Platonic, Hegelian, Husserlian, Heideggerian) of what he called the "metaphysics of presence." And even if he spoke of "les acquisitions les plus incontestables de la doctrine saussurienne" (*De la grammatologie* 81), his acknowledgement of indebtedness was manifestly deficient. This has led, in part, to a general downplaying, among professional philosophers, of the role that language plays in Derrida's grand philosophical narrative, visible, for instance, in the ingenious essay "La différence" that Vincent Descombes devotes to Derrida and Deleuze in his book *Le même et l'autre*, where the part that signs play in the production of *différance* as "retard originaire" (*Le même* 170–171) is preposterously marginal. True enough, literary scholars compensated for this neglect by perhaps overemphasizing Derrida's exclusive qualification as philosopher of language, but many, including Vickers, were dismayed by what he had to say, or by what others (Culler, Norris) had him say, about language. The title Vickers gave to the long chapter where he jointly considers Saussure and Derrida was "The Diminution of Language: Saussure to Derrida" (*Appropriating* 3–91).

---

(41). At one point he registers a shock—"This deliberate emphasis on separating writing from speech raises an interesting question: why is such conspicuous reiteration necessary?" (42)—that exactly captures the rationale of Derrida's critical approach, one he will later dismiss as gratuitous. It is evident that by 1987 Harris had either not read Derrida or read Derrida and erased the tracks. He will later, at a critical juncture of his book, speak of "perhaps the most fundamental—'hidden premiss' of Saussurean linguistics," to wit, "that the spoken word is 'invisibly' organized on exactly the same lines as the 'visible' organization of the written word" (78). Given, moreover, the manifest linear organization of written language, Harris concludes in a Delphic manner that "both arbitrariness and linearity spring conceptually from a single source. It is a source which subtly infuses Saussurean linguistics, in spite of lip-service paid to the primacy of speech, with all the latent scriptism of a pedagogic tradition in which writing was taken as the model to which language must—or should—conform" (78). Replace "scriptism" with "logocentrism" and you get an impeccable ventriloquizing of the famous Derridean claim. Needless to say, I think Harris is right.

6

I have argued that the naturalization of reason—what Levinas called, indistinctly, the naturalization or reification of consciousness (*Théorie de l'intuition* 32)—is an implicit precondition for the successful re-phenomenalization of Shakespeare, and that this precondition rests largely upon the relegation of Ferdinand de Saussure's linguistic theory. However, this relegation is not enough. A next precondition must be met: the parallel exorcism of Jacques Derrida's contribution to hermeneutics. In work published after 1990, this exorcism is often performed by simply setting your arguments on deco-silent mode, disabling the vibrating alerts and sonic alarms through which a deconstructive claim might threateningly respond to them. This of course if the scholar has been trained in deconstruction, however defectively. If, as is increasingly the case, the critic is not familiar with Derrida's work, then the deco-silent mode is a preloaded app in her critical prose. In fact, "Ignorance of Derrida" has become a resource handed down from one generation of literary scholars to the next, and it can hardly be denied that it works as an excuse.

At best, and this is very common among neo-phenomenological Shakespeare scholars like Paul Kottman, Julia Lupton, Kevin Curran, such ignorance is replaced with familiarity with Derrida's very late work, with essays published after 1990 that show a growing penchant for themes, like the human-animal divide, that are now frequent appearances in the neo-phenomenological radar screen. The most cited texts are *L'animal que donc je suis* (2006) and the seminar *La bête et le souverain* (2008). Also popular among phenomenology-inclined literary scholars with an interest in ethics, politics, and political theology, are of course Derrida's texts on friendship, hospitality, and faith, respectively *Politiques de l'amitié* (1994), *De l'hospitalité* (1996) and *Acts of Religion* (2002), which includes the piece "Hostipitality." Finally, it is not unlikely to find academics who would describe themselves as materialists, normally reluctant heirs of neo-historicism or cultural materialism, that resort to Derrida's 1994 essay *Spectres de Marx*. It is the case of Jonathan Gil Harris and Peter Stallybrass.[43]

---

[43] In the collection of essays edited by Campana and Maisano, *Renaissance Posthumanism*, the Derrida texts alluded to are *The Animal that therefore I am* (12), *Archive Fever* (c176), and *The Beast and the Sovereign* (306). Exceptionally, Julian Yates cites *Of Grammatology* (176). This is all, in a book whose "Introduction" invests strongly on his name, along with those of Descartes, Heidegger, and Agamben. In *Politics of the Scene*, Paul Kottman salutes Derrida as a teacher but cites only from Derrida's essay on *Romeo and Juliet*, and from "The White Mythology" (*Margins of Philosophy*). No reference to Derrida can be found in his next book, *Tragic Conditions in Shakespeare*. Julia Lupton cites *The Other*

This is the standard corpus, which could be re-edited in a single volume with the title *Phenomenal Derrida: Reconstructing the Good Life*. Surprisingly, scholars who apply Levinas to Shakespeare very often fail to consider Derrida's two other important texts on Levinas, the long essay published in 1964, and the set of essays published under the title *Adieu à Emmanuel Levinas*. The reason is obvious: for a thematic approach to hospitality—the only approach that matters to the phenomenological critic—the 1996 essay-interview is enough: let us not make things more complicated than they already are, let us not de-thematize and dialecticize too much. Also surprising is how Derrida's very long and conscientious reading of Jean-Luc Nancy in the book titled *On Touching*, where a prominent place is given to Merleau-Ponty's phenomenology of the flesh has gone under the radar of body-mindful early modern scholars. Or not surprising, for this Derrida would hardly flatter their interests.

I have vaguely delineated the reduced Derrida corpus tailored for the interests of a generation of academics that started publishing in the mid-1990s. Literary academics of an older generation, like Brian Vickers and Bruce Smith, have a different kind of grasp of Derrida's work, more centered on a set of texts—*Of Grammatology*, the 1966 John Hopkins lecture, "La différance," the first essay on Freud, the piece on Plato's pharmacy—that made up, in the 1980s, the standard deconstructive *vademecum* for post-graduate trainees in English and Comparative Literature Departments in the Anglo-American world. Of course, not all doctoral candidates read them all, or read them well. Most read Culler and Norris on Derrida. This led to a progressive simplification of Derridean arguments to the school-text theorems of the *disruption of fixed binarism*, the *inescapability of/from language*, the *critique of the fetishism of origins*, and the

---

Hearing: Reflections on Today's Europe in *Citizen-Saints*, and *The Animal that therefore I am* and *Of Hospitality* in *Thinking with Shakespeare*. In her latest book, *Shakespeare Dwelling*, she cites from *Of Hospitality* and *Specters of Marx*. In the collection *Shakespeare and Hospitality*, edited by Lupton and Goldstein, the Derrida texts cited by are, predictably, those dedicated to hospitality and Levinas (including in this case *Adieu à Emmanuel Levinas*), along with *Specters of Marx*, *Politics of Friendship*, *Acts of Religion*, and "Monolingualism of the Other." In the collection *Face-to-Face-to-Face in Shakespearean Drama*, edited by Lupton and Matthew Smith, the texts are the first essay on Derrida, described as a "long animadversion on Levinas' thought" (254), and, quite surprisingly, "Signature, Event, Context." Also unforeseen is a reference to Derrida's readings of Husserl in one of the essays included in *Entertaining the Idea*, edited by Lupton, Gallagher and Kearney, but the allusion is limited to *Margins of Philosophy*. More predictable is the reference to "Hospitality, Justice and Responsibility: A Dialogue with Jacques Derrida" included in *Questioning Ethics* (1999).

critique of the metaphysics of presence.[44] Since the last two demanded philosophical training to be fully grasped, they gradually fell off the menu. Only sophisticated and informed scholars like Marjorie Garber, Jonathan Goldberg, Stephen Orgel, Margreta de Grazia, and Peter Stallybrass managed to adapt correctly deconstructive claims to the parallel problems of the original author and the original text. But not without problems, as I have tried to show in section 9, "What Matters in Shakespeare." The problem, I implied, is not whether there is one or three *King Lears*. The problem is rather that there are earlier texts—including a *King Leir*—ghosting, double-voicing, and predetermining *King Lear*. The question is not whether Shakespeare is Oxford or Shakespeare, the question is rather how much of Ovid, or Chaucer, or Marlowe, or Spenser comes into the constitution of the auctor Shakespeare—how extensively they ghost-write what Shakespeare writes.[45] The problem, then, lies not in the impossibility of successfully retracing his traces to a unique name or text, but rather in the difficulty of assessing how extensively his traces retrace other traces. The inscriptive materiality of textual traces, their survival, their hauntological post-existence, their reemergence in subsequent textuality, are also major concerns in Derrida's work which, however refined and amplified by critics like Paul de Man, many literary scholars have incomprehensibly neglected. Derrida's essay on *Romeo and Juliet* is precisely about the determining power of an "old story" ("Conversation with Derek Attridge," *Acts of Literature* 66), about subtextual anteriority, about textual-serial repetition, about the overtaking of words and deeds by sheer pre-textual precedence, about, in short, the way *Romeo and Juliet* is predetermined by "all the *Romeo and Juliets* that came before it" ("Aphorism Countertime," *Acts of Literature* 417), and it is no accident that even a perceptive scholar like Jonathan Gil Harris should completely misrepresent the aim of the essay when he argues that "Derrida choses to read *Romeo and Juliet* independent of its sixteenth-century contexts" (54). This is wrong: Derrida is constantly asking his reader to assess the *dependence* of Shakespeare's play on his immediate and prior contexts, especially to the context of related texts that repeat *Romeo and Juliet*. The fact that he doesn't perform such reading is obvious: he himself is not a source-alert philological reader of English sixteenth-century literature. But Jonathan Goldberg, for instance, is that kind of scholar, and he shows no reservations in arguing that "Hamlet, burdened by memory, encounters a ghost, stages a play, both haunted

---

[44] For an express formulation of the first two, see Jonathan Gil Harris' *Shakespeare and Literary Theory*, 42–45.

[45] This kind of problem has been constantly addressed by Patrick Cheney in his remarkable books on sixteenth-century literature.

by the memory of earlier scripts" (*Shakespeare's Hands* 111). So did Harold Bloom in his splendid essay on *Romeo and Juliet* in his book on Shakespeare.

One reason for the neglect of the Derrida that acts as instigator of philological research (on sources, subtexts, intertexts), for the hermeneut that reminds us, with Harold Bloom, that "the meaning can only be another poem" (*The Anxiety of Influence* 70), is of course the scholar's lazy reliance on an *antica fiamma* kindled by romantic-phenomenological premises of expressive originality and spontaneous creativity. Another reason is the pressure that other more resounding deconstructive theorems, like the disruption of binarism, exerted in their mindset. Theoretical paradigms, in their dwarfed, streamlined, and bowdlerized adaptation to Anglo-American academia, tend to accommodate solely one central idea. The presence of two ideas is proof of somebody's sloppiness—whether the inventor of the paradigm or the author of the handbook. To reduce deconstruction to the childish trick of upsetting binary oppositions, reversing hierarchies, and erasing boundaries is, of course, a convenient expedient that allows the scholar to have her cake and eat it—to remain post-deconstructive while showing she can also play the game. Another informed scholar who was aware of the need to confront Derrida on his own best terms was Simon Palfrey, but the confrontation proved disappointing. In his excellent first monograph, *Late Shakespeare* (1997), to which I will return in section 18 of my book, Palfrey includes three Derrida titles (*Dissemination*, *Positions*, *Writing and Difference*). But none of these books are ever mentioned in his text. His vague allusions to Derrida and deconstruction strongly depend on the work of others, especially Eagleton. Expository work on deconstruction, whether sympathetic (Norris) or not (Felperin), is also referenced in the Bibliography, and yet never used in the book. It is only the sophistication of Palfrey's sustained argument that evinces familiarity with deconstructive approaches. But, even in his case, this is surely not enough. If you allow me this counterfactual, if Palfrey had been trained at Yale or John Hopkins twenty years before he published his first book, this would have received a different title: *Belated Shakespeare: Unworlding Old Words*. Although his *Late Shakespeare* came too late to become a classic of negative-dialectical hermeneutics, it remains one of the few masterpieces of literary interpretation that Shakespeare studies has ever produced.

7

In what follows I will consider Brian Vickers' and Bruce Smith's very critical approach to Derrida, and I will begin with Vickers. His central claim is that

Derrida has misread both Husserl and Saussure. Misreading originates in the fact that Derrida, Vickers argues, underhandedly resorts to the very concepts (presence, meaning) his "deconstructive" readings of these thinkers set out to discredit. This would be evidence of contradictory thought. And the charge extends, he believes, to other "founding fathers" (sic) of American deconstruction. Actually, one of Vickers' most memorable findings is the incongruity lodged in de Man's statement that "sign and meaning can never coincide," for, "if sign and meaning can never coincide," he points out, "how can we even understand what de Man has written?" (*Appropriating* 172). Gotcha! Well, actually, Vickers errs on the side of presumption: he fails to understand de Man, let alone Derrida. Vickers is of course a learned and expert scholar in the field of Renaissance literature. The section he devotes to deconstructionist readings of Shakespeare's work from the early 1980s through 1993 is therefore rich in insight and good sense. His dissatisfaction with second-hand deconstructionist appropriations of Shakespeare's work is in many cases totally justified, especially when he accuses critics of overlooking the wider frame of the text under study (the Shakespeare play or poem) in the interest of maximizing, on the evidence of very partially selected textual fragments, a patently overblown philosophical claim. This is something that has been celebrated even in negative reviews of Vickers's book.[46] But to conclude from this that such mode of partial reading illustrates the standard exegetic methodology of Derrida and de Man, "a combination of selective quotation and misreading" (172), is simply inaccurate. Not only because nobody should be held accountable for the blunders perpetrated in one's name. More important, because *all* textual exegeses are a combination of selective quotation and misreading: Derrida and de Man went to great lengths precisely to attest such claim, and they never took offence in being called *misreaders*, a category Harold Bloom (another proud *misreader*) did much to propagate. The difference is therefore not between reading and misreading, but rather between a *good* and a *bad misreading*. And this oscillation largely depends on the capacity to select your quotes and manufacture, through the deployment of good concepts, a convincing case. The good case will last longer and will possess a wider field of application. If no quotes are selected or all are frenziedly selected, criticism fades away into, respectively, complete silence (Wittgenstein) or unconditional rewriting (Borges). The best *misreader*, in sum, is much closer to the philologically exact and exacting critic than Brian Vickers is willing to realize. Vickers pokes fun at the

---

46 See for instance Michael Dobson's review in *The London Review of Books* (18 November 1993), which prompted an interesting exchange.

deconstructionist pride in over-close reading, but he only manages to defuse it in very local moments of his commentary, especially when dealing with soi-disant deconstructionist readers of Shakespeare. He excels at spotting fake closeness to Shakespeare's texts because he is himself very close to them. But things change quite a bit when he deals with Derrida's and de Man's readings of important thinkers like Plato, Rousseau, Kant, Hegel, Husserl, or Heidegger. In these cases he is at a loss to discern the closeness of a reading, and not only because he is no expert in the work of these philosophers. The reason is that he doesn't even seem to have bothered to read first-hand Derrida's close readings of their philosophical texts. His "closeness" here is merely presumed, and upon close inspection turns out to be made of distance, both the distance of his prejudice and the added interval of someone else's gloss of Derrida's gloss. If therefore we decide to follow Vickers's lead, we are at least at three removes from the original text whose elucidation Derrida offers. Maybe we shouldn't expect, after all, Vickers to be conversant with Husserl. I myself hold differently: if you aim fairly at understanding Derrida you must be extremely familiar with the Western philosophical tradition. Thus Vickers fails on both counts: he neither aims fairly nor is sufficiently familiar. The same may be applied to de Man's distinctively demanding canon: Rousseau, Kant, Hegel, Nietzsche, Kleist, Shelley, Mallarmé, Proust ... It is no accident that Vickers, who surely passed "Romantic poets" with honors, should only single out de Man's "close reading" of *The Triumph of Life* to corroborate his exegetical aptitude. He hardly had a choice.

It is, however, with Derrida that he chiefly takes issue. And, let me insist, there is a marked disproportion between the extension, volume, and pitch of his critical comments on Derrida and the flimsiness of the textual evidence adduced to enforce his censure. To wit: in the sixty-one pages or so (*Appropriating* 36–49; 165–213) he dedicates to deconstruction and to deconstructionist interpretations of Shakespeare, he only makes use of four texts, three essays—"La structure, le signe et le jeu dans le discours des sciences humaines" (1966), "La différance" (1968) and "Sémiologie et grammatologie" (1971)—and the opus magnum *De la grammatologie* (1967). The shorter pieces are either lectures (the first two) or a very concise interview (the third). They feature, moreover, among the standard—frowned upon, recited, over-quoted, and largely unread—textual loci in the Derrida canon, ever available for malcontents and enthusiasts to come along, glance, and vandalize, ripping off a sensational sentence or two. None of the three is organized as a diligent close reading of a particular text—notoriously an uncongenial choice for a lecture or an interview. This notwithstanding, Derrida does carefully quote from Saussure and Husserl in the interview with Julia Kristeva, looks into Heidegger's *Der Spruch des Anaximander* in the closing section of "La différance," and enters into explicit dialogue with Levi-Strauss's essays in the famous John Hopkins lecture. He hardly ever talks—or reads: his interview responses were normally written, and his lectures always written and read aloud—without a text at hand. Of *De la grammatologie* Vickers only mentions the schoolbook rebus "il n'y a pas de hors-texte" (*Appropriating* 46) along with some lines in the same page—and this to prove, one feels, he had a copy of the book by his elbow. There was no need for that, however, as he quotes extensively from Spivak's introduction to the book. This much is crystal-clear: Vickers has read Spivak on Derrida. And we also know that he has read the work of a handful of critics who are less obliging than Spivak to Derrida's philosophical position: Perry Anderson, Vincent Descombes, John Searle, Manfred Frank, Marc August, Wendell V. Harris, Luc Ferry, Alain Renault, Ernest Gellner ... In fact, the first subchapter he devotes to deconstruction, titled "Neo-structuralism: Emptying the System," cannot be said to be about Derrida's ideas: it is rather about these people's ideas about Derrida, and about Vickers's joy in having read these fantastic people. One final note about this fantastic people. Considering the meagre attention Vickers really pays to Derrida's work, one wonders at the motivation that may have led him to read so much on Derrida and so little by Derrida. Of course reading Anderson, Searle, Spivak or Descombes on Derrida is extremely rewarding, an intellectual treat in its own right. But investing your time and brains in the work of some of the other, less rewarding, critics, rather than in Derrida's work doesn't seem particularly wise, especially if what you seek to understand is the latter. Who is afraid of Ferdinand Derrida?

Nor can we really applaud Vickers on his choice of *ad hominem* aspersion as the sub-textual rhetorical device organizing his pages on deconstruction. It becomes embarrassingly obvious that he must have had a very hard time in accepting that a French philosopher called Jacques Derrida deservedly became a very prestigious intellectual during the 1960s and 1970s. He backs in and out from this admission a number of times, and the reader is treated to the shameful spectacle of seeing a powerful intellectual performing simultaneously salutations and vindictive antics to a much better known—and much stronger—intellectual. We are constantly reminded of Derrida's two founding vices: being French and belonging to a generation of "Parisian iconoclasts" who achieved notoriety in the 1960s under the more or less accidental banner of post-structuralism.[47] None of these things Derrida could exactly help, although his Frenchness was multiculturally enriched and his post-structuralism not

---

47 "Parisian iconoclasts," "French iconoclasts," "1960s iconoclasts": these phrases recur in Vickers' book. He also uses the first one in his first "Letter" written as a response to Dobson's review in *The London Review of Books*.

seldom disowned. The third related vice is that he thinks badly, writes loosely, and reduces argument to a "three-card trick" (40). The last claim, vested in a phraseology probably lifted from Descombes, who spoke of "double jeu," "stratagem" and "ruse" apropos of Derrida's master argument (*Le même et l'autre* 162–163), is never proved, as Vickers invites the reader, in a footnote, to confirm for himself Derrida's sorcery by reading the opening paragraphs of the 1966 lecture "La structure, le signe et le jeu dans le discours des sciences humaines." I have just reread them, and I fail to see the third-card trick. Is it so difficult, for Vickers, to accept that the center of what Western philosophy has called a structure simultaneously opens and closes, enables, and disables, the game that results from that structure? Or that the centre of a structure of substitutions cannot itself be substituted, and that therefore the centre is both inside and outside the structure? The answer, of course, is that good old philologists don't believe in structures. In that case, your target is not Derrida, but the whole tradition of Western thought. When we turn to his treatment of the man de Man the arbitrariness of *ad hominem* aspersion is increased by a degree. We open Chapter 3, ready to absorb what Vickers has to say about "Deconstruction: Undermining, Overreaching" and the first strong claims that come our way grow out of phrases like "vague connotations of subverting existing order," "subversive attitudes" and, to crown it all, "pro-Nazi journalism" (165). We are rapidly given a piece of liberal, mundane insouciance—"My dissatisfaction with deconstruction long antedated these disclosures"—but the venom has been effectively inoculated. All subsequent references to the darkness of de Man's personal mindset—and there are a few pearls like "De Man, you feel, really lived with a void" (176)—are open invitations to connect the dots. Derrida the French, De Man the pro-Nazi: Vickers is extremely helpful in returning the debate on the suitability of deconstructing Shakespeare to significant outbreaks of cultural xenophobia that punctuated the history of England between 1789 and 1945. Edmund Burke and Jane Austen probably marveled at the sinister laud to the "fortress built by Nature for her self / Against infection and the hand of war" (*Richard II* 2.1.43–44). To describe, moreover, people like Geoffrey Hartman and Paul de Man as members of "the American clan" of the "founding fathers" (182) of deconstruction takes a great deal of bad taste. The cultural-historical connection between America and founding fathers nursed in agrarian gentility and groomed for neoclassic rationalism makes scant room for the prototype of the Continental intellectual expatriate that these two critics—the German "Jew" and the Belgian "Nazi"—so eminently epitomize. To be sure, they spoke English with an accent. Who doesn't? In the mid-eighties, Terry Eagleton rightly implied that Shakespeare spoke (and thought) English with a French (poststructuralist) accent. Adieu, adieu, adieu, remember him.

In his tiresome analysis of what he takes to be Derrida's misunderstanding of Saussure, there is a strain that can only be accounted for in terms of prejudice. Why does Vickers keep assuming that a French thinker trained in the best academic institutions, who is intimately conversant with the Western philosophical tradition, and in particular with those sections of it that deal with the problem of language from Plato to Wittgenstein, who has bothered to read modern linguists like Jakobson or Hjemslev, why should Vickers assume that this man would so radically misinterpret Saussure? Especially if we consider that a good many dense pages in the Derrida corpus of the 1960s are openly dedicated to elucidate the meaning of the *Cours*. Why should Vickers, a remarkable English-speaking intellectual very probably trained in a rather rich indigenous tradition of linguistics (Sapir, Firth), who probably came to the *Cours* only because the work of Levi-Strauss, Barthes and Derrida prompted him, why should he be so sure that he can understand Saussure better than a French-speaking philosopher schooled in Continental traditions of linguistics and philosophy of language who showed, in addition, a compelling interest during the central and most productive years of his professional career in elucidating the meaning of the *Cours*, a text to which he came once and again, in different contexts and with varying degrees of intensity, with interviewers and before audiences perfectly trained in the history of theoretical linguistics? Wherefore are we invited to accept such improbability? The whole of his dismantling of deconstruction rests on the razor edge of such improbability. I have already pointed out that Derrida made some mistakes in his reading of the *Cours*, and that he was closefisted in his recognition of indebtedness to Saussure's very original conception of language. But Vickers, whose reading of Ferdinand de Saussure is defective and second-hand, is not the person to call Derrida to task form misreading the Swiss linguist.

Let me now briefly consider some of Vickers' errors of interpretation in his supposedly direct confrontation with the work of Jacques Derrida:

1. We first hear of Derrida as someone who "invoked Nietzsche as a talisman for the rhetorical (or Utopian) vision of a future for language and thought beyond all constrains of good and evil" (*Appropriating* 37). This is not true. Derrida's positing of writing as the object of a new scientific field (*grammatologie*) was always conjectural, tentative, and calculated to provoke critical *travail*—a Marxian concept he employs often in his writings of the 1960s. Grammatology is an open-ended project that hinges on the prior deconstruction of metaphysical (logocentric) texts rather than a closed discipline with a fixed set of rules, a limited number of concepts, and a pre-determined cluster of objects. However extensive and plural in its virtual modes of implementation—indeed it has to it, like the final abridgment in *Cymbeline*,

"circumstantial branches, which / Distinction should be rich in" (*Cymbeline* 5.5.384–85)—Derrida's grammatology is narrow in its "scientific" scope: to unmask logocentric bias and to allow *écriture* to emerge. No Utopian inflexion urges the project, and certainly no ethics of transvalorization animates its local effects. The fact that, as Lukacher as elegantly formulated, "the overcoming of metaphysics and logocentrism is, at its most elemental, the recognition that language cannot account for its own effects" (Lukacher, *Primal* 180) doesn't mean that something else (the empirical world, referents, emotions, affects, energy, a transcendent force) can successfully step in to effect such accounting. "Une monde de signes sans faute" is not an anarchic realm of force hurled *jenseits Gute und Böse*, but rather a semiotic game un-tormented by the—pastoral, Rousseaunian, Romantic—drive to regress to position one in the board: the pre-lapsarian, sin-free, original paradise. Vickers makes a similar misjudgment when he attributes to Derrida the nostalgic imagination of "a prelapsarian state in which man experienced 'full presence,' the 'transcendental signified' being there to be consumed, expended, touched, known" (43). If you read the second part of *De la grammatologie*, titled "Nature, Culture, Écriture," and draw the inference I have just transcribed, then you are either a very dense person or Brian Vickers himself. There is no other option, for we must assume that Vickers, who is anything but dense, has read it. Or mustn't we? At any rate, why he reaches such conclusion, he alone knows. But one may surmise that Vickers is not particularly adept at bearing the ironic-dialectical stance of a philosophical argument that ventriloquizes the position of the text it scrutinizes in order not only to bring to light and undo its unformulated claims and unconscious premises but also to prove that reason (the reason of *all* arguments) is dialectical, and therefore ironic, because it is forced to internalize (an re-echo) the claims and premises of the arguments it intends to sublate. The position thereby achieved is one of superiority, and Vickers and others—Descombes, Abrams, quoted by Vickers (170)—are wrong to conclude from Derrida's comprehensibly communicative construction of arguments against the stable significance of situated acts of intentionally communicative language (literary and philosophical texts) that he falls into contradiction. Derrida never says that *all* speech acts are inherently self-defeating: only those that purport to *mean* otherwise or differently from the way they may surely end up meaning—those that *intend* to mean purely, mean presently, mean immediately, mean fully, mean exactly, mean naturally, mean properly, mean the thing itself, mean the empirical *transcendens* or the transcendental idea—are likelier to become subject to their own—or someone else's—deconstruction. I guess what I am trying to say is that you need some dialectical tolerance of what is wrongly called "contradiction" in order to tolerate Derrida's very noble and forthcoming philosophical game. Drawing heavily on Descombes, Vickers sharpens his criticism into the outrageous claim that Derrida not only misconstrues Husserl but ends up embracing the Husserlian faith in the *transcendental signified*. This is wrong. Derrida retains from Husserlian phenomenology a strong penchant for transcendental accounts of significance—justifications of *the conditions of possibility* of meaning. But whereas in Husserl the accounts of meaning creation are both undialectical and confined to ideal essences or noemata, Derrida favors dialectical accounts of meaning production as reinscription confined to the formal materials of language. While Husserl's can be called an *ideal* (not idealist) *transcendentalism* mapping out a tendentially nontemporal field of intentional *signifieds*, Derrida's is a just a *textualist transcendentalism* playing itself out in the fully temporalized "archi-scène" of contingent *signifiers*. To sum up, Derrida has no interest in consuming, expending, touching, or knowing the transcendental signified, as Vickers claims. His only concern is to track the doings and undoings of the *transcendental signifier* as it enters—overdetermines and sabotages—the metaphysical-cultural chain of meaning production.

2. We later read that "Derrida ignored Saussure's careful (albeit ultimately obscure and unsatisfactory) distinction between the constituent parts (abstractions) and the whole linguistic sign (an entity)" (38). This claim is also wrong: Derrida didn't ignore this distinction, he merely found fault in it. Moreover, Derrida denies that a sign can be called an "entity" precisely because it lacks the metaphysical condition of substantial fixity and self-determining presentation we expect from the particular kind of existing entities Vickers unconsciously considers signs to be. Derrida would not dispute Vickers's commonsensical description of signs (words) as "material objects actually existing" (38). *Différance* can surely put up with this combination of materiality and existence, to which contingency may be readily added. But he would object to the implicit premise that underpins Vickers argument, one he is blind to because he takes it absolutely for granted: that signs enjoy self-sustaining (original, invariable, truthful) presence along metaphysical lines of changelessness (Aristotle), clarity and distinctness (Descartes). For Derrida, the composite sign is always-already contaminated by the differential logic that makes its constituent parts possible in the first place: the point of intersection between two differing sequences does not set up, as Saussure implies, a resting place. It inscribes rather, always along the sequence of the signifier (the other sequence is only mentally presumed), a caesura of enhanced differing. Vickers believes otherwise and argues that "each linguistic sign is a unique correlation of a distinct signified with a distinct signifier" (38). In the annotation of any of Vickers's excellent critical editions one can find ample evidence

of the contrary: distinct signifiers are given multiple possible meanings and indistinct signifiers are editorially stabilized according to choices made across the semantic spectrum each solution affords. In his edition of Bacon's *Essays*, for instance, many terms are annotated with alternative terms (signifiers) that supposedly explain, clarify, elucidate, or complete the "meaning" (signified) implied in the original term. What is the point of annotating "mummeries" with "splendors, shows" (Bacon, *The Essays* 3) if "mummeries" is a "unique correlation of a distinct signified with a distinct signifier"? Why do you then violate such sacred correlation by associating your distinct signifier (mummeries) with other signifiers (splendors, shows)? If Vickers believes that the footnote merely exhibits signifieds (a natural belief, after all, for a commonsensical scholar), then the correlation is violated on the side of the signified. In the first case, three signifiers share the one and selfsame signified: this unmoors the signifier fomenting its contingent slipperiness (Lacan). In the second case, three signifieds share the one and only signifier: this we call the inexorable figurative aberrancy or equivocalness of meaning (de Man). In his action of editorial "stabilization" of meaning, Vickers the philologist unwittingly espouses post-structuralist dogma, for his work openly presupposes both that signs are not unique correlations and that meanings are not stable. But Vickers the critical polemicist works strongly against his own presupposition.

3. Further down Vickers contends that Derrida tries "to dazzle us into thinking that language can never make meanings or referents 'present,' *in the same way as words can never make things appear*" (40). Vickers finds the claim outrageous and counter-attacks with the stiletto of common-sense: "But whoever thought that language could or should do that?" (40). Well, I can think of many people who thought exactly that.[48] Starting with Vickers himself, who argues four pages later that "*meaning* is *fully realized* in language through the joint *operations* of semantics, grammar and syntax, *vital* linguistics elements" (44; emphases added) supposedly ignored by Saussure and his structuralist and post-structuralist heirs. *Fully realized meaning through the vital operations of elements*: diverse but interconnected romantic (*Leben*, life, organic, vital), phenomenological (*lebendige, erfüllen, meinen*) and functionalist (operations) tropes come together to operate the miracle of *presence*: as Hölderlin

---

48 If Vickers has read Plato's *Phaedrus* and has not abstained from reading Derrida's impressive essay on that dialogue in "La pharmacie de Platon" (not included in the bibliographical list of his book), he is then merely playing the role of the sophistic eiron, the person who pretends to know less than he actually knows. Is it that hard to understand that by stating that in the Western cultural tradition "the sign is usually said to be put in place of thing itself" Derrida is merely stating a fact?.

proclaimed, "Wörte, wie Blumen, enstehen." Apparently, Vickers fails to realize the implications of his own claims, a startling outcome that serves to confirm the undying relevance of deconstruction. But this is not the worse. His claim that the French philosophers seeks "to dazzle us into thinking that language can never make meanings or referents 'present,' *in the same way as words can never make things appear*" is based upon his reading of the passage, in "La Différance," where Derrida offers a rather orthodox characterization of the traditional, even banal, linguistic conception whereby "the sign is usually said to be put in place of the thing itself, the present thing, 'thing' here standing equally for meaning or referent" and that therefore "the sign, in this sense, is deferred presence" (*Margins* 9). Vickers seems to overlook 1) that Derrida is recording a conventional cultural belief, not giving an opinion, and 2) that in the logic of this belief, "referent" (*Bedeutung*, extension) and "meaning" (*Sinn*, intension), although holding a position of equidistance with respect to the signifier, tend to be construed as the *real presences* (Steiner), the former (the referent)—what Vickers calls the thing—because it may actualize itself as an empirical *donnée* to justify the semiotic transaction, and the latter (the meaning) because, according to phenomenology, meaning is the noematic presence whose intentional projection sets the expressive-communicative act in motion. Vickers often mentions "phenomenology," but he appears to be unaware of its basic conceptual assumptions. He defiantly states that "the concept of 'presence' is irrelevant here" (40). Well, it may be irrelevant for him, but it was certainly not for Husserl, whose entire theory of intentionality and meaning turns around the concept of presence, and less so for Derrida, who spent more than a decade turning around Husserl's circumvolutions.

4. Vickers is very distraught with Derrida's attention to *langue* rather than to *parole*, and believes that such misplaced attention betokens a complete misinterpretation of the Saussurean dichotomy. He argues that "in fact Derrida *never* mentions *parole*, writes as if this part of the dichotomy does not exist" (41; emphasis added). This is ostensibly wrong. In point of fact, Derrida mentions and discusses at length the Saussurean concept of *parole* both in *De la grammatologie* (42–52, 74–78) and in *Positions* (14–41; 58–60). Furthermore, in *Marges de la philosophie*, *parole* is significantly mentioned in the opening essay, "Tympan," and discussed in tandem with *langue* and *écriture* in "La différance" (4, 5, 12, 16), the essay from which Vickers is quoting. In this particular essay, a great deal of attention is paid to the "alliance de la parole et de l'être dans le mot unique, dans le nom enfin propre" (29) apropos of Heidegger's "Der Spruch des Anaximander," often translated as "The Saying of Anaximander." Vickers has either not read Derrida or is consciously lying. You choose. He has

evidently leafed through the opening pages of "La différance," and his shock at what he sees leads him to wholesome apercus like the following:

> Quoting a passage from Saussure, Derrida takes it as proving that the subject is inscribed in language, is a 'function' of language (ibid., p.15). But this is exactly the opposite of what Saussure says, namely that *langue* is 'not a function of the speaking subject,' and *parole* is 'an individual act involving will-power and intelligence' (CLG, p.30). (41)

Vickers' argument is manifestly inconsistent. A careful reading of what Derrida actually says suffices to reveal the magnitude of the former's error:

> Or, si nous nous référons encore une fois à la différence sémiologique, qu'est-ce que Saussure, en particulier, nous a rappelé? Que 'la langue [qui ne consiste donc qu'en différences] n'est pas une fonction du sujet parlant.' Cela implique que le sujet (identité à soi ou éventuellement conscience de l'identité à soi, conscience de soi) est inscrit dans la langue, est 'fonction' de la langue, ne devient sujet parlant qu'en conformant sa parole, même dans ladite 'création,' même dans ladite 'transgression,' au système de prescriptions de la langue comme système de différences, ou du moins à la loi générale de la différance, en se réglant sur le principe de la langue dont Saussure dit qu'elle est 'le langage moins la parole.' 'La langue est nécessaire pour que la parole soit intelligible et produise tous ses effets.'
>
> *Marges* 16

Vickers makes one omission and one mistake: 1) he omits to mention that it is Derrida who takes into consideration Saussure's idea that "language is not a function of the speaking subject" and 2) he mistakenly contends that this idea is "exactly the opposite" of Derrida's claim that "the subject (in its identity with itself, or eventually in its consciousness of its identity with itself, its self-consciousness) is inscribed in language, is a 'function' of language" (*Margins* 15). Curiously, Vickers has decided to withhold the parenthetical clarification about the subject. This, and what can only qualify as obtuseness, prompts him to see *opposition* where there is just a risky inference. Broadly taken, the opposite of "language is not a function of the speaking subject" could be said to be its contrary, "language is a function of the speaking subject" or its actual *opposite*, "the speaking subject is not a function of language." It is certainly not, as Vickers argues, "the speaking subject is a function of language." This is Derrida's hypothetical inference, logically inconsistent, but dialectically laden with rich implications, none of which, by the way, *completely* disables the subject as an active participant exercising her will-power and intelligence. It merely sets limits of transcendental-formal possibility to what the speaker can say, will and understand.

5. Further ahead, Vickers states that

> Derrida energetically continued his distorting destruction of Saussure (while simultaneously accusing him of contradiction), postulating the existence of "a concept signified in and of itself, a concept simply present to thought, independent of a relationship to language, that is of a relationship to a system of signifiers," and suggesting that in fact "every signified is also in the position of a signifier" (Derrida 1981, pp. 19–20). As every reader of the *Cours* will recognize, these ideas are wholly foreign to Saussure, would indeed be impossibilities in his system. (41)

As the reader may have noted, we stumble again upon Vickers' resistance to accept the existence of the Western-metaphysical prejudice that conceptual meaning befalls as *present* to the mind. Derrida, of course, fights that prejudice by confounding the silent speech of the mind—"I have ne'r a tongue in my head" (*The Merchant of Venice* 2.2.142)—and devolving to "music, letters" (*Pericles* 15.8). What Vickers calls a "distorting destruction" is merely the contrastive placing of Saussurean arguments along a chain of philosophical and linguistic versions of language that assume similar unspoken postulates about the relation between mind, language, and reality. Through this contrastive work, Derrida tentatively makes Saussure speak in the languages of Plato, medieval philosophers, or Husserl. And Derrida is very seldom unmindful of the difference between what Saussure says and what he makes him say by means of an exogenous projection. As it happens, in this particular case, this is what Derrida says, with the context that Vickers has carefully removed:

> Le maintien de la distinction rigoureuse—essentielle et juridique -entre le *signans* et le *signatum*, l'équation entre le *signatum* et le concept (p. 99) laissent ouverte en droit la possibilité de penser un concept signifié en lui-même, dans sa présence simple à la pensée, dans son indépendance par rapport à la langue, c'est-à-dire par rapport à un système de signifiants.
>
> Positions 29–30

Quite evidently, Vickers is wrong in arguing that Derrida is "postulating the existence" in Saussure's arguments of this "concept signifié." Derrida is postulating rather the *possibility* of the existence, outside Saussure's arguments but cued by them, of signified concepts that are present to the mind independently of the role they might play in the relational meshes of langue. This Saussure never says, but, as Derrida sharply and correctly notes, his binary conception of the nature of the linguistic sign "leaves *de iure* open the possibility of thinking a signified concept in itself." This is a problem of modality (existence versus possibility) in argumentative prose, and if Derrida speculatively *modalizes* the *facta bruta* of Saussure's arguments it is because they are themselves highly speculative and "energetically" (I use Vickers' adverb) open to re-descriptive possibilities. If one reads Saussure, like Vickers, as someone notarizing an affidavit, then not much is accomplished by way of interpretation. If one reads the *Cours*, like Derrida, actualizing the philosophical possibilities that the critical points of the argument constantly instigate, then of course one may risk, here and there, some overinterpretation, but one is certainly treating Saussure's text as a major contribution to the Western tradition of philosophy of language, to which thinkers like Husserl also greatly, and quite often in ways not dissimilar to Saussure, contributed. Of course to read the latter way—to *modalize* Saussure's discourse by elaborating dormant possibilities—you must know something about the Western tradition of philosophy of language, and you must have read Husserl's *Logical Investigations*.

6. Still harping on "La différance," Vickers argues that "Derrida's theory of deferral cites no empirical evidence, and once again a spatialized metaphor substitutes for argument" (44). Let me start with the second complaint—Vickers seems to be unaware of a tradition of thought, ranging from Vico to Blumenberg, and from Hegel and Nietzsche to Derrida himself, that has indisputably demonstrated that philosophical argument is simultaneously propped and checked by tropes, and that very often what look like stretches of syllogistic logic and dialectical progress are merely conceptual narratives sustained and animated by tropes of contiguity or substitution. Now, let us consider the first complaint: "Derrida's theory of deferral cites no empirical evidence." This is hilarious. It is like demanding of a paranoid that he shows us, empirically, the weapons that he believes his neighbor hides in his flat, like asking Jane Austen to prove, empirically, that there are *truths universally acknowledged*. Ideological opinion and unconscious perception cannot be demonstrated empirically, but they *exist*. They are like the law in Derrida's interpretation of the famous Kafka tale: "there is some law, some law which *is not there but which exists*" ("Before the Law" qtd. Lukacher, *Daemonic* 36). They enjoy the formal-transcendental life of a structural effect, not the positive life of a stone, but they are as real as a stone in that they produce other (perlocutionary) reality-changing effects. "Deferral" is a formal-transcendental category, not a stone. It

is, like "différance," a "(non)concept" (Goldberg, *Shakespeare's Hand* xiv) rather than a concept. You cannot see it, but it is there: there as the unconscious, hauntological, transcendental structure of many things that are there—things like time, language, or life.

7. Finally, let me consider the claim, put forward in the section "Deconstruction: Undermining, Overreaching," that "to Derrida's followers [...] ambivalence in a literary work is neither a virtue nor a facet of character, but proof of the innate weakness of language" (169). Vickers must have very silly followers in mind. In general, both Derrida and his strong followers (the early Bloom, de Man, Hartman, Hillis Miller), including strong critics working in the Shakespeare field (Fineman, Garber, Goldberg), never speak of the "innate weakness of language." What they would take for a weakness is the subjection of language to a law other than the creative rule of contingency, arbitrariness, and dissemination that Derrida helped to formulate: language is impoverished and weakened when its built-in productivity is submitted to the exogenous rules of ideal transcendentalism, rigid logicism, positive empiricism, strict functionalism. The pragmatic effectiveness of these rules depends on the standing (*present*) authority of a *transcendens* (noemata, ideal signifieds, cognitive competence, pure logical realms, grammar, sensorial evidence, social action) to which the immanent power of language is ingloriously deflected. But Vickers misconstrues the valence of their valorization of language, and mistakes celebratory liberation for diminution. He writes: "It is therefore rather simple-minded of deconstructionists to imagine that the detection of ambivalences, however frequent, in any way threatens language, or philosophy, or literature, for detecting them is not an innocent act" (169). Derrida has never maintained that ambivalence threatens language. Ambivalence may threaten the author or interpreter who believes to be unthreatened by the inherently ambivalent dimension of language. As simple as that. And since there have been, are, and will be, writers and readers, speakers and listeners, that profess to write and read, speak and hear, invariably mono-semantic and literal statements, in the wild belief that they can master language's disseminative drive, then it is salutary to remind *them*—not language—that ambivalence will turn back, with a vengeance, to threaten and undo their most pious expectations and intentions. There is, in Derrida, no diminution of language. There is rather the diminution of naïve users of language. It is very surprising that so eminent a philologist like Brian Vickers should expose himself to be so ruthlessly diminished in a debate with Ferdinand Derrida.

I will now consider Bruce Smith's fisticuffs confrontation with Derrida. I have already pointed out that some of Bruce Smith's misconstructions of Husserl originate in his inability to give up the "natural standpoint." This natural standpoint is, already in Hegel's *Phenomenology of Spirit*, what spirit must abandon in its rational pursuit of itself. The Cartesian overtones of this formulation cannot be avoided, nor can we seek to camouflage—as many soi-disant phenomenological critics seem to do—the degree of Husserl's direct commitment to Descartes. Throughout the opening chapters of *Phenomenal Shakespeare*, Smith expresses his commitment to the literal ("the literal sense," xvi), to the natural ("the natural world," 22) to the common (the "common experiences" xv), and to the "visceral presence" (2). This way he endorses what Derrida would call the *empiricist* expression of a *metaphysics of presence*, whose most banal delusion is epistemological *naturalism*. One can easily grasp what Smith is up to, and one can even be sympathetic with it: he wants to replace a model of text-and-drama hermeneutics based on the "rational mind" (xviii) with alternative models of meaning-construction that rely on new attention to the body—its emotions and affections. But this can be done without undertaking the ridiculous task of confuting Saussure, structuralism, post-structuralism, Lacan, Derrida, and the linguistic turn.

Smith's efforts at controverting some of the principles that underlie Saussure's major paradigm-shift may impress uneducated postgrad students, who are in passing given the bonus exemption from having to read some important texts like *Of Grammatology, Blindness and Insight* or *Philosophy and the Mirror of Nature*, but it doesn't really work on audiences with a basic grasp of contemporary philosophy and theory. The question actually arises: did Smith read Derrida? In *Phenomenal Shakespeare* he manages to grab a floating sentence from *La voix et le phénomène*, and successfully identifies the page in the book where it belongs (*Phenomenal Shakespeare* 27; *Speech and Phenomena* 86). The rest of his allusions to Derrida and deconstruction, including several references to the title *Of Grammatology*, are all vague, school-text, platitudes. In some cases, he makes basic errors, like assuming that in reading one is confronted with a choice—either to be attentive to gesture and the origin of communication in the human body, or to be attentive to words and to Derrida's 'arche-writing' (55), as if this archi-writing were readily accessible to the standard (framing) phenomenological reader. This is like asking someone to choose between his conscious and his unconscious self, between his rational motives and his ideology, or between smoking and breathing. But let us consider for a moment the passage from *La voix et le phénomène* to which Smith alludes, one directly concerned with the problematic relationship between reduction and temporality:

> The externality of space, externality as space, does not overtake time; rather, it opens as pure "outside" "within" the movement of temporalization. If we

recall now that the pure inwardness of phonic auto-affection supposed the purely temporal nature of the "expressive" process, we see that the theme of a pure inwardness of speech, or of the "hearing oneself speak," is radically contradicted by "time" itself. The going-forth "into the world" is also primordially implied in the movement of temporalization. "Time" cannot be an "absolute subjectivity" precisely because it cannot be conceived on the basis of a present and the self-presence of a present being. Like everything thought under this heading, and like all that is excluded by the most rigorous transcendental reduction, the "world" is primordially implied in the movement of temporalization. As a relation between an inside and an outside in general, an existent and a nonexistent in general, a constituting and a constituted in general, temporalization is at once the very power and limit of phenomenological reduction. Hearing oneself speak is not the inwardness of an inside that is closed in upon itself; it is the irreducible openness in the inside; it is the eye and the world within speech. *Phenomenological reduction is a scene, a theater stage.*

Speech 86

In my commentary in an earlier chapter of Sanford Budick's article on Hamlet's "now," I already argued that, as Derrida here explains, temporalization poses a limit to phenomenological reduction. Since the spacing-logic or movement of temporalization (retention, protention, delay, absence, difference, trace) presumes the outside of the supposedly reduced world, temporalization and speech, the supposedly "inward" gains obtained after the reduction, are necessarily beholden to the contingent law of the excluded world. The inside is violated by the irreducible openness of the outside. Therefore silent speech unfolds in the likeness of "the externality of space." Since the phenomenological reduction facilitates access to this inward external space, it can be compared to "a scene" or a "theatre stage." This metaphorical use is confirmed in another passage where Derrida argues that

> Intersubjectivity is inseparable from temporalization taken as the openness of the present upon an outside of itself, upon another absolute present. This being outside itself proper to time is its spacing: it is a *proto-stage* [*archi-scène*]. This stage, as the relation of one present to another present as such, that is, as a nonderived re-presentation (*Vergegenwärtigung* or *Repräsentation*), produces the structure of signs in general as "reference," as being-for-something (*für etwas sein*), and radically precludes their reduction.
>
> Speech 84, n9

What both passages taken together submit is that the theatrical stage prompted by the phenomenological reduction—the scene of temporalized silent speech—is inexorably underwritten by a more basic scene—the *archi-scène*—where the continuous inward flows of temporality and speech are actually stripped down to the discontinuous spacing that characterizes externality.[49] Let us now see what Smith infers from the passage:

> Far from being "pure," Derrida says in a rare moment of italicized directness, "*Phenomenological reduction is a scene, a theater stage*" (Derrida 1973: 86, emphasis original). With this aperçu I take Derrida to be referring to the secondhand status of the impressions that Husserl regards as just *being there*, "at hand." About those impressions, Derrida insists, there is nothing "natural" at all. What gets framed in Husserl's acts of *epoché*, images as well as words—are not natural givens—things out there in the world—but man-made fabrications.
>
> Phenomenal 22

Smith does well to advertise his exegetic uncertainty ("I take Derrida to be referring"), for his interpretation is profoundly mistaken. He decontextualizes the Derrida passage, located in a section centered on the relation between speech and inward temporality, and places it alongside the Husserl passage from *Ideas I* §27 which he wrongly interpreted, as we saw in an earlier section, as the description of an act of reductive "framing." Derrida is not saying that in the scene of the mind, after the reduction, images and words are only derivatively imprinted, as if unable to enter the stage in their full natural splendor—indeed, their dressing up for that stage would determine the theatrical nature of the reduction. Not at all. This is taken for granted and would even be the case before the reduction. What he is saying is that the phenomenological reduction fails to secure the eviction of a worldly externality whose necessary contingency makes itself most visibly felt in the differential production—the constitution through spacing—of the very dubious aural and temporal presences that glide across to the mind's inward stage. The fact that the phenomenological reduction predisposes the mind to become a scene, a theater stage, a kind of intra-scopic re-presentation of the outside world, betokens the failure of the reduction as a purely transcendental, prophylactic measure: the mind inadvertently reproduces what it aims to cancel.

---

49   For l'Oedipe as dramatic structure of *machine théâtrale*, see Althusser, *Écrits sur la psychanalyse*, 45.

One certainly doesn't need Derrida's dismantling of phenomenological metaphysics to fathom that "knowing-in-place-in-time is a theatrical scene," that "speeches and the props in that scene [are] artifacts, not natural givens" and that "presence is an illusion made with those speeches and props" (Smith, *Phenomenal* 27). A superficial reading of some texts by Plato, Cicero, Francis Bacon, and Giordano Bruno, would suffice for this notion to take shape. Shakespeare, for one, could have found in their work enough inspiration to write something like *The Tempest*. Smith radically under-interprets the nature, scope, and significance of Derrida's engagement with Husserl. What Derrida argues is that the props that set up the illusion for the theatre of the mind are in fact *external*, but decidedly not in the natural—naturalistic and phenomenal—sense implied by Smith. There are more things in earth—to wit, contingency, accidentality, extension, exteriority, discontinuity, scansion, separateness—than are dreamt of in his philosophy.

At bottom, Smith makes the basic mistake of seeking to frame an *emotional theory* of language—something like trying to devise a cordial theory of the heart, or a fluid theory of blood. Emotions are the opposite of theory. There are theories of emotion, but they are not emotional—remember, with Spinoza, that "The concept of a 'dog' doesn't bark," which we could rephrase as "The concept "Shakespearean body" does not feel."[50] To try to make room for a renewed attention to affection and emotion in Shakespeare studies is of course legitimate, but it is not necessary to de-theorize the theoretical paradigms in order to achieve that goal. This is very much what Smith does in his essay on "Premodern Sexualities," where he reengages critically with Derridean thought. But again the force of his arguments is undercut by the fact that he relies exclusively on Culler's book *On Deconstruction*. No Derrida or de Man text is included in the list of bibliographical references. This is striking, as this long section covers nearly one third of the article. This neglect may account for some extravagant pronouncements, like:

> A more troubling problem with deconstruction, perhaps, is its assumption that all texts pretend to wholeness. The representation of sexualities in Shakespeare's *Measure for Measure*, for example, is already so full of faultlines that a truly deconstructive reading would be a wholistic reading. (325)

---

50   Spinoza's comment was repeated often by Althusser, whose war against "phenomenological idealism" was frequently waged with Spinozian weapons. See, Knox Peden, *Spinoza contra Phenomenology*, 161–162.

The problem here is not that Smith finds holistic readings problematic. There is nothing inherently wrong in trying to account hermeneutically for every nook and cranny of a text, for nothing prevents you from concluding that all the text's parts work against unity, harmony, continuity, stability, integration, even holism. Take, for instance, Barthes' holistic reading of Balzac's *Sarrasine* in *S/Z*, or Bourdieu's comprehensive analysis of Flaubert's *L'éducation sentimentale* in *Les règles de l'art*. The real problem lies in the assumption that deconstruction holds "that all texts pretend to wholeness." I ignore where did Smith lift this notion from, but the notion is wrong. Maybe he misremembers de Man's critique of the "intent at totality of the interpretive process" (*Blindness and Insight* 31), which Culler evokes on page 199 of his book. The pretense to wholeness is a critical vice that deconstruction repeatedly exposes, but wholeness is here construed as unity achieved through the pressure exerted by intentional meaning (Husserl's *Meinen*). Thus there is always a measure of interpretive distortion in the author who believes that his text is united, and therefore whole, by virtue of an intention that, in the expectation it be fulfilled (*erfüllt*), he strives to project on it. Not all texts pretend to wholeness, only those whose authors (poets, novelists, philosophers) are partly or completely deluded by the intentional fallacy. An auto-deconstructed text makes no such assumptions and falls under no delusion. *Measure for Measure*, perhaps. But there is still more:

> In practice what a deconstructive critic finds in aporia is the need for more text, for the mediating text that is being provided by none other than the critic. Deconstruction shares, then, with new historicism-cultural materialism a radical objectification of the subject of inquiry, a distrust of sense experience, of which erotic desire is surely an extreme example.
> "Premodern Sexualities" 325

There are two concerns here. On the one hand, Smith forgets that there are many ways, especially in the case of the reader Shakespeare, in which *the mediating texts* (let us use the plural, for the sake of accuracy) are a constitutive part of the text, are built into the text as its sublated intertextual anteriority. The critic activates already existing mediations. The correctness of a critical exercise is therefore very much a function of the critic's breath of readings: the best way to start understanding Shakespeare is by reading all he read, by internalizing, that is, all his *textual mediations*. It is certainly not enough, but it is the best starting point. In this sense, eros for Shakespeare is less a raw, immediate thing (staring at his penis or fondling with a girl by the river Avon) than an experience mediated by, say, texts by Ovid or Marlowe. On the other hand, what is, for Smith, "the subject of inquiry"? Is it a textual reality or an experience supposedly predating the text? Well, Smith's subject is nominally *eros* or *premodern sexuality*, which he construes as an experience that refuses to be objectified, even by scientific or intellectual inquiry:

> Eros resists that kind of objectification. It can be given a scientific name, *sexualitas*, and thus be turned into an object of systematic investigation, but for the historical subjects who felt it, no less than for the critic who reads its textual record, eros remains a subjective experience. (325)

On this logic, heart-attacks are also subjective experiences—especially, I guess, of "historical subjects" proud of their "embodiedness" (325)—for they start with an embodied historical subject that feels (shortness of breath, chest discomfort). Does that make the experience immune to clinical-diagnostic objectification? Fortunately, not. Language, Saussure rightly argues, also begins as a subjective experience in a bi-personal scene of speech (*le circuit de la parole*), but that doesn't prevent it from becoming "an object of systematic investigation." The fact that in both cases the objective findings map out a transcendental realm of systemic normativity that may account (genetically or causally) for the experience doesn't rule out the fact that heart-attacks and speech remain, in (phenomenological) principle, subjective experiences. Smith's comment is shockingly naïve. I return to Roy Harris' example (*Reading Saussure* 10): playing tennis is, yes, a subjective experience where players share the trajectory of the ball between one racket and another, but it presupposes (is mediated by) an abstract system of conventional rules, let alone the emulative pressure of precedents. This is where a paradoxical *transcendental wholeness of non-totalization* calls for the *finite infinity* that inheres in the concept of the game (*jeu*):

> If totalization no longer has any meaning, it is not because the infiniteness of a field cannot be covered by a finite glance or a finite discourse, but because the nature of the field—that is language, and a finite language—excludes totalization. This field is in effect that of a *play*, that is to say, a field of infinite substitutions only because it is finite [*dans la clôture d'un ensemble fini*], that is to say, because instead of being an inexhaustible field [*un champ inépuisable*], as in the classical hypothesis, instead of being too large, there is something missing from it: a center which arrests and grounds the play of substitutions.
> DERRIDA *Writing* 289; *L'écriture* 423

The minute *eros* begins its human play, it becomes the part of a finite game of infinite possibilities. Sartre used to say that it was impossible to think dialectically without consciously identifying your thought as dialectical. That is, too, the prerogative of *eros* as a cultural event in human interaction: when it happens it is because you know that it happens and are able to identify it as such. It is surrounded by competing categories (philia, agape, infatuation, etc.) also at work in the field. The rest is the more or less joyous business of body proximity and sex. Derrida never said that the metaphysical drive to organize semantic-conceptual material along binary oppositions is something that he found particularly pleasing, whence the foolishness of accusing deconstruction of binding us humans to "cut-and-dried distinctions" (Egan, *The Struggle for Shakespeare's Text* 165). Also preposterous is to allege that deconstruction is unable to assume the position of the "among" (326), and to propose instead a phenomenological turn to what Michel Serres called the priority of prepositional coordinates. This reveals considerable ignorance of Derrida's work, as the motif of the "among" is explicitly discussed in *Passe-Partout*, and a figurative equivalent (*hyphen*) is a recursive presence in essays like *Cartouches, The Beast and the Sovereign, Monolingualism of the Other, Archive Fever, On the Spirit, Adieu to Emmanuel Levinas*, and *Death Penalty*, to mention only some.

Smith oscillates between a scholastic adherence to primary deconstructive theorems obtained from secondary sources—"If, as Derrida claims, all meanings are a product of *différance*, neither half of a binary male/female, heterosexual/homosexual, legitimate/ illegitimate can claim ontological priority. Neither is natural (Culler 131–34)" ("Premodern Sexualities" 323)—and what is at bottom a wholesale forsaking of meanings, products, differences and binaries in exchange for the joyous business of natural life. This is, I fear, not exactly an anti-deconstructive gesture—it is rather a recusation of *all* kinds of formalism, structuralism, and post-structuralism. I would risk a stronger claim: to find fault in literary scholarship that "objectifies" the subject of inquiry, resorts to the "mediating text," and rejects "sense experience" as a reliable source of textual signification, is to object to modern philology as a discipline. Smith believes that "texts not only represent bodily experience; they imply it in the way the ask to be touched, seen, heard, even smelled and tasted" (326). If you decide to give up mediation and trade the givenness of the text for the sensorial donations and phenomenal deliveries of sensibility, if you subjectify the subject of inquiry and become a truster of sense experience, then you may as well also give up Shakespeare and flee the metropolis, seize the blooming lilacs, and buy a cottage in Concord. We cannot ask a text to give us what a text cannot give. There is plenty of life outside the text, and outside language.

As the immediate context clarifies, what Derrida meant with the famous phrase "Il n'y a pas de hors-texte" (*De la grammatologie* 227), is that we cannot search outside the text for the meaning that is produced in the text, that we cannot transgress the immanence of the text (and of language) in search for a transcendent confirmation of the significance that has been verbally constituted inside the text.[51] The phrase resonates with many other phrases in the book where the same radical rejection of the *transcendent* existence of a pure presence-origin of meaning is being asserted: "il n'y a pas de parole plein" (102), "il n'y a pas de musique avant le langage" (280), "il n'y a pas de musique animale " (280), " il n'y a pas de signe comme tel " (281), "Il n'y a pas d'institution sociale avant la langue" (313), " Il n'y a pas de parole, donc, nous le savons, pas de chant, et par conséquent pas de musique, avant l'articulation " (345), "il n'y a pas d'écriture *vraie*" (412), "il n'y a pas de chose même" (412) "Il n'y a pas de langage avant la différence locale" (355), "il n'y a pas de presence" (437), "il n'y a pas d'essence de la présence ni de présence de l'essence" (439). Note that what Derrida, whether through Rousseau or in his own terms, is saying is that these things—pure speech, pure music, the full-fledged sign, true writing, the thing itself, essence, and presence—exist only on condition they are factored in as conventional conceptual delusions (tropes) whose congruence is subject to the strictures (arbitrariness, difference, negativity, relationality) of grammatological constitution, and therefore beholden to the infinite slipperiness of the finite transcendental field/game of writing. Similarly, in the famous apothegm—*il n'y a pas de hors-text*—Derrida implies that there is no presence (no transcendent "referent" and no "transcendental signified") that, being outside the text, is meaningful *in* the text.[52] Furthermore, he is not saying what he is normally taken to say: that no meaning-giving reality exists outside the transcendental field of writing and textuality. On the contrary, for Derrida, reality is there, it is immense, it is nearly everything that really exists and matters, but the non-textualized ontic *plenty* it may possess is something that escapes us altogether, as *meaning*. To violate and confound the immanence of textual

---

51   Compare my interpretation of the phrase with Jonathan Gil Harris' in *Shakespeare and Literary Theory*, 43–44.
52   He would have conceded that certain transcendent presences are meaningful *to* the text, in line with a materialist determinism he learnt from Althusser. It is also important to stress that even Derrida mentions the "signifié transcendantale" (*De la grammatologie* 227) as something that is absent from the text, this doesn't imply that the text is not produced through and in a transcendental field—that of writing. This formalist condition Derrida doesn't himself emphasize much, but there is a sense in which his concept of archi-writing can be construed as a transcendental field.

significance with presumptions of non-textual significance is an outrageous (Quixotesque and Flaubertian) move—as fatuous as trying to marry the white queen of a chess-set, as silly as mistaking Snout for a wall. There is reality, no end of reality, only not for us.

CHAPTER 13

Doing Shakespeare

To the Things Themselves

1

In the "Prologue" to *The Human Condition,* Arendt explains that what she proposes is "a reconsideration of the human condition from the vantage point of our newest experiences and our most recent fears," and specifies: "What I propose, therefore, is very simple: it is nothing more than to think what we are doing. 'What we are doing' is indeed the central theme of this book" (5). So what are we doing? Well, Simon Palfrey, Paul Kottman, and Julia Lupton would speedily reply: *we are doing Shakespeare.* And we are doing him and his things for no other reason than because he helps us to think about our life and our politics, us, who reconsider the human condition from the vantage point of our newest experiences and our most recent fears. As impressive as it sounds.

Years later, in her unfinished book, *The Life of the Mind,* Arendt paid cursory attention to Husserl, alluding quite correctly to the theory of essences and the importance of intentionality. There is however a more cryptic reference to a Husserl prepositional phrase, which she interestingly leaves in the original German. After a meditation on the traditional tension in Western philosophical discourse between the pull of thought and the pull of sensible things, she portends that

> the crisis of philosophy and metaphysics came to an end when the philosophers themselves began to declare the end of philosophy and metaphysics. By now this is an old story. (The attraction of Husserl's phenomenology sprang from the anti-historical and anti-metaphysical implications of the slogan '*Zu den Sachen selbst*' [...])
>
> *The Life of the Mind* 9

This was not the first time Arendt used the phrase. In a 1948 essay titled "What is Existential Philosophy?" she praised the reconstructive dimension of Husserl's philosophy, aimed at taking side with "'the little things' [Hofmannsthal's phrase in letter to Stefan George] and against big words because it is in those little things that the mystery of reality lies hidden" (*Essays in Understanding* 165). Husserl's philosophy couldn't be further from such romantic-pietistic gibberish. But Arendt concludes, undaunted, tracing a line that I see running from George Eliot to Nathalie Sarraute:

> Husserl's phrase "to the things themselves" is no less a magic formula than Hofmannsthal's "little things." If we still could achieve anything by magic—in an age whose only good is that all magic fails in it—we would indeed have to begin with the smallest and seemingly most modest of things, with unpretentious "little things," with unpretentious words (165).

Four years before she published this paper, Adorno and Horkheimer were talking about the *disenchantment of the world* (Horkheimer & Adorno, *Dialectic* 1–3) brought about by the Enlightenment. Arendt appears to have responded to this diagnosis with a primitivist and potentially reactionary call to return to animism and spiritualism. It is hard to see what role Husserl could have played in this debate other than that of the sailor who, in the face of encroaching irrationalist tendencies like existentialism, tied himself to the sinking mast of radical rationalism. Fascism, recall, was around the corner, with its heap of broken shadows. Legend has it that Arendt attended Husserl's lectures in Freiburg in the winter semester of 1926–1927, "but does not seem to have been particularly impressed" (Moran 294). Did she read the *Logical Investigations*, the 1901 book where the slogan appears in print, albeit surely not as a slogan? Or did she merely read Heidegger's *Basic Concepts of Phenomenology*, also published that year of 1927, where the phrase is mentioned and correctly applied (140, 174). She probably read neither book, for she misinterprets the phrase as a call to veer away from philosophical abstractions and metaphysical concepts to *things*, what she calls "objects of sensation" (*The Life of the Mind* 8) in contradistinction to words and concepts. This confusion, which is not exclusively Arendt's, is the subject of this section. *Doing Shakespeare* has become *doing the Shakespeare things themselves*, and this development partly hinges upon a misunderstanding of the nature of Husserl's phenomenological project that Arendt distinctly foreshadowed.

In "Parergon" Derrida reiterates that the first question in any philosophical interrogation of art is the question of the factual existence of the work, of "le fait qu'*il y a* des oeuvres d'art" (*La vérité en peinture*, 38). Not so much the question of *things* as of *works*—of works, that is, that occur in a mode of existence that is not exactly factual or natural. We may wish to ignore Hegel, Heidegger, and Derrida, when discussing art, including Shakespeare's textual art, but if we do so we run the risk of exiting a *hermeneutic circle* that alone guarantees the intelligibility of most of the terms—concepts like sense, meaning, form, content, signifier, signified—in our discussion.[1] The hermeneutic circle, a central concept in the Heidegger-Gadamer-Szondi tradition, is animated by the *mediatedness* (Derrida, *La verité* 41) that articulates "le ressort de la dialectique spéculative" (31).[2] Dropping from the rotating wheel involves, first and foremost, the all-out removal of the frame or boundary separating inside from outside, art from life, and next the promotion of the *un-arting* of art, i.e. its final ontological collusion with the framing ecosystem of things, objects and actants. This some may find liberating. I personally find Derrida's advice to shun the risks of exiting such circle through "la fausse sortie, le bavardage empirique" (*La verité* 37) far more revolutionary. For here we are, in the involutionary standstill of the natural standpoint, freed from the prison-house of structures (including language and power), at the foot of the wheel, liberated from the masturbatory habits of formalism, doing Shakespeare by going at last to the things themselves. At what cost? In *The Many Faces of Realism*, Hilary Putnam explains that

> We can and should insist that some facts are there to be discovered and not legislated by us. But this is something to be said when one has adopted a way of speaking a language, a "conceptual scheme." To talk of "facts" without specifying the language to be uses is to talk of nothing; the word "fact" no more has its use fixed by Reality Itself than does the word "exist" or the word "object." (36)

The same applies to the word "thing," probably the most misunderstood noun in the phenomenological traditions.

In the "Introduction" to the *Criticism* issue dedicated to "Shakespeare and Phenomenology" (2012), Kevin Curran and David Kearney remind the reader that "one of Husserl's maxims is an attempt to recover 'things themselves.'" And they continue: "Phenomenology provides a way to address material culture, to attend to the things of the early modern world, without losing sight of the fact that there is no intelligible object world divorced from the subject" (359). Despite the proviso in the coda ("without losing"), their take on phenomenology with a view to addressing material culture and attending to things

---

1   Stephen Thomson sees in Derrida's mixed attitude to Descartes a similar realization of the inescapability of, in this case, the vicious circle of Cartesian filiation: "Jeu d'écarts."
2   Derrida: "Le *Mitte*, tiers, élément milieu, veille à l'entrée dans le cercle herméneutique ou dans le cercle de la dialectique spéculative. L'art joue ce rôle. Chaque fois que la philosophie détermine l'art, le maîtrise et l'enclôt dans l'histoire du sens ou dans l'encyclopédie ontologique, elle lui assigne une fonction de médium" (*La vérité* 41).

is inescapably naïve and brazenly wrong. Their earlier attempt at glossing Husserl's thought was already unpromising: "Consciousness, Husserl argued, was always directed toward an object of some sort. Consciousness was always consciousness *of* something or other. The life of the mind could not, therefore, be discussed in terms distinct from the material world" (356). The first two sentences are correct. But there is a *non sequitur* in the third. For one, Husserl seldom speaks of the *material world*: the world out there is the realm of the transcendent, the fact-world of nature (*Naturwirklichkeit*), at most a *lifeworld* (*Lebenswelt*). Phenomenological disinterest in confronting the *res materialis* (*Ideas I* §149, 314), the sensible ὕλη, the hyletic data or *Stoffe* (§85, 175–176), is a fact that some early modern scholars should look carefully into.³ Second, and more important, the whole point of phenomenology is that the life of the mind *must* be discussed in terms *distinct* from the transcendent world, the natural world, including psychological descriptive terms. This distinction is a prerequisite of transcendental separateness, facilitated by the reduction. Any other mode of investigation is a naturalized (anthropologized, psychologized) mode of research, and Husserl's life-long project involved breaking away from that and drawing—or redrawing, by returning to Descartes and Kant—a transcendental line.

Curran's and Kearney's understanding of the Husserl phrase is standard enough in critical parlance. It doesn't differ much from the intended meaning of the same phrase in, say, the Henry James remark on Baudelaire to the effect that "he cares more for his process—for making grotesquely-pictorial verse—than for the things themselves" (*Literary Criticism II* 154). But Husserl and James didn't mean the same thing, or *things*. Husserl's phrase *to the things themselves* has taken a rare life of its own, as culturally felicitous as based on deep misunderstanding, one no doubt aggravated by Merleau-Ponty's mandarin call to an "ontological rehabilitation of the sensible" (*Signes* 165). In the light of some of the turns, changes and developments that have helped reshape Shakespeare criticism in the last twenty years or so, Curran and Kearney's use of the phrase reads as an apposite slogan—a kind of promotional war call summoning disperse critical commandos to enter in action. In their footnote

---

3   The terms "matter" and "material" are not included in any of the detailed conceptual indexes of the following introductory books to phenomenology: Dan Zahavi's *Husserl's Phenomenology* (2003) and *Phenomenology: The Basics* (2019), David Woodruf Smith's *Husserl* (2013), and Dermot Moran's *Introduction to Phenomenology*. For the phenomenological imperviousness to materialist assumptions, especially as regards the problem of perception, see Zahavi, *Husserl's Legacy*, 190–194. This should work as a reminder for early modernist scholars who invoke *phenomenology* to dabble in *physiology*—and end up doing neither.

to the phrase, they observe that "'Things themselves' is also an apt description of early modern and Shakespeare studies of the past twenty years," and they link it to "the material turn" in the same discipline (364, n20). They are very right to single out the phrase to denote what has happened in the discipline in the last two decades, but they very wrongly estimate the grounds of cogency and appropriateness subtending their choice of phrase.

To state it clearly at the outset: the turn, in Husserl, to things themselves is anything but a *materialist turn*. To interpret Husserl's appeal to stand by the things themselves as a call to save "the natural unsophisticated standpoint of positive reality (*Positivität*)" (*Ideas I*, "Preface to the English Edition" 39) is an error of positively natural and unsophisticated readers of Husserl. The temptation to become exactly that is of course strong. After decades of boring textualism (close reading, deconstruction) and boring historicism (cultural materialism, new historicism, feminism) the time has finally come to roll up our sleeves and get things seriously done. Going to the things themselves and doing them, in our particular context, means nothing less than *Doing Shakespeare*, whatever that means, the title of a landmark study by an eminent scholar, Simon Palfrey. working partly in this revisionary tradition. Although it openly invokes the procedural routines of phenomenology, the mistranslated Husserl motto smacks of *plumpes Denken*, a crude, unprincipled empiricism—what Sartre called "empirisme sans principes" (Sartre, *Critique de la raison dialectique I* 28)—whose necessary finale is but a vulgar re-ontologization of critical thought.

Phenomenology, to be sure, has been deservedly charged with this volatile empiricism and with much more. But what I want to stress here is that a return to the sensible, material, or empirical things themselves is inimical to the transcendental spirit of Husserl's phenomenology and consequently has no place in its program. It may have become a convenient motto for a reprogrammed phenomenology—for instance, Merleau-Ponty's—but one wonders how far phenomenology can be revamped and redeployed in empiricist directions without stopping to deserve the name. It is evident that Curran's and Kearney's appeal draws part of its force from the intellectual prestige attached to the names of phenomenology and Husserl. But one should be respectful with the arguments, labels, and names one musters in order to advance a case or further a claim. The notion of a *return to the things themselves* is utterly incompatible with Husserl's appeal to bring "the essence of a material thing to primordial givenness," and then, within the racket of an "object-giving consciousness" to complete "the mental steps required for the 'insight' [*Einsicht*], for the primordial givenness, that is, of the essential content [*die originäre Gegebenheit des Wesensverhaltes erfordert*]" (*Ideas I* §6 17; *Ideen I* 16). The process carefully described by Husserl deals with the—insightful—givenness of essences, not with the—exsightful, if you wish—return to things. No sense is here involved other than the *mind's eye*. In the "Introduction" to *Ideas I*, Husserl argues that "pure or transcendental phenomenology will be established not as a science of facts but as a science of essential Being (as eidetic science), a science which aims exclusively at establishing 'knowledge of essences' and absolutely no facts [*und durchaus keine Tatsachen*]" (*Ideas I* 3). Are these essences the *facta* (4) he later mentions? Obviously not. The laying down of an essential ground is manifestly an act of transcendental prudence, not an invitation to an ontic-factual bacchanalia.[4] Even the honest and informed Merleau-Ponty feels bound to record the fact that Husserl conceived of phenomenology as an "étude des essences," (*Phénoménologie* 7), and that landing *unmittelbar* on existential facticity was a supervening move (and mode) not envisioned by the rules of the game.[5]

Going to the things themselves, in Husserl, is an operation that only gets started once the *epoché* has been effectively completed, but what is bracketed in the *epoché* is precisely both the natural attitude about external reality and the belief in the very existence of the local things one aims to phenomenologically experience. Husserl goes as far as stating that "the whole of Absolute Being [...] is essentially independent of all Being of the type of a world or Nature, and it has no need of these for its existence. The existence of what is natural cannot condition the existence of consciousness since it arises as the correlate of consciousness" (*Ideas I* §51 98).[6] So, if, as Sanford Budick suggests, following Kermode, to "realize experience" ("Shakespeare's Now" 135) is the ultimate goal of Shakespearean art, then we must be ready to countenance the paradox—or absurdity—that the experience *cannot* be performed: "If, on the one hand, the phenomenologist leaves the 'natural attitude' and brackets

---

4   In *Ideas I* he argues that in the *pure sciences of essential being*, to which phenomenology aspires, "*no experience qua experience*, i.e. *qua* consciousness that apprehends or sets up reality or concrete being, *can take over the function of supplying a logical ground*" (18).
5   Merleau-Ponty rushes in his "Introduction" to *Phénoménologie de la perception* to qualify his assertion with a call to *existence* and *facticité*. His book was published in 1945, when the impact of existentialism (Heidegger's included) forced thinkers of a younger generation to compromise. We shouldn't forget, however, that by 1929 Husserl already felt dejected by the advent of Heideggerian existentialism. He lamented "the faddish swing to a philosophy of 'existence,' the abandonment of 'philosophy as rigorous science.'" See Bruzina's "Introduction" to Fink's *Sixth Cartesian Meditation* (XII).
6   According to Derrida, *absolute existence* is accorded only to pure consciousness: "" il est difficile de le négliger, Husserl pré-détermine si peu l'être comme objet que, dans *Idées I*, l'existence absolue n'est reconnue qu'à la conscience pure" (*L'écriture* 126). He adds later that a noème "n'est pas un moment réel (*reell*) pour Husserl" (179).

his corresponding existence-belief, he cannot at the same time perform the perceptual experience he wishes to investigate" (Christian Beyer "Edmund Husserl"). The existence-belief, in short, is a precondition of perception, but so is too, in a certain sense, the natural standpoint that ensures our effective (sentient, intuitive, immediate, prerational) belonging to a fact-world. When suspending it through *epoché*, we do not abandon the thesis of the natural standpoint, "we make no change in our conviction," insists Husserl, but merely place it "out of action" (*Ideas I* 57). It is hard to understand how we can hold fast to a conviction while disconnecting or bracketing it, but this difficulty testifies to Husserl's bold readiness to play by transcendental rules. At any rate, the upshot is that for phenomenology the beginning of knowledge or science is beholden to a distrust (if not fear) of the real world of things: *timor mundi initium sapientiae*. Whereas in Hegelian dialectic ineffective reality is at least respectfully reckoned as reality, in phenomenological *askesis* the real becomes positively spectralized. As Marx would say, "the actual situation is expressed [...] as appearance, as phenomenon" (*Critique of Hegel's Philosophy of Right*, 7). It is like the difference between, say, an old mole and a ghost.

2

So, to come to the point, what did Husserl mean then when he summoned us to return *to the things themselves*? Let us move slowly, with some texts open on the table. To lend textual support to their reading of the phrase, Curran and Kearney mention in the footnote some pages of *Logical Investigations*, inviting the reader to confront "characteristic formulations of this idea" ("Introduction" 364). The page numbers are correctly transcribed, but it is not clear that they have read the content of the pages. Going to the things themselves is to allow things to appear as they are originally *given*. Husserl distinguished between objective (logical) conditions and subjective (noetic) conditions of knowledge. Whereas the former involve the fundamental principles, structures and laws that constitute the a priori foundation of any theory, the noetic conditions invoke our "ability to distinguish between truth and falsity, validity and nonvalidity, fact and essence, evidence and absurdity" (Zahavi, *Husserl's Phenomenology* 11). Thus, phenomenology demands a logicist purification of psychologism, and this in turn requires, Zahavi explains, "a return to the things themselves, to base our considerations on that which is actually *given*. To phrase it differently, if we are to examine in a nonprejudicial manner what ideality or reality is, we need to pay attention to its experiential givenness" (11–12). So returning to the things themselves means confronting in a valid, truthful, essential, and evident manner the givens—whether the perceived things of reality or the intuited truths of ideality—as they are experienced in our mental life, not as they are in themselves. The *things themselves* of the phenomenological refrain are immanent and potentially transcendental objects (immanent to the experience of consciousness) not transcendent things. What Zahavi doesn't here say is that Husserl favored *ideality* over *reality*, and that the experiential givenness that mattered for him was, at the time he wrote *Logical Investigations*, the *givenness* of the good old Cartesian *cogitata*. Later the expedient of *epoché* allowed him to remain in transcendental orbit without considerations of actual empirical perception—the kind of considerations that occupy the mind trapped in the natural standpoint. Later still, he devoted himself, in his study of noemata, to the ideality behind the transcendental constitution of reality, before he entered a late period of attention—no empirical return, in any case—to intersubjectivity, otherness and the body. So to return to the things themselves is to avoid reflective confusion and metaphysical presuppositions in the act of receiving the givens of mental experience. It is, in fact, a near-Cartesian call to remain *presuppositionless* (Zahavi 13). Derrida, let me recall, defines phenomenology as a "passage à l'essentialité," driven by the constant anticipation of the *esse* of essence (*L'écriture* 196).

The first important use of the phrase "an die Sachen selbst" can be found in *Logical Investigations* §41, in the section titled "*Prolegomena zur reinen Logik*," a rather unpromising rubric for scholars, like Curran and Kearney, interested in "material practices" and "material culture" ("Introduction" 355, 359). There the phrase occurs as the prepositional object of the verbs *consider, return, reconsider,* and *look* more attentively *at*. In a nutshell, what the philosophical narrator asks the reader is to reconsider the issues at hand, the matter that is being, in each case, discussed. The invitation to turn to "the 'things themselves'" (101) is a call to focus the debate on the specific topic at hand, which Husserl distinguishes from the tendency to argue in a general manner: "Die Täuschung verschwindet, sowie man, statt im allgemeinen zu argumentieren, *an die Sachen selbst* herantritt" (*Logische* 159; emphasis added). Interestingly, Findlay, the English translator, deviates from the German original by putting the phrase in inverted commas, thus calling attention to its emblematic fate. No reference is made in the immediate context of this excerpt to things as material things or factual objects. The only "things" we can trace in the textual environs are the hardly factual "logical laws" (*die logische Gesetze*). In section 64 of the "Prolegomena," "Sachen selbst" (236) alludes to whatever falls in the realm of the objective (*sachliche*) and is explicitly opposed to the normative:

> Talk of "mutual belongingness as regards subject-matter" is most naturally taken to mean a belongingness grounded in things, in subject-matters themselves [*in den Sachen selbst gründet*]. Here only a unity in terms of theoretical law or of the concrete thing will be relevant, and our conception will place normative unity over against unity of subject-matter in a single opposition.
>
> *Logical* 149; *Logische* 236

The next important appearance of the phrase is the one cited by Curran and Kearney. I quote the whole passage in order to provide the phrase with its context:

> Our great task is now to bring the Ideas of logic, the logical concepts and laws, to epistemological clarity and definiteness [*Klarheit und Deutlichkeit*]. Here phenomenological analysis must begin. Logical concepts, as valid thought-unities, must have their origin in intuition [*Anschauung*]: they must arise out of an ideational intuition [*ideierende Abstraktion*] founded on certain experiences, and must admit of indefinite reconfirmation, and of recognition of their self-identity, on the reperformance of such abstraction. Otherwise put: we can absolutely not rest content with "mere words," i.e. with a merely symbolic understanding of words [*Wortverständnis*], such as we first have when we reflect on the sense of the laws for "concepts," "judgements," "truths" etc. (together with their manifold specifications) which are set up in pure logic. Meanings [*Bedeutungen*] inspired only by remote, confused, inauthentic intuitions [*uneigentlichen Anschauungen*]—if by any intuitions at all— are not enough: we must go back to the "things themselves" [*Wir wollen auf die "Sachen selbst" zurückgehen*]. We desire to render self-evident [*zur Evidenz bringen*] in fully-fledged intuitions [*vollentwickelten Anschauungen*] that what is here given [*Gegebene*] in actually performed abstractions is what the word-meanings in our expression of the law really and truly stand for. In the practice of cognition we strive to arouse dispositions in ourselves which will keep our meanings unshakably the same, which will measure them sufficiently often against the mark set by reproducible intuitions [*reproduziblen Anschauung*] or by an intuitive carrying out of our abstraction.
>
> *Logical Investigations II* 168; *Logische II* 10

Husserl, in the role of stern logicist, submits a strong opposition between, on the one hand, dealing with mere words (*blossen Worten*) about concepts

(*Begriffe*), an activity that is wont to vaporize in remote, confuse and inauthentic intuitions, and get lost in dense particularities, and, on the other, dealing with the concepts, judgements and truths that constitute the realm of logical concepts (*logischen Begriffe*). That Husserl held the belief that we can effectively abstain from getting lost in verbal-conceptual confusion is a powerful sign of his anti-dialectical vein—for dialectical thought assumes an inevitable traverse through verbal confusion.[7] Of course, in order to achieve the latter, we must, to an extent, engage in *Wortverständnis*: Husserl's position here is not far from the positivist view, partly shared by Wittgenstein, of philosophy understood as *Sprachkritik*, and it paves the way to Heideggerian *Auslegung*.[8] The final goal is a purification (a Cartesian clarification) of the real philosophical matters. It is with these logical concepts that Husserl seeks to converse in a way that is pure, i.e. uncontaminated both by the genetic realm of psychological experiences (*psychischen Erlebnissen*) and by linguistic impurities. Husserl's gesture repeats Spinoza's attempt to divest Cartesian philosophy from its narrative, expository, analytical quality, saving only, as Derrida explains, "the content, the topics [*les matières*], the very matters" (Derrida, "Language and the *Discourse of Method*" 62). Husserl seeks an interpretation of logical objectivities (*einer Interpretation der logischen Objektivitäten*). His starting assumption is the fact that all forms of thought and cognition refer

---

7   Jameson argues that we can "grasp the nature of the dialectical effect—indeed the dialectical shock—more clearly as we follow the process through which we are led to a critical and negative position, then brutally cancelled in a second moment to which we are less likely to lend our absolute credence, having now learned the experience of the linguistic and conceptual untrustworthiness of such positions in general" (*Valences* 57). We may also recall Badiou's impatience with linguistic philosophizing à la Derrida, a slightly anti-dialectical hostility that can be traced back to Foucault's response to Derrida's essay on the former's book on madness. Žižek has elevated the dialectical motif of the *traverse* (the traverse of phantasies and of contradictions) to near-mythical proportions.

8   Frege was also examining similar problems some decades earlier, when laying down his *Foundations of Arithmetic* (1884), where numbers joined the list of problematic concepts in need of a gradual purification, for he was aware that "knowledge of a concept in its purity (*Reinheit*) is achieved" only "by peeling off the alien clothing (*fremde Umhüllungen*) that conceals it from the mind's eye (*dem geistigen Auge*)" (*The Frege Reader* 88). Michael Beaney, the editor and translator of this particular Fregean fragment, obviously had Shakespeare at his fingertips. *The mind's eye*: *dem geistigen Auge*. Or maybe Frege had Hamlet in mind, in his mind's eye. Or maybe Horatio and Hamlet where already seeing through the ghost, peeling off that "portentous figure" (*Hamlet* 1.1.106.2) and its attendant rhetoricity, and thus foreseeing the advent of modernist logicism (Frege, Husserl, Wittgenstein). Only on this rationalist logic of depuration can the king (any king) be deemed a *thing*, a flabby concept to be refined by "the inward service of the mind and soul" (*Hamlet* 1.3.13). To the things themselves—in the mind's eye.

to objects and objective situations—"die Tatsache nämlich, das alles Denken und Erkennen auf Gegenstände bzw. Sachverhlte geht" (8). Note the lexical continuity between these *Sachverhlte* (objective situations) and the *Sachen* of the refrain, and recall that objectivity presupposes but is neither empiricalness nor materiality, and that matters of *logical objectivity* are handled at the Home Office and not in the Foreign Affairs department. Husserl uses again the phrase in the "Vorwort" to the second edition (1913) of the first volume of *Logical Investigations*, titled *Prolegomena zur reinen Logik*:

> if these Investigations are to prove helpful to those interested in phenomenology, this will be because they do not offer us a mere programme (certainly not one of the high-flying sort which so encumber philosophy) but that they are attempts at genuinely executed fundamental work on the immediately envisaged and seized things themselves [*den unmittelbar erschauten und ergriffenen Sachen*]. Even where they proceed critically, they do not lose themselves in discussions of standpoint, but rather leave the last word to the things themselves, and to one's work upon such things [*vielmehr den Sachen selbst und der Arbeit an ihnen das letzte Wort belassen*].
>
> Logical Investigations 4; Logische Untersuchungen x

In conclusion, *auf die Sachen selbst zurückgehen* is not, as Curran and Kearney imply, an invitation to return to sensorial, material, empirical things themselves. Husserl would have judged that step as a pre-philosophical reversion. When later in *Ideas I* §19 he discusses naturalist misconstructions, he will make it very clear that

> the fundamental defect of the empiricist argument lies in this, that the basic requirement of a return to the 'facts themselves' [*die Grundforderung eines Rückganges auf die 'Sachen selbst'*] is identified or confused with the requirement that all knowledge shall be grounded in *experience*. Accepting the intelligible naturalistic limitation of the field of knowable 'facts,' he takes for granted without further question that experience is the only act through which facts themselves are given. But facts (*Sachen*) are not necessarily *facts of nature* (*Natursachen*) the factworld in the ordinary sense, not necessarily the fact-world (*Wirklichkeit*) in general, and it is *only with the fact-world of nature* (*Naturwirklichkeit*) that the primordial dator act which we call experience is concerned. (36)

Let me repeat: "facts (*Sachen*) are not necessarily *facts of nature.*" In the meshes of his expository prose, the things themselves are certainly non-natural facts, but rather the things (concepts, ideas, notions) that matter to Husserl at each stage of the exposition. Also in *Ideas I*, Husserl closes section 87 with the summons, "Doch nun zu den Sachen" (*Ideen I* 180), meaning "But now to the matters themselves!" (*Ideas I* 184). The matters he will deal with in the next section are the immanent (*reele*) and intentional factors of experience, the proper and the intentional correlates of intentional experience, as a preparatory meditation conducive to the discussion of the actual matter at hand—the noema. The fact, however, that the thing or matter (*Sache*) of Husserl's analytical disquisition is, in this particular case, the noema doesn't mean of course that the noema is a thing (*Ding*), a material, empirical, sensuous thing. Consider, for instance, Curran's rash reconstruction of Husserlian ideas in his essay on *Macbeth*:

> In the simplest sense, criminality in *Macbeth* is phenomenological because it deals with the intentional dimension of infraction. The doctrine of intentionality—the cornerstone of Husserlian phenomenology—states that every act of consciousness, every thought, is directed towards an object of some sort. That is to say, consciousness is always consciousness *of* something or other: the thought and the thing are never readily separable. Indeed, the thing—what Husserl would call an "intentional object," or noema—creates the thought, creates the very conditions of sentience, not the other way around. In Macbeth's soliloquy, the dagger takes on the role of the intentional object. It catalyzes Macbeth's consciousness of his own criminality and at the same time teeters playfully on the frontier between idea and object.
>
> "Feeling Criminal in Macbeth" 393

There are two major concerns here. The first is that the noema cannot be simply identified with the "intentional object." Husserl was rather ambiguous in his treatment of the noema—one of his most memorable philosophical creations—but he certainly intended it to denote the ideal content, or ideal meaning, of an act of consciousness (Zahavi, *Husserl's Phenomenology* 65; Smith, *Husserl* 253–260; 448). In *Ideas I* §89, Husserl distinguishes between the thing *simpliciter* (the natural tree that bears fruit and burns) and the perceived tree as such, the tree as perceived, or object as intended. This distinction rehearses another he made in *Logical Investigations* between "the object as it is intended, and *simpliciter* the object which is intended" (*Logical Investigations* v, §17; qtd. by Smith, *Husserl* 255). As David W. Smith explains, "the *way* an object is intended in an act is encapsulated in the sense of the object in the experience, and that *sense* is the core of the *noema* or *intentional content* of the act" (*Husserl* 256). So the noema is a modal determination of ideal content, and it cannot be simply identified, as Curran does, with the "intentional object." Especially when this intentional object is invited to collapse, indistinctly, with the "thing" or the "object" in opposition to the "thought." Here lies Curran's central misrepresentation—to conceive of the noema as a thing/object that can be opposed to thought when the case is that noema is a transcendental category of thought. In short, neither the *simpliciter* physical thing dagger nor the intentional object dagger creates "thought" or "the conditions of sentience": it is only the sense of the ideal content of the object dagger as intended (the noema dagger) that determines the intentional mental activity oriented toward the intentional object dagger. Let me recall what Husserl states in *Ideas I* §51: "The existence of what is natural cannot condition the existence of consciousness since it arises as the correlate of consciousness" (*Ideas I* 98). The sense of the ideal content of an intentional object—the noema—lies at no less than three removes from the physical *thing*. Curran's claim that "the dagger's intentional quality marks it as substantial rather than phantasmic" (393) is egregiously wrong. Nothing "substantial" (hyletic, material) is allowed to set foot in the transcendental Eden. Curran's phenomenological account of the dagger scene makes no sense. There is no playful teetering on the frontier between idea and object. There is never the question of the real object (*Gegenstand*), but only the hallucinatory speculation on the concept of the object (*Gegenstandsbegriff*), which probably triggers the hallucination.[9] There is only a mental fixation on the idea—the intentional object dagger. This is not to say that no phenomenological account of the scene can be proposed. On the contrary, Husserl has some interesting things to say about sensorial "hallucination" (*Ideas I* §39, §46, §88, §112) and the "visual phantom" (*visuelles Phantom*) (*Ideas I* §15 30).[10] Whether this correct phenomenological account is actually more interesting, or more correct, than other possible—for instance rhetorical, dialectical, or both—interpretations of the scene is an altogether different matter. What I am discussing is the theoretical congruency of Curran's particular adoption of Husserlian phenomenology, not building a case against all phenomenological readings of Shakespeare. And I submit that his incongruency hinges on

---

9 See Enzo Melandri, *Le* Ricerche Logiche *di Husserl*, 136–38.
10 Still, Husserl admits that "concerning hallucinations, illusions and perceptual deception of whatever sort, it may be that phenomenology has something to say, and perhaps even a great deal: but it is evident that here, in the role which they played in the natural attitude, they undergo exclusion" (*Ideas I* §88, 21).

the misrepresentation of the role that objects, construed as empirical things or material substances, play in Husserl's projected system. Since, therefore, the things that matter for Husserl, both in *Logical Investigations* and *Ideas 1*, are certainly not physical objects or empirical things, and since, furthermore, the matters the return to which he encourages are things that matter and mean precisely because they are argumentatively exposed to analytical discriminations that strip them of verbal trappings and protect them from discursive ambushes—this is of course Husserl's delusive wishful thinking—there is then a predictable overlap in the term *Sache* between what is the object of discussion and what is, *tout court*, a tendentially nonverbal logical-conceptual object.

3

I can see the reader's eyebrows raising at what she sees as an over-the-top rendition of the Husserl phrase.[11] Let me simply recall that Adorno—a German philosopher who devoted his early academic efforts to exposing the "immanent contradictions" of phenomenology, which he described as a "formal ontology" (Letter to Benjamin 6 November 1934)—translated in a 1940 article titled "Husserl and the Problem of Idealism" the phrase "Zu den Sachen selbst" as "getting back to the subject-matter itself [...] back to the materials themselves" (18).[12] These materials he describes as "the pure acts of thinking and meaning," unbiased by "the fallacies of arbitrary conceptual construction" (18). These fallacies originate, in Husserl's account, we have seen, in tricky words that instill

---

11   The misunderstanding remains. David Woodruff Smith in the *Stanford Encyclopedia* entry for "Phenomenology" argues that Heidegger, in *Sein und Zeit*, "explicitly parodies Husserl's call, 'To the things themselves!,' or 'To the phenomena themselves!,'" without clarifying the original meaning or explaining the sense of Heidegger's supposed "parody." Smith mentions again the refrain in his book on Husserl, without citing a reference: "Pure phenomenology, we might well assume, appraises structures of consciousness (including noema and horizon) without making use of metaphysical or ontological commitments. 'To the facts of experience alone!' might be the mantra, echoing Husserl's prescription 'To the things [*Sache*] themselves!'" (*Husserl* 281).

12   That a careful scholar like Gerhard Schwepeenhäuser misrepresents Adorno's use of the phrase in *Aesthetic Theory* as a Husserlian echo testifies to the persistence of the confusion (*Theodor W. Adorno* 110). The excellent "Analytical Index" to the English edition of Husserl's *Ideas 1* (Routledge, 2012), modelled on Ludwig Landgrebe's index included in the 1928 edition of the German original reads: "*Matter (Sache):* —*Subject-matter, affair, fact, matter-of-fact. A return to the matters themselves*" (357). For a confirmation of this use of *Sache* (as subject-matter, business, concern, case) one can turn to Kleist's *Michael Kolhaas*, where the protagonists *Rechstsache* (legal case) is often reduced to "seine Sache".

conceptual confusion—literally, other concepts (*andere Begriffe*)—in the realm of pure concepts. This way, the chronic inadvertent error (*unbemerkter Äquivocation*) of undesired word meanings (*Wortbedeutungen*) risks obscuring the clarity of essential (ontological) meditation. Husserl strives to expel from the logical investigation the more or less wavering meaning of words (*mehr oder minder schwankende Wortbedeutung*). To return to things themselves is not to regress to the tooth and claw of reality: it is rather to throw words overboard when ballooning one's way to the eidetic *empireum*. O for a muse of fire!

But if Adorno, whose anti-Husserlian animus was never particularly concealed, is considered an unreliable witness to the meaning of the phrase, let us place Husserlian textuality inside its inmost context of relevance—on the one side, Hegel, and on the other Heidegger—and see how the phrase is redefined by contrast. A decontextualized use of the standard translation of Husserl's famous phrase *an die Sachen selbst* as *to the things themselves* misleads the reader towards the kind of meaning that is actually implied, in Hegelese, in the phrase "das Irdische," translated by Miller as "worldly things" or "things of this world" (*Phenomenology of Spirit* 5). In Hegelese, too, *Sache* very often stands for "matter" or "issue at hand." In the "Preface" to *Phenomenology of Spirit*, "die Sache selbst zu umgehen" is translated by A.V. Miller as "evading the real issue" (2), and the section titled "Das geistige Tierreich und der Betrug, oder die Sache selbst" is rendered as "The spiritual animal kingdom and deceit, or 'the matter in hand' itself" (237). Further, in the "Preface" to the second edition of Hegel's *Science of Logic*, for instance, the sentence "Insofern also das subjektive Denken unser eigenstes, innerlichstes Thun ist, und der objektive Begriff der Dinge die Sache selbst ausmacht" is translated by George di Giovanni as "Inasmuch as subjective thought is our own most intimately inner doing, and the objective concept of things constitutes what is essential to them" (16). *Die Sache selbst* means then what is essential to the things, not the things themselves. Further down, we read: "By thus introducing content into logical consideration, it is not the things, but what is rather the fact [*Sache*], the concept of the things, that becomes the subject matter [*nicht die Dinge, sondern die Sache, der Begriff der Dinge, welcher Gegenstand wird*]" (19). *Sache* is however in this edition sometimes translated as "substance." Of this translation, Pippin says: "'Fact' doesn't help much as a translation; he doesn't seem to mean anything like *Tatsache*, or what is the case. He is moving in the opposite direction from anything empirical, anything having to do with things or facts about existence" (*Hegel's Realm of Shadows* 85). So is Husserl, always moving—not genetically in the immanence of the argument, but methodologically in the logic of his program—from the thing toward the concept of thing, to later, of course, reverse the direction in moves of transcendental constitution. Let me give another Hegel example, this time filtered through one of his eminent interpreters. In the first section of *Genèse et structure de la Phénoménologie de l'esprit de Hegel* (1946), Jean Hyppolite measures the originality of Hegel's conception of phenomenology as a history of consciousness that leaves behind the rigidity of Fichte's *deduction of representation* and Schelling's *transcendental idealism* by risking a comparison between Hegel's and Husserl's comprehension of *phenomenology*:

> Commentators have been struck by this characteristic tack of Hegel's phenomenology: to describe rather than to construct, to present the spontaneous development of an experience as it offers itself to consciousness and in the way it offers itself. This characteristic could lead us to compare Hegel's phenomenology to the phenomenology of Husserl if the differences between the two were not much deeper than their similarities. It is truly by going "to the things themselves," by considering consciousness as it presents itself directly, that Hegel wishes to lead us from empirical to philosophical knowledge, from sensuous certainty to absolute knowledge.
> *Genesis and Structure* 10

Two points must be stressed: 1) for Hyppolite, the comparison between these phenomenologies barely holds and 2) it is an experience, not a thing, that in Hegel's phenomenology presents itself to consciousness, and the mode of this presentation ("the way it offers itself") is there always-already mediated in ways (dialectical ways) that are incompatible with Husserl's vision. So what is the rationale of the Hegel-Husserl comparison? Well, Hyppolite is relying on the recent memory of her reader, who has been treated in the preceding paragraph to a quotation from the *Phenomenology of Spirit* that prefigures the actual transcendental frame of Husserl's evoked formula—*and die Sache selbst*—where *Sache* is less a thing than a matter at hand, a matter in hand, a matter involved (in this particular case, the experience of consciousness). This is the Hegel fragment in Miller's translation:

> But the essential point to bear in mind throughout the whole investigation is that these two moments, "Notion" and "object," "being-for-another" and "being-in-itself," both fall *within* that knowledge which we are investigating. Consequently, we do not need to import criteria, or to make use of our own bright thought during the course of the inquiry; it is precisely when we leave these aside that we succeed in contemplating the matter in hand as it is *in and for itself*. (51–52)

In the Cambridge UP edition of *The Phenomenology of Spirit*, Terry Pinkard gives us "the matter at issue" (56) rather than "the matter at hand." Do you want to know what original Hegel phrase is being translated as "the matter in hand" and "the matter at issue"? Yes: "die Sache." And note that Hegel here couldn't be further from making a plea for empirical immediacy: he is rather staking the kind of claim for watertight immanence—"within," "no imported criteria"—that we found in Husserl's *Logical Investigations*. But this Hyppolite doesn't say. In conclusion: *an die Sachen selbst* spells an appeal to argumentative immanence within the transcendental parameters of consciousness. But then, why does Hyppolite decide to use Husserl's refrain in order to capture the specificity of Hegel's phenomenology? Simply, what he asserts is that whereas Husserl's phenomenology is still entangled in empiricist delusions, an error that, Hyppolite believes, the call to return to the things themselves ostensibly evinces, Hegel's phenomenology made a correct use of the refrain, construing this return in terms of the self-presentation of consciousness. Note the phrasing: "it is truly [*véritablement*] by going 'to the things themselves'" (*Genèse et structure* 15). So there is an erroneous return (Husserl's) to external things, and a true, *véritable* return (Hegel's) to matters as they experientially present themselves in thought. Needless to say, Hyppolite is wrong about Husserl, but his mistake is instrumental because it furnishes us with a Hegelian redescription of Husserl's refrain, with the proviso that for Husserl self-presentation is not a teleological narrative. Also mistaken is John Heckman in his "Introduction" to the English edition of Jean Hyppolite's book on Hegel, when he observes that "phenomenology [...] appeared serious, down to earth. The famous call for a 'return to the things themselves' appeared like a call to relevancy. It offered 'something to believe in' (Levinas), and that was both its strength and its weakness" (XVIII). Although he seems to contemplate, through the use of the verb *appear*, the possibility of a misunderstanding, nothing in the immediate context of the passage suggests that he believes Levinas and others were misconstruing the call. Interestingly, nearly forty years after Heckman claimed that "phenomenology appeared [...] down to earth," Curran and Kearney are going to stray into that "appearance" and claim a return to Shakespeare's earth.

4

Let us move on now to Heidegger. We must bear in mind that, as we have already noted in a previous section, both in the introductory sections to *Being and Time* and in the early chapters of *The Fundamental Problems of Phenomenology*, Heidegger tries to assimilate the "method" of phenomenology, freshly minted by his mentor Edmund Husserl, to his own neo-ontological program. He decides to favor phenomenology as a propaedeutic procedure that allows the thinker to discard conceptual irrelevance and metaphysical pseudo-problems and to focus on what really matters, the self-showing of Being. The fact that the Greek word *fainomenon* could be translated as self-showing offered an additional ground for an assimilation or cooptation whose rationale hinged however elsewhere, in the critical force of phenomenology as a method of discrimination of the conceptually relevant, of concentration and focus on what really (conceptually, notionally, argument-wise) matters—which is never physical matter. In the second chapter of the "Introduction" to *Sein und Zeit*, Heidegger explains:

> The expression "phenomenology" signifies primarily a *concept of method*. It does not characterize the what of the objects of philosophical research in terms of their content, but the *how* of that research. The more genuinely effective a concept of method is and the more comprehensively it determines the fundamental conduct of a science, the more originally is it rooted in confrontation with *the things themselves* and the farther away it moves from what we call a technical device—of which there are many in the theoretical disciplines. The term "phenomenology" expresses a maxim which can be formulated: *"To the things themselves!"* [*zu den Sachen selbst*] It is opposed to all free-floating constructions and accidental findings; it is also opposed to taking over concepts only seemingly demonstrated; and also to pseudo-questions which often are spread abroad as 'problems' for generations.
>
> 26; emphases added

Heidegger's explication proves that the *things themselves* are the real problems, the concepts that are truly demonstrated, the firm constructions and the substantial findings. Their thinghood (*Sachheit*) is their content, not their empirical physicality. Heidegger would later repudiate the idea of method in a number of places, but here he is defending a phenomenological program that allows the thinker to sift through the conceptual materials and pick out only what is a real conceptual problem, a genuine question, and extrude pseudo-problems and accidental questions. The things themselves are the real problems. The first translators of *Sein und Zeit* into English, John Macquarrie and Edward Robinson, included an interesting footnote:

> The appeal to the "Sachen selbst," which Heidegger presents as virtually a slogan for Husserl's phenomenology, is not easy to translate

without giving misleading impressions. What Husserl has in mind is the "things" that words may be found to signify when their significations are correctly intuited by the right kind of *Anschauung*. (Cf. his *Logische Untersuchungen*, vol. 2, part 1, second edition, Halle, 1 913, p. 6.) We have followed Marvin Farber in adopting "the things themselves." (Cf. his *The Foundation of Phenomenology*, Cambridge, Mass., 1943, pp. 202–3.) The word "Sache" will, of course, be translated in other ways also. (50)

Macquarrie and Robinson suggest that it was Heidegger who first turned the refrain into a kind of "slogan for Husserl's phenomenology." Maybe they are right. One can adduce, in confirmation of this suggestion, that Heidegger often singled out the phrase for representative purposes. In the same "Introduction" to *Being and Time*, he contends that his elucidation of the preliminary concept of phenomenology shows "that its essential character does not consist in its *actuality* as a philosophical 'movement.'" Higher than actuality, he argues, "stands *possibility*." And concludes: "We can understand phenomenology solely by seizing it as a *possibility*." The footnote to this enigmatic sentence is very revealing:

> If the following investigation takes any steps forward in disclosing "the things themselves" the author must above all thank E. Husserl, who by providing his own incisive personal guidance and by very generously turning over his unpublished investigations familiarized the author during his student years in Freiburg with the most diverse areas of phenomenological research.
> *Being and Time* 36

For Heidegger, then, phenomenology is neither an actual doctrinal system nor a complete and closed method. It is rather an open program of investigation and research (*Untersuchung, Forschung*) that allows the researcher to disclose, through situated acts of analytical reading and interpretation (*Auslegung*), the matters that are, in each case, relevant to philosophical discussion. This understanding of the "slogan" is confirmed by the detailed description of the methodological ambition of Husserl's phenomenology that Heidegger made in his course *Introduction to phenomenological research*. It is worth quoting in full:

> The *Logical Investigations* are not motivated by the ambition of working out anything like a new textbook in logic. Instead the principal purpose is *to make the objects with which logic is preoccupied into the theme for once in such a way that research related to this is put into a position of being able*

> *actually to work on the subject matters—that the specific objects of this discipline* are brought to *a specific intuition that identifies them*. "Intuition" here means simply: to make present to oneself the object in itself, just as it presents itself. The basic tendency of the *Logical Investigations* is to make this "presentation" one that is methodically secured. Such a tendency could only be genuinely effective through research that *discloses the subject matter*. The "results" of these investigations are so replete that they have born fruit in contemporary philosophy in a way that can no longer be measured today. Even the very ones "stimulated" by the investigations are only slightly conscious of the extent of their effect. The entire course of our examinations starts from the *prospect of getting at the matters themselves*, working its way through a merely verbal knowledge to the things. (37–38)

The interpretation of "matters" [*Sachen*] as entities insofar as they are encountered (English version 213) is a recurrent heuristic motif in his book. How far this "merely verbal knowledge of the things" is from the standard neo-phenomenological craze to seize the empirical things themselves the reader can reckon for herself. It is the difference between reading the word dagger and seeing the actual dagger, the difference between hearing the word dagger pronounced by an actor and seeing the actor seeing the dagger. You decide. But keep in mind that the character behind the actor, and the author behind the character, were probably drawn to the word dagger, not to the thing itself. Shakespeare had, let me recall, a "verbal knowledge" of the "things," and he was very likely, and very happy, to "work his way through a merely verbal knowledge to the things."

5

Sir Toby asks Sir Andrew, "Art thou good at these kickshawses, knight?" (*Twelfth Night* 1.3.96), referring to masques and revels. The term *kickshawses* is a corruption of the French *quelque chose*, here meaning a trifle, that is, a something that has degenerated into a nothing. Like the knight, the phenomenological scholar is much pleased by masques and revels, but finds it incumbent, once and a while, to thrust away his abandon *at these quelques choses* and go *to the things themselves*, wrongly interpreted as material *Dinge*. The test of critical aptitude measures the ability to forego the pleasure of phenomena for the examination of material things, managing, that is, to outgrow the playgoer and become a historical phenomenologist. Here the adjective "historical" is the unconscious alibi that licenses her to undertake the de-transcendentalizing of phenomenological assumptions. What the historical phenomenologist drawn to performance studies or to the materiality of writing has to offer is therefore less a predictably formal ontology than a fallaciously materialist ontology, an outcome that even Levinas would have forcefully repudiated.[13] We are offered, in the exact terms of Jean Howard and Scott Cutler Shershow, "forms of criticism that fetishize the local, the particular, and the unmediated materiality of books, objects, and 'things' at the expense of considering the 'big picture'" ("Marxism Now, Shakespeare Now" 3). We are offered things themselves.

Curran's and Kearney's misreading of the Husserl motto is unwittingly indebted to Merleau-Ponty's systematic attempt to lessen the rigors of Husserl's "early" logicism in order to underscore the importance of a "later" period marked rather by what they deem a "retour au phénomène" (*Phénoménologie* 76, note 1). But it is far from clear that Husserl, despite his increased awareness of notions like configuration or *Gestalt*, ever actually left behind what Merleau-Ponty calls his "philosophie des essences" (76). Still, I insist, Merleau Ponty's persistent misreading of Husserl's phrase—"Revenir aux choses mêmes c'est revenir à ce monde avant la connaissance dont la connaisance *parle* toujours" (9)—did much to propagate the error amongst those—the happy many— already predisposed to be deceived. And yet, Merleau-Ponty was at least alert to the distance between the phenomenon and the empirical-material thing. In Curran's reading of the dagger scene in *Macbeth*, he misrepresents the concept of *intentionality* by stating that Husserl subordinates the mental to the thing. Curran neglects the mediatory status of the *phenomenon*, central to Kant's correlationist position. Merleau Ponty correctly stated that in phenomenology "les phénomènes [...] sont le berceau des choses" (85). Thus, only the "analyse intentionnelle" of an "expérience des phénomènes" construed as the "explicitation ou mise au jour de la vie préscientifique de la conscience" (86) may provide us with the key to intentional signification and transcendental constitution. Merleau-Ponty's problem was precisely his reluctance to accept the sealed-off immanence of this transcendental process, where noemata enjoyed a purely mental existence. In fact, a noema (*cogitationes*) is the intentional object of a noesis (*cogitation*), considered in its purity, "stripped of everything empirical and every reference to actual existence" (Moran, "Introduction" to *Ideas I*, xvi). Husserl insists that "transcendentally purified [*gereinigten*]

---

13 Levinas acknowledges the conceptual dimension of the things to which the phenomenological call directs us, when he speaks of the equivalence between the phenomenological horizon that is privileged over the being whose reality is under examination and the idealist concept (*Totalité* 35).

'experiences' are non-realities, and excluded from every connexion with the 'real world'" ("Introduction" to *Ideas I* 4).

Curran and Kearney are not the only Shakespeare scholars who misread the Husserl motto. Recently, in the essay titled "Theatre and Speculation" and included as an afterword to the collection of essays edited by Matthew Smith and Julia Lupton, *Face-to-Face in Shakespearean Drama* (2019), William West traces a "phenomenological" genealogy of thinkers that, in response to Descartes' solipsistic turn, tried "to restore thinking to the world from its seclusion in introspection." The face-to-face encounter, championed by Levinas, would have thus been anticipated by Hegel, who did much to blast solipsism by "staging a series of encounters in which Spirit recognizes itself in the semblance of another" (252). This seriously misrepresents Hegel's thought, but I will move ahead.[14] For West, the challenge faced by post-Cartesian thinkers was "to overcome the threat of solipsism and to seek community, whether with the world or with other selves in the world" (252). This comes closer to Hegel's original thought, but it is miles away from Husserl's, which makes up the destination of his argument:

> This genealogy might be that of phenomenology itself [...] But Hegelian thinking could seem to be a trick of rediscovering everywhere and forever the self, and other thinkers responded in a series of propositions and negations about coming face to face. In 1901 Edmund Husserl declared "We want to go back to the 'things themselves.'" Husserl's phenomenological minimum for ensuring that the self is not merely interrogating itself but encountering the world turned out to be something like coming face to face. In his later *Cartesian Meditations*, he proposed that at its barest, phenomenology and the evidence on which it is constructed are a refusal of abstraction, and embrace of experience and, literally, "a spiritual coming-to-face with It itself" (*ein Es-selbst-geistig-zu-Gesicht-bekommen*). Heidegger's explorations of Being turn away from the attempted

---

14 There is no other or Other to *Geist*. There are plural others to the multiple consciousness making up the objective We of World Spirit. *Geist* cannot be *personally* confronted. The scene of mutual recognition that Hegel describes in the famous section on Mastery and Servitude describes one stage in Spirit's rise from sensuous immediacy to absolute knowledge, but the agents in the near-allegorical scene are just separate consciousnesses. There is, in short, to face-to-face with Spirit because Spirit has no face. For the facelessness of the Other, see Lukacher: "In turning toward the face of death, of being, of finitude, of poetry, or of conscience, Freud seems to assume that what the poet addresses (in Shakespeare at least) no longer has a human face" (*Daemonic* 22).

immediacy of Husserl's phenomenology, seeing in Husserl's intent facing towards particular beings a blindness to Being. (252)

Husserl's maxim is again misinterpreted: Husserl is not stipulating a "phenomenological minimum" for "ensuring" a turn from solipsism to an "encountering the world" that should be "something like coming face to face." There is nothing "spiritual" or "ethical" in the mental seeing that Husserl is talking about.[15] The things themselves are *not* the world: they are just clearly defined mental concepts. And no *faces*, not even figurative faces, are involved in the turn to *die Sache selbst*, not even that of the phenomenological investigator.

Louis Althusser reminded Levi-Strauss that "ce n'est pas en produisant la possibilité d'un réel existant que tu en donnes l'intelligence, mais un produisant le concept de sa nécessité" ("Sur Lévi-Strauss", *Écrits philosophiques et politiques II* 426). He thus stressed the difference between the empirical thing (*un réel existent*) and the produced concept (*le concept*), and called Levi-Strauss to task for neglecting the transcendental field in favor of the field of transcendence. In a similar spirit, Adorno formulated in *Negative Dialectics* a warning that fitly depicts an all-too-common situation in Shakespeare studies today:

> Delusion is boundless in the field in which the official culture canon deposits its assets, in the supposedly sublime field of philosophy. Its most urgent need today appears to be the need for something solid. This need inspires the ontologies. (93)

The drive to ontology is old, and it can be seen a symptom of a vaster chronic logocentric impetus that accompanies Western culture since Plato. Ontology is of course an inclusive category that allows for a wide range of possibilities, from the transcendental ontologies of Husserl and Heidegger, to the more existentialist ontologies of Heidegger and Sartre, to Heidegger's mystical-textual ontology of Being, to Merleau-Ponty's ontology of the body. What all ontologies tend to share is confidence in the absolute unassailability of origin and presence. Ontology's reliance on transcendence is a much more complex issue. In

---

15 West quotes and translates from section five of the first meditation: "Evidenz ist in einem allerweitesten Sinne eine *Erfahrung* von Seiendem und So-Seiendem, eben ein Es-selbst-geistig-zu-Gesicht-Bekommen." His free version over-interprets the idiomatic German expression, and contrasts with that of Dorion Cairns, much closer to the only spirit that really matters here, the spirit of Husserl's contextualized letter: "Evidence is, in an *extremely broad sense*, an 'experiencing' of something that is, and is thus; it is precisely a mental seeing of something itself" (*Cartesian Meditations* 12).

fact, as Adorno sharply observed, this reliance prompts a contradiction that is the stock-in-trade of this philosophical discipline: "the exigency that ontology cannot do without its opposite, the ontical—the ontological principle's dependence on its counterpart, the inalienable *skandalon* of ontology—becomes an element of ontology" (*Negative Dialectis* 116). Depending on the type of ontology, however, the scandal will be differently felt. Part of the singularity of Husserlian phenomenology was that it managed to remain an ontology while resisting the lure of transcendence—of the ontic, of facticity, of materiality.

Derrida has noted that the repression of the haunting arch-original mediation of *écriture* has always resulted in the *ontologization* of any system likely to exhibit the latter's (literal) traces (*Positions* 100). The stigmatization of *écriture* is a common enough motif in Shakespeare's plays, where written communication easily degenerates into artificial praise or "forged letters" (*Cymbeline* 4.2.315). "To write, and read / Be henceforth treacherous" (*Cymbeline* 4.2.216–17) screams Imogen, but we know that this repudiation hides a deeper reliance on *writtenness* as the inescapable horizon and palimpsestal substratum of all things, including *kickshawses* and things themselves. At bottom, all characters are as anxious as Olivia to have the inside text brought to the open: "What is your text?" "Where lies your text?" (*Twelfth Night* 1.5.224–226). In the "Introduction" to her Penguin edition to *Much Ado About Nothing*, scholar Janette Dillon asked: "Is there a text in this play?" In the next section I take this puzzle to be a perplexity that riddles the entire Shakespeare dramatic corpus.

CHAPTER 14

Reading Shakespeare

Is There a Text in This Play?

1

Reading Plato (Szlezák) and *How to read Plato* (Kraut) are standard titles of books that concomitantly query an exacting conception: why should the first problem confronted by the interpreter of Plato's philosophy be to discover the adequate way of approaching to his *texts*—if that is the right way to name a voice-oriented and dialogue-shaped textuality that makes such a fuss about the incompetence of writing, about the "incompatibilité de l'*écrit* et du *vrai*" (Derrida, *La dissémination* 76), about the need, in order to safeguard truth, of "ne pas écrire mais apprendre par coeur" (Derrida, *La carte postale* 88). In 1964 Leo Strauss called attention to the "logographic necessity" Plato stipulates as a condition for good writing: like a healthy, breathing animal, the good writing must be composed of non-superfluous parts, and it must "talk to some readers and be silent to others" (53). Although Strauss frames this brief meditation on the *Phaedrus* as a methodological introduction to his reading of Plato's *Republic*, the comment takes on a distinctive speculative power. Three years later Jacques Derrida publishes *De la grammatologie*, and the strong thesis on logocentrism therein advanced would receive further textual support in a long 1968 article, "La pharmacie de Platon" first published in *Tel Quel* and later included in *La dissémination*. The fact that this essay examines in depth the same speculative ground covered by Strauss in his reflection on the *Phaedrus* is revealing. Many years later, in a 2012 interview, Derrida will speak of "la nécessité phonocentrique" ("La deconstruction et l'autre" 17) to describe the ineluctability of a regime of cultural subjection to the priority of (spoken, mental) logos over writing. Phonocentric and logocentric are synonymous in Derrida's work: both designate the cultural centrality of logos, broadly understood as the implicit identification of *mens* (semantic intention) and *vox* (voice) at the expense of writing. Derrida undoes the centrality of eidetic intention—that phenomenological monster—over (tropic, subtextual, intertextual, differential) retention and protection. Note the parallelism: logographic necessity, phonocentric necessity.

Within a very short period of time, Leo Strauss and Jacques Derrida feel a similar need to register the dominance of a *necessity*, which they call logographic, logocentric and phonocentric. This kindred testimony is driven by a parallel desire to unpack the metaphysical implications of the polarity orality-writing as it is made explicit in Plato's vexed textuality. The apparent coincidence doesn't stop there. Both Strauss and Derrida seek to discredit this denounced (logographic, logocentric) necessity by proclaiming the pressing rights of a deeper, more genuine, necessity. Strauss calls it *nature*. Derrida speaks of *arche-writing*, an "archi-écriture dont nous voulons ici indiquer la *nécessité*" (*De la grammatologie* 83). He later specifies the transcendental *necessity* of the related *archi-trace* (90). Both nature and *écriture* outline a prior realm of inescapable *anagké* (necessity) which preempts, and ultimately forecloses, the cultural effects produced by attempts at specious cultural foundation—in vocal agreements, politic-dialogic compacts, mental intentions, sensible distributions, or social conventions. These phenomenal aspirations glean their force from the effacement of an a priori necessity—from the fact, in Hegelese, that the immediate indeterminacy of Being has "*always already* [...] 'gone over' into *Nichts*" (Pippin, *Hegel's Realm of Shadows* 187).

An akin desire for reconstructed foundationalism drives a 1940 essay by Heidegger titled "Plato's doctrine of truth," whose closing paragraph reads:

> What is first required is an appreciation of the "positive" in the "privative" essence of *aletheia*. The positive must first be experienced as the fundamental trait of being itself. First of all what must break in upon us is that exigency (*Not*) whereby we are compelled to question not just beings in their being but first of all being itself (that is, the difference). Because this exigency (*Not*) stands before us, the original essence of truth still lies in its hidden origin (*in seinem verborgenen Anfang*).
> *Pathmarks* 182

The exigency or necessity (*Not*) Heidegger refers to is similar to Srauss's and Derrida's deeper necessity in that it aims to revive the "recollection" of what he calls, in reference to *aletheia*, "the original essence of truth as 'unhiddenness' (*Unverborgenheit*)." This original essence Plato decisively altered by introducing the notion of idea as the monitoring precondition in the process of truth-revelation, and by suggesting that *correctness* (*Richtigkeit*) and *agreement* (*Übereinstimmung*) are the criteria that superintend the epistemic attestation of metaphysical truth (Heidegger, *Wegmarken* 218, 230). Thus Plato metaphysically departed—that is, in deviating he initiated the error of metaphysics—from an earlier conception of truth wrought in pre-Socratic philosophy. This is a well-known Heideggerian fable whose hermeneutic accuracy need not concern us here. Suffice it to point out that in heralding the need to abide by an exigency that compels us to reconsider a prior foundation, to refurbish a primitive concept of truth/being based on disclosure and difference, Heidegger is, like Strauss and Derrida, indicting the cultural futility of specious, supervened foundations (historicism, contractualism, noematic intentionalism, metaphysics, representational epistemology, aestheticism).

To sum up, the three thinkers (Heidegger, Strauss, Derrida) similarly urge the pre-eminence of a prior necessity—a kind of "external necessity," to use a Hegel phrase much ab-used by Marx—in the context of an elucidation of the original problem "How to read Plato."[1] This necessity, which for Derrida is structural (or transcendental) despite its origin in factual contingency (the catastrophe of the historical arrival of writing as supplement), also taps the irrelevance of a pseudo necessity—what Heidegger called *die Not der Notlosigkeit* (*Wegmarken* 238). In his interpretation of Rousseau's *Essai sur l'origine des langues*, Derrida had similarly called attention to the "nécessité d'une non-nécessité" (367). Adorno, who never reached that far back (Plato, Rousseau) because he enthroned Kant as the Baron Munchhausen of philosophy, did however pretty much the same thing in an equivalent essay titled "Skoteinos, or How to Read Hegel," written in 1963, only one year before Strauss published his essay on Plato. Needless to say, for the dialectical tradition Adorno so stringently upholds, Plato and Hegel name but two versions of a single speculative conduct. *Speculative* is no doubt a disputed adjective. Discussing Feuerbach's alleged "speculative anthropology," Louis Althusser dismissed it as one of "convenience and ignorance which nonetheless resounds in so many disputes" ("Marx's Relation to Hegel," *Politics and History* 176). And yet, predictably, he never quite discarded it. In his essay, Adorno first argues that Hegel's "linguistic praxis follows a slightly archaic conception of the primacy of the spoken over the written word" (118) and then goes on to state that "Hegel's texts are antitexts" (119). In calling attention to the way such binarism—spoken word-written word—erodes the tendentially idealistic assurances of dialectical thought, in a manner congenial to De Manian deconstruction, Adorno rehearses the same conflict that Strauss, Derrida, and Heidegger had separately outlined.[2]

---

1 For Marx's discussion of external necessity, see the opening section of his *Critique of Hegel's 'Philosophy of Right,'* 5–6.
2 For De Man's reading of Hegel's conception of language, see "Sign and Symbol in Hegel's Aesthetics" in *Aesthetic Ideology*, 91–104.

2

I have made, I apologize, a long story long. What is the moral of this coincidence? Well, to start with, that it may not be a coincidence. And what is the bearing of this no-coincidence on the understanding of Shakespeare's poetic-dramatic work? First, that the problem "How to Read Shakespeare" is unamenable to evasion; that, as Nicholas Royle has pointed out, the *"experience of reading"* Shakespeare's "writing" should always take centre-stage ("Preface" to *How to Read*); that, however tendentially trans-textual (dramaturgical, theatrical), his texts remain texts; that, however dialogic, they are also profoundly anti-doxal and mock-dialogic: recall the Bastard's opening soliloquy in *King John*, where a psychodrama of interiority is underwritten and pre-empted by an actual "dialogue of compliment" between Question and Answer (1.1.180–216), and where the dialogue dramatizes a dialectical script whereby "to avoid deceit, I mean to learn" (215). And this because it is simply untrue "that truth is truth" (1.1.105) in unmediated, concept-less, sensorial, factual, non-verbal ways. So, can Shakespeare be accused of nostalgia for primitive foundations? Not really. In *King John*, for instance, the most primitive of his really historical plays, we never get to see Robin Hood scribbling under an oak-tree the opening articles of *Magna Carta*. But we do see a *natural* Bastard fighting his ambiguous life-path through various (written) wills—his stepbrother's father's will, with no force to dispossess him (*King John* 1.1.132), and his true father's will, with no force to dispossess his false king (*King John* 2.1.192). We are also treated to a great deal of bickering over an (issued, read, misread, finally ignored) warrant fating the legitimate heir to death. Through this subtle overlap of natural right and written-legal legitimacy Shakespeare oversees the inception of a moral necessity that the play never fully actualizes—the Bastard's natural *potentia*, alive in his comic outreach, undergoes a progressive dilution, and the disputed wills and warrants remain throughout an invisible *écriture*. Still, both nature and writing are binding enough to orient the plot in a distinctively anti-political and mock-social direction—a downright satire of diplomatic compromise—which exposes the futility of superfluous necessity, the necessity of the lack of *bad necessity*—in Shakespeare's parlance: *commodity, need, addition*—the irrelevance of yielding to "more than nature needs" (*King Lear* 2.4.261). This way such orientation spells a deeper, primordial, necessity: that of the *bastard course* (Derrida, *Glas* 12).

The problem of *how to read Shakespeare*—an arch-author spooked by the abiding refractoriness of *foul papers* and *bad quartos*—is not unlike that of how to read Plato, Rousseau and Hegel, arguably the most original and volatile thinkers of the Western tradition. The three sought to obviate the transcendental, yet materially inscribed, mediation of writing—what Fineman called "the 'languageness' of language" (*Shakespeare's Perjured Eye* 27)—while pressing conceptual syntheses and concocting ideological wholes to which our Western culture willy-nilly lies still in thrall. Hegel's offhand contention that "a truth cannot lose anything by being written down [*eine Wahrheit kann durch Aufschreiben nicht verlieren*]" (*Phenomenology* 60) betrays the anxiety of this massive, cultural, *refoulement*. The fact that we are still trying to figure out how to read them is proof that they largely managed to get away with it—with the obviation. The same applies to Shakespeare. Only "till [we have] passed necessity" (*Pericles* 2.0.6)—until we have, that is, simultaneously overthrown and preserved necessity—can we begin to make out the stakes involved in the business of understanding his work, which is the same thing as catching on with his experience. This, his experience, in turn resembles Pericles's—that of "a man thronged up with cold" (2.1.71). It is hard to suppress the suspicion that Shakespeare not Wilkins penned that phrase. It has the same formulaic ring we encounter in other renderings of the similar notion of human exposure to a trying existential ordeal: "a man much wrong'd" (*The Comedy of Errors* 5.1.333), "a man so breathed, that certain he would fight" (*Love's Labours Lost* 5.2.640), "a man that Fortune's buffets and rewards / Hath ta'en with equal thanks" (*Hamlet* 3.2.60–61), "a man / More sinned against than sinning" (*King Lear* 3.2.57–58). The experience of cold as a grounding necessity is implied in the words of Thelonius Monk used by Pynchon as an epigraph to *Against the Day*: "It's always night, or we wouldn't need light." The fact that we in fact need light in order to read Shakespeare and that we are prone to mistake as light any form of fake effulgence (the shine of his voice, the fulgor of his bodies, the glare of his compromise, the glints of his intention, the glitter of his sensorium, the very radiance of his immediate particulars) is proof enough of the need to—in Heideggerian dynamics—return (*Rückkher*) to the night of the original necessity, or, if you wish, into the necessity of the original *night* that *is*, and remains, *always*: it's always night, indeed, and only artificial light is likely to penetrate such darkness.[3] Romeo's voluntary seclusion in his "artificial night" (*Romeo and Juliet* 1.1.133) and Juliet's premonitory vision "that all the world will be in love with night" (*Romeo and Juliet* 3.2.24) cannot forestall the natural wisdom, formulated by Polonius, that true things follow "as the night the day" (*Hamlet* 1.3.79), and yet Shakespeare invests a lot, and not only in *Romeo and Juliet*, *Hamlet* and *Macbeth*, in the exoneration of humans draped in "nightly

---

3 A book of interviews with Jacques Derrida published in Spanish uses as title his remark "I don't write without artificial light".

colour" (*Hamlet* 1.2.68). Hamlet returning to the night of his father's apparition, Hamlet stuck in that night, Macbeth murdering sleep, Romeo in his artificial night. These accidents name a necessity. Pericles unriddling himself as the son of his sun-like father and therefore "like a glow-worm in the night" (2.3.42) echoes Hamlet's father's parallel farewell to his son and to the "glow-worm" that "shows the matin to be near" (*Hamlet* 1.5.89). But the son knows better: it's always night. It is always, that is, unphenomenal night.[4]

Refusal to cash in the necessity of such unphenomenal night has no doubt countless benefits. A sensational reward of marvelous possessions showers on the phenomenological critic. But he can see (phenomenally) what he reads—the lion, the moonlight, the casement in the window in the chamber, the cranny in the wall, the dog, the lanthorn, and the bush of thorn—largely because he doesn't read. Otherwise, he would realize that Shakespeare's characters "speak a language that [we] understand not" (*The Winter's Tale* 3.2.78), that even if an effort has to me made to "to understand" someone "in another tongue" (*Hamlet* 5.2.102.20) the task of dispelling misunderstanding cannot be carried out simply by feeling (seeing, listening to) the tongue, holding the hand, touching the mirror. And that whatever it is we manage to understand it cannot be properly translated into visual, acoustic, tactile, or phenomenal terms. If we believe it is cold when the prince says it is cold, or hot when he complains it is hot, then we are either dupes or ultra-refined valets. In either case we are unfit for critical discrimination.

In her essay on *Pericles*, Julia Lupton teaches a precious moral lesson: we need to "acknowledge our dependencies on other people as well as our capture within surroundings beyond our control" (152). *The sea, the sea*—as Iris Murdoch would say. Whether Shakespeare in *Pericles* also aims at teaching that, or any other thing, is another matter. But Lupton is confident he does. Her heuristic exigence is twofold, combining a plain anti-liberal emotion—best conveyed by Dicken's critique in chapter 43 of *Oliver Twist* of the utilitarian ethics of "number one"—and the anti-rationalist position (*res cogitans*

---

4   Ned Lukacher's speculative elaboration on the role of the dark lady, partly inspired by Joel Fineman's arguments, captures this sense: "The dark lady is the name of the instability within the sun; if the friend is stained, it is her fault, for it is her will that manipulates the wills of both the poet and the friend and draws them beyond the sun, beyond the world of phenomenality, and into the language beyond the language of consciousness" (*Daemonic* 120). Lukacher rightly insists on the relevance of "the materiality of language" and "the letter of the law" in *The Merchant of Venice*, and on the "enigmatic materiality that underlies the apophantic power of language" (121), on "the dark night of language […] the enigma of language as such" (122), and on the way the relation of friendship in the Sonnets draws the friends "ineluctably toward the dark mystery of language" (123).

is indissociable from *res extensa*) that Wordsworth impressed upon many Victorians, including Mill and Dickens. The seaside autobiographical evocations in *David Copperfield* show sufficient traces of this moral-emotional education, and these beautiful chapters work as an accompanying text to Lupton's piece. They provide the perfect Romantic-Victorian background for everything that went missing in *Pericles*, everything that slipped through the fishermen's net, and Lupton phenomenally rescues back to light:

> So the fortnight slipped away, varied by nothing but the variation of the tide, which altered Mr. Peggotty's times of going out and coming in, and altered Ham's engagements also. When the latter was unemployed, he sometimes walked with us to show us the boats and ships, and once or twice he took us for a row. I don't know why one slight set of impressions should be more particularly associated with a place than another, though I believe this obtains with most people, in reference especially to the associations of their childhood. I never hear the name, or read the name, of Yarmouth, but I am reminded of a certain Sunday morning on the beach, the bells ringing for church, little Em'ly leaning on my shoulder, Ham lazily dropping stones into the water, and the sun, away at sea, just breaking through the heavy mist, and showing us the ships, like their own shadows. (39)

If this is not sublime, what can be? Steven Marcus describes Dickensian *transcendence* as "a representation of life which fulfills that vision, which men have never yet relinquished, of the ideal possibilities of human relations in community, and which, in the fulfillment, extends our awareness of the limits of our humanity" (*Dickens* 17). I concur with Lupton that Shakespeare's maritime romances *can* be sentimentally, transcendentally redescribed. But maybe they *should* not be so easily allowed to be reformed into the "wonderful aesthetic fables of the Christians" (Lukacher, *Daemonic* 48) that Lupton takes them to be. For what gets lost in the ideal redescription is the playtext's literalness, a contingent instance that subjects all "ideal possibilities" to the obscene law of tyranny and incest, whence Pericles' masochistic overreaction: "O Helicanus, strike me, honoured sir, / Give me a gash, put me to present pain, / Lest this great sea of joys rushing upon me / O'erbear the shores of my mortality" (*Pericles* 21.177–180). The (ideal) joy and the (material) gash are incompatible. Something must give.

Moran has pointed out that Merleau-Ponty's endorsement of Husserl's take on pre-reflective and antepredicative meaning was largely spurred by the former's inability to let go of his happy childhood memories (391). The problem with Lupton's neo-romantic and neo-Victorian lesson is that is proffered in almost complete abstraction of the playtext titled *Pericles*. Lupton is not asking us to *read* the play. She has just singled out some stage directions, quoted brief fragments of the play referring to some objects and things—a net, a garment, a shed, a house—and, more importantly, she has recorded the names of the cities and islands that the characters visit or inhabit. And from this material—stage indications referring to action, lexical references to made-man things, and toponyms endowed with extraordinary cultural implications—she produces an imaginary hologram of autopoietic messianic community that is then devolved to the text, on the assumption that it works as its *representation*. At some points, her interpretation applies much better to parts of *David Copperfield* or to *Four on Our Island* (1892) Margaret Meade's girl Robinsonade than to *Pericles*. Critics of Meade's novel have highlighted a rezoning of Victorian domesticity through the dynamic openness to adventure that is also pertinent to *Pericles*. Further, Jane's courageous questioning in *Tarzan of the Apes*—"What horrible place are we in?' murmured the awestruck girl. But there was no panic in her fright" (121)—could be placed in productive oppositional contrast to Lupton's reading of Thaisa's and Marina's dauntless ability to reconfigure their environment: "Where am I? Where's my lord? What world is this?" (*Pericles* 12.103). This is all fine, I guess, but teaching and reading *Pericles* involves, I believe, a verbal sensibility attuned to other latitudes of experience and signification. Is there a text in this Shakespeare class? The student may ask. Well, if the answer is "not necessarily" or, at best, "purchase copies of *David Copperfield, Four on Our Island* and *Tarzan of the Apes*," then we have a problem. I am not saying that this is Lupton's problem, for she probably makes no such recommendation, but her interpretive moves license this mode of evasion. Having students read, for pedagogic purposes, a text other than the one you are teaching can always draw them closer to the text in question, but one ought to choose properly, for there are intertexts and intertexts. You may even suggest a challenging game of sorts. Rather than asking them to provide a sequel to, say, *Macbeth*, as Ewan Fernie and Simon Palfrey so brilliantly did, you may want to ask them to write a prequel to *Hamlet*, asking them to dramatize in prose what may have happened before the play's action actually commences. Then one of your students stands up and hands you the following story:

> It happened that green and crazy summer when Hamlet was sixteen years old. This was the summer when for a long time he had not been a member. He belonged to no club and was a member of nothing in the world. Hamlet had become an unjoined person who hung around in doorways, and he was afraid. In June the trees were bright dizzy green,

but later the leaves darkened, and the town turned black and shrunken under the glare of the sun. At first Hamlet walked around doing one thing and another. The sidewalks of the castle were gray in the early morning and at night, but the noon sun put a glaze on them, so that the stone burned and glittered like glass. The sidewalks finally became too hot for Hamlet's feet, and also he got himself in trouble. He was in so much secret trouble that he thought it was better to stay at home—and at home there was only Marcellus and Horatio. The three of them sat at the kitchen table, saying the same things over and over, so that by August the words began to rhyme with each other and sound strange. The world seemed to die each afternoon and nothing moved any longer. At last the summer was like a green sick dream, or like a silent crazy jungle under glass. And then, on the last Friday of August, all this was changed: it was so sudden that Hamlet puzzled the whole blank afternoon, and still he did not understand.

"It is so very queer," he said. "The way it all just happened."
"Happened? Happened?" said Horatio.
Marcellus listened and watched them quietly.
"I have never been so puzzled."
"But puzzled about what?"
"The whole thing," Hamlet said.
And Horatio remarked: "I believe the sun has fried your brains."
"Me too," Marcellus whispered.

Hamlet himself almost admitted maybe so. It was four o'clock in the afternoon and the kitchen was square and gray and quiet. Hamlet sat at the table with his eyes half closed, and he thought about a wedding. He saw a silent church, a strange snow slanting down against the colored windows. The bridegroom in this wedding was his uncle, and there was a brightness where her face should be. The bride (his mother) was there in a long white train, and she also was faceless. There was something about this wedding that gave Hamlet a feeling he could not name.

"Look here at me," said Horatio. "You jealous?"
"Jealous?"
"Jealous because your mother going to be married?"

> "No," said Hamlet. "I just never saw any two people like them. When they walked in the house today it was so queer."
> "You jealous," said Horatio. "Go and behold yourself in the mirror. I can see from the color in your eye."
>
> There was a watery kitchen mirror hanging above the sink. Hamlet looked, but his eyes were gray as they always were. This summer he was grown so tall that he was almost a big freak, and his shoulders were narrow, his legs too long. He wore a pair of blue black shorts, a B.V.D. undervest, and he was barefooted. His hair had been cut like a boy's, but it had not been cut for a long time and was now not even parted. The reflection in the glass was warped and crooked, but Hamlet knew well what he looked like; he drew up his left shoulder and turned his head aside.[5]

The gifted student is called Carson McCullers, you suggest she continues the story; she does, introduces some changes, and publishes, two years later, *The Member of the Wedding* (1946). Years later talented students with the names Tom Stoppard, Ian McEwan and Maggie O'Farrell sign up for your course. Your text—*Hamlet*—will always be served by the deepest necessity, such that if you leave your copy of the play at home, you can always resort to the writing of students that are necessarily bound to "the 'writtenness'" of your Shakespeare text (Erne 49–50). You are the happiest teacher alive.

Lupton's interpretation evinces, perhaps unwittingly, the same disinterest in the textual dimension of the text that is now fashionable among practitioners of so-called *surface reading*. The opposition between *symptomatic reading* and *surface reading* rehearses at bottom the contrast, reactivated by Badiou in his lectures on Plato, between the *long circuit* and the *petit circuit* or *circuit court*. He traces this contrast back to Deleuze, and argues:

> Il y a toujours le grand circuit par lequel vous repassez finalement par la profondeur du virtuel, dans l'intelligibilité de l'actualisation. Et puis il y a le petit circuit où vous coupe droit vers les conséquences de l'actualisation, mais sans avoir l'intelligibilité profonde que seul le virtuel détient, en tant que substance véritable de l'actualisation.
>
> PLATON 56[6]

---

5 I have introduced some minor changes (of names, gender, and kinship names) in the opening of McCullers' novel.
6 It is in *L'image-temps* (1985) where Deleuze distinguishes, following Bergson, between a "circuit large" and a "circuit petit" (92–110).

The tendency, among Arendt-inspired phenomenological critics, to reduce actualization to action and thereby to occlude the mediated determinacy of the virtual renders altogether dispensable the travails of symptomatic reading: "il suffit de chercher et trouver la bonne mesure" (56) and this measure "est déjà la," ever awaiting the theatrical actualization of the play in the surface of a text whose oceans remain sadly unsounded. To be sure, in *Pericles* some very important things (humans and chests) are cast by the ocean on the shore, but the scholar cannot merely *receive* these actualizations: she is bound to follow the long verbal circuit through which the experiences of errancy, loss and deliverance are meticulously scripted. Our "first business," Eliot demurred in his essay on *Hamlet*, is "to study a work of art" and he protested against great minds who used the petit circuit in order to achieve *immediate* self-projection:

> These minds often find in Hamlet a vicarious existence for their own artistic realization. Such a mind had Goethe, who made of Hamlet a Werther; and such had Coleridge, who made of Hamlet a Coleridge; and probably neither of these men in writing about Hamlet remembered that his first business was to study a work of art. The kind of criticism that Goethe and Coleridge produced, in writing of *Hamlet*, is the most misleading kind possible. For they both possessed unquestionable critical insight, and both make their critical aberrations the more plausible by the substitution—of their own Hamlet for Shakespeare's—which their creative gift effects. We should be thankful that Walter Pater did not fix his attention on this play.
> ELIOT, *Selected Prose* 45

Discussing the retroactive infiltration of phenomenology in pre-Husserlian work, Merleau-Ponty alludes to Hegel, Kierkegaard, Marx, Nietzsche and Freud, and adds, warily: "Une commentaire philologique des textes ne donnerait rien: nous ne trouvons dans les textes que ce que nous y avons mis " (*Phénoménologie* 8). Starting with Bruce Smith, who accused Derrida of finding in texts what he placed there and exhorted us not to be afraid of Merleau-Ponty, and continuing with a host of faithful partisans, Merleau-Ponty's injunction not to carry out philological commentaries is near-unanimously adhered to in the phenomenology-oriented sub-fields of Shakespeare studies.

In his acceptance speech for the National Book Award in Fiction for *JR*, April 1976, American novelist William Gaddis said:

> I feel like part of the vanishing breed that thinks a writer should be read and not heard, let alone seen. I think this is because there seems so often

today to be a tendency to put the person in the place of his or her work, to turn the creative artist into a performing one, to find what a writer says about writing somehow more valid, or more real, than the writing itself.
>
> *The Rush for Second Place* 122

Indeed, overthrowing bardolatry is easier said than done.

CHAPTER 15

If Caliban Is a Chimpanzee and Other Posthumanist Conditions

1

Philosophical incompetence is widespread in Shakespeare studies today. This is not, however, an uncommon situation in a field where very remarkable research has been produced, from the seventeenth century down to the present moment, quite often without the faintest sign of philosophical or theoretical elaboration. So, what is then the problem? The problem is the growing frequency with which we are offered, in essays on Shakespeare, a combination of philosophical incompetence and the pretence and affectation of philosophical elaboration. This is surely a more recent complication, and it has been particularly aggravated in the post-theoretical age that began in the mid-eighties. In certain sub-disciplines of the field it has become common to drop, in the course of a routinely thematic description of a Shakespeare play, the name of Husserl, or Merleau-Ponty, or Latour, to juggle one or two—quite often, one—"phenomenological" concepts, having read some Latour, only a little Merleau-Ponty, and no Husserl, and to proceed to project the concept on the reading without much sense of hermeneutic relevance and proportion. This is normally done by giving undue salience to often marginalized textual passages in order to accommodate them to the concepts at hand, passages whose actual significance is best ascertained through more standard exercises of exegetic (comparative, intertextual, philological) interpretation. One need not be a professional philosopher to discern unprofessional co-optations of philosophical ideas and philosophers' names in Shakespeare Studies today. This is particularly common in the subfield of research known as Posthumanism. Take, for instance, Karen Raber's recent book *Shakespeare and Posthumanism* (2018), published in the prestigious *Arden Shakespeare and Theory* series. The introductory chapter suffers from the same theoretical discombobulation and methodological *petitio principii* that characterizes all critical work about posthumanism. The angst of self-determination (What is Posthumanism?) stupefies the argument at the very outset, turning whatever comes next into a melancholy record of unfinished take-offs, lost chances, and reiterated dross. In general, writings on posthumanism are theoretically inconsistent because they are unable to determine the object (humanism) they supposedly catch up to, run over, and outpace. Their official reply to the question—posthumanism is an ongoing "deconstruction of humanism" (Herbrechter 3; Raber 21)—is, on the face of it, a self-defeating proposition, for deconstruction is the acme of the rationalist-dialectical tendency running through the humanist-liberal tradition. Much more honest, and truer to the facts, would be to admit that posthumanism is an internal modulation of humanism, and that as such it necessarily accompanied the latter, as an inside position of revision and contestation, from its very inception in Greek philosophy and literature. Calling it posthumanism mistakenly suggests a complete and undialectical overthrowing of humanism. Determining humanism entails, first and foremost, ascertaining the multiple anti-humanist claims that the assertion of—the decision on—*the human* necessarily incorporates. As a theoretical tendency, it will only become authoritative and perhaps coherent when it bothers to carefully scan the entire Wester humanist-liberal-rationalist archive and proceed to retrieve the rich and strange anti-humanist lesson that lies, often dormant, in the very texts that dare to posit the human being as a tenable, worth-fighting-for hypothesis. But this challenge remains unmet.

Glossing Stacy Alaimo's thought, Raber explains that "Human and non-human are open to one another, constitute one another; the human is not therefore an absolute, a pre-existing condition of being" (*Shakespeare* 65). This is the standard ersatz-dialectical trick or schoolbook deconstructive theorem I described in an earlier section under the name of *the disruption of fixed of binarism*. It is ersatz because it underhandedly institutes the fixity of one of the members of the polarity while professing to disable the opposition. Let us read carefully what Raber states: "the human is not therefore an absolute, a pre-existing condition of being." True enough, but *neither* is the non-human. The greater the fluidity you grant to one side of the opposition, the greater are the chances you absolutize it as an indefinite plastic order while rigidly essentializing the *other* side that is inextricably (dialectically) bound up with it: "excess of facticity becomes the vehicle for denying its own facticity. Hypostatized fact (*Faktum*) and hypostatized essence murkily merge" (Adorno, *Against* 105). Whereas the humanist tradition can be accused of having produced a fluidly heterogenous and indeterminate figure of the *transcendental* human at the cost of occasionally sub-producing a rigidified conception of the non-human, posthumanist scholars tend to fluidify the *transcendent* non-human into an absolute order at the expense of congealing the human trope into a relative fixed essence. The former point of course the posthumanist scholar would not concede—she would not acknowledge that the humanist conception of the human is the rhetorical outcome of an imaginative literary-cum-philosophical effort. Posthumanist scholars behave as if the dialectical phase of rationalism had never taken place, as if there was no awareness that abstract notions like "human" or "ability" were inherently informed and deformed by their opposites ("non-human" and "disability"), as if they were the first to knock at the door of reason and to be taken aback when unreason greets them in the hallway. This is something that happened to Plato, Montaigne, and Descartes, to mention only three important names. Envisaged in this way, anti-humanism becomes a necessary dialectical energy inscribed in the humanist project. If its adherents take the time to read Ficino, and Montaigne, and Bruno, and Descartes, and Hobbes, and Milton, and Locke, in some detail, in some depth, with the necessary delay, they will lose arrogance and gain respect. It is very easy to say that car engines are liable to breakdown, but very difficult to invent, and put together, a car engine. When Raber argues that "ontologically, there is no such thing as a 'human being'" we all assent, but when she adds that the process of manufacturing the human "relies on the constant oscillation between whatever 'we' humans are, and whatever we imagine 'animals' to be" (95) we can only protest: 1) because "whatever 'we' humans are" is the problem in the first place, it is already the product of cultural imagination, and therefore never a *fixed* relative *variable* (if you allow the oxymoron) awaiting to be factored in: William Empson once shrewdly pointed that Hamlet *must* be a problem "because he says he is" (*Essays* 80) and it is, let me insist, the resolve *to be a problem* that characterizes the human condition; and 2) "whatever 'we' humans are" is also something we imagine ourselves to be—Heidegger made it clear that the ownmost property of *Dasein* is to misinterpret its own being through "inquiry" ("Introduction," *Being and Time* 7–13)—and everything turns around this imaginative misprision (this is something Greenblatt formulated very aptly in *Renaissance Self-fashioning*). Indeed, posthumanist disinclination to regard conceptual language (terms like "human" or "reason" or "mind") in terms of technical prosthetic expansions of the human body is shocking, as this is indeed a major suggestion in all major deconstructive writing (Derrida's and de Man's work of the 1960s and 1970s). Such disinclination evinces a neglect of natural language, an oblivion of the role it plays in sparking human exceptionality. For posthumanists, *logos*, understood both as language and as reason, can be immediately sponged back into the body, reabsorbed into embodied *haecceitas*, leaklessly naturalized. For the dialectical-idealist tradition, *logos* originates before (alongside) nature and cannot be naturalized. For the dialectical-materialist tradition, *logos* originates with (inside) nature and yet—and *so much depends* on that *yet*—cannot be naturalized. Dialectics, originally an idealist tool, was the poisoned chalice Hegel passed on to Marx. Any materialism worth of that name should bow in gratitude, cherish the gift, and learn to go on living after drinking the poison. Otherwise it runs the risk of misconstruing the grounds of its indisputable potential.[1] Posthumanists show no pride in our human ability to believe ourselves to be human, and in the process of thus turning—through this very imaginative-conceptual belief, however delusional—into an exceptional kind of animal. Nowhere is the exhilarating contingency of this process better formulated than in Althusser's description of the Freudian account of the transition from baby to human child. According to the French thinker, the object of psychoanalysis is not the therapy itself, not the dual situation

> où la première phénoménologie ou morale venue trouve à satisfaire son besoin—mais les 'effets,' prolongés dans l'adulte survivant, de l'extraordinaire aventure qui, de la naissance à la liquidation de l'Œdipe, transforme un petit animal engendré par un homme et une femme, en petit enfant humain.
> *Écrits sur la psychanalyse* 34–35

The object of psychoanalysis is rater the *unconscious*—described by Althusser as one of the "effects" of the becoming-human of this small biological being (*petit être biologique*) issuing from human childbirth. Cocteau's memorable description of Victor Hugo captures the dialectical nature of this mechanism of self-creation, "Victor Hugo était un fou qui se prenait pour Victor Hugo," which we can translate as "a human is a madman who thinks she is a human," or, if you wish, "a human is a mad animal that thinks it is a human." Of course the madness, however boosted by the belief's feedback, is to be there in the first place, and such madness is the rationalist dementia of logos—from Parmenides to Heidegger, Kojève, or Derrida. It was in fact Derrida who brought to our attention the language-induced internal dislocation of some basic metaphysical oppositions, especially the nature-society and nature-culture oppositions in his sustained debate with Lévi-Strauss. When Raber quotes Agamben to the effect that "the state of nature to which civilized human man might 'return' is not a state that he ever left. Rather it is an idea produced

---

1 Being a materialist doesn't imply blaming matter for everything (spirit, polity, culture). Being a materialist is knowing that the explanatory practice of apportioning blame (determination, cause, dependence) is called upon *only* when there is perception of clinamen or disjointedness—"our state to be disjoint and out of frame," "the time is out of joint" (*Hamlet*) or the unlikelihood of the State as a stand-in for civil society in Marx's work—and there is disjointedness alone when material things fail to match their concepts. The existence of concepts is, therefore, a precondition of materialist critique. To protest that concepts are always embodied, a dogmatic and disputable view, does little to mitigate the scandal of their existence.

in and by the civilized order it is deemed to precede" (*Shakespeare* 43) and dates such finding to 2004, the year in which *L'aperto: L'uomo e l'animale* was published, we feel that posthumanists are, once more, reinventing the wheel. The most sustained deconstruction of the cursory parameters undergirding the polarity is to be found in Derrida's *De la grammatologie* (149–202), published in 1967. This doesn't mean Derrida throws the opposition overboard: no other philosopher has insisted so forcefully on the fact that we are inescapably social and cultural, inescapably inside the house of language, irreparably "human." No other contemporary thinker has so radically questioned the authenticity of nature as a pre-cultural datum. Agamben—whose undialectical and micrologic hermeneutics feeds on Benjamin's messianism—fails to cite him at his own risk.

2

As I anticipated in the section on Descartes, posthumanists are out there to repair what they call the Cartesian "error"—the priority of the mind over the body within an oppositional and split conception of the human, the so-called mind-body composite. They oppose to it a phenomenology of porosity, interpenetration, and reconstructed bridges, but they all too often limit themselves to retaining the dreaded opposition (mind-body) and reversing the valence. To assert that the body is prior to the mind involves the same metaphysical violence, the same ontological faith in notions like transcendence, origin, and presence, that radical mentalists employ when they try to impose their alternative version. Furthermore, posthumanists cling to the categories of mind and body with schoolboy tenacity, without realizing that the dialectical modes of criticism which trace their lineage to Plato and Hegel, but also to Descartes, have little faith in the factual existence of something called the mind, let alone the body. In other words, Plato, Descartes, Kant, Hegel, and Derrida were neither radical mentalists nor internalists. *Body*, *mind*, and a host of related categories like *reason*, *judgement*, *imagination*, or *will*, are so many personages in their speculative narratives or dialectical μῦθοι. When Kant, in his theorization of the sublime, loss awareness of this tropological fact, he made himself vulnerable to critique:

> How can faculties, themselves a heuristic hypothesis devoid of any reality—for only people who have read too much eighteen-century psychology and philosophy might end up believing that they have an imagination or a reason, the same way they have blue eyes or a big nose [...]?

> We are clearly not dealing with mental categories but with tropes, and the story Kant tells us is an allegorical tale.
>
> DE MAN, *Aesthetic* 87

So was Descartes' story. Posthumanist scholars also insist on the idea that "prior to Descartes, the status of human vs. animal was vexed" (Raber, *Shakespeare* 91) implying that the human-exceptionalist thesis arose with Descartes, and that the "vexing" was therefore successfully discontinued in the post-Cartesian age. But this is a very inaccurate implication. Talking about the elevation, in Kant's theorization of the sublime, from the natural to the supernatural, de Man argued that

> this transposition [never] allows for the condition of totality that is constitutive of the sublime, and it can therefore not supersede the failure by becoming, as in a dialectic, the knowledge of this failure. The sublime cannot be defined by the failure of the sublime, for this failure deprives it of its identifying principle.
>
> *Aesthetic* 75

Well, unlike the sublime, the human being—who remains however more sublime than beautiful—is itself the *failure* of its *becoming human* (Freud's *Menschwerdung*). The human is not only the mortal illness of nature, as Kojève memorably argued (*Introduction* 555). The human is primarily *the very failure of the human*. It is therefore the dialectical creature par excellence. When Lear suddenly exclaims, "O, I have ta'en / Too little care of this!" (*King Lear* 3.4.33–34), he is beginning to humanize himself through the *recognition* of his failure to raise up to the humanist challenge. He is not just a magistrate acknowledging professional negligence. He is a beast becoming human through the realization of his persistent inhumanity, and this inhumanity is, incidentally, not merely a question of ethical care, but also a matter of the understanding (of the totality of others, of the world at large, of the mandate of the universal) that genuine ethical care presupposes. But posthumanist readers of *King Lear* are, of course, uninterested in this pathetic figure. They are busy enough smelling the wind and searching for the snail.

I insist: Descartes tells us a story of "human" faculties, and so does Kant. There is no need to believe it to become a humanist. In fact, if you disbelieve it, and still remain tolerably open to the humanist delusion, then you become an ironic-liberal humanist, which is what Shakespeare, Montaigne and Derrida probably were. Only posthumanists believe in the literality of the Cartesian and idealist fables. That is why they behave like Platonic realists and Puritan allegorists, planning to destroy a dystopian Gehenna populated with clearly defined symbolic creatures (Reason, Will, Mind) with an army of antagonistic opponents (Sense, Affection, Body). Current consumers of the present-day equivalents of eighteenth-century psychology and philosophy—tracts on cognitivism, musty issues of *Scientific American*, and film versions of Jane Austen's novels—are here to tell us that they have more sensibility than sense, more animality than sensibility, that their bodies shape their minds, that their animal spirits flush their bodies, and they tell us this and other charming things with an intensity of conviction that is utterly disarming. In its current formulations, posthumanism comes through as an explosive blend of arrogance and ignorance, a typical teenager indisposition. Indeed, it shares many symptoms with adolescence: bizarre affectivism, absorbing pet-devotion, techno-craziness, invincible resentment against authority, and a freakish knack at coining code terms and ganging around the neologism in endless debates over its adequacy. I refer the reader back to Ray Brassier's comment about the organized foolishness of speculative-realist debates, quoted in full at the end of section 6. We may actually stretch the target of his aspersion to include some posthumanist debates, without much risk of disfiguration. In fact, as I mentioned above, a conceited meta-methodological digressiveness conducted as an interminable quibble over the dubiously useful term "posthumanism" is posthumanism's most distinctive intellectual gesture. There is ample proof of this in the three introductory chapters to Stefan Herbrecher and Ivan Callus' *Posthumanist Shakespeares* (2012), in Scott Maisano's and Joseph Campana's edited collection *Renaissance Posthumanism* (2016), and in Karen Raber's *Shakespeare and Posthumanism* (2018).

The wheel is also rediscovered when posthumanist scholars remind us, and insist that the reminder is also Shakespeare's, that "in an important sense all meat-eating is potentially an invitation that some other alien thing to take up residence within one" (Raber, *Shakespeare* 119) or that "every human also [resides] within external layers of animality, namely furs and leathers" (120). O the shock! Thank God Shakespeare was there to open our eyes and intimate this important ecomaterialist lesson before bad men like Descartes and Locke—who of course believed chickens were made of flavored energy bars and wool garments were manufactured with polyacrylonitrile fiber—came along and erased all traces of animality from the human, turning the latter into "the inmost centre of the earth" (*Titus Andronicus* 4.3), into "the centre of my sinful earth" (Sonnet 146.1). And imagine the shock for Elizabethan playgoers who, temporarily exiled from their daily ideological misprision—their aseptic, odorless, incorporeal routines of ethereal interaction, pure thought, emotional elevation, and spiritual absorption—entered the Globe to be reminded, at last, "of their animality" (Raber 100). Silly people that had no idea their bodies were like those of the animals they fed and ate, made of the bodies of the animals they swallowed, digested and excreted (they didn't even know they excreted, they had to confront a strange play titled *Coriolanus* to discover they had an anus), and had to attend a performance of *A Midsummer Night's Dream* to discover that their neighbors were also asses, that sex-seeking humans were almost brutes, and that sex-making humans were actually brutes. The resolve to turn a characteristically human-fashioning practice like Renaissance drama into an institutionalized memento of human bestiality is wondrously nonsensical.[2] It reminds me of a child asking his parents when do master chess-players pee during a long game. The question is fine, for a laugh, or the beginning of a Kafka tale, or a Nabokov novel. But something is lost if our analysis of a chess game—the arbitrary geometry, the strategy, the brutal intelligence of the players—is restricted to this particular concern, or to the fact that the board is made of wood and knights represented as horses' heads. Everything human beings do has a material basis (this we've always known), including spiritual and intellectual things (this we've known since Lucretius, Darwin, or Marx), but this doesn't mean that the meaning of these things is completely beholden to the material basis. The fact that a talking human animal is also a hungry, lusty, or sick animal, doesn't reduce the significance of his talk to the determinants of corporal precarity. Omitting these determinants is wrong (this was a common ideological distortion, not exclusively imputable to humanism), but taking alone these determinants into account is even more perverse.

---

2 When I made this same point some years ago, Karen Raber responded in a review published in the *Shakespeare Quarterly*: "Although Heffernan generally approves Andreas Höfele's recent *Stage, Stake and Scaffold: Humans and Animals in Shakespeare's Theater* (2011), he notes that it doesn't take into account, by his lights, the obvious fact that early moderns would have been exposed on a daily basis to 'morbid contingency and corporal decadence' (22) in their intimate proximity to animals. O the irony: an insight into the lived experience of early moderns and their creaturely status, delivered as a corrective to a scholar of the field who has made such observations possible in the first place" (527). Raber's sarcasm would be very effective if she were able to demonstrate, with some textual evidence, that my observation (not the vague "observations" she refers to) is actually somewhere in print, authored by Höfele or by someone working in his footsteps. But she doesn't. Raber, let me insist, fails to prove that Höfele or any other scholar has made that particular observation—that Elizabethan people were so enmeshed in their own animality that they certainly did not need institutionally organized animal abuse or Shakespeare's plays to be reminded of it. And she fails to prove it because Höfele never makes that observation, or any other one anywhere near it. In fact, his book strongly suggests the opposite, that only through proximity to stake, scaffold and stage, can the early modern subject gain awareness of "the human possibility of inhumanity" (*Stage, Stake and Scaffold* 167). I still find this suggestion ridiculously unrealistic, and I still believe my opinion remains what Raber very correctly calls a "corrective".

As perverse, or more, as reducing the (perhaps) universal power of Heidegger's philosophy to the mediocrity of his local Nazism.³ Adorno once proclaimed that "thought is no protector of springs whose freshness might deliver us from thinking [*Denken vollends hütet keine Quellen, deren Frische es von Denken befreite*]" (*Negative Dialectic* 15; *Negative Dialektik* 26). He was very right: similarly, to pretend to use critical thought to deliver us from the need to reengage with the thinking habits of "humanists" like Descartes, Hegel, Heidegger, Adorno, and Derrida is simply absurd. Much more honest would be, in their case, to remain ever silently fresh by the spring, under the greenwood tree, glancing at the fish and the otter, untouched by the greyness of theory.

3

Karen Raber is very able to conceive, against the icy drift of Augustan irony, a "virtuous hose" (Hume, *An Enquiry Concerning Human Understanding* 13). But she is averse to theoretical discussion. Her arguments against opposing views take on a distinctively evasive form. In a review of an earlier book of mine on Shakespeare published in *Shakespeare Quarterly* she argued that my discussion of the relevance of animalist and posthumanist arguments to Shakespeare studies boiled down to the aperçu that Shakespeare didn't like dogs (526–527). This proves little beyond the fact she didn't like my joke, which is probably the only thing she understood in my "Introduction," surely the only thing she read. The other prong of her criticism was that my theoretical argument was vitiated by the fact that I had turned "Shakespeare into a prescient reader of Heidegger, Nietzsche, Wittgenstein, Derrida, and a *host of other Great Men*" (526, emphasis added). Maybe she was right, maybe not, but one thing is certain: somebody in my book (Shakespeare or myself) had bothered to read those *men*. Can she say the same? Who knows? What is indubitable is that her refutation of a *theoretical position* boiled here down to this very remarkable feat of *gender identification*: Heidegger, Nietzsche, Wittgenstein, and Derrida are men. Interestingly, the opening chapter of her recent book traces a genealogy of posthumanism that includes the names of Kant, Hegel, Marx, Freud, Husserl, Heidegger, Foucault, and Derrida. No woman philosopher, not even Arendt, is mentioned, and no horse-philosopher either. The difference, at any rate, is that Raber is at pains to prove that she has read any of these male

---

3   For this perverse operation, see Alain Badiou and Barbara Cassin, *Heidegger: Le nazisme, les femmes, la philosophie*, 56.

philosophers. Considering the scant familiarity she shows of their work, and in view of things like her mind-blowing belief that "smart phones change the *structure* of our thinking and redefine what it is possible for us to think" (71), it is no surprise that, for Raber, the only thing that Kant, Heidegger, Husserl, and Derrida have in common is that they are not women.

On page 10 Raber gives us a textbook fourteen-line synthesis of the history of philosophy from Descartes to Heidegger that I will spare the reader, not without remarking that she places the debate between Husserl and Heidegger "by the nineteenth century:" one of the thrills of post-posthumanist life must be to see the past fade away at a much greater speed, inducing sensations of post-past. Raber characterizes this antediluvian dispute as a "debate between Husserl's view that only the perception of objects and events counts for constituting the real vs. Heidegger's conception of 'being in the world,' or the social connection of the subject" (10). Let me clarify two things: 1) In Husserl the constitution of the real (real things, objects) is secondary to the axiomatic stabilization of a "transcendental ideality" (Kant, *Critique of Pure Reason* 65) he deferred to (pure logical) realm of the eidetic. He was only interested in *the constitution of the ideal*. Husserl didn't lose any sleep over the bearing of the noumenal real on the process of its own objectal constitution. As I have already argued in another section, in *Ideas I* he went as far as denying the methodological relevance of the existence of the real world;[4] and 2) The only Heidegger argument that may be chosen to confront in a versus-like manner Husserl's ontological positions is the former's argument about Being, about the ontological difference (Being versus beings) and about truth as *aletheia*, not his temporal and social construal of the human being (*Dasein*). The analysis of Heidegger's "corrections" of Husserl calls for an entirely different orientation.

The conjunction Shakespeare *and* Posthumanist Theory is not aimed at bringing about a new reading of Shakespeare's poems and plays in the light of a given theory. It rather aims at scavenging his texts in search for fragments that may sustain the impressions and opinions of a number of scholars who are extremely confused about the scope, definition, and goals of what they take to be a sub-discipline in the humanities. They do not know whether posthumanism is the theory of an object (the posthuman), the deconstruction of the theory of an object (the human), a blending of freakish euphoria (technological, positivist, cyborg, neo-materialist) or a pro-animalist sentiment fueled by eco-civic

---

4 "Reality, that of the thing taken singly as also that of the whole world, essentially lacks independence. And in speaking of essence we adopt here our own rigorous use of the term. Reality is not in itself something absolute, binding itself to another only in a secondary way, it is, absolutely speaking, nothing at all ..." (Husserl, *Ideas* 96).

sanctimoniousness. Since by their own admission they make the theory of the object (the posthuman) depend on the deconstruction of an older theory of another object (the human), one would expect in a book titled *Shakespeare and Posthumanist Theory* to find a sizable number of critical allusions to landmarks in the textual construction of humanism. In Raber's book we find plenty of references to the names of Descartes and Kant as the true founders of the rational exceptionalism that subtends humanist hubris, and yet no single text of either author is actually quoted. Raber limits herself to repeating textbook simplifications about the latter thinker that stand, in their squalor, considerably below wikipedic levels. In her two near-identical references to Kant she repeats, without mistaking the subject-object order, that the German philosopher asserted that the "subject required objects" (10, 69). Kudos. In the introductory chapter, she keeps referring to the essential role certain posthumanist critics (Neil Badmington, Cary Wolfe) assign to Derrida and Foucault. But she only quotes twice from one Derrida text, predictably *L'animal que donc je suis*, and never from Foucault. She also mentions Althusser and Lacan without citing their texts. Of course she wouldn't call this scholarly sloppiness or scientific incuriousness, but rather post-theoretical coolness. Neither would Stefan Herbrechter, who, in his Introduction to *Posthumanist Shakespeares*, claims that posthumanism has managed to manufacture a kind of "theory no longer entrenched in ideological dogmatism but a much more relaxed and open-minded theoretical approach" (5). I have serious doubts about their open-mindedness, but nobody questions, I think, their sensational relaxation. Still, I cannot help puzzling over Raber's disinterest in reading these Great Men. For all the weight Raber seems to place on the bearing "anti-humanist" contestation has on the determination of the posthumanist theoretical credentials, she doesn't seem to have spent much time reading post-structuralist thinkers or their current heirs. This relaxed scholarship may cause trouble, and it inevitably trivializes the matters under discussion. Her summary of Meillassoux's criticism of *correlationism* is a case in point. She reduces the latter philosophical position to "the premise that I only know the thing that hit me on the head because I can think in the first place" (*Shakespeare* 15). Following instructions of "relaxed scholarly approach," she mentions the book but identifies no page. The idea of the head being hit by an object she must have taken from Levy Bryant's allusion to her daughter being hit by a toy on the head in *The Democracy of Objects* (154).[5] Subject requires object, but toy requires girl's head, you get the

---

5 Raber quotes from Bryant's book shortly before she mentions Meillassoux (*Shakespeare* 15). As it turns out, Bryant devotes a long didactic section to explain the core ideas of *After*

idea. This is more or less the level of the discussion. Perfect for "unconstant children" (*King John* 3.1.169) and Houyhnhnms.

Raber is not the only posthumanist scholar to show a very unfirm grasp of the relevant theoretical sources. The use of Derrida's texts, for instance, in the edited collection *Renaissance Posthumanism* is also surprisingly meager, considering how often the name is dropped in Campana's and Maisano's "Introduction," along with those of Descartes, Heidegger, and Agamben. There are, on the whole, four direct quotations, from *The Animal That Therefore I Am* (12), *Archive Fever* (176), *The Beast and the Sovereign* (306), and *Of Grammatology* (176). The rest is either silence or Derrida according to others (Cary Wolfe, Donna Haraway, Matthew Calarco). Considering that, in the long humanist tradition, Derrida qualifies first and foremost as *the reader* (no pun intended), the informed commentator of—and privileged witness to—the human-exceptionalist opinions of others (Plato, Descartes, Hegel, Husserl, Heidegger), to reference Derrida through others involves a progressive distancing from the alleged ground of vexation and source of trouble—the *homo sum* narrative.[6] This way posthumanism, gradually turned post-post-post-posthumanism, joyfully recedes towards a glamorous future of illiterate relaxation.

4

The problem with posthumanism lies not only in its phenomenal re-humanization of the non-human but also in its very inane de-humanization of the human. If there is a human register—posthumanists would speak of the sedimented logos of a humanist archive, and I am ok with that—then the problem of posthumanists is that they willingly fail to raise to the exceptionality of that standard. Or not willingly: ignorance—of Giotto, Dostoyevsky, Alban Berg ...—would explain a lot. But it is hard to believe, for many scholars working in the posthumanist paradigm (Yates, Campana) are particularly sophisticated readers. When, in the "Introduction" to a collection of essays published under the title *The Return to Theory in Early Modern English Studies*, Paul Cefalu and Bryan Reynolds extol "an inclusive, non-anthropocentric conception of life that subverts [...] the Aristotelian supposition that man

---

Finitude. It is from these pages (*The Democracy of Objects* 54–57) that Raber may have taken her account of *correlationism*.

6   The essays edited by Stefan Herbrecher and Ivan Callus under the title *Posthumanist Shakespeares* show, in general, a much firmer grasp of some theoretical sources, particularly of Derrida.

is unique in being both rational and linguistically capable" (2) they seem to mean what they say. They do not appear to realize that alone this supposed uniqueness permits the ironic undoing of logocentric rationality that is the true mark of our exceptional and distinctive status vis-à-vis the rest of animate or inanimate things.[7] I am not merely advancing the standard sophistic claim that their statement (their being able to perform, through rational-verbal means, their argument) belies their premise (that humans are unique in being both rational and linguistically capable). What I suggest is that human uniqueness consists in *deciding* to be unique, in ethically and politically acting upon that decision, and in being sublimely undone in the dialectical process of its unlikely demonstration. The human is the only animal that can *pretend*, not only to be a human, as we have already seen, but also to be an animal—without ever actually ceasing to be an animal. Think of Edgar in *King Lear*. Heidegger said the rational animal—the human—is the animal that is capable of confrontation, of face-to-face presentation: "A mere animal, such as a dog, never confronts anything, it can never confront anything *to its face*; to do so the animal would have to perceive *itself*. It cannot say 'I,' it cannot talk at all" (*What is Called Thinking* 61). The human is the only animal that wants to be something different from an animal, can decide to be a human animal, can pretend to be an animal, and knows to be a thing—"for man is a giddy thing, and this is my conclusion" (*Much Ado About Nothing* 5.4.105–106). These are rare feats of ironic meta-rationality, earned at the cliff-edge of ontological difference (*this* thing is *a* man), unlikely to be reached by apes or stones. They are also "instances of the tragic disjunction between what has been and what could or should have been" (Lukacher, *Daemonic* 23). Terry Pinkard has lucidly condensed the dialectical-rationalist lesson that "only in self-conscious life is the species aware of itself as the species it is. The self-conscious subject has a knowledge from the inside of what it is to live a life of this genus, specifically, the self-conscious life of a rational animal" ("Introduction" to *Phenomenology of Spirit*, 22). Without the leap to self-consciousness we would remain in the morass of sense-certainty, happily touching, smelling, feeling, unaware of the speculative contradictions that beset our unexamined generalizations, including those about pre-human forms of life. We would be stuck in day one of *2001 Space Odyssey*, gazing at flying bones. In a passing aside, Fredric Jameson pungently specifies: "since 'consciousness,' when it is human and worth talking about" (*Valences* 120). And Derrida's rerun of an old Hegel theme, timely

---

7 For the notion of being more and less than human, rising above and sinking below the human level, see Ricoeur, *Finitude et culpabilité*.

revitalized by Kojève, reads: "la maladie de l'animal est le devenir de l'esprit" (*Glas* 125). Even Terry Eagleton is ready to concede such human exceptionality.[8] There are no Orlandos, no Edgars, no Timons, in non-human nature. Those among the posthumanists who boast of their animal condition, who claim to leave open the gates for the risky encounter with the non-human, are no meta-rational ironists at that. They rather practice a "courtesan-like painted affectation" (Sidney, *Apology for Poetry* 113), acting rather like Malvolios or arty moralists. I doubt that any early modern literary scholar working in the Anglo-American academia and holding her place in the demographic tank of the "bourgeois éco-responsables" (Houellebecq, *Sérotonine* 48) will ever forget her first-world passport when travelling around unsheltered areas of the world, or leave behind the substantial written testimonial (ids, passports, visas, vaccine cards) accrediting her exceptional human status—*hominibus, dico, non belluis* (Descartes, *Regulae* 332)—as subject to multiple-civil-rights entitlement and citizen of a liberal democracy, radically distinguishing her from everything—things, animals and very often from the less privileged humans inhabiting the shopworn political ecologies she gloriously glides through on her way to the next World Shakespeare Congress.

5

I opened this section with the observation that many theory-precarious "phenomenological" readings of Shakespeare's plays and poems, including posthumanist readings, give undue salience to often marginalized textual passages with a view to accommodating them to the concepts the scholar has bargained in the post-theory fly-market, passages whose actual significance is best ascertained through more standard exercises of exegetic (comparative, intertextual, philological) interpretation. Let me give two of examples of this particular kind of hermeneutic fiasco.

The first is Scott Maisano's "reading" of *The Comedy of Errors* and *The Tempest* in his essay "Rise of the Poet of the Apes," published in *Shakespeare Studies* in 2013. Building on a blatant misreading of Dromio of Syracuse's reply—"I am an ape" (*The Comedy of Errors* 2.2.198)—and searching methodological support in mixed assortment of theories—Lacan's idea of the mirror's stage, the putative

---

[8] In *Why Marx was Right*, Eagleton endorses Marx's defense of a (largely unchanging) human nature in terms I would readily subscribe to: "Change, in other words, is not the opposite of human nature; it is possible because of the creative, open-ended, unfinished beings we are. This, as far as we can tell, is not true of stoats" (81).

existence of a "Reversed Darwinism" of the Renaissance, odds and ends of cognitivist and anthropological chatter, some decontextualized observations of late-Derrida's ironic animalist-reverie, all conveniently spiced with a dash of Baboon metaphysics—Scott Maisano reaches the astonishing conclusion that the Ape-Poet Shakespeare calls the human-animal "differences and distinctions" into question, and that he proceeds to such questioning by lavishing on some of his apparently human characters, like Dromio of Syracuse, the ability to frame "a first-person subjective report of how it feels to be a nonhuman primate, how it feels 'something like' personhood, subjectivity, and language only to have others deny that you have any thoughts or feelings at all" (69). This is not all. His interpretation of *The Tempest* in this same essay is based upon the outrageous assumption that the 1873 critical identification of Caliban as—take a deep breath—a chimpanzee is correct. There is actually a sentence that opens, conditionally, "If Caliban is a chimpanzee," drags along a bit in a flub of nonsense, to conclude, portentously, "then, Caliban, I want to suggest, is Shakespeare" (71). So Caliban and Shakespeare are chimpanzees. This is not exactly news to us: we have already seen Julia Lupton compare the challenge of thinking with Shakespeare to the habits of living with cats and children. But Maisano presses his claim one inch farther. The spectacular absurdity of his conjecture would be fine in a Kafka story or a Deleuze meditation, but the problem is that Maisano is neither being ironic nor speculative: he is being smart and posthumanist. Is this really something he would tell his students in a class? Or is it the kind of esoteric wisdom reserved for fellow cognoscenti? Hey, Joe, listen, I discovered yesterday that Falstaff is a lazy bear.

I would like to invoke Nietzsche's diatribe against doctor Rée, who, having read Darwin, managed to produce the hypothesis that "the Darwinian beast and the ultra-modern and restrained weakling, who no longer bites [*nicht mehr beisst*], shake hands" (*Zur Genealogie* 13). But I guess the humor—the meta-rational irony—is inexorably lost on dog-fearing and owl-abiding posthumanists who are anxious to convey the intelligence that *Shakespeare in Bits* bites. The fact that this article was published in *Shakespeare Studies* shows the extent to which the infiltration of neo-Victorian sentimentalism, with its sub-branch of deistic Anglican naturalism, in the mainstream orthodoxy of the discipline seems an irreversible fact. A childish fascination with Disney's Quasimodo, Dr Moreau, Mougly and Elephant Man—we are all there, variously allured by those charms—is perfectly compatible, I believe, with the realization that Shakespeare's world only makes sense on the recognition of the human-exceptional difference. Let me state it clearly: Shakespeare doesn't call, in *The Comedy of Errors* and *The Tempest*, the animal-difference into question. He may do it (he does it) in other plays, like *King Lear* or *Coriolanus*, but to an effect that deviates markedly from Maisano's glittering inference. In *The Tempest*, Caliban is always a *man*. In *The Comedy of Errors*, Dromio of Syracuse claims to be a stupid man, not a monkey. Maisano discards the customary meanings of "ape" in the sentence "I am an ape"—ape as counterfeit and ape as dupe or fool—to conclude, in a rapid and broadly unwarranted move, that Dromio claims to be a "Barbary ape," the tailless monkey of proverbs (67–68). But this involves, in Maisano's recitation, no stigma at all. And therefore no meta-rational irony either. This is all very serious: "Dromio offers a first-person subjective report of how it feels to be a nonhuman primate, how it feels to possess 'something like' personhood, subjectivity, and language only to have others deny that you have any thoughts or feelings at all" (69). Wow.

The suggestion is daring enough to demand some philological support and contextual collation. But none is offered. If the reader bothers to examine the twenty occurrences of "ape" in the Shakespeare corpus she will be unsurprised to discover that none is complimentary to the beast that wants discourse of reason, and that most are in fact deeply unflattering.[9] The ape is a "little" (*Richard III* 3.1.130) and "busy" beast (*A Midsummer Night's Dream* 2.1.181) that plays with apples in its mouth (*Hamlet* 4.2.17), a stupid animal, inferior to a man as a man is inferior to a doctor (*Much Ado About Nothing* 5.1.193). However, like the parrot, it is characterized by an imitative disposition—it is a "mad-headed" animal (*1 Henry IV* 2.4.70)—that often goes in search of novelty (*As You Like It* 4.1.130), by imitating flying birds and eventually falling to death (*Hamlet* 3.4.177). More often still, this (unconscious) imitative disposition encourages the ape to ostentatiously present itself as what it is not, boastfully pretend to be what it is not, like a roguish pretentious imbecile (*2 Henry IV* 2.4.191), a cowardly beast (*The Merry Wives of Windsor* 3.1.72), a foolish creature that *imitates* its "keeper" or "master" (*Love's Labour's Lost* 4.2.117) and learns by imitation the magician's tricks (*Romeo and Juliet* 2.1.16). In *2 Henry IV*, Prince Harry mentions that Falstaff may have "transformed" the boy he gave him into an "ape," meaning someone ridiculously dressed in imitation of his masters and betters. At this point, the meaning of the word "ape" has been near-totally displaced to the figurative sense of "mimic." In *Cymbeline*, "ape of death" (2.2.31) is image, imitation, or mimic of death. In *Love's Labour's Lost*, Boyet, the Lord attending to the French Princess, is described by Biron as "the ape of form" (5.2.325), meaning a mimic of fashion. In *Measure for Measure*, the "glassy essence" of the human soul is compared by Isabella to an "angry ape" (2.2.123), a figure of

---

9 In *The Winter's Tale* and in *Cymbeline* the occurrences of the term "ape" coincide with its usage in *The Comedy of Errors*. In the three cases *ape* means fraudulent counterfeit.

grotesque mimicry. And in *The Winter's Tale*, the sculptor is an "ape" or imitator of Hermione (5.2.90).

With this comparative context in mind, the word "ape" in Dromio of Syracuse's statement, "I am an ape" can only mean what Stephen Greenblatt, in the Norton edition of the play, makes it mean: "An imitation (of myself); a fool" (738). Yet the sense "an imitation of my master; a fool" cannot be effaced in a comedy where status difference matters, foreshadowing Stoppard's rehearsing of the trope in *Travesties*: "but if the servant classes are going to ape the fashions of society, the end can only be ruin and decay" (30–31). Recall that when Luciana corrects Dromio, stating he is an ass, implying a duller beast, he concedes "'Tis so, I am an ass" (2.2.198–201). Antipholus admits to using him "for my fool" (2.2.27), implying jester, and speaks later of his "foolery" (4.3.31). The resulting dialectical spectrum of semantic valences ranging from the witless beast to the discerning fool, covering stark animal stolidity, stupid animal mimicry, foolish humanity, sharp humanity, fool-and-animal imitating humanity, is of course the cultural spectrum where Erasmus, Montaigne, Cervantes, and Shakespeare pasted their unforgettable ironic figures of feigned madness, artificial wildness, and intelligent imbecility. It is important to stress that while the imitative capacity of the beast is regarded—*pace* Aristotle—as a constant source of derision, the imitative ability of the human is, by contrast, in this carnivalesque tradition, regarded as a sign of ironic meta-rational perspicacity. This may be prejudiced, but most Western traditions were. What Maisano cannot do is simply misread the sentence through the lights of an alternative tradition, through the pious cant of a non-human-exceptionalist tradition—a sympathetic, pious, eco-ethical, *tierfreundlich*, broadly phenomenological, human-nonhuman reciprocal understanding—that is nowhere to be found in Shakespeare's plays. It takes some contrastive reading to awaken the posthumanist scholar from his dream. Surprisingly, Maisano and Campana ask naïve posthumanist critics "to read a bit more closely" ("Introduction" 5) the wrongly stigmatized documents of Renaissance humanism. Yes, but only a bit—lest you spoil your brilliant realization that Caliban is a chimpanzee, or that "Dromio offers a first-person subjective report of how it feels to be a nonhuman primate." Detractors of Richard Rorty have been chasing their own tail: the most eloquent refutation of *Philosophy and the Mirror of Nature* is lodged in Maisano's memorable sentence, concealed in an apparently modest paper on Renaissance drama. Who said research is unexciting?

The second example of posthumanist misreading I want to consider is Karen Raber's interpretation of *King Lear* in the second chapter, titled "Posthuman Cosmography" of her book *Shakespeare and Posthumanist Theory*. Her declared aim is "to offer a posthumanist reading of *King Lear* that arises from the proposition that it is 'about' a set of hyperobjects—land, weather, and the conflict between or within the two as it is expressed through one of the period's more disruptive experiences, the earthquake" (37). I will not lose time considering the theoretical sources that equip her with her posthumanist terminology. Suffice it to say that discussing the good old "natural elements" in *King Lear* in terms of "hyperobjects" will not make your reading necessarily more "disruptive." In fact, Raber's constant reliance on Bradley's 1904 commentary of *King Lear* (38–42) deliciously betokens a romantic-humanist sentimentalism of the sublime (from Burke to Coleridge, from Rousseau to Kleist) that is at odds, anyway, with Raber's call elsewhere in the same book to "dampen utopian idealism." But this is not my chief concern. What intrigues me is the apparent specificity Raber and her supporting posthumanist scholar, Laurie Shannon, attach to the comportment and significance of natural phenomena, like storms and seismic movements, in *King Lear*. The rain in the play, for instance, "is queer. It confuses, violates distinctions, rejects binarisms" (41). But—I rub my eyes in astonishment—rain and storms in tragedies are *always* queer.[10] Take the storm scenes in Aeschylus' The Persians. Or what the Chorus has to say in Sophocles' *Oedipus at Colonus* (1220–1248)

> Not to be born, by all acclaim,
> Were best; but once that gate be passed,
> To hasten thither whence he came
> Is man's next prize—and fast, Oh fast!
> For, once he has unloosed his hand
> From Youth and Youth's light vanities,
> What blow can from his path be banned?
> What griefs will not be surely his?
> Strife, envy, falseness, blood and hate,
> Till, last, the curse of curses, lone,
> Despised, weak, friendless, desolate,
> Old age hath claimed his own.
>
> We are old and know suffering; but dread
> Is the doom of this stranger at the door.
> Like a wave-lashed and winter-beaten shore,
> By the tempests of the North overrun,

---

10   Apropos of the *inscapes* and falling snow recorded in Hopkins' journals, Derrida states that "to be is to be queer," and Royle concludes that "deconstruction queers being and time" (*In Memory* 126–27).

> The cold storms beat upon his head:
> There is storm from the sinking of the sun,
> And storm from his first going forth,
> Storm from the noon-tide's light,
> Storm from the mountains of the night,
> And the wild winds of the north.

Rain and storm in Western tragedy are highly conventional codified tropes. So is the seismic imagery of earthquakes. Any interpretive claim we may want to advance about the significance of these tropes within a single play must take into consideration this wider generic, subtextual and intertextual horizon. One basic point: Seneca's tragedies, particularly *Medea* and *Agamemnon*, are drenched in storm imagery. In addition, drawing on Virgilian imagery from the *Aeneid*, Seneca wrote about earthquakes in the sixth book of his *Natural Questions*, and the trope plays an important role in *Hyppolitus*, where we hear Nurse read ask: "And yet, / Suppose that by our craft and guile we hide / This crime from him: what of thy mother's sire, / Who floods the earth with his illuming rays? / And what of him who makes the earth to quake, / The bolts of Aetna flashing in his hand, / The father of the gods?" (1.152–157). The rhetoric of the Messenger's speech later—"The grove begins to tremble, earth to quake, / And all the palace totters with the shock, / And seems to hesitate in conscious doubt / Where it shall throw its ponderous masses down" (1.695–698)—informs the tradition of the Lucanian sublime that reached Marlowe, who passed it on to Shakespeare. Let me quote some lines from Marlowe's translation of the First Book of the *Pharsalia*:

> The Fates are envious, high seats quickly perish,
> Under great burdens falls are ever grievous;
> Rome was so great it could not bear itself.
> So when this world's compounded union breaks,
> Time ends and to old Chaos all things turn,
> Confused stars shall meet, celestial fire
> Fleet on the floods, the earth shoulder the sea,
> Affording it no shore, and Phoebe's wain
> Chase Phoebus, and enraged affect his place,
> And strive to shine by day, and full of strife
> Dissolve the engines of the broken world. (70–80)[11]

---

11   I use Stephen Orgel's edition of Marlowe's *The Complete Poems and Translations*. For an excellent study of the Lucanian sublime, see Patrick Cheney, *Marlowe's Republican Authorship: Lucan, Liberty, and the Sublime*.

There is a very clear relation between these passages from Seneca and Lucan and the cataclysmic imagery of natural disorder in *King Lear*. The quote from *Oedipus*, moreover, bears on Shakespeare's play's overall significance in more than one way. For a trained philologist, it takes less than ten minutes to consider these sources and identify the relevant passages. There is nothing wrong with the postulation that *King Lear* is "about" disruptive weather and earthquakes. Nothing wrong either with the redescription of common phenomena (land, weather) with a specialized language—"a set of hyperobjects." This is just pedantic and pretentious, and only misguided if the scholar implies that a hidden significance is thereby, through the application of the terminology, being disclosed. What is particularly wrong is to pretend that *King Lear* is singularly inflected by this atmospheric-sublime, thematic or tropological bias. To argue in this manner is to ignore the tradition of the Western tragedy. In *King Lear* and *The Tempest* Shakespeare limits himself to radicalizing a possibility of nature-psyche figural transference centered around natural disorder that is a stock-in-trade device in the received literary tradition of the tragedy inside which he decided to fashion his authorial persona. Any scholar who seeks to examine the role the device plays in *King Lear* must do it by assessing the originality of Shakespeare's use of the device, and this can only be done contrastively—comparatively, dialectically—against a subtextual background characterized, like all inscriptive materiality, by sheer anteriority. The queer tragic rain started to pour long before Shakespeare sat down to write *King Lear*.

6

I would like to close this section with a brief consideration of the role that the attention to objects and animals plays in the phenomenological tradition. Predictably, posthumanists find it hard to discover philosophical support in Husserlian phenomenology and need to move to Merleau-Ponty for help with animals, and to historical phenomenology for insight on the human-things relation. In Karen Raber's book, for instance, we read about "new phenomenologies" (16), like "queer phenomenology" (16) and "historical phenomenology" (67), but also Ian Bogost's "alien phenomenology" (162), whose areas of research comprise "meteorology, shipwreck, the lithic environment, geohumoralism, foods and eating practices, physical prostheses, farmyard relations" (162). This reminds me of a character in a novel by Cuban writer Alejo Carpentier, described by the narrator as a woman who "had acquired her intellectual formation in the Great Surrealist bargain basement [*se había formado intelectualmente en el gran baratillo surrealista*]" (*Los pasos perdidos* 34).

Fine for a satirical remark or for expansive elaboration in a Raymond Roussel or George Perec novel, this kind of steampunk eclecticism hardly works as a "phenomenological" method, especially if the bricoleur intends to use it to read Shakespeare. The overlap of methodological approaches—like object-oriented studies, historical phenomenology, actor-network theory, assemblage theory, Merleau-Ponty's phenomenology of the body, ecocriticism, speculative realism, animal studies—animated by sometimes incompatible assumptions and aimed at often incompatible heuristic ends, is a standard practice among experienced scholars like Bruce Smith, Jonathan Gil Harris, and Julia Lupton. Needless to say, this obtuse ecumenism is also a stock feature of the posthumanist critical paradigm.

The role the animal plays in the phenomenological tradition is very limited. To be sure, Husserl conceded in *Ideas I* §152 that the "experiencing subject itself is constituted in experience as something real, as *man* or *beast*, just as the *intersubjective communities* are constituted as animal communities" (320), thus making a dialectical observation that is also implied in the way Hobbes retains the supposedly sublated state of nature within the higher-order political community. But this concession doesn't take us very far. In section 53 of the same book, titled "Animalia and Psychological Consciousness," Husserl clearly claims that "the consciousness that is naturally apperceived" has inexorably leaped beyond the level of mere appearing that characterizes "Corporeal Being." Apperceptive consciousness is simultaneously (dialectically) both a "very part of Nature" and much more than Nature: "a state of consciousness appears which is the state of a self-identical *real* ego-subject" (105). This second mode of appearance is closed to "*animal realities*" (104). Predictably, Merleau-Ponty's phenomenology of the flesh is more compromising. As Dillard-Wright has studied in a relevant monograph, he proposed in *Le visible et l'invisible* a thesis of "interanimality," a concept that included humans. This thesis, however, violates the transcendental limits of Husserlian phenomenology, which is anything if not human-exceptionalist. The case of Levinas is worth considering more carefully, for his concern with radical Otherness is often misconstrued as a blank cheque for posthumanists consecrated to the animal other.

Levinas modulates the difference between the human and the non-human in a very Heideggerian manner. He relates repressive violence to animality. Moreover, the human superiority over the animal is codified in cognitive terms (*savoir*) before it obtains a moral qualification—the disinterest of the good:

> Mais être homme, c'est savoir qu'il en est ainsi. La liberté consiste à savoir que la liberté est en péril. Mais savoir ou avoir conscience, c'est avoir du temps pour éviter et prévenir l'instant de l'inhumanité. C'est

> cet ajournement perpétuel de l'heure de la trahison—infime différence entre l'homme et le non-homme—qui suppose le désintéressement de la bonté, le désir de l'absolument Autre ou la noblesse, la dimension de la métaphysique.
> *Totalité* 24

The humanity of the human is predicated upon its ethical freedom, and freedom is here—in a Platonic and Spinozian manner—beholden to knowledge. The conditions Levinas stipulates for an authentic rapport with the Other to take place are extremely demanding, and it is unrealistic to assume that ecocritical thinking in general is likely to step out of the representative-proprietorial access to external reality that characterizes most of the relations established by the *Même* (27). The other face of Levinas' suffocatingly petit-bourgeois domestic conception of the feminine is this heroic-aristocratic exigence of nobility. On both counts, of course, he fails to pass the moralist posthumanist test. But the actual reason why he cannot be co-opted by posthumanist scholars is the standard of rational knowledge (*conscience, savoir*) he conspicuously sets for the ethical relation to unfold. The standard face-à-face, cheek-to-cheek picture of the scholar with her dog or cat in her arms (an image not seldom found in institutional websites) perfectly emblematizes both the principle of possessiveness organizing the relation and the drive to representation that prompts the whole affair in the first place. Possessiveness and representation: nothing could be further from the ethical relation. Levinas' onslaught on rationality and mediation in the section titled "Le discours instaure la signification" of *Totalité et infini* is interrupted by intriguing observation, this time on the inability that Hegelians show to explain how a rational animal is possible:

> The Hegelians may attribute to human animality the consciousness of tyranny the individual feels before impersonal law, but they have yet to make understandable how a rational animal (*un animal raisonnable*) is possible, how the particularity of oneself can be affected by the simple universality of an idea, how an egoism can abdicate?
> *Totality* 208; *Totalité* 229

This question, which Levinas believes unanswerable, is the only real question of a philosophy—from Plato to Badiou—that dares to speak its name. The fact that most of Shakespeare's self-centered characters have minds so uncouth or "fine no idea could violate" them, as Eliot opined of James (*Selected Essays* 151), does not necessarily leave them unaffected by impersonal, universal *ideas*. This of course sends us back to Descartes, whose mind was "violated" by the idea of infinity. And therefore to the difference, not so much between animals and humans generally, for Descartes explicitly "attributed all sort of perceptual, sensory and emotional state to animals" (Cottingham, *Cartesian Reflections* 28), not even the transcendental difference (later exacerbated by Hegel and Husserl) between the conscious and the non-conscious domain, but rather the difference between "thinking (rational, language-using) human beings and non-human animals." Let me quote at length from Cottingham's excellent book on Descartes:

> In many passages both here in the *Discourse* and elsewhere, Descartes approaches things from the outside, and asks how various kinds of observable phenomena (in humans and in animals) can be explained. Thinking, in one sense, is a publicly manifested phenomenon, something revealed in the astonishing and infinitely varied outputs of the human language user; and it is not some modernist behaviorist or linguistic theorist, but Descartes, the supposed "privacy" theorist, who underlines the point. It is of course true that, since he was unable to envisage any plausible physical mechanism that could account for thought, and its linguistic manifestation, Descartes ended up attributing the relevant capacities to an immaterial "rational soul." Many modern readers may regard such a move with distaste; but one moral of the chapter under discussion is that they should not allow such distaste to divert them from recognizing Descartes's remarkable philosophical and scientific insights into the unique (and objectively accessible) character of our human capacities for thought, reason, and language. (21)

If we happen to grant Shakespeare some insight into this unique character of our human capacities for thought, reason, and language, then we might rest satisfied with the age-old arrogation of a humanist Shakespeare. But of course if you read Shakespeare in search of animal affections and mineral emotions you might also get somewhere. Some travelers have in fact returned from the bourns of that undiscovered country. I believe I saw Deckard pass by in the street, under the queer rain, accompanied by a Nubian goat and a loquacious chimpanzee.

CHAPTER 16

The Aesthetic Ideology

1

In the remainder of this book I plan to discuss three hermeneutic fallacies—the *fallacy of representation*, the *fallacy of immediacy* and the *presentist fallacy*. They are all, in part, related misconstructions imputable to Husserl's own version of phenomenology, passed on to conscious or unsuspecting followers. The three are tightly interrelated and can be held to derive from what Paul de Man called *the aesthetic ideology*. To be sure, an important implication of my argument is that this ideology (the ideology of the aesthetic) is largely a phenomenological elaboration of an originally idealist-romantic motif. The three fallacies are omnipresent in current work on Shakespeare. Before I turn to examine each one in some detail, I will devote this brief section to the expression of the aesthetic ideology in Shakespeare studies today. But first I will try to elucidate, using Husserl's texts and the work of some commentators (Moran, Smith, Zahavi) the philosophical arguments that have helped articulate this ideology and encourage the related hermeneutic fallacies. Most of these argument were first laid out in Husserl's *Logical Investigations*, and received further development in *Ideas I* and *Ideas II*.

The whole theoretical apparatus of Husserl's phenomenology turns around six groundwork notions (*intuition, evidence, presentation, intentionality, fulfillment, givenness*) whose immanent relatedness renders it very difficult to provide autonomous definitions of each. The risk of circularity is constant. One could actually start anywhere.

1.1 *Intuition*

Let us begin with the notion of *intuition* (*Anschauung*). Already integral to Kant's epistemology, the notion was transformed by Husserl beyond recognition.[1] In the Glossary to his study *Husserl*, David W. Smith describes it as

---

[1] For Kant, intuition was originally "the capacity [...] to have singular and immediate representations of particular objects by means of the senses," a capacity different from the human ability to "form abstract and general representations, or concepts, by means of the intellect" (Guyer and Wood, "Introduction" to Kant, *Critique of Pure Reason*, 36). "Intellectual intuition," Kant points out often in his first *Critique*, is not something that we, *finite* beings, can afford. Husserl received the notion filtered through Dilthey, Bergson, and William James. Bergson's

"direct, self-evident experience" and distinguishes between "empirical intuition," as "sensory perception of things and events in space and time," and "eidetic intuition," which is the "comprehension of essences (especially as achieved by eidetic variation)" (466).[2] Husserl held that the same kind of clear intuition we have in the act of *seeing* that "2 + 2 = 4" we also have when we *see* a blackbird outside our window. As Moran explains, in both cases "I have an intuition which is fulfilled by certainty," in one case that of a mathematical truth and in the other that of "the bodily presence of the blackbird presenting itself to me" (10). From these succinct descriptions we realize that the concept of intuition is not primary or foundational enough, as it is predicated on the prior notion of certainty or "evidence." But let us proceed anyway. In *Ideas I*, the notion of intuition takes on a more transcendental significance and becomes "essential seeing." In phenomenology, Husserl avers, "the principle of all principles" is that *"every primordial dator* [or presentive] *Intuition* [*originär gebende Anschauung*] *is a source of authority for knowledge, that whatever presents itself in 'intuition'* (as it were in its bodily reality [*leibhaften Wirlkichkeit*]), *is simply to be accepted as it gives itself out to be, though only within the limits in which it then presents itself"* (*Ideas I* §24 43). Note the recurrence of verbal forms indicating *presentation* (*gebende, darbietet*): intuition is a seeing or comprehending that presents something to the mind. The principle is laden with relevant implications for Shakespearean hermeneutics: the immediacy of intuitive grasping, the unquestionability of what is given or present, its bodily reality, and its immanent limitation to what is presented/given.

1.2 Evidence

If intuition is self-evident experience, what is self-evidence? And what is evidence? David Smith describes evidence (*Evidenz*), often translated as self-evidence, as "intuitive or evidential support for judgements or knowledge claims, providing intuitive fulfillment." The notional circularity is rendered elliptical by the insertion of a further notion, that of fulfillment (*Erfüllung*). A constellation of notions (*Evidenz, Anschauung, Erfüllung*) emerges, all gravitating around the first. In *Ideas I*, Husserl implies that self-evidence is a "process of insight [*Einsehen*]" that should be brought *"into essential relations* with ordinary seeing [*gewöhnlichen Sehen*]." Anyone who has brought "some case of

---

  particular inflection of the notion as a mode of intellectual sympathy elicited accusations of irrational mysticism that also reached Husserl (Moran 9–11).
2 In *Logical Investigations* we read: "One ought not to confuse the assertoric inner evidence for the existence of a single experience, with the apodeictic inner evidence for the holding of a general law" (63).

self-evidence into view as a really given object of vision [*zu wirklich schauender Gegebenheit*]" (§21, 40), Husserl argues, will know what evidence is. Evidence is therefore self-confirming: it cannot be taught, you must first experience it, and you only know of it *a posteriori*. Just like an orgasm. And what you experience and know is that it is indeed the case: both the case itself of evidence and the evidence of something given (call it presence). Husserl is at pains to dissociate evidence from the lived experience of a feeling (Zahavi, *Husserl's Phenomenology* 32): evidence transpires as a confirmatory sensation of visual clarity and distinctness, most often related to the validity of judgements.[3] The Cartesian precedent is manifest. More radically stated, "inner evidence is nothing but the 'experience' of truth" (*Logical Investigations* 121). Because it is a necessary condition of the validity of judgements, knowledge and truth, there is a risk in describing evidence primarily as subordinate to these complex epistemological questions—the risk of overlooking the radical undecidability (the undemonstrability) upon which the entire cognitive process rests. No appeal to the intersubjective validation of a feeling can be scientific enough. This is the path followed by Zahavi, where the determination of evidence is contingent on the prior determination of intuition, intention, and fulfillment:

> For Husserl evidence in the strict sense of the term designates the ideal of a perfect synthesis of fulfillment where a signitive existence-positing intention (typically a claim) is adequately fulfilled by a corresponding perception, thus providing us with the very self-givenness of the object.
> HUSSERL's *phenomenology* 32

This is nonetheless an excellent summary. Evidence comes forth here as a synthesis of fulfillment. To grasp the implication of this definition we must obviate the ungrounded ground upon which the whole edifice rests. Recall the absurdity of Smith's definition: "Evidence is [...] evidential support for knowledge claims ...." The trees are so various (intuition, evidence, intention, sign, fulfillment) that there is a risk of missing the forest.

---

3 Early Husserl argued: "Judgement, however, is only recognized as true when it is inwardly evident. The term 'inner evidence' stands, it is said, for a peculiar mental character, well-known to everyone through his inner experience, a peculiar feeling which guarantees the truth of the judgement to which it attaches" (*Logical Investigations* 115). But Husserl insists later that inner evidence cannot be reduced to psychological factors, that "it depends also on ideal conditions" (119).

1.3   Intentionality

According to Husserl, all *cogitata* (sensations, perceptions, thoughts, judgements, valuations, wishes) are intentional experiences of things in that they imply orientation, directedness, and even consciousness, however vague or pre-flective, of things. The basic character of intentionality is the "property" of being a "consciousness of something [*Bewusstsein von etwas*]" (*Ideas I* §36 68). "In every wakeful *cogito*," he explains later, "a 'glancing' ray from the pure Ego is directed upon the 'object' of the correlate of consciousness for the time being, the thing, the fact, and so forth, and enjoys the typically varied consciousness *of* it" (*Ideas I* §84, 171). In an ontological sense, there are objects, which may be real, like a blackbird, or ideal, like a mathematical formula. The existence of the latter does not depend on psychological factors. Apart from the ontological fact of the existence of objectivity, there is, in the human mind, a capacity to act meaningfully or intentionally towards these objects. The variety of potential actions is large: there are sensations, evaluations, judgements, recollections, thoughts, and many others. Intentionality is a form of directedness that characterizes these mental acts, which Husserl describes as sense-giving or meaning-intending. These acts are however different from the meanings intended in them and from the objects of these meanings. We have, then, three elements in an intentional act: the act, the meaning, the object. Husserl's greatest concern was to safeguard the autonomy of both the meaning and the object with respect to the act that could intentionally grasp it. This way, since cognitive acts make up a large portion of our intentional experience (consciousness), his assertion of the autonomy of the object was his bulwark against accusations of idealism. But there are, of course, objects and objects, that is to say, real objects and more or less unreal objects—"*absent* objects, *impossible* objects, *nonexisting* objects, *future* objects or *ideal* objects" (Zahavi, *Husserl's Phenomenology* 14). This variability doesn't affect intentionality much. As Dan Zahavi argues, "my intention does not cease being intentional if it turns out that its object doesn't exist" (15). Ideal objects are, for instance, laws of logic or mathematical formulae. Husserl believed that in both cases they remained transcendent objects, even when they had no real existence. The problem with ideal objects becomes soon apparent: what is their consistency, if they are neither natural nor naturalized (psychological) entities? Husserl resorts here to a mode of Platonic self-sufficiency: well, they are *ideal*. But then, if we look at the assortment of objects that normally fall under the category of ideal objects we notice something surprising. Take, for instance, Zahavi's choice of objects in a passing comment about the status of ideal objects: "When one speaks of a law of logic or refers to logical truths, principles, sentences, and proofs" (*Husserl's Legacy* 9). The "object" that stands out in this list is "sentences," as this is manifestly a linguistic object whose verbal facticity no amount of terminological disguise (*Satz*, proposition, assertion) can do away with. One may delude oneself in the belief that logical truths, principles, and proofs exist without verbal assistance (Husserl's logic idealism is one such delusion, in my opinion), but it is hard to see how a sentence is not a real object. I will come back to this problem later. Suffice it to say that the position of language in the phenomenological "system"—to indulge Smith's persuasion that phenomenology is systematic—is at best *very* problematic. Aware of the problem, Husserl turned soon to language in his *Logical Investigations*. Some think he actually started there, upon the bank and shoal of language. But let us proceed step by step.

An intentional object is the object of an intention. In the case of the perception of an object—looking at something—that something, the object of my intentional act of seeing, is a real object, and not a representation. This way, as I anticipated in the section on Descartes, who prefigures this critique, Husserl flouts the *representative theory of perception*. The directedness of intentionality is literally "direct, that is, unmediated by any mental representations. So, rather than saying that we experience *representations*, one could say that our experiences are *presentational*, and that they *present* the world as having certain features" (Zahavi, *Husserl's Phenomenology* 19). Zahavi's excellent gloss is deliberately thick with emphasized allusions to *presence* and its cognates—to *present, presentation, representation*. If one wishes to characterize phenomenology as a metaphysics of presence, the section on intentionality (fifth Investigation) in *Logical Investigations* is a good place to start: Husserl argues that a presentation (*Vorstellung*, sometimes translated as *representation*) refers to a certain object in a certain manner, and this presenting, this putting forward, "is not due to its acting on some external, independent object, 'directing' itself to it in some literal sense, or doing something to it or with it [...] It is due to nothing that stays outside of the presentation, but to its own peculiarity alone" (qtd. in Zahavi, 21). Where does the spontaneity of the intentional presentation of unreal objects come from? Is spontaneity not, according to Kant, a defining feature of conceptual work? Can we have *intelligible intuitions*?

The miracle of intentionality is to warrant the unmediated or immediate presentation. Husserl may have been right in discarding the mediation of small-scale, delegate, representations, but his trust on *directedness* prevented him from considering the interference (mediation) of other potential surrogates of real things—like words, tropes, and concepts. But not completely. As Moran explains, Husserl was careful to distinguish between the presentation (*Vorstellung*) of an object in acts of visual perception from the representation (*Repräsentation*) "of the object in acts of fantasy or symbolization" (*Phenomenology*, 97). This critical discrimination forces us to reconsider the three elements making up an intentional act: 1) the *immanent content* of the act (the psychological process, which determines its *quality*: perception, desire, knowledge, assertion); 2) the *intentional content* (the meaning of the experience, which determines its *matter*); and 3) the *intentional object* (what is intended, what the agent is conscious of: if I look at a tree, the object is the real tree).[4] Let us consider the second. The fact that an intentional act has an intentional content that can also be called a meaning or sense (*Bedeutung*) implies that *meaning something* is a special kind of intentional act, as it is somehow presupposed in all others. In some more than others, though, as it is difficult to see how I can possibly *mean* when I *look at* a tree. And because meaning is a central component of linguistic signification, Husserl is forced to make room, in his *Logical Investigations*, for considerations about language: "Phenomenological analysis aims, in the first place, at clarifying and purifying our intuitions of the meanings of words and concepts. Only thus can we proceed to the analytic exploration of the connections between 'meaning-intentions and meaning fulfillments'" (*Logical Investigations* 168).

This centrality of meaning to the phenomenological project is underscored by Moran, who argues that "phenomenology is concerned with concrete acts of meaning, meaning-intendings, not as empirically occurring facts in the world or in terms of the ideal meanings they articulate, but in so far as they have essential, intentional, a priori structures" (93). But, of course, the transcendental structure of meaning-intendings presumes the existence of, on the one hand, empirical objects and facts in the world working as objects of intention and, on the other hand, of ideal meanings that are the content of the intention. At any rate, for Husserl's distinctions to obtain, *intentional meaning* is ideal or is nothing. Zahavi, who tends to dismiss Derrida's critique of Husserl, explains that the German thinker conceives of "the concrete act of meaning (the subjective process of intending something) as a relation between an ideality and a concrete instantiation thereof," with "ideal meaning" as the "*essence* of the concrete intention" (*Husserl's Phenomenology* 25).

1.4 *Meaning-Filling*

In the intentional act of knowing, the presentation of an intention can be direct or indirect. It is direct when the object is given "in the flesh, with full 'bodily presence' (*leibhaftig*)" (Moran, *Phenomenology* 117) or when it is

---

4   I here follow closely Zahavi's exposition: *Husserl's Phenomenology*, 22–23. Note, incidentally, that the meaning or sense (*Bedeutung*) is not the reference (*Beziehung*). In *Logical Investigations* Husserl has not yet adopted the Fregean distinction between *Bedeutung* and *Sinn*.

presented to us immediately or authentically in intuition: for instance, the lower numbers. It is indirect, if the object is presented through the inauthentic mediation of symbols: the case of the higher numbers. Because a symbol is the "empty presentation," the intention that deploys it is an "empty intending" (*Leermeinen*) which needs to be filled. Knowing, for Husserl, is an intentional act that presupposes the distinction "between the empty presentation and the various forms of 'filling' (*Erfüllung*) it can undergo" (Moran, *Phenomenology* 97). The problem, inherited from Brentano, of the ideal mental content—the intentional content—in the case of *empty* or *objectless presentations* forces us to reconsider the status of linguistic signs: could the ideal intentional content be reduced to the very symbol that encodes the empty presentation? Husserl would obviously reject such suggestion, which demands a contingent (material, external) contamination of the necessary (ideal, internal). The intimate correlation, in Husserl's logics-stirred unconscious, between meaning, sense, content and essence (*Logical Investigations* §37, 82) prompts a water-sealed immanence against the accidental alterities of language. Intentional acts are intuitions of experience where essences are viewed. And the viewing of essences (*Wesenserschauung*) is the viewing of *meanings*. Meanings are therefore "essential concepts and their governing formulae of essences" that are made themselves "known in intuition" (*Logical Investigations* 166). Husserl distinguishes, in the fifth logical investigation, between "the object which is intended" and "the object as it is intended." The distinction recalls Frege's between *Bedeutung* and *Sinn*, but Husserl prefers to speak of a distinction between semantic essences and *ideal meanings* (*Logical Investigations* V §17–21, 578–590). The need to purify further the rarefied entities of logical ideality (from object to content, from content to meaning, from meaning to essence), a process which will induce him to coin the term *noema*, leads Husserl to propose a return to things themselves in the sense we have examined in a previous section. In Moran's terms:

> By going back to the things themselves, Husserl means we cannot be satisfied with employing concepts whose evidential basis has not been properly clarified by being brought back to their original sources of intuition. The "things themselves," then, are the immediately intuited essential elements of consciousness, viewed not as psychological processes, but in terms of their essential natures as meaning-intentions (*Bedeutengsintentionen*) and their interconnected meaning-fulfillments (*Bedeutungserfüllungen*), essential structures involved in all understanding. (108)

But what is a meaning-fulfillment? How does the fulfillment of an intended meaning occur? Well, a meaning-intention is a sense-giving act. Consider, say, the intentional act of seeing a bridge. It is hard to see how seeing can be an intentional act, but this is the privileged example for Husserl and his interpreters. "When I see a bridge," explains Moran, "I have a fulfilled intuition of the bridge" (119). The assumption is that the meaning or sense of the bridge was "intended" in the act of seeing it, an act which can be alternatively understood in terms of a passive synthesis. But here's the rub of phenomenological epistemology—the tenacity with which it clings to the transcendental, ideal, antecedence of essential meanings even in acts of perception. This is, let me add in passing, what Kevin Curran misinterprets in his reading of the dagger scene in *Macbeth*, discussed in a previous section. And such misinterpretation rehearses the "naturalistic fallacy" that "besets reflection about world-directedness as such, whether knowledgeable or not" (McDowell, *Mind* xiv). Moran explains that Husserl modelled his "phenomenological account of truth in terms of adequation or fulfilment," that is, as an "account of the relation between perception and its fulfilment" (119). This—and this Moran doesn't say—obviously instils a prejudicial bias (knowledge as perception) which can only be aggravated by the prior contamination of perception by language (perception as linguistic meaning). In conclusions, meaning-intending acts (perception, knowledge) achieve their fulfilment or accomplishment (*Leistung*) when they win "an intuition of objectivity." A paradigmatic case of a fulfilled intentional act would be seeing a bridge, because the meaning intended is fulfilled by "the bodily presence of the object thought about" (Moran 119). This is, Moran continues, "an act of 'adequate self-presentation' (*adäquate Selbstdarstellung*) which is the paradigm of all genuine knowledge" (119). The adequacy of this self-presentation depends on the evidence of the objective presence that is presented with the strongest "sense of presence and immediacy" (119). Note the continuity between the following terms: *presentation, meaning, fulfilment, intuition, immediacy, presence*. When I remember or daydream about the bridge, the sense of presence and immediacy is less intense, but the content remains the same: I merely see it "in my mind's eye," I see it "in an intuition which presents itself" in ways different to perception. When I use the word "bridge" to refer intentionally (meaningfully) to a bridge that is not perceptively present, the ideal presentation of the meaning (the intentional content) is supposedly in my mind and therefore the form of intending is fulfilled. My own presence of mind, we assume, stretching the idiom, fulfils the meaning-intending of my act of expression, communication, assertion. But verbal expressions can be empty forms of intending: for instance, "when I talk about a bridge without really thinking about it" (Moran 119). For Husserl,

Moran argues, "signitive or empty intending is a basic feature of human intentionality through which we grasp things not 'autentically' (*eigentlich*) as in the paradigmatic case of perception" (120). Yet it is language that helps us to use categorial intuitions allowing us to see (essentially) not only objects, but also facts and states of affairs. So language inserts inauthenticity in intentionality, preventing us to cognize things in one blow, in acts of immediate givenness, but at the same time it provides the categorial structure that enables categorial intuition to take place. The latter claim Husserl obviously doesn't acknowledge, just as Kant didn't recognize that the entire set of concepts and schemata of the understanding was probably a mere sublimation of verbal categories. Zahavi tries to settle this issue by reminding us that there are *degrees of fulfilment*, but his view of the *signitive intention* is—like Husserl's—beguiled by conceptual idealism: the intuitive givenness of an object in perception fulfils the thought of that object in whatever intentional act (search, recollection, nostalgia) draws me towards it. He quotes Bernhard Rang to explain that in a relation of fulfilment "two intentions directed at the same object coincide in such a fashion that a purely signitive, conceptual intention fulfils 'itself' in another intuitive intention which is directed at the same object" (*Husserl's Phenomenology* 31). In both cases, the content (sense, meaning, noema) is the same: the intuition in one intentional act (perception) confirms the intuition in another intentional act (recollection, search, nostalgia) which ultimately rests on an act of judgement (thought). The difference between both objects is one of "modes of givenness"—in one case (thought) the conception of the object is empty, in the other (perception) it is filled. The intentional essence is the same in both cases (the meaning, content, or noema of the object), but only the perception of the object adds its "intuitive fullness (*Fülle*)" (Zahavi 31). This way of presenting what Smith calls the "narrative" of Husserl's "system" is however very tricky. Manifestly, the orientation is here empiricist, and perception is given pride of place: this approach is dominant in Merleau-Ponty. Smith's approach privileges rather the epistemic moment of the narrative and makes the whole system hinge upon the intentional act of the judgement that underpins the problems of knowledge and truth. A third approach would choose language as the original problem, the expression of an utterance as the primary intentional act containing the structural logic that makes intentionality work in the first place. This third approach is genetically the one that Husserl took: the *Logical Investigations* is, first and foremost, a study of language, and more specifically an attempt to explain why (the hell) language *is not* logic.

Imagine I say "The rose is red." This is a sentence. It is an utterance in an act of presumably communicative expression. The act is intentional: I want to express or communicate that the rose is red. But I do not communicate redness or express the rose: I utter a sentence. According to Husserl's philosophy of language, drafted in the first of his *Logical Investigations* (181–234), we may distinguish here between: 1) the intentional act of the expression, with a sentence as form of expression; 2) the intentional act of consciousness that underlies the expression—the form of whose act is a thought, of the kind "I think < The rose is red >"; 3) the meaning or sense of my sentence, the form of whose sense is a proposition < The rose is red >; and 4) the object, a state of affairs, which is articulated through the predicative structure of an individual (a rose) plus a property (redness). Note that the propositional meaning of the sentence and the thought are the same, or, more correctly expressed: the intentional act of expression and the intentional act of thought that supposedly underlies it share the proposition as their ideal meaning. Since Husserl believed that language expressed thought, this apparent coincidence spells a relation of subordination: the meaning of the sentence—that is, the proposition—derives from the judgement (thought) that is presupposed in the expression. Thus, any speech act (I wish the rose were red) involves an assertion (the rose is red), and every assertion (the rose is red) presupposes a judgement (< the rose is red >). The superiority of knowledge over speech is echoed in the superiority of ideal senses, meanings or noemata over words or symbols. The utterance of sentences leaves the contingent configurations of words, marshalled in intentional acts, open to more or less adequate fulfilment. But the fulfilment (*Erfüllung, Fülle*) of speech acts (sentences) remains a particularly vexed question in Husserl's alleged system, regardless of the narrative path we choose to account for it. What is the fulfillment of the sentence "The red is rose"? To be sure, the speaker's and listener's simultaneous perception of a red rose would give a sense of satisfactory completion to the speech act. But in the absence of a similar presentive perceptive intuition, what else could fulfil the intentional act of expressing or communicating that "the rose is red"? In the context of Husserl's transcendental idealism, the mere act of intending the expression and having the form of the expression (the sentence) *coincide* with the content of the expression (the ideal meaning or proposition) would be enough: we would have a self-confirming mechanism whereby the ideal *presentation* (*Vorstellung*) of the noema is fulfilled in the verbal presentation. If the listener understands the ideal meaning, and draws the proposition from the sentence, then we would add a further fulfilment in the form of intersubjective ratification. That the sense of a sentence can be fulfilled in the absence of the object to which the sentence refers my appear odd, but this is implied in Husserl's constant argument that the noema not only "embodies the way the object is intended in the act" (David Smith, *Husserl* 257), but that, as the content of my experience, it may even "*prescribe*—present or represent—the object of my perception" (200). When I see a rose the noema "rose" is prescribing—presenting to me in inner intuition—the ideal features of the object rose I have before me. The possibility of an internal noema presentation without the actual perception of the intentional object may explain the hallucinatory experience of the floating dagger in *Macbeth* (I personally don't think so, but this kind of unfulfilled or manqué perception would be the way to construct a *phenomenological* account of the incident). The presentation (*Vorstellung*) is first internal, eidetic: my mind transcendentally sets (*stellen*) forth (*vor*) or puts (*stellen*) forward (*vor*) the ideal content (the noema rose) that is later confirmed as a transcendent object through the act of perceptive intuition. This confirmation is *Erfüllung*. Such epistemic schema is supposedly built into the simple intentional acts that may branch out of the simple proposition "I see a rose," but as soon as noetic modes begin to inflect the content of this original intentional act, and the minute language contributes to these successive inflections through the modal possibilities of speech acts, then the nature of the fulfilment becomes more and more elusive. What is the fulfilment of a verbalized promise? The sincerity of the promise or the effective keeping of the promise? If I say, truthfully, sincerely, "I promise I will come tomorrow," but fail to come due to external reasons, the speech act of the promise is still felicitous, because I *meant* my promise. If I utter the same promise without the intention of keeping it, but end up coming the next day for reasons out my control, then the intention of the speech act remains unfulfilled, however successfully I happen to keep the promise.

2

The role language plays in phenomenology is extremely problematic, as Derrida has tirelessly denounced. Phenomenological scholars tend to obviate this problem and pull ahead as if Husserl's system basically worked. Still, the only way to make it work in an unproblematic manner is to obviate what makes it problematic, to overlook, that is, the interference of language. And language interferes in the epistemic-ontological transactions of transcendental idealism because speech acts cannot be fulfilled insofar as they are, more often than not, equivocal, empty, or merely echoic (quotations of other speech acts). Take these statements from *Hamlet*: "Methinks I see my father" (1.2.183), or "I see a cherub that sees them" (4.3.50), or "There's a special providence in the fall of a sparrow" (5.2.157). What can a phenomenological critic do with them? Let me consider the third statement. As any intentional act, the assertion that "There's is a special providence in the fall of a sparrow" contains three elements:

1) The *immanent content*, that is, the psychological process involved in the act of asserting. This would obviously involve some attention to the processual dimension of individual linguistic usage, which we could tentatively identify with parole. The transcendental parameters of the system of langue organizing the sentence produced in the assertion would be neglected in this approach.
2) The *intentional content*, that is, the meaning of the assertion. This would move us away from linguistic considerations toward the ideal sense (*Inhalt*), the semantic essence, the noematic content of the speech act.
3) The *intentional object*, that is, the external referent that the assertion intends. This transcendent approach excludes considerations of language.

How do we *fulfill* the intended meaning of Hamlet's sentence? Can "There's a special providence in the fall of a sparrow" enjoy the confirmation and corroboration of fulfilment? What is the *presentation* (ideal meaning, proposition) of the locution (sentence) that articulates the speech act? And how is this internal presentation fulfilled? Through the embodied intuition of perception? Or is it merely validated by the internal intuition? There is no clear answer to these questions: they merely suggest that Husserlian phenomenology is a philosophical attitude that fools the critical mind into believing in the immediate *presentation* of meaning, enjoining it to perform the immediate *fulfilment* of linguistic utterances that remain, alas, utterly unfulfilled. Confronted to sentences in a Shakespeare playtext, the phenomenology-oriented scholar tends to *realize* the *givenness* of its *presentation* by recognizing the fulfilment of the putative contents of the intentional act of expressing or asserting them. In the event that the scene of fulfillment is not properly encountered, the critic can always stage it herself. Shakespeare, they say, wanted to tell us something—and he succeeded because we understand it. This is the starting point and inaugural delusion. Through presentation, his sentences advance propositions or ideal meanings whose fulfilment it is the task of the scholar to identify or recognize. But since, as I argue, the fulfilment doesn't easily occur, the critic is bound to perform what is missing in the script. The critical performance of fulfilment may take three basic forms, which I will exemplify with the *Hamlet* quote. Each form corresponds to one of the components of the expressive-communicative sequence, phenomenologically understood:

Intentional CONTENT → Intentional PROCESS → Intentional OBJECT

1. *The Intentional content (the fallacy of representation)*. The scholar may focus on the intentional content, the ideational meaning of the assertion. The fall of the sparrow is mentally seen through the eye of the mind, or through the dator presentative givenness of the presentation (*Vorstellung*) implied in

the opening of the sentence: "There's a special providence": there before (*vor*) is set (*stellen*) a pro (*vor*) vidence (*videre, see*). The German term *Vorstellung* captures the shade of meanings involved: image, presentation, idea, illusion. A more philosophical sense of the term would describe it as a mental image or idea produced by prior perception of an object, as in memory or imagination, rather than by actual perception. This obviously suits the phenomenological requirement of intentional anteriority that goes into the meaning of noema, deferring fulfilment to an ulterior scene of perception. So a phenomenological take on Hamlet's assertion would merely establish that the sheer presentation of the intentional content—the ideational image of the falling sparrow—suffices as a mode of fulfilment. The imagined idea seen through the eye of the mind is simultaneously presentation and fulfilment. The assertion precariously mediates an unlikely transit between intentional meaning-*presentation* and fulfilled *representation*.[5] The transit is unlikely because— immediate, spontaneous—it barely takes place (the place of deferral). The assertion, in short, is unnecessary. The phenomenological scholar can dispose with statements, assertions, sentences, she can give up language altogether, relinquish the playtext, and flow immediately between cognition and perception, between presentation and representation—presuming the idea (mental presentation) and resuming the show (stage representation). There is no need, in this case, to assume the role of language. This is the *aesthetic fallacy of representation*, very common in the work of Paul Kottman and Julia Lupton, but also in that of Richard Wilson, a scholar always intrigued by "the tension that drives so many Shakespeare plays, between the symbolic *representation* of some impersonal abstract ideal and the embodied *presence* of a concrete personal reality" (*Free Will* 35; emphases in the original). It is thrilling to see Hegel's aesthetics and Husserl's phenomenology match so gracefully as late as 2013, nine years after Derrida left us. In an ideally representative conception of that collection of assertions and statements called *Hamlet* there would probably be a fallen sparrow on stage. I am sure phenomenological scholars *see*

---

5 For Brentano's take on "presentation," and its influence in Husserl, see Moran 46–47. Moran paraphrases Brentano to the effect that "no judgement can occur without some presentation; for example, my decision to go on a journey requires the presentation of the journey" (46). Or my decision to become a king requires the presentation of myself as king (Macbeth). The meaning, Husserl insists, should not be confused with the object itself. This is particularly important when we deal with an ideal object. Meanings are present in intentional acts, including, of course, acts of expression or assertion like: "All hail, Macbeth, thou shalt be king hereafter!" (*Macbeth* 1.3.48).

the noema *passer*, while other readers, me included, keep repeating the word "Ophelia."

2. *The intentional process (the fallacy of immediacy)*. By decoding the linguistic process in dynamic terms the scholar stresses the creative—or literally, creationist—dimension of Shakespeare's speech acts—acts that are constitutive in their ability to produce (present) the possibility (ideal meaning or content) they index. The formal actions of language, construed as *expressive parole*, posit creatively an ideal meaning that was not determinately contemplated a priori in the mind's eye, only indeterminately adumbrated and feelingly intuited. This is *presentation* a posteriori, with intentional content displaced from the pre-linguistic to the post-linguistic realm. Language provides the medium for the creationist embodiment of ideal meaning. However experimental, dynamic, and tentative the verbal process of the expressive-creationist intention—the intention to create preexist, in the ignorance of its object—becomes self-fulfilling. The intentional process produces simultaneously the presented content of the speech act and its fulfillment. in one single flash of immediate self-presentation, the act creates meaning and performs its fulfilment. This delineates the fallacy of immediacy as per Simon Palfrey, for whom the mocking of providence is the mocking of mental and creative anticipation, and it signals the bankruptcy of fixed intentional contents. In Palfrey's creationist universe, the sparrow is neither as static as the changeless metal of Yeat's golden bird nor as deciduous as Hamlet's falling bird—"an accident of mocking providence" (*Doing Shakespeare* 125). The sparrow, in other words, is still flying, still ascending the brightest heaven of invention. For the scholar in the grip of *the fallacy of immediacy*, the letter of the assertion is less important than the spirit that internally shaped it. The determinate signifier of the assertion only imperfectly reveals the dynamic indeterminacy of an expressive intention that it is the task of the scholar to reconstruct and retrace. This intention, however, does not present itself as a stable, immutable, intentional content, but rather as an intentional action. The formal-material mediation of language plays no significant role. The contingent concretion of the play's signifiers can only offer a schoolboy map of the treasure island of meanings boiling underneath, or above. Ultimately, the playtext is sacrificed in favor of *play*—less of textual play than of meaning play.

3. *The intentional object (the fallacy of presentism)*. Here, the fulfilment of the intentional process of Shakespeare's communication is deferred to the historical emergence of an object that may or may not have been there, historically present, at the time of Shakespeare's utterance. Alone the sensorial appearance to relevant witnesses (Shakespeare himself, his characters, the contemporary playgoers attending his plays, his contemporary readers) and to interested

parties (subsequent playgoers, readers, and scholars) of the intentional object can secure the fulfilment of the assertion. The structure of the prophetic statement, which modalizes our *Hamlet* assertion, makes room for all these possibilities: "If it be now, 'tis not to come. If it be not to come, it will be now. If it be not now, yet it will come. The readiness is all." The strict neo-historicist scholar contemplates only one scenario: since it was then, and is not to come, let us search for traces of this intentional object in the early modern textual archive broadly understood. This is reductive for the presentist scholar: whether it was then or not is irrelevant, she argues, what matters is that it will always come, there will always be an occasion to attest the presentist fulfilment of the intentional object aimed at in the Shakespeare assertion. A compulsive empiricist drive spurs the ambitions of the presentist scholar: her aim is to identify the object, the present thing, that fulfils the past communicative intention. This aim rests on the assumption that language has always functioned as a harmonious communicative tool in human societies, and this naïve transtemporal assumption is typically phenomenological, very visible in Levinas, but also in Arendt: "Men in the plural, that is, men in so far as they live and move and act in the world, can experience meaningfulness only because they can talk with and make sense to each other and to themselves" (*Human Condition* 4). The fall of the sparrow can be variously corroborated: *falling man* (De Lillo) in the 9/11 terrorist attacks, the effects of ecosystem destruction in our post-industrial age, right-winged neo-liberal fatalism, male impotence in the age of chemicals, you name it. This is the presentist fallacy, to which the recent work of Richard Wilson is increasingly spellbound. In the faulty—and partly phenomenological—logic of this fallacy, the language of the assertion is also negligible: if the signifier fully denotes the thing, then it can be traded for the thing; if it doesn't, if it lacks the denotative, referential, representational power they expect of a signifier, then they turn to a signified (a referent, a thing, an intentional object) that can be either more rewarding in the way of linguistic exactitude (terror is a presentist favorite, and so is tyranny) or sufficiently broad to cover various verbal occurrences, and reverse the heuristic traction: on the presentist evidence of the present thing, say, pandemia, they track the past text in search for signifieds (infection, plague, masks) that may fit the object. And, good Lord, it works!

These three "phenomenological" fallacies rely upon a non-Saussurean understanding of meaning and language. Whereas the fallacies of representation and presentism appeal to significance by zooming in on the abstracted signified, respectively on the intentional meaning and the referent, the fallacy of immediacy steps out entirely of the musty system of *langue* to freshly engage *parole*. In both cases, however, the signifier is lost, and so is, more importantly, the structural principle that "considers reference as a function of language and not necessarily as an intuition" (de Man, *Aesthetic* 8). The congruence of this deconstructive principle may take some unpacking, for which I enlist Warminski's help. Take a deep breath:

> What does this mean? Exactly what it says: that is, that a no longer non-linguistic (e.g., historical or aesthetic) terminology, and thus a properly *linguistic* terminology, is one which considers reference as precisely a referential *function of language*—that is, produced by the workings of structures proper to language as such, in the case of Saussurian linguistics, to language as *langue* or a system of signs made up of signifiers and signifieds whose relation is arbitrary and whose constitution is relational— and *not* as an "intuition"—that is, *not* produced by the structures proper to consciousness, its determinations, and its logic, which is always a *phenomeno*-logic, a logic of appearances that does indeed always designate the referent prior to designating reference (again, reference as the referential function of *language* and determined by *its* structures and not those of consciousness).
> *Material Inscriptions* 195–196

What Warminski here conveys with dialectical exactitude is a kind of intelligence very few today are willing to hear, I know. A most unwonted delivery of this critical formulation is the identification of a *phenomeno*-logic that Brian Vickers and Bruce Smith—prima facie, most unlikely bedfellows—heartily share. And it is within the parameters stipulated by this critical *phenomeno*-logic—intuition, referent—that the Shakespeare scholarship of critics like Jonathan Gil Harris, Paul Kottman, Julia Lupton, Simon Palfrey, Richard Wilson, and Christopher Pye similarly unfolds.

CHAPTER 17

The Aesthetic Fallacy

1

According to Martin Jarvis, "the standpoint of a sober materialism from which art's illusion could be dispelled right now is not available, because thinking itself as yet remains ineliminably entangled with idealism" (*Adorno* 115). This is taken from Jarvis's book on Adorno, particularly from the chapter he devotes to the German thinker's theory of truth, art, and ideology, possibly the most succinct and lucid commentary on *Asthetische Theorie* to date. The prose is chiefly expository and therefore prone to assume free-indirect-thought conditions of sympathetic presentation. So, on the face of it, "as yet" in Jarvis' exposé means 1969, the year Adorno died, presumably working on the materials that went into the book. Interestingly, also de Man died working on a book on, or better, against, the aesthetic ideology. But the echoic assimilation of Jarvis's prose stretches the temporal marker all the way up to 1998, the date when his monograph was published. Can we stop there? I don't think so. We are still, conceivably, under the umbrella of this *as yet*, for "thinking itself as yet remains ineliminably entangled with idealism." But Jarvis's astute point takes a narrower focus and makes a sharper claim, to wit, that *materialism* erects a standpoint from which *the illusion of art* cannot be dispelled. The first to suffer the burden of this condition was Adorno himself, whose theory of art is materialist but also dialectical, and therefore unsettlingly pledged to idealism. But there is of course idealism and idealism, just as there is, say, a Hegel for girl scouts, on aesthetics and civil society, and a Hegel for misfits, on antagonism and the void. Adorno, I think, belonged to the second group. He believed in the inevitability of the illusion of art, which is not exactly thinking all art must be illusive. "Philosophical critique," he argued as early as 1956, "has no other measure than the ruin of illusion," and illusion is largely the outcome of a farewell to concepts and their replacement with images (*Against* 39–40). Adorno, in his late age, was surrounded by delusions of various kinds, and turned back to Goethe. It was after all the 1968 student movement that forced him to interrupt his lecture on *Iphigenie auf Tauris* and step down from the podium.[1] Quite a

---

1 See the objective account of the appalling incidents describing the last days of Adorno as an academic lecturer in Stefan Müller-Doohm, *Adorno: A Biography*, 453–455, 474–475.

symbolic moment. Phenomenological scholars working under the influence of the first Hegel resemble more the semi-naked woman student that accosted Adorno at the lectern, with flowers and a teddy bear, a pastoral grotesquerie out of *A Midsummer Night's Dream*.

Flower power. Ici on spontane. Make love not war. Youkali. O the illusion, the illusion of art, that thing of the past. In general, phenomenological criticism makes the same mistake made two hundred years ago by romantic artists and scholars who sought to unearth and restore the music, sound, and speech of the cultural past as the essence of the (national) people involved in the spontaneous creation of that culture. *Volkgeist, Ursprache, folklore*—these were the abracadabra of a spiritualist-romantic ideology (Herder, Hartman) whose hidden agenda was to overpass the mediation of language conceived as difference, discontinuity, arbitrariness, and negativity. The romantics professed to be fighting the positivism of the nascent modern sciences, but they were secretly confederated against language. On this view of romanticism, Husserl is a romantic—and so is Heidegger, insofar as he refused to see the role that language played both in the transcendental determination of the ontological difference and in the constitution of the realm (ontology) that makes such determination possible. Also Badiou, in this respect, is an unrepentant, conservative romantic. The reactive, anti-phenomenological work of Adorno and Derrida, both of whom started their brilliant philosophical careers exposing the shortcomings of Husserl's system, marks the re-start of modern *criticism* proper, an intellectual program with roots in Montaigne, Bacon, Shakespeare, and Descartes, that has been greatly bolstered by Kantian criticism and inflected by Hegelian *speculative negativity*.[2] For all their anti-foundationalist stance, which targets alike notions like absolute, origin, or presence, the work of Adorno and Derrida partake decisively of the dialectic.[3] Their work, moreover, can be described as genuinely Kantian, paving the way to the mode of dialectical or *antithetical criticism*—this is Bloom's fitting coinage—we tend to identify with both symptomal reading and deconstruction. While Adorno's debt to Kant has always existed perfectly in the open, the way Derrida followed

---

2 Harold Bloom: "Iago may be nothing if not critical; Hamlet is criticism itself, the theatrical interpreter of his own story" (*Shakespeare* 423).
3 See Adorno's "Introduction" to *Against Epistemology*, especially the first section, "Procedure and Object," where "the power of contradiction" (4), which inheres in the dialectic, is opposed to phenomenological drive to the uncontradictable assurance of system. The complexity of Derrida's explicit response to dialectical thought rests largely on the difficulty to tell his reading methods during the 1960s and 1970s from traditional dialectical critique.

in Kant's tracks is less obvious. Discussing the figure of Cohen in the context of the neo-Kantian school, Derrida pointed out that

> it is too often forgotten, when one is interested in Husserl and Heidegger, that this neo-Kantian sequence has largely determined the context in which, that is to say also against which, Husserl's phenomenology, later the phenomenological ontology of the early Heidegger (who, besides, succeeded Cohen in his Marburg chair-and this also marks an institutional context in the strictest sense), in a way arose: against neo-Kantianism and in another relation to Kant.
> "Interpretations at War," 41

This confirms the pertinency of Cutrofello's decision to read contemporary continental philosophies as an array of orthodox (same) and unorthodox (other) *relations to Kant* (*Continental Philosophy* 1–5). Derrida's historicist notation reveals moreover the extent to which he believed that phenomenology had deviated from the critical path, initiating a dangerous neo-ontologization of philosophy. Let me repeat it once again: Husserl and Heidegger shared the conviction that phenomenology is an ontology. Adorno and Derrida in turn denounced the massive *refoulement* upon which this ontology was founded, but whereas Adorno spotted the silencing of historical materiality and contingency, Derrida detected the sacrifice of contingent-material linguisticity. To resist phenomenological scholarship, one needs therefore to expose its failure as criticism, and to vindicate a stronger mode of truly anti-ontological critique best represented by the work of Adorno, Derrida, and de Man. And insofar as phenomenological scholarship flourishes on critical grounds depleted by the organized *resistance to theory* (de Man), to resist phenomenological scholarship is to resist a resistance. Still, rather than seeking to force others to overcome their resistance to dialectical (anti-phenomenological) criticism—no such ambition guides my thoughts—I hope merely to state (denounce is too strong a word) that such resistance exists. And I do it because I believe it exists, because I believe its existence has a negative effect on the ways we are today understanding Shakespeare, and, last but not least, because I don't see anyone around anywhere near stating it exists. I find this unalertness daunting.

2

Phenomenological-aestheticist criticism of Shakespeare (Kottman, Lupton, Pye) is prisoner to the delusion that, contra Kant, the sublime can be represented, and the infinite can be made apparent (*anschaulich*). But Kant made the pleasure of the imagination depend precisely on this "failure to constitute the sublime." As de Man argues, the congruity of the law of the imagination (which is a law of failure) with the law of our suprasensory being cannot be transposed to the sensory. Precisely, moreover, "its failure to connect with the sensory would also elevate it above it. This law does not reside in nature but defines man in opposition to nature; it is only by an act of what Kant calls 'subreption' (p. 180; 96) that this law is fallaciously attributed to nature" (*Aesthetic* 76). I believe this subreption is at work in the critical pretense to de-transcendentalize and de-dialectize the *scene of representation* (in particular, Shakespeare's scene of representation) by assigning it powers that are exclusively metaphysical, which is to say ideological. The result is a *naturalization of the imagination* that is as harming, or more, than the naturalization of reason championed by cognitivists. The terms of the problem remain Kantian through and through. What we witness is a regressive attempt to reschedule modernity in aesthetic-phenomenal terms that Kant's textual system simply doesn't authorize. It was Foucault who argued that Kantian critique marks the threshold of our modernity because it questions representation on the basis of its rightful limits, it marks, therefore, "la retrait du savoir et de la pensée hors de l'espace de la représentation" (*Les mots et les choses* 255).[4] Contra Foucault, what scholars like Kottman, Lupton and Pye try to do is to force thought—Shakespeare's literary thought—back into the space of representation, back into the stage of illusion. The revels are not ended. Show's not over. Even the orchestra is beautiful.

What I find troublesome is the inevitable sacrifice of literary thought that this attempt to force thought entails. Let me make a controversial contention: if we aim to understand Shakespeare's literary production, rather than probing the highlights of aesthetic philosophy—Kant's third *Critique*, Hegel's *Lectures on Aesthetics*, and Adorno's *Aesthetic Theory*—one should read the works these thinkers devoted to questions of knowledge: the first *Critique*, the *Phenomenology of Spirit*, the first *Logic*, and *Negative Dialectics*. In doing this we don't exactly deny Shakespeare's corpus the status of aesthetic work. We do rather three things: 1) we lower the euphoria of scholars who strive to retrieve an early modern aesthetics; 2) we question the amenability of Shakespeare's things (scripts, playtexts, performed plays) to arguments both of mimetic purpose and of aesthetic autonomy; and, more importantly, 3) we construe the act of interpretation as an attempt to elucidate the logic of the actual

---

4 De Man returns to this dictum in his essays on Kant: *Aesthetic Ideology*, 70, 120.

experience dramatized in the playtext—a strictly verbal-conceptual experience of moral embarrassments only defectively overcome by cognitive and recognitive work. Sensorial failure and cognitive error prompt wrong moral decisions whose negative effects are only partly repaired by new-cognitive or re-cognitive work, and this work is realized through the resources of figurative-conceptual language. This is the standard dialectical-cum-experiential pattern in a Shakespeare poem and play. The faculties at stake are those of desire and knowledge. The feelings of pleasure and plain steering judgements about the agreeable, the beautiful and the sublime are of course presupposed as a ground that sustains other experiences, but in Shakespeare this ground does not *determine in the last instance*: moral experience—the experience of doing when we do not know, and of knowing that we do not know: the properly human experience—is much more beholden to the trials of verbal-conceptual understanding than to the deliveries of aesthetic sensibility. In this he differs from Spenser and Marlowe, who always seem to write from a site that is across the conceptual and into the sensual, across the river and into the trees. Even when, very rarely, strictly aesthetic experience is isolated inside a Shakespeare play as the object of focused contemplative attention or dialogic elaboration (*A Midsummer Night's Dream, Love's Labour's Lost, Hamlet, Macbeth, Cymbeline, The Tempest, The Winter's Tale*), this experience has less to do with sensorial pleasure than with cognitive misunderstanding. A case in point is Juliet, who is more interested in the cogency of the rational operation subsuming the particular rose under the word and concept "rose" than in assessing the agreeableness of its particular smell. Juliet's puzzle takes the following heuristic form, "What's in a name? that which we call a rose / By any other name would smell as sweet" (*Romeo and Juliet* 2.1.85–86), and not the form of the judgement of taste, "The rose is agreeable (in its smell) [*die Rose ist (im Geruche) angenehm*]" (*Critique* §8, 59), by means of which Kant illustrated the universality of the liking. Whereas Juliet interrogates a *Sache*, Kant elucidates the sensorial features of a *Ding*.

A fierce nominalist, Shakespeare refuses however to throw concepts—broadly understood, *pace* Brandom, as words and tropes—overboard. By contrast, the aesthetic domain stands guard against the speculative work of concepts. For all protestations to the contrary, aesthetics remains *the* empiricist's bulwark, a residual field surveyed by precritical rangers: an Arden forest where you may like or dislike the phenomenal, beyond considerations of desire and knowledge. If desire crops up, the attending morality is the beautiful (the communal, the embodied, the phenomenal) for its own sake: "Speak what we feel, not what we ought to say" (*King Lear* 5.3.323). And if knowledge hems in, its elemental maxim is "See it feelingly" (*King Lear* 4.6.145). *Universality not based on concepts*, a central tenet of Kantian aesthetics, is a perfect solution for the phenomenological scholar consumed with an old-Left respect for principles of "universal communicability [*allgemeine Mitteilbarkeit*]" (*Critique of Judgement* 61). The "indeterminate [*unbestimmt*]" and "indeterminable [*unbestimmbar*]" concepts (*Critique* 212) on which judgements of beauty rest are hardly concepts upon which speculative-dialectical work can be erected. And Shakespeare's plays stage *conflicts of understanding*, not *debates of taste*. We can of course treat them as objects of taste and frame judgements of beauty around their parts and wholes, but this eludes their singularity as verbal-conceptual dramatizations of experience, dramatizations to which we can best respond with critical work attuned to a speculative texture that is transcendentally mediated by concepts—and contaminated by words. This is not, moreover, what scholars dealing with the aesthetic—more often, political-aesthetic—dimension of Shakespeare's work are doing: they rather examine these plays as if they had been composed with an aesthetic intention (the intentional content) in mind and they are always in a rush to see the intention representatively *fulfilled* in the arena of the stage. The fact that Stanley Cavell and other important philosophers have responded to Shakespeare's plays in the former way, treating them as interpretations of the kind of experience philosophy, especially epistemology, is an interpretation of, is further evidence of their complex status as objects whose internal critique overspills matters of beauty and taste to engage issues of knowledge, recognition, and acknowledgement.[5] But let us see what Kant has to say:

> Now, on the other hand, a judgment of taste does deal with objects of sense-though not so as to determine a *concept* of these objects for the understanding, since it is not a cognitive judgment. Rather, this judgment is a singular intuitive presentation referred to the feeling of pleasure, and hence is only a private judgment; and to this extent its validity would be restricted to the judging individual: The object is an object of liking *for me*; the same may not apply to others: Everyone has his own taste. (212)

For the phenomenology-inspired early modern literary scholar this is of course paradise: a phenomenal combination of ontic presentative particular immediacy (*anschauliche einzelne Vorstellung*) and self-centered affective relativism (*der Gegenstand ist* für mich). As you like it. Who could ask for anything more? Well, one could actually ask for the kind of *transcendental* scruples that

---

5   See Cavell, *Disowning Knowledge*, xv, and 5–6.

preserve the standards of effective universality. To charge Kant with neglect of transcendental vigilance would appear untoward, to say the least, but the third *Critique* reads after all as a desperate attempt to smuggle through the backdoor those very guests (the sensible and empirical) that had been originally banned from a critical party run by transcendental norms. And they return with a vengeance. Kant's *indeterminate concepts* gesture towards the supersensible (*Übersinnliche*) that supposedly grounds all intuitions, and, as Werner S. Pluhar explains, "if we use [...] transcendental principles to make judgments about something supersensible, something beyond all possible experience, then our use of them is *transcendent*" ("Introduction" to *Critique of Judgement* xxxvii). Indeed, the confusion between the *transcendental* and the *transcendent*—the tendency to overlook the former and enthrone the latter, or even to reify the former into the latter—is a rather common lapse among phenomenological scholars.

3

The collection of essays titled *Political Aesthetic in the Era of Shakespeare* (2020), edited by Christopher Pye is a case in point. The spirit of the whole project betrays the acknowledged influence of Graham Hammill's and Julia Lupton's edited collection of essays, *Political Theology and Early Modernity* (2012). This link is not casual, as the implied formula *Political Theology* ↔ *Political Aesthetic* serves not only to turn aesthetics into a version of theology—the beautiful into a version of the supersensible—but also to discount real politics altogether from the calculus. In fact, in neither book is politics the matter at hand—or *Sache selbst*. Both projects are driven by a nostalgia for *phenomenal immediacy* that only pre-rational aesthetics and post-rational religion seem ready to relieve. Their drive is primarily moral: the *fulfillment* of "the promise of a fully relational sociality embodied ultimately in the audience's vicarious [...] theatrical engagement" (Pye, "Introduction" 16) or the courage to make "imaginative formulations with the power to reveal and constitute new norms, communities, and forms of life" (Hammill and Lupton, "Introduction" 7). These fantasies of embodied togetherness, in part inspired in Rancière's confidence in the political-aesthetic "promise of unrealized forms of life and community" (Pye, "Introduction" 6) are not only a far cry from Adorno's notion that art is "the social antithesis [*gesellschaftliche Antithesis*] of society" (*Aesthetic Theory* 8), but also *political* only in accordance with a very diluted—and very post-sixties, situationist, spontaneist—understanding of the term political. The fact that a certain philosophical Left (Badiou, Rancière) considers this understanding *strong* (or pure, or radical) rather than *diluted* is another kind of problem, albeit one that helps explain the rationale of Pye's misinterpretation of Kant. For one particularly questionable feature of his argument is the dubious assumption that the aesthetic philosophies of Adorno and Rancière are compatible, and that both conceive their philosophies "as a means for reconceiving possibilities of social rapport as well as the most fundamental phenomenological organization of the world" (3). Adorno was never interested in philosophy as means to effectuate a "most fundamental phenomenological organization of the world," and he certainly cared very little for "the communal dimensions of phenomenal experience" (3). He was alert to the communal distortions of objectal experience—empiricism and phenomenology being particularly baneful modes of ideological distortion—and was of course keenly aware of the effect that the democratic-capitalist system of production and distribution had on the reification and commodification of cultural values and artistic products, but he would have puzzled over a phrase like "sensible politicity" (Rancière, *Politics of Aesthetics*, 14). He never took part in "the grand aesthetic-political endeavour to have 'thought' become 'world'" (Rancière, *Politics of Aesthetics* 10): he didn't sacrifice the subject in order to save the object, which means that, for him, utopian redemption was either critical (dialectical, conceptual, thought) or nothing, and *nothing if not critical*. He valorized the utopian dimension of art, as Pye rightly argues, but he linked it to the negative, not to the phenomenal: "Art is no more able than theory to concretize utopia, not even negatively" (*Aesthetic Theory* 32). The notion that an aesthetic redistribution of the sensible can bring about emancipatory political change he would have judged profoundly naïve, based on a non-dialectical conception of the aesthetic—a "concept-free pseudopluralism" (Schweppenhäuser 95)—whose only terminus would be the hypostasis of the empirical. Rancière claims that in the aesthetic regime artistic phenomena adhere to a "regime of the sensible, which is extricated from its ordinary connections and is inhabited by a heterogenous power, the power of a form of thought that has become foreign to itself" (*Politics of Aesthetics* 23). This is both inaccurate and overstated, as Kant's aesthetic judgement does not have "the power of a form of thought," but the universally communicable power of a *sensation* or *mental state* cued by a sensible presentation (*Darstellung*) and prompted by a momentary (recreative) diversion of faculties (imagination, understanding) normally involved in the production of knowledge. "A form of thought" doesn't need to "become foreign to itself" in order to lose its power, because this power is exclusively sensorial, affective, sentimental: it is *flower power*, "the perfume and suppliance of a minute" (*Hamlet* 1.3.8). *Die Rose ist (im Geruche) angenehm*. The notion, therefore, that the aesthetic regime is characterized, as Rancière maintains, by "knowledge transformed into non-knowledge" (23) is wrong because there is no *knowledge* to begin with.[6] This couldn't be further from Adorno's negative aesthetics, staked on radical claims to knowledge and truth. The epistemic distinction Adorno ascribes to art would appear to turn it historically back to the age of the representative or poetic regime where determinations of *dignity* obtain. We may call this elitist nostalgia, but the truth is that the standards of dialectical relationality that Adorno stipulates for artworks both vis-à-vis reality and in relation to other artworks are incompatible with Rancière's Foucauldian celebration of sensorial positionality, and they account much better for the verbal *poiesis* practiced by Shakespeare or Beckett: How can Rancière explain the persistence of *King Lear* in *Waiting for Godot* and *Engame*? Would his be an *aesthetic* explanation? All of this notwithstanding, the unquestionable brilliance of Pye's reading of *King Lear* rests on a deep-seated adherence to Adorno that his flashy commitment to Rancière fails to compromise.

Pye argues that "political aesthetics" shows "concern with minimal levels of sensory apprehension" and holds this concern "consistent with the recent preoccupation in literary studies generally and Renaissance studies in particular with embodiment, affect, and bodily sensation" (7). This *willy nilly* places *political aesthetics* within the purview of phenomenology, specifically the phenomenologies of embodiment and empathy. In the "Introduction," Pye avoids the term, not always successfully, but the phrasing reeks of *phenomenological* sulfur. The cloven hoof, fully visible in his essay on *King Lear*, can be discerned

---

6 In *The Aesthetic Unconscious*, Rancière rehearses again the micro-narrative of the constitution of aesthetic thought, from Baumgarten to Hegel, that is scattered in many of his writings. Here he reiterates his persuasion that aesthetics "designates a mode of thought that develops with respect to things of art and that is concerned to show them to be things of thought" (4–5) but is careful enough to qualify the exceptional role of Kant in the narrative. Rancière argues rightly that Kant cautioned against the confusion between the sensible and the intelligible, and that he would not have conceived aesthetics as "a theory of indistinct knowledge" (5). By contrast, aesthetics, for Rancière, provides knowledge—*confused knowledge*—which he describes paradoxically, if not ridiculously, as "*the thought of that which does not think*" (6). Moreover, he describes those who seek to return aesthetics to "a critique of the judgement of taste, as Kant had formulated it" as actually promoting the relapse "to some impossible prerevolutionary paradise of 'liberal individualism'" (7, footnote). So, if you seek to keep sensibility and knowledge apart, cautioning against the pitfalls of "sensuous cognition," then you are a liberal individualist, one of those "solid citizens for whom art can never be irrational enough" (Adorno, *Minima Moralia* 75). Maybe not. Maybe you are simply indifferent to the cognitive claims of certain forms of art (especially the non-verbal) and respectful of the conceptual rationality of knowledge. For an alternative narrative of the genealogy of the aesthetic, that begins with Baumgarten's theorization of aesthetics as "a doctrine of nonconceptual knowledge" and Adorno (the bourgeois citizen, the liberal materialist, the Marxist individualist) not Rancière at the point of denouement, see Schweppenhäuser, 94–102.

in the "Introduction," where he quotes Catherine Craik and Tonya Pollard to the effect that "by situating the politics of phenomenal experience in relation to the inescapable problem of grounds, political aesthetics" would

> bring to view the unacknowledged stakes of such work [that of Renaissance studies, we suppose] insofar as that work is committed to a claim for 'the mind's embeddedness in the body,' or a fluid 'reciprocity between books, bodies and selves,'with all such formulations imply of a transparent rapport or direct translatability between material sensation and cognition. (7)

Prima facie, and given that the whole sentence is preceded by a difficult phrase, "At the same"—possibly a typo—it is hard to say whether Pye is taking an ironic distance from such supposedly anti-Cartesian "claim" and its attendant "formulations." If the phrase is "At the same time," then the implication is that political aesthetic simultaneously strives to warrant "minimal levels of sensory apprehension" *and* to expose the contradictions of a phenomenology-oriented scholarship with stakes in sensory apprehension. The resulting critical distance of, we assume, Pye the political aesthetician, would be confirmed by a sharp aside against the inconsistency of materialist critics—he cites De Grazia and Stallybrass—who claim to seek a vantage "outside of metaphysics" while metaphysically hypostatizing the thingness of material books (7). This is, I insist, very fine: but is Pye's argument free of *metaphysical* assumptions? How far does he turn his argument over to the "politics of phenomenal experience"? What are the "*minimal* levels of sensory apprehension" (emphasis added)? If early modern society is, as he assumes, following Carlo Galli, first constituted "as a phenomenal form" (11) or realized "in phenomenal form" (12), what are the exact proportions of phenomenality and form making up this mixed object? For it is not clear that "appearances [*Erscheinungen*]" or "beings of sense (*phenomena*) [*Sinnenwesen (Phänomena)*]" (Kant, *Critique of Pure Reason* 250) are at all "formal," and to argue that formalism entails phenomenality is a stretch. The questionable object at hand—phenomenal form—presents the two determinations (transcendence and transcendentality) whose confusion produces the unassimilable remainder of phenomenality that haunts political aesthetics, turning it into another hip version of phenomenology. Pye argues that "theology becomes political theology by suspending a fixed transcendental reference, by becoming, in Walter Benjamin's terms, a messianism without messiah" (13). I guess he meant a *transcendent* reference. God and its delegates are all metaphysical creatures, transcendent entities whose uncertain ontological status calls for the policing work of Kantian critique. There is nothing transcendental in a Messiah. One may of course object that what Pye means by "transcendental reference" is just "supernatural reference," and we can always reply that to favor this usage in an essay whose aim is to lay out the ultimately Kantian theoretical coordinates, supposedly valid for the entire collection it introduces, of the notion "political aesthetics" is a sign of sloppiness, if not of ironic perversity. Since sloppiness is improper of a sophisticated scholar like Pye, who elsewhere in the essay speaks of the "transcendental claims" of "Kantian aesthetics" (3), irony cannot be discounted. But is this irony "communicable"? Let us go step by step. In his essay on *King Lear*, Pye uses again the phrase "transcendental reference":

> Constitutive and yet without fixed transcendental reference, a function of its own creative divisions, the self-exceeding space of modern sociality is the space of an emergent aesthetic consciousness, for it is anesthetization that makes those formative negations—the inaugurating "nothing" of social relationality—available to phenomenal consciousness, even as it inevitably conjures the untoward limits of such a process of wrong creation (59–60).

To understand this we must bear in mind Pye's earlier claim that "it is the burden of the political-aesthetic to make that impossible ground [the inscriptive demarcation through which sovereignty, and a resulting political domain, seeks to constitute itself] phenomenally available, to make sheer difference cognizable at all" (52). On deManian logic, this attempt is of course doomed to failure, and the ensuing fiasco is the very birthmark of the *aesthetic ideology*. This logic is implied in Pye's brilliant argument, with only a brief note to acknowledge his debt to the Belgian thinker. But his reticence to defer to deconstructive authority may not be inattentive. For Pye's argument is not *stricto sensu* deconstructive. If he is aware of it, then his ambivalent use of the term "transcendental" is deliberately ironic. If he isn't, then there is sloppiness. In the above passage, "transcendental reference" can only mean "transcendent reference": an external thing (even a *Ding-an-sich*) that lends metaphysical support to the political-aesthetic game that is immanently unfolding. What is not autonomous—and the political-aesthetic field aspires to be autonomous—is heteronomous, and sources of normative authority external to a given field can only be described as transcendent. Whereas autonomy presupposes immanence—the immanence, of course, of the formal and *transcendental*—heteronomy presupposes *transcendence*. Again only by assuming that Pye actually means "supernatural reference" can we avoid the confusion. But can we assume that? Ten lines before the one where the phrase "transcendental reference" occurs, Pye speaks of Edgar's "transcendental consciousness" (59). Does he mean "supernatural consciousness"? The fact that he is discussing the scene in *King Lear* (4.6.69–72) where an "demon" is summoned and exorcised, where Edgar has, in Pye's terms, "internalized" the "supersensory" (59), would make this reading possible. But the fullness of the original sentence—"The dispersive scene suggests the horizonless opening from and against which transcendental consciousness—Edgar's consciousness—must seek to constitute itself" (59)—clearly suggests otherwise. In Kantian philosophy, a consciousness is either transcendental or nothing at all, openings and horizons are either spatial, and therefore related to space as an a priori (transcendentally ideal) form of sensible intuition, or nothing at all, and constitution, even self-constitution, is a transcendental endeavor or nothing at all. Therefore, Edgar's "transcendental consciousness" conforms to Kantian semantics or is a meaningless phrase.

In conclusion, the meaning of the term *transcendental* in the apparently concomitant phrases "transcendental reference" and "transcendental consciousness" is not uniform or consistent. Whether carelessly or ironically, Pye has conflated both meanings (supernatural and immanent-formal-constitutive) of the term *transcendental*, and the rationale of this confusion can be sought in the aesthetic ideology, which has led the scholar to phenomenalize—along exorbitant theological lines—the supersensible or supersensory, whereas Kant makes it very clear that the concept of the *Übersinnlich* is a transcendental rational concept (*transzendentale Vernunftbegriff*) (*Critique* §57, 212). The terminological confusion is a symptom of a larger problem, the two-stage procedure that sponsors 1) the constant upgrading of the aesthetic to a mode of cognition; and 2) the mimetic phenomenalization, and subsequent positing as an embodied transcendence, of a formal concordance that is immanent to the mind's faculties, and therefore transcendental. Let me start with the second stage: the purporsiveness that is formally entertained, transcendentally constituted, and solely communicable as state of spirit or sensation of concordance (*Übereinstimmung*) is devolved to nature as the harmony (*Harmonie*) of an embodied society. Pye argues that

> aestheticization implies an insistent movement beyond the hand of those who would instantiate it, though in the case of the aesthetic, that's an exorbitant movement that nevertheless remains radically immanent—thus the proximity between political aesthetics and Merleau-Ponty's project of imagining subjectivity neither as a function of an embodied community nor via transcendental reference but as constituted within the at once internal and external 'flesh of the social.' (13)

Note that "transcendental reference" cannot be understood in a Kantian sense, for it is here opposed to the "immanent movement" whose paradoxical exorbitance Pye seeks to explain, a movement that, we deduce, does not stretch out to the absolute exteriority of the transcendent, which the argument, laced by theological motifs, possibly inflects as theological or supernatural. If the movement of aestheticization is, as he argues, internal and immanent, then we expect it to be formal and *transcendental* in the Kantian sense. But our expectation is wrong: Pye suggests that it may not be so external as to become an "embodied community" but sufficiently external, referential, or transcendent (Pye says "transcendental") to become the "flesh of the social." In the footnote we read that the phrase can be found on page 149 of Merleau-Ponty's *The Visible and the Invisible*, but this is not the case. The phrase is neither in the original nor in the translation. The French expression "la chair du social" must be attributed to Claude Lefort, political thinker and disciple of Merleau-Ponty that Pye quotes elsewhere in abundance.[7] By contrast, "la chair du monde," conceived as "ségrégation, dimensionnalité, continuation, latence, empiètement" is a common enough expression in *Le visible et l'invisible*, and receives full attention in one of the May 1960 entries under the heading "Chair du monde—Chair du corps—Être" which cover the pages 248–251 in Alphonso Lingis' English version published in 1968. This is the same Merleau-Ponty, let me recall, that conflates the experience of my body with the experience of the other, that conceives of both as necessarily transcendent, that demands powers of hyper-reflection to postulate "the transcendence of the world as transcendence" (*The visible* 38) and that concludes—contra Levinas, but not Adorno and Deleuze, who eschew all provisions of uncooked transcendence—that "transcendence is identity within difference" (225). Only someone like Merleau-Ponty would construe Pye's assertion that Edgar's is a "transcendental consciousness" as a reference to a "transcendent consciousness": the phrase "conscience transcendante" occurs in his book in response to Husserl's attempt to explain the retentive conception of time along immanent lines (*The visible* 225).

---

7 It is specifically used in his essay "La question de la démocratie," included in *Essais sur le politique xixe-xxe siècles*, and in the book *Écrire. À l'épreuve du politique*. For the relation between Merleau-Ponty and Lefort, see Gilles Labelle.

4

Let us now examine the sections of Pye's argument where he resorts to Kant. First, he misrepresents the goal of Kant's project in the third *Critique* when he states that the German philosopher "sought to explain the means through which the sheer particulars of sensible apprehension become available to a form of comprehension that is communicable to others yet no mediated by established cognitive norms" ("Introduction" 3). The phrasing equivocates insofar as it leads us to believe that Kant sought, first and foremost, to explain the way the empirical becomes available to comprehension, when that particular search had been completed, more or less successfully, in the first *Critique*. If what he means to say is that Kant sought to explain the form of comprehension involved in aesthetic experience then he is wrong, first because this experience is not only unmediated by cognitive norms, but also non-cognitive *tout court*, and second because Kant certainly doesn't concern himself generally in the third *Critique* with the "the means through which the sheer particulars of sensible apprehension become available" to comprehension. When he does, briefly at §14, the result is a commitment to *aesthetic formalism* that falls foul of Pye's emphasis on empirical phenomenality. Pye argues, for instance, that the aesthetic judgement, is "bound up with the conditions of phenomenal experience as such" and "situated beyond the spheres of cognitive understanding on the one hand and the purely formal, nonempirical imperatives of reason that underpin ethical action on the other" (3). The former assertion is inaccurate, for aesthetic judgement, in Kant, is bound up with the faculties or powers (imagination, judgement) that procure "phenomenal experience," but not with its "conditions," especially its necessary condition: the use of concepts. The latter assertion is incorrect: the aesthetic judgement is prompted by transcendent forces (the empirical given) but plays itself out in the immanent sphere of pure forms. In Introduction VII, Kant describes the apprehension of forms characteristic of aesthetic judgements:

> When pleasure is connected with mere apprehension (*apprehensio*) of the form of an object of intuition, and we do not refer the apprehension to a concept so as to give rise to determinate cognition, then we refer the presentation not to the object but solely to the subject; and the pleasure cannot express anything other than the object's being commensurate with the cognitive powers that are, and insofar as they are, brought into play when we judge reflectively, and hence [expresses] merely a subjective formal purposiveness of the object.
>
> *Critique of Judgement* 29–30

To be sure, this pleasure is not produced by the *moral* concept of freedom, and therefore "we cannot possibly gain insight into by means of concepts, as necessarily connected with the presentation of an object" (30). But this doesn't necessarily imply that the judgement that accompanies such pleasure, i.e. the aesthetic judgement, is not *of necessity* formal. Aesthetic pleasure, continues Kant,

> is a pleasure that must always be recognized only through a perception upon which we reflect [and] that must be recognized as connected with the perception. Hence [a judgment of taste, which involves] this pleasure, is like any empirical judgment because it cannot proclaim objective necessity or lay claim to a priori validity; but, like any other empirical judgment, a judgment of taste claims only to be valid for everyone, and it is always possible for such a judgment to be valid for everyone despite its intrinsic contingency. (30–31)

Pye is not completely unaware of this tension, but he insists on parsing the "aesthetic judgement" as a "form of comprehension" (3). Two Kant concepts—*reflective judgment* and *sensus communis*—make up the munition he needs to advance his case:

> That "reflective judgement" is, for Kant, irreducible: it amounts to the precondition for all phenomenal perception. At the same time, precisely because it is a purely formal and relational enactment aesthetic judgement implies a heteronomy and sociality at subjectivity's core, a constitutive sociality unmediated by normative categories that Kant terms *sensus communis*. Aesthetic judgement involves, then, a form of communicability in advance of communicated content, and an other-directedness inherent in the most intimate forms of phenomenal apprehension.
>   Pye 4

The deployment here of notions like phenomenal perception, phenomenal apprehension, un-mediation, and other-directedness (a pale version of Brentano's and Husserl's *intentionality*) betrays Pye's endorsement of phenomenological doctrine. Some of these notions are, to be sure, implied in Kant's own writing—the writing that provided Husserl with a technical vocabulary. But it is their strategic alignment that smacks of phenomenologism. This transpires in the consecration of "an other-directedness inherent in the most intimate forms of phenomenal apprehension." Yet this is a minor distortion, if compared with the leap to communitarianism (Husserlian intersubjectivity) implied in the evocation, already rehearsed by Arendt, of *sensus communis*. I will come back to this later. For now let me just clarify two points.

First, the above passage and its immediate context construe the aesthetic judgement as a kind of reflective judgement, and this is correct. There are two reasons why one should feel impelled to redeploy the Kantian notion of the *reflective judgement*, which, unlike the *determinative judgement*, where the universal is given and the particular is subsumed under it, presupposes the givenness of the particular, "and judgment has to find the universal for it" (*Critique* 19–20). The first reason is that the *reflective judgement* originally unravels the dialectical thread that leads to Hegel's *speculative sentence*. As a precedent to critical-speculative work, nothing could be more promising. But the second reason, implicit in Pye's recourse to the notion, is less inviting: the reflective judgement is prompted by the central event in the phenomenological myth of the given: the givenness of the particular (*ist aber nur das Besondere gegeben: if only the particular is given*). So much depends on that *if only*. For what is less correct in Pye's construal is to assume that since reflective judgement is "a precondition for all phenomenal perception," so is the judgement of taste. Nowhere does Kant say that what reflective judgements can do for understanding—to classify natural things into hierarchical taxonomies of genera and species and to form empirical concepts (*Critique*, "Introduction" IV, 27)—aesthetic judgements can also accomplish. Aesthetic reflective judgements foster feelings of pleasure in a nonconceptual consciousness that are *not* presupposed in the phenomenal perception that serves as the basis of knowledge. Not even the free play of the imagination is definitely construed by Kant as a precondition for perception. Kant is adamant. The sense of finality or purporsiveness implied in aesthetic judgements and posited in a bold leap of *as-if* cognition is never a property of the object:

> Now a thing's purposiveness, insofar as it is presented in the perception of the thing, is also not a characteristic of the object itself (for no such characteristic can be perceived), even though it can be inferred from a cognition of things. Therefore, the subjective [feature] of the presentation which cannot at all become an element of cognition is the purposiveness that precedes the cognition of an object and that we connect directly with this presentation even if we are not seeking to use the presentation of the object for cognition. (29)

Purporsiveness has a transcendent origin—it is cued by the primitive, crude givenness of nature—and a transcendental destination—it is constituted via the formal concordance (*Übereinstimmung*) between the combination or unity (*Zusammensetzung*) of the diversity of the intuited in the faculty of the imagination and the unity (*Einheit*) of the concept that joins together the representations in the faculty of understanding (*Critique* §9, 62). It is the latter, transcendental destination that lends it a sort of *objective* dignity (as something really constituted out there) and a semblance of *cognitive* authority (as something giving rise to knowledge). But the aesthetic judgement is *not* a form of understanding. Knowledge, for Kant, is no *freien Spiele*. The fact that it is predicated upon a free play conducive to the harmony of the faculties of knowledge or cognitive powers—"*der Harmonie der Erkenntnisvermöge*"— meaning imagination and understanding (*Critique* §9, 62), does not make the aesthetic judgement meet the standards of true knowledge. Kant repeats the idea *ad nauseam*: purporsiveness precedes the knowledge of an object, but as a subjective not objective feature of presentation "it cannot at all become an element of cognition" (*Critique*, "Introduction" VII, 29); since the judgement of taste "decides by feeling rather than by a harmony with concepts" it follows that "aesthetic judgment [...] contributes nothing to the cognition of its objects" ("Introduction" VIII, 34–35); because in aesthetic judgements we do not use understanding to refer the presentation (*die Vorstellung*) to the object, but rather "we use the imagination (perhaps in connection with understanding) to refer the presentation to the subject and his feeling of pleasure or displeasure" we can safely state that "a judgement of taste is not a cognitive judgement" (*Critique* §1, 44); the feeling of pleasure or displeasure is "a very special power of discriminating and judging" that nevertheless "does not contribute anything to cognition" (44). We could go on quoting indefinitely. One may protest that Kant's dogged insistence betrays an anxious realization that there is something in the aesthetic judgement that is conducive to knowledge, albeit of an indistinct nature. But Kant is inflexible: "an aesthetic judgment is unique in kind and provides absolutely no cognition (not even a confused one) of the object" (§15, 75).

As Andrew Cutrofello and Paul Livingston observe, Kant brought Leibniz to task for "intellectualizing appearances by treating sensible intuitions as confuse thoughts" (*Problems* 8). Thus to uphold that "aesthetics is a philosophical procedure" (Pye, "Introduction" 5) betrays a naïve confidence. Aesthetics can be philosophically discussed, yes, but as a discursive field it produces judgements (Foucault would say statements) that fall short of philosophical—cognitive, critical, or dialectical—dignity. To claim that "aesthetic judgement for Kant sought to explain the means through which the sheer particulars of sensible apprehension become available to a form of comprehension that is communicable to others" (3) is wrong insofar as what he calls a "form of comprehension" is for Kant merely a "sensation [*Empfindung*]" (§9, 63) or "mental state

[*Gemütszustand*]" (§9, 61). This sensation is the quickening of the two powers (understanding and imagination) to an activity that is "required for cognition in general," but since the objective relation is missing insofar as there are no concepts to subsume the intuited presentation under properties or predicates, then the effect is wholly subjective—we are only left with a sensation of transcendental concordance, "the facilitated play of the two mental powers (imagination and understanding) quickened by their reciprocal harmony [*wechselseitige Zusammenstimmung*]" (§9, 63)—something similar to the lulling cadences of a washing machine that runs its laundry cycle with everything inside it (water jets, detergent, softener) save the laundry. You may call that washing, but it isn't. In choosing the term "comprehension" rather than "understanding" or "cognition," Pye is obviously trying to keep aesthetic knowledge within the boundaries of "sensory apprehension." But comprehension (*Zusamenfassung*) is for Kant a concept-dependent business, and it is the faculty of judgement that is in charge of it:

> Every empirical concept requires three acts of the spontaneous cognitive power: (1) *apprehension* (*apprehensio*) of the manifold of intuition; (2) *comprehension* of this manifold, i.e., synthetic unity of the consciousness of this manifold, in the concept of an object (*apperceptio comprehensiva*); (3) *exhibition* (*exhibitio*), in intuition, of the object corresponding to this concept. For the first of these acts we need imagination; for the second. understanding; for the third, judgment, which would be determinative judgment if we are dealing with an empirical concept.
> KANT, "First Introduction" to the *Critique of Judgement* 408

But the judgement of taste cannot deploy the concept of an object. It only empowers to feel pleasure in the contemplation of the object:

> A judgment of taste, on the other hand, is merely contemplative, i.e., it is a judgment that is indifferent to the existence of the object: it (considers) the character of the object only by holding it up to our feeling of pleasure and displeasure. Nor is this contemplation, as such, directed to concepts. for a judgment of taste is not a cognitive judgment (whether theoretical or practical) and hence is neither based on concepts. nor directed to them as purposes. (51)

Note the profound similarity between Kant's "indifference to the existence of the object" and Husserl's bracketing of the thesis of the existence of the natural world in *Ideas 1*.⁸ The difference is that whereas Husserl receded into the backroom with a flashlight, in search of transcendental concepts that could lend a semblance of knowledge to the intentional *cogitata*, Kant forces the aesthetic judgement to remain stranded at the cave mouth, enjoying a show it cannot comprehend.

So, is the aesthetic a cognitive realm? Kant's answer is no. We may believe otherwise (I personally do) but we would then deviate from the Kantian source. If our deviation is towards Adorno, then we must reconcile ourselves with the fact that "art militates against the concept as much as it does against domination, but for this opposition it, like philosophy, *requires concepts*" (*Aesthetic Theory* 96; emphasis added). Adorno himself puzzled over the apparent "aporia of the concept of aesthetic intuition" at the core of the *Critique of Judgment*— at the fact that judgements of taste "have reference" to the understanding and yet beauty pleases universally without a concept—but explains the aporia away as "the contradiction between [art's] spiritual and mimetic constitution." Adorno's claim is somewhat unconvincing, because the "reference" that aesthetic judgements "have"—or, better, the relation the judgements include (*eine Beziehung* [...] *enthalten*)—to the understanding is not binding or essential enough to turn these into cognitive judgements. Still, his argument exhibits a profound anti-mimetic hostility that is an un-renounceable trade-in-stock feature of his aesthetic theory.⁹ Fredric Jameson has rightly spoken of a crisis or critique of *Schein* (illusion, aesthetic appearance) that very often is invested with the Puritan force of a *Bilderverbot* (Jameson, *Late Marxism* 165–66). This

---

8 Adorno noted that "Kant was the first to achieve the insight, never since forgotten, that aesthetic comportment is free from immediate desire; he snatched art away from that avaricious philistinism that always wants to touch it and taste it" (*Aesthetic Theory* 10).

9 Adorno: "The 'Analytic of the Beautiful' concerns the 'Elements of the Judgment of Taste.' Of these Kant says in a footnote to section 1: 'I have used the logical functions of judging to help me find the elements that judgment takes into consideration when it reflects (since even a judgment of taste still has reference to the understanding). I have examined the element of quality first, because an aesthetic judgment about the beautiful is concerned with it first.' This flagrantly contradicts the thesis that beauty pleases universally without a concept. It is admirable that Kant's aesthetics let this contradiction stand and expressly reflected on it without explaining it away. On the one hand, Kant treats the judgment of taste as a logical function and thus attributes this function to the aesthetic object to which the judgment would indeed need to be adequate; on the other hand, the artwork is said to present itself 'without a concept,' a mere intuition, as if it were simply extralogical. This contradiction, however, is in fact inherent in art itself, as the contradiction between its spiritual and mimetic constitution. The claim to truth, which involves something universal and which each artwork registers, is incompatible with pure intuitability. Just how fateful the insistence on the exclusively intuitable character of art has been is obvious from its consequences" (*Aesthetic Theory* 97).

anti-phenomenal animus informs Adorno's celebration of spirit (Geist)—of what is "utterly unthinglike [*dem schlechterdings Undinglichen*]"—as "the force or the interior of works, the force of their objectivation; spirit participates in this force no less than in the phenomenality [*Phänomenalität*] that is contrary to it" (87); and his oracular assertion that "because artworks are not the unity of a multiplicity but rather the unity of the one and the many, they do not coincide with phenomenality [*Erscheinenden*]" (*Aesthetic Theory* 307). This foreshadows de Man's constant underlining of the non-coincidence of the linguistic and the phenomenal. Furthermore, Adorno's critique of the phenomenological myth of concept-free *intuititability* in *Aesthetic Theory* submits the relevant observation that the term (*Anschaulichkeit*) denoting such myth "conceals [*verdeckt*]" the "rational element in art by "dividing off the phenomenal element [*das phänomenale*] and hypostatizing it" (97). This is hard to swallow even for devoted readers of Adorno like Hugh Grady. His reading of *A Midsummer Night's Dream* posits a utopian re-naturalization of society and culture that can only be achieved through the elision of the negative and conceptual dimension of Shakespeare's most impure aesthetics.[10] Grady's aesthetics, by contrast, posits a notion of "*mimesis* as the artwork's ability to reproduce within itself aspects of nature which conceptual thought as such, and certainly ideology, are blind to" (*Shakespeare and Impure Aesthetics* 77). In my opinion, there are very few "aspects," if any, of human experience, including the human experience of nature, that, in Shakespeare's work, are not *conceptually seen*. The blindness (to the particular) of a concept is in Shakespeare always indirectly compensated by the dialectical intervention of other concepts, never by the aesthetic representation of the eluded thing.

Although Pye is not unaware of this context of anti-phenomenological critique, other Shakespeare scholars who, consciously or not, seize the aesthetic judgement for hermeneutic purchase, ignore or discount it to their own risk. Their take on Kantian aesthetics dismisses the *formalist* compulsion that organizes sections of the *Critique of Judgement* and appears to focus mostly on the inevitably "sensible" and phenomenal implications of what Kant calls, rather ambivalently, the *aesthetic idea* and describes as a "presentation [*Vorstellung*] of the imagination which prompts much thought, but to which no determinate though whatsoever, i.e. no determinate concept, can be adequate, so that

---

10 In his reading of *A Midsummer Night's Dream* included in *Shakespeare's Impure Aesthetics*, Grady doesn't mention, I think, Adorno's comments in letter of 28 May 1936 to Benjamin about Max Reinhardt's film "A Midsummer Night's Dream" (1935). Adorno points out that in trying to attain an auratic dimension the film inevitably leads to the destruction of aura (*The Complete Correspondence* 137).

no language can allow us to express it completely and allow us to grasp it" (*Critique* §49, 182). The aesthetic idea would be something like Husserl's intentional content, but devoid of the "sense-giving" (*sinngebende*) work that goes into the making of *noetic* experience. In phenomenological terms, the judgement of taste swings between the imaginative presentation and the sensible object, without the mediation, arbitration, or assistance of concepts:

$$\text{IMAGINATIVE PRESENTATION} \;\; \rightrightarrows \;\; \text{(CONCEPTS)} \;\; \rightleftarrows \;\; \text{SENSIBLE OBJECT}$$

The withholding of conceptual work, isolated from the relational flow between imagination and object, signals of course a failure, and this failure grounds in turn the triumph of presence—the sensorial presence of the object, the presentation of the object in the imagination. A counterpart of a rational idea, the aesthetic idea shares with it this sense of impending cognitive failure. In the case of the rational idea, however, it is the intuition or imaginative presentation that is missing, for Kant describes it "is a concept to which no intuition [*Anschauung*] (presentation of the imagination) can be adequate" (182). The everyday secular miracle that the aesthetic idea operates is to overcome cognitive confusion, ideational turbulence, and intuitive inadequacy by producing a representation that fleshes out, in sensible form, the very rational idea whose imaginative nonappearance caused conceptual havoc in the first place. More concretely, the aesthetic ideas "strive toward something that lies beyond the bounds of experience, and hence try to approach an exhibition of rational concepts [*Darstellung der Vernunftbegriffe*] (intellectual ideas), and thus [these concepts] are given a semblance of objective reality [*den Anschein einer objektiven Realität*]" (182). *Darstellung*, here translated as *exhibition*, can also be rendered as *representation*, and even as *presentation*. When phenomenology-oriented Shakespeare scholars co-opt Kantian aesthetics for hermeneutic purposes they seem to imply that Shakespeare is striving toward something that lies beyond the bounds of experience—the political sublime (Pye), a polity of friends (Lupton), shared human freedom (Kottman)—and that he effectively manages to *exhibit* an imaginative *presentation* of that something through the aesthetic re-*presentations* that his plays turn out to be. The play's the thing in which he catches (*fulfils*) the intuition, imaginative presentation, or intentional content. Theatrical exhibition is fulfilment. The reading of the text, where conceptual *Auslegung* is presumed, becomes unnecessary—or only *once* necessary, as *immediate* reading. The performance representation of the play unloads the visual givens in the imaginative presentation. Everything locks up in harmony, the time returns to joint, concordance is achieved. Since the aesthetic-phenomenological interpretation of a Shakespeare play is overly comedic due to its drive to symmetric shape and harmonious resolution, we may describe it as the comedy of comedy. But since Shakespeare's plays are most uneager and conflicted comedies, the aesthetic interpretation becomes the *true* concordant comedy of a *strange* discordant comedy: "Tis strange my Theseus, that these lovers speak of" (*A Midsummer Night's Dream* 5.1.1). Indeed, 'tis irreparably strange.

5

In *Dissensus*, Rancière describes aesthetic ideas as "inventions" that give art "its sensible quality," what we might call its "ontology" (211). This way, "the ontology of art under the aesthetic regime is what is weaved by the inventions of art [...] by placing one sensible world in another: the sensible world in which the imagination obeys the concept, in the sensible world in which understanding and imagination relate to each other without concept" (211). What is the meaning here of the phrase *sensible world*? Does the imagination obey a concept *in* a *sensible world*? Do imagination and understanding relate *in* a *sensible world*? Not exactly. All that Rancière describes occurs in a transcendental world—the formal world of the operation of the faculties. Ontologies have nothing to do with the sensible. Maybe Rancière's "general indifference to phenomenology" (Rockhill and Watts, "Introduction" to Rancière, *History, Politics, Aesthetics*, 2) may have something to do with his flagrant overinterpretation of Kant, but I would speak more of an indifference to Husserl's transcendental-ontological phenomenology than of a general indifference to phenomenology, for some of his assumptions loom large in the work of Merleau-Ponty.

In *Dissensus* Rancière argues that the oscillation in modern aesthetic theory between claims to autonomy and the realization of heteronomy takes the syntactical form, in the arguments of those who describe it (Flaubert, Mallarmé, Adorno, Lyotard), of the "basic emplotment of an *and*, the same knot binding together autonomy and heteronomy" (116). Pye's two essays in the collection, the "Introduction" and his piece on *King Lear*, are underwritten by the same conjunctive logic, although in his case the adversative formula "A (autonomy) *but* B (heteronomy)" seems more appropriate: "aesthetics is a philosophical procedure founded over and against itself, one that repeatedly undoes [through heteronomy] the ideology [of autonomy] it enables" (5); "the play unsettles [through heteronomy] the story of political-aesthetic origination [of autonomy] it sets forth" (15); "Such a figural and material aesthetic resists [through heteronomy] secularization even it symptomizes it [as autonomy]" (17); "the aesthetic concerns the way in which a discursive field institutes itself 'from within,' as it were, instituting its limits [as autonomy] in precisely the movement by which it exceeds itself [through heteronomy]" (48). The overall impression is that of a nicely done deconstructive exercise in which an aporetic contradiction is exposed. But on close inspection the argument appears to be flawed. Pye assumes that phenomenal objectification is a required entailment of art's autonomy, and this assumption is possibly prompted by his faith in "Rancière's exploration of the communal dimensions of phenomenal experience" ("Introduction" 3). For how communally and politically constituting can the dissolution—not distribution—of the sensible be? Can a better polity of equals gather at Dover, as apostolic witnesses Gloucester's sublime infinity and Edgar's demonic vision? I doubt it.

In the very remarkable essay that Christopher Pye contributes to the collection he edits, titled "'No cause, no cause': *King Lear* and the Space of the World," the rational idea is that of sovereignty, and Shakespeare's tragedy is read as an implicit attempt to flesh it out through aesthetic means that work, consciously or not, to undo this very intention. Implied in his argument is both the assumption that political sovereignty is an aesthetic concept within a field (politics) that is also already "a field of representation" ("Introduction" 1) and therefore aesthetically scripted, if not constituted, and the claim that *King Lear* posits itself as a cultural object informed by the aesthetic operation of abolishing phenomenality at the very moment it is *presented* for (political) action. The impasse of phenomenalization that Pye detects in *King Lear* would be a negative consequence of the play's drive to an autonomy, that comes with the vengeance of mimetic exigencies—the *aesthetic ideas*. But is this requirement of aesthetic-phenomenal *fullfilment* something operative in Shakespeare's art and in Adorno's vision of art? I doubt it too.

Terry Eagleton rightly called attention to the paradox that Marx "is accused of being outdated by the champions of a capitalism rapidly reverting to Victorian levels of inequality" (*Why Marx* 3). Likewise, Derrida is accused of being outdated by the champions of phenomenological-and-moralistic ideological practices that revert to Victorian levels of aesthetic sentimentalism, by those who, for all their "phenomenological" professions, are more led by "assurance morale" than by metaphysical "certitude" (Descartes, *Meditationes* 27). The strong interest in visual art shared by some phenomenology-inclined readers of Shakespeare—scholars like Lupton, Kottman, even Greenblatt—shows how relevant the *ästhetische Erziehung* remains for anyone intending to prove that, despite its occasional squalor, Shakespeare *imagined* a world that is "more fairer than fair, beautiful than beauteous, truer than truth itself" (*Love's Labour's Lost* 4.1.63). In the "Introduction" to *The Insistence of Art*, Kottman comments on the way "artworks and practices of the early modern period show the essentiality of aesthetic experience for philosophical reflection" (2). The "essentiality"? Is this Rancière's "ontology of art"? I don't think so. Kottman uses essentiality as the quality or state of being essential, that is, extremely important and necessary. But he could have picked another word, for his choice evinces a potential "phenomenological" (in both senses, Hegelian and Husserlian) inflection of his observation: art simultaneously supplies philosophy with new "essences" (imaginative ideas, noemata, intentional contents) and, more importantly, exhibits (fulfils) those essences in the show and *Schein* of aesthetic representation. What is lost, again, is the dialectical work of concepts, the dissemination of signifiers, the instance and insistence of the letters. Thus Kottman's comment, whose validity is endorsed by Lupton in a review, draws part of its force from the scarcely accidental juxtaposition of essentiality and aesthetics. The force indeed of Kottman's and Lupton's work on Shakespeare stems too from their reluctance to concede that such overlap betrays the bankrupt fiction denounced by de Man as *aesthetic ideology*—the *aesthetic* springing from the Schillerian misappropriation of Kant, with the dialectical moment utterly effaced, and *ideology* being "the confusion of linguistic with natural reality, of reference with phenomenalism" (*Resistance* 11). This is de Man replying to M. H. Abrams:

> But there is a dialectic, there is only dialectical force when there is encountered a negation; that is, the labor of the negative is absolutely essential to the concept of the dialectical. It is there in Kant, it is there in Fichte in a complicated way, it is there certainly in Hegel. It is not there in Schiller, to the extent that the harmony is not to be disturbed, to the extent that the opposites [...] are to compose with each other in a way which is not mediation, which is not certainly a negation of the one by the other.
>
> *Aesthetic* 157

The immediate composition of form and content—the forcing of the formal soul to its conceit (*Hamlet* 2.2.486)—is the keystone of an aesthetic ideology of representation, implied by Kant in the notion of concordance (*Übereinstimmung*), is now advocated by Lupton and Kottman, who emphasize the delights of hylomorphic reciprocity and symbolic congruence. In Shakespeare and Hegel "content and form are realized together'" writes Lupton in her review of Kottman, apparently unbothered by the scandal of such pragmatic confluence. She forgot to say that they are realized together in a synthetically (*synthetisch*) harmonious (*einstimmig*) fashion (Husserl *Cartesianischer* 144). If content and form are jovially realized together, then two questions arise. The fist, with Yeats, how can we know the dancer from the dance? There would be no way, and this undecidability sharply contrasts with Lupton's and Kottman's resolve to establish that the dancer (the intentional content: the pastoral polity of friends and shared personal freedom) comes first, and is fulfilled in the dance. The second, what is the point of modernist art?[11] Why didn't art stop at the stage of Virgil's *Georgics*, of Racine's *Phèdre* or of Goethe's *Romischen Elegien*? Why didn't art, that thing of the past, pull the break at one of those glorious neoclassical stages? Why did Shakespeare go on writing after something so disarmingly perfect as *Julius Caesar*? Go on, that is, to produce something so unspeakably imperfect but perfectly disarming and brilliant as *Antony and Cleopatra*? Only for money? Let me rephrase these questions: why did romantic and post-romantic writers decide, in general, with exceptions, to favour disharmony over harmony, discordance over concordance, indeterminacy over closure, and analysis over synthesis? Why did so many relevant Western writers of that period return to the Shakespeare of the great tragedies and late romances for inspiration? To see "content and form realized together"? Come on. The (aesthetic) peace resulting from the common realization of content (the manifold of intuition) and form (schematism, categories, concepts) serves merely to occlude the tension—the fissures and frictions, the antagonism—tending all occurrences, so common in Shakespeare's "experience," of temporalized mediation. Reflecting on Kant's debts to Rousseau, Dieter Henrich singles out the part of the priest from Savoy's profession of faith that starts with "observations on predicaments faced in a morally oriented human life: our conscience requires a certain order of things that is constantly violated by the course of the world" (Henrich, *Aesthetic Judgement* 11). So *tant pis* for the world, is the reaction of the aesthetic critic, blind to the fact that "the course of the world"—never "a certain order of things"—is what really counts for Shakespeare, and that this course, rife with antagonism and dissent, discordance, and semblance, maps a place where "wicked persons succeed and flourish whereas the just man remains repressed and persecuted" (Henrich, *Aesthetic Judgement* 11). Maps, that is, inside comedy, a tendentially tragic space, both unphenomenal and unamenable to harmonious phenomenalization. An anti-pastoral space where, for

---

11 I recommend the reading of de Man's analysis of the Yeats line in "Semiology and Rhetoric" (1973).

instance, Adonis is molested by Venus: a place therefore that is, as Empson suggests, characterized by an impressiveness and final solidity that turn, in the last instance, "upon not being 'nice'" (*Essays* 5). In Lockean logic, "it is a duty to seek peace, not a duty to deny the lessons of experience" (Dunn 59). Nor should we deny the findings of critical analysis: according to Kant, the powers of the mind (the separate faculties of sensibility and judgement) constitute an aggregate and not a system. Any attempt to cancel such distinction and bring about a fusion, a bid commonly made in the name of *Bildung*, results in the metaphysical absolutism described by Cutrofello:

> The idea of a being for whom sensibility and understanding would not be distinct faculties is the idea of a being for whom possibility and actuality would coincide, which is to say that, for such a being, nothing would exist but the necessary. Thus we can only ascribe intellectual intuition (such as we are capable of thinking it at all) to a being whose own existence would have to be cognized as necessary (CPJ 272–3). In other words, we can only ascribe it to a divine knower.
>
> *Continental Philosophy* 14

Call this knower Shakespeare, his continuously-created-known world the Shakespeare world. And call lesser knowers aspirants to this intellectual intuition. The upshot reflects the situation of aesthetic-phenomenological critics kneeling before the idol of *esse est necesse*. Theirs is a critical medium where essences, intentional contents and noemata would spontaneously spring in the mind, Shakespeare's capacious mind, awaiting the fulfilment that only aesthetic representation can grant. In the section on spontaneism I already anticipated the hermeneutic relevance of an intellectual intuition that Werner Pluhar describes in the following way:

> Such an understanding's intuition would thus not be a mere receptivity (which is passive), and hence not a sensibility as our intuition is, but would be an *intellectual* intuition, a complete *spontaneity* (i.e., it would be completely active): it would determine objects completely. It would not require for this determination (and cognition) a harmony between itself and some other, separate cognitive power (an imagination dealing with a passive intuition), but would determine objects in terms of the harmony within this understanding itself.
>
> "Introduction" to Kant, *Critique of Judgement* XCII

A complete spontaneity, like Juliet's maiden blush. The theological motif of spontaneous creation finds support in Lupton's celebration of the "affective territory shared by art with religion," a territory, to be sure, greatly compromised by the allegorical discontinuities of the scriptural tradition.[12] This Lupton knows well, but her recent work seems to mollify tropic ruggedness, to overlook hermeneutic antagonism and abate unrest. From the sublime new deal to an ethics of performance and a phenomenology of human action, ruled by the motif of the "multimedia performance space" (Lupton, "*Macbeth's* Martlets" 367), is a very short step. Lupton asks us to look for hospitality, both as a theatre of persons and a theatre of things—something like Latour's "Parliament of Things," but with things that "talk" (*We Have Never* 144)—in the "local traffic patterns and transcendental convocations of Shakespearean drama" (367). No reference to the playtext.[13] In fact, the playtext is rather surprisingly the only thing that fails to talk in this phenomenal talk show. The argument is clogged with terms like "environment," "affection," "entertainment," and, more importantly, "transcendental." Let me quote in full the eloquent description of her "phenomenological" project:

> Hospitality, I argue, is at once *a theater of persons and a theater of things*; indeed, it hosts these two dimensions of phenomenological access and asks them to break bread together. The ritual scripts, spatial routines, object inventories, and physical settings of hospitality integrate the sensible and the ethical platforms, as well as the historical and transcendental aspects of the phenomenological project, within a single environment of entertainment. Hospitality is a sequence of sociosymbolic actions that links the world of objects and the provisional persons who tend them (including women, servants, and children) to dramatic action. Phenomenological analysis calls us to unlock (not simply to analyze, but also to perform and reinvent) the affective labor, self-disclosing risks, and creaturely dependencies disclosed by hospitality events as they are themselves invited to appear in the local traffic patterns and transcendental convocations of Shakespearean drama. (367)

---

12   An essay by Victoria Kahn moves Lupton to raise the question: "Is the aesthetic necessarily the insistence of art against religion, or does the aesthetic also allow the affective territory shared by art with religion to insist and persist in new ways?" ("Review" 282).

13   The attention posthumanist critics give to the Shakespeare text also tends to be minimal, but they depend more on the playtext's semiotic encryption of the way the human subject dissolves before the nonhuman other: Raber actually alludes to "what matters in a given text" (94), which reveals a salutary hermeneutic deference.

The use of the adjective "transcendental" is a bit confusing. In the first occurrence, the phrase "transcendental aspects of the phenomenological project" appears orthodox enough, but the context of enunciation and the co-occurrence of the phrase "transcendental convocations," and the initial claim about "phenomenological access," presumably to persons and things, leaves little room for doubt. In the term transcendental, Lupton amalgamates the meanings of the terms "transcendent," implying the "physical settings" of actual, empirical persons and things, and "transcendental" in the sense of "supernatural." The latter meaning is confirmed by the copresence of two factors. First, the "Heaven's breath" in the *Macbeth* lines she examines. And second, the allusion to the gods in the final paragraph: "Hospitality is phenomenology as social theater: a way of soliciting and orchestrating forms of appearing that gather humans, objects, and animals, as well as deities and dust bunnies" (373). Phenomenology is here used as a methodological pretext to legitimate a very simple goal: "to integrate the sensible and the ethical platforms." The other pretext is, alas, Shakespeare's text. Lupton is only interested in the ethical payoff her aesthetic redescription of a *Macbeth* scene in terms of the distribution of the sensible may deliver. And she reads the scene, and by synecdochic extension the entire play, as a set of objectal-human materials in thrall to an organizing aesthetic idea of "entertainment." This aesthetic idea, in turn, would provide the *rational idea* (Kant) of hospitality (we would call it an ethical trope) a local habitation and a name: "theatre." At bottom, Lupton's interpretation—the idea that *Macbeth* realizes the conditions of theatre—is quite original, but the problem is that it is carried out in near-total abstraction of the playtext. From the intentional content of hospitality (the rational-ethical idea) we rush to the convocation of things and persons (the intentional objects) that, under the law of a rite of entertainment (the aesthetic idea), which law amounts to the form-content concordance (*Übereinstimmung*), convene the interactive encounter (theatre) that defines their newly realized (fulfilled) aesthetic-political identity: they become the (intentional and fulfilled) process of their own becoming. Thus described in phenomenological terms, the interpretation gains a kind of inelegant complexity that is absent, however, from Lupton's critical formulation, which inclines to stylistic virtuosity. All in all, what we get is a traditional allegorical reading, with the trope of hospitality mechanically superimposed on a playtext that recedes, unheeded, with the bat, "in cloistered flight" (*Macbeth* 3.2.42). I will examine the second version of this same essay in some detail in the next section. For now, let me insist on the fact that what goes missing in Lupton's energetic and eloquent invitation to join in an—embodied, represented, performed—party called *Macbeth* that unfolds exclusively in the critic's mind eye—is of course the very text *Macbeth*, and its attending bat. The distinction between the transcendental and the transcendent was, let me recall, for Husserl, "the most fundamental distinction of Being [*die radikalsten aller Seinsunterscheidungen*]," meaning ontological distinction (*Ideas I* 146). The "Santa Casa" whose *heiligen Registern* is charted in Lupton's phenomenology of domus-oriented hospitality—itself a revival of the ancient "neighbourhood self-government" still alive in Locke's vision of English local administration—thus supplies the domestic *Logik* orienting most returns of phenomenology: they speak about the planet but mean their front garden, speak about zombies and mean their toaster, prattle about non-human exceptionalism with their dog in mind and cat on lap.[14]

"Family, faith, flag, neighbourhood, and, for some at least, white privilege": these were, according to Barack Obama, the five ingredients of American conservatism at the end of the 1960s (*Audacity* 29). Interestingly, three of these ingredients (family, faith, neighbourhood) remain the tenets around which turns much of today's phenomenological and political-theology oriented criticism of early modern literature. This is not to say that neighbour-minding and hospitality-oriented critical imaginaries are inherently conservative. This is just to say that the phenomenology underwriting the turn to political theology is overdetermined with the *Sittlichkeit* ideologemes of civic-life religion of the common and the shared, a mode of faith not exactly untroubled by the phantoms of *Eigentlichkeit*:

> Ideality, the product of *Aufhebung*, is thus an onto-economic 'concept.' The eidos, philosophy's general form, is properly familial. It produces itself as oikos: house, habitation, apartment, room, residence, temple, tomb, hive, possessions, family, race, etc. If there is a common same in all this, it is the guardianship over the 'proper': which retains and inhibits, consigns absolute loss or consumes it only the better to watch it return into self, even as the repetition of death. Spirit is the other name of this repetition.
>
> DERRIDA, *Glas* 152

In Hegelese, Spirit is the "affective territory shared by art and religion" (Lupton, "Review," 282), a territory marked by oikos-nomic categories like "house, habitation, apartment, room, residence, temple, tomb, hive, and family"—implicitly or openly omnipresent in Lupton's book and other similar phenomenological criticism. I have removed "possessions" and "race" from Derrida's list, to avert

---

14   In the *Critique of Hegel's Philosophy of Right*, Marx ridicules the "holy register of the Santa Casa (the Logic)" (15), referring to Hegel's *Logic*. For neighborhood self-government see Mark Goldie, "Introduction," p. xxv.

the perilous threats of possessive individualism and racist communitarianism. But does this mean that the remaining categories are totally harmless. I fear not. Fascination with these figures, a common feature of Levinas' philosophical prose, spells a turn away from deterritorialization (*érrance*, dissemination, *Heimatlosigkeit*) towards reterritorialization. And this turn betrays the sacred nostalgia (*Heimkehr*) that Heidegger found in Hölderlin's poetry. In his essay on Derrida's *Spectres de Marx*, Fredric Jameson warned against the demarxification of aesthetics, marked by an inevitable return to religion, to the "religion of art" as the new "religions of the polis" (*Valences* 170). The latter phrase—*religions of the polis*—perfectly captures the destination of Kottman's and Lupton's religion of art. Shakespeare's secular text holds an uncertain middle place in between both extremes. If read, they are used for illustration of an allegorical idea, the*aesthetic idea*. The mediation of allegory is fully absorbed into the consonances of symbolic diction. No tropic leak, no contingent leftover, no material remainder, no dissonance escapes. Mediation becomes immediacy, and the Baroque *Trauerspiel* becomes a Swinburne poem.

6

Lupton and Kottman share a conception of art that is eminently representational in that allows for the re-instantiation of presence—to call it *presentational* would not be a disservice. The presence of the other—here, the work of art—is contingent on the ability of this other to travesty its dubious nature into some form of figurative—if possible, personified—presentation. Once formal dissonance is properly discounted, and fragmentation resynthesized, once the other-object is transmogrified into a convenient—harmonious—other, that is, into another as the other of the critic, then a set of analogical transferences ruled by an unfailing intentionality will make sure this other is brought—home—into the appropriate appropriation of the critic's (present to herself) property. No mediation obstructs the flow of intention. There is simply no room, in this expressive traffic, for text-based ideological interference.[15] Only translucid self-analogies ground this immediate transaction, and the critic's self serves as original *Ich-pole* because she apprehends "the originality of something included in [her] particular ownness [*die Originalität*

---

15   The *fils intentionnelles* (Merleau-Ponty, *Phénoménologie* 100, 115) secure the continuous connexion—"un courant d'existence" (116)—between *l'être au monde* and its *entourage* or life-horizon. Merleau-Ponty speaks of an "adhésion prépersonnelle à la forme générale du monde" (113).

des Eigentlichkeiten], something directly accessible [*direct Zugänglichen*] in original explication of [*her*] own self [*durch ursprungliche Auslegung meiner selbst*]" (Husserl, *Cartesianische* 152). Recall Lupton's claim that phenomenology grants "access," and my related question: why read *Hamlet* at all if you believe you are Hamlet? The answer: I do Shakespeare because I do myself, I know Shakespeare because I know myself, I think with Shakespeare because I think. To be sure, this feat of self-transparency is unknown to many critics, not only of a liberal tradition (Wilson, Matthiessen, Levin, Trilling, Marcus) awash in Freud or Dostoevsky, but also of a speculative-dialectical tradition, scholars acquainted with the work of Lacan, Adorno, Foucault, Althusser, Deleuze and Derrida. I am talking of scholars, in short, who turned to literary texts because they did not know themselves, and, more importantly, because they knew that literature would not give them the answer. Literature, for them, was a matter of questions, not of answers. It is hard to conceive of critics like Sedgwick, Goldberg, Bersani, Jameson, or Spivak stating or implying that they *possess* an original *explication* (*Auslegung*) of their own selves. Listen to Foucault: "I am no doubt not the only one who writes in order to have no face. Do not ask who I am and do not ask me to remain the same: leave it to our bureaucrats and our police to see that our papers are in order. At least spare us their morality when we write." (*Archeology* 17).[16] *Spare us their morality*.

That is all very nice in (French) theory, the aesthetic-moral scholar of the religions of the polis may reply. But when I am transfixed by the assurance that I know myself and celebrate my home and sing my pets, then there is no denying Shakespeare's "prodigal portion" (*As You Like It* 1.1.32), because his gift "[confirms] the crown to me and to my heirs" (*3 Henry VI* 1.1.173). There arises, amid the glories of self-confirming joy, a fast-withdrawal-no-receipt mode of drawing the bard plays' richness. Multiple cash withdrawal options are devised that leave no written trace behind once the aesthetic transaction is completed. The play's embodied visual bounty is absorbed without residue or remain, without unassimilated remnant. No words are necessary when form and content coincide, the latter effectuating, achieving, fulfilling—Husserl would say *erfüllen* (*Cartesianischer* 144)— the former and exposing it as a temporary distraction. The progress of the phenomenological critic who scans the Shakespeare thing—be it a noematic dress rehearsal, an intentional presentation or the objective representation, the real phenomenal performance—is a

---

16   In the original we read: "Plus d'un, comme moi sans doute, écrivent pour avoir plus de visage. Ne me demandez pas qui je suis et ne me dites pas de rester le même: c'est une moral d'état-civil; elle régit nos papiers. Qu'elle nous laisse libre quand il s'agit d'écrire" (*L'archéologie* 28).

fulfilling and verifying progress. This fulfilling process or progress—Husserl's "erfüllend Fortgang" (*Cartesianische* 144)—is the opposite of a hermeneutic *Auslegung*: whereas the former synthesizes (fuses), the latter analyses (separates). The foreign, strange body of the Shakespeare thing is assimilated through strategies of analogic transference that reel out in a synthetic (*synthetisch*) and concordant or harmonious (*einstimmig*) manner (*Cartesianische* 144). The problem, again, is concordance (*Übereinstimmung*), and the mad critical attempt to mend what in Shakespeare is fractured, to join what is disjoint, to musicalize what is very often "*a strange, hollow, and confused noise*" (*The Tempest* 4.1.143).[17] Rather than allowing the strange body of the Shakespeare thing to remain an inaccessible and strange entity (original *Unzugänglichen*) prescribing an unfulfillable experience (*unerfüllbaren Erfahrung*), the phenomenological critic inhabits the illusion that such experience is attainable because the thing is originally self-given (*original selbstgebenden*). *Thinking with Shakespeare*, *Doing Shakespeare*—these books are belied however by their phenomenological greed to appropriate the strange and familiarize the other under the delusion that the strange-other is in fact right there as a *presence* we can think with, perform with or dwell in, by means of corporal actions, fractions, interactions. Analytical or deconstructive reading (*Auslegung*) is discarded as ultra-formalist meandering and traded for fulfilling progress (*Fortgang*). The Shakespeare thing becomes a "non-originary presentation within the sphere of my ownness [*Vergegenwärtigungen in meiner eigentlichen Sphäre*]" (Husserl, *Cartesianische* 145). Under the auspices of Husserl's playful handling of the term *Paarung* (pairing)—he speaks of a contrastive pairing (*kontrastierende Paarung*) between original body and perceived body, between ego and alter ego (*Cartesianische* 141–5)—I here propose another title for a daring scholar to flesh out: *Making out with Shakespeare*. Or, more chastely, *Flushing with Shakespeare*.

7

The critical operation of cashing in the phenomenal cheques Shakespeare incessantly delivers hinges on the figure, familiar to admirers of Martin Luther King, of the unfulfilled contract:

---

17   Much has been said about music, voice, and rumour in Shakespeare, but a critical study of "noise" in his plays and poems (its connection with what Levinas calls "war" and Derrida "polemos," for instance) has not yet been written, I think. Adorno would be a good guide for that study.

> The most enlightened epistemology still participates in the myth of the first in the figure of the contract which is never fulfilled and therefore in itself endless, self-repeating without respite. Its metacritique presents it with its promissory note and forces from it the external insight, gained from society, that equivalence is not truth and that a fair trade-off is not justice. The real life process of society is not something sociologically smuggled into philosophy through associates. It is rather the core of the contents of logic itself.
>
> ADORNO, *Against Epistemology* 26

Adorno insists here on the unconscious of capitalist reification that undergirds, and ultimately undoes, the abstractions of transcendental-epistemological philosophy. He thus follows a path of demystification first broken by Hegel, Marx, and Nietzsche. And like his three forerunners, Adorno is particularly sensitive to the way in which the tropological investment of philosophy betrays its unconscious subservience to the infrastructures of myth (Hegel), real history (Marx) or moral-religious culture (Nietzsche). Thus, Husserl's unwitting construal of epistemology "analogously to a legal contest" is revealed in his use of "archaizing supplements from the language of law, such as 'demesne' (*Domäne*) and 'endowment' (*Stiftung*)" (26). Mercutio's conjuring of Romeo showcases a comparable demystification:

> The ape is dead, and I must conjure him.
> I conjure thee by Rosaline's bright eyes,
> By her high forehead and her scarlet lip,
> By her fine foot, straight leg, and quivering thigh
> And the demesnes that there adjacent lie,
> That in thy likeness thou appear to us.
>
> ROMEO *and* JULIET 2.1.16–21

Rosaline's phenomenal-aesthetic, perhaps sublime, superstructure (bright eyes, high forehead, scarlet lip) is gradually undone by elements of a sequence that have manifestly crossed the line, moving down to the infrastructural unconscious: fine foot, quivering leg, "and the demesnes that there adjacent lie." These demesnes are to *Romeo and Juliet*'s idealized erotoscape what the bat is to *Macbeth*'s soft ecology of martlets: a disruptive pharmakon, a material supplement that threatens to undo the generic symmetries of these two uncanny comedies. In Mercutio's homosocial logic, this (feminine) domain (*demesne*) also *lies* because it is untrue to the passion he expects, and deserves, from Romeo, perhaps also untrue to Romeo's desire. But in phenomenological logic, the absolute, and absolutely unfulfillable, irrepresentable, and unphenomenal givenness of these demesnes symbolize both the inexhaustible bounty of libido and the affluence of estates-rooted capitalist accumulation. Mercutio is a materialist because he calls attention to these two infrastructural reserves, and because he is very much alert to the odds of exhaustion—both sexual and economic. Phenomenological critics, by contrast, construe the Shakespearean demesne as protected by contract against consumption—without positive fulfillment (*Erfüllung*) or negative draining-out. They consequently erase it, and move on to phenomenalize other, more accessible funds, or pliable contents. What place is given to real demotic sex—the crude affair of open *et caeteras* and *poperin pears*—and to the contingent play of the arbitrary signifier—to the wild instance of the letter—that invariably constitutes it, in the aesthetic readings of *Romeo and Juliet* produced by Kottman and Lupton? None. Mercutio is absent from their readings, and if you discount Mercutio you completely misrepresent the text, because bad man (perhaps batman) Mercutio *is* the text—in one of the sources (Bandello) he literally mediates the hand-holding encounter scene in the Capulet party, thus preventing immediate fusion from ever taking place, and confirming Lacan's wild formula that the sexual relation doesn't exist. If you really want *aesthetic fulfilment* to prevail, you don't wait until act 3 to kill Mercutio. You simply deny him access to the play.

Lacan reminded his seminar audience that, according to Kabbalah, the designation of one of the modes of divine manifestation was identified with the *pudendum*, i.e. the *demesne*: "Il serait tout de même extraordinaire que, dans un discours analytique, ce soit au *pudendum* que nous nous arrêtions. Les fondements ici, sans doute, prendraient la forme de dessous, si ces *dessous* n'était pas déjà quelque peu à l'air " (*Les quatre* 14). With the assistance of *un discours analytique* we could also stop at the pudendum (the demesne, the nothing) that there adjacent lies. In his extraordinary readings of *Romeo and Juliet*, Jonathan Goldberg has indeed started to do exactly that. His deconstructive *Auslegung* of *Coriolanus* conducted literally through Caius Marcius' *anus* is another brilliant exercise in de-phenomenalization.[18]

Refusal to bear in mind the negative dimension of Shakespeare's contingent and signifier-bound poetics—its reluctance to become transposed into a visual aesthetics of imaginative synthesis and actor-network reconciliation—provokes an interesting critical slippage. Can we see Rosaline's nothing and Coriolanus' anus? I myself am not even interested (Mine is rather

---

18   See the essays, "'What? in a names that which we call a Rose': The Desired Texts of *Romeo and Juliet*," "Romeo and Juliet's Open Rs," and "The anus in Coriolanus" in *Shakespeare's Hand*.

the kind of perversion that makes me see Orielan(u)s where others read Rosaline: I am sorry). To use an Adorno antithesis, the phenomenological critic reads Shakespeare as Tchaikovsky or Stravinsky rather than as Schoenberg (Jameson, *Marxism and Form* 31–32), Shakespeare as ballet in lieu of atonal Shakespeare. The first option delivers a mode of false (undialectical) reconcilement, described in *Negative Dialectic* as follows:

> Reconcilement would release the nonidentical, would rid it of coercion, including spiritualized coercion; it would open the road to the multiplicity of different things and strip dialectics of its power over them. Reconcilement would be the thought of the many as no longer inimical, a thought that is anathema to subjective reason. (6)

It would be anathema because the many and the different and the multiple are necessarily "inimical" in that they cannot be ontologically or phenomenally reconciled in an aesthetic figure of concordance and entertainment or in an ethical-rational figure of mutuality or hospitality. Only a conventional, arbitrary, empty decision to reconcile can institute equality and universality in a field (the ontic material field) where everything is unequal and particular. Through force of (empty) law—as empty as nothing. We call that legal-political reconcilement, and we go on living, if we can, a less than good life. Phenomenal (moral-aesthetic) reconcilement is a less necessary fiction—the motion picture titled *The Best Life*, featuring mutuality and hospitality as best actor and actress (rational ideas), and entertainment and reconciliation as supporting actor and actress (aesthetic ideas)—and it is dangerous because it trades for natural what is also conventional. Kottman and Lupton idealize and sacralize the phenomenalized matter of Shakespeare, into which anyone is free to tap into and snack on. Scandalized with the academic idealistic glorification of the bard, they respond with strategies of standard demeaning commodification. In doing so, they are unwittingly, I believe, sheltering Shakespeare from thinkers like Marx, Nietzsche and Freud, described by Althusser as "naturals" or "bastards"—"enfants 'naturels,' au sens où la nature offense les moeurs, le bon droit, la morale et le savoir-vivre" ("Freud et Lacan," *Écrits sur la psychanalyse* 26).

Brian Vickers prophesized, we have seen, that phenomenology would outlive deconstructive formalism. He also had a soft spot for form-content reconcilement, and for moving *Bilder*—the Shakespeare *motion pictures*. In fact, in an approving review of *Appropriating Shakespeare*, Grace Tiffany states that "'aesthetic' is another word which Vickers restores to dignity by pointing to its humanistic as well as its artistic signification" (253). So the show's not over.

Sit down and relax. But recall that the lights will only go off when Ferdinand Derrida, invited by the usher to leave, exits the projection room with a book inside his raincoat pocket, the smoking pipe inside the other. Adorno waits for them outside, under the queer tragic rain, with a bat on his left shoulder. He touches his inside pocket to check that he carries the dagger, confirms it is not there, and mutters to himself, "dagger, dagger, dagger." The bat repeats the same words, in the same order. He greets his friends with a smile and says, this time in German, "*Wird sie strikt ästhetisch wahrgenommen, so wird sie ästhetisch nicht recht wahrgenommen.*"[19] They walk down a dirty wet street. The noise of passing traffic becomes gradually louder. Fade to black. The end.

---

19 The sentence is taken from *Ästhetische Theorie*, 17. The meaning is: "Art perceived strictly aesthetically is art aesthetically misperceived" (*Aesthetic Theory* 6).

CHAPTER 18

The Fallacy of Representation

1

Did Macbeth say "dagger"? There is no need to go back to the text, we could even give up the speech and have the actor mime it. If you read "dagger," and he says "dagger," he obviously meant "dagger." What is this whole fuss about? Make sure the fucking dagger goes on stage and find a way to make it hang. And don't forget to release the martlet when Banquo speaks at 1.6. This is not intended as a parody. Many similar requests must have been made by stage directors in productions of *Macbeth*. And good for them, for no one is asking them to produce *critical readings* of the play. The problem only arises when the critical reader behaves as a stage or artistic director, assuming that Shakespeare and his people have already *imagined* (*vorgestellt*) in their minds, through intentional *presentation*, what it is now their task to *represent* (*vortstellen*) through *performance*. On this assumption, the critical work becomes the phenomenalization of intentional contents into intentional objects, with the proviso that the martlet is not to be hurt by the dagger, the best way to avoid which is to leave your copy of the play at home. This critical view, once regarded as naïve, is not unpopular today among Shakespeare scholars:

> What it authentic here is something that is not in the text; it is something behind it and beyond it that the text is presumed to represent: the real life of the characters, the actual history of which the action is a part, the playwright's imagination, or the hand of the master, the authentic witness of Shakespeare's own story. The assumption is that the texts are representations or embodiments of something else, and that it is that something else which the performer or editor undertakes to reveal.
>
> ORGEL, *Authentic* 256

Fortunately, this view doesn't go unchallenged. There have always been penetrating readers and perceptive witnesses alert to the many ways in which the playtexts manage "to evade or disrupt the space of representation" (Lukacher, *Primal* 229). On 31 December 1660, Samuel Pepys wrote in his diary:

> At the office all the morning. And after that home; and not staying to dine, I went out and in Paul's churchyard I bought the play of *Henry the*

fourth. And so went to the new Theatre (only calling at Mr. Crew's and eat a bit with the people there at dinner) and there saw it acted; but my expectation being too great, it did not please me, as otherwise I believe it would; and my having a book, I believe did spoil it a little. (105)[1]

"All that is fine in the play, was lost in the representation," wrote Hazlitt after attending a production of *A Midsummer Night's Dream*. And he went on to conclude: "Poetry and the stage do not agree together" (*Characters* 103). What Hazlitt called *the representation* is of course the theatrical performance of the play, but the term encompasses too the wider meaning of artistic likeness or image we associate with the mimetic arts. In his "Introduction" to his Penguin edition of the comedy, Stanley Wells underlined the undying relevance of Hazlitt's judgement. But he did so in 1967, when this sort of thing could be said without causing much stir. Today it would be inconceivable to open a critical edition of a Shakespeare play with a sneer at its stage life. Today, in fact, all that is fine in a play is located in the *representation*—be it the play's theatrical performance or its inherent mimetic qualities. Few or no scholars are interested in displaying the difference between being and being "in show" (*A Midsummer Night's Dream* 3.2.151).

In the "Introduction" to *Face-to-Face in Shakespearean Drama*, Julia Reinhard Lupton & Matthew James Smith use *The Winter's Tale* to illustrate a point:

> In other words, Leontes treats the face as static and absorptive rather than dynamic and reflective. The somatic and spatial contortions of the face—masquerading as retreats of the face—is particularly clear in Shakespearean ballet. Here the face appears as an articulation in itself, always on the cusp of but never crossing into verbal speech, and so relying forthrightly on the audience's active interpretation of gesture, prop, musical movement and pantomime. (4)

This is an expedient way of showing their hand: if the Shakespeare playtext doesn't deliver the desired *representation*, then it is both convenient and legitimate to move on to Shakespearean ballet where meanings never cross "into verbal speech." In other words, when, with a view to the "clear" representation, the playtext is not sufficiently de-textualized, then one may theatricalize it further by, for instance, choreographing it into ballet. Recall that Rancière greeted the "figures of community" (17) as so many instantiations of "the

---

[1] I want to thank Estrella Baena for calling my attention to this Pepys passage.

theatrical paradigm of *presence*" and characterized the Platonic conception of theatre as "the *choreographic* form of the community than sings and dances its own proper unity" (*Politics of Aesthetics* 14–17). The good thing, of course, about choreography is that it eliminates all memory of graphs. And this erasure proves as phenomenal as the theatrical piece in *Nicholas Nickleby*, with "a characteristic dance by the characters, and a *castanet pas seul* by the Infant Phenomenon" (627). Lupton's and Smith's argument is moreover attended by pragmatic *common sense*, a faculty that purportedly applies itself through "observational judgements in which subjects," here the two scholars and their trusting readers, "respond directly to perceptible states of affairs" (Brandom, *A Spirit of Trust* 111). We thus remain safely in the ground precincts of empirical immediacy.[2] Shakespearean pantomime or ballet (a certainly refined version of "entertainment") is posited as the asymptotic ideal—the *aesthetic idea*—for representation, and if the plays themselves don't work towards it—Smith's and Lupton's assumption is that some comedies and most romances do—then it is the critic's task to force the reduction, to efface speech and bring to surface, through sensuous representation, the intentional object—the phenomena intended by Infant Phenomenon Will Shakespeare. From noemata to phenomena without solution of continuity: this is the blessing of representative immediacy. There follows a predictable list of hermeneutic reparations: the plural theatrical response (an audience not a reader), the active intervention (the audience is not a passive admirer but an active designer of meaning), the relevance of the non-verbal (gesture, prop, music, movement, pantomime), etcetera. The choreographication of Shakespeare drama is also very much at work in Lupton's readings of *Romeo and Juliet*, where scenes are invariably read, following Lawrence Manley, "in a nearly musical sense" (qtd. in Lupton & Smith 8).[3] Lupton and Smith claim to be interested in the "larger philosophical questions raised by drama as an art form and by Shakespeare as a dramatic poet" (6), and in the wake of their claim they give us a definition of drama as an "art form" (6). They are right: drama is a distinct and distinguished art form. But drama designates only one way of responding to a playtext. Reading is another one, and they are not incompatible. The notion that we must choose between conceiving of Shakespeare as someone who wrote to be read and someone who

---

2 The Brandom quotation in the previous sentence is taken from the section on the "Two Senses of 'Immediacy'" of his recent book on Hegel (*A Spirit of Trust* 110–115).
3 See her "Introduction" to *Romeo and Juliet: A Critical Reader*, and the articles "'Cut him out in little stars': Juliet's Cute Classicism" and "Making Room, Affording Hospitality: Environments of Entertainment in Romeo and Juliet." Chapter 1 of her book *Shakespeare Dwelling* is an enlarged version of the second of these essays.

wrote to have his playtexts used in stage productions is false. In both cases the playtext is being *read*—in the first case silently by a lonely reader with the text in her hand, in the second case aloud by a group of people with the text in their minds. It is always reading, but the chances of mistaken phenomenalization are greater, of course, in the second case.[4] We call that mistake *drama*, and we enjoy it. I do.[5]

2

Paul Kottman has recently published a fascinating article on *The Winter's Tale* where he engages provocatively with Stanley Cavell's reading of this play. I will not go into the details of Kottman's argument, which, drawing heavily on Hegel's *Lectures on Art* and aided by visual materials (paintings and sculptures) is sophisticated and successful within the bounds of its own terms. The problem is this limitation, these terms. Kottman aims to prove that *The Winter's Tale* is an artistic work that prefigures (by enacting) Hegel's diagnosis about the end of art and its post-life as religion. And he proves it, to be sure, in the logic of his own argument. The fact that the logic is itself Hegelian lends an affable but vicious circularity to the whole affair. This is the limitation: Kottman fails to take distance from Hegelian aesthetics. At the beginning of the essay proper he announces: "In what follows, I also want to offer some thoughts about the inseparability of form and meaning in the trial scene of *The Winter's Tale*" ("Why Shakespeare" 186). Was the tortuous overcoming of formalist (structuralist, post-structuralist, deconstructive) methods solely aimed at this classical destination—*the inseparability of form and meaning*? Such *phenomenal* achievement is accomplished by accompanying Hegel along a narrative of spiritual self-presentation whose climax is the "[making] visible ([making] 'shine') the liveliness of subjectivity as self-relatedness," to make "human self-consciousness *affectively*, compellingly visible—in a 'lively' way," to permit that "self-related subjectivity," which is "the subject matter or content," be "sensuously grasped" (186). This climax is first aesthetic—Christian painting and sculpture are instanced—and subsequently religious. I will not consider here what the celebration of this climax occludes but let me recall

---

4 There are cases, of course, of mistaken phenomenalization in the first case: Don Quijote's experience is one such case.
5 Novels tend to be the (critical) chronicles of people who mistake their life for the mistake of drama. I enjoy them even more. See Peter Brooks' wonderful study, *The Melodramatic Imagination*.

that the co-implication of shine and *Schein* (as deception) is a contingency that Shakespeare constantly earmarks, and that we encounter it in his plays in the form of the duplicity of appearance.[6] The transit, in Hegel's argument, from art to religion is caused by the insufficiency of the former realm to fulfill "the task of sensuously embodying the logic of mutual subjectivity" (189). When this insufficiency or failure is inscribed in the artistic work as one of its compositional moments, then this work becomes instructive "with respect to the demands of 'the modern logic of social subjectivity'" (189). This is, Kottman argues, the case of Shakespeare's play. I will not discuss here the opportunity of extrapolating from Hegel's "modern logic" of social *Sittlichkeit* to the Renaissance period—his alibi (Shakespeare's foreshadows Hegel) is a persuasive hermeneutic presumption. The real problem involves the wayward application of aesthetic principles of form-and-content concordance and sensuous embodiment of the ideal—the *rational idea* of "mutual subjectivity"—to Shakespeare's particular version of Renaissance and Baroque art. The narrative of the anthropogenetic *phenomenology* of Spirit becomes at some advanced point self-reflectively anthropo-performative, and the form of art that best expresses the telos of spiritual freedom is "dramatic-poetic *presentation*" (emphasis added), which Hegel, according to Kottman, posits as the artistic form best suited to "manifest" painting's failure to "sensuously comprehend love as the logic of mutual subjectivity" (188–89). A teleology of artistic stages is outlined, according to which drama sublates painting by internalizing the latter's failure—the inability, that is, of "painting's *presentations*" (188, emphasis added) to *sensuously comprehend*. This turns The Winter's Tale into something of a dialectical sublation of painting, with "failure" dislodged and *sensuous comprehension* restored. The *picture* becomes *motion picture*. And although the very idea of motion bears dialectical implications, this restoration is an essentially non-dialectical affair, for *sensuous comprehension* is a contradiction in terms: in Kant, the *apperceptio comprehensiva* (*Zusammenfassung*) involves the application of at least one concept. Therefore, the mode of sublation enabled by sensuous comprehension is the undialectical trope of *reconcilement*. To make this reading possible, Kottman is forced to occlude the *literariness*—the *writtenness*—of the play-text and aggrandize past recognition its pictorial-figurative proportions. For

---

6 Since Hegel and Nietzsche, but very especially for Husserl and Heidegger, philosophy has been more or less anxiously resigned to put up with the givenness of appearance (*Schein*), of phenomena. But there are many ways of accommodating appearance, and not all of them are guided by the rational idea or moral trope of radical hospitality. Hegel points out that Hegel: "Shine, the 'phenomenon' of skepticism, and also the "appearance" of idealism, is thus this immediacy which is not a something nor a thing" (*Logic* 343).

all the play's strong investment in figurative art (Hermione's sculpture), the play is encoded in a natural language (English): the totality of its phenomenal (shining) possibilities of sensuous embodiment is therefore contingent on the (negative, differential, relational, arbitrary) instances of the English letter. The occlusion of literary textuality begins when Kottman grudgingly concedes that Hermione "speaks" lines 3.2.89–109 rather than wordlessly projecting her very (figurative) presence. "She does not appear, silently, as in a painting of the 'blissful' Madonna" (189), Kottman demurs. What a pity that Shakespeare characters are not silent! Their speechlessness would make the work of the phenomenological critic so much easier. Nothing reveals better Kottman's unconscious wish to reduce the play to a motion picture than this passing comment. But Shakespeare's play is not a mime, it is not even "dramatic-poetic presentation" in the aesthetic sense Kottman borrows from Hegel. *The Winter's Tale* is rather *poetic writing* and what is scripted therein should not be instrumentalized as the mere index to higher modes of phenomenal (re)presentation. Kottman's reading of Hermione's phrase "the flatness of my misery" as if it had been coined to mean the "two-dimensional picture of her state" (190) is simply preposterous. In Shakespeare's plays, the five adverbial occurrences of *flatly* convey the meaning of "absolutely" or "utterly" and *flat* is very often used to mean "absolute" and "stupid"—"flat rebellion" (*King John* 3.1.224), "flat treason" (*Love's Labour's Lost* 4.3.289), "flat blasphemy" (*Measure for Measure* 2.2.134), "flat transgression" (*Much Ado About Nothing* 2.1.193), "flat perjury" (*Much Ado About Nothing* 4.2.37), "flat burglary" (*Much Ado About Nothing* 4.2.46), "flat knavery" (*The Taming of the Shrew* 5.1.31). It is in the context of this usage that Hermione's phrase "the flatness of my misery" reads like a variation on the more standard formula, "my flat misery." As in the case of Scott Maisano's "ape," the instance of the letter is recalcitrant, inimical to facile attempts at content-form (signified-signifier) reconcilement that render phenomenal representation possible.

But let us probe deeper into the unsaid premises of Kottman's "philological" observation. To suggest that Hermione wished to impart "the two-dimensional picture of her state" presupposes her awareness of being a three-dimensional body. This is of course plausible within the parameters of realistic verisimilitude that the natural standpoint affords fictional characters, and more than viable if we decide as readers or playgoers to accept the phenomenology of the flesh that the natural standpoint permits. But if we, as readers, take distance from this standpoint, or altogether disconnect it, and remain accordingly inside the transcendental-formal horizon of one-dimensional signifiers, then it makes little sense to underline the relevance, to the meaning of *The Winter's Tale*, of three dimensions becoming two, of the sculpture becoming a picture. If you are seeing the play, you may notice the suggestion of that particular transformation (depth becoming flatness), but if you are reading it, or listening to it, then the suggestion loses some relevance. Remember that the play is *The Winter's Tale*, and that *tales* are written, told, read, and listened to. *Seeing the tale* is a phenomenological transgression examined by James in "The Turn of the Screw" and Conrad in *Heart of Darkness*. If we wish to *see* a winter's *tale*, we might need some deconstructive guidance: Shoshana Felman, Peter Brooks, J. Hillis Miller, Nicholas Royle. I am afraid Hegel is not enough. The current attempt to replace enlightened rationality with religious art promotes an inevitable demotion from *Thinking* to *Picture-thinking with Shakespeare*. The joint effect of Kottman's Hegelian-aesthetic approach and the attention to political theology in early modern studies revives the need, strongly felt by the Young Hegelians, to "sever the identification between philosophy and religion" (Cutrofello, *Owl* 60).

3

Lacan rightly accused Merleau-Ponty of haughtily forcing phenomenological research to restore the purity of the presence of an embodied *Dasein* (*la pureté de cette presence*) to the root of the phenomenon (*à la racine du phénomène*).[7] The overlap here of romantic-metaphysical tropes of root and purity, and phenomenological motifs of presence and phenomenon delivers the toxic blend that is so characteristic of Merleau-Ponty's reprogramming of Husserl's philosophy. Lacan ironically highlighted the wrong phenomenological resolve to affix onto the Heideggerian "l'Être-là" the "présence (ou Être-là) -dans-par-à travers-un-corps." This is exactly what Kottman turns Hermione into, a "presence (or There-being)-in-by-through-a-body" ("Merleau-Ponty: In Memoriam" 75). By focusing on "la presence par le corps" rather than on the instance of the letter, the original mediation (let us not call it givenness) of the playtext is radically overlooked:

> But it is clear that phenomenology, with its main emphasis on an analysis of perception, insofar as it is articulated within the obscure or lucid drive of the body [*la poussée obscure ou lucide du corps*], can never account for the privilege of the fetish in a secular experience nor for the castration

---

7 I quote from the essay "Maurice Merleau-Ponty" in http://espace.freud.pagesperso-orange.fr/topos/psycha/psysem/merleau.htm.

complex in the Freudian discovery. Yet, the two invite us to face the function of signifier of the organ [*la fonction de signifiant de l'organe*] that is always hinted at in a veiled way in the human statue [*le simulacre humaine*]. (77)

Is the function of the *signifiers* "the flatness of my misery" that Lacan is inviting us to consider from the standpoint of the secular fetish and the castration complex, the phrase? Well, if we accept both Kottman's suggestion and Lacan's invitation, then the result is that the signifier ineluctably steers (and strays) clear from the scene of the body, from the mock-body, from the simulacrum or statue. It may also be worth noting that the final truth lying behind all simulacra, bodies, statues, and appearances is *read* (not *seen*) midway through the play. Leontes asks the Officer to "Break up the seals and read," and later asks for confirmation, "Hast thou read truth?" (*The Winter's Tale* 3.2.136). Not much is seen at the end anyway, for the last scene consists of Paulina's art-expert description of the statue and performative spell, working as a meticulous voice-over account of the statue's apparent vivification, followed by a constant promise of more tales—spring tales, perhaps—that may help explain the apparent miracle.

Hegel argued that "ordinary life [*das gemeine Leben*] has no concepts, only representations of the imagination, and to recognize the concept in what is otherwise mere representation [*blosse Vorstellung*] is philosophy itself" (*Science of Logic* 628). Therefore to expose insubstantiality and baselessness in the fabric of our visions and to state that our little life is simultaneously inhabited by the "wide gap of time" (*The Winter's Tale* 5.3.155) and "rounded with a sleep" (*The Tempest* 4.1.158) is no doubt *die Philosophie selbst. The Winter's Tale* is no mere representation of ordinary life, but a philosophical tale. No mere phenomenal drama, but a critical story.[8]

4

But then, of course, drama is action, and this determination would appear to justify everything. The current sacralization of action among Shakespeare scholars, nominally bounden to Arendt, and only vaguely inspired in serious

---

8   The representative dramatization of action as action tends to efface the critical and speculative dimension that is always present in narration—the framing of plot, the estrangement of narrative voice, the perspectivism, the reflexive elaboration (commentary) of the pragmatic-diairetic, etc. See Fredric Jameson, *Valences* 31.

attempts (Sartre, Althusser) to revitalize practice and praxis as viable counter-ideological tools, risks losing sight of the fact that, as Lenin put it, there is spontaneity and spontaneity, action and action, there are *good actions* as well as *bad actions*, and a great deal of—Badiou reminds us—irrelevant *pseudo-actions* (Ruda, *For Badiou* 48).[9] Acting is one of them, and acting out the very essence of acting—a metadramatic *pli* that is very common in Shakespeare—betokens a defiantly ironic exercise of *mauvaise foi*, a concept, incidentally, that Sartre probably learnt from Hamlet.[10] The situationist slogan painted in May 1968 in the walls of the Sorbonne, *Ici, on spontane*, guarantees neither the social benefit of what is spontaneously generated through action nor its significance. But the new academic version of the old "snobbish and party-going anarchism" (Badiou, *Communist* 50) is here to celebrate the collective-founding affordances of Shakespeare's radical dramaturgy—what Althusser would have called "les promesses sacrées de l'intersubjectivité" (*Écrits sur la psychanalyse* 29). This is not far from what a young Badiou, commenting on the French academic "aristocraticism" before and during the events of 1968, called "the meticulous organization of ideological stupidity" (*Communist* 74). I personally take all this fuss about collective action and mutuality in Shakespeare to be an undiscerned version of the "leftist hermeneutics" (*Communist* 199) that Badiou himself despises. An example of this kind of hermeneutics can be found in Julia Lupton's parallel reading of *The Winter's Tale*, which focuses exclusively on the masquerade, Whitsun pastoral and Pentecostal script of the "sheep-shearing feast" (4.3.37) (*Shakespeare Dwelling* 210–220).

---

9   Despite such useful reminder, Badiou's often sinister political choices leave too many things in the dark. For instance, in an essay strenuously constructed as an apology of Mao's Cultural Revolution, he finds the time to deplore the excesses of the Red Guards—"the persecution of people of futile motives, a sort of assumed barbarism." And he adds the following sentence: "This is also an inclination of youth left to its own devices" (*Polemics* 307), which reads like the cynical wisdom of ultra-conservatives like Duke of Athens in *A Midsummer Night's Dream*. The phrase reappears in *The Communist Hypothesis*: "The Red Guards of the Cultural Revolution were—as young people so often do when they are left to their own devices and obey the herd instinct—already committing countless crimes ..." (17). This is—to say the least—an odd resort to basic group-psychology and crude anthropology (Badiou would dismiss them as discourse of empiricist humanism) for a thinker professedly pledged to the meta-ontological reduction of social realities. Besides, History gives us plenty of examples of "young people left to their own devices" in situations potentially conducive to an emancipatory politics that produced no deaths (May 68 in Paris, 15–May in Madrid).

10 The fictional situation Sartre examines in *L'être et le néant* (87–98) in order to explain the concept of *mauvaise foi* resembles closely, with the gender roles reversed, Hamlet's conversation with Ophelia in *Hamlet* 3.1.

THE FALLACY OF REPRESENTATION 511

In Mailer's *The Armies of the Night* (1967), the narrator describes the way a play is spontaneously generated through the interaction of some of the young men and women gathered in protest against the Vietnam War:

> Well, let us move on the hear the music. It was being played by the Fugs, or rather—to be scrupulously *phenomenological*—Mailer heard the music first, then noticed the musicians and the costumes [...] they were dressed in orange and yellow and rose colored capes and looked at once like Hindu gurus, French musketeers and Southern cavalry captains, and the girls watching them, indeed sharing the platform with them were wearing love beads and leather bells—sandals, blossoms and little steel-rimmed spectacles abounded and the music, no rather the play, had begun, *almost Shakespearean* in its sinister announcement of great pleasures to come.
>
> 481; emphases added

Lupton believes that the humanities can recover some of this pastoral spirit, and "help us learn how to rezone spaces, reorganize scripts and services, to reoccupy forgotten forms of life so that our settings for work and for dwelling afford more opportunities for acknowledgement, creativity, and action" (220). There is of course nothing sinister in that belief, but the way the desired reorganization and reoccupation may actually take place is another matter. Everything depends, of course, on the exact nature of the scripts and services chosen for resurrection.

The prestige of aesthetic representation in phenomenological scholarship is based, as I have pointed out, on the notion that the intentional content—a rational-ethical ideal or trope like mutuality or hospitality—is fulfilled in the embodied interactions of drama. The notion of embodiment, developed by Husserl in *Ideas I* and *Ideas II*, shifted from its solipsistic seclusion in "bodily selfhood [*leibhaftigen Selbstheit*]" (*Ideen*, "Allgemeine Einführung in die reine Phänomenologie" 15), through Merleau-Ponty's speculative correlation between corporality and alterity, to scenarios of interpersonal corporality—call it entertainment, call it dance. But the figurative-representational embodiment in the social scene of appearance—what Lupton calls "human appearing"—is predicated upon the redemptive and reconciliatory replenishment (*Erfüllung*) into phenomenal object of a meaning (*intentional content*) that is only incompletely given or symptomal in the signifier. Alone the phenomenal apparition can flesh this meaning out—through a correspondence between "content and form" (Hegel, Kottman) and "word and deed" (Arendt, Lupton, Kottman). The correspondence (*Überenstimmung*), of content and form, of the faculties of imagination and judgement, is an unscripted entertainment, a party, a dance. The critic's task is to provide a description of this dance, whence her role as Paulina, both enchanter and over-voice, perhaps *enchanting over-voice*, reporting on what she *believes* she *sees*. This is surely not the "immanent description" (*Ideas 1*, "Introduction" 2) Husserl demanded of phenomenology, but rather a transcendent description. Thinking with Shakespeare thus amounts to engaging the politics of his scene by entering the stage of representation, stalking his dwellings, breaking into them, reporting what happens—like Norman Mailer or Joan Didion, but without, of course, the critical distance. From a metaphysics of presence in Husserl, we moved to a metaphysics of copresence in Merleau-Ponty, and a new journalism is afoot with reporters giving us the facts of Shakespeare's "drama of proximity and co-presence," his "art of co-presence" (Smith and Lupton, "Introduction" to *Face-to-Face* 8).[11] Matthew Smith and Julia Lupton state that "Shakespeare's most powerful scenes of face-to-face encounter [...] restore co-presence between characters" (12). Very true and accurate, as critical report. But Kottman forgets to mention that Leontes does not hug Hermione, that it is Hermione that hugs him, that Leontes does not address Hermione or speak to her directly in the closing scene of the play, after the "resuscitation." I very much doubt there is co-presence or mutual recognition in that scene. When reference is made to the possibility of touching and holding hands, he recoils and claims to be satisfied with seeing and, more importantly, hearing what Paulina has to say about his wife. In fact, the final, crowning, recognition occurs between Leontes and Paulina.

5

Commenting on an epistolary remark by Cezanne, Derrida observes that "il écrit, dans un langage qui ne montre rien. Il ne donne rien à voir, ne décrit rien, représente encore moins " (*La vérité en peinture* 7). So a *tale told* by an idiot, full of this and that, *representing nothing*. For Adorno, the similarity between good philosophy and good art springs from their shared respect of and fidelity to their contents, which in both cases are grasped oppositionally, "art by making itself resistant to its meanings [*gegen ihre Bedeutungen*], philosophy by refusing to clutch at any immediate thing [*kein Unmittelbares*]" (*Negative Dialectic*

---

11 The first phrase appears in the one-sentence description of the book in the Publisher's website. For copresence see also Lupton, *Shakespeare Dwelling*, 15, 82.

15, 27). So a tale told, meaning nothing, clutching at no immediate thing. These are of course Samuel Beckett's conditions of literary production, probably foreshadowed by Shakespeare. So the *double-voicing* (Royle) of *twice-told tales* (Hawthorne), *et caeteras*, and *popperin pears, e via dicendo*. Adorno's anti-mimetic argument was less an iconoclastic drive than a defense of the labor of the negative and the work of the concept.[12] The dialectical rapport between mimesis and conceptuality led him therefore to acknowledge a mimetic dimension in the concept: "To represent the mimesis it supplanted, the concept has no other way than to adopt something mimetic in its own conduct, without abandoning itself" (*Negative Dialectic* 14; *Negative Dialektik* 26). The translator has omitted something in his version: the concept [*Begriff*] aims to represent the cause [*Sache*] of the mimesis it supplanted [*verdrängte*]. This brings us to the circularity denounced by Fineman, that of "an idealizing language [that] figures itself as specifically specular language because such a visual logos, in its visibility and visuality, simulates the ideal such language speaks about" (13). In Adorno's narrative, the ideal conceptuality takes revenge by supplanting—through representation—the very figuration that had tried to "simulate" (that is, to supplant) it in the first place. At any rate, in both related accounts the two participants (visual figuration and ideal, mimesis and concept) exist only through their dialectical interaction. The agon names a Platonic moral of disputed precedence—poetry or philosophy.[13] I am interested in Adorno's suggestion of *concepts that adopt something mimetic in their own conduct,* for it evokes the situation of Platonic dialogue on the verge of becoming Aristophanean comedy. This is, I would submit, a dialectical situation Shakespeare invariably favors in his plays, from *1 Henry IV* onwards, with the proviso urged by Althusser that, in Marxian logic, if a concept designates a reality, then it is not the concept of that reality ("Marxism and Humanism," *For Marx* 207).[14] The

---

12   Fredric Jameson insisted on Adorno's anti-representational drive (*Late Marxism* 119), on his search for an imageless materialism. Maybe Shakespeare re-allocated Puritan-Platonic iconoclastic tendencies at the heart of his dialectic program, positing them as so many recursive moments of determinate negation that accompanied all mimetic transports of his drama. One may well speak of a dangerous supplement to representation, reminding producers, actors and spectators of the ruination undoing the mimetic project from within.

13   Unlike Badiou, who focuses exclusively on the banishment of the poets, Lukacher calls attention to other passages in Plato's *Republic* to conclude that "the poet is more tolerant of the daemon's unpredictability and its irreducible exteriority" (*Daemonic* 74–77).

14   Althusser here opposes a view that was somehow defended by early Marx, when the latter insisted, contra Hegel, that "ordinary empirical existence" should have "its own mind" or that family and civil society "should owe their existence to a mind [not] other that their own" (*Critique* 8–9).

discordance between reality and concept, thing and word, produces the echoic irony that is so characteristically Shakespearean: *Can honor set to a leg? I know not seems. Why bastard? Wherefore base? There would have been a time for such a word. I heard myself proclaimed. Romeo, doff thy name.*

The conflicted relation between mimesis and conceptuality can of course be read as an episode in the deconstructive narrative of repressed linguisticity or tropology. The Kantian and post-Kantian philosophical elaboration of figurative-tropological notions like the symbolic or the sublime hinged precisely upon the question of representation:

> This reading of the duplicity of Hegel's Aesthetics allows de Man to reconcile the two main statements of the text—"Art is the sensory appearance of the Idea"/"Art is for us a thing of the past"—for they turn out to be in fact the same statement: "Art is 'of the past' in a radical sense, in that, like memorization, it leaves the interiorization of experience forever behind. It is of the past to the extent that it materially inscribes, and thus forever forgets, its ideal content."
> WARMINSKI, "Introduction" to de Man, *Aesthetic* 6

The relinquishment or experience in the material inscription of the letter (language) spells the sacrifice of the sensorial/empirical and the resulting impossibility of reconciling the aesthetic judgement—and by extension the moral and political judgement—with a reason that steers clear of phenomenal representation. Kant's failure, in the section on the sublime of the third *Critique*, to properly theory the faculty of the imagination is borne out in the way his argument

> establishes the loss of the symbolic in the failure to represent, by sensory means, the infinite powers of inventive articulation of which the mind is capable. The faculty of imagination is itself beyond images; *Einbildungskraft* is *bildlos*, and the absurdity of its own name records it failure.
> *Aesthetic* 122

De Man's rendering of Kant's concept of the imagination as shot through with negativity and failure due to its very inability to represent in response to the demands of the sublime offers one possible version of the *dialectical aesthetics* (Adorno, Szondi) that the *phenomenological aesthetics of representation* is programmed to ignore.

Paul Kottman is intimately conversant with Hegel's lectures on aesthetics, but he shows no interest in taking over the hermeneutic position of distance this dialectical aesthetics demands. His excellent essay on "Hegel and Shakespeare on the Pastness of Past" uncritically assumes that some Hegelian expectations about art already inform the intentional program of Shakespeare's dramaturgy. He aims to prove that "the significance of Shakespearean drama for Hegel just is Shakespeare's artistic registration of art's historical loss of vocation" (281). Shakespeare thus "embedded art's loss of vocation into his own drama" (281). This obviously implies that Shakespeare assumed at some point that art had at some point reached its own vocation. The workings of a prior *Versöhnung* (reconciliation) or plenitude is thus presumed. Maybe what really happened is that Shakespeare always-already grasped the inappropriateness of art—its inherent distance from any putative vocation. With Spenser and Marlowe as phenomenal precursors, as authors who produced a literary art committed to sensuous representation, it wouldn't have been hard for Shakespeare to believe that he was late, or that art was something of the past. It may have been Shakespeare's distinctive gesture to capitalize—via rewriting and parodic mimesis—on such *dépassement*, and to ironically dialectize the phenomenal ground opened by his precursors. But this Kottman doesn't say. His essay opens with an implicit celebration of the specific "sharing" and "collective acknowledgement" that characterize a performative and temporal artistic expression like drama. The importance of *enactment* is also intermittently asserted. On this logic, Kottman is understandably reluctant to admit that de-materialization and de-sensuousness are fully necessary conditions for the achievement of the highest mode of fine art, that (Shakespeare's) in which its highest "vocation" is presented.

In two related essays, de Man called attention to the way Kant outgrew his faith in the role of affectivity by enthroning *apatheia* and *phlegma* as noble purveyors of sublimity. But these two unemotional emotions educe their force from their independence from the empirical and the senses: "What makes the sublime compatible with reason is its independence from sensory experience; it is beyond the senses, *übersinnlich*. This is what makes the junction of cognition with morality possible" (*Aesthetic* 125). And de Man adds, with some humor: "A curious misprint, in the first edition of the third *Critique*, spelled *Sittlichkeit* for *Sinnlichkeit* (p.202), thus confusing with one stroke of the typesetter what it took Kant thirty years of philosophizing to tear asunder" (125). I believe that nothing carries better the weight of Kottman's and Lupton's mystified reading of Shakespeare's (deduced, civic) ethics into his (supposed, representational) aesthetics than the confusion of *Sittlichkeit* as *Sinnlichkeit*. Kottman assumes that Shakespeare's late plays, and especially *The Tempest*, already mourn "the *pastness* of the hope that the sensuous embodiment of unacknowledged claims on mutual recognition could be directed at a beholding audience in the hope of identifying or rectifying failures of mutual intelligibility" (280). According to this assumption, Shakespeare comes through as a moralist who hopes to rectify human conduct through the *sensuous embodiment* of an intentional content (the ethical-rational idea of mutuality). This is quite an assumption: we are dealing after all with an *upstart crow*. But Kottman is resolved:

> Whether in *Hamlet* or *The Tempest*, grasping that the challenges of mutual recognition and mutuality are open-ended—seeing our own understanding of these challenges as incomplete, even lacking reflective form—requires seeing that the intelligibility of these challenges is not adequately 'formed' by art, not adequately apprehended by the relationship that art installs between audience and performer (281).

My concern here is not with the stress on the "relationship" between "audience and performer," as if such nexus were Shakespeare's art's real *telos*. What I find distinctly confusing is the assumption, again, that Shakespeare aspired to "adequately 'form'" the intelligibility of moral claims about recognition and mutuality. Wasn't he rather *deforming* the *phenomenal* pictures of a prior literary praxis, the symbolic and sublime pictures of his two strong precursors, Spenser and Marlowe, respectively?

When the art-work is not adequately formed, the phenomenological critic comes to the rescue with a strong resolution to *reform*. I have already mentioned, in section 3, the futility of Bruce Smith's conception of criticism as the *reconstruction* of sense experience. The hermeneutic reformation of the play's flawed textual presentation is a parallel move. Lupton, for instance, praises the messianic "incompleteness" and "vulnerability" of the world in *Pericles* (*Shakespeare Dwelling* 121), but the fact is she attempts to actualize the incomplete by redeeming it through a strategy of *immanenten Transzendenzen* (Husserl, *Cartesianische* 175). The transcendent is here the text as an alien reality that is always incomplete, fragmentary, disjointed. The redemptive reformation of the incomplete text is a filling out of the empty: redemption, in this sense, is a sort of if supervened de-emptying or re-de-emption. Transcendence becomes immanent through an act of meaning-giving closing out: a suturing replenishment leading to interpretive closure. To read is to fulfill, to replenish, to fill out—to *erfullen*. The two-dimensional graphs wax into the three-dimensional figure of the portable hologram or intentional content: an illusion of embodied representation emerges. We no longer read scene 5 of the playtext

Pericles: we see actual fishermen throwing their nets overboard, we see their "action [...] in a tactile, corporeal, and immediately instrumental direction" (*Shakespeare Dwelling* 130) combined to create "cooperative rhythms of labor and affect" (131). Husserl compared the relation of phenomenology with psychology to the relation that exists between geometry and natural science (*Ideas I* 2). Lupton works indeed "in der reinen Geometrie" (*Ideen I* 14) of environmentally embedded human actions. The contingency and facticity (*Tatsächlichkeit*) of the text are redeemed in the *Wesens-Notwendigkeit* (Husserl *Ideen I* 9) of the hologrammatic intentional content. The hologram is no experiential ground supplied by the natural philosopher, but an ideal *logical ground* supplied by the phenomenologist (*Ideen I* 16). But this ideal space is no transcendental normative realm, but rather an ethical-rational idea, and therefore allegorically transcendent. Following T.S. Eliot, Lupton invites us to read for "the phenomenology of spatial experience as the means by which transcendence becomes world in the late plays" (118). *World-becoming transcendence*—this is an apt phrase to describe the phenomenological process of embodiment or incarnation in *religious representation*. The potential negativity of imagination is suppressed. The challenge of collective, community-building labor demands solely a constructive focus—"the mise-en-scène of a dramatically imagined locale for labor" (Lupton, *Shakespeare Dwelling* 130). No deconstruction, no critical denouement, will threaten the fishermen's "net work" (129). According to Paul de Man,

> In the laborious, businesslike world of morality, even the free and playful imagination becomes an instrument of work. Its task, its labor, is precisely to translate the abstractions of reason back into the phenomenal world of appearances and images whose presence is retained in the very word imagination, Bild in the German *Einbildungskraft*.
> DE MAN, *Aesthetic* 84

6

In the remaining part of this section, I intend to examine Lupton's essay "*Macbeth* against Dwelling," included in *Shakespeare Dwelling*. This is an expanded version of the article "*Macbeth*'s Martlets: Shakespearean Phenomenologies of Hospitality" that was published in the 2012 *Criticism* issue on "Shakespeare and Phenomenology." Lupton openly presents her reading as political: "The play is *biopolitical* in its wresting of political ends (the crown) from pre- or protopolitical scenes of dormancy and *political-theological* in its tendency to sacralize the slumbering life exposed to this violence" (*Shakespeare Dwelling* 86). But it is actually moral, or moralistic, in its implicit commendation of "dormancy" and the "slumbering life." If waking hours lead to "the feast of life, a hospitable gathering that is at once subjective, sumptuary, and sociable," sleep "allows us to digest the day by resting but also by dreaming" (95). *The feast of life*? Whose *life* is Lupton talking about? The life of the murderers, placed by Macbeth at the "worst rank of manhood" (*Macbeth* 3.1.104)? Obviously not: Lupton refers only to noble, aristocratic life. What do the tropes of slumbering life and dormancy mean for people whose lives are the very opposite of "a hospitable gathering," including "aristocrats" like Julius Caesar, Coriolanus, Hamlet, or Edgar? Someone could object by arguing that Lupton is assuming the social constraint of tragedy in the Western tradition. Still, this genre-based rationalization, seldom if ever offered by the scholar, would overlook the following moralistic claim:

> Guiding our attention to this distribution [*the sensorial distribution of thought and sleep*], however, does not decrease our sense of the characters' moral agency, but rather heightens our awareness of the forms of trust required to maintain a world in which we depend on other persons and things for our dwelling as well as for the forms of acknowledgement that make dwelling worth pursuing. (96)

Our? We? Who depends? Who are we? This presentist extrapolation can only be done from the standpoint of a moral absolute. Can we say of all human beings that they trust to maintain a world in which they depend on other persons and things for their dwelling? I very much doubt it. Lupton's communitarian faith, mildly inflected by Kottman's worship of Hegelian mutuality and recognition, is at odds with much that is still meaningful in the liberal credo. Is depending on other people an asset or a liability? This remains, I fear, an open question. These tropes of mutuality and recognition depend on the master-trope of dwelling-hospitality, which the scholar identifies as constitutive of drama. Lupton speaks of the "residential origins of dramatic action" (87). The *good life*, now redescribed as the "slumbering life," is predicated upon conditions of rest that alone hospitable dwelling affords, and drama is the collective action that enforces these conditions. Lupton *imagines* an ideal society based on the communal affordances of dwelling (this is her *intentional content* or rational-ethical idea) and measures the play according to its capacity to adequately *conform* to it. If and where the text doesn't *conform*, she will *reform*. Since Macbeth murders sleep, and revokes dwelling, Macbeth is a bad person, and the play showcases his threat to the ideal society. Lupton's task is formidable: she has to demonstrate that the play does in fact advance "the slumbering life" exposed to Macbeth's violence. She needs to prove that there is an actual intimation or presentation of the intentional content—the ideal society based on the communal affordances of dwelling.

The whole essay is therefore an effort to visually *represent* what the play textually fails to *present*. In phenomenology, it is evidentiary *intuition* that makes something present, and Lupton, troubled by the nonappearance of the bower of bliss in the play, is compelled to resort to intuitive grasping: "The play's haunted house aesthetics, whether *intuited* through the reading process, teased out by theatrical production, or allowed to gather and lurk on the bare stage, arise from the disturbances visited by the Macbeths on dwelling" (87, emphasis added). If the "haunted house aesthetics" is "intuited through the reading process," so is the original house aesthetics, and if the reading process fails to *present* it, then we can turn to the theatrical production, and its bare sunlit stage, to *represent* what is missing. Given the scarcity of phenomenal-mimetic indications of slumbering life, Lupton has to resort to the notion of atmosphere. The play, she argues, is "a commentary on the genesis of atmosphere" (86). In drama, she contends, "atmosphere emulsifies mood and setting, an inmixing powered in this play by the deeds against dwelling" (86). She speaks about "the play's atmospheric invitations" tapped by successive productions, and argues that, instead, she will "seek out the play's commentary on the genesis of atmosphere as neither a technical addition to drama nor a merely semantic cushion of meaningfulness" (86). This means that "the genesis of atmosphere" is an end in itself, and it is the ultimate goal of the play. Poetical atmosphere? Obviously not. That is a philological absurdity concocted by liberal-humanist scholars who believed, alas, that *Macbeth* was a *poem limited*. Thus, for instance, in a bold move against late-romantic and Victorian conceptions of "atmosphere," William Empson had the nerve to reduce it to "the consciousness of what is implied in meaning" (*Seven Types* 37). Consciousness? Implication? Meaning? Ambiguity? This of course has little to with the scenic kind of atmosphere Lupton has in mind. Considering the physical conditions of theatrical production in Shakespeare's time, such scenic conception appears unrealistic. But anyway. "Atmosphere" emerges "in *Macbeth* as a floating feature implied and produced by the actions of the characters, actions that occur as substantial speech (Arendt) and in locales cultivated by routines of habitation (Heidegger)" (87). Lupton here obviously displays the very conservative-romantic *Heimweh* that informs so many sections of Levinas' *Totalité et infini*. At work in both cases is an evident *embourgeoisement* of aristocratic distinction. But the key term in the quotation is "implied," which reinforces the idea of "intuition"? What are the limits of this non-rational implication? Who is the agent of implication? What is "substantial speech"? How can we differentiate the speech from the locales, if the locales are only *given* through speech (dialogue and stage directions)?

Her essay is strained by the attempt to allegorically project onto the play a personal fascination with entertainment planning, interior design, clothing design, and outdoor party décor. The aesthetic "atmosphere" of this ethical idea conjures a content that is intentional only in Lupton's mind, not in Shakespeare's. Dwelling, a symbol of the homed-in *Gemeinschaft*, determines a particular "house aesthetic," and it is the goal of her essay, we have seen, to analyze "the play's haunted house aesthetic" (87). The political, the moral, and the aesthetic are glued together in the phenomenon of dwelling. So, Macbeth murders the sleep that is presented by *Macbeth* and intuited by Lupton. The goal of her essay is to stage—to represent—this intuition. This, let me insist, is no easy task. Lupton gives importance to one particular incident, Duncan's murder, which, by her own admission, "occurs offstage" (88). But this is no disincentive. We need only "think of the murder as *imaginatively* rezoning the curtained space as a canopied bed of state, its heavy drapery protecting the sleeping king from the prying eyes of the assembled audience" (89, my emphasis). The critic openly places herself as a member of the "assembled audience"—the assembled *spectatorship* would do more justice to the stress on seeing, as *audience* is premised on hearing. This imaginative projection encourages the *presence* of meaningful (symbolic) representation under the auspices of sight—"présence de la chose au regard comme *eidos*" (Derrida, *De la grammatologie* 23)—and labors to secure the actualization of a scenographic conception of space (outfitting, layout, lighting) "by the actors, in collaboration with the audience's attention and imagination" (105), in "co-présence," that is, "de l'autre et de soi, intersubjetivité comme phénomène intentionnel de l'ego" (23).

The scholar, who sees with "prying eyes," "imaginatively" collaborates in the rezoning of the observed symbol (the curtained space) standing for the "canopied bed of state." All the emphasis of this argument falls on the act of seeing and imagining—quite an exploit, considering that the murder occurs offstage, and that its only indisputable phenomenal appearance is verbal (aural, graphic), unfolding, vestigially, as in a dark mirror, in the exchange between Lady Macbeth and her husband in 2.2. The fact then that the "canopied bed of state" is not part of the setting, is not onstage and is never described in the play (curtains and blankets appear only metaphorically) is, however, no hindrance to Lupton's visionary excursion into the play's phenomenal "affordances":

> This sovereign softscape affords, without prescribing, a variety of scenographic possibilities that resonate with contemporary scenes of

> displacement, encampment, and occupation, the appareled halls of Inverness flowing into present-day fabric architecture designed to host refugees and migrant workers. (89)

This *presentist* vagary holds some beauty, but little exegetic accuracy. Nothing in *Macbeth* licenses this resonant analogy. One may either move back from *Macbeth* to *Beowulf* or *The Battle of Maldon* to track the precedence of makeshift military architecture (the ravaged mead-hall), or forgo *Macbeth* altogether and reach out to *Sir Thomas More* in order to pay a humanist tribute to the victims of post-deportation mobility: "Imagine that you see the wretched strangers, / Their babies at their backs, with their poor luggage / Plodding to th' ports and coasts for transportation" (Add.II.D 81–83). Imagine. And imagine the further challenge this harsh reality would pose to the aesthetic celebration of the transience of furniture and dwelling. There is nothing inherently praiseworthy in living, let alone dying, under an open tepee. It may be beautiful to think about it, sublime even to see it in Lars von Trier's extraordinary *Melancholia*, but being *forced* to live on the road, under the volcano, surfacing, into the wild, or breaking the waves has nothing necessarily beautiful or sublime about it, even before forty. At any rate, this *moral diversion* prompted by the religious-political "affordances" of aesthetic *entertainment* shouldn't divert us from our play. Suffice it to say that, as Lupton is implicitly bound to acknowledge, the travails of *Heimatlosigkeit*, itinerancy, precarity and exposure are much more effectively conjured up in *King Lear* (18–19). *Macbeth* is decidedly not a play about the *transience of residence*, not a play whose central aim is to "imagine dwelling as an improvisatory orchestration of spatial and temporal remainders" (91). Lupton taps here, perhaps unwittingly, into the imaginative resources of the diasporic American sublime—existential displacement from Poe, Twain and Melville to Faulkner's *As I Lye Dying*, DeLillo's *Americana*, Auster's *The Music of Chance*, or Pynchon's *Mason and Dixon*—although she mostly courts the situationist aesthetics of Guy Debord.

The essay mentions the "play" and "*Macbeth*" from the outset, but we don't know what exactly is Lupton referring to: the playtext or an imagined performance? And what are the conditions of the imagined performance? In the first section of the essay there is no reference to the text. In the second section, titled "Investitures," four lines are showcased (1.4.45–48), and Lupton focuses on the term "harbinger." But this focus is short-lived, as the critic infers from it the notion of "appareling," nowhere to be found in the playtext. Much attention is given to this second notion: "Such appareling belongs to the hospitable softscape, the mobilization of fabrics, foliage, and furnishings for the shaping, lining, canopying, dividing, and outfitting of spaces for entertainment" (88).

From there we move on to "investing," derived from "invest," a term which appears in the play only in a context of political-power inheritance (1.4.41). Lupton teases out, quite correctly, the etymological sense of "enrobement," but the truth is that the passage favors the "stars" as the adequate signs of nobleness:

> My plenteous joys,
> Wanton in fulness, seek to hide themselves
> In drops of sorrow. Sons, kinsmen, thanes,
> And you whose places are the nearest, know
> We will establish our estate upon
> Our eldest, Malcolm, whom we name hereafter
> The Prince of Cumberland; which honour must
> Not unaccompanied invest him only,
> But signs of nobleness, like stars, shall shine
> On all deservers. From hence to Inverness,
> And bind us further to you. (1.4.33–44)

The fact moreover that the signifier "Inverness" may have cued the (material) instance of the letter "invest" should also give us pause, and make us reconsider the real, if any, semantic motivation in the choice of the verb. What I am trying to say is that the semantic realm of clothing is neither explicitly nor implicitly invoked in these lines. The borrowed robes, the old robes and giant's robes can be found elsewhere in the play, but Lupton doesn't open that particular commode.

But let us move on to the *Macbeth* lines (1.6.3–10) that prompt the longest exegetical elaboration in Lupton's reading. This is Banquo speaking:

> This guest of summer,
> The temple-haunting martlet, does approve
> By his loved mansionry, that the heaven's breath
> Smells wooingly here. No jutty, frieze,
> Buttress, nor coign of vantage, but this bird
> Hath made his pendent bed and procreant cradle:
> Where they most breed and haunt I have observed
> The air is delicate.

Lupton has been forced to admit that "the readying of spaces for rest is not detailed in the text itself" (89). But who cares about the text? We get instead, she argues, "several allusions to the kind of soft implements that help support sleep [...] to create a sense of security," and one such reference "of the investiture of space" is Banquo's description of "avian artistry" (89). Lupton calls this description an "image" and she goes on to explain that "the image visualizes the building of a contexture of affordances" (90). From the *text* in formalist criticism we moved to the *context* in neo-historicist criticism, and now to *contexture* in phenomenological criticism. So *the image visualizes*, which sounds like Heidegger's *die Sprache spricht*. If the image visualizes, the image acts as an agent of vision, unless we take her to mean that the image facilitates someone's visualization of the "building of a contexture ..." Both meanings are implied in the phenomenological account of the noematic constraint of perceptive processes, whereby the intentional content predetermines (in fact, produces) the perceptive act of grasping the intentional object. The intentional content, in Kant's aesthetics, could be a rational idea, a tendentially allegorical ethical trope. Here, the "ideals" are the "values of medieval hospitality" (90). The martlet's nesting (the aesthetic idea) concretizes the rational-ethical idea through symbolic means: "the image of nesting begins to visualize dwelling as an improvisatory orchestration of spatial and temporal remainders" (91). The form-meaning concordance (*Übereinstimmung*) is perfect. Shakespeare's meaningful art needs no religion to replace it. If only he had been a bit more careful in the visual concretization of this "improvisatory orchestration." "None of this," Lupton is bound to admit, "appears before us as a prop or picture on stage" (91). This is quite an admission. But, like Kottman and Smith, Lupton will *reform* the play by *reconstructing* its bidimensional *pictures*. No effort must be spared when the *Erfüllung* of aesthetic representation is at risk: "instead, the crenellated composite of birds, nests, and castle emerge and dissolve on the scrim of the imagination" (91). Again, of whose imagination? Whose imagination (Shakespeare's, Banquo's, ours) makes the "crenellated composite" emerge? "I have observed," says Banquo. Lupton lets us know she has observed too. But shall we enlist Shakespeare among the observers of *this bird*'s nesting? Shakespeare gives us verses, not observations. Do we all see the bird and the nest through the nets of the word? Lupton assumes we do, and assumes much more:

> In gazing at the loose tapestry formed by the martlets' nests and shaping it into a more formal image of human accommodation, Duncan and Banquo are imagining their own rooms at the inn. And as we gaze with these visitors at these conjured nests, we gain a passing phenomenological access to our own coigns of vantage, pendant beds, and pleasant seats in theater, inn, great hall, nursery, and dormitory. (91)

She assumes that Duncan and Banquo, the two of them, are "gazing" at something (the loose tapestry formed by the nests) that is there, when in fact only Banquo states he has observed. Duncan's prior remark concerns exclusively the sweet quality of the air. Lupton also assumes that this thing they are seeing (the intentional object) is but an instantiation of a "formal image of human accommodation," the symbol or aesthetic idea that reveals the presiding ethical trope or rational idea (hospitality). She assumes both characters are catachrestically "imagining" their own rooms. She assumes, in a further tropological concordance, that "we" (whoever we are) can gaze at what they gaze. These are the blessings of "phenomenological access" to things themselves (intentional objects), and what they stand for (intentional contents). The role of language in this immediate transaction is negligible: like all perfect symbols, the "formal image" of nesting is asked to "emerge and dissolve" without contingent leftover or material remainder. But can this be argued without doing violence to the text? The symbolic office of the martlet's nest would indeed be impeccable if only there was a nest to be seen. But is there? Lupton's phrasing is hesitant: from "in gazing at the loose tapestry formed by the martlet's nests" we move, in the next sentence, to our gazing at "the conjured nests." *Conjured nests*? To conjure is to make something appear or seem to appear by using magic, and by extension to create or imagine something. So is Banquo observing, gazing, or conjuring? Adorno once observed that in Husserl's philosophy, "staring magically transforms all becoming into being" (*Against* 152). Maybe this is just a magical-phenomenological trick. And yet, if the nests are conjured, and Banquo is already imagining, what is the bird that Shakespeare is "making appear" through verbal *presentation*? The martin or martlet, whose etymology leads, rather arbitrarily, as most etymologies, to Mars and war? And with equal arbitrary slipperiness, we slide along the scene's phenomenal horizon, from the house-martin to the Queen herself, war-bird Lady Macbeth: "See, see, our honored hostess!" is Duncan's reply to a conjuration, Banquo's, whose only effect has been to make the Queen appear: "*Enter Lady Macbeth*" (1.6.10). I am not merely indulging in signifier fantasy: what the audience and the characters only and surely *see* is the apparition of the Queen. Lupton is reluctantly alive to "the ghostliness of all phenomenological concretion" (Adorno, *Against* 85), and mobilizes a phenomenological vocabulary of imagination, intuition, and concept-free "apprehension"—understood both as "broad intuiting" and "anxiety" (91)—to account for the mode of presentation of an aesthetic idea (nesting) that is not to be discarded for lack of phenomenal support. The whole tropological event unfolds via episodes of concordant fusion, first the merging of witnesses—"Banquo engages in an act of ekphrasis that merges several subjects (Duncan, the audience, himself) as they approach diverse objects" (91–92)—and next through the harmonious reciprocity between intentional content and intentional object, idea and symbol, symbol and thing: "if the image *reflects on* hospitality as theme, it is also *produced by* hospitality as a spatial routine" (92). Further, "conscience" is said to "[merge] with atmosphere" (94). The final merging is that of Hegel and Husserl into the composite presiding genius of the aesthetic ideology that undergirds Lupton's romantic reading. The resulting effect is one of utter concordance (*Übereinstimmung*), perfect for good rest, tight sleep, sweet dreams. Needless to say, Freud has no say in this economy of complete repair and fulfilling restoration. But neither would a scholar like Jonathan Goldberg, who has argued, discussing *Hamlet*, that "seeing is reading" and that "the embodied characters is a scriptive formation" (*Shakespeare's Hand* 112). If the character is, imagine the bird. Imagine the emblematic, scriptural bird, in Chaucer, Milton, Yeats or Stevens.

The bed, the curtains, the enrobing garments, the martlet's nest—Lupton *sees* these and other absent things and calls them "the play's object world" (92). They are, she adds, proof that they play "is indeed phenomenological in soliciting such *Umwelt*-ing" (111). But no amount of stylized redescription— "the soft implements that support sleep," "a homelier inventory of objects," "the play's atmospheric architecture" (93)—will manage to *conjure* them into phenomenal presence or stage representation. The play's textual materiality is a stubborn thing, and it resists immediate aesthetic phenomenalization and representation. Still, Lupton's reconstructive and reforming scholarship is tenacious. In the section of her article titled "Revoking Prayer," she organizes a commentary around lines 2.2.20–34, where Macbeth tells his wife about the blessings exchanged by the sleepers. This scant reported material is enough for the scholar to construct a meditation on the role of prayer within structures of dwelling and hospitality. She had already anticipated that "bedtime prayers provide another repertory that configure somatic processes, affective attitudes, and poetic speech in the scenes of dwelling; constituting at once a liturgy, a dramaturgy, a scenography, bedtime prayers ..." (86), and now she examines this repertory in some depth. Her whole commentary, nonetheless, hinges upon a figment, the conjecture that "Duncan may have intoned such a sequence of prayers before climbing to his bed at Inverness" (97). But the stubborn textual fact is he didn't. We know, with Pierre Macherey, that much can be hermeneutically surmised from the plain fact of textual omissions. But this is different: Lupton is relocating verbal clues and making crossed assumptions in order to prove that the royal bed was a canopied haven and laborious nest of blessed rest where the King was slumbering in the cadenzas of half-conscious prayer before he was brutally assassinated by the upstart bat. The strategy here is not that of decoding a textual omission, but of performing the kind of textual transmission that allows the play's intentional content to be fulfilled, and the inexistent *presentation* therefore to be reformed and reconstructed through her ideal representation: "Duncan may have intoned." Actualizing dormant possibilities and suggesting counterfactuals is a fine critical strategy only when both feet are on the ground, and the text lies open on the desk. Lupton's interest in prayer deepens further the phenomenological diminution of language in which her essay invests so much. Since "bedtime prayers integrate ritualized speech with physical gestures" (97), prayers can be said to offer the scholar an illustration of the power of fleshy, performative *parole* abstracted from the formal-transcendental structure of langue. Prayer, described as "metabolic" (97) and "somatic" (86), instantiates a naturalization of language best exemplified in the allusion to "the biosemantic soup of the witching hour" (110). *Biosemantic*? I can hear Saussure's canonized bones bursting their cerements. This diminution of language, the neglect of the playtext's signifiers, is a symptom of a larger problem in her reading—the contraction of thought to a corporal function. Lupton quotes Curran to the effect that "knowledge and thought [form] part of a larger sensual experience that extends beyond the mental or spiritual into a real, material world of things and actions'" (95). If we accept this naturalization of thought, we must either reject Descartes or reform him. Lupton chooses the latter: "A kind of immanent and affective Cartesianism draws the melting into air undergone each time we fall asleep into a knot of something permanent (thought, mind, soul)" (101). Note the telescoping of the tropes of *melting into* and *drawing into a knot*. The latter figure is another variation on the motif (the aesthetic idea) of *concordance*, itself a prerequisite, we saw, in Kant, for the existence of an aesthetic idea. Lupton's entire essay is a display of variations (*nesting, merging, netting*) around the notion of concordant fusion that organizes the larger idea of hospitality. Her conception of hospitality, condensed in a prepositional phrase she keeps repeating in the essay—"in concert with" (107, 112, 115, 116)—has fully obliterated the traces of antagonism and hostility that inform the concept: "Hospitalité, hostilité, *hostipitalité*" (Derrida, *De l'hospitalité* 45). If the Macbeths ruin the stage of hospitality it is because hospitality, to Lupton's mind, is not a figure open to internal contestation or deconstruction. But this is not the case in Levinas, who rejects the notion of intentionality (central to the receptiveness inherent to hospitality) as based on *adequation* and *representation*.[15]

---

15 Levinas readjusts the concept of *intentionality* to describe the subjective protention of receptiveness, which he characterizes as *not* based on adequation: "Toute savoir en tant qu'intentionnalité suppose dejà l'idée de l'infini, l'inadequation par excellence" (*Totalité*

Lupton insists on the cognitive potential of prayer, praising the fusion of "thought and sound" (101) and the "visible forms of thinking-with that belong to prayer as life practice" (103), but her analysis submits no clear instance of thought-in-prayer, not only because no such thing is very likely to occur (repetition, invocation, ritual and liturgy are inimical to rational thought) but especially because it simply doesn't occur in *Macbeth* at all. At any rate, this reliance on absent prayers evinces Lupton's tacit endorsement of the "medieval metaphysics of the play" (104), a kind of creationist worldview where sounds immediately conjure thought and reality, without the apparent intervention of language, and where the habits of "knitting together social and biological processes in the bundled sleeve of care" produce a "theological economy that posits God as just distributor" (111). Is this reported thought? Who believes this? Macbeth? The porter? The second witch? The doctor? Macduff's son? The temple-haunting martlet? All of them? I ignore the answer. But it very much looks as if Lupton herself upholds both this economy and this metaphysics.

Lupton's piece is not an essay in interpretation of Shakespeare's playtext. It is a moral admonition whose doctrine is illustrated through a mental representation of a couple of scenes in a Shakespeare play. At its most eloquent, the piece reads like a transcendentalist sermon, with Donne's and Emerson's tropes (the beetle, cultivation, invitation, gifts, covenant love) informing philosophical figures, whether by Husserl (scan, offerings) or Hegel (bond of trust, respect):

> Does the shard-born beetle inhabit the landscape of blessings or the landscape of curses? The beetle's flight reveals them as the same landscape. To dwell is to cultivate a mindfulness that builds resilience by anticipating precarity, to encourage independence by practicing gratitude, and to exercise ingenuity by responding to affordances as invitations, to see feelingly. Blessings are a form of dramatic poetry that scan the environment for its offerings, not in order to maximize them as resources or standing reserve but to receive them as gifts that come with strings attached: the

---

12). We may thus argue that his reliance on *inadequacy* disables the symbolic harmony of representation defended by Lupton and Kottman. The vocabulary of excess is in keeping with poststructuralist assumptions in Lacan, Badiou and Žižek. "L'idée de l'infini qui n'est pas à son tour une représentation de l'infini est la ssource commune de l'activité et de la théorie" (13). Levinas rejects the vocabulary of *representation* and *adéquation* which presumably subtends Heidegger's investment in the notion of evental disclosure or revelation. (13). Levinas turns away from Husserl largely because he sees him as the philosopher of intentionality and interpretation, or, rather, of "intentionality understood as representation" (Moran 345).

bond of trust and accountability oiled by virtues of respect, pity, and covenant love. (111)

This is very nicely argued but is sadly irrefutable. Popper famously pointed out that "a theory that is not refutable by any conceivable event is non-scientific. Irrefutability is not a virtue of a theory (as people often think) but a vice" (*Conjectures and Refutations* 36). Describing Lupton's as a non-scientific theory is inaccurate. It is not a theory, and she is not aiming at being scientific. We may say, however, that her essay is built upon a non-critical argument. Lupton identifies an interesting theme (sleep and repair in the perspective of hospitality) that the playtext only fragmentarily and relatively sustains. She reads too much into it, I believe, and too much that is irrelevant to the actual interpretation of the playtext. But she is not reading the playtext. She is morally meditating before a mental representation of the play. Reading Lupton meditate is a most rewarding experience, but it has little to do with the Shakespeare experience.

In *What is Called Thinking?*, Heidegger suggested an escape route from our traditional way of thinking through "representational ideas" (213), which led, of course, to some primeval soup of apocalyptic meaning. As I tried to explain in sections 2 and 12 on Descartes and Saussure respectively, there are other ways of resisting the phenomenal lures of mental representation. A negative, relational, and dialectical conception of thought may help. Fredric Jameson has very recently argued that "the problem of representation today eats away at all the established disciplines like a virus, particularly destabilizing the dimension of language, reference, and expression (which used to be the domain of literary study), as well as that of thought (which used to be that of philosophy)" (*Representing* Capital 4). In the case of phenomenological scholarship, representation, reference and expression make stable bedfellows. Representation is, Jameson avers, "an essential operation in cognitive mapping and in ideological construction" (6). This Spenser and Marlowe knew very well. And so did Shakespeare, who put much effort into un-mapping and deconstructing. In the book with Macbethian title *The Seeds of Time*, Jameson had already portended that "contradiction is always one step before representation" (5). The bat one step before the martlet, the borrowed robes one fold deeper into the sumptuous robes, insomnia in advance of sleep, noise before prayer.

CHAPTER 19

The Fallacy of Immediacy

1

In the third of his *Metaphysical Meditations*, Descartes distinguishes between the two ideas a human being can have of the sun. The first, drawn from the senses, construes the sun as a small circle in the sky; the second, drawn from rational evidence—"prise des raison de l'astronomie, c'est-à-dire des certaines notions nées avec moi" (147)—, conceives of the sun as a huge sphere, many times bigger than the earth. Descartes concludes: "Certes, ces deux idées que je conçois du soleil, ne peuvent pas être toutes deux semblables au même soleil; et la raison me fait croire que celle qui vient immédiatement de son apparence, est celle qui lui est le plus dissemblable" (147). The phrase "celle qui vient immédiatement de son apparence" was originally rendered in Latin as "quae quam proxime ab ipso videtur emanasse." Descartes, who authorized the translation, rested therefore content with the adverbial "immédiatement." In the sixth *Meditation* he repeatedly warns against the cognitive deceptions of the immediate and direct (*ad immediate dignoscendum, per se immediate istas ideas*, see *Meditationes* VII 79, 83), and it is with these adverbials—*proxime, immediate*—that I am concerned in the present section. The moral of Descartes' apercu is simple: we should not trust whatever is *immediately given in appearance,* as it may prove the most unreliable appearance of the original thing whose knowledge we are after. As a champion of mediation, Descartes contributed greatly to institute the *pathos of distance* so warmly praised by Nietzsche. A truly Cartesian meditation, therefore, should stipulate the undoing of immediacy. This is one of the foundational embarrassments of phenomenology, a self-styled science of essences that gleans its data from immediate evidence.

Kant, we know, maintained that "intuitions without concepts are blind" (*Critique of Pure Reason* A51/B75), and Robert Brandom has recently stated that, in Hegel's *Phenomenology of Spirit*, "immediacy is ultimately unintelligible apart from its relation to universals" (*A Spirit of Trust* 121). *Intuitive immediacy* unattended by concepts and universals is, for the idealist tradition, a chimera. But not for phenomenology. In *Ideas I*, Husserl unabashedly assumes the possibility of an intuition of essences or essential intuition, and "the datum of essential intuition is a pure essence [*das Gegebene der Wesensanschauung ein reines Wesen*]" (*Ideas I* §3 12). Intuition moreover is inherently presentive (*gebende*), and the evidence it supplies is *immediate* evidence. Phenomenological wisdom draws, in sum, from the stunning productivity of "an immediately presentive intuition [*unmittelbar gebende Anschauung*]" (*Ideas I* §18 34).[1] From this high-water mark follows a downward inferential scale of lessening immediacy. The whole spectrum is thus firmly rooted in radical *Unmittelbarkeit*.[2] Feel the confidence:

> Confessedly all mediate grounding leads back to the immediate [*auf unmittelbare zurück*]. *The primary source of all rightness*, in respect of all domains of objects and the positing acts related to them, lies in immediate and more narrowly specified *primordial self-evidence*, or in the primordial givenness which motivates it.
>
> *Ideas I* §141 295

What Husserl calls "mediate self-evidence [*mittelbarer Evidenz*]" (296) is a delegated flash that can hardly pass the test of dialectical mediation. Immediate intuition is not however to be identified with immediate sensorial intuition: "*Immediate seeing* [*Das unmittelbare 'Sehen'*] not merely the sensory seeing of experience, but *seeing in general as primordial dator of consciousness* of any kind whatsoever, is the ultimate source of justification for all rational statements" (*Ideas I* §19 36). Husserl constantly reminds his readers of the need to outmatch empiricism, and this can only be accomplished through an *epoché* enabling the thinker to deal with the real *Punkte*—ideas, essence and knowledge of essential being—"on a basis of immediacy [*einer unmittelbaren Feststellung*]" (*Ideas I* §18 34). And yet the firmness of the evidence obtained is unquestionable—"Through acts of immediate intuition we intuit a 'self'" (*Ideas I* §43 81)—and the intuited is not to be taken as sign or image of anything else. To sum up:

---

1 I use here F. Kersten's translation of *Ideas I*.
2 On section 7 of the "General Introduction" to *Ideas*, we read: "Grounded on the predicatively formed eidetic affair-complexes (or the eidetic axioms), seized upon in immediate insight, are the mediate, predicatively formed eidetic affair-complexes which become given in a thinking with mediated insight—a thinking according to principles, all of which are objects of immediate insight. Consequently each step in a mediate grounding is apodictically and eidetically necessary. The essence of purely eidetic science thus consists of proceeding in an exclusively eidetic way; from the start and subsequently, the only predicatively formed affair-complexes are such as have eidetic validity and can therefore be either made originarily given immediately (as grounded immediately in essences originarily seen) or else can become 'inferred' from such 'axiomatic' predicatively formed affair-complexes by pure deduction" (16–17).

> It is the distinctive peculiarity of phenomenology to include all sciences and all forms of knowledge in the scope of its eidetic universality, and indeed in respect of all that which is *immediately* transparent [*unmittelbar einsichtig*] in them, or at least would be so, if they were genuine forms of knowledge. The meaning and legitimacy of all the *immediate* starting-points possible and of all immediate steps in possible methods come within its jurisdiction.
>
> *Ideas I* §62 120, emphases added

This kind of confidence—this arrogance of immediacy—has no place in dialectical thought. In Kant intellectual intuition was obtained at a much higher speculative cost. It is worth noting that Levinas' original immersion in phenomenology resulted in a book-length study dedicated to that very miracle—Husserl's *Wesensschauung* or *Ideation* (*Ideen* 10)—and that his life-long explorations in ethics and metaphysics is characterized by a constant determination to frame an *immediate* ethical experience untroubled by language or metaphysical difference. Immediacy was, moreover, along with intuition and evidence, a concept that Merleau-Ponty received untouched from Husserl's phenomenology, without the need to reprogram it. What could be more immediate that the holding of hands? Although Merleau-Ponty strongly objects to Bergson's reliance in the "données immédiates de la conscience" (*Phénoménologie de la perception* 84) he refuses to give up immediacy as such and contents himself with transforming it: "est désormais immédiat non plus l'impression, l'objet qui ne fait qu'un avec le sujet, mais le sens, la structure, l'arrangement spontané des parties" (85). Impressions are not immediately given, but spontaneous meaning (*le sens*) is.

The phenomenological scholar couldn't agree more. In current Shakespeare studies, *immediacy* takes many forms. "If Caliban is a chimpanzee [...] then Caliban, I want to suggest, is Shakespeare" (Maisano, "Rise of the Poet" 71). This is one. Another is: "Shylock is Shakespeare" (Kenneth Gross). These equations are sampled out from a logic of character-author conflation that is of course traditional. It is, in addition, legitimate when the equivalence is the outcome of speculative work. "Hamlet is Shakespeare" is a common enough solution to the play's riddled significance, and it results effortlessly from hermeneutic enterprises that are characterized by dialectical brio. Greenblatt's suggestion that Shakespeare sides with (almost is) the witches in Macbeth is another example, although in this case the argument is insufficiently dialecticized.[3]

---

3 See Greenblatt, "Shakespeare Bewitched."

The difference between arguing that Shakespeare is a chimpanzee or a witch and arguing that Shakespeare is Shylock or Hamlet is evident. In the former comparison we place ourselves above Shakespeare, whom we reduce to a case of immediate *stoliditas*, whereas in the latter we consider the superiority over us of a text-produced transcendental consciousness threatened by the destructive mediation of its own (verbal) nothingness. The former equation submits a clear answer in the form and matter of an immediate thing; the latter solely furnishes a question, that is, a problem.[4] In the former case, the sublime *homo noumenon* (the scholar as agent of moral freedom) asserts his superiority of the grotesque *homo phenomenon* (Shakespeare as natural ape of bag lady). In the latter case the valence is reversed: it is the scholar who shows, before the incomprehensible, sublime "respect for his own determinacy" or limitation (*Achtung für unsere eigene Bestimmung*) (Kant *Critique of Judgement* §27).

The author as character is one of the versions of immediacy. But there are others. A word is a thing. Intention is meaning. A trope is an image. Form is content. These are all forms of concertation or concordance that rely on the logic of immediate (symbolic) representation. In phenomenological criticism, *immediacy* encrypts the advantages of the fast food diner round the corner— it delivers without delay. Ideal for fast, unclose reading. The many virtues of immediacy percolate all levels of the hermeneutic experience: 1) the immediate reading of the play-text gives up reading altogether and embraces the text's symbolic phenomenalization of reference (in an imagined or a real production of the play); 2) the immediate understanding of the genesis of the playtext lays aside the biographical motif of Shakespeare reading others' texts and intuits him as a man directly intuiting fresh life experiences; 3) the immediate understanding of our reception of the playtext turns down the playtext and invokes the author's transtemporal presence and his phenomenal things as a reliable display of objects placed directly before us for potential ego-projection. The upshot is the ideological reduction of a complex reading process.

Consider the second process: a text is born through the author's sensorial apprehension of external phenomena. Take, for instance, James Shapiro's reflection in his book *1599: A Year in the Life of William Shakespeare*:

> When scholars talk about the sources of Shakespeare's plays, they almost always mean printed books like Holinshed's *Chronicles* that they themselves can read; but Shakespeare's was an aural culture, the music of

---

4 In response to a friend who asks him about the relation between ideology and the unconscious, Althusser writes in 1975: "Toute question n'implique pas forcément sa réponse" (qtd. in Oliver Corpet and François Matheron, "Présentation" to *Écrits sur la psychanalyse*, 12).

which has long faded. Lost to us are the unrecorded sounds reverberating around him—street cries of vendors, church bells, regional and foreign accents, scraps of overheard conversation, and countless bits of speech and noise that filled the densely packed capital. (93)

Alas the scholars! These grey people, who talk about sources, and read them! They miss the real life, the *Lebenswelt* and *Umwelt* surrounding and embracing William's senses. This romantic fantasy of unregistered *parole*, of unrecorded sounds and regional accents, is unwittingly indebted to Merleau-Ponty. If Shapiro believes he is eluding the grasp of theory by inviting us, with Whitman, to close the book and open the window, he is wrong. His comment is laden with theoretical assumptions (orality, aurality, origin, intuition, evidence, presence, spontaneity), all of which lead ultimately to the notion of *immediacy*. The sounds are lost to us, but not to Shakespeare, who managed to immediately record some of them. "Some of these" adds Shapiro, "made their way into Shakespeare's writing, others impeded it, and still others were a kind of precondition for it" (93). The coda reveals Shapiro's best poststructuralist instincts, as he is probably thinking of transcendental infrastructural preconditions, but the confidence with which he asserts that cries, bells, accents, and bits of speech "made their way into Shakespeare's writing" is simply appalling. The poet as mechanical bricoleur, as "flower arranger and sous chef" (Lupton, *Shakespeare Dwelling* 115), of things themselves as they directly land atop his desk—this is indeed another version of immediacy, and one that informs a great deal of biographical work on Shakespeare—from Park Honan to Stephen Greenblatt. Most scholars who undertake to write about his life make the very mistaken assumption that reading is not a part of life. In the case of Shakespeare, it was very likely one of the most, if not the most, important.[5] Shapiro suggests that Shakespeare's truth is what happened at the other side of his room window. Adorno would have told him that "wahr ist nur, was nicht in diese Welt passt" (*Ästhetische Theorie* 93). Shapiro's book is caught in the critical enchantment of art's unmediated sensual *presence* or immediacy (*unmittelbare sinnliche Gegenwart*, 93). It is, and will remain, a very popular book. Perfect for a *present*.

The ideological pressure of immediacy can be attested in the relevance that the notion of "presence-effects" has gained among scholars, like Bruce Smith, Julia Lupton, and Matthew James Smith. The notion may owe part of its purchase to the neo-historicist empiricist drives—Greenblatt's turn to

---

5 Honan's way of opposing book-learned rhetoric and eloquence to "the experience of life" (57, 82, 121) is simply ridiculous. Grammatical instruction, verbal memorization, absorbed reading, these were all *life experiences* for Shakespeare.

history in order "touch the effect of the real" (*Learning to Curse* 7)—but has been redeployed "to capture the range of pre-semantic, rhythmic, affective, gestural, respiratory and other embodied aspects of face-to-face encounters that actors realise on stage" (Lupton & Smith, "Introduction" to *Face-to-Face* 6). As I have already noted in a previous section, the idea of "presence-effects" is taken from Hans Ulrich Gumbrecht (*Production of Presence: What Meaning Cannot Convey*) who in turn claims to derive it, through Jauss and Gadamer, from the German masters of phenomenology (Heidegger and Husserl). The lure of immediacy is here portentous: "Between faces in conflict there is no strict divide between form and content, intention and constraint" (Lupton & Smith 10). One senses again the idealist-aesthetic prejudice that runs through Kottman's work. What is content if not formalized? Where do we find unconstrained (immediate, unmediated) intention? This is all a delusion. In literature, everything is constraint and form, *force et signification*. The rest (contents, intentions, presences) is bad literature, pride, metaphysics, prejudice, religion, ideology, sense and sensibility.

Constraint and form spell, for instance, the functional conditions of any trope, including prosopopoeia. It is very surprising that in a book dedicated to the face-to-face in Shakespearean drama there is no single reference to this trope. Or not surprising, for Derrida sharply demonstrated that the very possibility of the Levinasian visage is predicated upon the effacement of material linguisticity, upon, that is, the oblivion of the trope: "Le visage n'est pas une métaphore, le visage n'est pas une figure. Le discours sur le visage n'est pas une allégorie, ni, comme on serait tenté de le croire, une prosopopée" (*L'écriture* 149). To argue in tropological terms about the transcendental-formal conditions of the face-to-face, intimating that the face is but another linguistic *figure*, would of course interpose mediation in a process that is—like touching the dagger or gazing at the martlet's nest—characterized by transcendent *immediacy*.

2

"Immediate" is an interesting adjective. First, because, in the course of its etymological evolution, it mutated its meaning from "intervening, interposed" in the late 14c to "with nothing interposed, direct" in the early 15c. This dramatic reversal was very likely produced through the mistaking of a spatial preposition (*in mediate* as in the middle or in the way) for a negative prefix (*in-mediate* as non-mediate). The latter meaning takes in modern English—including Shakespeare's—a variety of modulations: immediate as resulting without delay, as pressing or urgent, as next in a sequence, and as nearest or close, both in spatial location and within a family.⁶ The fact that the slippery instance of the letter (*in mediate* > *in-mediate*) again draws our attention to semantic contradictions, inconsistencies, and flat reversals reads like a fabular demonstration of the need to take stock of the materiality of signifiers and tropes in the act of interpretation. Nothing, not even immediacy, proves immediate enough.

Perhaps the most spectacular version of Shakespearean scholarship sponsoring the enchantments of immediacy can be found in the work of Simon Palfrey. The version is spectacular both by virtue of the critic's very remarkable critical talents and because of the steadfastness of his commitment to this phenomenological notion. Let me quote the closing sentence of his and Tiffany Stern's "Introduction" to *Shakespeare in Parts*:

> But by looking at parts we not only discover a newly active, choice-ridden actor; we discover a new Shakespeare, whose part-based understanding and experimentation lead to remarkable innovations in creating subjectivity and engineering dramatic affect, producing on-stage drama of *unprecedented immediacy*. (12)

This *unprecedented immediacy*, which Palfrey elsewhere places at the service of Shakespearean ontological *possibility*, resembles the *unpredictable spontaneity* that Kottman and Lupton discover in Shakespearean interpersonal action.

Simon Palfrey is a contemporary scholar who reads Shakespeare baroque poetics through the lenses of a romantic, late-modernist expressionism. His conception of Shakespeare poetics is dominated by *multum-in-parvo* notions of multiplicity, recursivity, and possibility, of conflation, confusion, and embodiment. He upholds a creationist aesthetics of multiple, many-sided incarnation, and the tropes he relies on most are the symbol and the metaphor. He sees language as an incessant, procreant, diffusive force, endowed with creationist potential—the power, that is, to generate world, meaning, possibility.⁷ The esemplastic imagination is, in his critical hands, exasperated

---

6 Shakespeare often uses the temporal adverbial "immediately," implying "promptly or without delay." "Immediate" as an adjective he uses more sparingly, with the adverbial sense of "without delay" (*Cymbeline*), or "next in the line to throne" (*2 Henry IV*, *Hamlet*). But immediate can also mean something "inmost or very internal": "I kiss thy hand, but not in flattery, Caesar, / Desiring thee that Publius Cimber may / Have an immediate freedom of repeal" (*Julius Caesar* 3.1.52–54). Or something spatially "very near".

7 Palfrey's trust on Shakespearean possibility is shared by Nuttall, who describes the poet as "the philosopher of human possibility" (*Shakespeare* 381).

into its reversal—the imaginative multiplication of the many out of the ever-emerging one. Language, for Palfrey, is no formal-transcendental structure, no system of constructive rules. Language is only language in action, speech act, *embodied parole*. His focus is on *energeia*, not *ergon*, and his disinterest in the *completed work* (as outcome or result) causes a great deal of terminological indecision: he seldom refers to "playtexts" or "texts," sometimes to "plays," very often to the fluid "medium" and the "playworlds." With this romantic conception of language, aesthetics, and poetics in mind, Palfrey set out in the mid-nineties to read Shakespeare's late plays, and he produced what remains, in my opinion, one of the most rare, acute, and original exercise of sustained critical reading produced in our post-theoretical age: *Late Shakespeare: A New World of Words* (1997). The strategy he employs is simple: since Shakespeare's language is this anomic, immanent, creationist force—something like Humboldt's ἐνέργεια—any external constraint that, in the form of explanatory systems, epochal genres, ruling ideas, critical paradigms, or literary categories, seeks to discipline the extant Shakespeare work (ἔργων) into stable meaning is bound to failure, and must be dismissed. A great deal is accordingly ousted, both in the way of critical frameworks (Foucault's epistemes, Marxian ideologies, the logocentric paradigm) and in the way of period cultural configurations (the category of romance, the Republican ideology of *vivere civile*, the monarchical ideology of the body politic, the scripted patterns of mythical heroism). Shakespeare's fecund and unpredictable *parole* navigates the space where these contextual or supervened structures of meaning would operate as obstacles and sirens, and the task of the critic is to track this dynamic adventure of resistance, contestation, and advance. One can only admire Palfrey's eloquent report of this exegetic trailing. The book is, however, not exempt of theoretical risks, the direst of which is the claim to give up theory altogether—and, in particular, deconstructive theory.

Palfrey's opening remarks delineate what appears to be a method of *antithetical criticism*. It invokes a standard interpretation of the Shakespearean late "romance" and proceeds to its meticulous undoing. If the standard is a straw-reading or bogey, the whole strategy will founder. If the undoing is specious or incomplete, the strategy is also at risk. Despite these perils, the reader is confronted at the very outset with what appears to be a self-conscious exercise in dialectical—mediation-sensitive—hermeneutic, not unlike the stock deconstructive reading. No reader can expect, at this prefatorial point, the onslaught of brine immediacy that will very soon flood and suffocate the exegesis. Palfrey opens with a heuristic determination of the revocable hermeneutic model that has wrongly appropriated the Shakespeare late play, speaks vaguely of "a reputation," of discovered "myths," of definitions that are "often thought."

Gradually, the misconstrued object (*The Tempest, Cymbeline, The Winter's Tale, Pericles*) emerges as a decorous courtly work marked by an aristocratic-ethic idealism where notions of grace, nature and beneficent destiny are asked to wait upon the ruling power. Palfrey adds that the Shakespearian romance is often regarded as an "amplification of some such idealism, with a vision not simply patriotic, but dream-sewn, hierophantic, celestial" (1). He then offers examples of traditional interpretations (Norbrook on *Cymbeline*, Edwards on *Pericles*) that would fit the standard, and denounces their shared limitations. He speaks of "the priority given to the pre-emptive master cribs over polysemous or performative liberties" (2). These *performative liberties* are, at the level of language, what the *unpredictable interpersonal action* identified by Kottman and Lupton is on a pragmatic plane. Pre-emptive readings, argues Palfrey, falsify the stylistic and ideological heterogeneity of the plays by forcing them to operate under imaginary rules of sublime propriety. This obscures the romances' inherent (figural and thematic) impropriety, subversion, and surprise. Palfrey shuns the hermeneutic recourse to ideas of lost innocence, providence, and destiny as mere expressions of critical repressive and rigid wishful thinking. And he denounces the privileging of teleology, stark contrast and rigid binarism—good and evil, misery and happiness—over conflation and confusion. In teleological or binaristic readings,

> there is little room for local detail, still less for subversion or surprise; the *material* qualities in history and language are effaced by a binarism which is never a mirror, never conflation or confusion, but at best a stark contrast framing unswerving loyalties and necessities.
> 3; emphasis in the original

This may not be the place to fully engage the question of Shakespeare's *strange art of necessities* (*King Lear* 3.2.68), of his loyalties to verbal antecedence, subtextual earliness and ideological priority, but let me recall that they still remain an open question. What is remarkable in Palfrey's comment is the period theoretical syncretism he achieves by connecting neo-historicist claims (to local detail, subversion, history), anti-deconstructive assumptions (to revoke the very existence of binarism), and neo-materialist aims (to attend to *material* qualities). What is left unformulated is the role language is asked to play in such hybrid reading method. What are the "*material* qualities of language" that facilitate "conflation or confusion"? Ideational, conceptual qualities, or material (acoustic and graphic) qualities? This is unclear. What is by contrast very apparent is that conflation and confusion evoke a romantic conception of language as a *synthetic* force of the imagination. While conflation spells *aesthetic concordance* (*Übereinstimmung*), confusion registers the opposite of (Cartesian, Hegelian, Saussurean) difference. Is this adhesion to a pre-modern conception of language in any way related to Palfrey's diffidence vis-à-vis deconstruction? One thing at a time.

The problem, of course, is how to celebrate impropriety (and subversion, and conflation, and confusion) without repairing to some version of *binarism*. Palfrey is alive to this predicament, and he evades it—at this prefatory stage, at least—by conjecturing that "it may be in disjunction itself that one identifies Shakespeare's *dialectical ambition* and political preoccupations" (4; emphasis added). In his reading of *The Winter's Tale*, he contends that "Shakespeare's disjunctive pastorals seem to ensure from just such a failure of authority, such a collapse of linguistic and conceptual wholeness" (*Late* 80). So there is binarism (part-whole, subversion-power), then, after all. To call it "disjunction" and attribute its operativeness to Shakespeare's openly "dialectical ambition" is not only a confirmation that a play of two (binarism) is actually in order. It is also a vigorous aggravation of the problem. The same applies to the claim that Shakespearean "body language" expresses itself disjunctively with respect to organic tropes of the body politic that seek to contain somatic excess: "Words undertake a constant battle to reconcile their fluidity with the unified, unitary social body. Such multiplicity cannot be contained and ordered in the idealized heroic body: hence the tragedy of organicist logos" (82).[8] The argument is manifestly antithetic and dialectical, if not plainly deconstructive. But what is exactly Palfrey trying to say? To begin with, who is the "one" that identifies Shakespeare's "dialectical ambition"? Probably the revamped hermeneut that has left behind the busted romance model. But then, what does that "leaving behind" mean? Is Palfrey to forget all he has learned about providence and deliverance in Wilson Knight, Frye, Norbrook and Edwards? Or is rather the memory of that reading to be inscribed as the precondition of his neoteric gloss? The latter would overly denote a dialectical procedure, which I believe to be perfectly sensible, but Palfrey has shifted the scene of dialectics from the act of decoding (reading) to the act of encoding (writing), as part, that is, of the author's own ambition. This I take too as a dexterous point, which obviously forces us to reconsider the nature and size of what Hans Robert Jauss, following Gadamer, would call the *Erwartungshorizont* or horizon of expectations. If Shakespeare is effectuating a disjunction within a paradigm, obviously this paradigm is less the heuristic construction of modern critics like Wilson Knight or Frye than the actual literary practice that *romance* stood for in Shakespeare's

---

8   He will later speak of "Shakespeare's reworking of the romance 'body politic'" (*Late* 94).

own time. Palfrey's apropos consideration of Ben Jonson's critical reaction to his rival's late art contributes to just this mode of appreciation—rightly called dialectical. And yet, this mode of appreciation is far from being the dominant one in a study that ultimately plumps for "a kinetic dialectic, unresolved and combative, between co-existing yet antinomic ideologies" (4). Sadly, however, this notion of a *kinetic dialectic*—in Palfrey's expert hands, a multi-button blender where everything and anything (tropes, ideas, themes, ideologemes, emotions) are invited to melt (to conflate and confuse) into a novel cipher of polymorphic subversion—is simply not a *dialectic*. In its pathos for effusively assertive indistinctiveness it is rather the opposite of a rational dialectic—it resembles much more a backsliding (because deprived of the virtual idea) *life-becoming course*. Thus, we are invited to infer, the plays' "antinomic appearance" (5) is not going to be interpreted as the effect of Shakespeare's conscious attempt at undermining the conventions of romance. This, which would make perfect sense as a starting hypothesis, is not however Palfrey's declared intention. It is perhaps too predictable and simple. And yet, once more, the platitudes of binarism are retained in the appeal to *antinomy*.

Let me analyze this conflict more closely. From the very beginning, Palfrey strives to distance himself from exegetic routines tied to dialectical servitudes—thesis and antithesis, subversion and containment. He invariably concentrates on the sovereign immanence of the plays' figural language, as an autonomous realm of meaning-production that is only obliquely involved in the intimation of transcendent (religious, political) meanings. This calls for a monistic metaphysics of *creatio continua*. No extraneous paradigm like Foucaldian power should deprive personal verbal performance from its creationist unpredictability: "Textualizing and aestheticizing political and semantic agency, the movement's predetermining paradigms rob both self and language of suppleness, surprise, and liberty" (9). In Bruce Smith and Brian Vickers we found a similar defense of the unprecedented quality of personal communication combined with a parallel critique of predetermining formal paradigms, like *langue*, ideology, or the unconscious. Note here the tacit equivalence between self and language: arguably, a libertarian expressionism controls the logic of this transaction. This is sharply thrown into relief whenever Palfrey pauses to, rather unclearly, determine the plays' political dimension. One senses the anxiety of the young scholar who fears imputations of ideological innocence, if not political quietism: to survive in the academic ecosystems of the late 1990s, close reading had to make room for the astute indictment of art's connivance with power—or cease to exist academically altogether. In its graceful combination of stylistics and ideological critique, Bakhtinian analysis—ever at hand in the book's sensational reports of disruptive corporal tropology—offers Palfrey the trapeze to perform his reading acrobatics while remaining "aloof from Marxist teleological commitments" (9). Of course, these teleological commitments, which are sorely real and wholly noticeable in all bland appropriations of materialism (new historicism, utopian materialism, eco-phenomenology, political theology, and messianic spiritualism) are never the necessary consequence of a dialectical procedure. Theodor Adorno and Slavoj Žižek are both right in tracing back all forms of critically informed materialism to their common origin in Hegelian—whether negative or not—dialectic. So in order not to land in the safety net, Palfrey goes political. He starts by reminding us that romantic readers were "aware, if also at times afraid, of the plays' potent mixture of symbolism and politics" (2). He later insists of the failure of panopticon methods—ideology-oriented and Foucauldian, or alert to "textual indeterminacy and materiality"—that "rarely tease of the politics of a particular phrase or character, or how the language operates 'in and around' its unique spoken moment" (10). This claim is crucial because it relegates (deconstructive) material-textual indeterminacy to the Hell of *framework methodologies*. This raises the question of the kind of materiality, if any, Palfrey favors in his attempt to erect a *playwork methodology*, one that allows the play to freely work out its ontology of possibility and surprise. One would expect "indeterminacy" to play a role in his romantic poetics of verbal creationism, but the word he has chosen, "confusion," is perhaps more appropriate because it eschews the dialectical (virtually binaristic) oscillation between the determinate and the indeterminate. Confusion, for Palfrey, is a sort of pre-Socratic principle or original amalgamation, something like the immediacy of pure Being that Hegel posits at the beginning of the *Science of Logic* (45–47). This is not exactly the immediacy of givenness and facticity, also detected by Hegel, which we encounter in other phenomenological aesthetics. It is more ontologically primeval, something as undetermined as the Greek ἄπειρον, a notion courted by Renaissance and Romantic Neoplatonists. But let us go back to the terms of Palfrey's claim. As noted above, the adequacy of phrase to character—more broadly construed, of language to self—spells a profound logocentric necessity, no doubt festooned with phenomenological trappings. The final focus on the "spoken moment" brings out more forcefully even the logographic compulsion noticed by Strauss: the Plato-Shakespeare text as a breathing animal that relates via "spoken moments" to the attentive reader. Supposedly, moreover, these explosions of unsystematic and unruly *parole* are likely to deliver "the politics of a particular phrase." What exactly this means is Greek to me. Obviously not the microphysics of power, as he has repeatedly abjured all Foucauldian methods. If, alternatively, Palfrey is trying to undermine a conception of politics as necessarily a master-narrative that

THE FALLACY OF IMMEDIACY   541

carries over its entire plot, vocabulary and syntax in each of its local manifestations, and to suggest that an isolated item of discourse can be immanently invested with political meaning regardless of the potential recuperation of a transcendental text that putatively frames it, then he should make explicit, ab initio, the number, names, and constitutive grammars of those dispersed *phrasal-politics*. But he doesn't. As it turns out, all the examples he gives—Jacobean theocracy, republic humanism—reveal an unbound confidence in historiographic master narratives as well as on Shakespeare's conscious ability to solicit and/or encounter them at micro-logical level. So, again, indeed, we are constantly being sent back to some mode of dialectic.

In his reading of *Pericles*, for instance, Palfrey insists on dropping the unnerving suggestion that republican forms of *vivere civile* and humanist versions of *virtu* crucially inform the play (51). Estates under pressure, virtue under pressure, these are phrases that help modulate the argument but receive no genuine explanation, let alone textual corroboration. To argue that *Pericles* upholds "the need for [...] reflexive public discourse" (67) is well intended (we feel Pocock and Habermas pressing in just this direction) but mystified, a desperate attempt to infuse upbeat (mildly iconoclast) cogency into a play whose stakes in state politics totals up to a blank and whose oppressive family (and sexual) politics strangles all inklings of alternative utopia in a delirious swing of psychic deferrals and domestic anticipations. But politics is not my direct concern in this reading. The real problem is language, as it is the romantic processing of language as exclusively speech-act or performative *parole* that is done through the unwitting implementation of phenomenological *immediacy*. Immediacy is also visible in the undoing of dialectical possibilities that his monistic metaphysics inevitably fosters. Despite his multiple efforts, Palfrey keeps relapsing into a vocabulary (dialectic, antinomy) that is, however adjectivally inflected, manifestly redolent of binarism. This spells an obstacle and the need to overcome it. It portends, too, the ultimate failure to carry out such subjugation, for the whole book is penetrated with what I would term a poorly operative dialectic. What Palfrey calls a *kinetic dialectic* is not convincingly construed as the result of Shakespeare's creative efforts. It emerges rather as Palfrey's perfunctory critical deployment of a genuine dialectic. However paradoxical this may seem, his *kinetic dialectic* resembles the *dialectique arrêtée* described by Sartre in *Critique de la raison dialectique* (63, n2) as one devoid of awareness of "dialectical time," i.e. the temporality—brilliantly analyzed by Husserl and neglected by Sanford Budick—of protention and retention. Thus what Palfrey tentatively envisages as Shakespeare's ambition (dialectical kinesis, disjunction, ambiguity) is but a cover for his own inability to make a reading dialectic work. And the only way to make it work is to assume the relational temporality of reading and writing. Only thus will the spontaneous creativity of the now be exposed for what it is—a mere delusion. What is the temporality of "networks of metaphor" characterized by "polytropical density" (115)? I ignore it, but in Palfreys' hands it is certainly not the temporality of allegory and narrative. Just like sex is not a concatenation of orgasms (three-in-a-row beyond forty is an optimistic prospect), and reproduction not a non-stop sequence of labors and births (triplets are uncommon), a play is not a succession of politics-inducing phrases and world-making tropes.

Through this putative liberation, he thus aims at re-focalizing attention to neglected areas of unexpected tropic significance, whence his focus on categories like "ambiguity and disjunction" (7) that have been shorn of dualistic underpinnings. But this purification is never successfully achieved: his penchant for the detection of analogical structures of figural return (metaphor, symbol) and fractal tropic repetition (controlled metonym) leads him to espouse a conception of the plays' rhetoric that is anything but ambiguous or disjunctive. If the tropes are at all deviant, straying or divisive, they are so with respect to the supposed normative figural behavior of the supposed normative romance. In the limited context of each play, these disjunctive figures unanimously labor for conjunction (conflation, confusion), and Palfrey sees to it that no confirming trope is left unturned. What we are never successfully given is a distinct cutout of this mysterious tiger paper he calls "conventional romance," along with its attending rhetorical structure.[9]

Let me summarize. Palfrey faults critical frameworks interested in "textual indeterminacy and materiality" with the implementation of "panoptical methods [that] rarely tease out the politics of a particular phrase or character" (10). He thus berates *en bloc* critical tendencies that through an "array of ideological-cum-linguistic master-codes" (10) and paradigms "rob both self and language of suppleness, surprise, and liberty" (9). His preliminary strategy of meta-critical denunciation allows him to break ground for his own critical work, which I would describe as a very successful attempt to restore for Shakespearean hermeneutics the notion of text-embodied spontaneous creative agency. This he achieves through a brilliant combination of incisive close reading and romantic expressionism. Still, the denunciation is unwarranted. To argue that "Foucauldian" interpretive paradigms rob language of

---

9   His construal of the paper tiger—the standard conception of the Shakespeare late romance—is open to further additions, scattered across the entire book, with no discernible aim at categorical comprehensiveness. The romance privileges Platonic monuments (nobility, virginity, divinity), it is haunted by Arcadian books and pastoral hillscapes, it remains watertight in its moral plenitude, etc.

suppleness, surprise and liberty is a very inaccurate guess: a detailed reading of Michel Foucault's book-length essay on *Raymond Roussel* would be enough to persuade Palfrey that Foucault is not "Foucaldian," and that Anglo-American college digests of French theory are as inherently unreliable as the field work of self-proclaimed proselytes. Palfrey endorses a conception of Shakespeare's plays as inherently multi-perspectival, heteroglossic, cross-generic, mongrelized, and makes his exegetic indecisiveness over the political nature of these plays depend on their *intentional* formal sloppiness and generic hybridity. The intention behind formal disjunction and rhetorical density is inseparable, he argues, from Shakespeare's "dialectical ambition." Palfrey strategically absolves his critical uncertainty by denouncing the play's political tepidness. I have already pointed out the central fault-lines in this reading: the unexamined romantic conception of language and the incapacity to formulate Shakespeare's distinct political argument. But the major objection is methodological: Palfrey purports to read dialectically (antithetically) and at the same time disavow what de Man would call "the mediating intercession" that language brings to dialectical processes. In other words, he wants to do deconstruction, but rather than asserting the ultimate triumph of difference within a binarism-ridden horizon of writing, he tries to eliminate dualistic thought in a primeval—pre-dualistic—pool of expressionist indifference and confusion. Palfrey doesn't seem to realize that the victory of *indeterminacy*, in deconstruction, hinges on the prevalence of *transcendental langue*, and seeks rather to make *confusion* reign via the antecedence of *transcendent parole*. The anxiety that organizes his responses to deconstruction is another episode in the deficient reception of Ferdinand Derrida in Shakespeare studies.

3

In the "Introduction" to *Late Shakespeare*, he warns the reader that his "project imposes necessary limits to the applicability of a deconstructionist critique," and he goes on to state, confidently, that "Derrida's early work assumes as its bogey a classical logocentrism which might be thought an inappropriate or unrealized 'metaphysic' for Shakespeare's unstable and inwardly shifting 'episteme' (to haul in Foucault's own inexact and contentious term)" (13). Palfrey is here mixing up irreconcilable categories. Logocentrism, on Derrida's view, is not a replaceable, disposable, episteme likely to be reached, entered, and abandoned by human generations projected across a historical continuum. Logocentrism is a chronic condition of Western thought. Derrida describes it as a "métaphysique de l'écriture phonétique" (*De la grammatologie* 11) which, via ethnographic domination, has imposed itself across human cultures. Thus logocentrism is another name for *phonocentrisme*, characterized as "proximité absolue de la voix et de l'être, de la voix et du sens de l'être, de la voix et de l'idéalité du sens" (23). It may be mitigated or resisted, but it cannot be properly transgressed, let alone dispensed with. Derrida makes this point very clear in an interview with Henri Ronse included in *Positions* (1972): "On ne s'installe jamais dans une transgression, on n'habite jamais ailleurs" (21). So the contention that because Shakespeare's unstable "metaphysic" is not "logocentric" we must impose limits on the applicability of a deconstructionist critique is wide of the mark. Such contention only serves to confirm the historical pervasiveness of a logocentric metaphysic (from Plato to Husserl and Palfrey himself) and the need to define the value of an author's "metaphysic" precisely against such inescapable horizon: a resistance to logocentrism that is contentiously aware of itself—"What's in a name?"—is a dialectical confirmation of logocentrism's powerful sway. To apply, therefore, a deconstructionist critique to Shakespeare is a perfectly safe and sound thing to do. Indeed, Palfrey's immediately following asseverations about Shakespeare's language's resistance to "univocal" meaning contribute merely to confirm that the poet probably resisted from within—from within *langue*'s formal-transcendental inside—the metaphysical persuasion that the mental-ideal presentation of meaning in the mind, to the mind (the intentional content), is *the* pre-condition of all meaning. Palfrey, we will see in a moment, deviates from this deconstructive view, and proposes an alternative conception of language where the only thing that holds empirical—and therefore metaphysical—*presence* is the *process* of signification proper. Palfrey coyly concedes that his "methodology is somewhat bastardized, lacking theoretical 'purity'" and he defensively avouches that "so too is life and language" (13). But this admission is uncalled for because unjustified: there is no such thing as a pure deconstructionist methodology, and no demand of doctrinal adhesion (I take that to be his "theoretical 'purity'") urges the work of Derrida, de Man, or any of their serious followers (Hillis Miller, Hartman, Hamacher, Chase, Warminski, Jacobs, Felman, Lukacher, Royle). As I have already denounced in this book, textbook deconstruction construed as a rigid schoolboy method is a convenient fantasy produced by the Anglo-American academia for the rapid consumption of its members: as such, it has proven a routine bogey for those among them that outgrew their post-graduate years with a sense that the method was silly, after all, largely because they understood it, and that therefore there was no point in reading Derrida—lest they should not understand him. Why take the risk?

Logocentrism exerts control over the history of metaphysics, which

> malgré toutes les différences et non seulement de Platon à Hegel (en passant même par Leibniz) mais aussi, hors de ses limites apparentes, des présocratiques à Heidegger, a toujours assigné au logos l'origine de la vérité en général: l'histoire de la vérité, de la vérité de la vérité, a toujours été, à la différence près d'une diversion métaphorique dont il nous faudra rendre compte, l'abaissement de l'écriture et son refoulement hors de la parole 'pleine'.
>
> *De la grammatologie* 11–12

For Derrida, dissension from this epistemic regime of phonetic logocentrism can only take place "within a logocentric epoch" which has not yet come to its end, even if we seem to be witnessing its *clôture* (14). He later mentions "three millennia" of subjection to logocentric metaphysics. Thus logocentrisme doesn's simply designate a metaphysical dispensation; it also nominates an epoch, "cette *époque* de la parole pleine" (64). Dissent from logocentrism, to which Shakespeare certainly contributed, is necessarily logocentric dissent (chronic decentering confirms the existence of a center), and it takes many forms. One of them is to denounce the shortcomings of "a science of writing reined in by (*bridéé par*) metaphor, metaphysics, and theology" (*De la grammatologie* 13). Thus logocentrism—the epistemic dispensation that subjects truth (logos) to phonetic interiority—comes into being through the strategic alliance of metaphor, metaphysics, and theology—precisely the three conditions determining a dominant set of interpretive protocols in the present-day field of Shakespeare studies, the three conditions, let me add, as we will see in a moment, that organize Palfrey's creationist conception of language. We must also recall that metaphysics and theology were inextricably conjoined by Heidegger in a decisive essay that argued the dependence of the metaphysics of identity upon the concrete *metaphorology* of the Greek term *auto*. To resist logocentrism is to defy and meet this formidable coalition of transcendent armies: proximity, immediacy, presence. Derrida underscores the logocentric implication of all philosophies of presence:

> le logocentrisme serait donc solidaire de la détermination de l'être de l'étant comme présence. Dans la mesure où un tel logocentrisme n'est pas tout à fait absent de la pensée heideggerienne, il la retient peut-être encore dans cette époque de l'onto-théologie, dans cette philosophie de la présence, c'est-à-dire dans la philosophie.
>
> *De la grammatologie* 23

Interestingly, however, Derrida will also argue that Heidegger's relation with *logocentrisme*, which he describes as a "metaphysique de la presence," is conflictual in that the (silent) voice of being is a metaphor that eschews the possibility of reliance on any form of articulate language. The resulting adoption of a "decalage metaphorique" (36; Spivak's rendition of this phrase as 'metaphoric discrepancy' is insufficient) makes it all the more evident that a full-fledged logocentric program can adopt *metaphor* as its expressive medium. And yet, despite the fact that Heidegger purports to ground the possibility of a true ontology in a pre-metaphysical site that is also immune to language constrains, his positing of an ontic-ontological difference is itself premised upon a more original grounding, i.e. that of the *différance* of writing (*De la grammatologie* 38). Such *différance* is no origin, no ground, and it needs to pass through the determination of the ontic-ontological difference before actually crossing it (*biffer*) as a determination. This paradoxical gyration, this circuitous turn, is itself a dialectical figure of Hegelian overcoming that Derrida calls *tour d'écriture*. Spivak's translation, *trick of writing*, retains only one figural sense of the term *tour*, and it neglects the sense of ride, turn, lap, that is contextually implicit in Derrida's *odological* argument: note the terms *plus proche, passage*. I want to retain this figure of the *tour d'écriture* because it aptly conveys the sense of mediation that, central to Hegelian dialectic, also underpins the deconstructive argument. Derrida may have rightly unmasked the metaphysical *immediacy* that governs the pivotal notions of Hegel's aesthetic (symbol, metaphor, representation). But his construal of the mediation of *écriture* is robustly Hegelian in its dialectical effectiveness. There is no overstating the importance that this *tour* has for many Shakespeare characters that undertake, more or less without a book, their "course of learning and ingenious studies" (*The Taming of the Shrew* 1.1.9). If tropes are turns (and tours, and detours, and courses), then metaphor and symbol, based on immediacy and transparency, on concordance and harmony, on exact content-form correspondence, on direct sublation and unsoiled substitution, are tropes that aspire to give up their arbitrary condition, inscriptive materiality and relational mediation, and become pure presences—or present processes.

"Language" in Shakespeare's age, according to Palfrey, "was not merely an instrument, but a *subject*, an agile, almost supra-notional, metaphor of evolving self-presence" (11). This view combines a phenomenological metaphysics of self-presence with a romantic poetics of metaphor and evolution and a politics of pragmatic agency. The focus is on the procreant agency of a process *with* a subject. Palfrey concurs with Eagleton that Shakespeare is proleptic in his anticipation of Marx, Freud, Nietzsche, Derrida, "and sundry other modern giants" (Raber's "host of eminent Men"). This approximates his position to a speculative-dialectical method, but there is a but. Actually, a "still":

> And while there are Cartesian speculations galore in Shakespeare, still his work remains in important senses free from the dichotomizing epistemologies which, from Descartes "cogito" on, have characterized the modern metaphysical tradition. It is indeed partly Shakespeare's very "primitivism"—for instance his unsentimental willingness to find root for both language and temperament in the desiring body—which makes him seem so "modern," so imminent. And this openness to novelty, in turn, suggests Shakespeare's scrupulous intimacy to his own historical moment. (13)

Everything is here: the anti-Cartesian animus, the phenomenology of the flesh inflected through Deleuzian echoes ("the desiring body"), the naturalization and embodiment of language, the neo-historicist attention to the moment. But here too we can find the romantic drive to a primitivism of roots and grounds that is so visible in metaphysical foundationalism. Metaphysics is not totally forsaken in the act of rejecting the Cartesian cogito: it regresses, with a vengeance, both in the primeval roots and in the transcendence of the body. Still harping on Derrida, Palfrey goes on to maintain that

> an awareness of philological, or indeed ideological, "différance" is useful mainly in so far as it might help to tap the strains and nuances within the political discourse of Shakespeare's time and place. The referents are there, the signs signify; it is just that they are neither straightforward nor univocal (13).

Palfrey seeks to come through as a scholar who uses deconstruction selectively and conditionally, but, in the turns and twists of his expostulation, he again misrepresents Derrida. First, *différance* has no other critical "use" than that of exposing strains and nuances in logocentric discourse. His use of it is therefore sadly unexclusive. Second, in a linguistic theory dominated by the work of *différance* there is no room for "referents" (this faith in intentional objects, characteristic of neo-historicism and historical phenomenology is a transcendent delusion) and signs never signify other than in deviated and equivocal ways. Palfrey claims that his "methodology is somewhat bastardized, lacking theoretical 'purity'; but so too is life and language" (13). His strategic reliance on deconstructive critique is not only belied by his faith in objectal transcendence (referents) but also by the methodological precedence he attaches to "impure" life and language. This reveals, as I have already noted, a metaphysical prejudice. It is no surprise therefore that he should construe "the critical challenge," like Bruce Smith, as one of reconstruction—"how best to reconstruct renaissance discourse" (13)—and not deconstruction. This drive to reconstruction mirrors, on the critical plane, the play's "polychronic search for repair" (77). Palfrey shuns frameworks and paradigms, but this deep homology is obviously controlled by the kind of "humanist" design we encounter in the work of Wilson Knight and Frye.

The aesthetic notion of concordance enters Palfrey's critical discourse through his sustained identification, across Shakespeare's "medium," of homology, analogy, and embodiment (18–19). Let me underline that such identification conflicts with his repudiation, elsewhere, of "secure analogies and elegant orders" (95) as the artificial outcome of repressive exegetic paradigms. "The analogic technique," he argues, "fosters the *creation*, through multiple displacements and parallels, of *shared bodies*" (19, emphasis added), a notion indebted to Merleau-Ponty's phenomenology of embodiment and intersubjectivity. But Palfrey goes a step further and considers that "these 'characters' become cumulative embodiments of 'unwilled,' lime-like language, the plastic semiotics of the particular crises at hand" (19). Thus homology and analogy prompt a dramaturgy of shared bodies that are, at bottom, the plastic emergence of "lime-like language"—something like the speech-thought "continuum" Bruce Smith wanted to discover in Saussure, or even the "couche spéciale dénommée matérielle ou *hylétique* faisant," according to Levinas, "l'objet d'une discipline phénoménologique" (*Théorie de l'intuition* 66). This emergence occurs through the "supra-characterological metaphoric energy which is Shakespeare's 'take' on his times" (19). It is the geological, spontaneous, magmatic, seismic, *immediacy* of this metaphorical energy that singularizes, according to Palfrey, Shakespeare's creationist poetics. At the end of his reading of *Pericles*, he states that "different 'characters' are needed to take up the unrecuperable energies of language which, in its metaphorical plenty, registers desire beyond strict precedent and decorum" (78). This libidinal construal of verbal *energeia* hinges on an exclusively positive and analogical conception of rhetoric: the choice of metaphor over any other trope betokens a metaphysical reliance on the immediate *presentations* of intentional content. As I have already noted, metaphor and symbol are the two (romantic) tropes that best conceal the aberrant mediation of their constitutive signifier: their very *raison d'être* is the sublation of contingent materiality.

It is hard to see what exactly the role of "referents" (intentional objects) is in a philosophy of language that locates the crisis of creation exclusively in the *intentional process*: "Shakespeare supplies metaphor-in-process" (26), he tells "[tales] of process and surprise" (162).[10] The object, we must assume, is something as theologically sudden and metaphysically heavy as "Caliban [rising] out of the mud" (24). In *Cymbeline*, Palfrey argues, "Shakespeare is developing that radical conception of theatrical metaphor—language given a metamorphic, almost coagulative potency to become as much 'mass' as that which empirically is physical—which finds consummate expression in Caliban" (97). To be sure, something in Shakespeare anticipates "the force that through the green fuse drives the flower" (Dylan Thomas 13), but to turn his work into an untimely bouquet of primordial expressionism is simply unrealistic. Palfrey shows no philosophical qualms in asserting the *transcendent* (empirical and physical) productivity of language, nor is he indecisive about the possibility of its "consummate expression." The expression is consummate, i.e. fulfilled, because "preparatory metaphor comes relentlessly true" (115). By "keeping its promises" (24), language produces *true metaphors, consummate expressions* and *concordant creations*: the process conforms to an intentional content which the process itself generates and retro-posits. Nothing explains better Palfrey's conception of the poetic language's capacity to created unprecedented meaning than Bloom's coda to his famous apothegm—"the meaning of a poem can only be another poem, but *another poem—a poem not itself*" (*Anxiety* 70)—for what Palfrey ultimately suggests is that the meaning of Shakespeare's textual parts are those very textual parts themselves. The Hölderlin simile—"Worte, wie Blumen, enstehen [*words originate like flowers*]" ("Brot und Wein")—examined by de Man in "Intentional Structure of the Romantic Image" conveys this notion of generative process: "The similarity between the two terms does not reside in their essence (identity), or in their appearance (analogy), but in the *manner* in which both originate" (emphasis added). The image, in short, "is essentially a kinetic process" (*The Rhetoric of Romanticism* 3). A *process* may be *kinetic*, no doubt, but a *kinetic process* is not a dialectic. When a dialectic becomes kinetic, linguistic mediation gets reabsorbed by the immediacy of a language that has become the very house of Being. To argue, as Heidegger does in his readings of Hölderlin, that "the immediate *is* itself the mediating intercession" (de Man, *Blindness and Insight* 261) is contradictory. De Man's reconstruction of the German thinker's argument puts forward an ontological thesis about origin that is, *mutatis mutandis*, what Palfrey unwittingly espouses in his readings of *Late Shakespeare*:

---

10   For the dialectic between a poetics of process (Mallarmé) and a poetics of the sensuous object (Baudelaire), see Paul de Man, "Process and Poetry" (1956), included in *Critical Writings 1953–1978*, 64–75.

> Heidegger's thesis can be considered as demonstrated if the following identification is granted: the intercession, which is language, is also the immediate itself: the law, the language that differentiates, is the intercession, the immediate or Being itself: everything is united at the plane of Being.
>
> *Blindness and Insight* 261

Everything (the Heraclitean τὰ πάντα) is united, conflated, confused, Palfrey would develop, at the plane and ground of slime and mud, in the original chaos.

4

The view of language that transpires in *Late Shakespeare* is confirmed and developed in Palfrey's subsequent monographs, especially in *Doing Shakespeare* (2005) and *Shakespeare's Possible Worlds* (2014). In the "Preface to the Second Edition" of the former book, language has become such a transparent (plastic, docile, fluid) medium of expressionist creation that there is no need to mention it:

> Let us imagine that we are entering these plays for the very first time. We have never been here before. We do not know what world we are in, its rules or coordinates, or where we are from moment to moment. We cannot be sure what counts as life. All we can trust is that every last part of this playworld is potentially animate with mind, motion, emotion. (XI)

What is missing in this conjectural scenario is the word "word." What is the role of words in Shakespeare's playworlds? Palfrey's is a perfect romantic fantasy of immediacy. By giving up the mediation of words—Palfrey mentions *mind, motion, emotion* and *playworlds*, but doesn't refer to *language*—he disencumbers the act of interpretation from what Walter Jackson Bate called *the burden of the past*—which is also de burden of the present, the weight of contexts and intertexts, the dense mediation of concepts and tropes, the pressure of scripted ideologies. As Althusser pointed out in 1965, in an essay on "Freud et Lacan" that paves the way to the best Derrida (1966–1975), "tout se joue dans la matière d'un langage formé précédemment" (*Écrits sur la psychanalyse* 42). The task of the critic, argues Palfrey, is to embody Shakespearean energeia—"Our job is to give body and motion to the Shakespeare-potential" (xi)—in the delusional conviction that this potential is primeval not secondary, not derived, that this energeia is not also ergon, this potential not outcome, and that our not being the first to enter these playworlds (Friday and Caliban are always-already there) turns prior hermeneutic mediation into a constitutive absence of the "playworld" at hand. But Palfrey doesn't care about *subtextuality* or *secondariness*. These modes of belatedness and determinism are inimical to his persuasion that "in Shakespeare, pretty much anything can bear life—not merely refer to life, but bear life, embody life" (xi). The life of words, conceived of as "storehouses or potentials" is not to be preempted or accounted for by the "inscription" of "media [...] in the text" (xii). The transcendental totality (of paradigm, of *langue*, of text) stoops to the sporogenous vibrancy of parts: "But what if each bit of the playworld is new, as life always is?" (xiii) To get at the excess and multi-form of Shakespeare's playworlds requires, he urges, "a combination of contextual knowledge, applied technique, and a feelingly sentient imagination." Predictably, "it is the last which is the most vital. However, it can only be released if it is applied to that is actually there in the dramatic phenomena" (xiv). There are no words, only potentials, no playtexts, only playworlds, no signifiers, only dramatic phenomena, and the chief response to them is, alas, "a feelingly sentient imagination." The task of the sentient, imaginative scholar is to follow the dynamic "traces" scattered in Shakespeare's "creations," the better to "apprehend the manifold life within. Such a response is not derivative, or second-hand, or a pale shadow of the primal source. It is the thing itself, felt and growing into futures" (xiv). All the relevant phenomenological assumptions are on deck: origin, spontaneity, concept-free apprehension, and "the thing itself," here identified less with the intentional object than with the intentional process that aims at it. And yet, I am taking for granted Palfrey's unproblematic endorsement of *intentionality*, a notion barely operative in his prior book, where even "dialectical ambition" played a notoriously insufficient role. As we progress in this second book, however, the notion begins to emerge. In the chapter on "Difficulty" he identifies "a powerfully directing authorial intention," even if there is "a passing of meaningful responsibility" (27) to the actors. Shakespeare, we are next told, "*intends* multiple possibilities" (28, emphasis in the original), and his "rhetoric is directed, intentional speech" (31). In strict aesthetic-representational logic, the direction of intentionality translates directly (immediately) into the direction of rhetoric, and this way intention spells the tension that effectuates the concordance—both *Übereinstimmng* and *Erfüllung*—between intentional content and intentional object. Shakespeare's procreative *parole* makes a new world visible: "language is not primarily there to describe what is already known and observed. Instead, it is itself finding out what might be *present*" (37, emphasis added). Otherwise put, "it is the words that do most of the work of making such dramatic words *visible to the mind*" (38, emphasis added). A world present and visible to the mind: Husserl, whose theory of noemata is a far cry from Palfrey's procreant words, would have rejoiced with this phenomenal prospect. Also Adorno, with a grin:

> The pure object of intention should be the ideal unity. The in-itself should appear in the act. Husserl will do justice to the desideratum, "Learn to see ideas," by introducing a type of act "in which the objects apprehended in these manifold forms of thought are self-evidently given, with the acts, in other words, in which our conceptual intentions are fulfilled, achieve self-evidence and clarity.
>
> *Against* 99[11]

In *Doing Shakespeare,* Palfrey asserts that "*aesthetic* form is history-in-*action,* just as it can *embody* a character's consciousness in *process*" (9, emphases added). Nine years later, in his book *Shakespeare's Possible Worlds* (2014) this phenomenological profession of aesthetic faith is reformulated in his theory of *formactions.* "Words," Palfrey contends, "work" both "as instruments in the theatre and as embodiers of meaning." But in theatre words are of course not alone. He sees, he adds, "every moving unit [textual and extratextual] as a potential mode or node of language" (11). Every single one of Shakespeare's instruments, "not only his figures of speech, is potentially endowed with multiple 'mimic actions.' It is these instruments that I will call 'formactions'" (12). This theory, and the exegetic use to which it is put in this extraordinary book, demands much more space and attention than I can give it here. Suffice it to say, by way of conclusion, that this creationist and pragmatic conception of language is but another variation on the transcendent-metaphysical resourcefulness of figurative *parole,* at the expense of the transcendental system of *langue,* and that the phenomenological notion that subtends the whole hermeneutic project is that of immediacy. Palfrey is now unafraid to proclaim his phenomenological faith. He reads *Macbeth* through Merleau-Ponty, and speaks openly of the play's "phenomenological facts" (access to sensations, witnessing or the sharing of guilt) (*Shakespeare's Possible Worlds* 39–41). And even if he asserts that "no hermeneutic strategy, or phenomenological rationale" can account for the cognitive and perceptive challenges posed by "Shakespearean playlife" (39), he will elsewhere claim, in the course of his rereading of *Pericles,* that "dramatic phenomenology is here worryingly antinomian" (309), and even

---

11 The quoted material inside Adorno's cited passage is drawn from Husserl's *Logical Investigations.*

speak unconditionally of Shakespeare's "bracingly modern aesthetic phenomenology" (234). And Shakespeare's is, for Palfrey, let me insist, a phenomenology of radical immediacy: the basic stuff of the play *Macbeth* is "passionate immediacy: the immediacy of emotions in action" (42); the actor's actions help "constitute a shivering emotional immediacy" (59); although often subverted, Shakespeare's "chosen media" is characterized by a "shared and galvanizing immediacy" (39). It is, in conclusion, "the most basic principle of Shakespeare's work that immediacy harbours things, felt but not articulated, intuited but not quite seen, heart but not understood" (330). *Immediacy* becomes the "storehouse"—likened elsewhere by Palfrey to the word—the "medium" where the concept-free *intuition* of *things* spontaneously eventuates. It may worth mentioning that the image of the storehouse was reserved by Saussure to langue, to the system of language. This re-assignment of energeia and potential—of ontological memory, if you wish—to *per-form-active parole* is perhaps Palfrey's most radical reaction-formation against the cultural authority of Ferdinand Derrida. His most genuine phenomenological gesture.

The celebration of the immediacy of the Shakespeare thing (instrument, playworld, playlife, formation, word, character) is done at great hermeneutic cost. It leaves behind the rich horizons of significance that alone the earliness and priority of formal-transcendental mediation can afford. Speculative dialectics is a method of production and analysis of experience whose basic goal is to expunge immediacy from attestations and justifications of meaning. In the section titled "La conception dialectique du néant" of his book *L'être et le néant*, Jean-Paul Sartre reminds his reader that if Hegel begins his *Science of Logic* in the void *immediacy* of Being—"la simple immédiateté vide" (47–48)—it is the better to reflectively constitute the very ground of all reflective constitution, i.e. mediation. Immediacy is speculatively posited in order to legitimate, among other things, the very retroaction of its own speculative position. Before it can be postulated as an empirical *transcendens* (apeiron, indeterminacy, primeval chaos, confusion, mass), immediacy is a rational trope, a speculative position of thought. This Hegelian proviso played an important part in Marx's resistance to the standard conception of *work*, alive in Proudhon, as a naturalized "objet immédiat" (*Misère de la philosophie* 106). In his *Critique of Hegel's Philosophy of Right*, moreover, he establishes a constant association between the immediate (*unmittelbar*) and the magic (*magisch*) (34). Here he closely follows his admired Hegel, who dissected, in the *Encyclopedia*, the fallacies of immediate knowledge, linking it to primitive religious thinking:

> A second corollary which results from holding immediacy of consciousness to be the criterion of truth is that all superstition or idolatry is allowed

to be truth, and that an apology is prepared for any contents of the will, however wrong and immoral. It is because he believes in them, and not from the reasoning and syllogism of what is termed mediate knowledge, that the Hindu finds God in the cow, the monkey, the Brahmin, or the Lama. (72)

Unattended by mediate knowledge, the Shakespeare scholar stands too by the lime, next to the pool of amniotic liquid, and finds God in the monkey, Shakespeare in the ape, and the original human creature in Caliban. Brave new world. Despite Palfrey's constant appeal to the disjunctive fragment, the Shakespeare playworld he contemplates is ruled by *analogy*, not *anomaly*, by the potential of the positive more than by the work of the negative, and his fragments (the parts of Shakespeare in parts) are always complete fractal mirrors of the whole.[12] At bottom, Palfrey rejects the "discontinuity, alienation and reflection" that are signature features of the dialectic (Adorno, *Hegel* 4). His still aesthetic conception of the harmonious totality is however not Hegel's, for the latter, according to Adorno, "does not make the parts, as elements of the whole, autonomous in opposition to it" (4). Nor does he make them autonomous *in confirmation* of the whole. All in all, in dialectic, the part-whole relation is not fractal or monadologic, if only because neither part nor whole enjoys the metaphysical consistency of the *transcendens*. It should come as no surprise, then, that in Levinas' metaphysical world immediacy should come to the fore. Derrida's predictable reaction was one of utmost impatience. Before phrases like "Face à face sans intermédiaire," Derrida glosses, in Hegelese : "sans intermédiaire et sans communion, sans médiateté, ni immédiateté " (*L'écriture* 134). Derrida insists on "la nécessité indépassable de la médiation" (182), even in attempts to construe (constitute) the other, as Husserl does in his fifth Cartesian meditation, via analogical apperception. But Levinas' adoption of phenomenology can do, we have seen, without transcendental considerations. Only the immediately transcendent matters. Derrida's moving description of the cultural significance of Levinas' thought deploys a tropology of seismic figures (*alluvia, eruption, volcano*) that reminds us of Palfrey's primeval mud:

> A thought for which the entirety of the Greek logos has already erupted, and is now a quiet topsoil deposited not over bedrock, but around a

---

12   For the oscillation of *analogy* and *anomaly* in modern poetry, see de Man's essays in *Romanticism and Contemporary Criticism*.

more ancient volcano. A thought which, without philology and solely by remaining *faithful to the immediate*, but buried nudity of experience itself, seeks to liberate itself from the Greek domination of the Same and the One (other names for the light of Being and of the phenomenon) as if from oppression itself-an oppression certainly comparable to none other in the world, an ontological or transcendental oppression, but also the origin or alibi of all oppression in the world.

> Writing 82–83; emphasis added

Groping *sans philologie* through the primal bliss of the *nudité immediate* (*L'écriture* 122): this is where Palfrey, "faithful to the immediate," has placed us. Face-to-face and body-to-body with Caliban. Facing his cave, contemplating the phenomena and the appearances. To be sure, no turning around towards the transcendental sun will do without that immediate experience of earth, but some turning around (some truly deviant tropism and disjunctive phototropism) must occur if experience (dialectical experience) is to get underway:

> Not every experience that appears as primary can be denied pointblank. If conscious experience were utterly lacking in what Kierkegaard defended as naïveté, thought would be unsure of itself, would do what the establishment expects of it, and would become still more naïve. Even terms such as "original experience," terms compromised by phenomenology and neo-ontology, denote a truth while pompously doing it harm. Unless resistance to the façade stirs spontaneously, heedless of its own dependencies, thought and activity are dull copies. Whichever part of the object exceeds the definitions imposed on it by thinking will face the subject, first of all, as immediacy; and again, where the subject feels altogether sure of itself—in primary experience—it will be least subjective. The most subjective, the immediate datum, eludes the subject's intervention. Yet such immediate consciousness is neither continuously maintainable nor downright positive; for consciousness is at the same time the universal medium and cannot jump across its shadow even in its *own données immédiates*. They are not the truth. The confidence that from immediacy, from the solid and downright primary, an unbroken entirety will spring—this confidence is an idealistic chimera. To dialectics, immediacy does not maintain its immediate pose. Instead of becoming the ground, it becomes a moment
>
> ADORNO, *Negative Dialectic* 39–40

The downright primary, the ground, is a chimera. Only a dialectical *Urgrund* (the gap) would do, but no aesthetic poetics of visual representation (and Palfrey's conception of Shakespeare's remains that very thing) can bear the truly disjunctive, negative and antagonistic work of the lacunar and the abyssal.

CHAPTER 20

The Fallacy of Presentism

1

Presentism was a party, we could say, with Hemingway's permission. But perhaps we should also alter the tense—*presentism is a party*—for it is all about presences in a present that is still rife with the good news, with the intelligence, that is, that Shakespeare is all about us, about you and me, about him and her and them, in our here and now and when. Like an endless birthday party of presents: think of the opulent 2012, 2014 and 2016 celebrations of Shakespeare, with everyone relating, everyone connected, everyone invited to commemorate. Everything—all that happened in the four intervening decades and got more or less registered—is there-here as a given or gift, as a presence or present, for the cultural historian to stockpile and reassemble. With his poems and plays at hand's reach, his corpus an instruction manual to guide us around our difficult times: if the stock market collapses, ask Timon; me too, protests Lucretia; Trump wins the election, liken him to populist Caesar; the pandemic breaks out, scan Romeo's skin for buboes. The game is so easy, so pleasant, so *immediately* rewarding. A redesigned conceptualization of "Shakespeare's *presence*" will enable us to better calibrate his *"immediacy* and power" (Fernie, "Action! *Henry V*" 96–97; emphasis added). The things themselves are here. They are the present intentional objects of what was once present, as intentional content, in Will's body-mind continuum: recall that in phenomenology, the subject *is* his intention (Levinas, *Théorie de l'intuition* 70), that to exist, for consciousness, is merely to be "continuellement *présente* à elle-même" (60; emphasis added), and that knowledge of the external thing (Arendt's *little thing*) amounts to confronting or facing the object: "dans sa *présence* en face de l'objet, se trouve le secret de sa subjectivité" (50; emphasis added). The ethical *face-à-face* was thus foreshadowed by the epistemological *face-à-chose*, and presentism curates the party where things (the intentional objects) are daily given as quotidian gifts. Furthermore, since nothing has ever been so immediately imminent that this present, our present, "so in the current state of the world, not to mention higher education, it seems especially urgent that the works of literary study interface with the *present* in its *immediacy*" (Linda Charnes, "Shakespeare, and belief, in the future," 65; emphases added). More *urgent* today than in 1790? More *urgent* today than in 1917? More *urgent* today than in 1945? I guess I should stop making irrelevant questions. The task of the presentist scholar is to proceed to the search of these objectal presences and retrace the direction of the intention back to the source in Shakespeare's embodied experience: this may involve some surface reading of one of the playtexts, but don't despair, it will not be long before you stumble upon a line like "But such is the infection of the time" (*King John* 5.2.20) to get you started in acrobatic exercises of immediate-presentist extrapolation.

In the chapter of his *Postmodernism* book titled "Nostalgia for the Present," Fredric Jameson reminded us of the necessarily dialectical understanding of the present that is the mark of genuine historicism:

> Historicity is, in fact, neither a representation of the past nor a representation of the future (although its various forms use such representations): it can first and foremost be defined as a perception of the present as history; that is, as a relationship to the present which somehow defamiliarizes it and allows us that *distance from immediacy* which is at length characterized as a historical perspective.
>
> *Postmodernism* 284; emphasis added

The presentist method recommends exactly the opposite relationship, for it is driven by a non-historicist attempt at familiarizing the past (Shakespeare's textual materials) by projecting over it a present gifted with (atoned by) allegedly transparent meanings. From "distance from immediacy" we move on to passionate immediacy. In short, we refamiliarize Shakespeare while he dignifies us. This simple and infinitely rewarding operation takes place under the auspices of immediate embodiment. For the presentist scholar, the present is not history—a dialectical narrative of necessary contingencies arrogated by a fiction of totality—but rather an unmediated collection of facts—or things. And the scholar is licensed to go, once again, to the things themselves.

One of the legacies new historicism has handed down to presentism is an undialectical understanding of social roles and ideological categories. Sartre said once that "Valery is a petit bourgeois intellectual [*intellectuel petit-bourgeois*], no doubt about it. But not every petit bourgeois intellectual is Valery" (*Search for a Method* 56; *Questions de méthode* 53). Admiringly, everyone nodded in agreement. With uncalled-for resentment against Foucault and others, Bloom implied something equivalent about Shakespeare in the mid-nineties (*The Western Canon* 53–56) and everybody complained. Specifically, Bloom observed that "if there is no canon, then John Webster, who wrote always in Shakespeare's shadow, might as well be read in Shakespeare's place, a substitution that would have amazed Webster" (52). By asserting that Shakespeare *is not* Webster, Bloom was opposing the immediacy that shores the mechanical rule of ideological equivalence. The dialectical density of things, what Adorno called *sedimented Geist* and Sartre the *practico-inert*, is to the ontic horizon of factual objects what the *damaged life* of the ideological unconscious is to the horizon of decentered subjectivities. Nothing is immediately equal or identical to anything else. No person to anyone else. Radical ontic difference overrules our horizons of existence. Whereas analogic equivalences may be proposed under rules of systemic totality, the wholesale empiricist equations of presentism imply a neglect of genuine ontic difference as well as a disdain of authentic dialectical collation. At its best, new historicism gave us local information about the material background of Renaissance life that was relevant to local aspects of the meaning of a play. More often, it amounted to a lethal mélange of pre-critical sociology, non-theoretical hyper-empiricism, and neo-Marxian ethicism. Presentist criticism is but an opportunist offshoot of the neo-historicist tree—*opportunist* because by locating Shakespeare's intentional object in the present they forsake the need to study the past. Of studying the present there is of course no question because we (you and me and them) are all presences in the present. We—me, Donald Trump, and the al-Qaeda terrorist—are the present. And it goes without saying that we can all talk about these things themselves, these people, us. On this logic, of course, a stone is the best qualified agent to discuss geological matters. But this idiocy is no objection to the presentist scholar. If a sophisticated critic like Simon Palfrey is capable of arguing that his methodology is bastardized and lacks theoretical purity because "so too is life and language" (*Late Shakespeare* 13), then anything in the way of empiricist-methodological exoneration can be expected: my scholarship is messy, for example, because (my) life is messy—so much is going on, I have to read the papers, watch tv, drive my kids to school, track my social networks, in search of the latest presentation, the latest human appearing, the latest intentional object. Without a sense of method, presentism follows the trail of the *vanishing present*, yet unmindful of the critical-dialectical significance Spivak pressed into this fascinating category. Terence Hawkes and Hugh Grady have recently argued that "the present is [...] a universal and inescapable factor" and that since "we can never, finally, evade the present" ("Introduction: Presenting Presentism" to *Presentist Shakespeares* 5), the neo-historicist agenda ought to be reversed so that we can "begin with the material present" (4). Not unmindful of the theoretical risks incurred, they observe that "taking one's present situation fully into account seems bound to complicate and foreground that dialectical relationship [the relation between historicism and presentism]" (3). But the problem is not so much the detection of that complication as the elision of the assumption of *an uncomplicated access to the present* that sustains their whole program. Was

France's present in 1789 an "inescapable factor" for Louis XVI? What kinds of access did that present afford? How immediate was it? What was it made of—things, phenomena, appearances, images, values, words? How many of those elements, and in what order, do you need in order to constitute the presence of a present? What is "the material present" Grady and Hawkes are talking about? The answer is either unclear or absent. Knowing the present is like doing phenomenology: you only need to be born—and see feelingly, of course, obeying the weight of this sad time—to accomplish it. Like Merleau-Ponty's phenomenology of the flesh, presentism has dismally "reconstituted an intuitionism of immediate access to the other" (Derrida, *On Touching* 191).

Geoffrey Bennington has rightly remarked that "post-theory has often become a thinly made-up return to pre-theoretical habits and a sort of intellectual journalism (preoccupied by the question of the *news*)" ("Inter" 105). In post-theoretical presentism, the reader is treated to a toxic blend of intellectual journalism, sham existentialism, and pre-reflective phenomenology. Moving from one scholar to the next doesn't alter the quality of the treat: one feels trapped in a *mond clos* of self-confirming allusions and self-serving evidence—assailed, like a Le Bruyère reader, by "phénomènes de clôture sociale" (Barthes *Essais* 235). Husserl pointed out with enviable candor that, phenomenologically speaking, the Other (*der Andere*) is a modification of myself (*Modifikations meines Selbst*) (*Cartesianische* 144), and this has become dogma among presentist scholars. A pretentious appeal to "risk, authenticity and the boundary situation" (Adorno, *Hegel* 50) has become the standard prelude to many current readings of Shakespeare. We hear a lot about Shakespeare in 9/11, Shakespeare and climate change, Trumping Shakespeare, Corona-Shakespeare will come soon, and the like. But full truth to the immediacy of the critic's experience cannot be bartered for a genuine appreciation of the mediation of Shakespeare's experience.

I have highlighted three equations that illustrate the theoretical misprisions of presentist readings: "Shakespeare is me," "Richard III is Donald Trump" and "Hamlet is an al-Qaeda terrorist." Let me consider them in some detail.

2

Adorno's moving defense of Hegel in the closing sections of his essay "Aspects of Hegel's philosophy" harbors a lesson that I find amenable to contemporary reapplication in the field of early modern studies. Adorno seeks to counter the prestige of a caricaturized version of Hegel's thought that stems from a calculated misreading perpetrated by late-romantic and proto-existentialist thinkers like Schopenhauer and Kierkegaard:

> Hegel's bourgeois unpretentiousness worked to the benefit of his immeasurable efforts, inscribed with their own impossibility, to think the unconditioned—an impossibility that Hegel's philosophy reflects itself as the epitome of negativity. In the face of that, the appeal to authenticity, risk, and the boundary situation is a modest one. If there is truly a need for thinking the subject in philosophy, if there can be no insight into the objectivity of the matter at hand without the element currently dealt with under the trademark of the existential, that moment achieves legitimacy not in showing off but in shattering that self-positing through the discipline imposed on it by the thing itself and extinguishing itself within it. Hegel is almost without peer in following this path. But as soon as the existential moment asserts itself to be the basis of truth, it becomes a lie. Hegel's hatred of those who ascribed the right of full truth to the *immediacy of their experience* is directed to this lie as well.
> HEGEL 50; emphasis added

Much of what passes today for Shakespeare studies is the result of a moral drive to sublimate elements in the scholar's proximate biographical entourage (ethnic-cultural-religious affiliation, hobbies, gender identity) through the use of more or less conscious phenomenological strategies and the added halo of prestige the name Shakespeare bestows on virtually anything it is attached to. In Adorno's very precise terms, these scholars "ascribe the right to full truth to the *immediacy of their experience*." What is present to them by way of internal or external presentation readily becomes the relevant extreme (the intentional object) of an immediate correlation that the critical operation calls presentist and whose other (accessory) extreme is the intentional content of Shakespeare's experience. Partly to blame for this mess is the phenomenological lifting of the prohibition to mistake confessional relief and emotional self-examination for philosophy: Merleau-Ponty's dismissal of neo-Cartesian psychological description *à la troisieme personne* (*Phénoménologie* 72, 86) has become a license to burble freely about oneself, about one's own narrowly eco-responsible petit-bourgeois domesticated *Lebenswelt*—a nest of relatively banal commitments and affections now widely advertised by the propagating effects of social networks, banal both because they tend to be sadly unexclusive, and formidably indifferent to the issues at hand—when what is due is nothing less, but also nothing more, than a reading of texts written by a third person called William Shakespeare. True enough, as Jameson pointed out summarizing a Lukácsian insight, "the forms of middle-class thought are dependent of the deep inner logic of the content of middle-class life" (*Marxism* 346), but scholars could do better both in detecting their own ideological limits and in mitigating the effect these may have on their interpretive work. Commenting on the ideological pressure of Aristotelian vraisemblance upon reactionary critical practices, Roland Barthes made fun of the delusive prejudice of traditional critics who would treat Racine's characters according to standards of psychological transparency derived from their own limited worldviews: "Cette clarté surprenante des êtres et de leurs rapports n'est pas réservés à la fiction: pour le vraisemblance critique, c'est la vie elle même qui est claire" (*Critique et vérité* 22). Julia Lupton's and Matthew Smith's reliance on what they call "the scripts of everyday experience" (7) to interpret the logic of face-to-face interaction in Shakespearean drama bespeaks a near-unwitting phenomenological reflex, the overrating of the enchantments of an everydayness—Heideggerian and Freudian *Alltäglichleit*—that is, in their view, shared by everyone and unsoiled by doxal or ideological mediation: the assumption is that a phenomenological script—"la vie elle même"—is a clear natural thing out there waiting to be equally retrieved by all of us. The Myth of the Received is but a variation on the Myth of the Given. The arch-expressionist and neo-romantic approach to the exercise of critique results in the routine syllogistic reduction: since "experience in this play is life itself" and "my experience is an experience of life itself," then it follows that "the experience of this play is my experience." Ergo: "This is me!" "Caliban is me!," "Shakespeare is me!" The distortion is not unlike Bruce Smith's mawkish commutation of *As You Like It* into *As It Likes You*, which means that, yes, Shakespeare likes you (Smith, *Phenomenal Shakespeare* 5). In my opinion, the syntactic affordances of the neutral "it" as agent are much better represented by Heidegger's "It gives" (*On Time and Being* 5), a gnomic aphorism whose meaning is cleverly unpacked by Cutrofello: "Just as Kant thinks being not as positedness but as the unpositable ground by which the positable is positable, so Heidegger ultimately thinks of being not as givenness but as that by which the given is given" (*Continental* 57). But to prioritize the condition of givenness over the given—the ground necessity of ontological prodigality (why being and not nothing?) over the specious needs of gifts (who cares? take and go)—is certainly not a priority among affectively regaling scholars. The strength of this distortion partly derives from the radicalization of assumptions of phenomenological intersubjectivity, which may lead the unalert scholar to the delusive program of transparent mind-reading: "Shakespeare's theater is the equivocal space where conventional explanations fall away, where one person can enter another person's mind, and where the phantastic and the bodily touch" (Greenblatt, *Will in the World* 355). Space, persons, minds, the phantastic, the bodily: where is the playtext? Let me recall, by the way, that this celebration of the fusion between the phantastic and the bodily contrasts with Greenblatt's condemnation, in 1987, of a president-cum-film-actor's indifference "to the traditional differentiation between fantasy and reality" (*Learning to Curse* 199). Poor Reagan. So how does it work? Is the differentiation good or bad? Good in some cases (literary activity) and bad in others (political praxis)? Can humans switch on and off, at wish, the fantastic-imaginative faculty? If they can, as Greenblatt appears to suggest, the human world is beautifully pastoralized to pre-Freudian and pre-Marxian conditions. Brave new world.

This delusive romantic assertion—"Shakespeare is me!"—only becomes hermeneutically productive when behind "me" there is somebody as talented as Emerson, Dickinson, Whitman, Woolf or Pollock (in the critical discipline, people like Matthiessen or Sedgwick). The problem with this is that even at their most radical and original, the scholars' lives (mine included) remain as flat and uninteresting as the lives of John Updike's or Jonathan Franzen's suburban personages. I wouldn't mind reading Ingeborg Bachmann, James Baldwin, Jean Genet, Jerzy Kosinski or Carson McCullers dilating—openly or not—on themselves while pretending to discuss Shakespeare, because these people are genuinely interesting. But I'd rather abstain from the moralism of what Houellebecq charmingly described as "un movement spirituel en plein developpement à base de fondamentalisme écologiste, matiné chez les uns d'altermondialisme gauchiste, chez les autres de cuculterie New Age" (*Ennemis* 169). Dubbing the arch-petit-bourgeois Western academic Left as "gauche caviar" would be however a flagrant mistake, given the ultra-healthy diet habits of the new environmentalists. It is highly symptomatic that no other than Fredric Jameson found it necessary, in his essay on Derrida's *Spectres de Marx*, to specify that the USA is a place "where intellectuals in general are not only by definition 'left' intellectuals, busy propagating theory and 'political correctness,' but are also invested with a symbolic upper-class value qua intellectuals, as over against the ordinary middle-class people" (*Valences* 161). This can be made extensive to most developed countries in the Western world. And part of the leftist unordinariness consists precisely in stressing how ordinary—how mundane, how corporal, how communal, how phenomenal—one's life is after all. But even Greenblatt on his life and ancestry can be as fatiguing as Philip Roth or Paul Auster tracing Newark genealogies. If we want a feel of the Central-European Jewish experience, then one might as well turn to the real thing—and that is the sublime Joseph Roth. There may be a sociological explanation to this state of affairs, with a focus on the hedonistic privatization of life rightly denounced by Lipotevsky as an apparently (but only so) contradictory effect of May 68 ("The Contribution of Mass Media" 133): the aftershocks of that non-event

(Aron's *revolution introuvable*) are all too visible in the ideological make-up of various generations of Western scholars, and not precisely because they were inappropriately treated to overdoses of French Theory.[1] Still the individualism *à la carte* identified by Lipotevsky is paradoxical in more ways than the French thinker predicted—the greatest contradiction being that the social-ideological menu predetermines fixed minority and group identities that fall foul of liberal notions of individualism. I agree with Ewan Fernie that *"the freedom to be yourself"* and *"the freedom to be different"* are two major and immensely estimable expressions of freedom in Shakespeare's work (*Shakespeare for Freedom* 2–4), but I never lose sight of the fact that there are many illiberal ways of construing those stirring slogans.

It is more correct to say that these generations of scholars were (are) simply badly trained in odds and ends of French theory, unable to reconcile its innermost speculative thrust with either the encroaching positivism of their academic ecosystems (close the book) or with the cool nonchalance of post-theoretical life (open the window). The rejection of liberal property led to a celebration of self-property—something already authorized by Locke and amply examined by Charles Taylor in his book on *The Ethics of Authenticity* (1991)—and the self-proper (the *eigen*) became the genuine object of desire. Taylor diagnosed a shift in modern times towards the need to acknowledge the recognition of identities, a recognition that more ancient social configurations took more or less for granted. Now, however, our hedonistic societies are intoxicated with calls to self-love, which Taylor illustrates with a quote from a book by Gail Sheehy that was popular in the sixties:

> If I could give everyone a gift for the send-off on this journey, it would be a tent. A tent for tentativeness. The gift of portable roots .... For each of us there is the opportunity to emerge reborn, authentically unique, with an enlarged capacity to love ourselves and embrace others .... The delights of

---

1 See Luc Ferry et Alain Renaut, *La pensée 68*, 21–125. The ideological contradictions of the sixties' protest movements have been scrutinized in many productive ways. I particularly relish David Hajdu's sharp formulation in *Positively 4th Street*: "By April 1962 the nascent discontent on college campuses (initially associated with civil rights and the cold war) was beginning to take form as a movement of sorts, one of a distinctly postwar American character—a mobilization in the name of political and moral principle that was also a fashion trend and a business opportunity" (116). Arguably, the political-moral Shakespeare construed by neo-phenomenological scholars is also a fashion trend and an extraordinary business-cum-career-promotion opportunity. No liberal should be scandalized by this: laissez faire! But maybe high-principled anti-liberals should be concerned about potential contradiction.

> self-discovery are always available. Though loved ones move in and out of our lives, the capacity to love remains.
>
> GAIL SHEEHY, *Passages: Predictable Crises of Adult Life*, 1976; qtd. in Taylor, 44

Traces of this kind of stuff, which infuriated Adorno during his residence in California (see his book *The Stars Down to Earth*), and their attending sentimental-romantic ideology of middle-class adventure, inform, unconsciously or not, the life expectations of many early modern literary scholars. Lupton's argumentative investment in the transience of *tents* in her reading of *Macbeth* is a case in point.[2] Acknowledgement of recognition easily degenerates, as Taylor implies, into demand of recognition:

> The projecting of an inferior or demeaning image on another can actually distort and oppress, to the extent that it is interiorized. Not only contemporary feminism but also race relations and discussions of multiculturalism are undergirded by the premiss that denied recognition can be a form of oppression. Whether this factor has been exaggerated may be questioned, but it is clear that the understanding of identity and authenticity has introduced a new dimension into the politics of equal recognition, which now operates with something like its own notion of authenticity, at least in so far as the denunciation of other-induced distortions are concerned. (49–50)

I am interested in the effects that this "new dimension" (Taylor was writing in 1991) and its attending "own notion of authenticity" has had on Shakespeare studies. From an interbellum world dominated by artistic and thought experiments that promoted a radically liberal image of humans with neither attributes nor identities, we have returned—after the exceptional lapse of the sixties and seventies—to a profoundly un-modernist world of *Menschen mit Eigenschaften*. For scholars awash in this post-hippy ethics of authenticity the greatest possession is the possession of her beautiful soul and self. The problem, one early denounced by Joan Didion in a memorable collection of articles, is that the *schöne Seele* very seldom escapes the tyranny of custom and ideology, and that inadvertent custom-holders tend to believe that their "feelings, on subjects of this nature, are better than reasons, and render them unnecessary" (Mill, *On Liberty* 9). "This is me" has become the unstated phrase

---

2 This reading, scarcely mediated by the playtext, as I observed above, is however modulated by a comparison with Lars von Trier's film *Melancholia*, whence the investment in the tent.

in the prolegomena to many lectures, papers, and books in the academic market of the Humanities. Some seminars in Shakespeare conferences are overly designed as occasions for group therapy, with discussion at pains to conceal the drift towards the confessional show. Nothing can stop "the upward production curve of maudlin narcissism" (Hughes, *Culture* 7), a tendency that overspills into the personal-life exhibitionism of academic output, increasingly outsourced to online venues like blogs, twitter, youtube, not rarely in the expansive acknowledgement section of their monographs, whose bottom-line—I have hundreds of supporting friends, innumerable nice colleagues, a wonderful family, two cats, love mountain-trekking, wrote part of my book in a room with a Tuscan view, came across old ladies dressed in black who gave much to think about—is so ridiculously similar to the life of the rest of colleagues across campus and page, that it can be spared without great loss. Hughes rightly emphasizes the "loss of dignity" consequent on the "belief that self-exposure confers distinction" and argues that such "consensus has arrived, in the immense social fallout from American post-therapeutics" (8). Note the dates of publication of these three highly diagnostic books: Taylor's *The Ethics of Authenticity* (1991), Hughes' *The Culture of Complaint* (1993) and Vickers' *Appropriating Shakespeare* (1993). A connected pattern can be discerned, a teleological design running from the assertion of personal property constituted through self-exposure to the demand of recognition partly satisfied through an *appropriation* of Shakespeare that is no longer a matter of methodological parochialism (Marxist criticism, psychoanalytic criticism, deconstructive criticism ...) but rather a matter of personal definition according to religious, ethnic, gender, and more vaguely ideological (spiritualist, eco-related, humanist-related, community-related, object-related) categories. What Vickers saw as the future and promise of phenomenology in Shakespeare studies in the wake of the post-structuralist debacle has very often taken the form of *personalist presentism*. I guess Vickers wasn't expecting that, but his crusade against theory dismally contributed to de-dialectize the critical soil. It was a matter of time that the leaves of grass should sprout to new life. In the "Introduction" to Ewan Fernie's *Spiritualist Shakespeares* we read that "Shakespearean spirituality promiscuously, irresistibly breeds with the spiritual possibilities of our own time" (18). This is the same scholar who believes in "the powerful imminence of sense—ineffably beyond thought" ("Action! *Henry V*" 97). *Shakespearean spirituality* is one presentist flower. Another can be found in Stefan Herbrechter's "Introduction" to the edited collection *Posthumanist Shakespeares*:

> No wonder that cognitive and neurosciences and increasingly called upon to explain the cognitive cultural 'map' of the early modern mind and

'Shakespeare's brain' (cf. Crane, 2000). All these are attempts to demonstrate the continued if not increasing relevance of Shakespeare and the privileged relationship between early and late modern culture" (12).

It is one thing to be interested in postmodern spirituality and the cognitive map of the brain. One fine thing. It is quite another to discuss Shakespeare's *spirituality* and Shakespeare's *brain*. This is unwise not only because anachronistic—Shakespeare would have been as puzzled by those words as Webster by the suggestion that he could usurp Shakespeare's place—but also because anachronism (very often a productive critical tool) is here the conduit of the scholars' drive to assert what Adorno called "the immediacy of their experience."

The desperate search for foundations in the endemically *grundlos* academic debate (no Author, no *signifié*, no History, no *hors-texte*) led many to discover in themselves the very place to start their critical narratives and to root their claims—whence the current chitchat about presentism and affection. As early as 1993, as I have already pointed out, art historian Robert Hughes diagnosed the cult of selfhood in American culture as both a hangover of Puritan calls to personal virtue and an instigator of collective infantilism and imbecility.[3] The bottom line is: I don't understand the thoughts of a past author, and I have little to add to the current discussion, but do I have emotions (sentiments of differential identity, tremors of civic belonging, passions of distinct sexual and political affiliation, ideological outlooks on existence, the mind, the beyond) and shall you know them! The scholar sounds as inanely excited about his self-discoveries as Dean Moriarty about the irrelevance of doubting the existence of God. In many cases, sadly, the personal exhibition feeds on and exhausts completely the academic piece. I find this a bit depressing. I am fine with people on the academic road who want to narcissistically talk about themselves, their biographical highlights, their community-work commitments, their domestic pets, and their grand ideas about the meaning of life. But they should learn to find the right place to relieve (themselves) of what remains, to critical practice, *things indifferent* (ἀδιάφορα). Coffee-breaks between seminar papers are, for instance, perfect for this. They may protest arguing that such things are not indifferent insofar as they constitute the very difference of the critical standpoint from which they interpret. But we may reply reminding them of our right to find their difference indifferent, that is, utterly irrelevant. It is always useful to remember that, according to Derrida, a radical mode of

---

3 "The self is now the sacred cow of American culture, self-esteem is sacrosanct [...] The vulgarity of confessional culture is stupefying [...] All you need is be yourself" (Hughes, *Culture* 6–10).

hospitality must dispense with the requirement of the name, and therefore with name-related, label-related identity: "l'hospitalité commence par l'accueil sans question, dans un double effacement, l'effacement de la question et du nom" (*De l'hospitalité* 31). And here I seek support in the much-maligned Alain Finkielkraut, whose personal experience as a Jewish-Polish boy entering the haven (for him a heaven) of French *secular indifference* through educational institutions in the 1950s is quite revealing. These institutions created the voice that sixty years later was raised against the affective, sentimental ground of our public demands for identity recognition, and proclaimed the need to re-institute indifference:

> Indifférence salutaire: c'est une chance et non une déchéance que toutes les relations entre les hommes ne soient pas soumises à la loi de l'amour. Heureusement pour l'humanité, d'autres sentiments sont possibles, ainsi d'ailleurs que des relations *asentimentales*. La transmission des savoirs a tout à perdre de la confusion du *cognitif* et de l'*affectif*.
> *L'identité malheureuse* 46

The demand for supposedly differential identity recognition is a sentimental and affective move that informs the presentist approach to Shakespeare. Although the affectivism behind current scholarly presentism is a matter of spontaneous immediacy, it is not exactly a matter of chance. It is rather—to deploy the Humean distinction—a matter of causes:

> When any causes beget a particular inclination or passion, at a certain time, and among a certain people; though many individuals may escape the contagion, and be ruled by passions peculiar to themselves; yet the multitude will certainly be seized by the common affection, and be governed by it in all their actions.
> "On the rise and progress of the arts and sciences," *Political Essays* 59

As I noted in a previous section, the authors of the V21 Collective Manifesto argued that the primary affective mode of positivist historicism was "the amused chuckle." To my mind, the common affection in today's ultra-positivist presentism is also this amused chuckle, even if the jollity can hardly repress the bitterness of social-ideological resentment. The current hysteria in the proclamation of identity as personal difference would not be culturally obtrusive if the self that sets out to proclaim her difference was really unique. The motto of an important recent movement of justified protest against the normalization of sexual harassment, "Me Too," could be said to epitomize the unconscious drive of presentist readings of Shakespeare: me too, my identity is also interpellated by Shakespeare, and I want it to be recognized—through Shakespeare. Liberal society, even anarcho-libertarian liberal society, would find no fault in a conception of society of finite singulars that fiercely strive to have their difference recognized, inasmuch, of course, as they do not use the few public resources available in the more or less minimal state to have their difference officially sanctioned: it is hard to dislike people like George Sand or Thoreau. The requirement of public recognition through official means in the sphere of the civil society—an exigency that is putatively mirrored in the understanding of dramatic art, including Shakespeare's, as a "cooperative competition" into which participants enter in "pursuit of acknowledgement" (Lupton & Smith "Introduction" 7)—becomes an issue only when the putatively different identity in search of recognition is a group-identity, an identity *à la carte* (only of course in cases of systemic and systematic oppression of a distinctive minority can a demand for recognition—and the ensuing strategic essentialism defining its identity—be political effective). And it is an issue because "a real politics knows nothing of identities" (Badiou, *Communist* 8).[4] It is therefore group-difference that inscribes itself in the public space in the form of pronoun stickers (he, she) and, eventually, adjective stickers (Jew, Muslim, Christian, feminist, neo-liberal, vegan) and noun stickers (cat-lover, runner, social activist, gun rights advocate). Imagine a James novel, say, *The Bostonians* or *The Princess Casamassima*, or think of *Billy Budd* or *Howards End* with characters carrying their identity buttons. Obviously, the narratives would fail to progress beyond the second page: there would be no such novels. Some would object that such scenario of cultural loss (a world without *Billy Budd* or *The Bostonians*) would not be that bad after all, as these novels are the product, however dissident, of liberal societies were difference (sexual and political, not only social) was being coercively invisibilized. They would have a point, no doubt. But the fact is that Billy Budd is there, hanging from the mast, and so is Kent, unfairly pilloried, and Kate, distastefully disciplined, and Shylock, unreasonably humiliated. In order to cope with them and to understand them it is not necessary to identify with them. It is better to take distance, both from them and from their lynchers.

In fact, I guess a balance can be achieved, a balance where personal difference and group-difference may coexist in the public space of civil society without a constant demand for an official recognition of difference. The

---

4 This plain statement, to which I subscribe, places unbearable strains on Badiou's near-Calvinist construal of politics, which I find unsavory.

omnipresence of the Hegelian category "recognition" in current Shakespeare scholarship by Kottman and Lupton raises suspicion that the semantics of the notion is erratic and ultimately unable, that is, to avert current political appropriation. Recognition and mutuality, today, in civil societies, is certainly not the tractable ontological affair that Hegel contemplated. These tropes have much to do with the *narcissism of small differences* that Freud warned us against:

> Lacan's systematic assault on American ego psychology and, beyond this, the 'American way of life' was in fact mounted in defense of a different notion of difference. Not one that demands to be attended to now, recognized now, but one that waits to be exfoliated in time and through the relation to others.
> COPJEK, *Read* 151

Demand for immediate recognition should be waived for two reasons. First, because true personal difference is never the outcome of a wish, never something you deliberately construct, and it is therefore always likely to be in any case recognized by others, even without the urgency of solicitation. True difference, like madness, simply occurs: recall Lacan's affiche "Ne devient pas fou qui veut" (*Écrits* 176).[5] In an akin contingent manner, Shakespeare is different from Webster, and Gregor Samsa from his sister. Second, the exigency to have your group-difference (being, say, a white Christian raw vegan heterosexual) necessarily recognized in institutional spaces like high-schools or academic conferences runs contrary to the standards of respect to deep personal difference (the necessary fluidity or plasticity of selves whose determinations *pass show*, are resistant to nomenclature and impervious to categorization: I do not know what or who I am) or merely indifference (I do not care who or what I am). At the juncture where a true radical difference meets the lone and level sands of indifference one is likely to encounter the inscription of real equality—we are equal because we are both completely different from one another and indifferent to that difference, because our difference (is so marked and yet unscripted that it) doesn't make any difference.[6] The problem arises when the differential "this is me" *immediately* degenerates into "Shakespeare is with me." It was Hume who averred that the education and politeness presumed in all

---

5   In his "Introduction" to Badiou's book on Wittgenstein, Bruno Bosteels recalls that Lacan is said to have posted this statement on the wall of his consultation room: *Wittgenstein's Antiphilosophy*, 47–48.
6   Jonathan Goldberg shows impatience with the consequences of Derridean "indifference of difference" (*Shakespeare's Hand* xviii).

modes of social conversation exacted the *attenuation* of one's personality in favor of another's—"mutual deference or civility, which leads us to resign our own inclinations to those of our companion."[7] And Benda later denounced the replacement of "la culture" with "ma culture," the latter understood exclusively in terms of "les gestes les plus simples de mon existence quotidienne" (qtd. in Finkielkraut, *La défaite* 16). Thus far, in this seemingly impressionistic excursus, I have sought support in Taylor, Hughes and Finkielkraut. This may render my rant all the more negligible, especially to self-styled progressive sensibilities, though these probably stopped reading many sections ago. In any event, let me now turn to one of Finkielfraut's most vociferous *bête-noires*, Alain Badiou, a Marxian philosopher whose ferociously critical stance on corporate (corporative, minority identity, particularized, communitarian) ethics and the *ethicization of politics*—including cultural politics—I greatly admire. This is part of point 33 in his provocative essay on the law on the Islamic headscarf. He critiques the pointlessness of positioning communitarian lifestyles as an urgent political target:

> Let people live as they wish, or can, eat what they are used to eating, wear turbans, dresses, headscarves, miniskirts, or tap-dancing shoes; let them prostrate themselves photographed bowing and scraping, or speak colourful jargons. Not having the least universal significance, these kinds of 'differences' neither hinder thought, nor support it. So there is no reason either to respect them or vilify them. That the 'Other' lives somewhat differently—as amateurs of discreet theology and portable mortality like saying after Levinas—is not an observation that costs much effort.
> *Polemics* 106

Badiou can recommend *indifference to innocuous difference* because he knows genuine and potentially harmful (evental) difference is something difficult to come by. In the case real difference emerges, unsettling the real situation, and creating a new present, then of course universal significance is at stake, and thought may occur as a truth process established in fidelity to the event. Shakespeare's texts were (are) one such difference, and *pastism*—not *eternalism*—would be the term that would best define our attitude of truthful formalization in accordance with them.[8] Presentism is marked by the arrogation of a personal difference (the significance of one's present) that is

---

7 Quoted in Finkielkraut, *L'identité malheureuse*, 195.
8 For the debate between presentism and eternalism in Husserl's philosophy of time, see Tarditi.

putatively measured over against Shakespeare's, and this is doubly erroneous: first, because it rests on a wild overestimation of private experience, and second, because it overlooks the fact that Shakespeare, through fidelity to his own traces, managed to create his own present. Otherwise put, Shakespeare didn't write newspaper chronicles. "A present," for Badiou, "is the set of consequences in a world of an eventual trace" (*Logic of Worlds* 592). A book should be written about the way Shakespeare read some of his texts (*1 Henry IV*, *Romeo and Juliet*, *As You Like It*) and, constructing in his world a present out of those traces, decided to be the author that had written those texts—to father his own identity by introjecting earliness—and moved ahead both to become that author and to expand that present by writing *Hamlet*, *King Lear*, *Troilus and Cressida*, and *Antony and Cleopatra*. These playtexts, in turn, constitute our present.

3

Stephen Greenblatt's *Tyrant: Shakespeare on Politics* (2018) opens with a glib rehash of period exotica—a rerun of *Elizabeth and Essex* spiced up with a truculent dash of Jesuit terrorism. Of course, if you prefer the grand style or the real thing, read Lytton Strachey and Richard Wilson. The first chapter is at pains to set the theme, as tyranny is solely construed as an impending scenario. Then we get two chapters on party politics and fraudulent populism, centered on *2 Henry VI*, with only aspiring tyrants (York and Cade) dishing out threats and gibes. One fourth of the book is behind and we are still without a tyrant or a definition of tyranny. There follows a farcical character assassination of Richard III, himself a stage cartoon, that is too close to the popular caricature of Trump (swimming, climbing, unbecoming, unfeeling) to serve any critical purpose, whether as a piece of political analysis or, more desirably, of literary exegesis. The suggestion of Shakespeare's prefiguration of what Greenblatt takes to be the 2016 US presidential elections conditions—"a whole county's collective failure" (66), a candidate who is "so obviously and grotesquely unqualified for the supreme position of power that they dismiss him from their mind" (67) who finds it "almost impossible to resist the big, bold lie, shamelessly reiterated" (69) and whose "climactic accession to the throne" is "the consequence of an election" (76)—is too flat and opportunistic to be true. The remaining chapters, on *Macbeth*, *King Lear*, *Julius Caesar*, *Coriolanus* and *The Winter's Tale* also fail to produce the monster. The only real tyrant is Leontes. The rest are a criminal chieftain, a foolish monarch, and two presumptive autocrats. The book delivers instead old-style character-centered glosses of the plays' plots, awash in psycho-pathological diagnostics—Macbeth's "sexual anxieties" (99), Leontes's "paranoia" (123), Lear's "personality disorder" (119)—and insipid transtemporal moral evaluation: York's Machiavellianism is "something so base" (36), Lear's game is "nauseating" (115) and Richard's conduct reeks with "utter shamelessness" (91). If you prefer the real doctor, read Bradley. And many a current Shakespeare critic can do better as priest.

The book's only theoretical adumbration appears in the first chapter: in order to safely frame a theatre that could work as a "key to understanding the crisis of the present," Shakespeare adopted a "lifelong strategy of indirection" (14) whereby current political events where disguised in ancient (Roman, Medieval) robes. But this *ex post facto* account of Shakespeare's self-fashioning into a master of chicanery is itself a chicane. No displacement argument holds when detached from comparative contexts: was Shakespeare any different from Aeschylus, Seneca, Marlowe or Racine in the way he displaced political representation? Is indirection not part of the very generic game (historical-tragic drama) he had decided to play? The book, moreover, doesn't fulfil its scant theoretical promise. What we get instead is an impromptu cumulative impressionistic account of tyranny that is embarrassingly exposed to the idiosyncrasies of character and plot. Since the author has aprioristically decided that the characters at hand are tyrants, his prose need only accommodate, here and there, for the sake of consistency, the adjective "tyrannical" or phrases like "the tyrant's soul" or "the tyrant's course," with an article (*the*) presupposing an analytical determination the book refuses to furnish. The resulting sham coherence is further finessed with platitudinous captions like "The tyrant, the playwright reflected, always and necessarily has powerful enemies" (138), ideal for a BBC documentary or a kindergarten presentation on *The Lion King*.

The book's subtitle, *Shakespeare on Politics*, is also misleading. No theoretical or materialist analysis of politics is attempted, and no historicization of the Renaissance power-game is hinted. We are given instead some exercises in old-style political history, what Marx mockingly referred to as "high-sounding dramas of princes and states [*hochtönende Haupt-und Staatsaktionen*]" (*The German Ideology* 57). Greenblatt's presentist resolve to (always) de-historicize brings about the perilous side-slippage and eventual confusion of concepts like party and partisan (or faction), class and rank. To allude to "common people" who "vote" in "parliamentary elections" (39) inside a discussion of mid-1400s English politics is at best distracting. More puzzling still is the neglect of La Boétie in a book about Renaissance representations of tyranny. But Greenblatt has bigger fish to fry. The book, he confesses, is an attempt to prove "Shakespeare's uncanny relevance to the political world in which we now find ourselves," meaning the USA in the wake of the 2016 presidential elections.

Let me quote in full the way in which Shakespeare's *intentional content*—the *tyranny* Greenblatt's book fails to conceptually and historically determine—dawned on the moral consciousness of a scholar who had already identified in his present the presence (Trump) of the corresponding and concordant *intentional object*, and was solely waiting for friends and relatives to prompt him to the keyboard:

> Not so very long ago, though it feels like a century has passed, I sat in a verdant garden in Sardinia and expressed my growing apprehensions about the possible outcome of an upcoming election. My historian friend Bernhard Jussen asked me what I was doing about it. "What can I do?" I asked, "You can write something," he said. And so I did. That was the germ of the current book. And then, after the election confirmed my worst fears, my wife Ramie Targoff and son Harry, listening at the dinner table to my musings about Shakespeare's uncanny relevance to the political world in which we now find ourselves, urged me to pursue the subject. And so I have. (191)

Uncanny relevance? To the political world in which we *now* find ourselves, and not in June 1976 in South Africa, not in India from 1942 to 1947? Weren't these not so old precedents (and more recent ones: Russia, Venezuela, the Arab Spring) enough to incite you to your scholarly contribution to the debate on Shakespeare's relevance to our political world?[9] Did you need Trump to become president in order to press the relevance and present the analogy? Shakespeare, let's face it, would have shown no interest in Trump: at best, he would have honored him with a cameo appearance in the opening pool-and-champagne party in *Timon of Athens*. (If Greenblatt wants to be relevant, and he has been immensely relevant in the past, he should stop treating Shakespeare's "rabble" as an adroit political actor and give us his thoughts on the American people, including of course those who voted for Trump).

By the time that, in his book, we read that Lear's fool is "the equivalent of a late-night comedian" (118) we know for sure it is not intended for a specialized readership. And when a sentence turgidly yawns "We would not have been able to survive as a species ..." (155) we begin to see the kind of readership he aims to impress. If Greenblatt is attempting to reach the Walhalla of paperback immortality by joining a coterie of savants—Pinker, Chomsky, Harari,

---

9 The original version of the manuscript was sent to the publisher in early February 2022. The Russian invasion of parts of Ukraine followed shortly after.

Nussbaum—in their up-to-the-minute cross-disciplinary appeals to human identity, universalism, rights, and reason, then this book may be a major push. As a piece of Shakespeare criticism, it is merely trivial. The idea of the book, we have seen, dawned on the author while he "sat in a verdant garden in Sardinia." In view of its impressive lack of scholarly support—no bibliography list and only 21 endnotes—*Tyrant* seems to have been written at that pastoral sitting. Et in Arcadia Greenblatt.

4

In my examination of Simon Palfrey's readings of Shakespeare I insisted that his method lacked dialectical rigor. His tracking of Shakespeare's "dialectical ambition" was accomplished through an *arrested dialectic* that inevitably turned *hermeneusis* into a monotonous bulletin of earthquake activity. In the case of Richard Wilson, an outstanding Shakespeare scholar whose *forte* is the framing and deployment of an eclectic sociological method, dialectic tends to be forsaken in favor of presentist *alegoresis*. This doesn't mean he is a textualist or formalist scholar. His remarkable book *Secret Shakespeare: Studies in theatre, religion and resistance* (2004) evinces no doubt the very "Puritan mania to expose the hidden meaning" (95) he himself attributes to a play like *Much Ado About Nothing*, but Wilson claims, quite rightly, to be writing "in our post-theoretical moment, with its return to real bodies in social sites" (36). This was a canny observation, for Wilson was writing six years before Bruce Smith published *Phenomenal Shakespeare*, a book whose disinterest in *social sites* was directly proportional to its engrossment with *real bodies*. Wilson, for his part, has a soft spot for *social bodies* as they interact with and in *textual sites*, and this explains a familiarity with the work of Jacques Derrida that is however confined to the post-1980s essays, those that examine the (moral-political) "projects of the impossible, such as forgiveness, freedom, friendship, hospitality, justice, mourning, pardon, rogues and gifts" (*Free Will* 422). This is an increasingly apocalyptic and political Derrida whose exercises in phenomenological *Auslegung* become more and more thematic, less interested in transcendental-normative conditions of meaning than in the *possibility* of implementing whatever semblance of useful transcendent meaning our flawed societies demand. Although tuned to a different scale, *possibility* is also the theme of the Shakespeare scholarship produced by Simon Palfrey and A.D. Nuttall.

But let us examine more closely Wilson's allegorical procedure, which begins with a semblance of empirical inference. A genetic scene is posited.

An element of his historical-political reality impinging, however indirectly, on Shakespeare's life, produces a psychic reaction-formation that is presently more or less explicitly sublimated into art. The private-psychic reaction forms a *primal scene* where the self engages the forces shaping the public space. For Wilson, it is commonly the literary author doing something—stooping before, recoiling from, offending, resisting—a figure of political authority. This primal scene—and emblematic Hegelian master-slave dumb show of dreamlike proportions where allowances for speech are of the essence—becomes in turn the key to open any Shakespeare text: this explanatory scheme organizes the essays in *Secret Shakespeare* (2004) and *Free Will: Art and Power on Shakespeare's Stage* (2013). The process is dominated by 1) a symbolic reduction: the contingencies of psycho-social interaction are transformed into a symbolic scene or emblem 2) an allegorical decryption: since the emblem is supposed to encode the plots and narratives of existing texts, their correct reading involves the decryption of the emblem. Any analogous situation in a Shakespeare play can allegorically retranslate into the (biographical, historical) terms of the primal scene, and so the allegorical reading can get started, and eventually play itself out, through instances of aesthetic (form-content) concordance and phenomenological (intentional content-intentional object) fulfilment. The presentist twist to this standard neo-historicist method involves the reallocation of the primal scene from Shakespeare's past to the scholar's present. The intentional object of the poet's art is no longer exclusively the phenomena of his historical, social, and political reality that come together in the past primal (symbolic) scene, but also equivalent *facta* in the scholar's present that happen to shape into a corresponding scene. This presentist twist was, as I have already noted, already at work in neo-historicist criticism: "Such connection could be made by analogy or causality; that is, a particular set of historical circumstances could be represented in such a way as to bring out homologies with aspects of the present" (Greenblatt, *Learning to Curse* 224).

The first concern with this method involves of course the value and significance, for the cultural historian, of these *facta*, slashed as *données immédiates* from the face of the Given: how un-dense, unscripted and "natural" are these social facts in their *givenness* (Marx and Engels, *The German Ideology* 53–55) before they enter the hermeneutic processor? An inevitable abstracting process rules the conversion of historical phenomena into the parts of a symbolic scene, and an additional abstraction follows when the scene is asked to correspond to its equivalent in the Shakespeare canon. Finally, presentist hermeneutics inserts a further de-particularizing torsion by extrapolating to the present scene. Manifestly, what lends stability to this mirror game is the relative fixity of the Shakespeare canon, which in neo-historicist and presentist readings takes the proportions and status of the secular Book. Complaining about the loss of reality caused by philosophical abstraction, Marx wrote:

> Ainsi, les métaphysiciens qui, en faisant ces abstractions, s'imaginent faire de l'analyse, et qui, à mesure qu'ils se détachent de plus en plus des objets, s'imaginent s'en approcher au point de les pénétrer, ces métaphysiciens ont à leur tour raison de dire que les choses d'ici-bas sont des broderies, dont les catégories logiques forment le canevas. Voilà ce qui distingue le philosophe du chrétien. Le chrétien n'a qu'une seule incarnation du Logos, en dépit de la logique; le philosophe n'en finit pas avec les incarnations.
> *Misère de la philosophie* 158

A distinction is suggested between the *materialist thinker* who is careful to assess the value, meaning, and mode of determination of "les choses d'ici-bas," the *philosopher* who postulates an endless sequence of incarnations (logical abstractions fleshing out things), and the *Christian thinker* who totalizes incarnation around the allegorical potency of *Logos*. The first thinker is of course Marx himself. The third thinker is any medieval scholastic intellectual, say, Dante. Only the second is problematic, for Marx targets a speculative philosopher who, in the logic of his pamphlet, should be Hegel and yet is much less totality-aware and mediation-sensitive than the author of *The Phenomenology of Spirit*. Anyway, adapting this distinction to our critical map, I would suggest that Simon Palfrey is to the philosopher what Richard Wilson is to the Christian thinker. Whereas the former favors a poetics of de-totalized and immediate symbolic incarnations, the latter champions an allegorical poetics of the (Shakespeare) Book. For all his attempts to come through as a literary scholar attuned to performance and alert to the broad cultural poetics of the Renaissance stage, Wilson's particular strength is that of the brash *glossatore* and impatient *reader*.

A second problem has already been denounced: the emblem or symbolic scene is often decided in advance by a literary-critic-cum-bad-historian who screens a section of the past in search of a historical anecdote that tropes—and totalizes—the social field at hand (Kastan, *Shakespeare After Theory* 30). There is no need for the symbolic *reduction* because what awaits reduction (the whole social field) is actually ignored, but also because the anecdotal scene imposes itself as an ineluctable given. What we get is a dwarfed, fractal reality, formalized into a text (Kastan 31) and perfectly adapted to intertextual collation and hermeneutic manipulation. At fault is not the allegorical hermeneutic procedure: *all* readings tend to become allegorical. The problem lies in suggesting that the process of encoding that goes into the making of the text is itself allegorical. As Kastan has observed, "Shakespeare's plays do not seem to me 'almost altogether Allegoricall' or even partly so" (*Will to Believe* 39). Another related problem in Wilson's handling of this hermeneutic schema lies in the arbitrariness with which he deals with the textual materials, without much attention to context. He sacrifices consistency for the sake of comprehensiveness. The mediation of the totally relevant canon is never fully addressed. The phrase, the line, the speech, or the scene (it is normally less than a line), are selected in complete isolation, without attention to their connectedness to other similar textual segments (in the play at hand or in other plays, by this or by another author) that inevitably contribute to their meaning—whether by way of analogy or sheer differential opposition. This is something a reader can do for the sake of occasional textual backup: a general notion the critic is trying to describe can be supported by a quote from the text or texts that are the more or less direct object of analysis. This is, in fact, something I myself have done in some parts of my book, at my own peril, for the sake of enhancing the Shakespearean relevance of my arguments. There is a problem, however, when this mode of ultra-selective quotation based on a more or less accountable recurrence—of a lexeme, of a notion, of a situation—is brought into play in readings where what is at stake is actually the understanding of one play. Take for instance *Hamlet*. In his most recent book, *Worldly Shakespeare: The Theatre of Our Good Will* (2016), Wilson reads Hamlet in the perspective of 9/11 "as a play about 'self-slaughter' [1.2.32] as a form of holy terror, and its most famous soliloquy, 'To be or not to be' [3.1.56] a deeply disturbing meditation on the absolute antagonism of the *jihad*" (18). With the slim speculative and rather unrehearsed argumentative evidence he draws from two articles, one by Foucault and the other by Emmanuel Le Roy Ladurie, Wilson undertakes an interpretation of *Hamlet* in which the tragedy is asked to conform to an overarching thesis on "the occult affiliation of al Qaeda with the Society of Jesus" (18). The paranoid search for *affiliations* delivers the stuff that popular-postmodern dreams are made off, all the way from Ken Follet and Dan Brown to Don DeLillo: post-grad students probably love it. Affiliation evokes both the logic of corresponding concordance, and the essentialist rigidity of group identity. Aesthetic and ideology go hand in hand in this presentist transaction. Wilson is asking us to reassess, with the *primal scene* of the present-day religious suicidal terrorist in mind, "the apocalyptic sacrificial imagery that fires Shakespeare's Jacobean tragedy" (18). In the chapter specifically devoted to that end, titled "Fools of Time: Shakespeare and the Martyrs," Wilson garners all the textual evidence *Hamlet* (the Book of Books) can offer on the topic of suicidal violence, which is surely not inconsiderable. And then he moves out to round up further confirming quotes from play-texts—*Julius Caesar, Titus Andronicus, Much Ado About Nothing, The Comedy of Errors*—chosen solely because verbal scraps in them appear to corroborate the thesis on free-willed violent martyrdom. As a reading strategy, this is effective, and Wilson is a master of making up a case. But effectiveness is not correction. Like posthumanist readings of Shakespeare, his allegorical *analysis* (this was Marx's term) lacks dialectical scope and consistency.

Wilson fails to mention that of the ten occurrences of the term "martyr" in the Shakespeare canon, only three concern English history, and none of them refer to Catholic martyrs. One is Oldcastle in the "Epilogue" to *2 Henry IV*, the Lollard rebel that Shakespeare turned into a genial rogue and Fox redeemed as proto-Protestant martyr. The next occurrence is Mowbray's figural reference to martyrs in love at *2 Henry IV* 4.1.191. And the third is to the first truly Protestant martyrs, Thomas Cromwell (*Henry VIII* 3.2.450). In conclusion, the two English *martyrs* Shakespeare openly alludes to are two worshiped and inaugural figures of English Protestantism. Of course, they were not exactly terrorists, and yet, Wilson could protest, Shakespeare was probably already playing tactical hide-and-seek: placing the eggs of his compulsion deliberately in the wrong basket, to erase traces. And yet, and yet. A further objection could take the following form: it is futile to determine the nature and intensity of this psychosocial compulsion, this irrepressible need to return to and reinstate the primal scene of Catholic terrorist self-sacrifice in Edmund Campion. Did Shakespeare see the "amputated thumb" (*Secret Shakespeare* 55)? Did he touch it? Ach! Did he see "the heads of Arden and Sommerville impaled on London bridge" (121)? But did he see them feelingly? Did he know his father kept a spiritual testament in the "roof" (50), one he could produce and touch? O the thumb, and the heads, and the rafter, and the roof: these are the givens, the little things *d'ici bas* always accessible to the scholar, ever present "at hand" for allegorical inference, the safest place to start "for the materialist analysis of Shakespeare" (*Secret* 27). It's very simply: you first screen the playtext in search of the relevant lexeme (say, "martyr"), but also of other terms, for the connoted significance can easily migrate to other related words and haunt other figures. Next, you step beyond your text into neighboring plays. It is Wilson after all who calls attention to the fact that *Titus Andronicus* is "the text in which the word 'martyr' occurs more than any other" (*Worldly* 132). So if the occurrence of the word is significant for analysis, and moving beyond *Hamlet* borders is deemed valid, then one is also forced to reckon with occurrences that controvert the thesis. This is a plain dialectical stipulation: the totality mediates and (negatively) determines the particular. Meaning only crops up *sub specie omnis*. Meaning tends to be, therefore, what eighteenth-century German scholar Johann Martin Chladenius would call a *mittelbarer Verstand*—a mediated sense (Szondi, *Introduction* 29). A good reading should elude the symmetries of perfect transcendent correspondence (intentional content-intentional object), recoil from the empirical scene into the formal-transcendental stage and confront whatever refutative material and contradictory information the relational scanning produces.

Let me give another example. For Wilson the person who decides to violently sacrifice his life for the sake of a holy cause is a holy suicide terrorist—be it the Jesuit or the Jihad terrorist. Hamlet himself, whose acts of terror amount to freaking Ophelia out a couple of times, is described by Wilson as "religious maniac" which must learn to see, post 9/11, "through the eyes of his victims" (*Worldly* 126). Honestly, I don't know what Wilson is talking about. Anyway, if Hamlet is a potential terrorist, what about plain English soldiers fighting in late-medieval English wars? Remember what exactly that means: it entails deliberately risking your life (the chances of dying were considerable) in the action of killing as many enemies as possible for the sake of an honor which could only be cashed in terms of national-religion immortality. Take the once lionized St Crispin Day's harangue. You have read it hundreds of times. Read it again:

>   What's he that wishes so?
> My cousin Warwick? No, my fair cousin.
> If we are marked to die, we are enough
> To do our country loss; and if to live,
> The fewer men, the greater share of honour.
> God's will, I pray thee wish not one man more.
> By Jove, I am not covetous for gold,
> Nor care I who doth feed upon my cost;
> It ernes me not if men my garments wear;
> Such outward things dwell not in my desires.
> But if it be a sin to covet honour
> I am the most offending soul alive.
> No, faith, my coz, wish not a man from England:
> God's peace, I would not lose so great an honour
> As one man more methinks would share from me
> For the best hope I have. O do not wish one more.
> Rather proclaim it presently through my host
> That he which hath no stomach to this fight,
> Let him depart. His passport shall be made
> And crowns for convoy put into his purse.
> We would not die in that man's company

> That fears his fellowship to die with us.
> This day is called the feast of Crispian.
> He that outlives this day, and comes safe home
> Will stand a-tiptoe when the day is named
> And rouse him at the name of Crispian.
> He that shall live this day and live t'old age
> Will yearly on the vigil feast his neighbours
> And say, 'Tomorrow is Saint Crispian."
> Then will he strip his sleeve and show his scars
> And say 'These wounds I had on Crispin's day.'
> Old men forget; yet all shall be forgot,
> But he'll remember, with advantages
> What feats he did that day. Then shall our names,
> Familiar in his mouth as household words—
> Harry the king, Bedford and Exeter,
> Warwick and Talbot, Salisbury and Gloucester—
> Be in their flowing cups freshly remembered.
> This story shall the good man teach his son,
> And Crispin Crispian shall ne'er go by
> From this day to the ending of the world
> But we in it shall be remembered,
> We few, we happy few, we band of brothers;
> For he today that sheds his blood with me
> Shall be my brother; be he ne'er so vile,
> This day shall gentle his condition.
> And gentlemen in England now abed
> Shall think themselves accursed they were not here,
> And hold their manhoods cheap whiles any speaks
> That fought with us upon Saint Crispin's day.
>
> HENRY V 4.3.18–67

If this is not an invitation to die killing for the sake of immortality uttered by a man who assumes he is going to die, then this is nothing. So is our "sweet Hal" an Al-Qaeda terrorist? I would never encourage the overlap, for I do not share the methodology tending such text-insensible transhistorical analogy. But Ewan Fernie, for instance, has ("Action! *Henry V*" 116–119), and I guess Wilson should have attempted the comparison with Hamlet if he had been bothered by dialectical scruples. The strength of Wilson's reading—which is in general maximal—may rest precisely on his ignoring these dialectical instigations. Perhaps I am missing something. Or I am too inclined to credit to my eyes. Before the final battle, the French Constable says that the soldiers "have said their prayers, and [...] stay for death" (4.2.56). How would Voltaire respond to that?

Let me return to the basic reading procedure identified above: a symbolic (inferential) reduction, gleaned from the empirical historical horizon, followed by an allegorical (deductive) decryption. This is standard practice in the psychoanalytic and sociological—at bottom phenomenological—hermeneutics of French and Swiss critics like Poulet, Starobinski, Mauron, Bachelard, Goldman, all the way up to Bourdieu. What Wilson adds to this simple schema is the aperture of the enclosed exegetical circuit to a supervened horizon of contemporary historical eventuation. This presentist urge seriously aggravates the tendency, peculiar to *alegoresis*, to erase the historical distance with the past. Merleau-Ponty once argued that "la vérité est un autre nomme de la sédimentation, qui elle-même est la présence de tous les présents dans le nôtre" ("Sur la phénoménologie du language," *Problèmes actuels* 107). Lyotard faulted this argument as prone to dialectical circularity (*La phénoménologie* 44), but what it lacks is precisely a dialectical (conceptual) comprehension of sediments. What follows, in Wilson's application of the method, is a flat short-circuit of immediacies: a past historical situation (say, war on violent Catholic martyrdom) resurfaces in a present historical situation (say, war on Islam terrorism). As in Biblical typological exegesis, the Old Testament prefigures the New, and so the past foreshadows the present: "*figura* is something real and historical which announces something else that is also real and historical [...] *figura* often appears in the sense of deeper meaning in reference to future things" (Auerbach, *Figura* 29–35). The Shakespeare text, itself a bed of sediments and mediations, is pawned as a provisional connector and vanishes in the process. In point of fact, discussing *Hamlet* is not exactly necessary for what Wilson has in mind, which amounts to denouncing past and present ideological settings. In this chapter, then, *Hamlet* is literally *not to be* considered, interpreted, or simply read.

At the end of his densely written "Introduction" to *Worldly Shakespeare*, Wilson comments briefly on a passage of Frank Kermode's memoirs where the British scholar attributes his mentor's interest in Shakespearean forms of absolutism not so much to a "taste for recondite and difficult scholarship" (these are Kermode's words) as to the fact that "'supreme authority' is 'something he would have liked himself.'" Wilson redirects this exercise in unmasking to his own personal experience: "As someone who came to literary criticism at the University of York in the 1970s through the grandiose art-historical door Kermode described, I recognize the astuteness of his story of the academic illusion of power" (25). This amalgam of resonating evocations reminds me of a similar one, albeit with reversed political valences, made by Richard Rorty in his "Remarks on Deconstruction and Pragmatism." The American philosopher interrogates the utility of deconstruction to literary departments entranced by leftist politics:

> On the contrary, by diverting attention from real politics, [this flurry of deconstructive activity] has helped create a self-satisfied and insular academic left which—like the left of the 1960s—prides itself on not being co-opted by the system and thereby renders itself less able to improve the system. Irving Howe's much-quoted jibe—'These people don't want to take over the government; they just want to take over the English Department'—seems to me to remain an important criticism of this academic left. (15)[10]

The ways to entry the board of power games are, of course, multiple. Many squares are numbered one, there are three caskets at least, but only one treasure at the center of the palace. The treasure is Power, and there are many trim gentlemen pressing at the gates. Shakespeare called this treasure Portia, and Portia in turn "temporal power" (*The Merchant of Venice* 4.1.185) and "earthly power" (4.1.191). The lesson on the compromised truth of this illusion is simple and circular, its attending cynicism hardly escapable: "As Lentricchia puts it, leftists whose only political outlets are sit-ins, picketing, and the like 'are being crushed by feelings of guilt and occupational alienation'" (Rorty, "De Man and the American Cultural Left," *Essays on Heidegger* 133). Shylock's desperate remonstrance—"by my soul I swear / There is no power in the tongue of man / To alter me: I will have my bond" (4.1.236–37) is very moving, and it may be garnished with as much biopolitical needlework as the hermeneut deems fit, but the fact is that the bond ends up defaced and outfaced by ducal power—very likely to Shakespeare's satisfaction. Yet Wilson wants us to know that *he* (Wilson) is immune to the illusion of power, a commendable fact apparently prefigured by the other *he* "at hand" (Shakespeare). Once again, we feel the thrill of prefiguration and one-to-one allegorical concordance. Once again, the weasel clash of immediacies. To turn Wilson's *immediate experience* of dislike of supreme authority into the *clé de tout* for Shakespeare's plays is trivial and probably mistaken. Not only because, as I have tried to show in this book, Shakespeare's writing—like Dante's and Milton's—congenitally stands up for any person's ambition to reach the *potentia* of supreme authority: "Thou, nature,

---

10   Rorty reruns the anecdote in his essay "De Man and the American Cultural Left," in *Essays on Heidegger*, 137.

art my goddess; to thy law / My services are bound [...] I grow, I prosper" (*King Lear* 1.2.1–23), "Gain, be my lord, for I will worship thee" (*King John* 2.1.599). *The upstart crow*, remember. Surely, he never forgot. But, more importantly, because Wilson's reading strategy, tributary to the extraneous aim of highlighting the advent of historical repetition, risks erasing its defiantly unrepeatable (textual) object. The adjusted velocities of critical reading may not be totally compatible with the longing to sponsor an enhanced immediate historical experience (*Erlebnis*). Although both were openly hostile to the crude allegorical (theological) reduction of Kafka's narratives, Adorno found fault in Benjamin's attempt at pressing too rapidly the linkage between proto-history and modernity. He believed Benjamin should have tried to "dialectize" the former and this way allow for a "conceptualization" of the relation (*Correspondence* 27). A blind adherence to the call to *always historicize* (Jameson) without taking stock of the parallel need to *periodically dialecticize* (Adorno) prompts a deficient application of the Derridean notion of difference, which in Wilson's work tends to fall under the spell of thematic historical-ideological oppositions informed by contingent incommensurability. What Wilson calls "incommensurable difference" (*Worldly* 3) is the outcome of the historical naturalization of ideological (party, partisan, faction, political, sectarian, religious) differentiation, not the expression of a true transcendental antagonism. *Différance*, in short, doesn't translate into empirical vocabularies of social dissension. Or translates only *sub specie omnis*, on a very temporary basis, and with the axiological valences open to reversion, or simply disconnected.

For all his advocacy of a universalism based on antagonistic toleration—at bottom, an arch-liberal goal—Wilson's critical position is characterized by a strong anti-nominalist belief in the reality of categorial (ideological, religious, political, national) identity. Whereas true liberals—including the late, apocalyptic Derrida—do not make much of identity essentialism, anti-liberals do invest a great deal in that kind of prefabricated determination. Terry Eagleton's lifelong inability to escape the plebeian-patrician dialectic is a case in point, and so is Dollimore's glib opposition between liberal-humanist-rationalist essentialism and subversion. Wilson's critical exercises are inclined to the swift category reduction of imaginary or real, past and present, opponents: Heidegger and de Man held Nazi ideas (*Shakespeare in French Theory*, 58), Schmitt is a "Catholic and Fascist jurist," "Hitler's crown jurist" (*Worldly* 5–6), Girard is a Catholic (*Shakespeare in French Theory* 53). What is the analytical gain in repeating that Schmitt was a Nazi? Or, for that matter, that Shakespeare was a crypto-Catholic? Apart from identifying the person who repeats the attributive sentence as a very progressive and sensible person—it functions as a political identity sticker—the analytical gain is dubious. I see it as a moralistic reflex, informed by phenomenological assumptions of clear-and-distinct empirical givenness. Castoriadis discovered the same zest for assignation in Plato's handling of Socrates' opponents in the dialogues. In the course of Plato's arguments, he argues, "la réfutation logique est complétée par l'assignation [...] ontologique, sociale, politique" (*Sur* Le politique 26). The many-sided subdivision of the social field implied in this mode of stigmatization plays a central role in Marlowe's social landscape—it is actually indispensable for a dramaturgy where giving offence is often the enabling action and triggering factor of the tragedy. But it may not be so relevant for Shakespeare. Kastan holds that "religious identities in early modern England [...] are characteristically far more eclectic and unstable than the polarized master categories of 'Catholic' and 'Protestant' allow" (*Will to Believe* 29). To confine Shakespeare's pragmatism to his ability to conceal his true faith under veils of undecidablity is to concede too little. He may have also been a *pragmatist*—and a *proto-liberal* too, these are my alternative stickers—in his deep-seated reluctance to *differ* on partisan concerns. It is one thing to suggest that Shakespeare consigned political, religious, and perhaps even national determinations to a private Elysium of indifference (*adiaphora*) (*Free Will* 11). It is another to state that he was a dissembler. Something must give. One must decide. At any rate, the decision can only be made by following textual traces whose tendency to differ is dolefully (or not) beyond our control. The attempt to trace the witness of Campion's hanging who "cut of a thumb and [carried] it away" (*Worldly* 132), and produce the macerated thumb, that little thing, is—I guess—out of the question. But maybe not.

Bibliographical References

Adorno, Theodor. "Husserl and the Problem of Idealism." *The Journal of Philosophy* 37.1 (1940): 5–18.
Adorno, Theodor. *Negative Dialektik*. Frankfurt am Main: Suhrkamp, 1970.
Adorno, Theodor. *Noten zur Literatur IV*. Frankfurt am Main: Suhrkamp, 1981.
Adorno, Theodor. *Hegel: Three Studies*. Trans. Shierry W. Nicholsen. Cambridge, Mass.: The MIT Press, 1993.
Adorno, Theodor. *Ästhetische Theorie*. Ed. Gretel Adorno & Rolf Tiedemann. Frankfurt am Main: Suhrkamp, 1995.
Adorno, Theodor. *Kant's* Critique of Pure Reason. Ed. Rolf Tiedemann. Trans. Rodney Livingstone. Cambridge: Polity, 2001.
Adorno, Theodor. *Zu einer Theorie der musikalischen Reproduktion*. Frankfurt am Main: Suhrkamp, 2001.
Adorno, Theodor. *Aesthetic Theory*. Trans. R. Hullot-Kentor. London: Continuum, 2002.
Adorno, Theodor. *Negative Dialectic*. Trans. E.B. Ashton. London: Routledge, 2004.
Adorno, Theodor. *Minima Moralia. Reflections from Damaged Life*. Trans. E.F.N. Jephcott. London: Verso, 2005.
Adorno, Theodor. *Against Epistemology: A Metacritique. Studies in Husserl and the Phenomenological Antinomies*. Trans. Willis Domingo. Malden: Polity, 2013.
Adorno, Theodor and Walter Benjamin. *The Complete Correspondence, 1928–1940*. Ed. Henry Lonitz. Trans. Nicholas Walker. Cambridge, Mass.: Harvard UP, 1999.
Agamben, Giorgio. *The Time that Remains*. Trans. Patricia Dailey. Stanford: Stanford UP, 2005.
Alexander, Michael, ed. *The Earliest English Poems*. London: Penguin, 1991.
Althusser, Louis. *Pour Marx*. Paris: Maspero, 1965.
Althusser, Louis. *Écrits sur la psychanalyse: Freud et Lacan*. Ed. Olivier Corpet et François Matheron. Paris: STOCK/IMEC, 1993.
Althusser, Louis. *Écrits philosophiques et politiques*. Tome I. Paris: STOCK, 1994.
Althusser, Louis. *Écrits philosophiques et politiques*. Tome II. Paris: STOCK, 1995.
Althusser, Louis. *For Marx*. Trans. Ben Brewster. London: Verso, 2005.
Althusser, Louis. *Politics and History: Montesquieu, Rousseau, Marx*. London: Verso, 2007.
Althusser, Louis, et al. *Lire le Capital*. Paris: Presses Universitaires de France, 1965.
Arendt, Hannah. *The Life of the Mind*. New York: Harvest Book, 1978.
Arendt, Hannah. *Lectures on Kant's Political Philosophy*. Ed. Ronald Beiner. Chicago: Chicago UP, 1982.
Arendt, Hannah. *Essays in Understanding 1930–1954*. Ed. Jerome Kohn. New York: Schocken, 1994.

Arendt, Hannah. *The Human Condition*. Introd. Margaret Canovan. Chicago: The U of Chicago P, 1998.
Arendt, Hannah. *The Origins of Totalitarianism*. Prologue by Samantha Power. New York: Schocken, 2004.
Ariosto, Ludovico. *Orlando Furioso*. Ed. Marcello Turchi. Milano: Garzanti, 1982.
Aristotle, *Metaphysics*. Ed. Hugh Lawson-Tancred. London: Penguin, 1999.
Ashbery, John. *The Mooring of Starting Out: The First Five Books of Poetry*. Hopewell: The Ecco Press, 1997.
Ashbery, John. *Your Name Here*. Manchester: Carcanet, 2000.
Auerbach, Erich. *Figura*. New York: Meridian Books, 1959.
Bacon, Francis. *The Advancement of Learning*. Ed. G.W. Kitchin. London: Dent, 1958.
Bachmann, Ingeborg. *Malina. Werke* 3. München: Piper, 1993.
Badiou, Alain. "Descartes/Lacan" (translated by Sigi Jöttkandt with Daniel Collins), *Umbr(a): A Journal of the Unconscious: On Badiou* (1996): 13–16.
Badiou, Alain. *Ethics: An Essay on the Understanding of Evil*. London: Verso, 2002.
Badiou, Alain. *Logiques des mondes. L'être et l'événement, 2*. Paris: Seuil, 2006.
Badiou, Alain. *Conditions*. Trans. Steven Corcoran. London: Continuum, 2008.
Badiou, Alain. *Theory of the Subject*. Trans. Bruno Bosteels. London: Continuum, 2009.
Badiou, Alain. *Being and Event*. Trans. Oliver Feltham. London: Continuum, 2011.
Badiou, Alain. *Wittgenstein's Antiphilosophy*. Ed. Bruno Bosteels. London: Verso, 2011.
Badiou, Alain. *L'aventure de la philosophie française depuis les années 1960*. Paris: La Fabrique, 2012.
Badiou, Alain. *L'immanence des vérités. L'être et lévénement, 3*. Paris: Fayard, 2018.
Badiou, Alain. *Théorie axiomatique du sujet. Le Séminaire 1996–1998*. Paris: Fayard, 2019.
Badiou, Alain. *Pour aujourd'hui: Platon! Le Séminaire 2007–2008*. Paris: Fayard, 2019.
Badiou, Alain and Barbara Cassin. *Heidegger. Les femmes, le nazisme et la philosophie*. Paris: Fayard, 2010.
Barad, Karen. "Quantum Entanglements and Hauntological Relations of Inheritance: Dis/continuities, SpaceTime Enfoldings, and Justice-to-Come." *Derrida Today* 3.2 (2010): 240–268.
Barthes, Roland. *Essais critiques*. Paris: Seuil, 1964.
Barthes, Roland. *Critique et vérité*. Paris: Seuil, 1966.
Barthes, Roland. *The Neutral: Lectures at the Collège de France (1977–1978)*. Trans. Rosalind E. Kraus and Denis Hollier. New York: Columbia UP, 2005.
Beckett, Samuel. "Three Dialogues." *Proust and Three Dialogues with George Duthuit*. London: Calder, 1987.
Belsey, Catherine. "Historicizing New Historicism." *Presentist Shakespeares*. Ed. Hugh Grady and Terence Hawkes. 27–45.
Belsey, Catherine. *Shakespeare in Theory and Practice*. Edinburgh: Edinburgh UP, 2008.

Benjamin, Walter. *Ursprung des deutschen Trauerspiels.* Frankfurt am Main: Suhrkamp, 1978.

Benjamin, Walter. *The Origin of German Tragic Drama.* Trans. John Osborne. London: Verso, 1998.

Bennett, Jane and Michael J. Shapiro, Ed. *The Politics of Moralizing.* London: Routledge, 2002.

Bennington, Geoffrey. "Inter." In *Post-Theory: New Directions in Criticism.* Ed. Martin McQuillan et al. Edinburgh: Edinburgh UP, 1999. 103–119.

Bercovitch, Sacvan. *The American Jeremiad.* Madison: The U of Wisconsin P, 2012.

Berlin, Isaiah and Jamin Jahanbegloo. *Conversations with Isaiah Berlin.* New York: Charles Scribner's Sons, 1991.

Berry, Philippa. "'Salving the mail': Perjury, grace, and the disorder of things in *Love's Labour's Lost*" in Fernie, *Spiritual Shakespeares.* 94–108.

Best, Stephen and Sharon Marcus. "Surface Reading." *Representations* 108.1 (2009): 1–21.

Bevington, David. *Shakespeare's Ideas: More Things in Heaven and Earth.* Oxford: Wiley-Blackwell, 2008.

Beyer, Christian. "Edmund Husserl." *The Stanford Encyclopedia of Philosophy* (Winter 2020 Edition), Edward N. Zalta (ed.), URL <https://plato.stanford.edu/archives/win2020/entries/husserl/>. Accessed 1 January 2022

Blanchot, Maurice. *The Writing of the Disaster.* Trans. Ann Smock. Lincoln: U of Nebraska P, 1995.

Bloch, Ernst. *Sujeto-Objeto (El pensamiento de Hegel).* Trans. Wenceslao Roses. México: Fondo de Cultura Económica, 1949.

Bloch, Ernst. *Vorlesungen zur Philosophie der Renaissance.* Frankfurt am Main: Suhrkamp, 1972.

Bloch, Ernst. *Filosofia del rinascimento.* Intr. Remo Bodei. Bologna: Il Mulino, 1981.

Bloom, Harold. *The Anxiety of Influence: A Theory of Poetry.* Oxford: Oxford UP, 1973.

Bloom, Harold. ed. *Caliban.* New York: Chelsea, 1992.

Bloom, Harold. *The Western Canon.* New York: Harcourt Brace, 1994.

Bloom, Harold. *Shakespeare: The Invention of the Human.* New York: Riverhead, 1998.

Blumenberg, Hans. *Shipwreck with Spectators. Paradigm of Metaphor for Existence.* Trans. Steven Rendall. The MIT P, 1997.

Bouissac, Paul. *Saussure: A Guide for the Perplexed.* London: Bloomsbury, 2010.

Bourne, Craig and Emily Caddick Bourne, Ed. *The Routledge Companion to Shakespeare and Philosophy.* London: Routledge, 2019.

Bradley, A.C. *Shakespearean Tragedy: Lectures on* Hamlet, Othello, King Lear *and* Macbeth. London: Penguin, 1991.

Brandom, Robert. *Tales of the Mighty Dead. Historical Essays in the Metaphysics of Intentionality.* Cambridge, Mass.: Harvard UP, 2002.

Brandom, Robert. *A Spirit of Trust. A Reading of Hegel's* Phenomenology. Cambridge, Mass.: Harvard UP, 2019.

Brassier, Ray. "I am a Nihilist Because I Still Believe in Truth: Interview with Marcin Rychter." *Kronos* 16.1 (2011) https://cengizerdem.wordpress.com/2011/03/05/ray-brassier-interviewed-by-marcin-rychte-r-i-am-a-nihilist-because-i-still-believe-in-truth/. Accessed 1 January 2022

Brooks, Peter. *The Melodramatic Imagination: Balzac, Henry James, Melodrama, and the Mode of Excess*. New Haven: Yale UP, 1996.

Budick, Sanford. "Hamlet's 'Now' of Inward Being." *Shakespeare's* Hamlet: *Philosophical Perspectives*, ed. Tzachi Zamir. Oxford: Oxford UP, 2018. 130–153.

Budick, Sanford. "Shakespeare's Now: Some Philosophical Perspectives on *King Lear* and *The Winter's Tale*." *Entertaining the Idea: Shakespeare, Performance and Philosophy*. Ed. Lowell Gallagher, James Kearney, and Julia Reinhard Lupton. Toronto. U of Toronto P, 2020. 135–164.

Burroughs, Edgar Rice. *Tarzan of the Apes*. New York: Ballantine Books, 1984.

Butler, Judith. *Gender Trouble*. London: Routledge, 1999.

Butler, Judith. "Restaging the Universal: Hegemony and the Limits of Formalism." *Contingency, Hegemony, Universality*. London: Verso, 2000. 11-43.

Campana, Joseph and Scott Maisano, Ed. *Renaissance Posthumanism*. New York: Fordham UP, 2016.

Caputo, John. *The Prayers and Tears of Jacques Derrida. Religion without Religion*. Bloomington: Indiana University Press, 1997.

Caputo, John. "Community without a Community." *Deconstruction in a Nutshell: A Conversation with Jacques Derrida*. New York: Fordham UP, 1997. 106–124.

Carpentier, Alejo. *Los pasos perdidos*. Madrid: Alianza, 2014.

Casement, William. "Husserl and the Philosophy of History." *History and Theory* 27.3 (1988): 229–240.

Cassin, Barbara. "Ab-sense, or Lacan from A to D." *There's No Such Thing as a Sexual Relationship: Two Lessons on Lacan*. Alain Badiou and Barbara Cassin. Trans. Susan Spitzer and Kenneth Reinhard. New York: Columbia UP, 2017. 3–44.

Castoriadis, Cornelius. *Sur* Le politique *de Platon*. Paris: Seuil, 1999.

Cavell, Stanley. *Disowning Knowledge in Seven Plays of Shakespeare*. Cambridge: Cambridge UP, 2012.

Charnes, Linda. "Shakespeare, and belief, in the future." *Presentist Shakespeares*. Ed. Hugh Grady and Terence Hawkes. London: Routledge, 2007. 64–78.

Cheney, Patrick. *Marlowe's Republican Authorship: Lucan, Liberty, and the Sublime*. London: Palgrave, 2008.

Cheney, Patrick. *Shakespeare's Literary Authorship*. Cambridge: Cambridge UP, 2008.

Christie, Agatha. *They Came to Baghdad*. London: HarperCollins, 2017.

Ciliberto, Michele. *Giordano Bruno*. Bari: Laterza, 1992.

Claeys, Gregory. *Marx and Marxism*. London: Pelican, 2018.

Clarke, Simon. *The Foundations of Structuralism. A Critique of Lévi-Strauss and the Structuralist Movement*. Sussex: The Harvester Press, 1981.

Coetzee, J. M. *Giving Offence: Essays on Censorship*. Chicago: The U of Chicago P, 1996.

Cohen, Tom, J. Hillis Miller and Barbara Cohen. "A 'Materiality without Matter'?" *Material Events: Paul de Man and the Afterlifes of Theory*. Minneapolis: The U of Minnesota P, 2001. vii–xxv.

Colebrook, Claire. "Matter without Bodies." *Derrida Today* 4.1 (2011): 1–20.

Colebrook, Claire. *Jacques Derrida: Key Concepts*. London: Routledge, 2014.

Comay, Rebecca and Frank Ruda. *The Dash—The Other Side of Absolute Knowing*. Cambridge, Mass.: The MIT Press, 2018.

Copjek, Joan. *Read My Desire: Lacan Against the Historicists*. 1994. London: Verso, 2015.

Copjek, Joan. "Psychoanalysis and its consequences: Joan Copjek interviewed by Colby Chubbs." *Chasma* 6.1 (2020): 189–203.

Cottingham, John. *Cartesian Reflections: Essays on Descartes' Philosophy*. Oxford: Oxford UP, 2008.

Cottingham, John. "The Mind-Body Relation." *The Blackwell Guide to Descartes' Meditations*. Ed. Stephen Gaukroger. Oxford: Blackwell, 2006. 179–192.

Crockett, Clayton. *Derrida and the End of Writing: Political Theology and the New Materialism*. New York: Fordham UP, 2018.

Cummings, Brian and Freya Sierhuis, Ed. *Passions and Subjectivity in Early Modern Culture*. Farnham: Ashgate, 2013.

Curran, Kevin. "Phenomenology and Law: Feeling Criminal in *Macbeth*." *Criticism* 54.3 (2012): 391–401.

Curran, Kevin. *Shakespeare's Legal Ecologies: Law and Distributed Selfhood*. Evanston IL: Northwestern UP, 2017.

Curran, Kevin and David Kearney. "Introduction." Special Issue on "Shakespeare and Phenomenology." *Criticism* 54.3 (2012): 353–364.

Cutrofello, Andrew. *The Owl at Dawn: A Sequel to Hegel's Phenomenology of Spirit*. Albay: SUNY Press, 1995.

Cutrofello, Andrew. *Continental Philosophy : A Contemporary Introduction*. New York: Routledge, 2005.

Cutrofello, Andrew. "On the Idea of a Critique of Pure Practical Reason in Kant, Lacan and Deleuze." *Symposium* 10.1 (2006): 91–102.

Cutrofello, Andrew. *All for Nothing: Hamlet's Negativity*. Cambridge, Mass.: The MIT Press, 2014.

Damasio, Antonio. *Descartes' Error: Emotion, Reason and the Human Brain*. 1994. London: Penguin, 2005.

Daniel, Drew. *The Melancholy Assemblage: Affect and Epistemology in the English Renaissance*. New York: Fordham UP, 2013.

Daylight, Russell. *What if Derrida was Wrong about Saussure?* Edinburgh: Edinburgh UP, 2011.
De Grazia, Margreta. "The Essential Shakespeare and the Material Book." *Textual Practice* 2.1 (1988): 69–86.
De Grazia, Margreta. Hamlet *without Hamlet*. Cambridge: Cambridge UP, 2007.
De Grazia, Margreta and Peter Stallybrass. "The Materiality of the Shakespearean Text." *Shakespeare Quarterly* 44.3 (1993): 255–283.
Deleuze, Gilles. *La philosophie critique de Kant*. Paris: PUF, 1963.
Deleuze, Gilles. *Différence et répétition*. Paris: PUF, 1968.
Deleuze, Gilles. *L'image-temps*. Paris: Minuit, 1985.
Deleuze, Gilles. *Foucault*. Ed. Seán Hand. Minneapolis: U of Minnesota P, 1988.
Deleuze, Gilles. *Deux régimes de fous: Textes et entretiens 1975–1995*. Ed. David Lapoujade. Paris: Minuit, 2003.
Deleuze, Gilles and Claire Parnet. *Dialogues*. Paris: Flammarion, 1996.
Deleuze, Gilles and Felix Guattari. *Mille Plateaux: Capitalisme et schizophrénie*. Paris: Minuit, 1980.
Deleuze, Gilles and Felix Guattari. *A Thousand Plateaus: Capitalism and Schizophrenia*. Trans. Brian Massumi. Minneapolis : U of Minnesota P, 1987.
Deleuze, Gilles and Felix Guattari. *Qu'est-ce que la philosophie?* Paris: Minuit, 1991.
De Man, Paul. "Semiology and Rhetoric." *Diacritics* 3.3 (1973): 27–33.
De Man, Paul. *Allegories of Reading*. New Haven: Yale UP, 1979.
De Man, Paul. *Blindness and Insight: Essays in the Rhetoric of Contemporary Criticism*. Ed. Wlad Godzich. London: Routledge, 1983.
De Man, Paul. *The Rhetoric of Romanticism*. New York: Columbia UP, 1984.
De Man, Paul. *The Resistance to Theory*. Ed. Wlad Godzich. Minneapolis: U of Minnesota P, 1986.
De Man, Paul. *Critical Writings 1953–1978*. Ed. Lindsay Waters. Minneapolis: The U of Minnesota P, 1989.
De Man, Paul. *Romanticism and Contemporary Criticism*. Ed. E.S. Burt, Kevin Newmark and Andrzej Warminski. Baltimore: The John Hopkins UP, 1993.
De Man, Paul. *Aesthetic Ideology*. Ed. Andrzej Warminski. Minneapolis: U of Minnesota P, 1996.
Dennett, Daniel. "Who's On First? Heterophenomenology Explained." *Journal of Consciousness Studies* 10–9–10 (2003): 19–30.
Derrida, Jacques. "Introduction" to Edmund Husserl, *L'origine de la géométrie*. Paris: PUF, 1962.
Derrida, Jacques. *La voix et le phénomène : Introduction au problème du signe dans la phénoménologie de Husserl*. Paris: PUF, 1967.
Derrida, Jacques. *De la grammatologie*. Paris: Minuit, 1967.
Derrida, Jacques. *L'écriture et la différence*. Paris: Seuil, 1967.

Derrida, Jacques. *Positions*. Paris: Minuit, 1972.

Derrida, Jacques. *Marges de la philosophie*. Paris: Minuit, 1972.

Derrida, Jacques. *La dissémination*. Paris: Seuil, 1972.

Derrida, Jacques. *Glas*. Paris: Galilée, 1974.

Derrida, Jacques. *Of Grammatology*. Ed. Gayatri Spivak. John Hopkins UP, 1977.

Derrida, Jacques. *La vérité en peinture*. Paris: Flammarion, 1978.

Derrida, Jacques. "La langue et le discours de la méthode." in *Recherches sur la philosophie et le langage* 3 (1983): 35–51.

Derrida, Jacques. *La carte postale. De Socrate à Freud et au-delà*. Paris: Flammarion, 1985.

Derrida, Jacques. *Psyché: Inventions de l'autre*. Tome I. Paris: Galilée, 1987.

Derrida, Jacques. *Memoires for Paul de Man*. New York: Columbia UP, 1989.

Derrida, Jacques. *Le problème de la genèse dans la philosophie de Husserl*. Paris: PUF, 1990.

Derrida, Jacques & Moshe Ron. "Interpretations at War: Kant, the Jew, the German." *New Literary History* 22.1 (1991): 39–95.

Derrida, Jacques. *Acts of Literature*. Ed. D. Attridge. New York: Routledge, 1992.

Derrida, Jacques. *Spectres de Marx. L'Etat de la dette, le travail du deuil et la nouvelle Internationale*. Paris: Galilée, 1993.

Derrida, Jacques. *Politiques de l'amitié*. Paris: Galilée, 1994.

Derrida, Jacques. *Points de suspension: Interviews: 1974–1994*. Ed. Elizabeth Weber. Trans. Peggy Kamuf et al. Stanford: Stanford UP, 1995.

Derrida, Jacques. *Adieu à Emmanuel Levinas*. Paris: Galilée, 1997.

Derrida, Jacques. *De l'hospitalité*. Ed. Anne Dufourmantelle. Paris: Calmann-Lévy, 1997.

Derrida, Jacques. "Typewriter Ribbon: Limited Inc (2)" in *Material Events. Paul de Man and the Afterlife of Theory*. Ed. Tom Cohen, J. Hillis Miller and Barbara Cohen. Minneapolis: The U of Minnesota P, 2001. 277–360.

Derrida, Jacques. "Language and the Discourse on Method." *Bamidbar* 1.2 (2011): 61–80.

Derrida, Jacques. "La déconstruction et l'autre." *Le temps modernes*, 3–4. 669/70 (2012): 7–29.

Descartes, René. *Le monde et le Traité de l'homme*. In *Œuvres philosophiques*. Tome I (1618–1637). Ed. Ferdinand Alquié. Paris: Garnier, 1963.

Descartes, René. *Discourse on Method and Meditations on First Philosophy*. Trans. Donald Cress. Indianapolis: Hackett, 1998.

Descartes, René. *Discourse on Method*. Trans. Ian Maclean. Oxford: Oxford UP, 2006.

Descartes, René. *Discours de la méthode et Essais (La Dioptrique, Les Météors, La Géométrie)*. *Œuvres complètes III*. Ed. Geneviève Rodis-Lewis *et al.* Paris: Gallimard, 2009.

Descartes, René. *Règles pour la direction de l'esprit*. *Œuvres compètes I*. Ed. Denis Kambourchner and Jean-Marie Beyssade. Paris: Gallimard, 2016.

Descartes, René. *Méditations métaphysiques*. *Œuvres complètes IV-1*. Ed. Jean-Marie Beyssade *et al.* Paris: Gallimard, 2018.

Descartes, René. *Méditations métaphysiques. Œuvres complètes IV-2*. Ed. Jean-Marie Beyssade et al. Paris: Gallimard, 2018.
Descombes, Vincent. *Le même et l'autre. Quarante-cinq ans de philosophie française (1933–1978)*. Paris: Minuit, 1979.
Descombes, Vincent. *Objects of All Sorts: A Philosophical Grammar*. Trans. L. Scott-Fox and J.M. Harding. Baltimore: John Hopkins UP, 1986.
DeVries, Willem A. *Wilfrid Sellars*. London: Routledge, 2005.
Dickens, Charles. *David Copperfield*. Ed. Nina Burgis and Andrew Sanders. Oxford: Oxford UP, 1997.
Dickens, Charles. *Nicholas Nickleby*. Ed. Paul Schlicke. Oxford: Oxford UP, 1999.
Dickens, Charles. *Oliver Twist*. Ed. Philip Horne. London: Penguin, 2007.
Dickinson, Emily. *The Complete Poems*. Ed. Thomas H. Johnson. Little, Brown & Company, 1976.
Di Giovanni, George. "Introduction" to Hegel, *The Science of Logic*. Cambridge UP, 2010.
Dillard-Wright, David. *Ark of the Possible: The Animal World in Merleau-Ponty*. Lanham: Lexington Books, 2009.
Dollimore, Jonathan. *Radical Tragedy: Religion, Ideology and Power in the Drama of Shakespeare and His Contemporaries*. 2nd ed. New York: Harvester Wheatsheaf, 1989.
Dollimore, Jonathan. "The Cultural Politics of Perversion: Augustine, Shakespeare, Freud, Foucault." *Textual Practice* 4.2 (1990): 179–196.
Dollimore, Jonathan. *Sexual Dissidence: Augustine to Wilde, Freud to Foucault*. Oxford UP, 1991.
Dollimore, Jonathan. "Wishful Theory and Sexual Politics." *Radical Philosophy* 103 (2000): 18–24.
Dollimore, Jonathan. "Then and Now." *Critical Survey* 26.3 (2014): 61–82.
Dreyfus, H. *Being-in-the-World: A Commentary on Heidegger's Being and Time*. Cambridge: MIT, 1991.
Dubouclez, Olivier. "Politique de l'invention. Derrida s'expliquant avec Descartes." *Methodos: Savoirs et Textes* 18 (2018). http://journals.openedition.org/methodos/4962; DOI: https://doi.org/10.4000/methodos.4962. Accessed 1 January 2022
Duncan-Jones, Katherine. *Ungentle Shakespeare: Scenes from his Life*. London: Bloomsbury, 2001.
Dunn, John. *The Political Thought of John Locke: An Historical Account of the Argument of the 'Two Treatises of Government.'* Cambridge: Cambridge UP, 1969.
Dunn, John. *Locke*. Oxford: Oxford UP, 1984.
Dworkin, Ronald. *Taking Rights Seriously*. Cambridge, Mass.: Harvard UP, 1978.
Eagleton, Terry. *Why Marx was Right*. New Haven: Yale UP, 2012.
Easthope, Antony. *Privileging Difference*. Ed. Catherine Belsey. London: Bloomsbury, 2001.
Egan, Gabriel. *The Struggle for Shakespeare's Text. Twentieth-Century Editorial Theory and Practice*. Cambridge: Cambridge UP, 2012.

Egan, Gabriel. "Homeostasis in Shakespeare." *Posthumanist Shakespeares*. Ed. Ivan Callus and Stefan Herbrechter. New York: Palgrave, 2012. 77–94.

Eliot, George. *Adam Bede*. Ed. Stephen Gill. London: Penguin, 1980.

Eliot, T.S. *Collected Poems 1909–1962*. London: Faber and Faber, 1974.

Eliot, T.S. *Selected Prose of T.S. Eliot*. Ed. Frank Kermode. London: Faber and Faber, 1975. 151–153.

Empson, William. *Some Versions of Pastoral. A Study of the Pastoral Form in Literature*. London: Penguin, 1966.

Empson, William. *Essays on Shakespeare*. Ed. David B. Pirie. Cambridge: Cambridge UP, 1986.

Empson, William. *Seven Types of Ambiguity*. London: Penguin, 1995.

Erne, Lukas. *Shakespeare as Literary Dramatist*. Second edition. Cambridge: Cambridge UP, 2013.

The Earliest English Poems. Ed. Michael Alexander. New York: Penguin, 1996.

Farrington, Benjamin. "Francis Bacon 1561–1626." *Impact of Science on Society* 12.1 (1962): 3–22.

Fearing, F. "René Descartes. A study in the history of the theories of reflex action." *Psychological Review* 36.5 (1929): 375–388. https://doi.org/10.1037/h0074868. Accessed 1 January 2022.

Felski, Rita. *The Limits of Critique*. Chicago: The U of Chicago P, 2015.

Fernie, Ewan, ed. *Spiritual Shakespeares*. London: Routledge, 2005.

Fernie, Ewan. "Action! *Henry V*." *Presentist Shakespeares*. Ed. Hugh Grady and Terence Hawkes. London: Routledge, 2007. 96–120.

Ferry, Luc and Alain Renault. *La pensée 68: Essai sur l'anti-humanisme contemporain*. Paris: Gallimard, 1988.

Filmer, Robert. *Patriarcha and Other Writings*. Ed. Johann P. Sommerville. Cambridge: Cambridge UP, 1991.

Finkielkraut, Alain. *La défaite de la pensée*. Paris: Gallimard, 1987.

Finkielkraut, Alain. *L'identité malheureuse*. Paris: Gallimard, 2013.

Firth, John R. "Personality and Language in Society," *The Sociological Review* 62 (1950). Reprinted in Firth, *Papers in Linguistics 1934–1951*. London: Oxford UP, 1957. 177–189.

Foster, John Bellamy. *Marx's Ecology: Materialism and Nature*. New York: Monthly Review Press, 2000.

Foucault, Michel. *Raymond Roussel*. Paris: Gallimard, 1963.

Foucault, Michel. *L'archéologie du savoir*. Paris: Gallimard, 1969.

Foucault, Michel. *The archeology of knowledge*. Trans. A.M. Sheridan Smith. New York: Pantheon Books, 1972.

Foucault, Michel. "La folie, l'absence d'œuvre." *Dits et écrits I. 1954–1975*. Paris: Gallimard, 2001.

Frege, Gottlob. *The Frege Reader*. Ed. Michael Beaney. London: Blackwell, 1997.

Gadamer, Hans Georg. *Hegel's Dialectic: Five Hermeneutical Studies*. Trans. P. Christopher Smith. New Haven: Yale UP, 1976.

Gadamer, Hans Georg. *Truth and Method*. Trans. revised by Joel Weinsheimer and Donald G. Mar. London: Continuum, 1975.

Gaddis, William. *A Frolic of His Own*. New York: Scribner, 1994.

Gaddis, William. *The Rush for Second Place: Essays and Occasional Writings*. New York: Penguin, 2002.

Gallagher, Lowell, James Kearney and Julia Reinhard Lupton. *Entertaining the Idea: Shakespeare, Philosophy, and Performance*. Toronto: U of Toronto P, 2021.

Garber, Marjorie. *Shakespeare's Ghost Writers. Literature as Uncanny Causality*. London: Routledge, 2010.

Gasché, Rodolphe. *The Tain of the Mirror: Derrida and the Philosophy of Reflection*. Cambridge: Harvard UP, 1986.

Goethe, Johann Wolfgang. *Faust*. Frankfurt am Main: Fischer, 1974.

Goldgaber, Deborah. *Speculative Grammatology: Deconstruction and the New Materialism*. Edinburgh: Edinburgh UP, 2020.

Goldie, Mark. "Introduction" to John Locke, *Political Essays*. Cambridge: Cambridge UP, 1997.

Goldstein, David B. and Amy L. Tigner, eds. *Culinary Shakespeare: Staging Food and Drink in Early Modern England*. Pennsylvania: The Penn State UP, 2016.

Grady, Hugh. *Shakespeare and Impure Aesthetics*. Cambridge: Cambridge UP, 2009.

Grady, Hugh and Terence Hawkes, Ed. *Presentist Shakespeares*. London: Routledge, 2006.

Greenblatt, Stephen. "Shakespeare Bewitched." In *Shakespeare and Cultural Traditions*. Ed. T. Kishi, R. Pringue, and S. Wells. Newark: U of Delaware P, 1991. 17–42.

Greenblatt, Stephen. *Will in the World: How Shakespeare Became Shakespeare*. New York: Norton, 2004.

Greenblatt, Stephen. *Learning to Curse*. London: Routledge, 2007.

Greenblatt, Stephen. *Tyrant: Shakespeare on Politics*. New York: Norton, 2018.

Greene, Donald. *The Politics of Samuel Johnson*. 1960. 2nd ed. Athens: The University of Georgia Press, 1990.

Gross, Kenneth. *Shylock is Shakespeare*. Chicago: The U of Chicago P, 2006.

Habermas, Jürgen. "Hannah Arendt's Communications Concept of Power." *Social Research* 44.1 (1977): 3–24.

Habermas, Jürgen. *The Philosophical Discourse of Modernity: Twelve Lectures*. Trans. Frederik Lawrence. Cambridge, Mass.: The MIT Press.

Habermas, Jürgen. *Wahrheit und Rechtfertigung*. Frankfurt am Main: Suhrkamp, 1999.

Hägglund, Martin. *Radical Atheism: Derrida and the Time of Life*. Stanford: Stanford UP, 2008.

Hajdu, David. *Positively 4th Street: The Lives and Times of Joan Baez, Bob Dylan, Mimi Baez Fariña, and Richard Fariña*. New York: Farrar, Strauss & Giroux, 2011.

Halliday, M.A.K. *An Introduction to Functional Grammar*. London: Arnold, 1985.

Hammill, Graham & Julia Reinhard Lupton, eds. *Political Theology and Early Modernity*. The U of Chicago P, 2012.

Harris, Jonathan Gil. *Shakespeare and Literary Theory*. Oxford: Oxford UP, 2010.

Harris, Jonathan Gil. *Untimely Matter in the Time of Shakespeare*. Philadelphia: The U of Pennsylvania P, 2011.

Harris, Roy. *Reading Saussure. A Critical Commentary on the* Cours de linguistique générale. London: Gerald Duckworth, 1987.

Harris, Roy. *Saussure and His Interpreters*. Edinburgh: Edinburgh UP, 2001.

Hatfield, Gary. *Descartes and the Meditations*. London: Routledge, 2003.

Hatfield, Gary. "René Descartes." *The Stanford Encyclopedia of Philosophy* (Summer 2018 Edition), Edward N. Zalta (ed.) URL = <https://plato.stanford.edu/archives/sum2018/entries/descartes/>. Accessed 1 January 2022

Haugeland, John. *Artificial Intelligence: The Very Idea*. Cambridge, Mass.: The MIT Press, 1985.

Hawthorne, Nathaniel. *The Scarlet Letter*. Ed. Leland S. Person. New York: Norton, 2005.

Hayat, Pierre. "Emmanuel Levinas: Une intuition du social." *Le Philosophoire* 2.32 (2009): 127–137.

Hazlitt, William. *Characters of Shakespeare's Plays*. Oxford: Oxford UP, 1955.

Heckman, John. "Introduction" to Jean Hyppolite, *Genesis and Structure of Hegel's* Phenomenology of Spirit. Trans. Samuel Cherniak and John Heckman. Evanston: Northwestern UP, 1974.

Hegel, G. W. F. *Phänomenologie des Geistes*. Werke 3. Frankfurt am Main: Suhrkamp, 1970.

Hegel, G. W. F. *Aesthetics. Lectures on Fine Arts*. Trans. T.M. Knox. London: Clarendon Press, 1975.

Hegel, G. W. F. *Phenomenology of Spirit*. Trans. A.V. Miller. Oxford: Oxford UP, 1979.

Hegel, G. W. F. *Outlines of the Philosophy of Right*. Ed. Stephen Houlgate. Trans. T.M. Knox. Oxford: Oxford UP, 2008.

Hegel, G. W. F. *The Science of Logic*. Ed. George di Giovanni. Cambridge: Cambridge UP, 2010.

Hegel, G. W. F. "The Spirit of Christianity and its Fate." https://www.marxists.org/reference/archive/hegel/works/fate/index.htm. Accessed 1 January 2022

Hegel, G. W. F. *Encyclopedia of the Philosophical Sciences in Basic Outline*. Ed. Klaus Brinkmann & Daniel O. Dahlstrom. Cambridge: Cambridge UP, 2015.

Hegel, G. W. F. *The Phenomenology of Spirit*. Ed. Terry Pinkard. Cambridge UP, 2018.

Heidegger, Martin. *Being and Time*. Trans. John Macquarrie & Edward Robinson. Oxford: Blackwell, 1962.

Heidegger, Martin. *Sein und Zeit*. Tübingen: Max Niemeyer, 1967.

Heidegger, Martin. *What is Called Thinking?* Trans. J. Glenn Gray. New York: Harper & Row, 1968.
Heidegger, Martin. *Identity and Difference.* Trans. Joan Stambaugh. New York: Harper & Row, 1969.
Heidegger, Martin. *On Time and Being.* Trans. Joan Stambaugh. New York: Harper & Row, 1972.
Heidegger, Martin. *Die Grundprobleme der Phänomenologie.* In *Gesaumtausgabe.* Vol. 24. Frankfurt am Main: Vittorio Klostermann, 1975.
Heidegger, Martin. *The Basic Problems of Phenomenology.* Ed. Albert Hofstadter. Bloomington: Indiana UP, 1982.
Heidegger, Martin. *Nietzsche.* Vols 1 and 2. Ed. David Farrell Krell. New York: Harper & Row, 1982.
Heidegger, Martin. *Unterwegs zur Sprache.* In *Gesamtsausgabe.* Vol. 12. Frankfurt am Main: Vittorio Klostermann, 1985.
Heidegger, Martin. *Hegel's Phenomenology of Spirit.* Trans. Parvis Emad and Kenneth Maly. Bloomington: Indiana UP, 1988.
Heidegger, Martin. *Kant and the Problem of Metaphysics.* Trans. R. Taft. Bloomington: Indiana University Press, 1997.
Heidegger, Martin. *Pathmarks.* Trans. William McNeill. Cambridge: Cambridge UP, 1998.
Heidegger, Martin. *Off the Beaten Track.* Ed. Julian Young & Kenneth Haynes. Cambridge: Cambridge UP, 2002.
Heidegger, Martin. *Being and Time.* Trans. Joan Stambaugh. Revised and with a Foreword by Dennis J. Schmidt. Albany: State U of New York P, 2010.
Heidegger, Martin and Eugene Fink. *Heraclitus Seminar 1966/67.* Trans. Charles H. Seibert. The U of Alabama P, 1979.
Henrich, Dieter. *Aesthetic Judgement and the Moral Image of the World. Studies in Kant.* Stanford: Stanford UP, 1992.
Henrich, Dieter. *The Unity of Reason: Essays on Kant's Philosophy.* Ed. Richard L. Velkley. Cambridge, Mass.: Harvard UP, 1994.
Hesse, M. B. "Francis Bacon's Philosophy of Science." *A Critical History of Western Philosophy.* Ed. D. J. O'Connor. New York: Free Press, 1964. 141–52.
Hobbes, Thomas. *On the Citizen.* Ed. Richard Tuck and Michael Silverthorne. Cambridge: Cambridge UP, 1998.
Hobbes, Thomas. *Leviathan.* Ed. C.B. Macpherson. London: Penguin, 1981.
Hobsbawm, Eric. "Identity Politics and the Left." *New Left Review* 217 (1996): 38–47.
Honan, Park. *Shakespeare: A Life.* Oxford: Oxford UP, 1998.
Horkheimer, Max and Theodor Adorno, *Dialectic of Enlightenment: Philosophical Fragments.* Ed. Gunzelin Schmid Noerr. Trans. Edmund Jephcott. Stanford: Stanford UP, 2002.

Houellebecq, Michel. *Sérotonine*. Paris: Flammarion, 2019.
Houellebecq, Michel & Bernhard Henry-Lévy. *Ennemis publics*. Paris: Grasset, 2008.
Hughes, Robert. *The Culture of Complaint: The Fraying of America*. London: Harvill, 1994.
Hume, David. *A Treatise of Human Nature*. Ed. Ernest Campbell Mossner. London: Penguin, 1969.
Hume, David. *Political Essays*. Ed. Knud Haakonssen. Cambridge: Cambridge UP, 1994.
Hume, David. *An Enquiry Concerning Human Understanding*. Ed. Peter Millican. London: Penguin, 2007.
Husserl, Edmund. *Philosophie der Arithmetik: Psychologische und logische Untersuchungen*. Halle-Saale: C.E.M. Pfeffer, 1891.
Husserl, Edmund. *Ideen zu einer reinen Phänomenologie und phänomenologischen Philosophie* (Erstes Buch). *Jahrbuch für Philosophie und phänemonologische Forschung*. Halle: Max Niemeyer, 1913.
Husserl, Edmund. *Cartesian Meditations. An Introduction to Phenomenology*. Trans. Dorion Cairns. The Hague: Martinus Nijhoff, 1960.
Husserl, Edmund. *Logical Investigations*. Trans. J.N. Findlay. London: Routledge, 1970.
Husserl, Edmund. *The Crisis of the European Sciences and Transcendental Phenomenology*. Trans. David Carr, Evanston: Northwestern UP, 1970.
Husserl, Edmund. *Cartesianische Meditationen und Pariser Vorträger*. Ed. S. Strasser, *Husserliana I*. Den Haag: Martinus Nijhoff, 1973.
Husserl, Edmund. *Logische Untersuchungen*. Ed. Elmar Holenstein. Den Haag: Martinus Nijhoff, 1975.
Husserl, Edmund. *Ideas pertaining to a Pure Phenomenology and to a Phenomenological Philosophy*. Trans. F. Kersten. *Collected Works*. Volume II. The Hague: Martinus Nijhoff, 1983.
Husserl, Edmund. *Ideas pertaining to a Pure Phenomenology and to a Phenomenological Philosophy, Second Book*. Trans. Richard Rojcewicz and André Schuwer. Foreword by John Scanlon. Dordrecht: Kluwer, 1989.
Husserl, Edmund. *Early Writings in the Philosophy of Logic and Mathematics*. Trans. D. Willard, Dordrecht: Kluwer, 1994.
Husserl, Edmund. *Ideas: General Introduction to Pure Phenomenology*. Trans. W.R. Boyce Gibson. London: Routledge, 2002.
Husserl, Edmund. *Philosophy of Arithmetic*. Trans. Dallas Willard. Springer Science, 2003.
Husserl, Edmund. *Méditations cartésiennes*. Trans. Gabrielle Pfeiffer et Emmanuel Levinas, Paris: Vrin, 2014.
Husserl, Edmund. *The Phenomenology of Internal Time-Consciousness*. Trans. James S. Churchill. Bloomington: Indiana UP, 2019.
Hyppolite, Jean. *Gènese et structure de la* Phénoménologie de l'esprit *de Hegel*. Paris: Aubier, 1946.

Hyppolite, Jean. *Genesis and Structure of Hegel's* Phenomenology of Spirit. Trans. Samuel Cherniak and John Heckman. Evanston: Northwestern UP, 1974.
James, Henry. *Literary Criticism*. 2 Vol. New York: The Library of America, 1984.
Jameson, Fredric. *Marxism and Form: Twentieth-Century Dialectical Theories of Literature*, Princeton: Princeton UP, 1971.
Jameson, Fredric. *Late Marxism: Adorno, or the Persistence of the Dialectic.* London: Verso, 1990.
Jameson, Fredric. *Postmodernism, or, the Cultural Logic of Late Capitalism*. Durham: Duke UP, 1991.
Jameson, Fredric. *The Seeds of Time*. New York: Columbia UP, 1994.
Jameson, Fredric. *Brecht and Method*. London: Verso, 1998.
Jameson, Fredric. *The Ideologies of Theory*. London: Verso, 2008.
Jameson, Fredric. *Valences of the Dialectic*. London: Verso, 2009.
Jameson, Fredric. *Representing* Capital. *A Commentary on Volume One*. London: Verso, 2011.
Jameson, Fredric. *The Antinomies of Realism*. London: Verso, 2013.
Jay, Martin. *Downcast Eyes. The Denigration of Vision in Twentieth-Century French Thought*. Berkeley: U of California P, 1993.
Johnson, Samuel *Selected Writings*. Ed. Patrick Cruttwell. London: Penguin, 1968.
Johnson, Samuel. *Lives of the Poets*. Ed. Roger Londsdale. Oxford: Clarendon Press, 2006.
Johnston, Adrian. "Where to Start?: Robert Pippin, Slavoj Žižek, and the True Beginning(s) of Hegel's System." *Crisis and Critique* 1.3 (2014): 371–418.
Joughin, John J., ed. *Philosophical Shakespeares*. London: Routledge, 2000.
Joyce, James. *Ulysses*. Ed. Declan Kiberd. London: Penguin, 1992.
Judt, Tony. *Past Imperfect: French Intellectuals, 1944–1956*. New York: New York UP, 2011.
Julian of Norwich. *Revelations of Divine Love*. Ed. A. Spearing and E. Spearing. London: Penguin, 1999.
Kant, Immanuel. *Critique of Judgement*. Trans. Werner S. Pluhar. Indianapolis: Hackett, 1987.
Kant, Immanuel. *Critique of Pure Reason*. Ed. Paul Guyer and Allen Wood. Cambridge: Cambridge UP, 1998.
Kant, Immanuel. *Critique of Pure Reason*. Trans. Marcus Weigelt. London: Penguin, 2008.
Kant, Immanuel. *Religion within the Boundaries of Mere Reason*. Ed. Allen Wood and George di Giovanni. Cambridge: Cambridge UP, 2018.
Kastan, David Scott. *Shakespeare After Theory*. New York: Routledge, 2013.
Kastan, David Scott. *A Will to Believe: Shakespeare and Religion*. Oxford: Oxford UP, 2014.
Kates, Joshua. *Fielding Derrida. Philosophy, Literary Criticism, History, and the Work of Deconstruction*. New York: Fordham UP, 2008.
Kleist, Heinrich von. *Sämtlichen Erzählungen*. Zurich: Diogenes, 1990.

Kohn, Jerome. "Hannah Arendt's Jewish Experience: Thinking, Acting, Judging." *Thinking in Dark Times: Hannah Arendt on Ethics and Politics.* Ed. Roger Berkowitz et al. New York: Fordam UP, 2010. 179–194.
Kojève, Alexandre. *Introduction à la lecture de Hegel.* 1947. Paris: Gallimard, 1968.
Kottman, Paul. *A Politics of the Scene.* Stanford: Stanford UP, 2008.
Kottman, Paul. *Tragic Conditions in Shakespeare. Disinheriting the Globe.* Baltimore, The John Hopkins UP, 2009.
Kottman, Paul. "No greater powers than we can contradict." *Criticism* 54.3 (2012): 445–454.
Kottman, Paul. "Duel." *Early Modern Theatricality.* Ed. Henry S. Turner. Oxford: Oxford UP, 2013. 402–422.
Kottman, Paul. "Hegel and Shakespeare on the Pastness of Art." *The Art of Hegel's Aesthetics. Hegelian Philosophy and the Perspective of Art History.* Ed. Paul Kottman and Michael Squire. Leiden: Wilhelm Fink, 2018. 263–302.
Kottman, Paul. "Why Shakespeare Stopped Writing Tragedies." *Journal of Medieval and Early Modern Studies* 49.1 (2019): 113–135.
Kymlicka, Will. *Liberalism, Community and Culture.* Oxford: Oxford UP, 1989.
Leo, Russ. "Affective Physics: Affectus in Spinoza's Ethics." *Passions and Subjectivity in Early Modern Culture.* Ed. Brian Cummings and Freya Sierhuis. 33–50.
Lacan, Jacques. "Maurice Merleau-Ponty." *Les Temps Modernes* 185–186 (1961) : 245–254. http://espace.freud.pagesperso-orange.fr/topos/psycha/psysem/merleau.htm. Accessed 1 January 2022
Lacan, Jacques. *Écrits I.* Paris: Seuil, 1966.
Lacan, Jacques. *Le moi dans la théorie de Freud et dans la technique de la psychanalyse. Le Séminaire II.* Ed. Jacques-Allain Milller. Paris: Seuil, 1973.
Lacan, Jacques. *Les quatre concepts fondamentaux de la psychanalyse.* Ed. Jacques-Allain Miller. Paris: Seuil, 1973.
Lacan, Jacques. "Merlau-Ponty: In Memoriam." Trans. Wilfried ver Eecke and Dirk de Schutter. *Review of Existential Psychology and Psychiatry* 18.1–2–3 (1985): 73–81.
Lacan, Jacques. *L'éthique de la psychanalyse. Le Séminaire VII.* Paris : Seuil, 1986.
Lacan, Jacques. *Écrits.* Trans. Bruce Fink. New York: Norton, 2006.
Lacan, Jacques. *Le séminaire de Jacques Lacan: D'un discours qui ne serait pas du semblant.* Paris : Seuil, 2006.
Labelle, Gilles. "Maurice Merleau-Ponty et la genèse de la philosophie politique de Claude Lefort." *Politique et sociétés* 22.3 (2003): 9–44.
Laqué, Stephan. "'Not Passion's Slave': Hamlet, Descartes and the Passions." *Passions and Subjectivity in Early Modern Culture.* Ed. Brian Cummings and Freya Sierhuis. Farnham: Ashgate, 2013. 267–280.
Laruelle, François. *Introduction to Non-Marxism.* Trans. Anthony Paul Smith. Minneapolis: U of Minnesota P, 2015.

Laslett, Peter. *The World We Have Lost, Further Explored*. London: Routledge, 2000.
Latour, Bruno. *We Have Never Been Modern*. Trans. Catherine Porter. Cambridge, Mass.: Harvard UP, 1993.
Latour, Bruno. *Politics of Nature: How to Bring the Sciences into Democracy*. Trans. Catherine Porter. Cambridge, Mass.: Harvard UP, 2004.
Lefort, Claude. *Essais sur le politique (xixe- xxe siècles)*. Paris: Seuil, 1986.
Lefort, Claude. *Écrire. À l'épreuve du politique*. Paris: Éditions Calmann-Lévy, 1992.
Levi-Strauss, Claude. *Tristes tropiques*. Paris: Plon, 1955.
Levi-Strauss, Claude. *Structural Anthropology*. Trans. Claire Jacobson and Brooke Grunfest Schoepf. New York: Anchor Books, 1967.
Levinas, Emmanuel. *Totalité et infini: Essai sur l'exteriorité*. The Hague : Nijhoof, 1961.
Levinas, Emmanuel. *Théorie de l'intuition dans la phénoménologie de Husserl*. Fourth edition. Paris: Vrin, 1978.
Levinas, Emmanuel. *Totality and Infinity*. Trans. Alphonso Lingis. The Hague: Martinus Nijhoff, 1978.
Levinas, Emmanuel. *Autrement qu'être ou au-delà de l'essence*. The Hague: Martinus Nijhoff, 1978.
Levinas, Emmanuel. "Paix et proximité." *Les cahiers de la nuit surveillé* 3 (1984): 339–345.
Levinas, Emmanuel. "La souffrance inutile." *Les cahiers de la nuit surveillé* 3 (1984): 329–338.
Levinas, Emmanuel. "The Paradox of Morality: An Interview with Emmanuel Levinas" in *The Provocation of Levinas: Rethinking the Other*. Ed. Robert Bernasconi and David Wood. London: Routledge, 1988. 168–180.
Levinas, Emmanuel. *De l'existence à l'existant*. Paris: Vrin, 2004.
Lewitscharoff, Sybille. *Blumenberg*. Frankfurt am Main: Suhrkamp, 2013.
Lipotevsky, Gilles. "The Contribution of Mass Media." *Ethical Perspectives* 7.2 (2000): 133–138.
Livingston, Paul and Andrew Cutrofello. *The Problems of Contemporary Philosophy*. Cambridge: Polity, 2015.
Llewelyn, John. "Levinas and Language." *The Cambridge Companion to Levinas*. Ed. Simon Critchley and Robert Bernasconi. Cambridge: Cambridge UP, 2002. 119–138.
Locke, John. *Two Treatises of Government*. Ed. Peter Laslett. Cambridge UP, 1994.
Loidolt, Sophie. *Phenomenology of Plurality: Hannah Arendt on Political Intersubjectivity*. New York: Routledge, 2018.
Lukacher, Ned. *Primal Scenes: Literature, Philosophy, Psychoanalysis*. Cornell: Cornell UP, 1988.
Lukacher, Ned. *Daemonic Figures: Shakespeare and the Question of Conscience*. Cornell: Cornell UP, 1994.
Lukács, Georg. *History and Class Consciousness: Studies in Marxist Dialectics*. Trans. Rodney Livingstone. Cambridge, Mass.: The MIT Press, 1971.

Lupton, Julia Reinhard. *Citizen-Saints: Shakespeare and Political Theology*. Chicago: The U of Chicago P, 2005.

Lupton, Julia Reinhard. *Thinking with Shakespeare*. Chicago: The U of Chicago P, 2011.

Lupton, Julia Reinhard. "*Macbeth*'s Martlets: Shakespearean Phenomenologies of Hospitality." *Criticism* 54.3 (2012): 365–376.

Lupton, Julia Reinhard. "Making Room, Affording Hospitality: Environments of Entertainment in *Romeo and Juliet*." *Journal of Medieval and Early Modern Studies* 43–1 (2013): 145–172.

Lupton, Julia Reinhard, ed. *Romeo and Juliet: A Critical Reader*. London: Bloomsbury, 2016.

Lupton, Julia Reinhard. "'Cut him out in little stars': Juliet's Cute Classicism." *Shakespeare Survey* 70 (2017): 240–48.

Lupton, Julia Reinhard. "Review of Paul Kottman's *The Insistence of Art: Aesthetic Philosophy After Early Modernity*." *Shakespeare Studies* 46 (2018): 279–284.

Lupton, Julia Reinhard. *Shakespeare Dwelling: Designs for the Theater of Life*. The U of Chicago P, 2018.

Lupton, Julia Reinhard. "Virtue in *Twelfth Night*: A Humanifesto" https://renaissance.indiana.edu/events/lupton-papers/Lupton_Virtues_Indiana.pdf. Accessed 1 January 2022.

Lupton, Julia and Kenneth Reinhard. *After Oedipus: Shakespeare and Psychoanalysis*. Ithaca: Cornell UP, 1993.

Lupton, Julia and David Goldstein, eds. *Shakespeare and Hospitality: Ethics, Politics, and Exchange*. London: Routledge, 2016.

Lyotard, Jean-François. *La phénoménologie*. Paris: PUF, 1954.

Lyotard, Jean-François. *Le différend*. Paris: Minuit, 1983.

Mailer, Norman. *Four Books of the 1960s*. Ed. J. Michael Lennon. New York: The Library of America. 2018.

Maisano, Scott. "Infinite Gesture: Automata and the Emotions in Descartes and Shakespeare." *Genesis Redux: Essays in the History and Philosophy of Artificial Life*. Ed. Jessica Riskin. Chicago: U of Chicago P, 2007. 63–84.

Maisano, Scott. "Rise of the Poet of the Apes." *Shakespeare Studies* 41 (2013): 64–76.

"Manifesto of the V21 Collective" http://v21collective.org/manifesto-of-the-v21-collective-ten-theses/. Accessed 1 January 2022

Mann, Thomas. *Der Zauberberg*. Frankfurt am Main: Fischer, 1991.

Mann, Thomas. *The Magic Mountain*. Trans. H.T. Lowe-Porter. London: Secker & Warburg, 1928.

Mann, Thomas. *Schopenhauer, Nietzsche, Freud*. Ed. Andrés Sánchez Pascual. Madrid: Alianza, 2000.

Marlow, Christopher. *Shakespeare and Cultural Materialist Theory*. London: Bloomsbury, 2017.

Marlowe, Christopher. *Doctor Faustus*. Ed. David Bevington and Eric Rasmussen. Manchester: Manchester UP, 1993.

Marcus, Steven. *Dickens from Pickwick to Dombey*. New York: Simon and Schuster, 1965.

Marx, Karl. *Critique of Hegel's 'Philosophy of Right.'* Ed. Joseph O'Maley. Ca,bridge: Cambridge UP, 1970.

Marx, Karl. "On the Jewish Question." *Early Political Writings*. Ed. Joseph O'Malley. Cambridge: Cambridge UP, 1994. 28–50.

Marx, Karl. *Misère de la philosophie*. Ed. Jean Kessler. Paris: Payot, 2002.

Marx, Karl and Friedrich Engels. *The German Ideology: Introduction to a Critique of Political Economy*. Ed. Christopher John Arthur. London: Lawrence & Wishart, 1970.

Marx, Karl and Friedrich Engels. *The Holy Family, or Critique of Critical Critique*. Trans. R. Dixon. Moscow: Foreign Language Publishing House, 1956.

McCullers, Carson. *The Member of the Wedding*. London: Penguin, 1962.

McDowell, John. *Mind and World*. Cambridge, Mass.: Harvard UP, 1996.

McIntyre, Alasdair. *After Virtue. A Study in Moral Theory*. Third edition. Notre Dame: U of Notre Dame P, 2007.

Melandri, Enzo. *Le* Ricerche Logiche *di Husserl. Introduzione e commento a la Prima ricerca*. Bologna: Il Mulino, 1990.

Menand, Louis. "Too Good for this World: What Do We Want from Great-books Courses?" *The New Yorker* December 20 (2021): 64–68.

Merleau-Ponty, Maurice. *Phénoménologie de la perception*. Paris: Gallimard, 1945.

Merleau-Ponty, Maurice. "Sur la phénoménologie du langage." *Les problèmes actuels de la phénoménologie*. Bruxelles: Desclée de Brower, 1952. 89–109.

Merleau-Ponty, Maurice. *Signes*. Paris: Gallimard, 1960.

Merleau-Ponty, Maurice. *Phenomenology of Perception*. Trans. Colin Smith. London: Routledge, 1962.

Merleau-Ponty, Maurice. *Le visible et l'invisible*. Ed. Claude Lefort. Paris: Gallimard, 1964.

Merleau-Ponty, Maurice. *The Visible and the Invisible*. Ed. Claude Lefort. Trans. Alphonso Lingis. Evanston: Northwestern UP, 1968.

Mill, John Stuart. *On Liberty and Other Essays*. Ed. Stefan Collini. Cambridge: Cambridge UP, 1989.

Milton, John. *The Major Works*. Ed. Stephen Orgel & Jonathan Goldberg. Oxford UP, 2008.

Moran, Dermont. *Introduction to Phenomenology*. London: Routledge, 2000.

Moran, Dermont. "Introduction" to Edmund Husserl, *Ideas*. London: Routledge, 2002.

Morrison, Toni. *Song of Solomon*. London: Picador, 1977.

Mounin, Georges. *Saussure ou le structuraliste sans le savoir*. Paris: Seghers, 1968.

Muller, Robin M. "Kant and Saussure." *Rivista Italiana di Filosofia del linguaggio* (2010): 130–146.

Müller-Doohm, Stefan. *Adorno: A Biography*, London, Polity, 2005.

Nail, Thomas. "What is Assemblage." *SubStance* 46.1 (2017): 21–37.
Nass, Michael. *Miracle and Machine*. New York: Fordham UP, 2012.
Nietzsche, Friedrich. *Beyond Good and Evil*. Ed. Walter Kaufmann. New York: Vintage, 1989.
Nietzsche, Friedrich. *Zur Genealogie der Moral: Eine Streitschrift*. Berlin: Goldmann, 1992.
Nozick, Robert. *Anarchy, State, and Utopia*. London: Blackwell, 1974.
Nozick, Robert. *The Nature of Rationality*. Princeton: Princeton UP, 1994.
Nussbaum, Martha C. *The Fragility of Goodness: Luck and Ethics in Greek Tragedy and Philosophy*. Revised edition. Cambridge: Cambridge UP, 2001.
Nussbaum, Martha C. "The Professor of Parody: The Hip Defeatism of Judith Butler." *The New Republic*. 22 February 1999.
Nuttall, A.D. *Shakespeare the Thinker*. New Haven: Yale UP, 2007.
Obama, Barack. *The Audacity of Hope: Thoughts on Reclaiming the American Dream*. Edinburgh: Canongate, 2007.
Olbromski, Cezary Józef. *The Notion of "lebendige Gegenwart" as Compliance with the Temporality of the "Now." The Late Husserl's Phenomenology of Time*. Frankfurt am Main: Peter Lang, 2011.
Orgel, Stephen. *The Authentic Shakespeare and Other Problems of the Early Modern Stage*. New York: Routledge, 2003.
Orgel, Stephen. *Spectacular Performances*. Manchester: Manchester UP, 2013.
Palfrey, Simon. *Late Shakespeare: A New World of Words*. Oxford: Oxford UP, 1997.
Palfrey, Simon. *Doing Shakespeare*. London: Bloomsbury, 2004.
Palfrey, Simon. *Shakespeare's Possible Worlds*. Cambridge: Cambridge UP, 2014.
Palfrey, Simon. *Poor Tom: Living* King Lear. Chicago: The U of Chicago P, 2014.
Palmer, Anthony. "Scepticism and Tragedy: Crossing Shakespeare with Descartes." *Wittgenstein and Scepticism*. Ed. Denis McManus. London: Routledge, 2004. 260–277.
Pascal, Blaise. *Oeuvres complètes*. Ed. Ch. Lahure. Paris: Hachette, 1858.
Pascal, Blaise. *Les provinciales*. Ed. Michel Le Guern. Paris: Folio, 1987.
Peden, Knox. *Spinoza Contra Phenomenology. French Rationalism from Cavaillès to Deleuze*. Stanford: Stanford UP, 2014.
Pepys, Samuel. *The Shorter Pepys*. Ed. Robert Latham. London: Penguin, 1987.
Petrarca, *Canzoniere*. Ed. Daniele Ponchiroli, Roberto Antonelli and Gianfranco Contini. Torino: Einaudi, 1992.
Pinker, Steven. *Enlightenment Now. The Case for Reason, Science, Humanism, and Progress*. New York: Penguin, 2019.
Pippin, Robert. *After the Beautiful: Hegel and the Philosophy of Pictorial Modernism*. Chicago: The U of Chicago P, 2013.
Pippin, Robert. *Hegel's Realm of Shadows. Logics as Metaphysics in The Science of Logic*. The U of Chicago P, 2019.
Plath, Sylvia. *Collected Poems*. New York: HarperPerennial, 1992.

Plato. *The Republic*. Ed. Desmond Lee. London: Penguin, 1974.
Plato. *Theaetetus and Sophist*. Ed. Christopher Rowe. Cambridge: Cambridge UP, 2015.
Poe, Edgar Allan. *Essays and Reviews*. Ed. G.R. Thompson. New York: The Library of America, 1984.
Popper, Karl. *Conjectures and Refutations: The Growth of Scientific Knowledge*. London: Routledge, 1963.
Popper, Karl. *The Poverty of Historicism*. London: Routledge, 2002.
Priest, Graham. *Beyond the Limits of Thought*. Oxford: Oxford UP, 2002.
Priest, Graham. *One. Being an Investigation into the Unity of Reality and of its Parts, including the Singular Object which is Nothingness*. Oxford: Oxford UP, 2014.
Proust, Marcel. *Sodome et Gomorrhe*. Ed. Antoine Compagnon. Paris: Gallimard, 1999.
Putnam, Hillary. *The Many Faces of Realism*. Open Court, 1988.
Pynchon, Thomas. *Gravity's Rainbow*. London: Vintage, 2000.
Quine, W.V. "Two Dogmas of Empiricism." *The Philosophical Review* 60.1 (1951): 20–43.
Raber, Karen. "Review of *Renaissance Posthumanism*, edited by Joseph Campana and Scott Maisano, and *Shakespeare's Extremes*, by Julián Jiménez Heffernan." *Shakespeare Quarterly* 67.4 (2016): 525–527.
Raber, Karen. *Shakespeare and Posthumanist Theory*. London: Bloomsbury, 2018.
Racine, Jean. *Bajazet*. Ed. Marc Douguet. Paris: Flammarion, 2015.
Raimondi, Ezio. "La prigione della letteratura" in Torquato Tasso, *Dialoghi*. Ed. Giovanni Baffetti. Milano: Rizzoli, 1998. 9–56.
Rancière, Jacques. *Le partage du sensible. Esthétique et politique*. Paris: La Fabrique, 2000.
Rancière, Jacques. *History, Politics, Aesthetics*. Ed. Gabriel Rockhil and Philip Watts. Durham: Duke UP, 2009.
Rancière, Jacques. *The Aesthetic Unconscious*. Trans. Debra Keates and James Swenson. London: Polity, 2010.
Rancière, Jacques. *The Politics of Aesthetics*. Trans. Gabriel Rockhill. London: Bloomsbury, 2013.
Rancière, Jacques. *Dissensus: On Politics and Aesthetics*. Ed. Steven Corcoran. London: Bloomsbury, 2015.
Rawls, John. *A Theory of Justice*. Revised edition. Cambridge, MA: Harvard UP, 1999.
Ricoeur, Paul. *Finitude et culpabilité*. Paris: Aubier, 1960.
Ricoeur, Paul. *De l'interprétation: Essai sur Freud*. Paris: Seuil, 1965.
Ricoeur, Paul. *Freud and Philosophy: Essay on Interpretation*. Trans. Denis Savage. New Haven: Yale UP, 1970.
Riffaterre, Michel. "Prosopopeia." *Yale French Studies* 69 (1985): 107–123.
Rimbaud, Arthur. *Poésies. Une saison en enfer. Illuminations*. Ed. Louis Forestier. Paris: Gallimard, 1965.

Rodríguez, Juan Carlos. *Theory and History of Ideological Production: The First Bourgeois Literatures (the 16th Century)*. Trans.Malcolm K. Read. Newark: University of Delaware Press, 2002.

Rorty, Richard. *Philosophy and the Mirror of Nature*. Oxford: Blackwell, 1980.

Rorty, Richard. *Contingency, irony, and solidarity*. Cambridge: Cambridge UP, 1989.

Rorty, Richard. *Essays on Heidegger and Others*. Cambridge: Cambridge up, 1991.

Rorty, Richard. "Remarks on Deconstruction and Pragmatism" in *Deconstruction and Pragmatism*. Ed. Simon Critchley and Chantal Mouffe. New York: Routledge, 1996. 13–18.

Rorty, Richard. *Achieving Our Country: Leftist Thought in Twentieth-Century America*. Cambridge, Mass.: Harvard UP, 1999.

Rossi, Paolo. *Francesco Bacone: Dalla magia allá scienza*. Torino: Einaudi, 1974.

Rothleder, Dianne. *Fraught Decisions in Plato and Shakespeare*. London: Rowman & Littlefield, 2021.

Rousseau, Jean-Jacques. *Discours sur l'origine et les fondements de l'inégalité parmi les hommes*. Ed. Blaise Bachofen & Bruno Bernardi. Paris: Flammarion, 2008.

Rousseau, Jean-Jacques. *Les Confessions*. Ed. F. Raviez. Paris: Livre de Poche, 2012

Rovelli, Carlo. *Reality Is Not What It Seems: The Journey to Quantum Gravity*. Trans. Simon Carnell & Erica Segre. London: Penguin, 2016.

Rovelli, Carlo. *The Order of Time*. Trans.Simon Carnell & Erica Segre. New York: Riverhead Books, 2018.

Royle, Nicholas. *The Uncanny*. Manchester: Manchester UP, 2003.

Royle, Nicholas. *How to Read Shakespeare*. New York: Norton, 2005.

Royle, Nicholas. *In Memory of Jacques Derrida*. Edinburgh: Edinburgh UP, 2009.

Royle, Nicholas. *Hélène Cixous: Dreamer, realist, analyst, writing*. Manchester: Manchester UP, 2020.

Ruda, Frank. *For Badiou: Idealism without Idealism*. Evanston: Northwestern UP, 2015.

Ruda, Frank. "Marx in the Cave." *Reading Marx*. Slavoj Žižek et al. London: Polity, 2018. 62–100.

Russell, Bertrand. *What I Believe*. Preface by Alan Ryan. London: Routledge, 2004.

Russell, Bertrand. *Sceptical Essays*. London: Routledge, 2004.

Ryle, Gilbert. *The Concept of the Mind*. Introduction by Julia Tanney. London: Routledge, 2009.

Sartre, Jean-Paul. *L'être et le néant. Essai d'ontologie phénoménologique*. Paris: Gallimard, 1943.

Sartre, Jean-Paul. *Critique de la raison dialectique précédé de Questions de méthode I*. Paris: Gallimard, 1960.

Sartre, Jean-Paul. *Critique de la raison dialectique II*. Paris: Gallimard, 1960.

Sartre, Jean-Paul. *Search for a Method*. Trans. Hazel E. Barnes. New York: Alfred A. Knopf, 1963.

Saussure, Ferdinand de. *Course in General Linguistics*. Trad. Wade Baskin. New York: Philosophical Library, 1959.

Saussure, Ferdinand de. *Cours de linguistique générale*. Ed. Rudolg Engler. Wiesbaden: O. Harrassowitz, 1967–1968.

Saussure, Ferdinand de. *Cours de linguistique générale*. Publié par Charles Bailly et Albert Séchehaye avec la collaboration de Albert Riedlinger. Ed. Tullio de Mauro. Paris: Payot, 1995.

Saussure, Ferdinand de. *Écrits de linguistique générale*. Ed. Simon Bouquet and Rudolf Engler. Paris: Gallimard, 2002.

Sawday, J. *The Body Emblazoned: Dissection and the Human Body in Renaissance Culture*. London: Routldege, 1995.

Schmidt, Jana V. *Arendt und die Folgen*. Stuttgart: Springer Verlag, 2018.

Schweppenhäuser, Gerhard. *Theodor W. Adorno: An Introduction*. Trans. James Rolleston. Durham: Duke UP, 2009.

Séchehaye, Albert. "Les problèmes de la langue à la lumière d'une théorie nouvelle." *Revue Philosophique de la France et de l'Étranger* 84 (1917): 1–30.

Sell, Annette. "Heideggers Gang durch Hegels *Phänomenologie des Geistes*." *Hegel-Studien* 39. Hamburg: Felix Mainer, 1998.

Sellars, Wilfrid. "Empiricism and the Philosophy of Mind." *Minnesota Studies in the Philosophy of Science, Volume 1: The Foundations of Science and the Concepts of Psychology and Psychoanalysis*. Ed. Herbert Feigl and Michael Scriven. Minneapolis: U of Minnesota P, 1956. 253–329.

Sellars, Wilfrid. *Science, Perception and Reality*. Atascadero: Ridgeview, 1991.

Seneca. *The Tragedies of Seneca*. Ed. Frank Justus Miller. Chicago: The U of Chicago P, 1907.

Serrano de Haro, Agustín. "Husserl en el pensamiento de Hannah Arendt." *Investigaciones fenomenológicas* 6 (2008): 299–308.

Shakespeare, William. *The Norton Shakespeare*. Ed. Stephen Greenblatt et al. New York: Norton, 2008.

Shakespeare, William. *Hamlet: The Texts of 1603 and 1623*. Ed. Ann Thompson and Neil Taylor. London: Bloomsbury, 2006.

Shakespeare, William. *The Merchant of Venice*. Ed. John Drakakis. London: Bloomsbury, 2011.

Shakespeare, William. *Sonnets*. Ed. Katherine Duncan-Jones. London: Bloomsbury, 2010.

Shakespeare, William. *Much Ado About Nothing*. Ed. Janette Dillon. London: Penguin, 2005.

Shapiro, James. *Shakespeare and the Jews*. Rev. ed. New York: Columbia, 2016.

Shapiro, James. *1599. A Year in the Life of William Shakespeare*. London: Faber & Faber, 2005.

Skinner, Quentin. *Reason and Rhetoric in Hobbes*. Cambridge: Cambridge UP, 1996.

Skinner, Quentin. *Liberty Before Liberalism*. Cambridge: Cambridge UP, 1998.
Slater, Michael D. "The Ghost in the Machine: Emotion and Mind–Body Union in Hamlet and Descartes." *Criticism* 58.4 (Fall 2016): 593–620.
Sloterdijk, Peter. *Kritik der zynische Vernunft*. Frankfurt am Main: Suhrkamp, 1983.
Smith, Bruce. "Premodern Sexualities." *PMLA* 115.3 (2000): 318–29.
Smith, Bruce. *Phenomenal Shakespeare*. Oxford: Wiley-Blackwell, 2010.
Smith, Bruce. "Phenomophobia, or Who's Afraid of Merleau-Ponty?" *Criticism* 53.3 (2012): 479–483.
Smith, David W. *Husserl*. New York: Routledge, 2013.
Smith, Matthew James and Julia Lupton, eds. *Face-To-Face in Shakespearean Drama: Ethics, Performance, Philosophy*. Edinburgh: Edinburgh UP, 2019.
Sontag, Susan. *Against Interpretation and Other Essays*. New York: Dell Pub, 1966.
Sophocles. *Oedipus at Colonus*. Trans. George Murray. London: George Allen & Unwin, 1948.
Spivak, Gayatri Chakravorty. *In Other Worlds. Essays in Cultural Politics*. New York: Methuen, 1987.
Stang, Nicholas. "Kant's Transcendental Idealism." *The Stanford Encyclopedia of Philosophy* (Spring 2021 Edition), Edward N. Zalta (ed.), URL = <https://plato.stanford.edu/archives/spr2021/entries/kant-transcendental-idealism/>. Accessed 1 January 2022
Stevens, Wallace. *The Collected Poems*. New York: Vintage, 1990.
Stevens, Wallace. *The Necessary Angel. Essays on reality and the imagination*. London: Faber and Faber, 1960.
Stoppard, Tom. *Travesties*. London: Faber and Faber, 1975.
Strauss, Leo. *The City and the Man*. Charlottesville: The U of Virginia P. 1994.
Szlezák, Thomas A. *Reading Plato*. London: Routledge, 1999.
Szondi, Peter. *Theorie des modernen Dramas 1880–1950*. Frankfurt am Main: Suhrkamp, 1965.
Szondi, Peter. *Introduction to Literary Hermeneutics*. Trans. Martha Woodmansee. Cambridge UP, 2010.
Swarbrick, Steven. "Materialism without matter: Deleuze." *Genealogy of the Posthuman*, 26 December 2017. https://criticalposthumanism.net/deleuze-gilles/. Accessed 1 January 2022
Tanney, Julia. "Rethinking Ryle: A Critical Discussion of *The Concept of Mind*" in Ryle, Gilbert. *The Concept of the Mind*. IX–LVII.
Tarditi, Claudio. "Reassessing Husserl's Account of the Time-continuum after the Debate on Presentism and Eternalism." *Philosophy Kitchen* 13 (2020): 35–48.
Taylor, Charles. *The Ethics of Authenticity*. Cambridge, Mass: Harvard UP, 1991.
Taylor, Charles. *Modern Social Imaginaries*. Durham: Duke UP, 2003.
Thomas, Dylan. *Collected Poems 1934–1953*. London: Everyman, 1991.

Thomson, Stephen. "Jeu d'écarts: Derrida's Descartes." *Oxford Literary Review* 39.2 (2017): 189–209.

Tiffany, Grace. "Review of Brian Vickers' *Appropriating Shakespeare*." *Comparative Drama* 28.2 (1994): 252–257.

Trilling, Lionel. *The Liberal Imagination*. Intr. Louis Menand. New York: NYRB, 2008.

Vickers, Brian. *Appropriating Shakespeare: Contemporary Critical Quarrels*. New Haven: Yale UP, 1993.

Warminski, Andrzej. *Material Inscriptions. Rhetorical Reading in Practice and Theory*. Edinburgh: Edinburgh UP, 2013.

Warminski, Andrzej. *Ideology, Rhetoric, Aesthetics: For De Man*. Edinburgh: Edinburgh UP, 2013.

Wells, Stanley. "Introduction" to *A Midsummer Night's Dream*. London: Penguin, 1981.

West, William. "Afterword: Theatre and Speculation." *Face-To-Face in Shakespearean Drama: Ethics, Performance, Philosophy*. 250–261.

Whitman, Walt. *The Complete Leaves of Grass*. Ed. William Moore. Taibundo: Tokyo, 1966.

William, William Carlos. *Selected Poems*. Ed. Charles Tomlinson. New York: Penguin, 1976.

Wilson, John Dover. *What Happens in Hamlet*. Cambridge: Cambridge UP, 1951.

Wilson, Richard. *Secret Shakespeare: Studies in theatre, religion, and resistance*. Manchester: Manchester UP, 2004.

Wilson, Richard. *Shakespeare in French Theory: King of Shadows*. London: Routledge, 2006.

Wilson, Richard. *Free Will. Art and Power on Shakespeare's Stage*. Manchester: Manchester UP, 2013.

Wilson, Richard. *Worldly Shakespeare: The Theatre of Our Good Will*. Edinburgh UP, 2016.

Wilson Knight, G. *The Wheel of Fire: Interpretation of Shakespeare's Tragedy*. London: Routledge, 2001.

Witmore, Michael. *Shakespearean Metaphysics*. London: Continuum, 2008.

Wittgenstein, Ludwig. *Tractatus Logico-Philosophicus*. Trans. C.K. Ogden. Intr. Bertrand Russell. London: Kegan Paul, 1922.

Wittgenstein, Ludwig. *Culture and Value*. Ed. G.H. von Wright. Chicago: The U of Chicago P, 1980.

Wordsworth, William. *Poetical Works*. Ed. Thomas Hutchinson. New edition by Ernest de Selincourt. Oxford University Press, 1936.

Yates, Julian. "'Hello Everything': Renaissance/Post/Human." *The Return of Theory in Early Modern English Studies*, Volumen 2. Ed. Paul Cefalu. London: Palgrave, 2014.

Young-Bruehl, Elisabeth. *Hannah Arendt: For Love of the World*. 2nd ed. New Haven: Yale UP, 2004.

Žižek, Slavoj. *The Sublime Object of Ideology*. London: Verso, 1989.
Žižek, Slavoj. *The Ticklish Subject: The Absent Centre of Political Ontology*. London: Verso, 1999.
Žižek, Slavoj. "Class Struggle or Postmodernism." *Contingency, Hegemony, Universality: Contemporary Dialogues on the Left*. London: Verso, 2000.
Žižek, Slavoj. "Introduction: Between the Two Revolutions" to V.I. Lenin, *Revolution at the Gates: A Selection of Writings from February to October 1917*. London: Verso, 2002. 1–14.
Žižek, Slavoj. *Organs Without Bodies: On Deleuze and Consequences*. London: Routledge, 2004.
Žižek, Slavoj. *The Parallax View*. Cambridge, Mass.: The MIT Press, 2006.
Žižek, Slavoj. *How to Read Lacan*. New York: Norton, 2006.
Žižek, Slavoj. *The Plague of Fantasies*. London: Verso, 2009.
Žižek, Slavoj. *Less Than Nothing: Hegel and the Shadow of Dialectical Materialism*. London: Verso, 2012.
Žižek, Slavoj. "Plato, Descartes, Hegel." *The Palgrave Handbook of German Idealism*. *The Palgrave Handbook of German Idealism*. Ed. M.C. Altman, Palgrave Macmillan: London. 2014.
Žižek, Slavoj. *Repeating Lenin*. Zagreb: Arkzin, 2001.
Žižek, Slavoj. "Marx Reads Object-Oriented Ontology." *Reading Marx*. By Slavoj Žižek, Frank Ruda and Agon Hamza. London: Polity Press, 2018, 17–61.

Index of Names

(*Some relevant topics and titles are listed alphabetically inside the entries of the most relevant names: Immanuel Kant, Hegel, Karl Marx, Edmund Husserl, Martin Heidegger, Emmanuel Levinas, Maurice Merleau-Ponty, Hannah Arendt, Louis Althusser, Theodor Adorno, Jacques Derrida, Paul de Man, Gilles Deleuze, Alain Badiou, Slavoj Žižek, Margreta de Grazia, Bruce Smith, Jonathan Gil Harris, Paul Kottman, Julia Lupton, Simon Palfrey, Richard Wilson, Christopher Pye, and others*)

Agamben, Giorgio   157, 191, 204, 276, 277, 290, 365n., 430, 431, 438
   L'aperto: l'uomo e l'animale   431
   The Time that Remains   158
Alexander, Michael   57
Adorno, Theodor   26, 70n., 102–103, 110, 111, 115, 115n., 143, 152, 158n., 166, 186, 216, 228, 263, 269, 286, 300, 308n., 323, 328, 342, 351, 473, 478, 488, 496, 497n., 514, 540, 552n., 559, 567
   anti-mimetic resistance   18, 513, 513n.
   and Benjamin   219–20, 280, 292, 329, 404, 584
   on constellation   297n.
   on critique   116
   De Man's reading of   217n.
   and Derrida   26, 153, 467–68, 501
   disenchantment of the world   392
   against *Eigentlichkeit*   207
   Entkustung, de-arting   20, 20n.
   and Husserl   26n., 466–67
   on *A Midsummer Night's Dream*   467, 485, 485n.
   philosophy versus science   327
   and Rancière   473–74, 487
   redemption   297–98, 300
   on *Romeo and Juliet*   142
   and Sloterdijk   58n.
   and strong theory   117
   Verstand   303
   zu den Sachen selbst   404–05, 404n.
   Aesthetic Theory   20, 52, 59, 142, 178n., 201, 216, 469, 472, 484–85, 484n., 533
   Against Epistemology   49n., 52, 57, 92, 103, 104n., 109, 216–17, 225, 276, 278n., 428, 466–67, 467n., 498, 524, 552
   Hegel: Three Studies   289, 554, 560–61
   Kant's Critique   108
   Minima Moralia   288, 474n.
   Negative Dialectic   18, 56, 78, 91, 121, 153, 231, 262, 285, 289, 300, 318–20, 413–14, 435, 469, 500, 512–13, 555
   Notes on Literature   27, 288
   "Skoteinos, or How to Read Hegel,"   417
   The Stars Down to Earth   565.
Althusser Louis   10, 24, 47n., 102–04, 104n., 111, 117, 121–22, 143, 164n., 208, 217n., 218, 228, 240, 243, 287, 290, 337, 351, 353, 387n., 389n., 437, 496
   determination in the last instance   1n.
   essentialized human being   106–07
   materialism and aleatory materialism   237, 258, 361
   materialist-dialectical generality   259–63
   against moral ideologies   7, 104, 104n., 173, 321
   overdetermination   89, 239
   against phenomenology   78
   process without a subject   77
   against spontaneity   161, 167
   Écrits sur la psychanalyse   118, 206n., 224n., 384n., 430, 500, 510, 532n., 550
   "L'internationale des bonnes sentiments"   104n.
   Machiavel et Nous   173
   For Marx   1n., 6–7, 106–07, 237, 259–61, 278n., 321, 513
   Politics and History   107, 417
   "La querelle de l'humanisme"   7, 158n., 219
   Reading Capital   169n., 236, 323
   "Sur Levi-Strauss"   413
Antonioni, Michelangelo   207
Arendt, Hannah   76, 139n., 145, 177, 181, 182, 185, 188–91, 193, 194, 198, 202n., 207, 217, 232, 276, 290, 293, 319, 326, 339, 358–59, 425, 435, 509, 511, 519

INDEX OF NAMES   613

on coercion-free
   communication   212, 227
on friendship   165
Habermas on   158n., 183, 197n., 227, 324n.
and Heidegger   158n., 164, 205, 392
on Jewish identity   135n.
on natality   224
and phenomenology   139
influence in Shakespeare studies   153–60
on St. Augustine   79, 164
on Kant's *sensus communis*   50, 138, 179, 481
on spontaneous action   161
on things themselves   138, 391–92
"What is Existential Philosophy?"   391, 557
The Human Condition   37n., 89, 89n., 156, 158n, 182, 229, 330, 391, 464
The Life of the Mind   242, 391–92
Origins of Totalitarianism   164
Ariosto, Ludovico   278
   Orlando Furioso   85
Aristotle   154, 170, 259, 276, 293, 375, 443
on ethics   195, 197, 206, 228n.
Categories   213
Metaphysics   170
Ashbery, John   87, 100, 218, 251
Asimov, Isaac   277
Attridge, Derek   117, 367
Auerbach, Erich *Figura*   582
Auster, Paul   563
   The Music of Chance   521

Bachmann, Ingeborg *Malina*   300
Bacon, Francis   62, 62n., 80, 228, 385, 467
on pastoral philosophy   221–22
The Advancement of Learning   310, 318
Essays   376
Badiou, Alain   4n., 54, 91, 117, 121, 166, 183, 235n., 239, 289, 448, 467, 472–73, 510n., 513, 527n., 569
on anti-philosophy   9n., 198, 570n.
on Descartes   61, 66, 74, 81n., 88, 97–101, 216
on democractic materialism   1
on difference   571
against finitude   28
on infinity   100
language in   94, 400n.

on leftist hermeneutics   210
on materialism versus idealism   77–78, 81, 267
on provisional morality   183, 183n.
on the present   572
on the subject   43, 43n.
on subtraction   49
on universality   286
L'aventure de la philosophie française   104n., 275, 297n.
Being and Event   114
The Communist Hypothesis   1n., 510, 569
Conditions   49, 270
Deleuze: La clameur de l'être   167n.
"Descartes/Lacan"   88, 118
Heidegger   435n.
The Immanence of Truths   1n., 74, 100, 109
Logics of Worlds   1, 100n., 103, 215, 572
Manifesto for Philosophy   114
Metapolitics   1n.
Pour aujourd'hui: Platon!   54n., 58n., 87n., 173, 424
S'orienter dans la pensée   88
Théorie axiomatique du sujet   81n.
Theory of the Subject   77, 93
Barad, Karen   274n.
Barthes, Roland   355, 373, 386
Critique et vérité   562
Essais critiques   213, 560
The Neutral   209, 300
Bate, Jonathan   171
Bate, Walter Jackson   550
Beckett, Samuel   32, 85, 341, 474, 513
Belsey, Catherine   24, 25, 31n., 105, 113, 171, 282, 350
Benjamin, Walter   20, 148n., 160, 191, 217n., 218, 255, 276, 290, 404, 431, 485
on constellation   297n.
on dialectics and Adorno's critique   194, 219–20, 280, 292, 329, 584
messianism   431, 475
on translation and linguistic nostalgia   14n., 136, 359
on redemption   297
Origin of German Tragic Drama   292, 297
Bennett, Jane   294
The Politics of Moralizing   178
Vibrant Matter   263n.

Bennington, Geoffrey   560
Bercovitch, Sacvan *The American Jeremiad*   39
Berlin, Isaiah   159–60
Bernhard, Thomas   272
Berry, Philippa   62–63
Bevington, David   285, 340n.
Beyer, Christian   317, 397
Blake, William   146, 200, 272
Blanchot, Maurice *The Writing of the Disaster*   29–30, 53
Bloch, Ernst   207
  Vorlesungen zur Philosophie der Renaissance   115, 177
  Subjekt-Objekt: Erläuterung zu Hegel   55, 55n
Bloom, Harold   115, 171n., 208, 235, 282, 291, 369, 381, 467
  Caliban   272
  The Anxiety of Influence   96, 368, 549
  Shakespeare: The Invention of the Human   26n., 32, 36, 68n., 82, 82n., 147n., 214n., 271n., 368, 467n
  The Western Canon   558
Blumenberg, Hans   166, 170, 380
  Lewitscharoff's novel about   32, 234
  Schiffbruch mit Zuschauer   32, 36, 42
Bosteels, Bruno   570n.
Bouissac, Paul   343, 358
Bourne, Craig   23
Bourne, Emily Caddig   23
Bradley, A.C.   115, 233, 235, 573
  Shakespearean Tragedy   15, 444
Brandom, Robert   70, 117, 119, 320, 325, 470
  Tales of the Mighty Dead   89, 169n.
  A Spirit of Trust   54, 54n., 194, 281, 283, 504, 504n., 529
Brassier, Ray   123–24, 433
Bristol, Michael   171
Brooks, Peter   117, 508
  The Melodramatic Imagination   505n.
Brown, Dan   578
Bruno, Giordano   5, 5n., 99, 258, 385, 429
Budick, Sanford   17, 100n., 138, 172, 301, 309
  on Hamlet's now and Husserlian temporality   311–17, 383, 396, 541
Burroughs, Edgar Rice *Tarzan of the Apes*   422
Burrow, Colin   171
Butler, Judith   105–107, 108n., 117, 183, 183n., 197n.

Campana, Joseph   17, 68, 117, 161, 365n., 433, 438, 443
Capote, Truman   104
Caputo, John   29, 53, 198n.
Carpentier, Alejo *Los pasos perdidos*   446
Carson, Rachel   103n.
Casement, William   308
Cassin, Barbara   56, 70n., 435n.
Castoriadis, Cornelius   285, 585
Cavell, Stanley   282, 283
  Disowning Knowledge   64, 99, 99–100n., 282, 284, 505
Charnes, Linda   557
Cheney, Patrick   244, 267, 367n., 445n.
Christie, Agatha *They Came to Baghdad*   59
Ciliberto, Michele   5n.
Claeys, Gregory   187, 299
Clarke, Simon   339, 339n., 343, 349–53, 352n.
Coetzee, J.M.   180
  Giving Offence   40, 173, 180, 202–03
Cohen, Barbara   267n., 269
Cohen, Tom   267n., 269
Colebrook, Claire   79, 239, 239n., 264, 269n., 273, 274, 274n.
Comay, Rebecca   117
  The Dash—The Other Side of Absolute Knowing   56
Copjek, Joan   123n., 141, 215n., 570
Cottingham, John   62–63, 68n., 449
Crockett, Clayton   274n.
Curran, Kevin   10, 17, 177, 179, 189, 202, 232, 270, 326, 362, 365, 526
  on communitarian moralism   173–176
  on Deleuzian *agencement*   263, 263n.
  on Descartes   73–74, 87
  on intentionality and the noema   402–404, 411–12, 457
  on Levinasian phenomenology and the ethics of exteriority   139, 144–51, 173
  to the things themselves   2, 138, 393–404
Cutrofello, Andrew   18, 25, 117, 139, 171, 282
  All for Nothing   4n., 41, 48–50, 120
  Continental Philosophy   86–87, 127, 176, 166–68, 468, 491, 562
  "On the Idea of a Critique"   319
  The Owl at Dawn   117, 508
  Problems of Contemporary Philosophy   482

INDEX OF NAMES 615

Damasio, Antonio   60, 61n., 66
Daniel, Drew   218–20, 299
Dante   577, 583
Daylight, Russel   363n.
De Grazia, Margreta   25, 27n., 117, 171, 213,
    238, 282, 291, 367
  on the materiality of the Shakespeare
    text   241–56.
Deleuze, Gilles   80n., 85, 117, 122, 123, 144,
    166–67, 200, 219, 243, 244, 270, 277, 296,
    364, 424, 441, 478, 496
  on dialectics   275
  on transcendental empiricism   167n.,
    239, 267, 269n.
  Deux régimes de fous   291
  Différence et répétition   54, 54n., 239n.,
    243, 297
  Foucault   2, 108n., 282n.
  L'image-temps   424n.
  *La philosophie critique
    de Kant*   7–8, 74
  Milles plateaux   263, 263–64n.
  Nietzsche   300
  Qu'est-ce que la philosophie?   307n.
DeLillo, Don   59, 578
  Americana   521
  Falling Man   464
De Man, Paul   3n., 10, 13, 27, 70n.,
    117, 167, 224, 253, 269–70, 277, 312, 349,
    367, 381, 385, 429, 485, 524, 543, 544,
    583, 584
  Vickers on de Man   369–70, 372, 376
  Aesthetic Ideology   53n., 55n., 83n., 84–85,
    116, 167–70, 209n., 213–14, 216–17, 217n.,
    254–55, 293, 296, 361, 417, 432, 451, 465,
    466–69, 489, 514–17
  Allegories of Reading   3, 33–34, 46–49,
    106, 199–200, 213n., 262, 350–51n., 490n.
  Blindness and Insight   386
  Critical Writings   216n., 549n.
  The Rhetoric of Romanticism   325,
    325n., 549
  *The Resistance to
    Theory*   75, 84, 255
  *Romanticism and Contemporary
    Criticism*   554
De Mauro   333n., 351–53, 358n., 360,
    361, 361n.
Dennett, Daniel   235
Derrida, Jacques   4, 9, 10, 12, 13, 16, 18, 20, 26,
    29, 31n., 45n., 49, 53, 55n., 66, 70, 79,

    85–86, 94, 97, 101–02, 196, 111, 114, 115n.,
    117, 121, 122, 133, 143, 157–59, 164n., 165n.,
    166–67, 170, 191, 200, 216, 223, 228, 233,
    239n., 240, 243, 244, 247n., 264, 269n.,
    270, 273–74, 277, 289, 294, 312, 316n.,
    319, 323–390, 400n., 425, 430–32, 435–
    36, 438, 441, 444n., 455, 460, 462, 467,
    467n., 488, 496, 501, 534, 547, 550, 553,
    575, 584
  on Levinas   4–6, 8, 28, 33–34, 96–98,
    100n., 148, 150, 205, 497n.
  on Shakespeare   26–27n., 210, 235–36,
    248n., 367
  Acts of Religion   365
  Adieu à Emmanuel Levinas   5n., 100n.,
    148, 148n., 152n., 153, 388
  L'animal que donc je suis   87, 118, 154, 365,
    365n., 437
  Acts of Literature   248n., 367
  La carte postale   245, 341, 416
  La bête et le souverain   365, 365n., 388
  "La déconstruction et l'autre"   415
  La dissémination   368, 376n., 416
  L'écriture et la différence   4–6, 33–34, 53n.,
    91, 92, 93n., 98–99, 152, 152n., 153n., 199,
    205–06, 254n., 261n., 273, 323, 323n.,
    336, 360, 368, 387, 396n., 398, 554–55
  Glas   42, 236, 279, 418, 439–40, 494
  Of grammatology   32, 42n., 47n., 51, 95–
    96, 224–25, 256, 268, 336, 363, 365n.,
    373–74, 377, 382, 389, 416–17, 431, 520
  De l'hospitalité   27, 35, 149, 365, 526, 543–
    46, 568
  "Interpretations at War: Kant, the Jew, the
    German"   468
  "Introduction" to *L'origine de la
    géométrie*   21n., 243n., 329n.
  "La langue et le discours de la
    méthode"   90, 109, 118n., 400
  Limited Inc.   252, 325
  Mal d'Archive   164, 205, 261,
    261n., 365n.
  *Marges de la
    philosophie*   36, 42, 252, 254, 280,
    365n., 377–78
  *Memories for Paul
    de Man*   55
  Points de suspension   178, 199n.
  Politiques de l'amitié   6n., 164–65, 365
  Positions   113, 285, 288, 321, 368, 377, 379–
    80, 414, 544

Derrida, Jacques (*cont.*)
  Le problème de la genèse dans la philosophie de Husserl   21n., 22, 140n., 163, 253n., 316
  Psyché: Inventions de l'autre I   14n., 210, 235–36, 388
  Spectres de Marx   79, 79n., 365, 495, 563
  A Taste for the Secret   122n.
  On Touching   8, 12n., 13n., 112, 112n., 137, 186, 186n., 242, 366, 560
  La vérité en peinture   20, 392–93, 393n., 512
  La voix et le phénomène   382–83
Descartes   9, 16, 19, 21n., 60–101, 103, 109, 116, 118n., 119, 136, 148, 160, 166, 183, 194, 215, 216, 233–34, 276, 304, 307, 308, 318, 331, 336, 342, 352, 365n., 375, 382, 393n., 394, 412, 429, 431–38, 448–49, 467, 526, 528, 547
  Dioptriques   19, 80
  Discours de la méthode   63, 67, 71–74, 183n., 448–49
  L'homme   72, 80
  Méditations métaphysiques   55n., 57–58, 63–66, 68, 71, 71n., 96, 96n., 97–98, 100n., 166, 321, 488, 530
  Le monde   19n., 89
  Les Météors   61
  Règles pour la direction de l'esprit   440
Descombes, Vincent   24–25, 24n., 345–46, 350, 358, 358n., 364, 371–72, 374–75
DeVries, Willem   83n.
Dickens, Charles   37, 136, 345, 421
  David Copperfield   246n., 421
  Nicholas Nickleby   504
  Oliver Twist   420
Dickinson, Emily   17, 29, 36, 146, 563
Di Giovanni, George   405
Dillard-Wright, David   447
Dollimore, Jonathan   24, 67, 103, 108, 108n., 114–15, 121–22, 122n., 161, 171, 217–18, 232–33, 329, 584
Dostoyevski, Fiódor   438, 496
Dreyfus, Hubert   218
Duncan-Jones, Katherine   50, 173n.
Dunn, John   223n., 491
Dworkin, Ronald   35, 40n., 42

Eagleton, Terry
Easthope, Anthony   108n.
Egan, Gabriel   17
  on Descartes   60–63, 66
  on Shakespearean textuality   243, 243n.
Eliot, George   40, 148, 190, 392
  Adam Bede   181
  Scenes of Clerical Life   148
Eliot, T.S.   100, 185n., 219, 448, 517
  Four Quartets   84
  "Hamlet and his Problems"   84–85, 209n., 425
  "Tradition and the Individual Talent"   344, 347
Empson, William   235, 283
  Essays on Shakespeare   429, 491
  Seven Types of Ambiguity   519
  Some Versions of the Pastoral   225n.

Farrington, Benjamin   221–22
Faulkner, William   42, 272
  As I Lye Dying   521
Fearing, F.   61
Felski, Rita   58n., 116, 208–09, 209n., 213, 215, 217n.
Fernie, Ewan on freedom   564
  on presentist immediacy   557, 581
  on shame   211
  on spirituality   79, 79n., 566
  Macbeth, Macbeth   422
Ferry, Luc   229, 371, 564n.
Filmer, Robert   222–23
Fink, Eugen *Heraclitus*   52–53
Finkielkraut, Alain *L'identité malheureuse*   568, 571n.
  La défaite de la pensée   571
Firth, John   348, 348n., 356, 373
Follet, Ken   578
Forster, E.M.   121, 122n.
  Howard's End   569
Forster, John *The Life of Charles Dickens*   246n.
Foster, John Bellamy   162
Foucault, Michel   2, 10, 90, 104, 111, 113, 115, 117, 122, 143, 167, 208, 219, 232, 240, 282, 287, 291, 400n., 435, 437, 536, 543, 558, 578

INDEX OF NAMES 617

L'archéologie du savoir 266, 273, 341, 482, 496
"La folie, l'absence d'oeuvre" 350
Les mots et les choses 469
Raymond Roussel 270, 543
Franzen, Jonathan 146, 563
Frege, Gottlob 244n., 339, 353, 361, 399n., 455n., 456

Gadamer, Hans Georg 21n., 393, 534, 538
Hegel's Dialectic 58, 271, 280, 329
Truth and Method 293, 293n.
Gaddis, William *A Frolic of His Own* 43
The Rush for Second Place 209, 272, 425–26
Garber, Marjorie 25, 27, 31–32, 31n., 32, 38, 45, 48–49, 171, 282, 367, 381
Gasché, Rodolphe 16, 94
Goethe, Johann Wolfgang 42, 80, 185n.
Faust 208
Iphigenie auf Tauris 288, 566
Romischen Elegien 490
Goldgaber, Deborah 274
Goldie, Mark 494n.
Gordimer, Nadine 180, 272
Grady, Hugh 24, 27, 37, 57n., 59, 113, 139, 164n., 177, 292, 299, 321, 485, 485n., 559–60
Graves, Robert *The Real David Copperfield* 246n.
Greenblatt, Stephen 4, 24, 113, 114–15, 115n., 171, 220n., 228, 305, 306, 312, 328, 429, 443, 488, 531, 531n., 533, 562–63, 576
presentism in *Tyrant: Shakespeare on Politics* 572–75
Greene, Donald 209n.
Gross, Kenneth 8n., 531

Habermas, Jurgen 75, 272, 541
on Arendt 158n., 183, 197, 197n., 227–28, 324n.
The Philosophical Discourse of Modernity 358n.
Truth and Justification 231n., 293
Hägglund, Martin 316n.
Hajdu, David 564n.
Halliday, M.A.K. 331, 348–50, 348n.
Halpern, Richard 18, 25, 117, 171

Harris, Jonathan Gil 17, 138, 171, 172, 177, 191, 237, 251, 447, 465
on deconstruction and Derrida 27n., 31n., 114, 366–67, 367n., 389n
on materialism 257–265, 268–70
Harris, Roy 14, 331, 339, 340n., 341, 343–45, 350, 354n., 355–56, 363n., 364n., 387
Hatfield, Gary 63, 68
Haugeland, John 89
Hawthorne, Nathaniel 39
The Scarlet Letter 38
Twice-Told Tales 513
Hayat, Pierre 151
Hazlitt, William 503
Heckman, John 407
Hegel, G.W.F. 4, 4n., 9, 16, 18, 20–21, 25, 27, 38, 41, 41n., 43, 47n., 53n., 54n., 55n., 58, 70n., 74, 76, 76n., 77, 80n., 85, 92–93, 103, 107, 109, 115–16, 117, 119n., 120–21, 135, 139, 146, 148–49, 150–53, 160, 166, 167, 189, 194, 201, 212–13, 214, 216, 217n., 225, 228, 232, 243, 244, 247n., 252, 278n., 279, 283, 284, 286, 286n., 288–90, 323, 325n., 326–27, 336, 342, 364, 370, 380, 392, 397, 412, 412n., 416–17, 417n., 418, 425, 429, 431, 435, 438–39, 448–49, 462, 466–67, 474n., 481, 489, 498, 504n., 511, 513n., 518, 525, 527, 540, 545–46, 553–54, 560–61, 570, 577
Aphorismen aus Hegels Wastebook 118n.
Encyclopedia of the Philosophical Sciences 280
Lectures on Fine Art 469, 504–08, 514–15
Outlines of the Philosophy of Right 142, 144, 144n., 220
Phenomenology of Spirit 82, 127–29, 139, 140–42, 157–58, 216, 278, 282, 285, 291, 329, 405–07, 419, 469, 530, 576
Science of Logic 38, 42, 116n., 118, 166, 218, 271, 327, 405, 469, 494n., 506n., 509, 540, 553
Heidegger, Martin 4, 6n., 21n., 25, 28, 53, 75, 79n., 87, 87n., 89, 97n., 98, 98n., 112, 126, 136, 145, 149, 152, 154, 158n., 159, 164n., 167, 181, 199, 206–07, 225, 236, 243, 275, 277, 290, 293, 318, 319, 342, 349, 362, 364, 365n., 370, 393, 396n., 400, 405, 419, 430, 435–36, 435n., 438, 457, 467,

Heidegger, Martin (*cont.*)
    468, 495, 506, 508, 519, 523, 527n., 534,
    545–46, 550–51, 562, 584
    on phenomenology   131–34
    Basic Problems of Phenomenology   132–
        33, 157, 392, 407
    "Bauen Wohnen Denken"   294
    Being and Time   131–34, 137, 146–47, 149,
        175, 217, 293n., 301–03, 405n., 407–
        10, 429
    Four Seminars   118n., 218
    Hegel's Phenomenology of Spirit   128,
        139, 216
    Heraclitus   43
    Identity and Difference   73
    Kant und das Problem der Metaphysik   95,
        100, 300
    Off the Beaten Track   278–79, 338,
        370, 377
    Pathmarks   53n., 416–17
    On Time and Being   562
    What is Called Thinking?   327, 439, 528
Henrich, Dieter *Aesthetic Judgement and the
        Moral Image of the World*   490
    *The Unity of Reason: Essays on Kant's
        Philosophy*   148
Hesse, Herman   232
    Siddhartha   78
Hesse, M.B.   62n.
Hobbes, Thomas   40, 154–55, 178, 181, 184,
        199, 228, 234, 271, 276, 429, 447
    Leviathan   162, 306, 306n.
    On the Citizen   215
Hobsbawm, Eric   121–22, 121n.
Honan, Park   533n.
Houellebecq, Michel *Sérotonine*   440
    Ennemis publics   563
Hughes, Robert *The Culture of Complaint: The
        Fraying of America*   207–08, 566–67,
        567n., 571
Hume, David   1, 21n., 24, 40, 62, 50–71
    *An Enquiry Concerning Human
        Understanding*   435
    Political Essays   568
    A Treatise of Human Nature   22–23
Husserl, Edmund (restricted to the
        most important references) on
        animals   447
    corporal reflection   319
    on dialectics   4, 21, 113, 198, 329
    on embodiment   112n., 138, 511
    on evidence   110, 451–52
    and existentialism   206
    on givenness   118, 167, 527
    and the history of
        philosophy   21n.
    historicism and origins   97, 186, 225,
        252–53, 253n.
    on immanence   98
    on intersubjectivity and the other   136,
        138, 156, 179, 447, 480, 554, 560
    on intentionality   12, 402–03, 453–55,
        460–65, 480, 486
    on immediate intuition   110, 127, 135, 168–
        69, 220, 450–51, 530–31, 534
    on language   12, 119, 339, 340–43, 359,
        379–80, 386, 421, 455–65
    on the material world, facticity, nature
        and phenomena   4, 16, 107, 132–33,
        273, 394–95, 436
    on meaning-filling   118, 455–60,
        497–98
    on mediation   21–22, 328n.
    on natural standpoint, the reduction and
        epoché   4, 58, 76, 107–110, 132, 279–80,
        297, 306–10, 381, 384, 483–84
    on noemata   278n., 402–03, 456–57,
        486, 522
    metaphysics of presence   112n.
    ocularcentrism   291n.
    on perception by delegation   19
    on phenomenology   129–31
    on psychology   21, 129, 352, 400, 517
    return to Descartes   81, 93n., 98, 100n.
    on spontaneity   163, 166, 167–68
    on temporality   269, 301, 311–17, 541
    "to the things themselves"   3, 21–22, 157,
        391–414
    on totality   285n.
    transcendental idealism, logical
        absolutism and theory of essences   4,
        8, 93, 104, 109, 111, 130–33, 138, 179, 206,
        252–53, 232, 266, 329–30, 375, 391–410,
        411–12, 449, 494
    misinterpretation of *Vorhandenheit*   11,
        301–05, 384

INDEX OF NAMES   619

    Cartesian Meditations   4, 25n., 98, 118,
       135–36, 179, 285, 314, 396, 412, 413n.,
       490, 496–97, 516, 560
    The Crisis of the European Sciences and
       Transcendental Phenomenology   81,
       97, 220, 253n.
    Ideas I   63n., 110, 130, 137, 160–67, 280,
       302–03, 306, 308–10, 314, 353, 384, 394,
       394–97, 401–03, 403n., 404m., 412, 436,
       447, 451, 453, 494, 511, 517, 529–31
    Ideas II   136–37, 156, 450, 511
    Logical Investigations   92, 129, 129n, 340–
       41, 341n., 359, 397–404, 409–10, 450–52,
       451n., 452n., 454–56, 459
    The Phenomenology of Internal Time-
       Consciousness   315–316, 316n.
Huxley, Aldous   200, 207
Hyppolite, Jean   406–07

Jackson, Shirley   104
James, Henry   19, 37, 41, 85, 100, 112, 394
    The Bostonians   569
    The Princess Casamassima   569
Jameson, Fredric   54, 116–17, 206–07, 215n.,
       233, 257, 287, 329, 351
    Antinomies of Realism   272
    Brecht and Method   298–99
    Late Marxism   297n., 484, 513n.
    Marxism and Form   330, 500, 561–62
    Postmodernism, or, The Cultural Logic of
       Late Capitalism   206, 558
    Representing Capital   214, 328n., 528
    The Seeds of Time   528
    Valences of the Dialectic   55, 56n., 114n.,
       116n., 161n., 215, 227, 276, 290n., 295–96,
       328, 400n., 439, 495, 509n., 563
Jay, Martin   116, 117
    Downcast Eyes   291n.
Johnson, Samuel   41, 209n., 233
    Lives of the Poets   123, 238
    "Preface" to *Shakespeare*   287
Johnston, Adrian   4
Joughin, John   79
Joyce, James   17, 26n., 123
    Ulysses   59
Judt, Tony   104n.
Julian of Norwich *Revelations of Divine*
       Love   58

Kafka, Franz   37, 106, 240, 272, 380, 434,
       441, 584
Kant, Immanuel   3, 4n., 16, 21n., 24, 29, 120,
       155, 194, 228n., 231, 319, 328
    Adorno's book on the first
       Critique   108, 411
    Adorno on Kantian
       mediation   289
    Adorno's and Derrida's debts to
       Kant   467–68
    aesthetic idea and rational idea   238,
       485–86, 493, 523, 526
    amor mundi   342
    apprehension and comprehension   479–
       80, 483
    Arendt on Kant's *sensus communis*   138,
       160, 179–80, 202
    Brandom on Kant   283
    correlationism   411
    critique   7–8
    Cutrofello on the first *Critique*   165–
       70, 468
    Deleuze on Kant's critical philosophy   7–
       8, 74
    de Man on Kant   116, 209n., 214, 217n.,
       255, 361, 370, 431–32, 468, 514–15
    and Descartes   87, 92, 94, 136, 160, 331,
       342n., 394, 432, 437
    finitude   148, 148n., 236
    formalism and transcendentality   239,
       255, 269, 273, 321, 336–37, 347,
       353, 360–61
    Foucault on Kant   469
    Heidegger's *Kantbuch*   95, 300
    immanence   160
    intuition   451, 451n.
    intellectual intuition   127, 167, 450n.,
       491, 531
    Kant-Hegel tradition   4n., 42, 109, 117,
       139, 323
    nature versus freedom   200–01
    Kantian phenomenology   126–27
    Kant and Hegelian and Husserlian
       phenomenologies   128–29
    manifold   276
    Putnam on Kant   193–94
    space   293
    spontaneity   165–70, 474

Kant, Immanuel (*cont.*)
  sublime   53, 85, 213–14, 293, 311, 313, 431–32, 468–69, 514
  Rancière on Kant   474n.
  reflective judgement   480–81
  taste and indeterminate concepts   471–72, 484
  transcendental rational concept   477
  transcendental deduction   311, 313
  transcendental schematism   361, 458
  Übereinstimmung   489, 493
  unpositable ground of being   562
  Žižek on Kantian ethics   225
  Critique of Judgement   20, 53, 53n., 179–80, 213, 238, 293, 469–501, 532
  Critique of Pure Reason   119, 165–70, 436, 451n., 475, 529
  Metaphysical Foundations of Natural Sciences   126
  Religion within the Boundaries of Mere Reason   221, 224
Kastan, David Scott   25, 171, 171n., 275, 282, 318, 578–79, 585
Kates, Joshua   16
Kermode, Frank   26n., 171, 282, 291, 396, 582
Kerrigan, John   171
Kleist, Heinrich von   232, 272, 370, 444
  Michael Kolhaas   404n.
Kohn, Jerome   124n.
Kojève, Alexandre   104n., 431, 440
  Introduction à la lecture de Hegel   432
Kottman, Paul Adorno legacy   27
  aesthetic idealism   172
  aesthetic ideology   465, 534
  aesthetic fallacy of representation   462, 469, 488–90, 495, 499–500, 515
  affective comprehension   194, 220
  affections in *Hamlet*   211–12
  Arendtian phenomenology, plurality and action   153–56, 158, 231
  care, cure, curation   175
  political community   181–189, 191
  content-form correspondence   510, 527n.
  critical consensus   23
  Derrida   365, 365n.
  doing Shakespeare   391
  dialectical thought   17, 172, 270, 282
  tragic diremption   225
  Hegelian end of art in *The Winter's Tale*   505–12
  shared freedom   486
  friendship in *Hamlet*   165
  Hegelian phenomenology   139–44
  intersubjectivity   138, 179, 232
  Levinasian Autrui   146, 150
  moralistic politics   178, 202
  natality   224n.
  pastoral romance   227
  phenomenological relationality   145
  social antagonism   226
  spontaneity   161–62, 230, 535
  Hegelian recognition   325n., 516–18, 570
  religion of art   495, 500
Kymlicka, Will   180n.

Lacan, Jacques   *D'un discours qui ne serait pas du semblant*   338
  Écrits   19, 88–89, 88n., 120, 143, 240n., 570
  L'étique de la psychanalyse   271
  Les quatre concepts fondamentaux de la psychanalyse   6, 499
  "Maurice Merleau-Ponty : In Memoriam"   167, 327, 327n., 508–09
  Séminaire II: Le moi dans la théorie de Freud   76, 76n., 115–16
Labelle, Gilles   478n.
Laqué, Stephan   76n.
Laruelle, François determination in the last instance   1
  Introduction to Non-Marxism   1
Laslett, Peter   177n., 224n.
Latour, Bruno   80, 204, 217, 257, 264, 277, 427
  Politics of Nature   318
  We Have Never Been Modern   492
Lefort, Claude   478, 478n.
Levi-Strauss, Claude   86, 86n., 223, 345–46, 355, 371, 373, 413, 430
  Structural Anthropology   86
  Tristes tropiques   320–21
Levinas, Emmanuel   3, 4–5, 8, 12, 28, 97, 93, 93n., 107, 127, 139–53, 154, 159, 159n., 169, 175, 176, 187, 205, 251, 273, 276, 285n., 297, 319, 319n., 321, 324, 326, 366, 366n., 407, 411, 478, 571
  on domesticity and reterritorialization   147–48, 292n., 495

INDEX OF NAMES 621

on eschatological ethics, infinite alterity,
    the Other and face-to-face   4–5, 7, 33,
    93, 97, 98, 101, 131, 134–35, 145, 160, 206,
    412, 535, 554
ethics of exteriority   144–45, 173
on immediacy   145–53, 554
on intentionality   526, 526–27n.
on language   6n., 98–99, 330, 340, 341n.,
    358–60, 359n., 464
on morality   198
on animality and the
    non-human   447–48
on phenomenality   4–6, 5n.
on society and plurality   33, 138,
    232, 233n.
on totality   276
on violence, ontology and war   6, 196–97,
    226, 233, 497n.
Autrement qu'être et au-delà de l'essence
De l'existence à l'existent   151
"The Paradox of Morality"   206
"Paix et proximité"   145
*Théorie de l'intuition dans la
    phénoménologie de Husserl*   135, 315,
    365, 531, 548, 557
"Le souffrance inutile"   153
Totalité et infini   4–6, 6n., 33, 97, 97n.,
    98n., 100n., 146–53, 148n., 149n., 151n.,
    160, 198, 232, 233n., 276, 411n., 448, 519
Lewitscharoff, Sybille *Blumenberg*   32, 234
Lipotevsky, Gilles   564
Livingston, Paul   482
Llewelyn, John   360
Locke, John   62, 176, 178, 182, 199, 223n., 224,
    234, 429, 433, 491, 494, 564
    Two Treatises of Government   39, 223–24
Lukacher, Ned   18, 25, 27n., 117, 171, 282, 545
    *Daemonic Figures: Shakespeare and the
    Question of Conscience*   6, 6n., 27,
    29, 30–31, 31n., 36n., 43–44, 86, 86n.,
    163–64, 169, 176, 200, 211n., 225n., 248,
    267n., 281n., 323, 331, 380, 412n., 420n.,
    421, 439, 513
    *Primal Scenes: Literature, Philosophy,
    Psychoanalysis*   36, 47n., 49n., 55,
    374, 502
Lukács, Georg   217n., 287, 292, 351, 561–62
    History and Class Consciousness   287–88

Lupton, Julia   36, 79, 217n.
    acknowledgement as political
        question   182, 182n., 569
    aesthetic fallacy   462, 468–69, 472, 488–
        92, 492n., 499
    animals   192, 441
    Arendtian phenomenology, plurality and
        action   153–58, 179, 219
    phenomenological bracketing   309
    care, cure, curation   175
    choreography and
        representation   503–04
    citizen-saint   153
    citizenship and the political
        community   186–194
    critical consensus   23
    collective utopian politics   36n.,
        37, 177–78
    and Derrida   365, 365n.
    doing Shakespeare, to the things
        themselves   391, 412
    dialectical thought   17, 172, 282, 295n.
    digestive reflection   299, 319
    domesticity   202n.
    embodiment   138
    face-to-face ethical interaction   512,
        534, 562
    Hegelian recognition   570
    Heideggerian *Zuhandendheit*   134
    hospitality and dwelling in
        Macbeth   492–95, 517–28, 565,
        565n.
    immediacy   57, 233, 535
    intersubjectivity   138, 179, 205
    Levinasian *Autrui*   146, 150
    and Merleau-Ponty   294
    miracle   182n.
    natality   224n.
    pastoral romance   226–27
    performance   324–26
    picture-book phenomenology   293
    phenomenological relationality   145–46
    political community and messianic
        domesticity in *Pericles*   420–24, 516
    presence effects   112, 533–34
    hologrammatic representation   517
    ritual community and political
        theology   205, 206n., 472, 510–12, 32

Lupton, Julia (*cont.*)
  spontaneity and friendship in
    Hamlet 164–65, 186, 486
  spontaneity and virtue in *Twelfth Night* 161–63, 195–97, 202, 228–29.
Lyotard, François 166, 200, 244, 292, 487
  Le différend 114
  La phénoménologie 582

Mailer, Norman *The Armies of the Night* 39, 511–12
Maisano, Scott on non-human apes 277, 441–44, 507
  on Derrida 365n., 438
  on Descartes 68, 68n.
  on immediacy 531
  on posthumanist meta-methodology 433
  on spontaneity 161
Mann, Thomas 31, 41, 41n.
  The Magic Mountain 56
  Mario und der Zauberer 46
Marcuse, Herbert 207, 351
Marlow, Christopher 114n.
Marlowe, Christopher 111, 135, 252, 278, 285, 367, 386, 445, 445n., 470, 515, 516, 528, 573, 585
Marcus, Steven 421
Marx, Karl 7, 77n., 79n., 106n., 115, 117n., 119, 162n., 165, 187, 214, 216, 217n., 238, 257, 259–61, 269n., 278n., 286n., 287, 299, 301, 319, 440n., 488, 513
  The Communist Manifesto 116
  Critique of Hegel's Philosophy of Right 221, 221n., 397, 444n.
  The German Ideology 116, 162–63, 225, 229–30, 573, 576
  The Holy Family 77–78n.
  Misère de la philosophie 18–19, 161–62, 228–29, 577
  Grundrisse 4, 21, 71, 285
  "On the Jewish Question" 176, 189–90
McCullers, Carson 563
  The Member of the Wedding 422–424, 424n.
McDowell, John *Mind and World* 14, 52n., 64, 70n., 113, 168, 186, 298, 457
McIntyre, Alasdair *After Virtue* 196, 203, 228
Meade, Margaret *Four on Our Island* 422

Melandri, Enzo 403n.
Melville, Herman *Billy Budd* 569
Menand, Louis 180–81, 181n.
Merleau-Ponty, Maurice undialectical phenomenology of the flesh and body 3, 7, 9, 12, 66, 83, 93, 98, 98n., 111, 112n., 126, 131, 134–34, 135–37, 140, 142, 143, 145, 152, 154, 158, 160, 167–68, 176, 187, 191, 217, 232, 242, 270, 276, 277, 279, 285n., 290n., 294, 303, 306, 319, 327n., 330, 358–59, 362, 366, 395, 413, 421, 427, 446–47, 458, 477, 478n., 487, 508, 511, 512, 533, 548, 553, 560
  on language 50, 358–59
  Phénoménologie de la perception 136–37, 158n., 168–69, 220, 319n., 327, 329, 396, 396n., 411, 425, 495n., 531, 561
  Les problems actuels de la phénoménologie 582
  Signes 50, 185, 359n., 394
  The visible and the Invisible 5n., 12, 12n., 160, 292, 294, 478
Mill, John Stuart *On Liberty* 40n., 179, 421
Milton, John 17, 38, 39, 146, 272, 277, 429, 525, 583
  Paradise Lost 38
Montaigne 85, 183, 216n., 429, 432, 443, 468
Moran, Dermont 124n., 129, 130–36, 145, 149n., 155–159, 158n., 164, 262n., 324, 392, 394n., 411, 421, 450–52, 454–58, 462n., 527n.
Morrison, Toni 104, 272
  Song of Solomon 209
Mounin, Georges 360
  Saussure 337, 340, 343, 343n., 355, 356n., 359n.
Muller, Robin M. 342, 342n.
Müller-Doohm, Stefan 26n., 466n.
Musil, Robert 232, 565

Nabokov, Vladimir 434
Nail, Thomas 263n.
Nass, Michael 274n.
Nietzsche, Friedrich 2, 4, 13, 20, 31, 31n., 37, 41, 41n., 42, 70n., 85, 117, 117n., 118, 119, 164n., 167, 177, 193, 209, 228, 253, 258, 269n., 300, 328, 349, 370, 371, 380, 425, 435, 441, 498, 500, 506n., 529, 548
  Beyond Good and Evil 41, 248

INDEX OF NAMES 623

Zur Genealogie der Moral   58, 119
Novalis   272
Nozick, Robert *Anarchy, State, Utopia*   198
   The Nature of Rationality   67, 70, 198
Nussbaum, Martha   162, 194, 206, 229,
   350, 575
   The Fragility of Goodness   197, 220, 228n.
   "The Professor of Parody: The Hip
     Defeatism of Judith Butler"   197n.
Nuttall, A.D.   25, 115, 117, 171, 282, 284, 284n.,
   535n., 575

Obama, Barack   494
Olbromski, Cezary Józef   317n.
Orgel, Stephen   18, 25, 117, 121, 171, 251, 253,
   282, 291, 367, 445n., 502

Palfrey, Simon   17, 23, 45, 57, 172,
   422, 559, 577
   on Derrida and deconstruction   368
   doing Shakespeare   45, 391, 395
   romantic expressionism and
     creationism   172, 463
   on linguistic embodiment   138
   on verbal immediacy   57, 465, 513–536
   on possibility   575
   undialectical thought   17, 575
   on *vita activa* and moral collective
     Utopia   177, 191–92
Palmer, Anthony   100n.
Pascal, Blaise   79, 85, 120, 213
   De l'esprit géométrique   120n.
   Pensées   213n., 229
   *Prière pour demander à Dieu le bon usage
     des maladies*   2, 2n., 62, 62n.
   Les provinciales   319
Pasolini, Pier Paolo   37
Peden, Knox   385n.
Pepys, Samuel   502–03
Petrarca *Canzoniere*   14
Pinker, Steven   117n., 118, 127, 330, 574
Pippin, Robert   117
   After the Beautiful   19
   Hegel's Realm of Shadows   271n., 286, 320,
     405, 416
Plath, Sylvia   59
Plato   5, 16, 21, 55n., 58n., 76, 96, 109, 113,
   115, 174, 196, 244, 145, 280–83, 285, 297,
   320, 329n., 364, 366, 370, 373, 379, 385,
   413, 415–18, 429, 438, 448, 504, 514, 540,
   542n., 544, 545, 585
   Phaedrus   376n., 415
   The Republic   53n., 87, 87n., 98, 415, 513n.
   The Sophist   213
Pocock, J.G.A.   328
Poe, Edgar Alan   41
Popper, Karl *Conjectures and
   Refutations*   528
   The Poverty of Historicism   324n.
Potter, Beatrix   277
Priest, Graham   70
   Beyond the Limits of Thought   95, 314
   One   94n., 245
Proust, Marcel   32, 85, 136, 272, 370
   Sodome et Gomorrhe   19
Putnam, Hillary *The Many Faces of
   Realism*   193–94, 343, 393
Pynchon, Thomas *Against the Day*   419
   The Crying of Lot   49, 207
   Gravity's Rainbow   206n.
   Mason and Dixon   521

Quine, W.V.   339, 349
   "Two Dogmas of Empiricism"   58

Raber, Karen   17, 20, 115, 115n., 172, 209–11,
   272, 298, 325, 492n., 547
   on Descartes   70–72, 87
   on posthumanism   427–38, 443–46
Racine, Jean   134, 272, 562, 573
   Bajazet   36
   Phèdre   490
Raimondi, Ezio   82
Rancière, Jacques   235, 281, 282, 472–
   74, 487–89
   The Aesthetic Unconscious   474n.
   Dissensus   487
   History, Politics, Aesthetics   587
   Le partage du sensible   155
   The Politics of Aesthetics   473–74, 503–04
Rand, Ayn   123
Rawls, John *A Theory of Justice*   226
Renault, Alain   229, 371, 564n.
Ricardo, David   278n.
Ricoeur, Paul *De l'interprétation*   338n., 352n.
   Finitude et culpabilité   439n.
Riffaterre, Michel   325n.
Rimbaud, Arthur   51, 166, 232

Rodríguez, Juan Carlos *Theory and History of Ideological Production* 164n.
Rorty, Richard 37, 349
  Achieving our Country 40n.
  Contingency, Irony, Solidarity 1, 41, 202, 262
  Essays on Heidegger and Others 169, 234, 583, 583n.
  Philosophy and the Mirror of Nature 89, 104, 203n., 238–39, 344, 443
  "Remarks on Deconstruction and Pragmatism" 582–83
Rossi, Paolo 62n.
Roth, Joseph 563
Roth, Philip 563
Rothleder, Dianne 165n., 281n., 283
Rousseau, Jean-Jacques 33, 182, 203, 225, 370, 374, 389, 418, 444, 490
  Confessions 33–35, 42n., 46–51
  Discours sur l'origine et les fondements de l'inégalité 234
  Essai sur l'origine des langues 417
Rovelli, Carlo 31, 32, 45
Royle, Nicholas 18, 25, 26, 28n., 117, 121–22, 171, 282, 508, 544
  Hélène Cixous 306n.
  How to Read Shakespeare 27n., 84n., 120, 134n., 272n., 418
  In Memory of Jacques Derrida 122n., 161, 224, 317, 444n.
  The Uncanny 32
Ruda, Frank 166
  For Badiou: Idealism without Idealism 56n., 81, 93n., 95, 97, 329n., 510
  The Dash—The Other Side of Absolute Knowing 56
  "Marx in the Cave" 287
Russell, Bertrand 48, 49, 244, 339, 349
  Sceptical Essays 173, 291
  What I Believe 40
Ryle, Gilbert *The Concept of the Mind* 61, 61n.

Sartre, Jean Paul 34, 117, 126, 148, 152, 158n., 167, 291n., 320, 388, 413, 510
  Critique de la raison dialectique I 290, 292, 395, 541

  L'être et le néant 93, 93n., 135–36, 510n., 553
  Search for a Method 558
Saussure, Ferdinand de 4, 9–12, 14, 50, 90, 96, 103, 112, 113, 151–52, 210, 224, 243n., 245, 273m, 275, 320, 331–64, 365, 369, 370, 373–80, 382, 387, 465, 526, 528, 538, 548, 553
  Cours de linguistique générale 332, 333n., 335, 336, 337n., 338, 340, 346, 348, 351, 352n., 354, 357, 363, 363n., 379
  Écrits de linguistique générale 332n.
Schweppenhäuser, Gerhard 300, 473–74
Séchehaye, Albert 356
Sellars, Wilfrid. "Empiricism and the Philosophy of Mind" 55, 55n., 57, 271, 299
  Science, Perception and Reality 83
Seneca 281, 445, 446, 572
  Agamemnon 445
  Medea 445
  Natural Questions 445
Shakespeare *All's Well that Ends Well* 290
  Antony and Cleopatra 16, 76, 84n., 272n., 284, 290, 490, 572
  As You Like It 37, 56, 112, 117, 196, 221, 291, 321, 325, 442, 440, 471, 496, 562, 572
  Coriolanus 147, 177, 233, 434, 443, 499, 499n., 518, 572
  Cymbeline 113, 272, 298, 373–74, 414, 442, 442n., 470, 535n., 537, 549
  The Comedy of Errors 419, 440–42, 579
  Double Falsehood 250
  Hamlet 4, 4n., 6, 15, 15n., 16, 18, 28n., 29–59, 68, 68n., 71, 75, 76n., 79–82, 82n., 84–87, 91, 95, 100n., 101, 120, 134, 146, 151, 161, 163–66, 169, 176–77, 184–88, 192, 198, 202, 209n., 211–14, 219, 220, 225, 233, 247, 248, 250, 252, 253, 266–67, 271n., 281, 281n., 287, 288, 292, 294, 306, 306n., 310–15, 316–18, 326, 328, 338, 340, 345, 346, 349, 367, 383, 400n., 419–20, 422–25, 429, 430n., 442, 460, 461–64, 467n., 471, 474, 489, 496, 510, 510n., 516, 518, 525, 531–32, 535n., 560, 572, 578–82
  1 Henry IV 61, 71, 285–88, 442, 513, 572, 579
  2 Henry IV 71, 442, 535n.

INDEX OF NAMES

Henry V 206, 290, 580–81
1 Henry VI 53, 192, 284, 330
3 Henry VI 192, 496
Henry VIII 579
Julius Caesar 147n., 280, 536
King John 23, 82, 284–85, 291, 418, 438, 507, 558, 584
King Lear 4n., 6, 10, 11, 15n., 16, 28, 32, 34, 45, 45n., 57–58, 64, 71, 95, 102, 134, 151, 177, 187–88, 202, 213, 214n, 220, 226, 233, 235–36, 243, 247–49, 252, 284, 287–89, 295–96, 298, 335, 341, 345, 350, 367, 418, 432, 439, 440, 441, 443–46, 470, 474, 476–78, 487–88, 518, 521, 537, 572
Love's Labour's Lost 62, 83, 219, 285, 310, 419, 442, 470, 489, 507
Macbeth 73, 99n., 120, 124, 178, 213, 271, 272, 280, 290, 402, 411, 419–20, 422, 457, 460, 462n., 470, 492–94, 498, 502, 517–28, 531, 552, 553, 565, 572–573
Measure for Measure 16, 119–20, 291–92, 297–98, 326, 385, 386, 442, 507
The Merchant of Venice 8n., 28, 56, 71, 144–45, 146, 149–50, 151, 175–76, 182, 202, 219, 233, 235, 278, 379, 420n., 569, 583
The Merry Wives of Windsor 442
A Midsummer Night's Dream 57, 177, 280, 285, 291, 390, 434, 442, 467, 470, 485, 485n., 487, 503, 510n.
Much Ado About Nothing 1, 285, 414, 439, 442, 507, 575, 579
Othello 8, 8n., 71, 99, 113, 204, 213, 235, 252, 264–65, 271, 278, 282, 285, 287, 288, 467n.
Pericles 56, 58, 76, 99, 177, 192, 222, 235, 297, 379, 414–25, 516–17, 537, 541, 548, 552
The Rape of Lucrece 82, 235
Richard II 58, 177, 222, 263, 263n., 372
Richard III 264n, 442, 560
Romeo and Juliet 15n., 26n., 56, 90, 94, 99, 142, 155n., 213, 248, 248n., 267, 290, 365n., 367–68, 419, 442, 471, 499–50, 504, 504n.
The Sonnets 13, 144–45, 149–50, 173, 420n.
The Taming of the Shrew 156, 215, 272, 318, 321, 325, 507, 546, 561

The Tempest 6, 6n., 16, 41, 43, 54, 56, 81, 86–87, 89–90, 99, 120, 188, 202, 222, 233, 233n., 272, 282, 285, 286, 288, 291, 338, 440–43, 449, 470, 509, 515, 516, 531, 537, 549, 551, 554–55, 562
Timon of Athens 19, 177, 193, 233, 440, 557, 575
Titus Andronicus 433, 579
Troilus and Cressida 6, 81, 92, 99, 214
Twelfth Night 18, 82, 163–64, 195–96, 202, 222, 227–29, 266, 280–82, 319, 414
The Two Gentlemen of Verona 44
Venus and Adonis 10–11, 13–15, 82, 285, 305
The Winter's Tale 99, 121, 222, 291, 311, 420, 442n., 443, 471, 503, 505–10, 537, 538, 572
Shapiro, James 171, 233, 284, 532–33
Shapiro, Michael 178
Skinner, Quentin *Liberty Before Liberalism* 209
 Reason and Rhetoric in Hobbes 215n.
Sloterdijk, Peter *Kritik der zynische Vernunft* 1, 20, 20n., 58, 58n.
Smith, Adam 278n.
Smith, Bruce 17, 24, 102, 134, 157, 171, 220, 447, 405, 516, 533, 548, 562
 on Derrida and deconstruction 9, 362, 366, 368, 381–90, 425, 439
 on embodiment, language and Saussure 9–10, 11–14, 15–16, 138, 331–39, 354–58, 548, 575
 the natural standpoint, framing and the epoché 4, 9, 14, 138, 301–10, 317–18
 on the ontic and sexuality 107–113
 Phenomenal Shakespeare 4, 9–10, 12n., 18, 57, 69, 112, 124, 154, 207, 210, 301, 308, 309, 331–32, 335, 338, 357, 382, 562, 575
 "Phenomophobia, or Who's Afraid of Merleau-Ponty?" 362
 "Premodern Sexualities" 107, 145, 285–90
Smith, David W. 98, 130n., 399n., 402–04, 404n., 450–54, 458–59, 516, 523
Smith, Matthew James 112, 233, 324n., 325, 326, 366n., 412, 503, 504, 512, 533, 534, 562, 569
Sontag, Susan *Against Interpretation* 112, 210
Sophocles 197
 Oedipus at Colonus 444–45

Spivak, Gayatri Chakravorty   34n., 86n., 106, 117, 371, 496, 546
   A Critique of Postcolonial Reason: Towards a History of the Vanishing Present   559
   In Other Worlds   54n., 106, 183
Stang, Nicholas   347
Stevens, Wallace   76, 525
   The Necessary Angel   239
Stoppard, Tom   424
   Travesties   443
Strauss, Leo *The City and the Man*   415–17
Szlezák, Thomas A. *Reading Plato*   320, 416
Szondi, Peter   117, 393, 514
   Introduction to Literary Hermeneutics   580
   Theorie des modernen Dramas 1880–1950   34
Swarbrick, Steven   80n.

Tanney, Julia   6n.
Tarditi, Claudio   571n.
Tasso, Torquato   82, 278
Taylor, Charles   176
   The Ethics of Authenticity   207, 564–66, 571
   Modern Social Imaginaries   177n.
Thomas, Dylan   549
Thomson, Stephen   81, 97, 393n.
Tiffany, Grace   340n., 500
Trilling, Lionel   496
   The Liberal Imagination   39

Updike, John   146, 563

Vickers, Brian *Appropriating Shakespeare*   9–10, 25, 27, 50, 170–77, 206, 331, 339–66, 369–81, 465, 500, 539, 566
Virgil   445, 490

Walser, Robert   123, 232
Warminski, Andrzej   117, 544
   "Introduction" to Paul de Man's *Aesthetic Ideology*   116, 256–57, 514
   Material Inscriptions   3n, 64n., 90, 114n., 465
Waugh, Evelyn *The Loved One*   207
Weiss, Peter   232

Wells, Stanley   57, 280, 503
West, Nathaniel *The Day of the Locust*   207
West, William   412, 413n.
Whitman, Walt   69, 122, 124–25, 161, 188, 318, 533, 563
Williams, William Carlos   84
Wilson, John Dover *What Happens in Hamlet*   267n.
Wilson, Richard   172, 220n., 572
   secrecy and resistance   15n.
   critical consensus   23
   deconstruction   27n., 114
   difference   54
   moralization of politics   114
   dialectical thought   17, 282
   immediacy   318
   embodiment and the aesthetic fallacy   462–65
   presentism   575–85
Wilson Knight, G.   235, 538–39, 548
   The Wheel of Fire   15, 217
Witmore, Michael   154, 191
Wittgenstein, Ludwig   4, 9n., 41, 41n., 300, 326, 339, 349, 375, 400n., 435, 570n
   Culture and Value   238
   Tractatus logico-philosophicus   326, 369, 400
Wordsworth, William   83, 136, 279, 421

Yates, Julian   217n., 365n., 438
Yeats, William Butler   262, 262n., 490, 490n., 525

Žižek, Slavoj   6n., 85, 87–88, 111, 117, 143, 151, 166, 183, 200, 228, 267, 352n., 400n., 527n.
   on antagonism, the infrastructure, and ideology   226, 293, 351
   on Descartes   67, 75–76, 87–88, 91–92, 95
   on dialectics and totality   275, 284, 294, 300–01, 328, 343, 540
   moralism versus Kantian ethics   225
   on science   79–80, 327, 342
   on spontaneity   161, 161n., 164
   on universality   121, 186, 286
   "Class Struggle or Postmodernism"   121–22n., 183n., 226
   How to Read Lacan   91, 186

Less than Nothing: Hegel and the Shadow of Dialectical Materialism   56, 284, 343
Organs without Bodies: Deleuze and Consequences   173
The Parallax View   19n.
The Plague of Fantasies   58, 79–80, 95, 104n., 122, 186n., 225
"Plato, Descartes, Hegel"   76
Reading Marx   85n., 119, 119n., 216, 275, 294, 298n., 300–01, 328
Repeating Lenin   161, 161n.
The Sublime Object of Ideology
The Ticklish Subject: The Absent Centre of Political Ontology   67, 75–76, 91–92, 164